Emerging Capabilities and Applications of Artificial Higher Order Neural Networks

Ming Zhang
Christopher Newport University, USA

A volume in the Advances in
Computational Intelligence and
Robotics (ACIR) Book Series

Published in the United States of America by
    IGI Global
    Engineering Science Reference (an imprint of IGI Global)
    701 E. Chocolate Avenue
    Hershey PA, USA 17033
    Tel: 717-533-8845
    Fax: 717-533-8661
    E-mail: cust@igi-global.com
    Web site: http://www.igi-global.com

Library of Congress Cataloging-in-Publication Data

Names: Zhang, Ming, 1949 July 29- author.
Title: Emerging capabilities and applications of artificial higher order
  neural networks / by Ming Zhang.
Description: Hershey, PA : Engineering Science Reference, an imprint of IGI
  Global, [2020] | Includes bibliographical references and index. |
  Summary: "This book explores the emerging capabilities and applications
  of artificial higher order neural networks in the fields of economics,
  business, modeling, simulation, control, recognition, computer science,
  and engineering"-- Provided by publisher.
Identifiers: LCCN 2019054311 (print) | LCCN 2019054312 (ebook) | ISBN
  9781799835639 (hardcover) | ISBN 9781799835646 (paperback) | ISBN
  9781799835653 (ebook)
Subjects: LCSH: Neural networks (Computer science)--Industrial
  applications. | Engineering--Data processing. | Business--Decision
  making--Data processing.
Classification: LCC QA76.87 .Z4745 2020 (print) | LCC QA76.87 (ebook) |
  DDC 006.3/2--dc23
LC record available at https://lccn.loc.gov/2019054311
LC ebook record available at https://lccn.loc.gov/2019054312

This book is published in the IGI Global book series Advances in Computational Intelligence and Robotics (ACIR) (ISSN: 2327-0411; eISSN: 2327-042X)

British Cataloguing in Publication Data
A Cataloguing in Publication record for this book is available from the British Library.

For electronic access to this publication, please contact: eresources@igi-global.com.

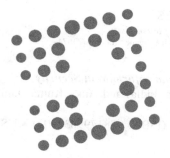

Advances in Computational Intelligence and Robotics (ACIR) Book Series

ISSN:2327-0411
EISSN:2327-042X

Editor-in-Chief: Ivan Giannoccaro, University of Salento, Italy

MISSION

While intelligence is traditionally a term applied to humans and human cognition, technology has progressed in such a way to allow for the development of intelligent systems able to simulate many human traits. With this new era of simulated and artificial intelligence, much research is needed in order to continue to advance the field and also to evaluate the ethical and societal concerns of the existence of artificial life and machine learning.

The **Advances in Computational Intelligence and Robotics (ACIR) Book Series** encourages scholarly discourse on all topics pertaining to evolutionary computing, artificial life, computational intelligence, machine learning, and robotics. ACIR presents the latest research being conducted on diverse topics in intelligence technologies with the goal of advancing knowledge and applications in this rapidly evolving field.

COVERAGE

- Fuzzy Systems
- Automated Reasoning
- Neural Networks
- Machine Learning
- Artificial Life
- Synthetic Emotions
- Cognitive Informatics
- Algorithmic Learning
- Natural Language Processing
- Brain Simulation

IGI Global is currently accepting manuscripts for publication within this series. To submit a proposal for a volume in this series, please contact our Acquisition Editors at Acquisitions@igi-global.com or visit: http://www.igi-global.com/publish/.

Titles in this Series

For a list of additional titles in this series, please visit:
http://www.igi-global.com/book-series/advances-computational-intelligence-robotics/73674

Machine Learning Techniques for Pattern Recognition and Information Security
Mohit Dua (National Institute of Technology Kurukshetra, India) and Ankit Kumar Jain (National Institute of Technology, Kurukshetra, India)
Engineering Science Reference • © 2021 • 300pp • H/C (ISBN: 9781799832997) • US $225.00

Driving Innovation and Productivity Through Sustainable Automation
Ardavan Amini (EsseSystems, UK) Stephen Bushell (Bushell Investment Group, UK) and Arshad Mahmood (Birmingham City University, UK)
Engineering Science Reference • © 2021 • 275pp • H/C (ISBN: 9781799858799) • US $245.00

Examining Optoelectronics in Machine Vision and Applications in Industry 4.0
Oleg Sergiyenko (Autonomous University of Baja California, Mexico) Julio C. Rodriguez-Quiñonez (Autonomous University of Baja California, Mexico) and Wendy Flores-Fuentes (Autonomous University of Baja California, Mexico)
Engineering Science Reference • © 2021 • 346pp • H/C (ISBN: 9781799865223) • US $215.00

Machine Learning Applications in Non-Conventional Machining Processes
Goutam Kumar Bose (Haldia Institute of Technology, India) and Pritam Pain (Haldia Institute of Technology, India)
Engineering Science Reference • © 2021 • 313pp • H/C (ISBN: 9781799836247) • US $195.00

Artificial Neural Network Applications in Business and Engineering
Quang Hung Do (University of Transport Technology, Vietnam)
Engineering Science Reference • © 2021 • 275pp • H/C (ISBN: 9781799832386) • US $245.00

For an entire list of titles in this series, please visit:
http://www.igi-global.com/book-series/advances-computational-intelligence-robotics/73674

701 East Chocolate Avenue, Hershey, PA 17033, USA
Tel: 717-533-8845 x100 • Fax: 717-533-8661
E-Mail: cust@igi-global.com • www.igi-global.com

This book is dedicated to my wife, Zhao Qing Zhang.

Table of Contents

Section 3
Artificial Higher Order Neural Networks for Modeling and Simulation

Section 4
Artificial Higher Order Neural Networks for Control and Recognition

Detailed Table of Contents

Section 1
Models of Artificial Higher Order Neural Networks

Chapter 1

This chapter introduces the background of the higher order neural network (HONN) model developing history and overviews 24 applied artificial higher order neural network models. This chapter provides 24 HONN models and uses a single uniform HONN architecture for all 24 HONN models. This chapter also uses a uniform learning algorithm for all 24 HONN models and uses uniform weight update formulae for all 24 HONN models. In this chapter, polynomial HONN, Trigonometric HONN, Sigmoid HONN, SINC HONN, and Ultra High Frequency HONN structure and models are overviewed too.

Chapter 2

This chapter introduces multi-polynomial higher order neural network models (MPHONN) with higher accuracy. Using Sun workstation, C++, and Motif, a MPHONN simulator has been built. Real-world data cannot always be modeled simply and simulated with high accuracy by a single polynomial function. Thus, ordinary higher order neural networks could fail to simulate complicated real-world data. But MPHONN model can simulate multi-polynomial functions and can produce results with improved accuracy through experiments. By using MPHONN for financial modeling and simulation, experimental results show that MPHONN can always have 0.5051% to 0.8661% more accuracy than ordinary higher order neural network models.

Real-world financial data is often discontinuous and non-smooth. Neural network group models can perform this function with more accuracy. Both polynomial higher order neural network group (PHONNG) and trigonometric polynomial higher order neural network group (THONNG) models are studied in this chapter. These PHONNG and THONNG models are open box, convergent models capable of approximating any kind of piecewise continuous function, to any degree of accuracy. Moreover, they are capable of handling higher frequency, higher order nonlinear, and discontinuous data. Results confirm that PHONNG and THONNG group models converge without difficulty and are considerably more accurate (0.7542% - 1.0715%) than neural network models such as using polynomial higher order neural network (PHONN) and trigonometric polynomial higher order neural network (THONN) models.

Section 2
Artificial Higher Order Neural Networks for Economics and
Business

This chapter delivers general format of higher order neural networks (HONNs) for nonlinear data analysis and six different HONN models. Then, this chapter mathematically proves that HONN models could converge and have mean squared errors close to zero. Moreover, this chapter illustrates the learning algorithm with update formulas. HONN models are compared with SAS nonlinear (NLIN) models, and results show that HONN models are 3 to 12% better than SAS nonlinear models. Finally, this chapter shows how to use HONN models to find the best model, order, and coefficients without writing the regression expression, declaring parameter names, and supplying initial parameter values.

This chapter develops a new nonlinear model, ultra high frequency trigonometric higher order neural networks (UTHONN) for time series data analysis. UTHONN includes three models: UCSHONN (ultra high frequency sine and cosine higher order neural networks) models, UCCHONN (ultra high frequency cosine and cosine higher order neural networks) models, and USSHONN (ultra high frequency sine and sine higher order neural networks) models. Results show that UTHONN models are 3 to 12% better than equilibrium real exchange rates (ERER) model, and 4–9% better than other polynomial higher order neural network (PHONN) and trigonometric higher order neural network (THONN) models. This study also uses UTHONN models to simulate foreign exchange rates and consumer price index with error approaching 10-6.

Chapter 6

This chapter develops two new nonlinear artificial higher order neural network models. They are sine and sine higher order neural networks (SIN-HONN) and cosine and cosine higher order neural networks (COS-HONN). Financial data prediction using SIN-HONN and COS-HONN models are tested. Results show that SIN-HONN and COS-HONN models are good models for some sine feature only or cosine feature only financial data simulation and prediction compared with polynomial higher order neural network (PHONN) and trigonometric higher order neural network (THONN) models.

Section 3
Artificial Higher Order Neural Networks for Modeling and Simulation

Chapter 7

This chapter develops a new nonlinear model, ultra high frequency sinc and trigonometric higher order neural networks (UNT-HONN), for data classification. UNT-HONN includes ultra high frequency sinc and sine higher order neural networks (UNS-HONN) and ultra high frequency sinc and cosine higher order neural networks (UNC-HONN). Data classification using UNS-HONN and UNC-HONN models are tested. Results show that UNS-HONN and UNC-HONN models are more accurate than other polynomial higher order neural network (PHONN) and trigonometric higher order neural network (THONN) models, since UNS-HONN and UNC-HONN models can classify data with error approaching 10-6.

Chapter 8

A new open box and nonlinear model of cosine and sigmoid higher order neural network (CS-HONN) is presented in this chapter. A new learning algorithm for CS-HONN is also developed in this chapter. In addition, a time series data simulation and analysis system, CS-HONN simulator, is built based on the CS-HONN models. Test results show that the average error of CS-HONN models are from 2.3436% to 4.6857%, and the average error of polynomial higher order neural network (PHONN), trigonometric higher order neural network (THONN), and sigmoid polynomial higher order neural network (SPHONN) models range from 2.8128% to 4.9077%. This suggests that CS-HONN models are 0.1174% to 0.4917% better than PHONN, THONN, and SPHONN models.

Chapter 9

Real-world data is often nonlinear, discontinuous, and may comprise high frequency, multi-polynomial components. Not surprisingly, it is hard to find the best models for modeling such data. Classical neural network models are unable to automatically determine the optimum model and appropriate order for data approximation. In order to solve this problem, neuron-adaptive higher order neural network (NAHONN) models have been introduced. Definitions of one-dimensional, two-dimensional, and n-dimensional NAHONN models are studied. Specialized NAHONN models are also described. NAHONN models are shown to be "open box." These models are further shown to be capable of automatically finding not only the optimum model but also the appropriate order for high frequency, multi-polynomial, discontinuous data. Rainfall estimation experimental results confirm model convergence. The authors further demonstrate that NAHONN models are capable of modeling satellite data.

Section 4
Artificial Higher Order Neural Networks for Control and Recognition

Chapter 10

This chapter develops a new nonlinear model, ultra high frequency polynomial and trigonometric higher order neural networks (UPT-HONN) for control signal generator. UPT-HONN includes UPS-HONN (ultra high frequency polynomial and sine function higher order neural networks) and UPC-HONN (ultra high frequency polynomial and cosine function higher order neural networks). UPS-HONN and UPC-HONN model learning algorithms are developed in this chapter. UPS-HONN and UPC-HONN models are used to build nonlinear control signal generator. Test results show that UPS-HONN and UPC-HONN models are better than other polynomial higher order neural network (PHONN) and trigonometric higher order neural network (THONN) models, since UPS-HONN and UPC-HONN models can generate control signals with error approaching 10-6.

This chapter develops a new nonlinear model, ultra high frequency sigmoid and trigonometric higher order neural networks (UGT-HONN), for data pattern recognition. UGT-HONN includes ultra high frequency sigmoid and sine function higher order neural networks (UGS-HONN) and ultra high frequency sigmoid and cosine functions higher order neural networks (UGC-HONN). UGS-HONN and UGC-HONN models are used to recognition data patterns. Results show that UGS-HONN and UGC-HONN models are better than other polynomial higher order neural network (PHONN) and trigonometric higher order neural network (THONN) models, since UGS-HONN and UGC-HONN models can recognize data pattern with error approaching 10-6.

Recent artificial higher order neural network research has focused on simple models, but such models have not been very successful in describing complex systems (such as face recognition). This chapter presents the artificial higher order neural network group-based adaptive tolerance (HONNGAT) tree model for translation-invariant face recognition. Moreover, face perception classification, detection of front faces with glasses and/or beards models of using HONNGAT trees are presented. The artificial higher order neural network group-based adaptive tolerance tree model is an open box model and can be used to describe complex systems.

Preface

Artificial Higher Order Neural Networks for Economics and Business was the first editing book published by IGI Global in 2009 in artificial Higher Order Neural Network (H)NN) area. In 2010, *Artificial Higher Order Neural Networks for Computer Science and Engineering* was published by IGI Global as the second editing book in this area. In 2013, *Artificial Higher Order Neural Networks for Modeling and Simulation* was the third editing book published by IGI Global. *Applied Artificial Higher Order Neural Networks for Control and Recognition* was the fourth editing book published by IGI Global in the Higher Order Neural Network area in year of 2016.

This book, *Emerging Capabilities and Application of Artificial Higher Order Neural Networks*, is the first solo author and multiple chapters book world widely published by IGI Global in the HONN area. This is a 12 chapter book which introduces Higher Order Neural Networks (HONNs) to people working in the fields of economics, business, modeling, simulation, control, recognition, computer science and computer engineering, and presents to them that HONNs are open box neural networks tools compared to the traditional artificial neural networks. This is the first sole author and multiple chapter book which includes details of the most popular HONNs models and applications, and provides opportunities for millions of people working in the economics, business, modeling, simulation, control, recognition, computer science and computer engineering areas to know what HONNs are, and how to use HONNs.

Artificial Neural Networks (ANNs) are known to excel in pattern recognition, pattern matching and mathematical function approximation. However, they suffer from several well-known limitations– they can often become stuck in local, rather than global minima, as well as taking unacceptably long times to converge in practice. Of concern, especially from the perspective of economics and financial time series predictions, is their inability to handle non-smooth, discontinuous training data, and complex mappings (associations). Another limitation of ANN is a 'black box' nature – meaning that explanations (reasons) for their decisions are not immediately obvious, unlike techniques such as Decision Trees. This then is the motivation for developing artificial Higher Order Neural Networks (HONNs), since HONNs are 'open-box' models and each neuron and weight are mapped to function variable and coefficient.

In recent years, researchers use HONNs for pattern recognition, nonlinear simulation, classification, and prediction in the computer science and computer engineering areas. The results show that HONNs are always faster, more accurate, and easier to explain. This is the second motivation for using HONNs in computer science and computer engineering areas, since HONNs can automatically select the initial coefficients, even automatically select the model for applications in computer science and computer engineering area.

Giles and Maxwell (1987) published the first paper on HONN. Bengtsson (1990) wrote the first book in the higher order (or higher-order, consistency) neural network area. Higher order correlations in the training data require more complex neuron activation functions (Barron, Gilstrap & Shrier, 1987; Giles & Maxwell, 1987; Psaltis, Park & Hong, 1988). Neurons which include terms up to and including degree-k are referred to as kth-order neurons (Lisboa & Perantonis, 1991). In addition, the increased computational load resulting from the large increase in network weights means that the complex input-output mappings normally only achievable in multi-layered networks can now be realized in a single HONN layer (Zhang & Fulcher, 2004). Currently the output of a kth-order single-layer HONN neuron will be a non-linear function comprising polynomials of up to kth-order. Moreover, since no hidden layers are involved, both Hebbian and Perceptron learning rules can be employed (Shin & Ghosh, 1991).

Several different HONN models have been developed by Zhang and Fulcher, during the past decade or so. A more comprehensive coverage, including derivations of weight update equations, is presented in Zhang & Fulcher (2004). The Neuron-Adaptive HONN (and NAHONN group) leads to faster convergence, much reduced network size and more accurate curve fitting, compared with P(T)HONNs (Zhang, Xu & Fulcher, 2002). Each element of the NAHONN group is standard multi-layer HONN comprising adaptive neurons, but which employs locally bounded, piecewise continuous (rather than polynomial) activation functions and thresholds. Now as with the earlier HONN groups, it is possible to provide a similar general result to that found previously by Hornik (1991) for ANNs – namely that NAHONN groups are capable of approximating any kind of piecewise continuous function, to any degree of accuracy (a proof is provided in Zhang, Xu & Fulcher, 2002).

Moreover, these models are capable of automatically selecting not only the optimum model for a time series, but also the appropriate model order and coefficients.

The objectives of this book are:

- This is the first sole author and multiple chapter book which introduces HONNs to people working in the fields of economics, business, modeling, simulation, control, recognition, computer science and engineering.
- This is the first sole author and multiple chapter book which introduces to researchers in economics, business, modeling, simulation, control, recognition, computer science and engineering areas that HONNs are open box neural networks tools compare to traditional artificial neural networks.
- This is the first sole author and multiple chapter book which provides opportunities for millions of people working in the economics, business, modeling, simulation, control, recognition, computer science and engineering areas to know what HONNs are, and how to use HONNs in control and recognition areas.
- This book explains why HONNs can approximate any nonlinear data to any degree of accuracy and allows researchers to understand why HONNs are much easier to use, and HONNs can have better nonlinear data recognition accuracy than SAS nonlinear (NLIN) procedures.
  - This book introduces the HONN group models and adaptive HONNs, and allows the people working in the control and recognition areas to understand HONN group models and adaptive HONN models, which can simulate not only nonlinear data, but also discontinuous and unsmooth nonlinear data.

The title of the Chapter 1 is "Models of Artificial Higher Order Neural Networks." This chapter introduces the background of Higher Order Neural Network (HONN) model developing history and provides an overview of 24 applied artificial higher order neural network models. This chapter provides 24 HONN models and uses a single uniform HONN architecture for all 24 HONN models. This chapter also use a uniform learning algorithm for all 24 HONN models and uses uniform weight update formulae for all 24 HONN models. In this chapter, polynomial HONN, Trigonometric HONN, Sigmoid HONN, SINC HONN, and Ultra High Frequency HONN structure and models are also discussed.

The title of the Chapter 2 is "Models of Artificial Multi-Polynomial Higher Order Neural Networks." This chapter introduces Multi-Polynomial Higher Order Neural Network models (MPHONN) with higher accuracy. Using Sun workstation, C++, and Motif, a MPHONN Simulator has been built. Real world data cannot always be modeled simply and simulated with high accuracy by single polynomial function. Thus, ordinary higher order neural networks could fail to simulate complicated real world data. But MPHONN model can simulate multi-polynomial functions, and can produce results with improved accuracy through experiments. By using MPHONN for financial modeling and simulation, experimental results show that MPHONN can always have 0.5051% to 0.8661% more accuracy than ordinary higher order neural network models.

The title of the Chapter 3 is "Group Models of Artificial Polynomial and Trigonometric Higher Order Neural Networks." Real-world financial data is often discontinuous and non-smooth. Accuracy will be a problem, if we attempt to use neural networks to simulate such data. Neural network group models can perform this function with more accuracy. Both Polynomial Higher Order Neural Network Group (PHONNG) and Trigonometric polynomial Higher Order Neural Network Group (THONNG) models are studied in this chapter. These PHONNG and THONNG models are open box, convergent models capable of approximating any kind of piecewise continuous function, to any degree of accuracy. Moreover, they are capable of handling higher frequency, higher order nonlinear and discontinuous data. Results obtained using Polynomial Higher Order Neural Network Group and Trigonometric Polynomial Higher Order Neural Network Group financial simulators are presented, which confirm that PHONNG and THONNG group models converge without difficulty and are considerably more accurate (0.7542% - 1.0715%) than neural network models such as Polynomial Higher Order Neural Network (PHONN) and Trigonometric polynomial Higher Order Neural Network (THONN) models.

The title of Chapter 4 is "SAS Nonlinear Models or Artificial Higher Order Neural Network Nonlinear Models?" This chapter delivers general format of Higher Order Neural Networks (HONNs) for nonlinear data analysis and six different HONN models. This chapter mathematically proves that HONN models could converge and have mean squared errors close to zero. This chapter illustrates the learning algorithm with update formulas. HONN models are compared with SAS Nonlinear (NLIN) models and results show that HONN models are 3 to 12% better than SAS Nonlinear models. Moreover, this chapter shows how to use HONN models to find the best model, order and coefficients, without writing the regression expression, declaring parameter names, and supplying initial parameter values.

The title of Chapter 5 is "Time Series Data Analysis by Ultra-High Frequency Trigonometric Higher Order Neural Networks." This chapter develops a new nonlinear model, Ultra high frequency Trigonometric Higher Order Neural Networks (UTHONN), for time series data analysis. UTHONN includes three models: UCSHONN (Ultra high frequency Sine and Cosine Higher Order Neural Networks) models, UCCHONN (Ultra high frequency Cosine and Cosine Higher Order Neural Networks) models, and USSHONN (Ultra high frequency Sine and Sine Higher Order Neural Networks) models. Results show that UTHONN models are 3 to 12% better than Equilibrium Real Exchange Rates (ERER) model, and 4 – 9% better than other Polynomial Higher Order Neural Network (PHONN) and Trigonometric Higher Order Neural Network (THONN) models. This study also uses UTHONN models to simulate foreign exchange rates and consumer price index with error approaching 10^{-6}.

The title of Chapter 6 is "Financial Data Prediction by Artificial Sine and Cosine Trigonometric Higher Order Neural Networks." This chapter develops two new nonlinear artificial higher order neural network models. They are Sine and Sine Higher Order Neural Networks (SIN-HONN) and Cosine and Cosine Higher Order Neural Networks (COS-HONN). Financial data prediction using SIN-HONN and COS-HONN models are tested. Results show that SIN-HONN and COS-HONN models are more accurate models for financial data prediction compared with Polynomial Higher Order Neural Network (PHONN) and Trigonometric Higher Order Neural Network (THONN) models.

The title of the Chapter 7 is "Data Classification Using Ultra-High Frequency SINC and Trigonometric Higher Order Neural Networks." This chapter develops a new nonlinear model, Ultra high frequency SINC and Trigonometric Higher Order Neural Networks (UNT-HONN), for Data Classification. UNT-HONN includes Ultra high frequency siNc and Sine Higher Order Neural Networks (UNS-HONN) and Ultra high frequency siNc and Cosine Higher Order Neural Networks (UNC-HONN). Data classification using UNS-HONN and UNC-HONN models are tested. Results show that UNS-HONN and UNC-HONN models are more accurate than other Polynomial Higher Order Neural Network (PHONN) and Trigonometric Higher Order Neural Network (THONN) models, since UNS-HONN and UNC-HONN models can classify the data with error approaching 10^{-6}.

The title of the Chapter 8 is "Data Simulations Using Cosine and Sigmoid Higher Order Neural Networks." New open box and nonlinear model of Cosine and Sigmoid Higher Order Neural Network (CS-HONN) is presented in this paper. A new learning algorithm for CS-HONN is also developed from this study. A time series data simulation and analysis system, CS-HONN Simulator, is built based on the CS-HONN models too. Test results show that average error of CS-HONN models are from 2.3436% to 4.6857%, and the average error of Polynomial Higher Order Neural Network (PHONN), Trigonometric Higher Order Neural Network (THONN), and Sigmoid polynomial Higher Order Neural Network (SPHONN) models are from 2.8128% to 4.9077%. It means that CS-HONN models are 0.1174% to 0.4917% better than PHONN, THONN, and SPHONN models.

The title of the Chapter 9 is "Rainfall Estimation Using Neuron-Adaptive Higher Order Neural Networks." Real-world data is often nonlinear, discontinuous and may comprise high frequency, multi-polynomial components. Not surprisingly, it is hard to find the best models for modeling such data. Classical neural network models are unable to automatically determine the optimum model and appropriate order for data approximation. In order to solve this problem, Neuron-Adaptive Higher Order Neural Network (NAHONN) Models have been introduced. Definitions of one-dimensional, two-dimensional, and n-dimensional NAHONN models are studied. Specialized NAHONN models are also described. NAHONN models are shown to be "open box". These models are further shown to be capable of automatically finding not only the optimum model but also the appropriate order for high frequency, multi-polynomial, discontinuous data. Rainfall estimation experimental results confirm model convergence. We further demonstrate that NAHONN models are capable of modeling satellite data. When the Xie and Scofield (1989) technique was used, the average error of the operator-computed IFFA rainfall estimates was 30.41%. For the Artificial Neural Network (ANN) reasoning network, the training error was 6.55% and the test error 16.91%, respectively. When the neural network group was used on these same fifteen cases, the average training error of rainfall estimation was 1.43%, and the average test error of rainfall estimation was 3.89%. When the neuron-adaptive artificial neural network group models was used on these same fifteen cases, the average training error of rainfall estimation was 1.31%, and the average test error of rainfall estimation was 3.40%. When the artificial neuron-adaptive higher order neural network model was used on these same fifteen cases, the average training error of rainfall estimation

The title of the Chapter 10 is "Control Signal Generator Based on Ultra-High Frequency Polynomial and Trigonometric Higher Order Neural Networks." This chapter develops a new nonlinear model, Ultra high frequency Polynomial and Trigonometric Higher Order Neural Networks (UPT-HONN), for control signal generator. UPT-HONN includes UPS-HONN (Ultra high frequency Polynomial and Sine function Higher Order Neural Networks) and UPC-HONN (Ultra high frequency Polynomial and Cosine function Higher Order Neural Networks). UPS-HONN and UPC-HONN model learning algorithms are developed in this chapter. UPS-HONN and UPC-HONN models are used to build nonlinear control signal generator. Test results show that UPS-HONN and UPC-HONN models are better than other Polynomial Higher Order Neural Network (PHONN) and Trigonometric Higher Order Neural Network (THONN) models, since UPS-HONN and UPC-HONN models can generate control signals with error approaching 10^{-6}.

The title of the Chapter 11 is "Data Pattern Recognition Based on Ultra-High Frequency Sigmoid and Trigonometric Higher Order Neural Networks." This chapter develops a new nonlinear model, Ultra high frequency siGmoid and Trigonometric Higher Order Neural Networks (UGT-HONN), for data pattern recognition. UGT-HONN includes Ultra high frequency siGmoid and Sine function Higher Order Neural Networks (UGS-HONN) and Ultra high frequency siGmoid and Cosine functions Higher Order Neural Networks (UGC-HONN). UGS-HONN and UGC-HONN models are used to recognition data patterns. Results show that UGS-HONN and UGC-HONN models are better than other Polynomial Higher Order Neural Network (PHONN) and Trigonometric Higher Order Neural Network (THONN) models, since UGS-HONN and UGC-HONN models to recognize data pattern with error approaching 10^{-6}.

The title of the Chapter 12 is "Face Recognition Based on Higher Order Neural Network Group-Based Adaptive Tolerance Trees." Recent artificial higher order neural network research has focused on simple models, but such models have not been very successful in describing complex systems (such as face recognition). This chapter presents the artificial Higher Order Neural Network Group-based Adaptive Tolerance (HONNGAT) Tree model for translation-invariant face recognition. Moreover, face perception classification, detection of front faces with glasses and/or beards, and face recognition results using HONNGAT Trees are presented. When 10% random number noise is added, the accuracy of HONNGAT Tree for face recognition is 1% higher that artificial neural network Group-based Adaptive Tolerance (GAT) Tree and is 6% higher than a general tree. The artificial higher order neural network group-based adaptive tolerance tree model is an open box model and can be used to describe complex systems.

This book, *Emerging Capabilities and Application of Artificial Higher Order Neural Networks*, is the first solo author and multiple chapters book world widely published by IGI Global in the HONN area. The mission of this book is to let millions of people working in the economics, business, modeling, simulation, control, recognition, computer science and engineering areas know that HONNs are much easier to use and can have better recognition results than SAS Nonlinear models, and understand how to successfully use HONNs models for nonlinear data control, recognition, and prediction. HONNs will challenge traditional artificial neural network products and change the research methodology that people are currently using in control and recognition areas for the control signal generating, pattern recognition, nonlinear recognition, classification, and prediction. This book will be the first book which collects chapters on HONNs for economic, business, modeling, simulation, control and recognition.

REFERENCES

Barron, R., Gilstrap, L., & Shrier, S. (1987). Polynomial and Neural Networks: Analogies and Engineering Applications. *Proceedings of International Conference of Neural Networks*, 2, 431-439.

Bengtsson, M. (1990). *Higher Order Artificial Neural Networks*. Diano Pub Co.

Giles, L., & Maxwell, T. (1987). Learning, Invariance and Generalization in High-Order Neural Networks. *Applied Optics*, 26(23), 4972–4978. doi:10.1364/AO.26.004972 PMID:20523475

Hornik, K. (1991). Approximation capabilities of multilayer feedforward networks. *Neural Networks*, 4(2), 251–257. doi:10.1016/0893-6080(91)90009-T

Lisboa, P., & Perantonis, S. (1991). Invariant pattern recognition usi9ng third-order networks and zernlike moments. *Proceedings of the IEEE International Joint Conference on Neural Networks*, 2, 1421-1425.

Psaltis, D., Park, C., & Hong, J. (1988). Higher order associative memories and their optical implementations. *Neural Networks*, 1(2), 149–163. doi:10.1016/0893-6080(88)90017-2

Shin, Y., Ghosh, J., & Samani, D. (1992). Computationally efficient invariant pattern classification with higher-order pi-sigma networks. In Intelligent Engineering Systems through Artificial Neural Networks (vol. 2, pp. 379-384). ASME Press.

Zhang, M. (2009). *Artificial Higher Order Neural Networks for Economics and Business*. IGI-Global. doi:10.4018/978-1-59904-897-0

Zhang, M. (2010). Artificial Higher Order Neural Networks for Computer Science and Engineering – Trends for Emerging Application. Hershey, PA: IGI Global.

Zhang, M. (2013). *Higher Order Neural Networks for Modeling and Simulation*. IGI-Global. doi:10.4018/978-1-4666-2175-6

Zhang, M. (2016). *Applied artificial higher order neural networks for control and recognition*. IGI Global. doi:10.4018/978-1-5225-0063-6

Zhang, M., & Fulcher, J. (2004). Higher order neural network for satellite weather predication. In Applied Intelligent Systems (pp.17-57). Springer-Verlag.

Zhang, M., Xu, S., & Fulcher, F. (2002). Neuron-adaptive higher order neural network models for automated financial data modeling. *IEEE Transactions on Neural Networks*, *13*(1), 188–204. doi:10.1109/72.977302 PMID:18244418

Acknowledgment

The author would like to acknowledge the help of all involved in the collation and the review process of the book, without whose support the project could not have been satisfactorily completed.

I would like to thank my supervisor, Dr. Rod Scofield, retired Senior Scientist of National Oceanic and Atmospheric Administration (NOAA), Washington DC, USA for supporting my artificial neural network research and awarding me USA National Research Council Postdoctoral Fellow (1991-1992) and Senior USA National Research Council Research Associate (1999-2000). I would like to thank Dr. John Fulcher, retired Professor of University of Wollongong in Australia, for a long time of research collaboration in the artificial neural network area since 1992.

I would like to thank Professor Dingbo Kuang, Fellow of Chinese Academy of Sciences, and Senior Scientist of Shanghai Institute of Technical Physics, Shanghai, China. Thank you for being my postdoctoral advisor from 1989 to 1991, when I was a postdoctoral researcher.

Thanks go to the publishing team at IGI Global, whose contributions throughout the whole process from inception of the initial idea to final publication have been invaluable. This project gave me the opportunity to publish this solo author and multiple chapter book of *Emerging Capabilities and Applications of Artificial Higher Order Neural Networks* first time in the artificial higher order neural network area in the world.

I would like to also thank IGI Global for giving me opportunities to publish my four editing books of Artificial Higher Order Neural Networks. They are:

Artificial Higher Order Neural Networks for Economics and Business (2009);

Acknowledgment

Artificial Higher Order Neural Networks for Computer Science and Engineering (2010);

Artificial Higher Order Neural Networks for Modeling and Simulation (2013);

Applied Artificial Higher Order Neural Networks for Control and Recognition (2016).

Special thanks go to my family for their continuous support and encouragement, and to my wife, Zhao Qing Zhang, for her unfailing support and encouragement during the years it took to give birth to this book.

Ming Zhang
Christopher Newport University, USA
January 1st, 2020

Section 1
Models of Artificial Higher Order Neural Networks

Chapter 1
Models of Artificial Higher Order Neural Networks

ABSTRACT

This chapter introduces the background of the higher order neural network (HONN) model developing history and overviews 24 applied artificial higher order neural network models. This chapter provides 24 HONN models and uses a single uniform HONN architecture for all 24 HONN models. This chapter also uses a uniform learning algorithm for all 24 HONN models and uses uniform weight update formulae for all 24 HONN models. In this chapter, polynomial HONN, Trigonometric HONN, Sigmoid HONN, SINC HONN, and Ultra High Frequency HONN structure and models are overviewed too.

INTRODUCTION

The contributions of this chapter will be:

- Introduce the background of HONN models' developing history.
- Overview 24 applied artificial higher order neural network models.
- Provide 24 HONN Models learning algorithm and weight update formulae.
- Using a single uniform HONN architecture for ALL 24 HONN models.
- Using a uniform learning algorithm for all 24 HONN models
- Using uniform weight update formulae for all 24 HONN models

DOI: 10.4018/978-1-7998-3563-9.ch001

This chapter is organized as follows: Section background gives the developing history of applied artificial higher order neural network (HONN) models. Section Higher Order Neural Network structure and Models introduces a single uniform structure for all 24 HONN modes. Section Learning Algorithm and Weight Update Formulae provides the uniform learning algorithm for all 24 HONN models and provides weight update formulae for all 24 HONN models. Section Future Research Directions predicts the future development direction in applied artificial higher order neural network area. Section Conclusion gives the summery of the 24 HONN models.

BACKGROUND

In 1995, Zhang, Murugesan, & Sadeghi (1995) develop very basic applied artificial higher order neural network model, called Polynomial Higher Order Neural Network (PHONN), for economic data simulation. PHONN can simulate data using higher order (order from 2 to 6) polynomial functions. In 1997, Zhang, Zhang, & Fulcher (1997) create a second very basic applied artificial higher order neural work model, called Trigonometric polynomial Higher Order Neural Network (THONN) models and THONN group models for financial prediction. PHONN models can model data by using higher order trigonometric functions, or by using groups of higher order trigonometric functions. In 1999, Zhang, Zhang, & Keen (1999) builds THONN system for analyzing higher frequency non-linear data simulation & prediction. The estimation errors are always around from 1% to 5%.

Starting from 2000, new applied artificial higher order neural network models are developed, based on PHONN and THONN models. Lu, Qi, Zhang, & Scofield (2000) study the PT-HONN models for multi-polynomial function simulation. Zhang, Zhang, & Fulcher (2000) apply higher order neural network group models for financial simulation. Qi, Zhang, & Scofield (2001) use M-PHONN model for rainfall estimation. Zhang (2001) tests the financial data simulation using A-PHONN model. Zhang, & Lu, (2001) also use M-PHONN model in studying financial data simulation. A-PHONN Model is also used in rainfall estimation (Zhang, & Scofield 2001).

From 2002, adaptive higher order neural network models are studied. And new HONN models continue to be developed. Xu, & Zhang (2002) present an adaptive activation function for higher order neural networks. Based on the different data, HONN adaptively chose the best function(s) for the special data. Zhang (2002a) investigates the rainfall estimation by using PL-HONN model. Zhang (2002b) also researches the financial data simulation by using PL-HONN model. Zhang, Xu, & Fulcher (2002) suggest the neuron-adaptive higher order neural network models for automated financial data modeling. Zhang, & Crane (2004) operate rainfall estimation using SPHONN model. Zhang, & Fulcher (2004) examine higher order neural networks for weather prediction.

New HONN models are developed from 2005. Crane, & Zhang (2005) generate data simulation system by using SINCHONN model. Fulcher, & Zhang (2005) introduce different higher order neural network models in the system and processing areas. Zhang (2005) build a data simulation system using sin(x)/x and sin(x) polynomial higher order neural networks. Fulcher, Zhang, & Xu. (2006) provide an overview the application of higher order neural networks to financial time series prediction. Zhang (2006) make a data simulation system using CSINC polynomial higher order neural networks. Zhang (2007) also build a data simulation system using YSINC polynomial higher order neural networks.

Starting from 2008, building new HONN models with the error approaching 0 became a hot research direction. Before 2008, the HONN error always is between 1% to 5%. For many applications, error between 1% to 5% is acceptable. But for nonlinear and discontinued data simulation, errors close to zero are welcomed. To solve this problem, Zhang (2008) design a higher order neural network nonlinear model and find the new HONN modes has better running result than SAS software. The simulation data error is close to zero. Zhang (Ed.) (2009a) edit a book called *Artificial Higher Order Neural Networks for Economics and Business*, in which includes new HONN model with error close to zero. Zhang (2009b) compares the running result between artificial higher order neural networks and SAS software for economics and business. The research results show that HONN model is better than SAS software if both simulate nonlinear and discontinued data. Zhang, M. (2009c) develop an ultra-high frequency trigonometric higher order neural networks for time series data Analysis. The key point is that the newly developed HONN can actually simulate 2 times higher than ultra-high frequency real word data. And newly developed HONN can let the simulating error approach to E-6. Zhang (2009d) also tries the time series simulation using ultra high frequency cosine and cosine higher order neural networks.

After 2010, adaptive higher order neural network models, high order neural network group models, and ultra-high frequency high order neural network models are continually developed.

Zhang (Ed.) (2010a) collects the HONN models and applications in *computer science and engineering areas*. Zhang (2010b) proposed higher order neural network group-based adaptive tolerance tree models. Zhang (2010c) shows the rainfall estimation results by using neuron-adaptive higher order neural networks. Zhang (2010d) publishes the time series simulation results by using ultra high frequency sine and sine higher order neural network models. Zhang (2011) studies a sine and sigmoid higher order neural networks for data simulation. Zhang (2012) use the polynomial and sigmoid higher order neural networks for data simulations and prediction. Zhang (Ed.) (2013a) collects the higher order neural networks for modeling and simulation. Zhang (2013b) develops the artificial multi-polynomial higher order neural network models. Zhang (2013c) also studies the artificial polynomial and trigonometric higher order neural network group models. Zhang (2014a) develops a SINC and sigmoid higher order neural network for data modeling and simulation. Zhang (2014b) uses an ultra-high frequency polynomial and sine artificial higher order neural networks for control signal generator.

Starting from 2015, ultra-high frequency HONN and other HONN models are continually developed. Zhang (2016a) creates the ultra-high frequency polynomial and trigonometric higher order neural networks for control signal generator. Zhang (2016b) studies ultra-high frequency sigmoid and trigonometric higher order neural networks for data pattern recognition. Zhang (2016c) also develops artificial sine and cosine trigonometric higher order neural networks for financial data prediction. Zhang (2016d) researches the ultra-high frequency SINC and trigonometric higher order neural networks for data classification. Zhang, M. (2016e) uses cosine and sigmoid higher order neural networks for date simulations. Above research results are shown in the book of "Applied Artificial Higher Order Neural Networks for Control and Recognition" edited by Zhang, M. (Ed.) (2016f).

HIGHER ORDER NEURAL NETWORK ARCHITECTURE AND MODELS

HONN Model Structure can be seen in Figure 1.

HONN Model formulae are:

- The input:

x: input variable

y: input variable (1)

- The first hidden layer:

$$net_k^{\ x} = c_k^{\ x}x$$
$$b_k^{\ x} = f_k^{\ x}\left(net_k^{\ x}\right) = f_k^{\ x}\left(c_k^{\ x}x\right)$$

(2)

$$net_j^{\ y} = c_j^{\ y}y$$
$$b_j^{\ y} = f_j^{\ y}\left(net_j^{\ y}\right) = f_j^{\ y}\left(c_j^{\ y}y\right)$$

(3)

- The second hidden layer:

$$net_{kj}^{\ h} = \left\{c_{kj}^{\ hx}b_k^{\ x}\right\}\left\{c_{kj}^{\ hy}b_j^{\ y}\right\}$$

(4)

$$i_{kj}^{\ c} = f^h\left(net_{kj}^{\ h}\right) = \left\{c_{kj}^{\ hx}b_k^{\ x}\right\}\left\{c_{kj}^{\ hy}b_j^{\ y}\right\}$$

(5)

- The output layer:

$$net^o = \sum\nolimits_{k,j=0}^{n} c_{kj}^{\ o} i_{kj}^{\ c}$$

(6)

Let:

$$f^o\left(net^o\right) = net^o$$

(7)

$$Z_c = f^o\left(net^o\right) = net^o = \sum\nolimits_{k,j=0}^{n} c_{kj}^{\ o} i_{kj}^{\ c}$$

(8)

Since:

Figure 1. HONN Architecture

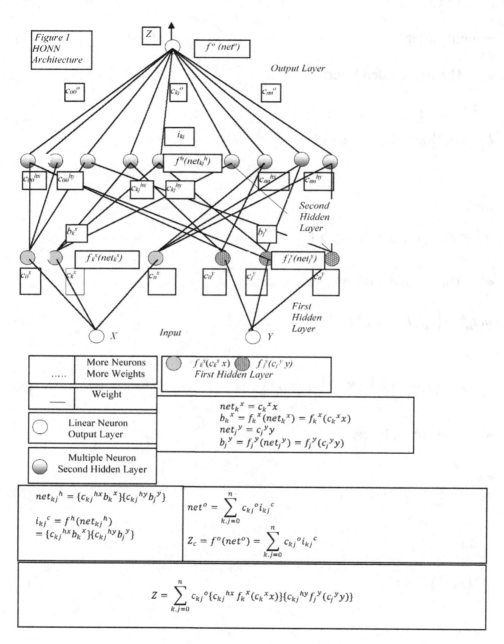

$$Z = Z_c = f^o\left(net^o\right) = net^o = \sum_{k,j=0}^{n} c_{kj}{}^o i_{kj}{}^c$$

$$= \sum_{k,j=0}^{n} c_{kj}{}^o f^h\left(net_{kj}{}^h\right) = \sum_{k,j=0}^{n} c_{kj}{}^o \left\{c_{kj}{}^{hx} b_k{}^x\right\}\left\{c_{kj}{}^{hy} b_j{}^y\right\}$$

$$= \sum_{k,j=0}^{n} c_{kj}{}^o \left\{c_{kj}{}^{hx} f_k{}^x\left(net_k{}^x\right)\right\}\left\{c_{kj}{}^{hy} f_j{}^y\left(net_j{}^y\right)\right\} = \sum_{k,j=0}^{n} c_{kj}{}^o \left\{c_{kj}{}^{hx} f_k{}^x\left(c_k{}^x x\right)\right\}\left\{c_{kj}{}^{hy} f_j{}^y\left(c_j{}^y y\right)\right\}$$

$$(9)$$

HONN general models are:

HONN General Model 0:

$$Z = \sum_{k,j=0}^{n} c_{kj}{}^o \{f_k{}^x\left(x\right)\}\left\{f_j{}^y\left(y\right)\right\}$$

$$(10)$$

$$where : \left(c_{kj}{}^{hx}\right) = \left(c_{kj}{}^{hy}\right) = 1 \; and \; c_k{}^x = c_j{}^y = 1$$

HONN General Model 1:

$$Z = \sum_{k,j=0}^{n} c_{kj}{}^o \{f_k{}^x\left(c_k{}^x x\right)\}\left\{f_j{}^y\left(c_j{}^y y\right)\right\} \; where \; \left(c_{kj}{}^{hx}\right) = \left(c_{kj}{}^{hy}\right) = 1$$

$$(11)$$

HONN General Model 2:

$$Z = \sum_{k,j=0}^{n} c_{kj}{}^o \{c_{kj}{}^{hx} f_k{}^x\left(c_k{}^x x\right)\}\left\{c_{kj}{}^{hy} f_j{}^y\left(c_j{}^y y\right)\right\}$$

$$(12)$$

PHONN Model

Zhang, Murugesan, and Sadeghi (1995) developed Polynomial Higher Order Neural Network (PHONN) model as follows:

$$Let: f_k^x\left(c_k^{\ x}x\right) = (c_k^{\ x}x)^k \tag{13}$$

$$f_j^y\left(c_j^{\ y}y\right) = (c_j^{\ y}y)^j \tag{14}$$

PHONN Model 0:

$$z = \sum_{k,j=0}^{n} c_{kj}^{\ o}(x)^k(y)^j \tag{15}$$
$$where: \left(c_{kj}^{\ hx}\right) = \left(c_{kj}^{\ hy}\right) = 1 \ and \ c_k^{\ x} = c_j^{\ y} = 1$$

PHONN Model 1:

$$z = \sum_{k,j=0}^{n} c_{kj}^{\ o}(c_k^{\ x}x)^k(c_j^{\ y}y)^j \ where \ \left(c_{kj}^{\ hx}\right) = \left(c_{kj}^{\ hy}\right) = 1 \tag{16}$$

PHONN Model 2:

$$Z = \sum_{k,j=0}^{n} \left(c_{kj}^{\ o}\right)\{c_{kj}^{\ hx}(c_k^{\ x}x)^k\}\{c_{kj}^{\ hy}(c_j^{\ y}y)^j\} \tag{17}$$

XSHONN Model

Zhang (2016g) develops the Polynomial and Sine Higher Order Neural Network (XSHONN) model as follows:

$$Let: f_k^x\left(c_k^{\ x}x\right) = (c_k^{\ x}x)^k \tag{18}$$

$$f_j^y\left(c_j^{\ y}y\right) = \sin^j(c_j^{\ y}y) \tag{19}$$

XSHONN Model 0:

$$z = \sum_{k,j=0}^{n} c_{kj}{}^{o} \left(x \right)^{k} \sin^{j} \left(y \right)$$

$$where : \left(c_{kj}{}^{hx} \right) = \left(c_{kj}{}^{hy} \right) = 1 \ and \ c_{k}{}^{x} = c_{j}{}^{y} = 1$$

(20)

XSHONN Model 1:

$$z = \sum_{k,j=0}^{n} c_{kj}{}^{o} \left(c_{k}{}^{x} x \right)^{k} \sin^{j} \left(c_{j}{}^{y} y \right) \quad where \ \left(c_{kj}{}^{hx} \right) = \left(c_{kj}{}^{hy} \right) = 1$$

(21)

XSHONN Model 2:

$$Z = \sum_{k,j=0}^{n} \left(c_{kj}{}^{o} \right) \{ c_{kj}{}^{hx} (c_{k}{}^{x} x)^{k} \} \{ c_{kj}{}^{hy} \sin^{j} (c_{j}{}^{y} y) \}$$

(22)

XCHONN Model

Zhang (2016g) develops the Polynomial and Cosine Higher Order Neural Network (XCHONN) model as follows:

$$Let : f_{k}{}^{x} \left(c_{k}{}^{x} x \right) = (c_{k}{}^{x} x)^{k}$$

(23)

$$f_{j}{}^{y} \left(c_{j}{}^{y} y \right) = \cos^{j} (c_{j}{}^{y} y)$$

(24)

XCHONN Model 0:

$$z = \sum_{k,j=0}^{n} c_{kj}{}^{o} \left(x \right)^{k} \cos^{j} \left(y \right)$$

$$where : \left(c_{kj}{}^{hx} \right) = \left(c_{kj}{}^{hy} \right) = 1 \ and \ c_{k}{}^{x} = c_{j}{}^{y} = 1$$

(25)

XCHONN Model 1:

$$z = \sum_{k,j=0}^{n} c_{kj}{}^{o} \left(c_k{}^x x \right)^k \cos^j \left(c_j{}^y y \right) \ where \ \left(c_{kj}{}^{hx} \right) = \left(c_{kj}{}^{hy} \right) = 1 \tag{26}$$

XCHONN Model 2:

$$Z = \sum_{k,j=0}^{n} \left(c_{kj}{}^{o} \right) \{ c_{kj}{}^{hx} (c_k{}^x x)^k \} \{ c_{kj}{}^{hy} \cos^j (c_j{}^y y) \} \tag{27}$$

SIN-HONN Model

Zhang (2016c) develops artificial sine and cosine trigonometric higher order neural networks for financial data prediction. Sine Higher Order Neural Network (SINHONN) model as follows:

$$Let: f_k{}^x \left(c_k{}^x x \right) = \sin^k (c_k{}^x x) \tag{28}$$

$$f_j{}^y \left(c_j{}^y y \right) = \sin^j (c_j{}^y y) \tag{29}$$

SIN – HONN Model 0:

$$z = \sum_{k,j=0}^{n} c_{kj}{}^{o} \sin^k (x) \sin^j (y) \tag{30}$$

where: $\left(c_{kj}{}^{hx} \right) = \left(c_{kj}{}^{hy} \right) = 1$ and $c_k{}^x = c_j{}^y = 1$

SIN – HONN Model 1:

$$z = \sum_{k,j=0}^{n} c_{kj}{}^{o} \sin^k (c_k{}^x x) \sin^j (c_j{}^y y) \ where \ \left(c_{kj}{}^{hx} \right) = \left(c_{kj}{}^{hy} \right) = 1 \tag{31}$$

SIN – HONN Model 2:

$$Z = \sum_{k,j=0}^{n} \left(c_{kj}{}^{o} \right) \{ c_{kj}{}^{hx} \sin^k (c_k{}^x x) \} \{ c_{kj}{}^{hy} \sin^j (c_j{}^y y) \} \tag{32}$$

COS-HONN Model

Zhang (2016c) develops artificial sine and cosine trigonometric higher order neural networks for financial data prediction. Cosine Higher Order Neural Network (COSHONN) model as follows:

$$Let: f_k^{x}\left(c_k^{x}x\right) = \cos^k(c_k^{x}x) \tag{33}$$

$$f_j^{y}\left(c_j^{y}y\right) = \cos^j(c_j^{y}y) \tag{34}$$

COS – HONN Model 0:

$$z = \sum_{k,j=0}^{n} c_{kj}^{o} \cos^k(x)\cos^j(y) \tag{33}$$
$$where:\left(c_{kj}^{hx}\right) = \left(c_{kj}^{hy}\right) = 1 \ and \ c_k^{x} = c_j^{y} = 1$$

COS – HONN Model 1:

$$z = \sum_{k,j=0}^{n} c_{kj}^{o} \cos^k(c_k^{x}x)\cos^j(c_j^{y}y) \ where:\left(c_{kj}^{hx}\right) = \left(c_{kj}^{hy}\right) = 1 \tag{34}$$

COS – HONN Model 2:

$$Z = \sum_{k,j=0}^{n} \left(c_{kj}^{o}\right)\{c_{kj}^{hx}\cos^k(c_k^{x}x)\}\{c_{kj}^{hy}con^j\left(c_j^{y}y\right)\} \tag{35}$$

THONN Model

Zhang, Zhang, & Fulcher (1997) and Zhang, Zhang, & Steve (1999) developed Trigonometric Higher Order Neural Network (THONN) model as follows:

$$Let: f_k^{x}\left(c_k^{x}x\right) = \sin^k(c_k^{x}x) \tag{38}$$

$$f_j^y \left(c_j^{\,y} y \right) = \cos^j \left(c_j^{\,y} y \right) \tag{39}$$

THONN Model 0:

$$z = \sum_{k,j=0}^{n} c_{kj}^{\,o} \sin^k (x) \cos^j (y) \tag{40}$$

$$where : \left(c_{kj}^{\,hx} \right) = \left(c_{kj}^{\,hy} \right) = 1 \ and \ c_k^{\,x} = c_j^{\,y} = 1$$

THONN Model 1:

$$z = \sum_{k,j=0}^{n} c_{kj}^{\,o} \sin^k (c_k^{\,x} x) \cos^j (c_j^{\,y} y) \ \ where : \left(c_{kj}^{\,hx} \right) = \left(c_{kj}^{\,hy} \right) = 1 \tag{41}$$

THONN Model 2:

$$Z = \sum_{k,j=0}^{n} \left(c_{kj}^{\,o} \right) \{ c_{kj}^{\,hx} \sin^k (c_k^{\,x} x) \} \{ c_{kj}^{\,hy} \cos^j (c_j^{\,y} y) \} \tag{42}$$

SINCHONN Model

Crane, & Zhang (2005) develop SINC Higher Order Neural Network (SINCHONN) model as follows:

$$Let : f_k^x \left(c_k^{\,x} x \right) = \left(\sin(c_k^{\,x} x) / \left(c_k^{\,x} x \right) \right)^k \tag{43}$$

$$f_j^y \left(c_j^{\,y} y \right) = \left(\sin(c_j^{\,y} y) / \left(c_k^{\,x} y \right) \right)^j \tag{44}$$

SINCHONN Model 0:

$$z = \sum_{k,j=0}^{n} c_{kj}^{\,o} \left(\sin(x) / x \right)^k \left(\sin(y) / y \right)^j \tag{45}$$

$$where : \left(c_{kj}^{\,hx} \right) = \left(c_{kj}^{\,hy} \right) = 1 \ and \ c_k^{\,x} = c_j^{\,y} = 1$$

SINCHONN Model 1:

$$z = \sum_{k,j=0}^{n} c_{kj}{}^{o} \left(\sin(c_k{}^x x) / \left(c_k{}^k x\right) \right)^k \left(\sin(c_j{}^y y) / \left(c_j{}^y y\right) \right)^j \; where : \left(c_{kj}{}^{hx}\right) = \left(c_{kj}{}^{hy}\right) = 1$$

(46)

SINCHONN Model 2:

$$Z = \sum_{k,j=0}^{n} \left(c_{kj}{}^{o}\right) \{ c_{kj}{}^{hx} \left(\sin(c_k{}^x x) / \left(c_k{}^x x\right) \right)^k \} \{ c_{kj}{}^{hy} \left(\sin(c_j{}^y y) / \left(c_j{}^y y\right) \right)^j \}$$

(47)

SSINCHONN Model

Zhang (2005) developed Sine and SINC Higher Order Neural Network (SSINCHONN) model as follows:

$$Let : f_k{}^x \left(c_k{}^x x\right) = \left(\sin(c_k{}^x x)\right)^k$$

(48)

$$f_j{}^y \left(c_j{}^y y\right) = \left(\sin(c_j{}^y y) / \left(c_k{}^x y\right)\right)^j$$

(49)

SSINCHONN Model 0:

$$z = \sum_{k,j=0}^{n} c_{kj}{}^{o} \left(\sin(x) \right)^k \left(\sin(y) / y \right)^j$$

(50)

$$where : \left(c_{kj}{}^{hx}\right) = \left(c_{kj}{}^{hy}\right) = 1 \; and \; c_k{}^x = c_j{}^y = 1$$

SSINCHONN Model 1:

$$z = \sum_{k,j=0}^{n} c_{kj}{}^{o} \left(\sin(c_k{}^x x) \right)^k \left(\sin(c_j{}^y y) / \left(c_j{}^y y\right) \right)^j \; where : \left(c_{kj}{}^{hx}\right) = \left(c_{kj}{}^{hy}\right) = 1$$

(51)

SSINCHONN Model 2:

13

$$Z = \sum_{k,j=0}^{n} \left(c_{kj}^{\ o} \right) \{ c_{kj}^{\ hx} \left(\sin(c_k^{\ x}x) \right)^k \} \{ c_{kj}^{\ hy} \left(\sin(c_j^{\ y}y)/\left(c_j^{\ y}y \right) \right)^j \} \qquad (52)$$

CSINCHONN Model

Zhang (2006) developed Cosine and SINC Higher Order Neural Network (CSINCHONN) model as follows:

$$Let: f_k^{\ x} \left(c_k^{\ x}x \right) = \left(\cos(c_k^{\ x}x) \right)^k \qquad (53)$$

$$f_j^{\ y} \left(c_j^{\ y}y \right) = \left(\sin(c_j^{\ y}y)/\left(c_k^{\ x}y \right) \right)^j \qquad (54)$$

CSINCHONN Model 0:

$$z = \sum_{k,j=0}^{n} c_{kj}^{\ o} \left(\cos(x) \right)^k \left(\sin(y)/y \right)^j \qquad (55)$$

$$where: \left(c_{kj}^{\ hx} \right) = \left(c_{kj}^{\ hy} \right) = 1 \ and \ c_k^{\ x} = c_j^{\ y} = 1$$

CSINCHONN Model 1:

$$z = \sum_{k,j=0}^{n} c_{kj}^{\ o} \left(\cos(c_k^{\ x}x) \right)^k \left(\sin(c_j^{\ y}y)/\left(c_j^{\ y}y \right) \right)^j \ where: \left(c_{kj}^{\ hx} \right) = \left(c_{kj}^{\ hy} \right) = 1$$

$$(56)$$

CSINCHONN Model 2:

$$Z = \sum_{k,j=0}^{n} \left(c_{kj}^{\ o} \right) \{ c_{kj}^{\ hx} \left(\cos(c_k^{\ x}x) \right)^k \} \{ c_{kj}^{\ hy} \left(\sin(c_j^{\ y}y)/\left(c_j^{\ y}y \right) \right)^j \} \qquad (57)$$

YSINCHONN Model

Zhang (2007) developed polynomial and SINC Higher Order Neural Network (YSINCHONN) model as follows:

$$Let: f_k^x\left(c_k^x x\right) = (c_k^x x)^k \tag{58}$$

$$f_j^y\left(c_j^y y\right) = \left(\sin(c_j^y y)/\left(c_k^x y\right)\right)^j \tag{59}$$

YSINCHONN Model 0:

$$z = \sum_{k,j=0}^{n} c_{kj}^{\ o}(x)^k \left(\sin(y)/y\right)^j \tag{60}$$
$$where:\left(c_{kj}^{\ hx}\right) = \left(c_{kj}^{\ hy}\right) = 1 \ and \ c_k^{\ x} = c_j^{\ y} = 1$$

YSINCHONN Model 1:

$$z = \sum_{k,j=0}^{n} c_{kj}^{\ o}(c_k^x x)^k \left(\sin(c_j^y y)/\left(c_j^y y\right)\right)^j \ where:\left(c_{kj}^{\ hx}\right) = \left(c_{kj}^{\ hy}\right) = 1 \tag{61}$$

YSINCHONN Model 2:

$$Z = \sum_{k,j=0}^{n}\left(c_{kj}^{\ o}\right)\{c_{kj}^{\ hx}(c_k^x x)^k\}\{c_{kj}^{\ hy}\left(\sin(c_j^y y)/\left(c_j^y y\right)\right)^j\} \tag{62}$$

SPHONN Model

Zhang, & Crane (2004) developed Sigmoid Polynomial Higher Order Neural Network (SPHONN) model as follows:

$$Let: f_k^x\left(c_k^x x\right) = \left(1/\left(1+\exp(c_k^x(-x))\right)\right)^k \tag{63}$$

$$f_j^y\left(c_j^y y\right) = \left(1/\left(1+\exp(c_j^y(-y))\right)\right)^j \tag{64}$$

SPHONN Model 0:

$$z = \sum_{k,j=0}^{n} c_{kj}{}^{o} \left(1/\left(1+\exp(-x)\right)\right)^{k} \left(1/\left(1+\exp(-y)\right)\right)^{j}$$

(65)

$$where: \left(c_{kj}{}^{hx}\right) = \left(c_{kj}{}^{hy}\right) = 1 \ and \ c_{k}{}^{x} = c_{j}{}^{y} = 1$$

SPHONN Model 1:

$$z = \sum_{k,j=0}^{n} c_{kj}{}^{o} \left(1/\left(1+\exp(c_{k}{}^{x}(-x))\right)\right)^{k} \left(1/\left(1+\exp(c_{j}{}^{y}(-y))\right)\right)^{j} \quad where: \left(c_{kj}{}^{hx}\right) = \left(c_{kj}{}^{hy}\right) = 1$$

(66)

SPHONN Model 2:

$$Z = \sum_{k,j=0}^{n} \left(c_{kj}{}^{o}\right)\{c_{kj}{}^{hx}\left(1/\left(1+\exp(c_{k}{}^{x}(-x))\right)\right)^{k}\}\{c_{kj}{}^{hy}\left(1/\left(1+\exp(c_{j}{}^{y}(-y))\right)\right)^{j}\}$$

(67)

SS-HONN Model

Zhang (2011) developed Sine and Sigmoid Higher Order Neural Network (SS-HONN) model as follows:

$$Let: f_{k}{}^{x}\left(c_{k}{}^{x}x\right) = \sin^{k}(c_{k}{}^{x}x)$$

(68)

$$f_{j}{}^{y}\left(c_{j}{}^{y}y\right) = \left(1/\left(1+\exp(c_{j}{}^{y}(-y))\right)\right)^{j}$$

(69)

SS – HONN Model 0:

$$z = \sum_{k,j=0}^{n} c_{kj}{}^{o} \sin^{k}(x)\left(1/\left(1+\exp(-y)\right)\right)^{j}$$

(70)

$$where: \left(c_{kj}{}^{hx}\right) = \left(c_{kj}{}^{hy}\right) = 1 \ and \ c_{k}{}^{x} = c_{j}{}^{y} = 1$$

SS – HONN Model 1:

$$z = \sum_{k,j=0}^{n} c_{kj}{}^{o} \sin^{k}(c_{k}{}^{x}x)\left(1/\left(1+\exp(c_{j}{}^{y}(-y))\right)\right)^{j} \; where : \left(c_{kj}{}^{hx}\right) = \left(c_{kj}{}^{hy}\right) = 1$$

(71)

SS – HONN Model 2:

$$Z = \sum_{k,j=0}^{n} \left(c_{kj}{}^{o}\right)\{c_{kj}{}^{hx} \sin^{k}\left(c_{k}{}^{x}x\right)\}\left\{c_{kj}{}^{hy}\left(1/\left(1+\exp(c_{j}{}^{y}(-y))\right)\right)^{j}\right\}$$

(72)

PS-HONN Model

Zhang (2012) developed Polynomial and Sigmoid Higher Order Neural Network (PS-HONN) model as follows:

$$Let : f_{k}{}^{x}\left(c_{k}{}^{x}x\right) = (c_{k}{}^{x}x)^{k}$$

(73)

$$f_{j}{}^{y}\left(c_{j}{}^{y}y\right) = \left(1/\left(1+\exp(c_{j}{}^{y}(-y))\right)\right)^{j}$$

(74)

SPHONN Model 0:

$$z = \sum_{k,j=0}^{n} c_{kj}{}^{o}(x)^{k}\left(1/\left(1+\exp(-y)\right)\right)^{j}$$

(75)

$$where : \left(c_{kj}{}^{hx}\right) = \left(c_{kj}{}^{hy}\right) = 1 \; and \; c_{k}{}^{x} = c_{j}{}^{y} = 1$$

SPHONN Model 1:

$$z = \sum_{k,j=0}^{n} c_{kj}{}^{o}(c_{k}{}^{x}x)^{k}\left(1/\left(1+\exp(c_{j}{}^{y}(-y))\right)\right)^{j} \; where : \left(c_{kj}{}^{hx}\right) = \left(c_{kj}{}^{hy}\right) = 1$$

(76)

SPHONN Model 2:

$$Z = \sum_{k,j=0}^{n} \left(c_{kj}^{\ o}\right)\{c_{kj}^{\ hx}(c_k^{\ x}x)^k\}\left\{c_{kj}^{\ hy}\left(1/\left(1+\exp(c_j^{\ y}(-y))\right)\right)^j\right\} \tag{77}$$

CS-HONN Model

Zhang (2016e) developed Cosine and Sigmoid Higher Order Neural Network (CS-HONN) model as follows:

$$Let: f_k^{\ x}\left(c_k^{\ x}x\right) = \cos^k(c_k^{\ x}x) \tag{78}$$

$$f_j^{\ y}\left(c_j^{\ y}y\right) = \left(1/\left(1+\exp(c_j^{\ y}(-y))\right)\right)^j \tag{79}$$

CS – HONN Model 0:

$$z = \sum_{k,j=0}^{n} c_{kj}^{\ o} \cos^k(x)\left(1/\left(1+\exp(-y)\right)\right)^j$$
$$where : \left(c_{kj}^{\ hx}\right) = \left(c_{kj}^{\ hy}\right) = 1 \ and \ c_k^{\ x} = c_j^{\ y} = 1 \tag{80}$$

CS – HONN Model 1:

$$z = \sum_{k,j=0}^{n} c_{kj}^{\ o} \cos^k(c_k^{\ x}x)\left(1/\left(1+\exp(c_j^{\ y}(-y))\right)\right)^j \ where : \left(c_{kj}^{\ hx}\right) = \left(c_{kj}^{\ hy}\right) = 1 \tag{81}$$

CS – HONN Model 2:

$$Z = \sum_{k,j=0}^{n} \left(c_{kj}^{\ o}\right)\{c_{kj}^{\ hx}\cos^k\left(c_k^{\ x}x\right)\}\left\{c_{kj}^{\ hy}\left(1/\left(1+\exp(c_j^{\ y}(-y))\right)\right)^j\right\} \tag{82}$$

NS-HONN Model

Zhang (2014a) developed SINC and Sigmoid Higher Order Neural Network (NS-HONN) model as follows:

$$Let: f_k^x\left(c_k^x x\right) = \left(\sin(c_k^x x)/\left(c_k^x x\right)\right)^k \tag{83}$$

$$f_j^y\left(c_j^y y\right) = \left(1/\left(1+\exp(c_j^y(-y))\right)\right)^j \tag{84}$$

NS – HONN Model 0:

$$z = \sum_{k,j=0}^{n} c_{kj}^o \left(\sin(x)/(x)\right)^k \left(1/(1+\exp(-y))\right)^j \tag{85}$$
$$where: \left(c_{kj}^{hx}\right) = \left(c_{kj}^{hy}\right) = 1 \ and \ c_k^x = c_j^y = 1$$

NS – HONN Model 1:

$$z = \sum_{k,j=0}^{n} c_{kj}^o \left(\sin(c_k^x * x)/\left(c_k^x * x\right)\right)^k \left(1/\left(1+\exp(c_j^y(-y))\right)\right)^j \ where: \left(c_{kj}^{hx}\right) = \left(c_{kj}^{hy}\right) = 1 \tag{86}$$

NS – HONN Model 2:

$$Z = \sum_{k,j=0}^{n} \left(c_{kj}^o\right)\{c_{kj}^{hx}(\sin\left(c_k^x x\right)/\left(c_k^x x\right))^k\}\{c_{kj}^{hy}\left(1/\left(1+\exp(c_j^y(-y))\right)\right)^j\} \tag{87}$$

UCSHONN Model

Zhang (2009c) developed Ultra High Frequency Trigonometric Higher Order Neural Network (UTHONN) models, which includes Ultra High Frequency Sine and Cosine Higher Order Neural Network (UCSHONN) model as follows:

$$Let: f_k^x\left(c_k^x x\right) = \cos^k(k * c_k^x x) \tag{88}$$

$$f_j^y\left(c_j^y y\right) = \sin^j(j * c_j^y y) \tag{89}$$

USCHONN Model 0:

$$z = \sum_{k,j=0}^{n} c_{kj}^{\ o} \cos^k (k*x) \sin^j (j*y)$$

(90)

$$where: \left(c_{kj}^{\ hx}\right) = \left(c_{kj}^{\ hy}\right) = 1 \ and \ c_k^{\ x} = c_j^{\ y} = 1$$

USCHONN Model 1:

$$z = \sum_{k,j=0}^{n} c_{kj}^{\ o} \cos^k (k*c_k^{\ x}x) \sin^j (j*c_j^{\ y}y) \ where: \left(c_{kj}^{\ hx}\right) = \left(c_{kj}^{\ hy}\right) = 1$$

(91)

USCHONN Model 2:

$$Z = \sum_{k,j=0}^{n} \left(c_{kj}^{\ o}\right) \{c_{kj}^{\ hx} \cos^k (k*c_k^{\ x}x)\} \{c_{kj}^{\ hy} \sin^j (j*c_j^{\ y}y)\}$$

(92)

UCCHONN Model

Zhang (2009d) developed Ultra High Frequency Cosine and Cosine Higher Order Neural Network (UCCHONN) model as follows:

$$Let: f_k^{\ x}\left(c_k^{\ x}x\right) = \cos^k (k*c_k^{\ x}x)$$

(93)

$$f_j^{\ y}\left(c_j^{\ y}y\right) = \cos^j (j*c_j^{\ y}y)$$

(94)

UCCHONN Model 0:

$$z = \sum_{k,j=0}^{n} c_{kj}^{\ o} \cos^k (k*x) \cos^j (j*y)$$

(95)

$$where: \left(c_{kj}^{\ hx}\right) = \left(c_{kj}^{\ hy}\right) = 1 \ and \ c_k^{\ x} = c_j^{\ y} = 1$$

UCCHONN Model 1:

$$z = \sum_{k,j=0}^{n} c_{kj}{}^{o} \cos^{k}(k*c_{k}{}^{x}x)\cos^{j}(j*c_{j}{}^{y}y) \ \ where: \left(c_{kj}{}^{hx}\right) = \left(c_{kj}{}^{hy}\right) = 1 \qquad (96)$$

UCCHONN Model 2:

$$Z = \sum_{k,j=0}^{n}\left(c_{kj}{}^{o}\right)\{c_{kj}{}^{hx}\cos^{k}(k*c_{k}{}^{x}x)\}\,\{c_{kj}{}^{hy}\cos^{j}(j*c_{j}{}^{y}y)\} \qquad (97)$$

USSHONN Mosdel

Zhang (2010d) developed Ultra High Frequency Sine and Sine Higher Order Neural Network (USSHONN) model as follows:

$$Let: f_{k}{}^{x}\left(c_{k}{}^{x}x\right) = \sin^{k}(k*c_{k}{}^{x}x) \qquad (98)$$

$$f_{j}{}^{y}\left(c_{j}{}^{y}y\right) = \sin^{j}(j*c_{j}{}^{y}y) \qquad (99)$$

USSHONN Model 0:

$$z = \sum_{k,j=0}^{n} c_{kj}{}^{o} \sin^{k}(k*x)\sin^{j}(j*y)$$
$$where: \left(c_{kj}{}^{hx}\right) = \left(c_{kj}{}^{hy}\right) = 1 \ and \ c_{k}{}^{x} = c_{j}{}^{y} = 1 \qquad (100)$$

USSHONN Model 1:

$$z = \sum_{k,j=0}^{n} c_{kj}{}^{o} \sin^{k}(k*c_{k}{}^{x}x)\sin^{j}(j*c_{j}{}^{y}y) \ \ where: \left(c_{kj}{}^{hx}\right) = \left(c_{kj}{}^{hy}\right) = 1 \qquad (101)$$

USSHONN Model 2:

$$Z = \sum_{k,j=0}^{n}\left(c_{kj}{}^{o}\right)\{c_{kj}{}^{hx}\sin^{k}(k*c_{k}{}^{x}x)\}\,\{c_{kj}{}^{hy}\sin^{j}(j*c_{j}{}^{y}y)\} \qquad (102)$$

UPS-HONN Model

Ming Zhang (2016a) developed Ultra high frequency Polynomial and Sine Higher Order Neural Network (UPS-HONN) model as follows:

$$Let: f_k^x\left(c_k^x x\right) = (c_k^x x)^k \tag{103}$$

$$f_j^y\left(c_j^y y\right) = \sin^j(j * c_j^y y) \tag{104}$$

UPS – HONN Model 0:

$$z = \sum_{k,j=0}^{n} c_{kj}^{o}\left(x\right)^k \left(\sin^j(j * y)\right) \tag{105}$$

$$where: \left(c_{kj}^{hx}\right) = \left(c_{kj}^{hy}\right) = 1 \ and \ c_k^x = c_j^y = 1$$

UPS – HONN Model 1:

$$z = \sum_{k,j=0}^{n} c_{kj}^{o}\left(c_k^x * x\right)^k \left(\sin^j(j * c_j^y y)\right) \ where: \left(c_{kj}^{hx}\right) = \left(c_{kj}^{hy}\right) = 1 \tag{106}$$

UPS – HONN Model 2:

$$Z = \sum_{k,j=0}^{n}\left(c_{kj}^{o}\right)\{c_{kj}^{hx}(c_k^x * x)^k\}\{c_{kj}^{hy}\left(\sin^j(j * c_j^y y)\right)\} \tag{107}$$

UPC-HONN Model

Ming Zhang (2016a) developed Ultra high frequency Polynomial and Cosine Higher Order Neural Network (UPC-HONN) model as follows:

$$Let: f_k^x\left(c_k^x x\right) = (c_k^x x)^k \tag{108}$$

$$f_j^y \left(c_j^y y \right) = \cos^j (j * c_j^y y) \tag{109}$$

UPC – HONN Model 0:

$$z = \sum_{k,j=0}^{n} c_{kj}^{\ o} \left(x \right)^k \left(\cos^j (j * y) \right)$$

$$where: \left(c_{kj}^{\ hx} \right) = \left(c_{kj}^{\ hy} \right) = 1 \ and \ c_k^{\ x} = c_j^{\ y} = 1 \tag{110}$$

UPC – HONN Model 1:

$$z = \sum_{k,j=0}^{n} c_{kj}^{\ o} \left(c_k^{\ x} * x \right)^k \left(\cos^j (j * c_j^{\ y} y) \right) \ where: \left(c_{kj}^{\ hx} \right) = \left(c_{kj}^{\ hy} \right) = 1 \tag{111}$$

UPC – HONN Model 2:

$$Z = \sum_{k,j=0}^{n} \left(c_{kj}^{\ o} \right) \{ c_{kj}^{\ hx} (c_k^{\ x} * x)^k \} \{ c_{kj}^{\ hy} \left(\cos^j (j * c_j^{\ y} y) \right) \} \tag{112}$$

UGS-HONN Model

Zhang (2016b) developed Ultra high frequency siGmoid and Sine Higher Order Neural Network (UGS-HONN) model as follows:

$$Let: f_k^j \left(c_k^j x \right) = \left(1 / \left(1 + \exp(c_k^{\ x} (-x)) \right) \right)^k \tag{113}$$

$$f_j^y \left(c_j^k y \right) = \sin^j (j * c_j^k y) \tag{114}$$

UGS – HONN Model 0:

$$z = \sum_{k,j=0}^{n} c_{kj}^{\ o} \left(1 / \left(1 + \exp(-x) \right) \right)^k \left(\sin^j (j * y) \right)$$

$$where: \left(c_{kj}^{\ hx} \right) = \left(c_{kj}^{\ hy} \right) = 1 \ and \ c_k^{\ x} = c_j^{\ y} = 1 \tag{115}$$

UGS – HONN Model 1:

$$z = \sum_{k,j=0}^{n} c_{kj}^{o} \left(1 / \left(1 + \exp(c_k^{x}(-x)) \right) \right)^k \left(\sin^j (j * c_j^{y} y) \right) \quad where : \left(c_{kj}^{hx} \right) = \left(c_{kj}^{hy} \right) = 1$$

(116)

UGS – HONN Model 2:

$$z = \sum_{k,j=0}^{n} \left(c_{kj}^{o} \right) \{ c_{kj}^{hx} \left(1 / \left(1 + \exp(c_k^{x}(-x)) \right) \right)^k \} \{ c_{kj}^{hy} \left(\sin^j (j * c_j^{y} y) \right) \}$$

(117)

UGC-HONN Model

Zhang (2016b) developed Ultra high frequency siGmoid and Cosine Higher Order Neural Network (UGC-HONN) model as follows:

$$Let : f_k^{j} \left(c_k^{j} x \right) = \left(1 / \left(1 + \exp(c_k^{x}(-x)) \right) \right)^k$$

(118)

$$f_j^{y} \left(c_j^{k} y \right) = \cos^j (j * c_j^{k} y)$$

(119)

UGC – HONN Model 0:

$$z = \sum_{k,j=0}^{n} c_{kj}^{o} \left(1 / (1 + \exp(-x)) \right)^k \left(\cos^j (j * y) \right)$$

$$where : \left(c_{kj}^{hx} \right) = \left(c_{kj}^{hy} \right) = 1 \ and \ c_k^{x} = c_j^{y} = 1$$

(120)

UGC – HONN Model 1:

$$z = \sum_{k,j=0}^{n} c_{kj}^{o} \left(1 / \left(1 + \exp(c_k^{x}(-x)) \right) \right)^k \left(\cos^j (j * c_j^{y} y) \right) \quad where : \left(c_{kj}^{hx} \right) = \left(c_{kj}^{hy} \right) = 1$$

(121)

UGC – HONN Model 2:

$$Z = \sum\nolimits_{k,j=0}^{n} \left(c_{kj}{}^{o} \right) \{ c_{kj}{}^{hx} \left(1 / \left(1 + \exp(c_k{}^x (-x)) \right) \right)^k \} \{ c_{kj}{}^{hy} \left(\cos^j (j * c_j{}^y y) \right) \}$$

(122)

UNS-HONN Model

Zhang (2016d) developed Ultra high frequency siNc and Sine Higher Order Neural Network (UNS-HONN) model as follows:

$$Let: f_k{}^j \left(c_k{}^j x \right) = \left(\sin(c_k{}^x x) / \left(c_k{}^x x \right) \right)^k$$

(123)

$$f_j{}^y \left(c_j{}^k y \right) = \sin^j (j * c_j{}^k y)$$

(124)

UNS – HONN Model 0:

$$z = \sum_{k,j=0}^{n} c_{kj}{}^{o} \left(\sin(x) / (x) \right)^k \left(\sin^j (j * y) \right)$$

$$where: \left(c_{kj}{}^{hx} \right) = \left(c_{kj}{}^{hy} \right) = 1 \; and \; c_k{}^x = c_j{}^y = 1$$

(125)

UNS – HONN Model 1:

$$z = \sum_{k,j=0}^{n} c_{kj}{}^{o} \left(\sin(c_k{}^x * x) / \left(c_k{}^x * x \right) \right)^k \left(\sin^j (j * c_j{}^y y) \right) \; where: \left(c_{kj}{}^{hx} \right) = \left(c_{kj}{}^{hy} \right) = 1$$

(126)

UNS – HONN Model 2:

$$Z = \sum\nolimits_{k,j=0}^{n} \left(c_{kj}{}^{o} \right) \{ c_{kj}{}^{hx} \left(\sin(c_k{}^x * x) / \left(c_k{}^x * x \right) \right)^k \} \{ c_{kj}{}^{hy} \left(\sin^j (j * c_j{}^y y) \right) \}$$

(127)

UNC-HONN Model

Zhang (2016d) developed Ultra high frequency siNc and Cosine Higher Order Neural Network (UNC-HONN) model as follows:

$$Let: f_k^{\,j}\left(c_k^{\,j}x\right)=\left(\sin(c_k^{\,x}x)/\left(c_k^{\,x}x\right)\right)^k \tag{128}$$

$$f_j^{\,y}\left(c_j^{\,k}y\right)=\cos^j(j*c_j^{\,k}y) \tag{129}$$

UNC – HONN Model 0:

$$z = \sum_{k,j=0}^{n} c_{kj}^{\;o}\left(\sin(x)/(x)\right)^k\left(\cos^j(j*y)\right))$$

$$where:\left(c_{kj}^{\;hx}\right)=\left(c_{kj}^{\;hy}\right)=1 \; and \; c_k^{\,x}=c_j^{\,y}=1 \tag{130}$$

UNC – HONN Model 1:

$$z = \sum_{k,j=0}^{n} c_{kj}^{\;o}\left(\sin(c_k^{\,x}**x)/\left(c_k^{\,x}**x\right)\right)^k\left(\cos^j(j*c_j^{\,y}y)\right)) \; where:\left(c_{kj}^{\;hx}\right)=\left(c_{kj}^{\;hy}\right)=1 \tag{131}$$

UNC – HONN Model 2:

$$Z = \sum_{k,j=0}^{n}\left(c_{kj}^{\;o}\right)\{c_{kj}^{\;hx}\left(\sin(c_k^{\,x}**x)/\left(c_k^{\,x}**x\right)\right)^k\}\{c_{kj}^{\;hy}\left(\cos^j(j*c_j^{\,y}y)\right)\} \tag{132}$$

Models of UCSHONN, UCCHONN, USSHONN, UPS-HONN, UPC-HONN, UGS-HONN, UGC-HONN, UNS-HONN, and UNC-HONN are ultra-high frequency higher order neural networks. The key feature of these models is that these models all can simulate nonlinear data with error close to zero.

The Nyquist–Shannon sampling theorem, after Harry Nyquist and Claude Shannon, in the literature more commonly referred to as the Nyquist sampling theorem or simply as the sampling theorem, is a fundamental result in the field of information theory, telecommunications and signal processing. Shannon's version of the theorem states:

"If a function x(t) contains no frequencies higher than B hertz, it is completely determined by giving its ordinates at a series of points spaced 1/(2B) seconds apart."

In other words, a band limited function can be perfectly reconstructed from a countable sequence of samples if the band limit, B, is no greater than ½ the sampling rate (samples per second).

In simulating and predicting time series data, the nonlinear models of ultra-high frequency HONN should have twice as high frequency as that of the ultra-high frequency of the time series data. To achieve this purpose, a new model should be developed to enforce high frequency of HONN in order to make the simulation and prediction error close to zero.

The values of k and j ranges from 0 to n, where n is an integer. The ultra-high frequency HONN models can simulate ultra-high frequency time series data, when n increases to a big number. This property of the model allows it to easily simulate and predicate ultra-high frequency time series data, since both k and j increase when there is an increase in n.

GENERAL LEARNING ALGORITHM AND WEIGHT UPDATE FORMULAE

Output Neurons in HONN Model (Model 0, 1, and 2)

The output layer weights are updated according to:

$$c_{kj}^{\ o}\left(t+1\right)=c_{kj}^{\ o}\left(t\right)-\eta\left(\partial E\,/\,\partial c_{kj}^{\ o}\right) \tag{133}$$

where η = learning rate (positive and usually < 1)

c_{kj} = weight; index k an j = input index
(k, j=0, 1, 2, ..., n means one of n*n input neurons from the second hidden layer)
E = error
t = training time
o = output layer

The output node equations are:

$$net^o = \sum_{k,j=1}^{n} c_{kj}{}^o i_{kj}$$

$$z = f^o\left(net^o\right) = \sum_{k,j=1}^{n} c_{kj}{}^o i_{kj} \tag{134}$$

where i_{kj} = input to the output neuron (= output from 2nd hidden layer)

z = actual output from the output neuron

f ^{o} = output neuron activity function

The error at a output unit (neuron) will be:

$$\delta + (d - z) \tag{135}$$

where d = desired output value
The total error is the error of output unit, namely:

$$E = 0.5 * \delta^2 = 0.5 * (d - z) \tag{136}$$

The derivatives $f^{o'}(net^o)$ are calculated as follows: The output neuron function is linear function ($f^o(net^o) = net^o$):

$$f^{o\,'}\left(net^o\right) = \partial f^o / \partial(net)^o = \partial\left(net^o\right) / \partial\left(net^o\right) = 1 \tag{137}$$

Gradients are calculated as follows:

$$\partial E / \partial c_{kj}{}^o = \left(\partial E / \partial z\right)\left(\partial z / \partial\left(net^o\right)\right)\left(\partial\left(net^o\right) / \partial c_{kj}{}^o\right) \tag{138}$$

$$\partial E / \partial z = \partial\left(0.5 * \left(d - z\right)^2\right) / \partial z = 0.5 * \left(-2\left(d - z\right)\right) = -\left(d - z\right) \tag{139}$$

$$\partial z / \partial \left(net^{o} \right) = \partial f^{o} / \partial \left(net^{o} \right) = f^{o'} \left(net^{o} \right) \tag{140}$$

$$\partial \left(net^{o} \right) / \partial_{kj}{}^{o} = \partial \left(\sum_{k,j=0}^{n} c_{kj}{}^{o} i_{kj} \right) / \partial c_{kj}{}^{o} = i_{kj} \tag{141}$$

Combining Eqns. (138) through (141), the negative gradient is:

$$-\partial E / \partial c_{kj}{}^{o} = (d-z) f^{o'} \left(net^{o} \right) i_{kj} \tag{142}$$

For a linear output neuron, this becomes, by combining Eqns. (137) and (142):

$$-\partial E / \partial c_{kj}{}^{o} = (d-z) f^{o'} \left(net^{o} \right) i_{kj} = (d-z)(1) i_{kj} = (d-z) i_{kj} \tag{143}$$

The weight update equations are formulated as follows: for linear output neurons, let:

$$\delta^{ol} = (d-z) \tag{144}$$

Combining Formulae (133), (143), and (144):

$$c_{kj}{}^{o}(t+1) = c_{kj}{}^{o}(t) - \eta \left(\partial E / \partial c_{kj}{}^{o} \right) = c_{kj}{}^{o}(t) + \eta (d-z) f^{o'} \left(net^{o} \right) i_{kj} = c_{kj}{}^{o}(t) + \eta \delta^{ol} i_{kj}$$

$$where : \delta^{ol} = (d-z) \quad f^{o'} \left(net^{o} \right) = 1 (linear\ neuron) \tag{145}$$

Second-Hidden Layer Neurons in HONN Model (Model 2)

The second hidden layer weights are updated according to:

$$c_{kj}{}^{hx}(t+1) = c_{kj}{}^{hx}(t) - \eta \left(\partial E / \partial c_{kj}{}^{hx} \right) \tag{146}$$

w here η = learning rate (positive & usually < 1)

k, j = input index ($k, j = 0, 1, 2, \ldots,$ n means one of 2*n*n input combinations from the first hidden layer)

$\quad$ E $\quad$ = error

$\quad\quad$ t $\quad\quad$ = training time

hx = hidden layer, related to x input

$c_{kj}{}^{hx}$ = hidden layer weight related to x input

The equations for the 2nd hidden layer nodes are:

$$net_{kj}{}^{h} = \left\{ c_{kj}{}^{hx} b_{k}{}^{x} \right\}\left\{ c_{kj}{}^{hy} b_{j}{}^{y} \right\} \quad i_{kj} = f^{h}\left(net_{kj}{}^{h} \right) \quad\quad (147)$$

where i_{kj} = output from 2nd hidden layer (= input to the output neuron)

$_{bk}X$ and $_{bj}{}^{y}$ = input to 2nd hidden layer neuron (= output from the 1st hidden layer neuron)

f^{h} = hidden neuron activation function

hy = hidden layer, related to y input

$c_{kj}{}^{hy}$ = hidden layer weight related to y input

We call the neurons at the second layer multiple neurons. Their activity function is linear, and their inputs are the multiplication of two outputs of the first layer neuron output and their weights.

The error of a single output unit will be:

$$\delta = (d - z) \quad\quad (148)$$

where d = desired output value of output layer neuron and z = actual output value of output layer neuron

The total error is the sum of the squared errors across all output units, namely:

$$E_{p} = 0.5 * \delta^{2} = 0.5 * (d - z)^{2} = 0.5 * (d - f^{o}\left(net^{o} \right))^{2} = 0.5 * (d - f_{k}^{o}(\sum_{j} c_{kj}{}^{o} i_{kj}))^{2}$$
$$(149)$$

The derivatives $f^{h}{}'(net^{h}{}_{pj})$ are calculated as follows, for a linear function of second layer neurons:

$$i_{kj} = f^h\left(net_{kj}^{\ h}\right) = net_{kj}^{\ h} \quad f^{h'}\left(net_{kj}^{\ h}\right) = 1 \tag{150}$$

The gradient ($E/c_{kj}^{\ hx}$) is given by:

$$\partial E / \partial c_{kj}^{\ hx} = \partial(0.5*(d-z)^2)/\partial c_{kj}^{\ hx} = \left(\partial\left(0.5*(d-z)^2\right)/\partial z\right)\left(\partial z / \partial\left(net^o\right)\right)$$
$$\left(\partial\left(net^o\right)/\partial i_{kj}\right)\left(\partial i_{kj} / \partial\left(net_{kj}^{\ h}\right)\right)\left(\partial\left(net_{kj}^{\ h}\right)/\partial c_{kj}^{\ hx}\right) \tag{151}$$

$$\partial(0.5*(d-z)^2)/\partial z = -(d-z) \tag{152}$$

$$\partial z / \partial\left(net^o\right) = \partial f^o / \partial\left(net^o\right) = f_k^{o'}\left(net^o\right) \tag{153}$$

$$\partial\left(net^o\right)/\partial i_{kj} = \partial\left(\sum_{k,j=1}^n (c_{kj}^{\ o} i_{kj})\right)//\partial i_{kj} = c_{kj}^{\ o} \tag{154}$$

$$\partial i_{kj} / \partial\left(net_{kj}^{\ h}\right) = \partial\left(f^h\left(net_{kj}^{\ h}\right)\right)/\partial\left(net_{kj}^{\ h}\right) = f^{h'}\left(net_{kj}^{\ h}\right) \tag{155}$$

$$\partial\left(net_{kj}^{\ h}\right)/\partial c_{kj}^{\ hx} = \partial\left(\{c_{kj}^{\ hx} b_k^{\ x}\}\{c_{kj}^{\ hy} b_j^{\ y}\}\right)/\partial c_{kj}^{\ hx}$$
$$= b_k^{\ x} c_{kj}^{\ hy} b_j^{\ y} = \delta_{kj}^{\ hx} b_k^{\ x} \quad where: \delta_{kj}^{\ hx} = c_{kj}^{\ hy} b_j^{\ y} \tag{156}$$

Combining Eqns. (151) through (156), the negative gradient is:

$$-\partial E / \partial c_{kj}^{\ hx} = (d-z) f^{o'}\left(net^o\right) c_{kj}^{\ o} f^{h'}\left(net_{kj}^{\ h}\right) \delta^{hx} b_k^{\ x} \tag{157}$$

The weight update equations are formulated as follows: let output neuron is a linear neuron:

$$\delta^{ol} = (d-z) f^{o'}_{k}(net^{o}) = (d-z) \tag{158}$$

Also let the second layer neurons be linear neurons, combining Formulae (146), (150), (157) and (158):

$$c_{kj}^{hx}(t+1) = c_{kj}^{hx}(t) - \eta\left(\partial E / \partial c_{kj}^{hx}\right)$$
$$= c_{kj}^{hx}(t) + \eta\left((d-z) f^{o}{}'(net^{o}) c_{kj}^{o} f^{h}{}'(net_{kj}^{hx}) c_{kj}^{hy} b_{j}^{y} b_{k}^{x}\right)$$
$$= c_{kj}^{hx}(t) + \eta\left(\delta^{ol} c_{kj}^{o} \delta_{kj}^{hx} b_{k}^{x}\right)$$
$$where: \delta^{ol} = (d-z) \quad \delta_{kj}^{hx} = c_{kj}^{hy} b_{j}^{y}$$
$$f^{o'}(net^{o}) = 1(linear\ neuron) \quad f^{h'}(net_{kj}^{hx}) = 1(linear\ neuron) \tag{159}$$

Use the same rules, the weight update question for y input neurons is:

$$c_{kj}^{hy}(t+1) = c_{kj}^{hy}(t) - \eta\left(\partial E / \partial c_{kj}^{hy}\right)$$
$$= c_{kj}^{hy}(t) + \eta\left((d-z) f^{o}{}'(net^{o}) c_{kj}^{o} f^{h}{}'(net_{kj}^{hy}) c_{kj}^{hx} b_{k}^{x} b_{j}^{y}\right)$$
$$= c_{kj}^{hy}(t) + \eta\left(\delta^{ol} c_{kj}^{o} \delta_{kj}^{hy} b_{j}^{y}\right)$$
$$where: \delta^{ol} = (d-z) \quad \delta_{kj}^{hy} = c_{kj}^{hx} b_{k}^{x}$$
$$f^{o'}(net^{o}) = 1(linear\ neuron) \quad f^{h'}(net_{kj}^{hy}) = 1(linear\ neuron) \tag{160}$$

First Hidden Layer x Neurons in HONN (Model 1 and Model 2)

For the x input part, we have following formula as learning algorithm.
The 1st hidden layer weights are updated according to:

$$c_{k}^{x}(t+1) = c_{k}^{x}(t) - \eta\left(\partial E_{p} / \partial c_{k}^{x}\right) \tag{161}$$

where:

$c_k^x = 1^{st}$ hidden layer weight for input x; $k = k$th neuron of first hidden layer
η = learning rate (positive & usually < 1)
    E   = error
      t   = training time

The equations for the kth or j^{th} node in the first hidden layer are:

$$net_k^x = c_k^x * x \quad b_k^x = f_k^x\left(net_k^x\right) \text{ or } net_j^y = c_j^y * y \quad b_j^y = f_j^y\left(net_j^y\right)$$

$$(162)$$

where:

i_{kj} = output from 2nd hidden layer (= input to the output neuron)
b_k^x and b_j^y= output from the 1st hidden layer neuron (= input to 2nd hidden layer neuron)
f_k^x and f_j^y =1st hidden layer neuron activation function
    x   and y = input to 1st hidden layer

The total error is the sum of the squared errors across all hidden units, namely:

$$E_p = 0.5 * \delta^2 = 0.5 * (d - z)^2 = 0.5 * (d - f^o\left(net^o\right))^2 = 0.5 * (d - f^o(\textstyle\sum_j c_{kj}{}^o i_{kj}))^2$$

$$(163)$$

The gradient is given by:

$$\partial E_p / \partial c_k^x = \partial(0.5 * \left(d - z\right)^2) / \partial c_k^x = (\partial\left(0.5 * \left(d - z\right)^2\right) / \partial z)\left(\partial z / \partial\left(net^o\right)\right)$$

$$\left(\partial\left(net^o\right) / \partial i_{kj}\right)\left(\partial i_{kj} / \partial\left(net_{kj}{}^h\right)\right)\left(\partial\left(net_{kj}{}^h\right) / \partial b_k^x\right)\left(\partial b_k^x / \partial\left(net_k^x\right)\right)\left(\partial\left(net_k^x\right) / \partial c_k^x\right)$$

$$(164)$$

$$\partial(0.5 * (d - z)^2 / \partial z = -\left(d - z\right) \tag{165}$$

$$\partial z / \partial\left(net^o\right) = \partial f^o / \partial\left(net^o\right) = f^{o'}\left(net^o\right) \tag{166}$$

$$\partial\left(net^{o}\right)/\partial i_{kj} = \partial(\sum\nolimits_{k,j=1}^{l}\left(c_{kj}{}^{o}i_{kj}\right)/\partial i_{kj} = c_{kj}{}^{o} \tag{167}$$

$$\partial i_{kj} / \partial\left(net_{kj}{}^{h}\right) = \partial\left(f^{h}\left(net_{kj}{}^{h}\right)\right)/\partial\left(net_{kj}{}^{h}\right) = f^{h'}\left(net_{kj}{}^{h}\right) \tag{168}$$

$$\partial net_{kj}{}^{h} / \partial b_{k}{}^{x} = \partial\left(\left(c_{kj}{}^{hx} * b_{k}{}^{x}\right) * \left(c_{kj}{}^{hy} * b_{j}{}^{y}\right)\right)/\partial b_{k}{}^{x} = c_{kj}{}^{hx} * c_{kj}{}^{hy} * b_{j}{}^{y} = \delta_{kj}{}^{hx} c_{kj}{}^{hx}$$
$$where : \delta_{kj}{}^{hx} = c_{kj}{}^{hy} * b_{j}{}^{y} \tag{169}$$

$$\partial b_{k}{}^{x} / \partial\left(net_{k}{}^{x}\right) = f_{x}'\left(net_{k}{}^{x}\right) \tag{170}$$

$$\partial\left(net_{k}{}^{x}\right)/\partial c_{k}{}^{x} = \partial\left(c_{k}{}^{x} * x\right)/\partial c_{k}{}^{x} = x \tag{171}$$

Combining Formulae (165) through (171) the negative gradient is:

$$-\partial E_{p} / \partial c_{k}{}^{x} = (d-z)f^{o}{}'\left(net^{o}\right)c_{kj}{}^{o} * f^{h}{}'\left(net_{kj}{}^{h}\right)\delta_{kj}{}^{hx}c_{kj}{}^{hx}f_{x}{}'\left(net_{k}{}^{x}\right)x \tag{172}$$

The weight update equations are calculated as follows. For linear output neurons:

$$f^{o}{}'\left(net^{o}\right) = 1 \quad \delta^{ol} = (d-z)f^{o'}\left(net^{o}\right) = (d-z) \tag{173}$$

r linear neurons of second hidden layer:

$$f^{h'}\left(net_{kj}{}^{h}\right) = 1 \tag{174}$$

The negative gradient is:

$$-\partial E_p / \partial c_k^{\ x} = (d - z) f^{o\,\prime}(net^o) c_{kj}^{\ o} * f^{h\,\prime}(net_{kj}^{\ h}) \delta_{kj}^{\ hx} c_{kj}^{\ hx} f_x^{\ \prime}(net_k^{\ x}) x$$

$$= \delta^{ol} * c_{kj}^{\ o} * \delta_{kj}^{\ hx} * c_{kj}^{\ hx} * f_x^{\ \prime}(net_k^{\ x}) * x$$

$$(175)$$

By combining Formulae (161), (164), and (175), for a linear 1st hidden layer neuron: For a function of x input side:

$$b_k^{\ x} = f_k^{\ x}(net_k^{\ x}) \quad f_x^{\ \prime}(net_k^{\ x}) = \partial b_k^{\ x} / \partial(net_k^{\ x})$$

$$c_k^{\ x}(t+1) = c_k^{\ x}(t) - \eta(\partial E_p / \partial c_k^{\ x})$$

$$= c_k^{\ x}(t) + \eta(d-z) f^{o\,\prime}(net^o) c_{kj}^{\ o} * f^{h\,\prime}(net_{kj}^{\ h}) c_{kj}^{\ hy} b_j^{\ y} c_{kj}^{\ hx} f_x^{\ \prime}(net_k^{\ x}) x$$

$$= c_k^{\ x}(t) + \eta * \delta^{ol} * c_{kj}^{\ o} * \delta^{hx} * c_{kj}^{\ hx} * \delta^x * x$$

$$(176)$$

where

$$\delta^{ol} = (d-z) f^{o\,\prime}(net^o) = d - z \,(linear\ neuron)$$

$$\delta^{hx} = f^{h\,\prime}(net_{kj}^{\ h}) c_{kj}^{\ hy} b_j^{\ y} = c_{kj}^{\ hy} b_j^{\ y} \,(linear\ neuron)$$

$$\delta^x = f_x^{\ \prime}(net_k^{\ x})$$

$$(177)$$

First Hidden Layer y Neurons in HONN (Model 1 and Model 2)

For the y input part, we have following formula as learning algorithm.
The 1st hidden layer weights are updated according to:

$$c_j^{\ y}(t+1) = c_j^{\ y}(t) - \eta(\partial E_p / \partial c_j^{\ y})$$

$$(178)$$

where:

$C_j^{\ y}$ = 1st hidden layer weight for input y; $j = j^{th}$ neuron of first hidden layer

η = learning rate (positive & usually < 1)

    E   = error

       t   = training time

The equations for the kth or j^{th} node in the first hidden layer are:

$$net_k^x = c_k^x * x \quad b_k^x = f_k^x\left(net_k^x\right) \text{ or } net_j^y = c_j^y * y \quad b_j^y = f_j^y\left(net_j^y\right)$$

(179)

Where:

i_{kj} = output from 2nd hidden layer (= input to the output neuron)

b_k^x and b_j^y= output from the 1st hidden layer neuron (= input to 2nd hidden layer neuron)

f_k^x and f_j^y =1st hidden layer neuron activation function

    x   and y = input to 1st hidden layer

The total error is the sum of the squared errors across all hidden units, namely:

$$E_p = 0.5 * \delta^2 = 0.5 * (d-z)^2 = 0.5 * (d - f^o\left(net^o\right))^2 = 0.5 * (d - f^o(\textstyle\sum_j c_{kj}^o i_{kj}))^2$$

(180)

The gradient is given by:

$$\partial E_p / \partial c_j^y = \partial(0.5 * \left(d-z\right)^2) / \partial c_j^y = (\partial\left(0.5 * \left(d-z\right)^2\right) / \partial z)\left(\partial z / \partial\left(net^o\right)\right)$$

$$\left(\partial\left(net^o\right) / \partial i_{kj}\right)\left(\partial i_{kj} / \partial\left(net_{kj}^h\right)\right)\left(\partial\left(net_{kj}^h\right) / \partial b_j^y\right)\left(\partial b_j^y / \partial\left(net_j^y\right)\right)\left(\partial\left(net_j^y\right) / \partial c_j^y\right)$$

(181)

$$\partial(0.5 * (d-z)^2 / \partial z = -\left(d-z\right)$$

(182)

$$\partial z / \partial\left(net^o\right) = \partial f^o / \partial\left(net^o\right) = f^{o'}\left(net^o\right)$$

(183)

$$\partial\left(net^o\right)/\partial i_{kj} = \partial(\sum_{k,j=1}^{l}\left(c_{kj}{}^o i_{kj}\right)/\partial i_{kj} = c_{kj}{}^o \tag{184}$$

$$\partial i_{kj}/\partial\left(net_{kj}{}^h\right) = \partial\left(f^h\left(net_{kj}{}^h\right)\right)/\partial\left(net_{kj}{}^h\right) = f^{h'}\left(net_{kj}{}^h\right) \tag{185}$$

$$\partial net_{kj}{}^h/\partial b_j{}^y = \partial\left(\left(c_{kj}{}^{hx}*b_k{}^x\right)*\left(c_{kj}{}^{hy}*b_j{}^y\right)\right)/\partial b_j{}^y$$
$$= c_{kj}{}^{hx}*c_{kj}{}^{hy}*b_k{}^x = \delta^{hy}c_{kj}{}^{hy} \quad where: \delta_{kj}{}^{hy} = c_{kj}{}^{hy}*b_k{}^x \tag{186}$$

$$\partial b_j{}^y/\partial\left(net_j{}^y\right) = f_y'\left(net_j{}^y\right) \tag{187}$$

$$\partial\left(net_j{}^y\right)/\partial c_j{}^y = \partial\left(c_j{}^y*y\right)/\partial c_j{}^y = y \tag{188}$$

Combining Formulae (182) through (188) the negative gradient is:

$$-\partial E_p/\partial c_k{}^x = \left(d-z\right)f^{o'}\left(net^o\right)c_{kj}{}^o * f^{h'}\left(net_{kj}{}^h\right)\delta_{kj}{}^{hy}c_{kj}{}^{hy}f_y'\left(net_j{}^y\right)y \tag{189}$$

The weight update equations are calculated as follows. For linear output neurons:

$$f^{o'}\left(net^o\right) = 1$$
$$\delta^{ol} = \left(d-z\right)f^{o'}\left(net^o\right) = \left(d-z\right) \tag{190}$$

For linear neurons of second hidden layer:

$$f^{h'}\left(net_{kj}{}^h\right) = 1 \tag{191}$$

The negative gradient is:

$$-\partial E_p / \partial c_j{}^y = (d-z) f^o{}'(net^o) c_{kj}{}^o * f^h{}'(net_{kj}{}^h) \delta_{kj}{}^{hy} c_{kj}{}^{hy} f_y{}'(net_j{}^y) y$$
$$= \delta^{ol} * c_{kj}{}^o * \delta_{kj}{}^{hy} * c_{kj}{}^{hy} * f_y{}'(net_j{}^y) * y$$

$$(192)$$

By combining Formulae (178), (181), and (192), for a linear 1st hidden layer neuron: For a function of *y* input part:

$$b_j{}^y = f_j{}^y(net_j{}^y)$$
$$f_y{}'(net_j{}^y) = \partial b_j{}^y / \partial(net_j{}^y)$$

$$(193)$$

Using the above procedure:

$$c_j{}^y(t+1) = c_j{}^y(t) - \eta(\partial E_p / \partial c_j{}^y)$$
$$= c_j{}^y(t) + \eta(d-z) f^o{}'(net^o) c_{kj}{}^o * f^h{}'(net_{kj}{}^h) c_{kj}{}^{hx} b_k{}^x c_{kj}{}^{hy} f_y{}'(net_j{}^y) y$$
$$= c_j{}^y(t) + \eta * \delta^{ol} * c_{kj}{}^o * \delta^{hy} * c_{kj}{}^{hy} * \delta^y * y$$

where

$$\delta^{ol} = (d-z) f^{o'}(net^o) = d-z \quad (linear\ neuron\ f^o{}'(net^o) = 1)$$
$$\delta^{hy} = f^{h'}(net_{kj}{}^h) c_{kj}{}^{hx} b_k{}^x = c_{kj}{}^{hx} b_k{}^x \quad (linear\ neuron\ f^h{}'(net_{kj}{}^h) = 1) \quad (194)$$
$$\delta^y = f_y{}'(net_j{}^y)$$

24 HONN MODELS LEARNING ALGORITHM AND WEIGHT UPDATE FORMULAE

PHONN Model First Layer Neuron Weights Learning Formula

$$Let: f_k^{\ x}\left(c_k^{\ x}x\right) = (c_k^{\ x}x)^k \tag{195}$$

$$f_j^{\ y}\left(c_j^{\ y}y\right) = (c_j^{\ y}y)^j \tag{196}$$

For a polynomial function of x input side:

$$b_k^{\ x} = f_k^{\ x}\left(net_k^{\ x}\right) = (net_k^{\ x})^k = (c_k^{\ x} * x)^k$$
$$f_x{}'\left(net_k^{\ x}\right) = \partial b_k^{\ x} / \partial\left(net_k^{\ x}\right) = \partial\left((net_k^{\ x})^k\right) / \partial\left(net_k^{\ x}\right) = k(net_k^{\ x})^{k-1} = k * (c_k^{\ x} * x)^{k-1} \tag{197}$$

$$c_k^{\ x}\left(t+1\right) = c_k^{\ x}\left(t\right) - \eta\left(\frac{\partial E_p}{\partial c_k^{\ x}}\right)$$
$$= c_k^{\ x}\left(t\right) + \eta\left(d-z\right) f^{o'}\left(net^o\right) c_{kj}^{\ o} * f^{h'}\left(net_{kj}^{\ h}\right) c_{kj}^{\ hy} b_j^{\ y} c_{kj}^{\ hx} f_x'\left(net_k^{\ x}\right) x$$
$$= c_k^{\ x}\left(t\right) + \eta * \delta^{ol} * c_{kj}^{\ o} * \delta^{hx} * c_{kj}^{\ hx} * k * (c_k^{\ x} * x)^{k-1} * x$$
$$= c_k^{\ x}\left(t\right) + \eta * \delta^{ol} * c_{kj}^{\ o} * \delta^{hx} * c_{kj}^{\ hx} * \delta^x * x \tag{198}$$

where

$$\delta^{ol} = \left(d-z\right) f^{o'}\left(net^o\right) = d - z \quad \left(linear\ neuron\ f^o{}'\left(net^o\right) = 1\right)$$

$$\delta^{hx} = f^{h'}\left(net_{kj}^{\ h}\right) c_{kj}^{\ hy} b_j^{\ y} = c_{kj}^{\ hy} b_j^{\ y} \quad \left(linear\ neuron\ f^h{}'\left(net_{kj}^{\ h}\right) = 1\right)$$

$$\delta^x = f_x'\left(net_k^{\ x}\right) = k * \left(net_k^{\ x}\right)^{k-1} = k * (c_k^{\ x} * x)^{k-1}$$

For a polynomial function of *y* input part:

$$b_j^y = f_j^y \left(net_j^y \right) = (net_j^y)^j = (c_j^y * y)^j$$

$$f_y '\left(net_j^y \right) = \partial b_j^y / \partial \left(net_j^y \right) = \partial \left(net_j^y)^j \right) / \partial \left(net_j^y \right) = j * (net_j^y)^{j-1} = j * (c_j^y * y)^{j-1}$$

$$(199)$$

Using the above procedure:

$$
\begin{aligned}
c_j^y(t+1) &= c_j^y(t) - \eta \left(\partial E_p / \partial c_j^y \right) \\
&= c_j^y(t) + \eta(d-z) f^o {}'\left(net^o \right) c_{kj}{}^o * f^h {}'\left(net_{kj}{}^h \right) c_{kj}{}^{hx} b_k{}^x c_{kj}{}^{hy} f_y {}'\left(net_j^y \right) y \\
&= c_j^y(t) + \eta * \delta^{ol} * c_{kj}{}^o * \delta^{hy} * c_{kj}{}^{hy} * j * (c_j^y * y)^{j-1} * y \\
&= c_j^y(t) + \eta * \delta^{ol} * c_{kj}{}^o * \delta^{hy} * c_{kj}{}^{hy} * \delta^y * y
\end{aligned}
$$

$$(200)$$

where

$$\delta^{ol} = (d-z) f^o {}'\left(net^o \right) = d - z \quad \left(linear\ neuron\ f^o {}'\left(net^o \right) = 1 \right)$$

$$\delta^{hy} = f^h {}'\left(net_{kj}{}^h \right) c_{kj}{}^{hx} b_k{}^x = c_{kj}{}^{hx} b_k{}^x \quad \left(linear\ neuron\ f^h {}'\left(net_{kj}{}^h \right) = 1 \right)$$

$$\delta^y = f_y {}'\left(net_j^y \right) = j * (c_j^y * y)^{j-1}$$

XSHONN Model First Layer Neuron Weights Learning Formula

Polynomial and Sine Higher Order Neural Network (XSHONN) model as follows:

$$Let: f_k^x \left(c_k^x x \right) = (c_k^x x)^k \tag{201}$$

$$f_j^y \left(c_j^y y \right) = \sin^j (c_j^y y) \tag{202}$$

For a polynomial function of *x* input side:

$$b_k^{\ x} = f_k^{\ x}\left(net_k^{\ x}\right) = (net_k^{\ x})^k = (c_k^{\ x} * x)^k$$

$$f_x'\left(net_k^{\ x}\right) = \partial b_k^{\ x} / \partial\left(net_k^{\ x}\right) = \partial\left(net_k^{\ x})^k\right) / \partial\left(net_k^{\ x}\right) = k(net_k^{\ x})^{k-1} = k*(c_k^{\ x}*x)^{k-1}$$

$$(203)$$

$$c_k^{\ x}\left(t+1\right) = c_k^{\ x}\left(t\right) - \eta\left(\partial E_p / \partial c_k^{\ x}\right)$$

$$= c_k^{\ x}\left(t\right) + \eta\left(d-z\right)f^{o'}\left(net^o\right)c_{kj}^{\ o} * f^{h'}\left(net_{kj}^{\ h}\right)c_{kj}^{\ hy}b_j^{\ y}c_{kj}^{\ hx}f_x'\left(net_k^{\ x}\right)x$$

$$= c_k^{\ x}\left(t\right) + \eta * \delta^{ol} * c_{kj}^{\ o} * \delta^{hx} * c_{kj}^{\ hx} * k*(c_k^{\ x}*x)^{k-1}*x$$

$$= c_k^{\ x}\left(t\right) + \eta * \delta^{ol} * c_{kj}^{\ o} * \delta^{hx} * c_{kj}^{\ hx} * \delta^x * x$$

$$(204)$$

where

$$\delta^{ol} = \left(d-z\right)f^{o'}\left(net^o\right) = d-z \quad \left(linear\ neuron\ f^{o\,'}\left(net^o\right)=1\right)$$

$$\delta^{hx} = f^{h'}\left(net_{kj}^{\ h}\right)c_{kj}^{\ hy}b_j^{\ y} = c_{kj}^{\ hy}b_j^{\ y} \quad \left(linear\ neuron\ f^{h\,'}\left(net_{kj}^{\ h}\right)=1\right)$$

$$\delta^x = f_x'\left(net_k^{\ x}\right) = k*\left(net_k^{\ x}\right)^{k-1} = k*(c_k^{\ x}*x)^{k-1}$$

For a sine function of *y* input part:

$$b_j^{\ y} = f_j^{\ y}\left(net_j^{\ y}\right) = \sin^j(net_j^{\ y}) = \sin^j(c_j^{\ y}*y)$$

$$f_y'\left(net_j^{\ y}\right) = \partial b_j^{\ y} / \partial\left(net_j^{\ y}\right) = \partial\left(\sin^j(net_j^{\ y})\right) / \partial\left(net_j^{\ y}\right) \qquad (205)$$

$$= j*\sin^{j-1}(net_j^{\ y})*\cos(net_j^{\ y}) = j*\sin^{j-1}(c_j^{\ y}*y)*\cos(c_j^{\ y}*y)$$

Using the above procedure:

$$c_j^{\ y}(t+1) = c_j^{\ y}(t) - \eta\left(\partial E_p / \partial c_j^{\ y}\right)$$

$$= c_j^{\ y}(t) + \eta(d-z)f^{o\,\prime}(net^o)c_{kj}^{\ o} * f^{h\,\prime}(net_{kj}^{\ h})c_{kj}^{\ hx}b_k^{\ x}c_{kj}^{\ hy}f_y^{\ \prime}(net_j^{\ y})y$$

$$= c_j^{\ y}(t) + \eta * \delta^{ol} * c_{kj}^{\ o} * \delta^{hy} * c_{kj}^{\ hy} * j * \sin^{j-1}(c_j^{\ y}*y)\cos(c_j^{\ y}*y)*y$$

$$= c_j^{\ y}(t) + \eta * \delta^{ol} * c_{kj}^{\ o} * \delta^{hy} * c_{kj}^{\ hy} * \delta^y * y$$

$$(206)$$

where

$$\delta^{ol} = (d-z)f^{o\,\prime}(net^o) = d-z \quad \left(linear\ neuron\ f^{o\,\prime}(net^o)=1\right)$$

$$\delta^{hy} = f^{h\,\prime}(net_{kj}^{\ h})c_{kj}^{\ hx}b_k^{\ x} = c_{kj}^{\ hx}b_k^{\ x} \quad \left(linear\ neuron\ f^{h\,\prime}(net_{kj}^{\ h})=1\right)$$

$$\delta^y = f_y^{\ \prime}(net_j^{\ y}) = j * \sin^{j-1}(c_j^{\ y}*y)\cos(c_j^{\ y}*y)$$

XCHONN Model First Layer Neuron Weights Learning Formula

Polynomial and Cosine Higher Order Neural Network (XCHONN) model as follows:

$$Let: f_k^{\ x}\left(c_k^{\ x}x\right) = (c_k^{\ x}x)^k \qquad (207)$$

$$f_j^{\ y}\left(c_j^{\ y}y\right) = \cos^j(c_j^{\ y}y) \qquad (208)$$

For a polynomial function of x input side:

$$b_k^{\ x} = f_k^{\ x}\left(net_k^{\ x}\right) = (net_k^{\ x})^k = (c_k^{\ x}*x)^k$$

$$f_x^{\ \prime}\left(net_k^{\ x}\right) = \partial b_k^{\ x} / \partial\left(net_k^{\ x}\right) = \partial\left((net_k^{\ x})^k\right) / \partial\left(net_k^{\ x}\right) = k(net_k^{\ x})^{k-1} = k*(c_k^{\ x}*x)^{k-1}$$

$$(209)$$

$$c_k^x(t+1) = c_k^x(t) - \eta\left(\partial E_p / \partial c_k^x\right)$$
$$= c_k^x(t) + \eta(d-z) f^{o'}\left(net^o\right) c_{kj}^o * f^{h'}\left(net_{kj}^h\right) c_{kj}^{hy} b_j^y c_{kj}^{hx} f_x'\left(net_k^x\right) x$$
$$= c_k^x(t) + \eta * \delta^{ol} * c_{kj}^o * \delta^{hx} * c_{kj}^{hx} * k * (c_k^x * x)^{k-1} * x$$
$$= c_k^x(t) + \eta * \delta^{ol} * c_{kj}^o * \delta^{hx} * c_{kj}^{hx} * \delta^x * x$$

$$(210)$$

where

$$\delta^{ol} = (d-z) f^{o'}\left(net^o\right) = d - z \quad \left(linear\ neuron\ f^{o\,'}\left(net^o\right) = 1\right)$$
$$\delta^{hx} = f^{h'}\left(net_{kj}^h\right) c_{kj}^{hy} b_j^y = c_{kj}^{hy} b_j^y \quad \left(linear\ neuron\ f^{h\,'}\left(net_{kj}^h\right) = 1\right)$$
$$\delta^x = f_x'\left(net_k^x\right) = k * \left(net_k^x\right)^{k-1} = k * (c_k^x * x)^{k-1}$$

For cosine function of *y* input part:

$$b_j^y = f_y\left(net_j^y\right) = \cos^j(net_j^y) = \cos^j(c_j^y * y)$$
$$f_y'\left(net_j^y\right) = \partial b_j^y / \partial\left(net_j^y\right) = \partial\left(\cos^j(net_j^y)\right) / \partial\left(net_j^y\right) = j\cos^{j-1}(net_j^y) * \left(-\sin(net_j^y)\right)$$
$$= (-j) * \cos^{j-1}(net_j^y) * \sin(net_j^y) = (-j) * \cos^{j-1}(c_j^y * y) * \sin(c_j^y * y)$$

$$(211)$$

Using the above procedure:

$$c_j^y(t+1) = c_j^y(t) - \eta\left(\partial E_p / \partial c_j^y\right)$$
$$= c_j^y(t) + \eta(d-z) f^{o\,'}\left(net^o\right) c_{kj}^o * f^{h\,'}\left(net_{kj}^h\right) c_{kj}^{hx} b_k^x c_{kj}^{hy} f_y\,'\left(net_j^y\right) y$$
$$= c_j^y(t) + \eta * \delta^{ol} * c_{kj}^o * \delta^{hy} * c_{kj}^{hy} * (-j) * \cos^{j-1}(c_j^y * y) * \sin(c_j^y * y) * y$$
$$= c_j^y(t) + \eta * \delta^{ol} * c_{kj}^o * \delta^{hy} * c_{kj}^{hy} * \delta^y * y$$

$$(212)$$

where

$$\delta^{ol} = (d-z) f^{o\,'}\left(net^{o}\right) = d-z \quad \left(linear\ neuron\ f^{o\,'}\left(net^{o}\right)=1\right)$$

$$\delta^{hy} = f^{h\,'}\left(net_{kj}{}^{h}\right) c_{kj}{}^{hx} b_{k}{}^{x} = c_{kj}{}^{hx} b_{k}{}^{x} \quad \left(linear\ neuron\ f^{h\,'}\left(net_{kj}{}^{h}\right)=1\right)$$

$$\delta^{y} = f_{y}{}'\left(net_{j}{}^{y}\right) = (-j)*\cos^{j-1}(c_{j}{}^{y}*y)*\sin(c_{j}{}^{y}*y)$$

SIN-HONN Model First Layer Neuron Weights Learning Formula

Sine Higher Order Neural Network (SIN-HONN) model as follows:

$$Let: f_{k}{}^{x}\left(c_{k}{}^{x}x\right) = \sin^{k}(c_{k}{}^{x}x) \tag{213}$$

$$f_{j}{}^{y}\left(c_{j}{}^{y}y\right) = \sin^{j}(c_{j}{}^{y}y) \tag{214}$$

For a sine function of x input side:

$$b_{k}{}^{x} = f_{k}{}^{x}\left(net_{k}{}^{x}\right) = \sin^{k}(net_{k}{}^{x}) = \sin^{k}(c_{k}{}^{x}*x)$$

$$f_{x}{}'\left(net_{k}{}^{x}\right) = \partial b_{k}{}^{x} / \partial\left(net_{k}{}^{x}\right)$$

$$= \partial\left(\sin^{k}(net_{k}{}^{x})\right) / \partial\left(net_{k}{}^{x}\right) = k*\sin^{k-1}(net_{k}{}^{x})*\cos(net_{k}{}^{x}) = k*\sin^{k-1}(c_{k}{}^{x}*x)*\cos(c_{k}{}^{x}*x)$$

$$\tag{215}$$

$$c_{k}{}^{x}(t+1) = c_{k}{}^{x}(t) - \eta\left(\partial E_{p} / \partial c_{k}{}^{x}\right)$$

$$= c_{k}{}^{x}(t) + \eta(d-z) f^{o\,'}\left(net^{o}\right) c_{kj}{}^{o} * f^{h\,'}\left(net_{kj}{}^{h}\right) c_{kj}{}^{hy} b_{j}{}^{y} c_{kj}{}^{hx} f_{x}{}'\left(net_{k}{}^{x}\right) x$$

$$= c_{k}{}^{x}(t) + \eta * \delta^{ol} * c_{kj}{}^{o} * \delta^{hx} * c_{kj}{}^{hx} * k * \sin^{k-1}(c_{k}{}^{x}*x)\cos(c_{k}{}^{x}*x)*x$$

$$= c_{k}{}^{x}(t) + \eta * \delta^{ol} * c_{kj}{}^{o} * \delta^{hx} * c_{kj}{}^{hx} * \delta^{x} * x$$

$$\tag{216}$$

where

$$\delta^{ol} = (d-z) f^{o\prime}\left(net^o\right) = d-z \quad \left(linear\ neuron\ f^{o\,\prime}\left(net^o\right)=1\right)$$

$$\delta^{hx} = f^{h\prime}\left(net_{kj}{}^h\right) c_{kj}{}^{hy} b_j{}^y = c_{kj}{}^{hy} b_j{}^y \quad \left(linear\ neuron\ f^{h\,\prime}\left(net_{kj}{}^h\right)=1\right)$$

$$\delta^x = f_x^{\prime}\left(net_k{}^x\right) = k*\left(net_k{}^x\right)^{k-1} = k*\sin^{k-1}(c_k{}^x * x)*\cos(c_k{}^x * x)$$

For a sine function of *y* input part:

$$b_j{}^y = f_j{}^y\left(net_j{}^y\right) = \sin^j(net_j{}^y) = \sin^j(c_j{}^y * y)$$

$$f_y^{\prime}\left(net_j{}^y\right) = \partial b_j{}^y / \partial\left(net_j{}^y\right)$$

$$= \partial\left(\sin^j(net_j{}^y)\right)/\partial\left(net_j{}^y\right) = j*\sin^{j-1}(net_j{}^y)*\cos(net_j{}^y) = j*\sin^{j-1}(c_j{}^y * y)*\cos(c_j{}^y * y)$$

$$(217)$$

Using the above procedure:

$$c_j{}^y(t+1) = c_j{}^y(t) - \eta\left(\partial E_p / \partial c_j{}^y\right)$$

$$= c_j{}^y(t) + \eta(d-z) f^{o\prime}\left(net^o\right) c_{kj}{}^o * f^{h\prime}\left(net_{kj}{}^h\right) c_{kj}{}^{hx} b_k{}^x c_{kj}{}^{hy} f_y^{\prime}\left(net_j{}^y\right) y$$

$$= c_j{}^y(t) + \eta*\delta^{ol} * c_{kj}{}^o * \delta^{hy} * c_{kj}{}^{hy} * j*\sin^{j-1}(c_j{}^y * y)\cos(c_j{}^y * y)*y$$

$$= c_j{}^y(t) + \eta*\delta^{ol} * c_{kj}{}^o * \delta^{hy} * c_{kj}{}^{hy} * \delta^y * y$$

$$(218)$$

where

$$\delta^{ol} = (d-z) f^{o\prime}\left(net^o\right) = d-z \quad \left(linear\ neuron\ f^{o\,\prime}\left(net^o\right)=1\right)$$

$$\delta^{hy} = f^{h\prime}\left(net_{kj}{}^h\right) c_{kj}{}^{hx} b_k{}^x = c_{kj}{}^{hx} b_k{}^x \quad \left(linear\ neuron\ f^{h\,\prime}\left(net_{kj}{}^h\right)=1\right)$$

$$\delta^y = f_y^{\prime}\left(net_j{}^y\right) = j*\sin^{j-1}(c_j{}^y * y)*\cos(c_j{}^y * y)$$

COS-HONN Model First Layer Neuron Weights Learning Formula

Cosine Higher Order Neural Network (COS-HONN) model as follows:

$$Let: f_k^x\left(c_k^x x\right) = \cos^k(c_k^x x) \tag{219}$$

$$f_j^y\left(c_j^y y\right) = \cos^j(c_j^y y) \tag{220}$$

For a cosine function of x input side:

$$b_k^x = f_k^x\left(net_k^x\right) = \cos^k(net_k^x) = \cos^k(c_k^x * x)$$
$$f_x'\left(net_k^x\right) = \partial b_k^x / \partial\left(net_k^x\right) = \partial\left(\cos^k(net_k^x)\right) / \partial\left(net_k^x\right)$$
$$= k * \cos^{k-1}(net_k^x) * \left(-\sin(net_k^x)\right) = (-k) * \cos^{k-1}(c_k^x * x) * \sin(c_k^x * x) \tag{221}$$

$$c_k^x(t+1) = c_k^x(t) - \eta\left(\partial E_p / \partial c_k^x\right)$$
$$= c_k^x(t) + \eta(d-z) f^o{}'\left(net^o\right)c_{kj}^o * f^h{}'\left(net_{kj}^h\right)c_{kj}^{hy}b_j^y c_{kj}^{hx} f_x{}'\left(net_k^x\right)x$$
$$= c_k^x(t) + \eta * \delta^{ol} * c_{kj}^o * \delta^{hx} * c_{kj}^{hx} * (-k) * \cos^{k-1}(c_k^x * x) * \sin(c_k^x * x) * x$$
$$= c_k^x(t) + \eta * \delta^{ol} * c_{kj}^o * \delta^{hx} * c_{kj}^{hx} * \delta^x * x \tag{222}$$

where

$$\delta^{ol} = (d-z) f^o{}'\left(net^o\right) = d-z \quad \left(linear\ neuron\ f^o{}'\left(net^o\right) = 1\right)$$
$$\delta^{hx} = f^h{}'\left(net_{kj}^h\right)c_{kj}^{hy}b_j^y = c_{kj}^{hy}b_j^y \quad \left(linear\ neuron\ f^h{}'\left(net_{kj}^h\right) = 1\right)$$
$$\delta^x = f_x'\left(net_k^x\right) = (-k) * \cos^{k-1}\left(net_k^x\right) * \sin\left(net_k^x\right) = (-k) * \cos^{k-1}(c_k^x * x) * \sin(c_k^x * x)$$

For cosine function of y input part:

$$b_j^y = f_y\left(net_j^y\right) = \cos^j(net_j^y) = \cos^j(c_j^y * y)$$

$$f_y{}'\left(net_j^y\right) = \partial b^y{}_j / \partial\left(net_j^y\right)$$

$$= \partial\left(\cos^j(net_j^y)\right) / \partial\left(net_j^y\right) = j\cos^{j-1}(net_j^y) * \left(-\sin(net_j^y)\right)$$

$$= (-j) * \cos^{j-1}(net_j^y) * \sin(net_j^y) = (-j) * \cos^{j-1}(c_j^y * y) * \sin(c_j^y * y)$$

$$(223)$$

Using the above procedure:

$$c_j^y(t+1) = c_j^y(t) - \eta\left(\partial E_p / \partial c_j^y\right)$$

$$= c_j^y(t) + \eta(d-z) f^o{}'\left(net^o\right) c_{kj}^o * f^h{}'\left(net_{kj}^h\right) c_{kj}^{hx} b_k^x c_{kj}^{hy} f_y{}'\left(net_j^y\right) y$$

$$= c_j^y(t) + \eta * \delta^{ol} * c_{kj}^o * \delta^{hy} * c_{kj}^{hy} * \delta^y * y$$

$$(224)$$

where

$$\delta^{ol} = (d-z) f^{o'}\left(net^o\right) = d - z \qquad \left(linear\ neuron\ f^o{}'\left(net^o\right) = 1\right)$$

$$\delta^{hy} = f^{h'}\left(net_{kj}^h\right) c_{kj}^{hx} b_k^x = c_{kj}^{hx} b_k^x \qquad \left(linear\ neuron\ f^h{}'\left(net_{kj}^h\right) = 1\right)$$

$$\delta^y = f_y{}'\left(net_j^y\right) = (-j) * \cos^{j-1}(c_j^y * y) * \sin(c_j^y * y)$$

THONN Model First Layer Neuron Weights Learning Formula

Let:

$$f_k^x\left(c_k^x x\right) = \sin^k(c_k^x x)$$

$$(225)$$

$$f_j^y\left(c_j^y y\right) = \cos^j(c_j^y y)$$

$$(226)$$

For a sine function of x input side:

$$b_k^{\ x} = f_k^{\ x}\left(net_k^{\ x}\right) = \sin^k(net_k^{\ x}) = \sin^k(c_k^{\ x} * x)^k$$

$$f_x{}'\left(net_k^{\ x}\right) = \partial b_k^{\ x} / \partial\left(net_k^{\ x}\right) = \partial\left(\sin^k(net_k^{\ x})\right) / \partial\left(net_k^{\ x}\right) \qquad (227)$$

$$= k * \sin^{k-1}(net_k^{\ x}) * \cos(net_k^{\ x}) = k * \sin^{k-1}(c_k^{\ x} * x) * \cos(c_k^{\ x} * x)$$

$$c_k^{\ x}(t+1) = c_k^{\ x}(t) - \eta\left(\partial E_p / \partial c_k^{\ x}\right)$$

$$= c_k^{\ x}(t) + \eta(d-z) f^o{}'\left(net^o\right) c_{kj}^{\ o} * f^h{}'\left(net_{kj}^{\ h}\right) c_{kj}^{\ hy} b_j^{\ y} c_{kj}^{\ hx} f_x{}'\left(net_k^{\ x}\right) x$$

$$= c_k^{\ x}(t) + \eta * \delta^{ol} * c_{kj}^{\ o} * \delta^{hx} * c_{kj}^{\ hx} * k * \sin^{k-1}(c_k^{\ x} * x)\cos(c_k^{\ x} * x) * x$$

$$= c_k^{\ x}(t) + \eta * \delta^{ol} * c_{kj}^{\ o} * \delta^{hx} * c_{kj}^{\ hx} * \delta^x * x$$

$$\qquad (228)$$

where

$$\delta^{ol} = (d-z) f^{o'}\left(net^o\right) = d-z \qquad \left(linear\ neuron\ f^o{}'\left(net^o\right)=1\right)$$

$$\delta^{hx} = f^{h'}\left(net_{kj}^{\ h}\right) c_{kj}^{\ hy} b_j^{\ y} = c_{kj}^{\ hy} b_j^{\ y} \qquad \left(linear\ neuron\ f^h{}'\left(net_{kj}^{\ h}\right)=1\right)$$

$$\delta^x = f_x'\left(net_k^{\ x}\right) = k * \left(net_k^{\ x}\right)^{k-1} = k * \sin^{k-1}(c_k^{\ x} * x) * \cos(c_k^{\ x} * x)$$

For cosine function of y input part:

$$b_j^{\ y} = f_y\left(net_j^{\ y}\right) = \cos^j(net_j^{\ y}) = \cos^j(c_j^{\ y} * y)$$

$$f_y{}'\left(net_j^{\ y}\right) = \partial b^y{}_j / \partial\left(net_j^{\ y}\right) = \partial\left(\cos^j(net_j^{\ y})\right) / \partial\left(net_j^{\ y}\right) \qquad (229)$$

$$= j\cos^{j-1}(net_j^{\ y}) * \left(-\sin(net_j^{\ y})\right) = (-j) * \cos^{j-1}(net_j^{\ y}) * \sin(net_j^{\ y})$$

$$= (-j) * \cos^{j-1}(c_j^{\ y} * y) * \sin(c_j^{\ y} * y)$$

Using the above procedure:

$$c_j^{\ y}(t+1) = c_j^{\ y}(t) - \eta\left(\partial E_p / \partial c_j^{\ y}\right)$$

$$= c_j^{\ y}(t) + \eta(d-z)f^{o}{}'(net^o)c_{kj}^{\ o} * f^{h}{}'\left(net_{kj}^{\ h}\right)c_{kj}^{\ hx}b_k^{\ x}c_{kj}^{\ hy}f_y{}'\left(net_j^{\ y}\right)y$$

$$= c_j^{\ y}(t) + \eta * \delta^{ol} * c_{kj}^{\ o} * \delta^{hy} * c_{kj}^{\ hy} * (-j) * \cos^{j-1}(c_j^{\ y} * y) * \sin(c_j^{\ y} * y) * y$$

$$= c_j^{\ y}(t) + \eta * \delta^{ol} * c_{kj}^{\ o} * \delta^{hy} * c_{kj}^{\ hy} * \delta^{y} * y$$

$$(230)$$

where

$$\delta^{ol} = (d-z)f^{o}{}'(net^o) = d - z \quad \left(linear\ neuron\ f^{o}{}'(net^o) = 1\right)$$

$$\delta^{hy} = f^{h}{}'\left(net_{kj}^{\ h}\right)c_{kj}^{\ hx}b_k^{\ x} = c_{kj}^{\ hx}b_k^{\ x} \quad \left(linear\ neuron\ f^{h}{}'\left(net_{kj}^{\ h}\right) = 1\right)$$

$$\delta^{y} = f_y{}'\left(net_j^{\ y}\right) = (-j) * \cos^{j-1}(c_j^{\ y} * y) * \sin(c_j^{\ y} * y)$$

SINCHONN Model First Layer Neuron Weights Learning Formula

Let

$$f_k^{\ x}\left(c_k^{\ x}x\right) = \left(\sin(c_k^{\ x}x)/\left(c_k^{\ x}x\right)\right)^k \tag{231}$$

$$f_j^{\ y}\left(c_j^{\ y}y\right) = \left(\sin(c_j^{\ y}y)/\left(c_k^{\ x}y\right)\right)^j \tag{232}$$

For a SINC function of x input part:

$$b_k^{\ x} = f_k^{\ x}\left(net_k^{\ x}\right) = \left[\sin(net_k^{\ x})/net_k^{\ x}\right]^k = \left[\sin(c_k^{\ x}x)/c_k^{\ x}x\right]^k$$

$$f_x'\left(net_k^{\ x}\right) = \partial b_k^{\ x} / \partial\left(net_k^{\ x}\right)$$

$$= k\left[\sin(net_k^{\ x})/\left(net_k^{\ x}\right)\right]^{k-1} * \left[\cos(net_k^{\ x})/\left(net_k^{\ x}\right) - \sin(net_k^{\ x})/\left(net_k^{\ x}\right)^2\right]$$

$$= k\left[\sin(c_k^{\ x}x)/\left(c_k^{\ k}x\right)\right]^{k-1} * \left[\cos(c_k^{\ x}x)/\left(c_k^{\ x}x\right) - \sin(c_k^{\ x}x)/\left(c_k^{\ x}x\right)^2\right]$$

$$(233)$$

$$c_k^{\ x}(t+1) = c_k^{\ x}(t) - \eta\left(\partial E_p / \partial c_k^{\ x}\right)$$

$$= c_k^{\ x}(t) + \eta(d-z)f^{o'}\left(net^o\right)c_{kj}^{\ o} * f^{h'}\left(net_{kj}^{\ h}\right)c_{kj}^{\ hy}b_j^{\ y}c_{kj}^{\ hx}f_x'\left(net_k^{\ x}\right)x$$

$$= c_k^{\ x}(t) + \eta * \delta^{ol} * c_{kj}^{\ o} * \delta^{hx} * c_{kj}^{\ hx} * f_x'\left(net_k^{\ x}\right) * x$$

$$= c_k^{\ x}(t) + \eta * \delta^{ol} * c_{kj}^{\ o} * \delta^{hx} * c_{kj}^{\ hx} * \left[k\left[\sin(c_k^{\ x}x)/\left(c_k^{\ k}x\right)\right]^{k-1} * \left[\cos(c_k^{\ x}x)/\left(c_k^{\ x}x\right)\right.\right.$$

$$\left.\left.-\sin(c_k^{\ x}x)/\left(c_k^{\ k}x\right)^2\right]\right] * x = c_k^{\ x}(t) + \eta * \delta^{ol} * c_{kj}^{\ o} * \delta^{hx} * c_{kj}^{\ hx} * \delta^x * x$$

$$(234)$$

where

$$\delta^{ol} = (d-z)f^{o'}\left(net^o\right) = (d-z) \qquad \left(linear\ neuron\ f^{o\,\prime}\left(net^o\right) = 1\right)$$

$$\delta^{hx} = f^{h'}\left(net_{kj}^{\ h}\right)c_{kj}^{\ hy}b_j^{\ y} = c_{kj}^{\ hy}b_j^{\ y} \qquad \left(linear\ neuron\ f^{h\,\prime}\left(net_{kj}^{\ h}\right) = 1\right)$$

$$\delta^x = f_x'\left(net_k^{\ x}\right)$$

$$= k\left[\sin(net_k^{\ x})/\left(net_k^{\ x}\right)\right]^{k-1} * \left[\cos(net_k^{\ x})/\left(net_k^{\ x}\right) - \sin(net_k^{\ x})/\left(net_k^{\ x}\right)^2\right]$$

$$= k\left[\sin(c_k^{\ x}x)/\left(c_k^{\ x}x\right)\right]^{k-1} * \left[\cos(c_k^{\ x}x)/\left(c_k^{\ x}x\right) - \sin(c_k^{\ x}x)/\left(c_k^{\ x}x\right)^2\right]$$

For a SINC function of *y* input part:

$$b_j^y = f_j^y\left(net_j^y\right) = \left[\sin(net_j^y)/net_j^y\right]^j = \left[\sin(c_j^y y)/c_j^y y\right]^j$$

$$f_y'\left(net_j^y\right) = \partial b_j^y / \partial\left(net_j^y\right)$$

$$= j\left[\sin(net_j^y)/\left(net_j^y\right)\right]^{j-1} * \left[\cos(net_j^y)/\left(net_j^y\right) - \sin(net_j^y)/\left(net_j^y\right)^2\right]$$

$$= j\left[\sin(c_j^y y)/\left(c_j^y y\right)\right]^{j-1} * \left[\cos(c_j^y y)/\left(c_j^y y\right) - \sin(c_j^y y)/\left(c_j^y y\right)^2\right]$$

$$(235)$$

Using above procedure:

$$c_j^y(t+1) = c_j^y(t) - \eta\left(\partial E_p / \partial c_j^y\right)$$

$$= c_j^y(t) + \eta(d-z)f^{o'}\left(net^o\right)c_{kj}^o * f^{h}{}'\left(net_{kj}^h\right)c_{kj}^{hx}b_k^x c_{kj}^{hy}f_y'\left(net_j^y\right)y$$

$$= c_j^y(t) + \eta * \delta^{ol} * c_{kj}^o * \delta^{hy} * c_{kj}^{hy} * f_y'\left(net_j^y\right) * y$$

$$= c_j^y(t) + \eta * \delta^{ol} * c_{kj}^o * \delta^{hy} * c_{kj}^{hy} * \left[j\left[\sin(c_j^y y)/\left(c_j^y y\right)\right]^{j-1} * \left[\cos(c_j^y y)/\left(c_j^y y\right)\right.\right.$$

$$\left.\left. -\sin(c_j^y y)/\left(c_j^y y\right)^2\right]\right] * y = c_j^y(t) + \eta * \delta^{ol} * c_{kj}^o * \delta^{hy} * c_{kj}^{hy} * \delta^y * y$$

$$(236)$$

where

$$\delta^{ol} = (d-z)f^{o'}\left(net^o\right) = (d-z) \qquad \left(linear\ neuron\ f^{o}{}'\left(net^o\right) = 1\right)$$

$$\delta^{hy} = f^{h'}\left(net_{kj}^h\right)c_{kj}^{hx}b_k^x = c_{kj}^{hx}b_k^x \qquad \left(linear\ neuron\ f^{h}{}'\left(net_{kj}^h\right) = 1\right)$$

$$\delta^y = f_y'\left(net_j^y\right)$$

$$= j\left[\sin(net_j^y)/\left(net_j^y\right)\right]^{j-1} * \left[\cos(net_j^y)/\left(net_j^y\right) - \sin(net_j^y)/\left(net_j^y\right)^2\right]$$

$$= j\left[\sin(c_j^y y)/\left(c_j^y y\right)\right]^{j-1} * \left[\cos(c_j^y y)/\left(c_j^y y\right) - \sin(c_j^y y)/\left(c_j^y y\right)^2\right]$$

SSINCHONN Model First Layer Neuron Weights Learning Formula

$$Let : f_k^x\left(c_k^x x\right)=\left(\sin(c_k^x x)\right)^k \tag{237}$$

$$f_j^y\left(c_j^y y\right)=\left(\sin(c_j^y y)/\left(c_k^x y\right)\right)^j \tag{238}$$

For a sine function of x input side:

$$b_k^x = f_k^x\left(net_k^x\right)=\sin^k(net_k^x)=\sin^k(c_k^x * x)^k$$
$$f_x{}'\left(net_k^x\right)=\partial b_k^x / \partial\left(net_k^x\right)$$
$$=\partial\left(\sin^k(net_k^x)\right)/\partial\left(net_k^x\right)=k*\sin^{k-1}(net_k^x)*\cos(net_k^x) \tag{239}$$
$$=k*\sin^{k-1}(c_k^x * x)*\cos(c_k^x * x)$$

$$c_k^x\left(t+1\right)=c_k^x\left(t\right)-\eta\left(\partial E_p / \partial c_k^x\right)$$
$$=c_k^x\left(t\right)+\eta\left(d-z\right)f^o{}'\left(net^o\right)c_{kj}^o * f^h{}'\left(net_{kj}^h\right)c_{kj}^{hy} b_j^y c_{kj}^{hx} f_x{}'\left(net_k^x\right)x$$
$$=c_k^x\left(t\right)+\eta*\delta^{ol}*c_{kj}^o*\delta^{hx}*c_{kj}^{hx}*k*\sin^{k-1}(c_k^x * x)\cos(c_k^x * x)*x$$
$$=c_k^x\left(t\right)+\eta*\delta^{ol}*c_{kj}^o*\delta^{hx}*c_{kj}^{hx}*\delta^x * x$$
$$\tag{240}$$

where

$$\delta^{ol}=\left(d-z\right)f^o{}'\left(net^o\right)=d-z \qquad \left(linear\,neuron\ f^o{}'\left(net^o\right)=1\right)$$
$$\delta^{hx}=f^h{}'\left(net_{kj}^h\right)c_{kj}^{hy} b_j^y = c_{kj}^{hy} b_j^y \qquad \left(linear\,neuron\ f^h{}'\left(net_{kj}^h\right)=1\right)$$
$$\delta^x = f_x'\left(net_k^x\right)=k*\left(net_k^x\right)^{k-1}=k*\sin^{k-1}(c_k^x * x)*\cos(c_k^x * x)$$

For a SINC function of y input part:

$$b_j^y = f_j^y \left(net_j^y \right) = \left[\sin(net_j^y) / net_j^y \right]^j = \left[\sin(c_j^y y) / c_j^y y \right]^j$$

$$f_y' \left(net_j^y \right) = \partial b_j^y / \partial \left(net_j^y \right)$$

$$= j \left[\sin(net_j^y) / \left(net_j^y \right) \right]^{j-1} * \left[\cos(net_j^y) / \left(net_j^y \right) - \sin(net_j^y) / \left(net_j^y \right)^2 \right]$$

$$= j \left[\sin(c_j^y y) / \left(c_j^y y \right) \right]^{j-1} * \left[\cos(c_j^y y) / \left(c_j^y y \right) - \sin(c_j^y y) / \left(c_j^y y \right)^2 \right]$$

$$(241)$$

Using above procedure:

$$c_j^y (t+1) = c_j^y (t) - \eta \left(\partial E_p / \partial c_j^y \right)$$

$$= c_j^y (t) + \eta (d-z) f^o{}' \left(net^o \right) c_{kj}^o * f^h{}' \left(net_{kj}^h \right) c_{kj}^{hx} b_k^x c_{kj}^{hy} f_y{}' \left(net_j^y \right) y$$

$$= c_j^y (t) + \eta * \delta^{ol} * c_{kj}^o * \delta^{hy} * c_{kj}^{hy} * f_y{}' \left(net_j^y \right) * y = c_j^y (t) + \eta * \delta^{ol} * c_{kj}^o * \delta^{hy} * c_{kj}^{hy}$$

$$* \left[j \left[\sin(c_j^y y) / \left(c_j^y y \right) \right]^{j-1} * \left[\cos(c_j^y y) / \left(c_j^y y \right) - \sin(c_j^y y) / \left(c_j^y y \right)^2 \right] \right] * y$$

$$= c_j^y (t) + \eta * \delta^{ol} * c_{kj}^o * \delta^{hy} * c_{kj}^{hy} * \delta^y * y$$

$$(242)$$

where

$$\delta^{ol} = (d-z) f^o{}' \left(net^o \right) = (d-z) \qquad \left(linear\ neuron\ f^o{}' \left(net^o \right) = 1 \right)$$

$$\delta^{hy} = f^h{}' \left(net_{kj}^h \right) c_{kj}^{hx} b_k^x = c_{kj}^{hx} b_k^x \qquad \left(linear\ neuron\ f^h{}' \left(net_{kj}^h \right) = 1 \right)$$

$$\delta^y = f_y{}' \left(net_j^y \right)$$

$$= j \left[\sin(net_j^y) / \left(net_j^y \right) \right]^{j-1} * \left[\cos(net_j^y) / \left(net_j^y \right) - \sin(net_j^y) / \left(net_j^y \right)^2 \right]$$

$$= j \left[\sin(c_j^y y) / \left(c_j^y y \right) \right]^{j-1} * \left[\cos(c_j^y y) / \left(c_j^y y \right) - \sin(c_j^y y) / \left(c_j^y y \right)^2 \right]$$

CSINCHONN Model First Layer Neuron Weights Learning Formula

$$Let: f_k^x \left(c_k^x x \right) = \left(\cos(c_k^x x) \right)^k \tag{243}$$

$$f_j^y \left(c_j^y y \right) = \left(\sin(c_j^y y) / \left(c_k^x y \right) \right)^j \tag{244}$$

For a cosine function of x input side:

$$b_k^x = f_k^x \left(net_k^x \right) = \cos^k (net_k^x) = \cos^k (c_k^x * x)$$

$$f_x'\left(net_k^x \right) = \partial b_k^x / \partial \left(net_k^x \right)$$

$$= \partial \left(\cos^k (net_k^x) \right) / \partial \left(net_k^x \right) = k * \cos^{k-1}(net_k^x) * \left(-\sin(net_k^x) \right) \tag{245}$$

$$= (-k) * \cos^{k-1}(c_k^x * x) * \sin(c_k^x * x)$$

$$c_k^x \left(t+1 \right) = c_k^x \left(t \right) - \eta \left(\partial E_p / \partial c_k^x \right)$$

$$= c_k^x \left(t \right) + \eta \left(d-z \right) f^o{}'\left(net^o \right) c_{kj}^o * f^h{}'\left(net_{kj}^h \right) c_{kj}^{hy} b_j^y c_{kj}^{hx} f_x'\left(net_k^x \right) x$$

$$= c_k^x \left(t \right) + \eta * \delta^{ol} * c_{kj}^o * \delta^{hx} * c_{kj}^{hx} * (-k) * \cos^{k-1}(c_k^x * x) * \sin(c_k^x * x) * x$$

$$= c_k^x \left(t \right) + \eta * \delta^{ol} * c_{kj}^o * \delta^{hx} * c_{kj}^{hx} * \delta^x * x$$

$$\tag{246}$$

where

$$\delta^{ol} = (d-z) f^o{}'\left(net^o \right) = d-z \qquad \left(linear\ neuron\ f^o{}'\left(net^o \right) = 1 \right)$$

$$\delta^{hx} = f^h{}'\left(net_{kj}^h \right) c_{kj}^{hy} b_j^y = c_{kj}^{hy} b_j^y \qquad \left(linear\ neuron\ f^h{}'\left(net_{kj}^h \right) = 1 \right)$$

$$\delta^x = f_x'\left(net_k^x \right) = (-k) * \cos^{k-1}\left(net_k^x \right) * \sin\left(net_k^x \right) = (-k) * \cos^{k-1}(c_k^x * x) * \sin(c_k^x * x)$$

For a SINC function of y input part:

$$b_j^{\,y} = f_j^{\,y}\left(net_j^{\,y}\right) = \frac{\left[\sin(net_j^{\,y})\right.}{net_j^{\,y}\,]^j} = \frac{\left[\sin(c_j^{\,y}y)\right.}{c_j^{\,y}y\,]^j}$$

$$f_y'\left(net_j^{\,y}\right) = \frac{\partial b_j^{\,y}}{\partial\left(net_j^{\,y}\right)}$$

$$= j\left[\sin(net_j^{\,y})/\left(net_j^{\,y}\right)\right]^{j-1} * \left[\cos(net_j^{\,y})/\left(net_j^{\,y}\right) - \sin(net_j^{\,y})/\left(net_j^{\,y}\right)^2\right]$$

$$= j\left[\sin(c_j^{\,y}y)/\left(c_j^{\,y}y\right)\right]^{j-1} * \left[\cos(c_j^{\,y}y)/\left(c_j^{\,y}y\right) - \sin(c_j^{\,y}y)/\left(c_j^{\,y}y\right)^2\right]$$

$$(247)$$

Using above procedure:

$$c_j^{\,y}(t+1) = c_j^{\,y}(t) - \eta\left(\partial E_p / \partial c_j^{\,y}\right)$$

$$= c_j^{\,y}(t) + \eta\,(d-z)\,f^{o\,'}\left(net^o\right)c_{kj}^{\,o} * f^{h\,'}\left(net_{kj}^{\,h}\right)c_{kj}^{\,hx}b_k^{\,x}c_{kj}^{\,hy}f_y'\left(net_j^{\,y}\right)y$$

$$= c_j^{\,y}(t) + \eta * \delta^{ol} * c_{kj}^{\,o} * \delta^{hy} * c_{kj}^{\,hy} * f_y'\left(net_j^{\,y}\right) * y = c_j^{\,y}(t) + \eta * \delta^{ol} * c_{kj}^{\,o} * \delta^{hy} * c_{kj}^{\,hy}$$

$$* [\,j[\sin(c_j^{\,y}y)/\left(c_j^{\,y}y\right)]^{j-1} * \left[\cos(c_j^{\,y}y)/\left(c_j^{\,y}y\right) - \sin(c_j^{\,y}y)/\left(c_j^{\,y}y\right)^2\right]\,] * y$$

$$= c_j^{\,y}(t) + \eta * \delta^{ol} * c_{kj}^{\,o} * \delta^{hy} * c_{kj}^{\,hy} * \delta^{y} * y$$

$$(248)$$

where

$$\delta^{ol} = (d-z)\,f^{o\,'}\left(net^o\right) = (d-z) \qquad \left(linear\ neuron\ f^{o\,'}\left(net^o\right) = 1\right)$$

$$\delta^{hy} = f^{h\,'}\left(net_{kj}^{\,h}\right)c_{kj}^{\,hx}b_k^{\,x} = c_{kj}^{\,hx}b_k^{\,x} \qquad \left(linear\ neuron\ f^{h\,'}\left(net_{kj}^{\,h}\right) = 1\right)$$

$$\delta^{y} = f_y'\left(net_j^{\,y}\right)$$

$$= j\left[\sin(net_j^{\,y})/\left(net_j^{\,y}\right)\right]^{j-1} * \left[\cos(net_j^{\,y})/\left(net_j^{\,y}\right) - \sin(net_j^{\,y})/\left(net_j^{\,y}\right)^2\right]$$

$$= j\left[\sin(c_j^{\,y}y)/\left(c_j^{\,y}y\right)\right]^{j-1} * \left[\cos(c_j^{\,y}y)/\left(c_j^{\,y}y\right) - \sin(c_j^{\,y}y)/\left(c_j^{\,y}y\right)^2\right]$$

YSINCHONN Model First Layer Neuron Weights Learning Formula

$$Let: f_k^x\left(c_k^x x\right) = (c_k^x x)^k \tag{249}$$

$$f_j^y\left(c_j^y y\right) = \left(\sin(c_j^y y)/\left(c_k^x y\right)\right)^j \tag{250}$$

For a polynomial function of x input side:

$$b_k^x = f_k^x\left(net_k^x\right) = (net_k^x)^k = (c_k^x * x)^k$$
$$f_x{}'\left(net_k^x\right) = \partial b_k^x / \partial\left(net_k^x\right) = \partial\left(net_k^x)^k\right)/\partial\left(net_k^x\right) = k(net_k^x)^{k-1} = k*(c_k^x * x)^{k-1}$$
$$\tag{251}$$

$$
\begin{aligned}
c_k^x\left(t+1\right) &= c_k^x\left(t\right) - \eta\left(\partial E_p / \partial c_k^x\right)\\
&= c_k^x\left(t\right) + \eta\left(d-z\right)f^{o'}\left(net^o\right)c_{kj}^o * f^{h'}\left(net_{kj}^h\right)c_{kj}^{hy}b_j^y c_{kj}^{hx}f_x'\left(net_k^x\right)x\\
&= c_k^x\left(t\right) + \eta*\delta^{ol}*c_{kj}^o*\delta^{hx}*c_{kj}^{hx}*k*(c_k^x * x)^{k-1}*x\\
&= c_k^x\left(t\right) + \eta*\delta^{ol}*c_{kj}^o*\delta^{hx}*c_{kj}^{hx}*\delta^x*x
\end{aligned}
\tag{252}
$$

where

$$\delta^{ol} = \left(d-z\right)f^{o'}\left(net^o\right) = d-z \qquad \left(linear\ neuron\ f^{o\ '}\left(net^o\right)=1\right)$$
$$\delta^{hx} = f^{h'}\left(net_{kj}^h\right)c_{kj}^{hy}b_j^y = c_{kj}^{hy}b_j^y \qquad \left(linear\ neuron\ f^{h\ '}\left(net_{kj}^h\right)=1\right)$$
$$\delta^x = f_x'\left(net_k^x\right) = k*\left(net_k^x\right)^{k-1} = k*(c_k^x * x)^{k-1}$$

For a SINC function of y input part:

$$b_j^y = f_j^y \left(net_j^y \right) = \left[\sin(net_j^y) / net_j^y \right]^j = \left[\sin(c_j^y y) / c_j^y y \right]^j$$

$$f_y' \left(net_j^y \right) = \partial b_j^y / \partial \left(net_j^y \right)$$

$$= j \left[\sin(net_j^y) / \left(net_j^y \right) \right]^{j-1} * \left[\cos(net_j^y) / \left(net_j^y \right) - \sin(net_j^y) / \left(net_j^y \right)^2 \right]$$

$$= j \left[\sin(c_j^y y) / \left(c_j^y y \right) \right]^{j-1} * \left[\cos(c_j^y y) / \left(c_j^y y \right) - \sin(c_j^y y) / \left(c_j^y y \right)^2 \right]$$

$$(253)$$

Using above procedure:

$$c_j^y (t+1) = c_j^y (t) - \eta \left(\partial E_p / \partial c_j^y \right)$$

$$= c_j^y (t) + \eta (d-z) f^o{}' \left(net^o \right) c_{kj}^o * f^h{}' \left(net_{kj}^h \right) c_{kj}^{hx} b_k^x c_{kj}^{hy} f_y' \left(net_j^y \right) y$$

$$= c_j^y (t) + \eta * \delta^{ol} * c_{kj}^o * \delta^{hy} * c_{kj}^{hy} * f_y' \left(net_j^y \right) * y = c_j^y (t) + \eta * \delta^{ol} * c_{kj}^o * \delta^{hy} * c_{kj}^{hy}$$

$$* [j [\sin(c_j^y y) / \left(c_j^y y \right)]^{j-1} * \left[\cos(c_j^y y) / \left(c_j^y y \right) - \sin(c_j^y y) / \left(c_j^y y \right)^2 \right]] * y$$

$$= c_j^y (t) + \eta * \delta^{ol} * c_{kj}^o * \delta^{hy} * c_{kj}^{hy} * \delta^y * y$$

$$(254)$$

where

$$\delta^{ol} = (d-z) f^o{}' \left(net^o \right) = (d-z) \qquad \left(linear\ neuron\ f^o{}' \left(net^o \right) = 1 \right)$$

$$\delta^{hy} = f^h{}' \left(net_{kj}^h \right) c_{kj}^{hx} b_k^x = c_{kj}^{hx} b_k^x \qquad \left(linear\ neuron\ f^h{}' \left(net_{kj}^h \right) = 1 \right)$$

$$\delta^y = f_y' \left(net_j^y \right)$$

$$= j \left[\sin(net_j^y) / \left(net_j^y \right) \right]^{j-1} * \left[\cos(net_j^y) / \left(net_j^y \right) - \sin(net_j^y) / \left(net_j^y \right)^2 \right]$$

$$= j \left[\sin(c_j^y y) / \left(c_j^y y \right) \right]^{j-1} * \left[\cos(c_j^y y) / \left(c_j^y y \right) - \sin(c_j^y y) / \left(c_j^y y \right)^2 \right]$$

SPHONN Model First Layer Neuron Weights Learning Formula

$$Let: f_k^x\left(c_k^x x\right) = \left(1/\left(1+\exp(c_k^x(-x))\right)\right)^k \tag{255}$$

$$f_j^y\left(c_j^y y\right) = \left(1/\left(1+\exp(c_j^y(-y))\right)\right)^j \tag{256}$$

For a sigmoid function of x input side:

$$b_k^x = f_k^x\left(net_k^x\right) = \left[1/\left(1+\exp(-net_k^x)\right)\right]^k = \left[1/\left(1+\exp(c_k^x*(-x))\right)\right]^k$$
$$f_x'\left(net_k^x\right) = \partial b_k^x/\partial\left(net_k^x\right) = \partial\left[1/\left(1+\exp(-net_k^x)\right)\right]^k/\partial\left(net_k^x\right)$$
$$= k*\left[1/\left(1+\exp(-net_k^x)\right)\right]^{k-1}*\left(1+\exp(-net_k^x)\right)^{-2}*\exp(-net_k^x)$$
$$= k*\left[1/\left(1+\exp(-c_k^x*x)\right)\right]^{k-1}*\left(1+\exp(-c_k^x*x)\right)^{-2}*\exp(-c_k^x*x)$$
$$\tag{257}$$

$$c_k^x\left(t+1\right) = c_k^x\left(t\right) - \eta\left(\partial E_p/\partial c_k^x\right)$$
$$= c_k^x\left(t\right) + \eta\left(d-z\right)f^o{}'\left(net^o\right)c_{kj}^o * f^h{}'\left(net_{kj}^h\right)c_{kj}^{hy}b_j^y c_{kj}^{hx}f_x'\left(net_k^x\right)x$$
$$= c_k^x\left(t\right) + \eta*\delta^{ol}*c_{kj}^o*\delta^{hx}*c_{kj}^{hx}*f_x'\left(net_k^x\right)*x = c_k^x\left(t\right) + \eta*\delta^{ol}*c_{kj}^o*\delta^{hx}*c_{kj}^{hx}$$
$$*[k*[1/\left(1+\exp(-c_k^x*x)\right)]^{k-1}*\left(1+\exp(-c_k^x*x)\right)^{-2}*\exp(-c_k^x*x)]*x$$
$$= c_k^x\left(t\right) + \eta*\delta^{ol}*c_{kj}^o*\delta^{hx}*c_{kj}^{hx}*\delta^x*x$$
$$\tag{258}$$

where

$$\delta^{ol} = (d-z)f^{o'}(net^o) = d-z \qquad (linear\ neuron\ f^{o\,'}(net^o)=1)$$

$$\delta^{hx} = f^{h'}(net_{kj}{}^h)c_{kj}{}^{hy}b_j{}^y = c_{kj}{}^{hy}b_j{}^y \qquad (linear\ neuron\ f^{h\,'}(net_{kj}{}^h)=1)$$

$$\delta^x = f_x{}'(net_k{}^x) = k*[1/(1+\exp(-c_k{}^x*x))]^{k-1}*(1+\exp(-c_k{}^x*x))^{-2}*\exp(-c_k{}^x*x)$$

For a sigmoid function of *y* input side:

$$b_j{}^y = f_j{}^y(net_j{}^y) = [1/(1+\exp(-net_j{}^y))]^j = [1/(1+\exp(c_j{}^y*(-y)))]^j$$

$$f_y{}'(net_j{}^y) = \partial b_j{}^y/\partial(net_j{}^y) = \partial[1/(1+\exp(-net_j{}^y))]^k/\partial(net_j{}^y)$$

$$= j*[1/(1+\exp(-net_j{}^y))]^{j-1}*(1+\exp(-net_j{}^y))^{-2}*\exp(-net_j{}^y)$$

$$= j*[1/(1+\exp(-c_j{}^y*y))]^{j-1}*(1+\exp(-c_j{}^y*y))^{-2}*\exp(-c_j{}^y*y)$$

$$(259)$$

$$c_j{}^y(t+1) = c_j{}^y(t) - \eta(\partial E_p/\partial c_j{}^y)$$

$$= c_j{}^y(t) + \eta(d-z)f^{o\,'}(net^o)c_{kj}{}^o * f^{h\,'}(net_{kj}{}^h)c_{kj}{}^{hx}b_k{}^x c_{kj}{}^{hy}f_y{}'(net_j{}^y)y$$

$$= c_j{}^y(t) + \eta*\delta^{ol}*c_{kj}{}^o*\delta^{hy}*c_{kj}{}^{hy}*f_y{}'(net_j{}^y)*y = c_j{}^y(t) + \eta*\delta^{ol}*c_{kj}{}^o*\delta^{hy}*c_{kj}{}^{hy}$$

$$*[j*[1/(1+\exp(-c_j{}^y*y))]^{j-1}*(1+\exp(-c_j{}^y*y))^{-2}*\exp(-c_j{}^y*y)]*y$$

$$= c_j{}^y(t) + \eta*\delta^{ol}*c_{kj}{}^o*\delta^{hy}*c_{kj}{}^{hy}*\delta^y*y$$

$$(260)$$

where

$$\delta^{ol} = (d-z)f^{o'}(net^o) = d-z \qquad (linear\ neuron\ f^{o\,'}(net^o)=1)$$

$$\delta^{hy} = f^{h'}(net_{kj}{}^h)c_{kj}{}^{hx}b_k{}^x = c_{kj}{}^{hx}b_k{}^x \qquad (linear\ neuron\ f^{h\,'}(net_{kj}{}^h)=1)$$

$$\delta^y = f_y{}'(net_j{}^y) = j*[1/(1+\exp(-c_j{}^y*y))]^{j-1}*(1+\exp(-c_j{}^y*y))^{-2}*\exp(-c_j{}^y*y)$$

SS-HONN Model First Layer Neuron Weights Learning Formula

$$Let: f_k^x\left(c_k^{\ x}x\right) = \sin^k(c_k^{\ x}x) \tag{261}$$

$$f_j^y\left(c_j^{\ y}y\right) = \left(1/\left(1+\exp(c_j^{\ y}(-y))\right)\right)^j \tag{262}$$

For a sine function of x input side:

$$b_k^x = f_k^x\left(net_k^x\right) = \sin^k(net_k^x) = \sin^k(c_k^{\ x}*x)^k$$
$$f_x'\left(net_k^x\right) = \partial b_k^x/\partial\left(net_k^x\right) = \partial\left(\sin^k(net_k^x)\right)/\partial\left(net_k^x\right) \tag{263}$$
$$= k*\sin^{k-1}(net_k^x)*\cos(net_k^x) = k*\sin^{k-1}(c_k^{\ x}*x)*\cos(c_k^{\ x}*x)$$

$$c_k^x\left(t+1\right) = c_k^x\left(t\right) - \eta\left(\partial E_p/\partial c_k^x\right)$$
$$= c_k^x\left(t\right) + \eta\left(d-z\right)f^o{}'\left(net^o\right)c_{kj}^{\ o}*f^h{}'\left(net_{kj}^{\ h}\right)c_{kj}^{\ hy}b_j^{\ y}c_{kj}^{\ hx}f_x{}'\left(net_k^x\right)x$$
$$= c_k^x\left(t\right) + \eta*\delta^{ol}*c_{kj}^{\ o}*\delta^{hx}*c_{kj}^{\ hx}*k*\sin^{k-1}(c_k^{\ x}*x)\cos(c_k^{\ x}*x)*x$$
$$= c_k^x\left(t\right) + \eta*\delta^{ol}*c_{kj}^{\ o}*\delta^{hx}*c_{kj}^{\ hx}*\delta^x*x$$

$$\tag{264}$$

where

$$\delta^{ol} = \left(d-z\right)f^o{}'\left(net^o\right) = d-z \qquad \left(linear\ neuron\ f^o{}'\left(net^o\right)=1\right)$$
$$\delta^{hx} = f^h{}'\left(net_{kj}^{\ h}\right)c_{kj}^{\ hy}b_j^{\ y} = c_{kj}^{\ hy}b_j^{\ y} \qquad \left(linear\ neuron\ f^h{}'\left(net_{kj}^{\ h}\right)=1\right)$$
$$\delta^x = f_x'\left(net_k^x\right) = k*\left(net_k^x\right)^{k-1} = k*\sin^{k-1}(c_k^{\ x}*x)*\cos(c_k^{\ x}*x)$$

For a sigmoid function of y input side:

$$b_j^y = f_j^y\left(net_j^y\right) = \left[1/\left(1+\exp(-net_j^y)\right)\right]^j = \left[1/\left(1+\exp(c_j^y*(-y))\right)\right]^j$$

$$f_y'\left(net_j^y\right) = \partial b_j^y / \partial\left(net_j^y\right) = \partial\left[1/\left(1+\exp(-net_j^y)\right)\right]^k / \partial\left(net_j^y\right)$$

$$= j*\left[1/\left(1+\exp(-net_j^y)\right)\right]^{j-1} * \left(1+\exp(-net_j^y)\right)^{-2} * \exp(-net_j^y)$$

$$= j*\left[1/\left(1+\exp(-c_j^y*y)\right)\right]^{j-1} * \left(1+\exp(-c_j^y*y)\right)^{-2} * \exp(-c_j^y*y)$$

$$(265)$$

$$c_j^y(t+1) = c_j^y(t) - \eta\left(\partial E_p / \partial c_j^y\right)$$

$$= c_j^y(t) + \eta(d-z)f^o{}'\left(net^o\right)c_{kj}^o * f^h{}'\left(net_{kj}^h\right)c_{kj}^{hx}b_k^x c_{kj}^{hy} f_y'\left(net_j^y\right)y$$

$$= c_j^y(t) + \eta*\delta^{ol}*c_{kj}^o*\delta^{hy}*c_{kj}^{hy}*f_y'\left(net_j^y\right)*y = c_j^y(t) + \eta*\delta^{ol}*c_{kj}^o*\delta^{hy}*c_{kj}^{hy}$$

$$*[j*[1/\left(1+\exp(-c_j^y*y)\right)]^{j-1}*\left(1+\exp(-c_j^y*y)\right)^{-2}*\exp(-c_j^y*y)]*y$$

$$= c_j^y(t) + \eta*\delta^{ol}*c_{kj}^o*\delta^{hy}*c_{kj}^{hy}*\delta^y*y$$

$$(266)$$

where

$$\delta^{ol} = (d-z)f^{o'}\left(net^o\right) = d-z \qquad \left(linear\ neuron\ f^o{}'\left(net^o\right)=1\right)$$

$$\delta^{hy} = f^{h'}\left(net_{kj}^h\right)c_{kj}^{hx}b_k^x = c_{kj}^{hx}b_k^x \qquad \left(linear\ neuron\ f^h{}'\left(net_{kj}^h\right)=1\right)$$

$$\delta^y = f_y'\left(net_j^y\right) = j*\left[1/\left(1+\exp(-c_j^y*y)\right)\right]^{j-1}*\left(1+\exp(-c_j^y*y)\right)^{-2}*\exp(-c_j^y*y)$$

PS-HONN Model First Layer Neuron Weights Learning Formula

$$Let: f_k^x\left(c_k^x x\right) = (c_k^x x)^k \qquad (267)$$

$$f_j^{y'}\left(c_j^{y}y\right)=\left(1/\left(1+\exp(c_j^{y}(-y))\right)\right)^{j} \tag{268}$$

For a polynomial function of x input side:

$$b_k^{x}=f_k^{x}\left(net_k^{x}\right)=(net_k^{x})^k=(c_k^{x}*x)^k$$
$$f_x'\left(net_k^{x}\right)=\partial b_k^{x}/\partial\left(net_k^{x}\right)=\partial\left(net_k^{x})^k\right)/\partial\left(net_k^{x}\right)=k(net_k^{x})^{k-1}=k*(c_k^{x}*x)^{k-1} \tag{269}$$

$$c_k^{x}\left(t+1\right)=c_k^{x}\left(t\right)-\eta\left(\partial E_p/\partial c_k^{x}\right)$$
$$=c_k^{x}\left(t\right)+\eta\left(d-z\right)f^{o'}\left(net^o\right)c_{kj}^{o}*f^{h'}\left(net_{kj}^{h}\right)c_{kj}^{hy}b_j^{y}c_{kj}^{hx}f_x'\left(net_k^{x}\right)x$$
$$=c_k^{x}\left(t\right)+\eta*\delta^{ol}*c_{kj}^{o}*\delta^{hx}*c_{kj}^{hx}*k*(c_k^{x}*x)^{k-1}*x \tag{270}$$
$$=c_k^{x}\left(t\right)+\eta*\delta^{ol}*c_{kj}^{o}*\delta^{hx}*c_{kj}^{hx}*\delta^{x}*x$$

where

$$\delta^{ol}=(d-z)f^{o'}\left(net^o\right)=d-z \qquad \left(linear\ neuron\ f^{o\,'}\left(net^o\right)=1\right)$$
$$\delta^{hx}=f^{h'}\left(net_{kj}^{h}\right)c_{kj}^{hy}b_j^{y}=c_{kj}^{hy}b_j^{y} \qquad \left(linear\ neuron\ f^{h\,'}\left(net_{kj}^{h}\right)=1\right)$$
$$\delta^{x}=f_x'\left(net_k^{x}\right)=k*\left(net_k^{x}\right)^{k-1}=k*(c_k^{x}*x)^{k-1}$$

For a sigmoid function of y input side:

$$b_j^{y}=f_j^{y}\left(net_j^{y}\right)=\left[1/\left(1+\exp(-net_j^{y})\right)\right]^{j}=\left[1/\left(1+\exp(c_j^{y}*(-y))\right)\right]^{j}$$
$$f_y'\left(net_j^{y}\right)=\partial b_j^{y}/\partial\left(net_j^{y}\right)=\partial\left[1/\left(1+\exp(-net_j^{y})\right)\right]^{k}/\partial\left(net_j^{y}\right)$$
$$=j*\left[1/\left(1+\exp(-net_j^{y})\right)\right]^{j-1}*\left(1+\exp(-net_j^{y})\right)^{-2}*\exp(-net_j^{y})$$
$$=j*\left[1/\left(1+\exp(-c_j^{y}*y)\right)\right]^{j-1}*\left(1+\exp(-c_j^{y}*y)\right)^{-2}*\exp(-c_j^{y}*y) \tag{271}$$

$$c_j^{\ y}(t+1) = c_j^{\ y}(t) - \eta\left(\partial E_p / \partial c_j^{\ y}\right)$$

$$= c_j^{\ y}(t) + \eta(d-z)f^{o}{}'\left(net^o\right)c_{kj}^{\ o} * f^{h}{}'\left(net_{kj}^{\ h}\right)c_{kj}^{\ hx}b_k^{\ x}c_{kj}^{\ hy}f_y{}'\left(net_j^{\ y}\right)y$$

$$= c_j^{\ y}(t) + \eta * \delta^{ol} * c_{kj}^{\ o} * \delta^{hy} * c_{kj}^{\ hy} * f_y{}'\left(net_j^{\ y}\right) * y = c_j^{\ y}(t) + \eta * \delta^{ol} * c_{kj}^{\ o} * \delta^{hy} * c_{kj}^{\ hy}$$

$$*\left[j*\left[1/\left(1+\exp(-c_j^{\ y}*y)\right)\right]^{j-1}*\left(1+\exp(-c_j^{\ y}*y)\right)^{-2}*\exp(-c_j^{\ y}*y)\right]*y$$

$$= c_j^{\ y}(t) + \eta * \delta^{ol} * c_{kj}^{\ o} * \delta^{hy} * c_{kj}^{\ hy} * \delta^{y} * y$$

$$(272)$$

where

$$\delta^{ol} = (d-z)f^{o}{}'\left(net^o\right) = d-z \qquad \left(linear\ neuron\ f^{o}{}'\left(net^o\right)=1\right)$$

$$\delta^{hy} = f^{h}{}'\left(net_{kj}^{\ h}\right)c_{kj}^{\ hx}b_k^{\ x} = c_{kj}^{\ hx}b_k^{\ x} \qquad \left(linear\ neuron\ f^{h}{}'\left(net_{kj}^{\ h}\right)=1\right)$$

$$\delta^{y} = f_y{}'\left(net_j^{\ y}\right) = j*\left[1/\left(1+\exp(-c_j^{\ y}*y)\right)\right]^{j-1}*\left(1+\exp(-c_j^{\ y}*y)\right)^{-2}*\exp(-c_j^{\ y}*y)$$

CS-HONN Model First Layer Neuron Weights Learning Formula

$$Let: f_k^{\ x}\left(c_k^{\ x}x\right) = \cos^k\left(c_k^{\ x}x\right) \qquad (273)$$

$$f_j^{\ y}\left(c_j^{\ y}y\right) = \left(1/\left(1+\exp(c_j^{\ y}(-y))\right)\right)^j \qquad (274)$$

For a cosine function of x input side:

$$b_k^{\ x} = f_k^{\ x}\left(net_k^{\ x}\right) = \cos^k(net_k^{\ x}) = \cos^k(c_k^{\ x} * x)$$

$$f_x'\left(net_k^{\ x}\right) = \partial b_k^{\ x} / \partial\left(net_k^{\ x}\right) = \partial\left(\cos^k(net_k^{\ x})\right) / \partial\left(net_k^{\ x}\right)$$

$$= k * \cos^{k-1}(net_k^{\ x}) * \left(-\sin(net_k^{\ x})\right) = (-k) * \cos^{k-1}(c_k^{\ x} * x) * \sin(c_k^{\ x} * x)$$

$$(275)$$

$$c_k^{\ x}\left(t+1\right) = c_k^{\ x}\left(t\right) - \eta\left(\frac{\partial E_p}{\partial c_k^{\ x}}\right)$$

$$= c_k^{\ x}\left(t\right) + \eta\left(d-z\right) f^{o'}\left(net^o\right) c_{kj}^{\ o} * f^{h'}\left(net_{kj}^{\ h}\right) c_{kj}^{\ hy} b_j^{\ y} c_{kj}^{\ hx} f_x'\left(net_k^{\ x}\right) x$$

$$= c_k^{\ x}\left(t\right) + \eta * \delta^{ol} * c_{kj}^{\ o} * \delta^{hx} * c_{kj}^{\ hx} * (-k) * \cos^{k-1}(c_k^{\ x} * x) * \sin(c_k^{\ x} * x) * x$$

$$= c_k^{\ x}\left(t\right) + \eta * \delta^{ol} * c_{kj} s^o * \delta^{hx} * c_{kj}^{\ hx} * \delta^x * x$$

$$(276)$$

where:

$$\delta^{ol} = (d-z) f^{o'}\left(net^o\right) = d - z \qquad \left(\text{linear neuron } f^{o'}\left(net^o\right) = 1\right)$$

$$\delta^{hx} = f^{h'}\left(net_{kj}^{\ h}\right) c_{kj}^{\ hy} b_j^{\ y} = c_{kj}^{\ hy} b_j^{\ y} \qquad \left(\text{linear neuron } f^{h'}\left(net_{kj}^{\ h}\right) = 1\right)$$

$$\delta^x = f_x'\left(net_k^{\ x}\right) = (-k) * \cos^{k-1}\left(net_k^{\ x}\right) * \sin\left(net_k^{\ x}\right) = (-k) * \cos^{k-1}(c_k^{\ x} * x) * \sin(c_k^{\ x} * x)$$

For a sigmoid function of y input side:

$$b_j^{\ y} = f_j^{\ y}\left(net_j^{\ y}\right) = \left[1/\left(1+\exp(-net_j^{\ y})\right)\right]^j = \left[1/\left(1+\exp(c_j^{\ y} * (-y))\right)\right]^j$$

$$f_y'\left(net_j^{\ y}\right) = \partial b_j^{\ y} / \partial\left(net_j^{\ y}\right) = \partial\left[1/\left(1+\exp(-net_j^{\ y})\right)\right]^k / \partial\left(net_j^{\ y}\right)$$

$$= j * \left[1/\left(1+\exp(-net_j^{\ y})\right)\right]^{j-1} * \left(1+\exp(-net_j^{\ y})\right)^{-2} * \exp(-net_j^{\ y})$$

$$= j * \left[1/\left(1+\exp(-c_j^{\ y} * y)\right)\right]^{j-1} * \left(1+\exp(-c_j^{\ y} * y)\right)^{-2} * \exp(-c_j^{\ y} * y)$$

$$(277)$$

$$c_j^{y}(t+1)=c_j^{y}(t)-\eta\left(\partial E_p / \partial c_j^{y}\right)$$

$$=c_j^{y}(t)+\eta(d-z)f^{o}{}'\left(net^{o}\right)c_{kj}^{o}*f^{h}{}'\left(net_{kj}^{h}\right)c_{kj}^{hx}b_k^{x}c_{kj}^{hy}f_y{}'\left(net_j^{y}\right)y$$

$$=c_j^{y}(t)+\eta*\delta^{ol}*c_{kj}^{o}*\delta^{hy}*c_{kj}^{hy}*f_y{}'\left(net_j^{y}\right)*y=c_j^{y}(t)+\eta*\delta^{ol}*c_{kj}^{o}*\delta^{hy}*c_{kj}^{hy}$$

$$*[j*[1/\left(1+\exp(-c_j^{y}*y)\right)]^{j-1}*\left(1+\exp(-c_j^{y}*y)\right)^{-2}*\exp(-c_j^{y}*y)]*y$$

$$=c_j^{y}(t)+\eta*\delta^{ol}*c_{kj}^{o}*\delta^{hy}*c_{kj}^{hy}*\delta^{y}*y$$

$$(278)$$

where

$$\delta^{ol}=(d-z)f^{o}{}'\left(net^{o}\right)=d-z \qquad \left(linear\ neuron\ f^{o}{}'\left(net^{o}\right)=1\right)$$

$$\delta^{hy}=f^{h}{}'\left(net_{kj}^{h}\right)c_{kj}^{hx}b_k^{x}=c_{kj}^{hx}b_k^{x} \qquad \left(linear\ neuron\ f^{h}{}'\left(net_{kj}^{h}\right)=1\right)$$

$$\delta^{y}=f_y{}'\left(net_j^{y}\right)=j*\left[1/\left(1+\exp(-c_j^{y}*y)\right)\right]^{j-1}*\left(1+\exp(-c_j^{y}*y)\right)^{-2}*\exp(-c_j^{y}*y)$$

NS-HONN Model First Layer Neuron Weights Learning Formula

Let

$$f_k^{x}\left(c_k^{x}x\right)=\left(\sin(c_k^{x}x)/\left(c_k^{x}x\right)\right)^{k} \tag{279}$$

$$f_j^{y}\left(c_j^{y}y\right)=\left(1/\left(1+\exp(c_j^{y}(-y))\right)\right)^{j} \tag{280}$$

For a SINC function of x input part:

$$b_k^{\ x} = f_k^{\ x}\left(net_k^{\ x}\right) = \left[\sin(net_k^{\ x})/net_k^{\ x}\right]^k = \left[\sin(c_k^{\ x}x)/c_k^{\ x}x\right]^k$$

$$f_x'\left(net_k^{\ x}\right) = \partial b_k^{\ x}/\partial\left(net_k^{\ x}\right)$$

$$= k\left[\sin(net_k^{\ x})/\left(net_k^{\ x}\right)\right]^{k-1} * \left[\cos(net_k^{\ x})/\left(net_k^{\ x}\right) - \sin(net_k^{\ x})/\left(net_k^{\ x}\right)^2\right]$$

$$= k\left[\sin(c_k^{\ x}x)/\left(c_k^{\ k}x\right)\right]^{k-1} * \left[\cos(c_k^{\ x}x)/\left(c_k^{\ x}x\right) - \sin(c_k^{\ x}x)/\left(c_k^{\ x}x\right)^2\right]$$

$$(281)$$

$$c_k^{\ x}(t+1) = c_k^{\ x}(t) - \eta\left(\partial E_p/\partial c_k^{\ x}\right)$$

$$= c_k^{\ x}(t) + \eta(d-z)f^{o'}\left(net^o\right)c_{kj}^{\ o} * f^{h'}\left(net_{kj}^{\ h}\right)c_{kj}^{\ hy}b_j^{\ y}c_{kj}^{\ hx}f_x'\left(net_k^{\ x}\right)x$$

$$= c_k^{\ x}(t) + \eta * \delta^{ol} * c_{kj}^{\ o} * \delta^{hx} * c_{kj}^{\ hx} * f_x'\left(net_k^{\ x}\right) * x = c_k^{\ x}(t) + \eta * \delta^{ol} * c_{kj}^{\ o} * \delta^{hx} * c_{kj}^{\ hx}$$

$$*\left[k\left[\sin(c_k^{\ x}x)/\left(c_k^{\ k}x\right)\right]^{k-1} * \left[\cos(c_k^{\ x}x)/\left(c_k^{\ x}x\right) - \sin(c_k^{\ x}x)/\left(c_k^{\ x}x\right)^2\right]\right] * x$$

$$= c_k^{\ x}(t) + \eta * \delta^{ol} * c_{kj}^{\ o} * \delta^{hx} * c_{kj}^{\ hx} * \delta^x * x$$

$$(282)$$

where

$$\delta^{ol} = (d-z)f^{o'}\left(net^o\right) = (d-z) \qquad \left(linear\ neuron\ f^{o'}\left(net^o\right)=1\right)$$

$$\delta^{hx} = f^{h'}\left(net_{kj}^{\ h}\right)c_{kj}^{\ hy}b_j^{\ y} = c_{kj}^{\ hy}b_j^{\ y} \qquad \left(linear\ neuron\ f^{h'}\left(net_{kj}^{\ h}\right)=1\right)$$

$$\delta^x = f_x'\left(net_k^{\ x}\right)$$

$$= k\left[\sin(net_k^{\ x})/\left(net_k^{\ x}\right)\right]^{k-1} * \left[\cos(net_k^{\ x})/\left(net_k^{\ x}\right) - \sin(net_k^{\ x})/\left(net_k^{\ x}\right)^2\right]$$

$$= k\left[\sin(c_k^{\ x}x)/\left(c_k^{\ x}x\right)\right]^{k-1} * \left[\cos(c_k^{\ x}x)/\left(c_k^{\ x}x\right) - \sin(c_k^{\ x}x)/\left(c_k^{\ x}x\right)^2\right]$$

For a sigmoid function of *y* input side:

$$b_j^y = f_j^y \left(net_j^y \right) = \left[1 / \left(1 + \exp(-net_j^y) \right) \right]^j = \left[1 / \left(1 + \exp(c_j^y * (-y)) \right) \right]^j$$

$$f_y'\left(net_j^y \right) = \partial b_j^y / \partial \left(net_j^y \right) = \partial \left[1 / \left(1 + \exp(-net_j^y) \right) \right]^k / \partial \left(net_j^y \right)$$

$$= j * \left[1 / \left(1 + \exp(-net_j^y) \right) \right]^{j-1} * \left(1 + \exp(-net_j^y) \right)^{-2} * \exp(-net_j^y)$$

$$= j * \left[1 / \left(1 + \exp(-c_j^y * y) \right) \right]^{j-1} * \left(1 + \exp(-c_j^y * y) \right)^{-2} * \exp(-c_j^y * y)$$

$$(283)$$

$$c_j^y (t+1) = c_j^y (t) - \eta \left(\partial E_p / \partial c_j^y \right)$$

$$= c_j^y (t) + \eta (d-z) f^{o'} \left(net^o \right) c_{kj}^o * f^{h'} \left(net_{kj}^h \right) c_{kj}^{hx} b_k^x c_{kj}^{hy} f_y' \left(net_j^y \right) y$$

$$= c_j^y (t) + \eta * \delta^{ol} * c_{kj}^o * \delta^{hy} * c_{kj}^{hy} * f_y' \left(net_j^y \right) * y = c_j^y (t) + \eta * \delta^{ol} * c_{kj}^o * \delta^{hy} * c_{kj}^{hy}$$

$$* \left[j * \left[1 / \left(1 + \exp(-c_j^y * y) \right) \right]^{j-1} * \left(1 + \exp(-c_j^y * y) \right)^{-2} * \exp(-c_j^y * y) \right] * y$$

$$= c_j^y (t) + \eta * \delta^{ol} * c_{kj}^o * \delta^{hy} * c_{kj}^{hy} * \delta^y * y$$

$$(284)$$

where

$$\delta^{ol} = (d-z) f^{o'} \left(net^o \right) = d - z \qquad \left(linear\ neuron\ f^{o\,'} \left(net^o \right) = 1 \right)$$

$$\delta^{hy} = f^{h'} \left(net_{kj}^h \right) c_{kj}^{hx} b_k^x = c_{kj}^{hx} b_k^x \qquad \left(linear\ neuron\ f^{h\,'} \left(net_{kj}^h \right) = 1 \right)$$

$$\delta^y = f_y' \left(net_j^y \right) = j * \left[1 / \left(1 + \exp(-c_j^y * y) \right) \right]^{j-1} * \left(1 + \exp(-c_j^y * y) \right)^{-2} * \exp(-c_j^y * y)$$

UCSHONN Model First Layer Neuron Weights Learning Formula

Let

$$f_k^x \left(c_k^x x \right) = \cos^k (k * c_k^x x) \qquad\qquad (285)$$

$$f_j^y \left(c_j^y y \right) = \sin^j \left(j * c_j^y y \right) \tag{286}$$

For an ultra-high frequency cosine function of x input part:

$$b_k^x = f_k^x \left(net_k^x \right) = \cos^k (k * net_k^x)$$

$$f_x' \left(net_k^x \right) = \partial b_k^x / \partial \left(net_k^x \right) = \partial \left(\cos^k (k * net_k^x) \right) / \partial \left(net_k^x \right)$$

$$= k \cos^{k-1} (k * net_k^x) * \left(-\sin(k * net_k^x) \right) * k = -k^2 \cos^{k-1} (k * net_k^x) \sin(k * net_k^x)$$

$$= -k^2 \cos^{k-1} (k * c_k^x * x) \sin(k * c_k^x * x) \tag{287}$$

$$c_k^x (t+1) = c_k^x (t) - \eta \left(\partial E_p / \partial c_k^x \right)$$

$$= c_k^x (t) + \eta (d-z) f^{o'} \left(net^o \right) c_{kj}^o * f^h \left(net_{kj}^h \right) c_{kj}^{hy} b_j^y c_{kj}^{hx} f_x' \left(net_k^x \right) x$$

$$= c_k^x (t) + \eta * \delta^{ol} * c_{kj}^o * \delta^{hx} * c_{kj}^{hx} * \left(-k^2 \right) \cos^{k-1} (k * c_k^x * x) \sin(k * c_k^x * x) * x$$

$$= c_k^x (t) + \eta * \delta^{ol} * c_{kj}^o * \delta^{hx} * c_{kj}^{hx} * \delta^x * x \tag{288}$$

where

$$\delta^{ol} = (d-z) f^{o'} \left(net^o \right) = d-z \qquad \left(linear\ neuron\ f^{o'} \left(net^o \right) = 1 \right)$$

$$\delta^{hx} = f^h \left(net_{kj}^h \right) c_{kj}^{hy} b_j^y = a_{kj}^{hy} b_j \qquad \left(linear\ neuron\ f^{h'} \left(net_{kj}^h \right) = 1 \right)$$

$$\delta^x = f_x' \left(net_k^x \right) = \left(-k^2 \right) \cos^{k-1} (k * c_k^x * x) \sin(k * c_k^x * x)$$

For an ultra-high frequency sine function of y input part:

$$b_j^y = f_j^y \left(net_j^y \right) = \sin^j (j * net_j^y) = \sin^j (j * c_j^y * y)$$

$$f_y' \left(net_j^y \right) = \partial b_j^y / \partial \left(net_j^y \right)$$

$$= \partial \left(\sin^j (j * net_j^y) \right) / \partial \left(net_j^y \right) = j \sin^{j-1} (j * net_j^y) * \cos(j * net_j^y) * j$$

$$= j^2 * \sin^{j-1} (j * net_j^y) * \cos(j * net_j^y) = j^2 * \sin^{j-1} (j * c_j^y * y) * \cos(j * c_j^y * y) \tag{289}$$

Using the above procedure:

$$c_j^{\ y}(t+1) = c_j^{\ y}(t) - \eta\left(\partial E_p / \partial c_j^{\ y}\right)$$

$$= c_j^{\ y}(t) + \eta(d-z) f^{o\,\prime}\left(net^o\right) c_{kj}^{\ o} * f^{h\,\prime}\left(net_{kj}^{\ h}\right) c_{kj}^{\ hx} b_k^{\ x} c_{kj}^{\ hy} f_y^{\ \prime}\left(net_j^{\ y}\right) y$$

$$= c_j^{\ y}(t) + \eta * \delta^{ol} * c_{kj}^{\ o} * \delta^{hy} * c_{kj}^{\ hy} * \left(j^2\right)\sin^{j-1}(j*c_j^{\ y}*y)\cos(j*c_j^{\ y}*y)*y$$

$$= c_j^{\ y}(t) + \eta * \delta^{ol} * c_{kj}^{\ o} * \delta^{hy} * c_{kj}^{\ hy} * \delta^y * y$$

$$(290)$$

where

$$\delta^{ol} = (d-z) f^{o\,\prime}\left(net^o\right) = d - z \qquad \left(linear\ neuron\ f^{o\,\prime}\left(net^o\right) = 1\right)$$

$$\delta^{hy} = f^{h\,\prime}\left(net_{kj}^{\ hy}\right) c_{kj}^{\ hx} b_k^{\ x} = c_{kj}^{\ hx} b_k^{\ x} \qquad \left(linear\ neuron\ f^{h\,\prime}\left(net_{kj}^{\ hy}\right) = 1\right)$$

$$\delta^y = f_y^{\ \prime}\left(net_j^{\ y}\right) = \left(j^2\right)\sin^{j-1}(j*c_j^{\ y}*y)\cos(j*c_j^{\ y}*y)$$

UCCHONN Model First Layer Neuron Weights Learning Formula

$$Let: f_k^{\ x}\left(c_k^{\ x}x\right) = \cos^k(k*c_k^{\ x}x) \tag{291}$$

$$f_j^{\ y}\left(c_j^{\ y}y\right) = \cos^j(j*c_j^{\ y}y) \tag{292}$$

For an ultra-high frequency cosine function of x input part:

$$b_k^{\ x} = f_k^{\ x}\left(net_k^{\ x}\right) = \cos^k(k*net_k^{\ x})$$

$$f_x^{\ \prime}\left(net_k^{\ x}\right) = \partial b_k^{\ x} / \partial\left(net_k^{\ x}\right) = \partial\left(\cos^k(k*net_k^{\ x})\right) / \partial\left(net_k^{\ x}\right)$$

$$= k\cos^{k-1}(k*net_k^{\ x})*\left(-\sin(k*net_k^{\ x})\right)*k = -k^2\cos^{k-1}(k*net_k^{\ x})\sin(k*net_k^{\ x})$$

$$= -k^2\cos^{k-1}(k*c_k^{\ x}*x)\sin(k*c_k^{\ x}*x)$$

$$(293)$$

$$c_k^{\ x}(t+1) = c_k^{\ x}(t) - \eta\left(\partial E_p / \partial c_k^{\ x}\right)$$

$$= c_k^{\ x}(t) + \eta(d-z) f^{o'}\left(net^o\right)c_{kj}^{\ o} * f^{h'}\left(net_{kj}^{\ h}\right)c_{kj}^{\ hy}b_{\ j}^{y}{}_j c_{kj}^{\ hx} f_x'\left(net_k^{\ x}\right)x$$

$$= c_k^{\ x}(t) + \eta * \delta^{ol} * c_{kj}^{\ o} * \delta^{hx} * c_{kj}^{\ hx} * \left(-k^2\right)\cos^{k-1}(k*c_k^{\ x}*x)\sin(k*c_k^{\ x}*x)*x$$

$$= c_k^{\ x}(t) + \eta * \delta^{ol} * c_{kj}^{\ o} * \delta^{hx} * c_{kj}^{\ hx} * \delta^x * x$$

$$(294)$$

where

$$\delta^{ol} = (d-z)f^{o'}\left(net^o\right) = d - z \qquad \left(linear\ neuron\ f^{o'}\left(net^o\right) = 1\right)$$

$$\delta^{hx} = f^{h'}\left(net_{kj}^{\ h}\right)c_{kj}^{\ hy}b_{\ j}^{y} = a_{kj}^{\ hy}b_j \qquad \left(linear\ neuron\ f^{h'}\left(net_{kj}^{\ h}\right) = 1\right)$$

$$\delta^x = f_x'\left(net_k^{\ x}\right) = \left(-k^2\right)\cos^{k-1}(k*c_k^{\ x}*x)\sin(k*c_k^{\ x}*x)$$

For an ultra-high frequency cosine function of *y* input part:

$$b_j^{\ y} = f_j^{\ y}\left(net_j^{\ y}\right) = \cos^j(j*net_j^{\ y}) = \cos^j(j*c_j^{\ y}*y)$$

$$f_y'\left(net_j^{\ y}\right) = \partial b_{\ j}^{y} / \partial\left(net_j^{\ y}\right)$$

$$= \partial\left(\cos^j(j*net_j^{\ y})\right)/\partial\left(net_j^{\ y}\right) = j\cos^{j-1}(j*net_j^{\ y})*\left(-\sin(j*net_j^{\ y})\right)*j$$

$$= -j^2 * \cos^{j-1}(j*net_j^{\ y})*\sin(j*net_j^{\ y}) = -j^2 * \cos^{j-1}(j*c_j^{\ y}*y)*\sin(j*c_j^{\ y}*y)$$

$$(295)$$

Using the above procedure:

$$c_j^{\ y}(t+1) = c_j^{\ y}(t) - \eta\left(\partial E_p / \partial c_j^{\ y}\right)$$

$$= c_j^{\ y}(t) + \eta(d-z)f^{o'}\left(net^o\right)c_{kj}^{\ o} * f^{h'}\left(net_{kj}^{\ h}\right)c_{kj}^{\ hx}b_k^{\ x}c_{kj}^{\ hy} f_y'\left(net_j^{\ y}\right)y$$

$$= c_j^{\ y}(t) + \eta * \delta^{ol} * c_{kj}^{\ o} * \delta^{hy} * c_{kj}^{\ hy} * \left(-j^2\right)*\cos^{j-1}(j*c_j^{\ y}*y)*\sin(j*c_j^{\ y}*y)$$

$$= c_j^{\ y}(t) + \eta * \delta^{ol} * c_{kj}^{\ o} * \delta^{hy} * c_{kj}^{\ hy} * \delta^y * y$$

$$(296)$$

where

$$\delta^{ol} = (d-z)f^{o'}\left(net^o\right) = d-z \qquad \left(linear\ neuron\ f^{o\,'}\left(net^o\right) = 1\right)$$

$$\delta^{hy} = f^{h'}\left(net_{kj}^{\ hy}\right)c_{kj}^{\ hx}b_k^{\ x} = c_{kj}^{\ hx}b_k^{\ x} \qquad \left(linear\ neuron\ f^{h\,'}\left(net_{kj}^{\ hy}\right) = 1\right)$$

$$\delta^y = f_y{}'\left(net_j^{\ y}\right) = \left(-j^2\right)*\cos^{j-1}(j*c_j^{\ y}*y)*\sin(j*c_j^{\ y}*y)$$

USSHONN Model First Layer Neuron Weights Learning Formula

Let

$$f_k^{\ x}\left(c_k^{\ x}x\right) = \sin^k(k*c_k^{\ x}x) \tag{297}$$

$$f_j^{\ y}\left(c_j^{\ y}y\right) = \sin^j(j*c_j^{\ y}y) \tag{298}$$

For an ultra-high frequency sine function of x input part:

$$b^x_{\ k} = f_k^{\ x}\left(net_k^{\ x}\right) = \sin^k(k*net_k^{\ x})$$

$$f_x{}'\left(net_k^{\ x}\right) = \partial b^x_{\ k} / \partial\left(net_k^{\ x}\right) = \partial\left(\sin^k(k*net_k^{\ x})\right) / \partial\left(net_k^{\ x}\right)$$

$$= k\sin^{k-1}(k*net_k^{\ x})*\cos(k*net_k^{\ x})*k = k^2\sin^{k-1}(k*net_k^{\ x})\cos(k*net_k^{\ x})$$

$$= k^2\sin^{k-1}(k*c_k^{\ x}*x)\cos(k*c_k^{\ x}*x) \tag{299}$$

$$c_k^{\ x}(t+1) = c_k^{\ x}(t) - \eta\left(\partial E_p / \partial c_k^{\ x}\right)$$

$$= c_k^{\ x}(t) + \eta(d-z)f^{o\,'}\left(net^o\right)c_{kj}^{\ o}*f^{h\,'}\left(net_{kj}^{\ h}\right)c_{kj}^{\ hy}b^y_{\ j}c_{kj}^{\ hx}f_x{}'\left(net_k^{\ x}\right)x$$

$$= c_k^{\ x}(t) + \eta*\delta^{ol}*c_{kj}^{\ o}*\delta^{hx}*c_{kj}^{\ hx}*\left(k^2\right)\sin^{k-1}(k*c_k^{\ x}*x)\cos(k*c_k^{\ x}*x) \tag{300}$$

$$= c_k^{\ x}(t) + \eta*\delta^{ol}*c_{kj}^{\ o}*\delta^{hx}*c_{kj}^{\ hx}*\delta^x*x$$

where

$$\delta^{ol} = (d-z) f^{o'}\left(net^o\right) = d - z \qquad \left(linear\ neuron\ f^{o}{'}\left(net^o\right) = 1\right)$$

$$\delta^{hx} = f^{h'}\left(net_{kj}^{\ h}\right)c_{kj}^{\ hy}b^y_{\ j} = a_{kj}^{\ hy}b_j \qquad \left(linear\ neuron\ f^{h}{'}\left(net_{kj}^{\ h}\right) = 1\right)$$

$$\delta^x = f_x{'}\left(net_k^{\ x}\right) = \left(k^2\right)\sin^{k-1}(k*c_k^{\ x}*x)\cos(k*c_k^{\ x}*x)$$

For an ultra-high frequency sine function of y input part:

$$b_j^{\ y} = f_j^{\ y}\left(net_j^{\ y}\right) = \sin^j(j*net_j^{\ y}) = \sin^j(j*c_j^{\ y}*y)$$

$$f_y{'}\left(net_j^{\ y}\right) = \partial b_j^{\ y} / \partial\left(net_j^{\ y}\right)$$

$$= \partial\left(\sin^j(j*net_j^{\ y})\right) / \partial\left(net_j^{\ y}\right) = j\sin^{j-1}(j*net_j^{\ y})*\cos(j*net_j^{\ y})*j$$

$$= j^2*\sin^{j-1}(j*net_j^{\ y})*\cos(j*net_j^{\ y}) = j^2*\sin^{j-1}(j*c_j^{\ y}*y)*\cos(j*c_j^{\ y}*y)$$

$$\tag{301}$$

Using the above procedure:

$$c_j^{\ y}(t+1) = c_j^{\ y}(t) - \eta\left(\partial E_p / \partial c_j^{\ y}\right)$$

$$= c_j^{\ y}(t) + \eta(d-z) f^{o}{'}\left(net^o\right)c_{kj}^{\ o} * f^{h}{'}\left(net_{kj}^{\ h}\right)c_{kj}^{\ hx}b_k^{\ x}c_{kj}^{\ hy}f_y{'}\left(net_j^{\ y}\right)y$$

$$= c_j^{\ y}(t) + \eta*\delta^{ol}*c_{kj}^{\ o}*\delta^{hy}*c_{kj}^{\ hy}*\left(j^2\right)\sin^{j-1}(j*c_j^{\ y}*y)\cos(j*c_j^{\ y}*y)*y$$

$$= c_j^{\ y}(t) + \eta*\delta^{ol}*c_{kj}^{\ o}*\delta^{hy}*c_{kj}^{\ hy}*\delta^y*y$$

$$\tag{302}$$

where

$$\delta^{ol} = (d-z) f^{o'}\left(net^o\right) = d - z \qquad \left(linear\ neuron\ f^{o}{'}\left(net^o\right) = 1\right)$$

$$\delta^{hy} = f^{h'}\left(net_{kj}^{\ hy}\right)c_{kj}^{\ hx}b_k^{\ x} = c_{kj}^{\ hx}b_k^{\ x} \qquad \left(linear\ neuron\ f^{h}{'}\left(net_{kj}^{\ hy}\right) = 1\right)$$

$$\delta^y = f_y{'}\left(net_j^{\ y}\right) = \left(j^2\right)\sin^{j-1}(j*c_j^{\ y}*y)\cos(j*c_j^{\ y}*y)$$

UPS-HONN Model First Layer Neuron Weights Learning Formula

$$Let: f_k^x\left(c_k{}^x x\right) = (c_k{}^x x)^k \tag{303}$$

$$f_j^y\left(c_j{}^y y\right) = \sin^j(j * c_j{}^y y) \tag{304}$$

For a polynomial function of x input side:

$$b_k{}^x = f_k^x\left(net_k{}^x\right) = (net_k{}^x)^k = (c_k{}^x * x)^k$$
$$f_x{}'\left(net_k{}^x\right) = \partial b_k{}^x / \partial\left(net_k{}^x\right) = \partial\left(net_k{}^x)^k\right) / \partial\left(net_k{}^x\right) = k(net_k{}^x)^{k-1} = k * (c_k{}^x * x)^{k-1} \tag{305}$$

$$c_k{}^x\left(t+1\right) = c_k{}^x\left(t\right) - \eta\left(\partial E_p / \partial c_k{}^x\right)$$
$$= c_k{}^x\left(t\right) + \eta\left(d-z\right) f^{o'}\left(net^o\right) c_{kj}{}^o * f^{h'}\left(net_{kj}{}^h\right) c_{kj}{}^{hy} b_j{}^y c_{kj}{}^{hx} f_x{}'\left(net_k{}^x\right) x$$
$$= c_k{}^x\left(t\right) + \eta * \delta^{ol} * c_{kj}{}^o * \delta^{hx} * c_{kj}{}^{hx} * k * (c_k{}^x * x)^{k-1} * x \tag{306}$$
$$= c_k{}^x\left(t\right) + \eta * \delta^{ol} * c_{kj}{}^o * \delta^{hx} * c_{kj}{}^{hx} * \delta^x * x$$

where:

$$\delta^{ol} = \left(d-z\right) f^{o'}\left(net^o\right) = d-z \qquad \left(linear\ neuron\ f^{o}{}'\left(net^o\right) = 1\right)$$

$$\delta^{hx} = f^{h'}\left(net_{kj}{}^h\right) c_{kj}{}^{hy} b_j{}^y = c_{kj}{}^{hy} b_j{}^y \qquad \left(linear\ neuron\ f^{h}{}'\left(net_{kj}{}^h\right) = 1\right)$$

$$\delta^x = f_x{}'\left(net_k{}^x\right) = k * \left(net_k{}^x\right)^{k-1} = k * (c_k{}^x * x)^{k-1}$$

For an ultra-high frequency sine function of y input part:

$$b_j^{\ y} = f_j^{\ y}\left(net_j^{\ y}\right) = \sin^j(j * net_j^{\ y}) = \sin^j(j * c_j^{\ y} * y)$$

$$f_y'\left(net_j^{\ y}\right) = \partial b_j^{\ y} / \partial\left(net_j^{\ y}\right)$$

$$= \partial\left(\sin^j(j * net_j^{\ y})\right) / \partial\left(net_j^{\ y}\right) = j\sin^{j-1}(j * net_j^{\ y}) * \cos(j * net_j^{\ y}) * j$$

$$= j^2 * \sin^{j-1}(j * net_j^{\ y}) * \cos(j * net_j^{\ y}) = j^2 * \sin^{j-1}(j * c_j^{\ y} * y) * \cos(j * c_j^{\ y} * y)$$

$$(307)$$

Using the above procedure:

$$c_j^{\ y}\left(t+1\right) = c_j^{\ y}\left(t\right) - \eta\left(\partial E_p / \partial c_j^{\ y}\right)$$

$$= c_j^{\ y}\left(t\right) + \eta\left(d - z\right) f^{o\,'}\left(net^o\right) c_{kj}^{\ o} * f^{h\,'}\left(net_{kj}^{\ h}\right) c_{kj}^{\ hx} b_k^{\ x} c_{kj}^{\ hy} f_y'\left(net_j^{\ y}\right) y$$

$$= c_j^{\ y}\left(t\right) + \eta * \delta^{ol} * c_{kj}^{\ o} * \delta^{hy} * c_{kj}^{\ hy} * \left(j^2\right)\sin^{j-1}(j * c_j^{\ y} * y)\cos(j * c_j^{\ y} * y) * y$$

$$= c_j^{\ y}\left(t\right) + \eta * \delta^{ol} * c_{kj}^{\ o} * \delta^{hy} * c_{kj}^{\ hy} * \delta^y * y$$

$$(308)$$

where:

$$\delta^{ol} = (d - z) f^{o\,'}\left(net^o\right) = d - z \qquad\qquad \left(linear\ neuron\ f^{o\,'}\left(net^o\right) = 1\right)$$

$$\delta^{hy} = f^{h\,'}\left(net_{kj}^{\ hy}\right) c_{kj}^{\ hx} b_k^{\ x} = c_{kj}^{\ hx} b_k^{\ x} \qquad \left(linear\ neuron\ f^{h\,'}\left(net_{kj}^{\ hy}\right) = 1\right)$$

$$\delta^y = f_y'\left(net_j^{\ y}\right) = \left(j^2\right)\sin^{j-1}(j * c_j^{\ y} * y)\cos(j * c_j^{\ y} * y)$$

UPC-HONN Model First Layer Neuron Weights Learning Formula

$$Let: f_k^{\ x}\left(c_k^{\ x} x\right) = (c_k^{\ x} x)^k \qquad\qquad (309)$$

$$f_j^{y}\left(c_j^{y}y\right) = \cos^{j}(j * c_j^{y}y) \tag{310}$$

For a polynomial function of x input side:

$$b_k^{x} = f_k^{x}\left(net_k^{x}\right) = (net_k^{x})^{k} = (c_k^{x} * x)^{k}$$

$$f_x'\left(net_k^{x}\right) = \partial b_k^{x} / \partial\left(net_k^{x}\right) = \partial\left(net_k^{x})^{k}\right)/\partial\left(net_k^{x}\right) = k(net_k^{x})^{k-1} = k * (c_k^{x} * x)^{k-1} \tag{311}$$

$$c_k^{x}\left(t+1\right) = c_k^{x}\left(t\right) - \eta\left(\frac{\partial E_p}{\partial c_k^{x}}\right)$$

$$= c_k^{x}\left(t\right) + \eta\left(d-z\right) f^{o'}\left(net^{o}\right)c_{kj}^{o} * f^{h}\left(net_{kj}^{h}\right)c_{kj}^{hy}b_j^{y}c_{kj}^{hx}f_x'\left(net_k^{x}\right)x \tag{312}$$

$$= c_k^{x}\left(t\right) + \eta * \delta^{ol} * c_{kj}^{o} * \delta^{hx} * c_{kj}^{hx} * k * (c_k^{x} * x)^{k-1} * x$$

$$= c_k^{x}\left(t\right) + \eta * \delta^{ol} * c_{kj}^{o} * \delta^{hx} * c_{kj}^{hx} * \delta^{x} * x$$

where:

$$\delta^{ol} = (d-z) f^{o'}\left(net^{o}\right) = d - z \qquad \left(\text{linear neuron } f^{o}{'}\left(net^{o}\right) = 1\right)$$

$$\delta^{hx} = f^{h}\left(net_{kj}^{h}\right)c_{kj}^{hy}b_j^{y} = c_{kj}^{hy}b_j^{y} \qquad \left(\text{linear neuron } f^{h}{'}\left(net_{kj}^{h}\right) = 1\right)$$

$$\delta^{x} = f_x'\left(net_k^{x}\right) = k * \left(net_k^{x}\right)^{k-1} = k * (c_k^{x} * x)^{k-1}$$

For an ultra-high frequency cosine function of y input part:

$$b_j^{y} = f_j^{y}\left(net_j^{y}\right) = \cos^{j}(j * net_j^{y}) = \cos^{j}(j * c_j^{y} * y)$$

$$f_y'\left(net_j^{y}\right) = \partial b_j^{y} / \partial\left(net_j^{y}\right)$$

$$= \partial\left(\cos^{j}(j * net_j^{y})\right)/\partial\left(net_j^{y}\right) = j \cos^{j-1}(j * net_j^{y}) * \left(-\sin(j * net_j^{y})\right) * j$$

$$= -j^{2} * \cos^{j-1}(j * net_j^{y}) * \sin(j * net_j^{y}) = -j^{2} * \cos^{j-1}(j * c_j^{y} * y) * \sin(j * y) \tag{313}$$

Using the above procedure:

$$c_j^y(t+1) = c_j^y(t) - \eta\left(\partial E_p / \partial c_j^y\right)$$

$$= c_j^y(t) + \eta(d-z)f^{o\,\prime}\left(net^o\right)c_{kj}^{\,o} * f^{h\,\prime}\left(net_{kj}^{\,h}\right)c_{kj}^{\,hx}b_k^{\,x}c_{kj}^{\,hy}f_y^{\,\prime}\left(net_j^{\,y}\right)y$$

$$= c_j^y(t) + \eta * \delta^{ol} * c_{kj}^{\,o} * \delta^{hy} * c_{kj}^{\,hy} * \left(-j^2\right) * \cos^{j-1}(j * c_j^y * y) * \sin(j * c_j^y * y) * y$$

$$= c_j^y(t) + \eta * \delta^{ol} * c_{kj}^{\,o} * \delta^{hy} * c_{kj}^{\,hy} * \delta^y * y$$

$$(314)$$

where:

$$\delta^{ol} = (d-z)f^{o\,\prime}\left(net^o\right) = d - z \qquad \left(linear\ neuron\ f^{o\,\prime}\left(net^o\right) = 1\right)$$

$$\delta^{hy} = f^{h\,\prime}\left(net_{kj}^{\,hy}\right)c_{kj}^{\,hx}b_k^{\,x} = c_{kj}^{\,hx}b_k^{\,x} \qquad \left(linear\ neuron\ f^{h\,\prime}\left(net_{kj}^{\,hy}\right) = 1\right)$$

$$\delta^y = f_y^{\,\prime}\left(net_j^{\,y}\right) = \left(-j^2\right) * \cos^{j-1}(j * c_j^y * y) * \sin(j * c_j^y * y)$$

UGS-HONN Model First Layer Neuron Weights Learning Formula

$$Let: f_k^{\,j}\left(c_k^{\,j}x\right) = \left(1/\left(1 + \exp(c_k^{\,x}(-x))\right)\right)^k \qquad (315)$$

$$f_j^{\,y}\left(c_j^{\,k}y\right) = \sin^j(j * c_j^{\,k}y) \qquad (316)$$

For a sigmoid function of x input side:

$$b_k{}^x = f_k{}^x\left(net_k{}^x\right) = \left[1/\left(1+\exp(-net_k{}^x)\right)\right]^k = \left[1/\left(1+\exp(c_k{}^x*(-x))\right)\right]^k$$

$$f_x{}'\left(net_k{}^x\right) = \partial b_k{}^x / \partial\left(net_k{}^x\right) = \partial\left[1/\left(1+\exp(-net_k{}^x)\right)\right]^k / \partial\left(net_k{}^x\right)$$

$$= k*\left[1/\left(1+\exp(-net_k{}^x)\right)\right]^{k-1}*\left(1+\exp(-net_k{}^x)\right)^{-2}*\exp(-net_k{}^x)$$

$$= k*\left[1/\left(1+\exp(-c_k{}^x*x)\right)\right]^{k-1}*\left(1+\exp(-c_k{}^x*x)\right)^{-2}*\exp(-c_k{}^x*x)$$

$$(317)$$

$$c_k{}^x(t+1) = c_k{}^x(t) - \eta\left(\partial E_p / \partial c_k{}^x\right)$$

$$= c_k{}^x(t) + \eta(d-z)f^{o}{}'\left(net^o\right)c_{kj}{}^o*f^{h}{}'\left(net_{kj}{}^h\right)c_{kj}{}^{hy}b_j{}^y c_{kj}{}^{hx} f_x{}'\left(net_k{}^x\right)x$$

$$= c_k{}^x(t) + \eta*\delta^{ol}*c_{kj}{}^o*\delta^{hx}*c_{kj}{}^{hx}*f_x{}'\left(net_k{}^x\right)*x = c_k{}^x(t) + \eta*\delta^{ol}*c_{kj}{}^o*\delta^{hx}*c_{kj}{}^{hx}$$

$$*\left[k*\left[1/\left(1+\exp(-c_k{}^x*x)\right)\right]^{k-1}*\left(1+\exp(-c_k{}^x*x)\right)^{-2}*\exp(-c_k{}^x*x)\right]*x$$

$$= c_k{}^x(t) + \eta*\delta^{ol}*c_{kj}{}^o*\delta^{hx}*c_{kj}{}^{hx}*\delta^x*x$$

$$(318)$$

where:

$$\delta^{ol} = (d-z)f^{o}{}'\left(net^o\right) = d-z \qquad \left(linear\ neuron\ f^{o}{}'\left(net^o\right)=1\right)$$

$$\delta^{hx} = f^{h}{}'\left(net_{kj}{}^h\right)c_{kj}{}^{hy}b_j{}^y = c_{kj}{}^{hy}b_j{}^y \qquad \left(linear\ neuron\ f^{h}{}'\left(net_{kj}{}^h\right)=1\right)$$

$$\delta^x = f_x{}'\left(net_k{}^x\right) = k*\left[1/\left(1+\exp(-c_k{}^x*x)\right)\right]^{k-1}*\left(1+\exp(-c_k{}^x*x)\right)^{-2}*\exp(-c_k{}^x*x)$$

For an ultra-high frequency sine function of y input part:

$$b_j^y = f_j^y\left(net_j^y\right) = \sin^j(j*net_j^y) = \sin^j(j*c_j^y*y)$$

$$f_y'\left(net_j^y\right) = \partial b_j^y / \partial\left(net_j^y\right)$$

$$= \partial\left(\sin^j(j*net_j^y)\right)/\partial\left(net_j^y\right) = j\sin^{j-1}(j*net_j^y)*\cos(j*net_j^y)*j$$

$$= j^2*\sin^{j-1}(j*net_j^y)*\cos(j*net_j^y) = j^2*\sin^{j-1}(j*c_j^y*y)*\cos(j*c_j^y*y)$$

$$(319)$$

Using the above procedure:

$$c_j^y(t+1) = c_j^y(t) - \eta\left(\partial E_p / \partial c_j^y\right)$$

$$= c_j^y(t) + \eta(d-z)f^{o'}\left(net^o\right)c_{kj}^o * f^{h'}\left(net_{kj}^h\right)c_{kj}^{hx}b_k^x c_{kj}^{hy}f_y'\left(net_j^y\right)y$$

$$= c_j^y(t) + \eta*\delta^{ol}*c_{kj}^o*\delta^{hy}*c_{kj}^{hy}*\left(j^2\right)\sin^{j-1}(j*c_j^y*y)\cos(j*c_j^y*y)*y$$

$$= c_j^y(t) + \eta*\delta^{ol}*c_{kj}^o*\delta^{hy}*c_{kj}^{hy}*\delta^y*y$$

$$(320)$$

where:

$$\delta^{ol} = (d-z)f^{o'}\left(net^o\right) = d-z \qquad \left(linear\ neuron\ f^{o'}\left(net^o\right)=1\right)$$

$$\delta^{hy} = f^{h'}\left(net_{kj}^{hy}\right)c_{kj}^{hx}b_k^x = c_{kj}^{hx}b_k^x \qquad \left(linear\ neuron\ f^{h'}\left(net_{kj}^{hy}\right)=1\right)$$

$$\delta^y = f_y'\left(net_j^y\right) = \left(j^2\right)\sin^{j-1}(j*c_j^y*y)\cos(j*c_j^y*y)$$

UGC-HONN Model First Layer Neuron Weights Learning Formula

$$Let: f_k^j\left(c_k^j x\right) = \left(1/\left(1+\exp(c_k^x(-x))\right)\right)^k \qquad (321)$$

$$f_j^y\left(c_j^{\,k}y\right)=\cos^j\left(j*c_j^{\,k}y\right) \tag{322}$$

For a sigmoid function of x input side:

$$b_k^{\,x}=f_k^{\,x}\left(net_k^{\,x}\right)=\left[1/\left(1+\exp(-net_k^{\,x})\right)\right]^k=\left[1/\left(1+\exp(c_k^{\,x}*(-x))\right)\right]^k$$

$$f_x'\left(net_k^{\,x}\right)=\partial b_k^{\,x}/\partial\left(net_k^{\,x}\right)=\partial\left[1/\left(1+\exp(-net_k^{\,x})\right)\right]^k/\partial\left(net_k^{\,x}\right)$$

$$=k*\left[1/\left(1+\exp(-net_k^{\,x})\right)\right]^{k-1}*\left(1+\exp(-net_k^{\,x})\right)^{-2}*\exp(-net_k^{\,x})$$

$$=k*\left[1/\left(1+\exp(-c_k^{\,x}*x)\right)\right]^{k-1}*\left(1+\exp(-c_k^{\,x}*x)\right)^{-2}*\exp(-c_k^{\,x}*x)$$

$$\tag{323}$$

$$c_k^{\,x}(t+1)=c_k^{\,x}(t)-\eta\left(\partial E_p/\partial c_k^{\,x}\right)$$

$$=c_k^{\,x}(t)+\eta(d-z)f^{o\,\prime}\left(net^o\right)c_{kj}^{\,o}*f^h\left(net_{kj}^{\,h}\right)c_{kj}^{\,hy}b_j^{\,y}c_{kj}^{\,hx}f_x'\left(net_k^{\,x}\right)x$$

$$=c_k^{\,x}(t)+\eta*\delta^{ol}*c_{kj}^{\,o}*\delta^{hx}*c_{kj}^{\,hx}*f_x'\left(net_k^{\,x}\right)*x=c_k^{\,x}(t)+\eta*\delta^{ol}*c_{kj}^{\,o}*\delta^{hx}*c_{kj}^{\,hx}$$

$$*\left[k*\left[1/\left(1+\exp(-c_k^{\,x}*x)\right)\right]^{k-1}*\left(1+\exp(-c_k^{\,x}*x)\right)^{-2}*\exp(-c_k^{\,x}*x)\right]*x$$

$$=c_k^{\,x}(t)+\eta*\delta^{ol}*c_{kj}^{\,o}*\delta^{hx}*c_{kj}^{\,hx}*\delta^x*x$$

$$\tag{324}$$

where:

$$\delta^{ol}=(d-z)f^{o\,\prime}\left(net^o\right)=d-z \qquad \left(linear\ neuron\ f^{o\,\prime}\left(net^o\right)=1\right)$$

$$\delta^{hx}=f^{h\prime}\left(net_{kj}^{\,h}\right)c_{kj}^{\,hy}b_j^{\,y}=c_{kj}^{\,hy}b_j^{\,y} \qquad \left(linear\ neuron\ f^{h\prime}\left(net_{kj}^{\,h}\right)=1\right)$$

$$\delta^x=f_x'\left(net_k^{\,x}\right)=k*\left[1/\left(1+\exp(-c_k^{\,x}*x)\right)\right]^{k-1}*\left(1+\exp(-c_k^{\,x}*x)\right)^{-2}*\exp(-c_k^{\,x}*x)$$

For an ultra-high frequency cosine function of y input part:

$$b_j^{\ y} = f_j^{\ y}\left(net_j^{\ y}\right) = \cos^j(j*net_j^{\ y}) = \cos^j(j*c_j^{\ y}*y)$$

$$f_y{}'\left(net_j^{\ y}\right) = \partial b^y{}_j \,/\, \partial\left(net_j^{\ y}\right)$$

$$= \partial\left(\cos^j(j*net_j^{\ y})\right)/\partial\left(net_j^{\ y}\right) = j\cos^{j-1}(j*net_j^{\ y})*\left(-\sin(j*net_j^{\ y})\right)*j$$

$$= -j^2*\cos^{j-1}(j*net_j^{\ y})*\sin(j*net_j^{\ y}) = -j^2*\cos^{j-1}(j*c_j^{\ y}*y)*\sin(j*c_j^{\ y}*y)$$

$$(325)$$

Using the above procedure:

$$c_j^{\ y}\left(t+1\right) = c_j^{\ y}\left(t\right) - \eta\left(\partial E_p\,/\,\partial c_j^{\ y}\right)$$

$$= c_j^{\ y}\left(t\right) + \eta\left(d-z\right)f^{o}{}'\left(net^o\right)c_{kj}^{\ o}*f^{h}{}'\left(net_{kj}^{\ h}\right)c_{kj}^{\ hx}b_k^{\ x}c_{kj}^{\ hy}f_y{}'\left(net_j^{\ y}\right)y$$

$$= c_j^{\ y}\left(t\right) + \eta*\delta^{ol}*c_{kj}^{\ o}*\delta^{hy}*c_{kj}^{\ hy}*\left(-j^2\right)*\cos^{j-1}(j*c_j^{\ y}*y)*\sin(j*c_j^{\ y}*y)*y$$

$$= c_j^{\ y}\left(t\right) + \eta*\delta^{ol}*c_{kj}^{\ o}*\delta^{hy}*c_{kj}^{\ hy}*\delta^{y}*y$$

$$(327)$$

where:

$$\delta^{ol} = \left(d-z\right)f^{o'}\left(net^o\right) = d-z \qquad\qquad \left(linear\ neuron\ f^{o}{}'\left(net^o\right) = 1\right)$$

$$\delta^{hy} = f^{h'}\left(net_{kj}^{\ hy}\right)c_{kj}^{\ hx}b_k^{\ x} = c_{kj}^{\ hx}b_k^{\ x} \qquad \left(linear\ neuron\ f^{h}{}'\left(net_{kj}^{\ hy}\right) = 1\right)$$

$$\delta^{y} = f_y{}'\left(net_j^{\ y}\right) = \left(-j^2\right)*\cos^{j-1}(j*c_j^{\ y}*y)*\sin(j*c_j^{\ y}*y)$$

UNS-HONN Model First Layer Neuron Weights Learning Formula

$$Let: f_k^{\ j}\left(c_k^{\ j}x\right) = \left(\sin(c_k^{\ x}x)/\left(c_k^{\ x}x\right)\right)^k \qquad\qquad (327)$$

$$f_j^{\,y}\left(c_j^{\,k}y\right)=\sin^j(j*c_j^{\,k}y) \tag{328}$$

For a SINC function of x input part:

$$b_k^{\,x} = f_k^{\,x}\left(net_k^{\,x}\right)=\left[\sin(net_k^{\,x})/net_k^{\,x}\right]^k =\left[\sin(c_k^{\,x}x)/c_k^{\,x}x\right]^k$$

$$f_x'\left(net_k^{\,x}\right)=\partial b_k^{\,x}/\partial\left(net_k^{\,x}\right)$$

$$=k\left[\sin(net_k^{\,x})/\left(net_k^{\,x}\right)\right]^{k-1}*\left[\cos(net_k^{\,x})/\left(net_k^{\,x}\right)-\sin(net_k^{\,x})/\left(net_k^{\,x}\right)^2\right]$$

$$=k\left[\sin(c_k^{\,x}x)/\left(c_k^{\,k}x\right)\right]^{k-1}*\left[\cos(c_k^{\,x}x)/\left(c_k^{\,x}x\right)-\sin(c_k^{\,x}x)/\left(c_k^{\,x}x\right)^2\right] \tag{329}$$

$$c_k^{\,x}(t+1)=c_k^{\,x}(t)-\eta\left(\partial E_p/\partial c_k^{\,x}\right)$$

$$=c_k^{\,x}(t)+\eta\,(d-z)\,f^{o\,\prime}\left(net^o\right)c_{kj}^{\,o}*f^{h\,\prime}\left(net_{kj}^{\,h}\right)c_{kj}^{\,hy}b_j^{\,y}c_{kj}^{\,hx}f_x^{\,\prime}\left(net_k^{\,x}\right)x$$

$$=c_k^{\,x}(t)+\eta*\delta^{ol}*c_{kj}^{\,o}*\delta^{hx}*c_{kj}^{\,hx}*f_x^{\,\prime}\left(net_k^{\,x}\right)*x=c_k^{\,x}(t)+\eta*\delta^{ol}*c_{kj}^{\,o}*\delta^{hx}*c_{kj}^{\,hx}$$

$$*[k[\sin(c_k^{\,x}x)/\left(c_k^{\,x}x\right)]^{k-1}*\left[\cos(c_k^{\,x}x)/\left(c_k^{\,x}x\right)-\sin(c_k^{\,x}x)/\left(c_k^{\,x}x\right)^2\right]]*x$$

$$=c_k^{\,x}(t)+\eta*\delta^{ol}*c_{kj}^{\,o}*\delta^{hx}*c_{kj}^{\,hx}*\delta^x*x \tag{330}$$

where:

$$\delta^{ol}=(d-z)\,f^{o\prime}\left(net^o\right)=(d-z)\qquad\left(linear\ neuron\ f^{o\,\prime}\left(net^o\right)=1\right)$$

$$\delta^{hx}=f^{h\prime}\left(net_{kj}^{\,h}\right)c_{kj}^{\,hy}b_j^{\,y}=c_{kj}^{\,hy}b_j^{\,y}\qquad\left(linear\ neuron\ f^{h\,\prime}\left(net_{kj}^{\,h}\right)=1\right)$$

$$\delta^x=f_x^{\,\prime}\left(net_k^{\,x}\right)$$

$$=k\left[\sin(net_k^{\,x})/\left(net_k^{\,x}\right)\right]^{k-1}*\left[\cos(net_k^{\,x})/\left(net_k^{\,x}\right)-\sin(net_k^{\,x})/\left(net_k^{\,x}\right)^2\right]$$

$$=k\left[\sin(c_k^{\,x}x)/\left(c_k^{\,x}x\right)\right]^{k-1}*\left[\cos(c_k^{\,x}x)/\left(c_k^{\,x}x\right)-\sin(c_k^{\,x}x)/\left(c_k^{\,x}x\right)^2\right]$$

For an ultra-high frequency sine function of y input part:

$$b_j^y = f_j^y\left(net_j^y\right) = \sin^j(j * net_j^y) = \sin^j(j * c_j^y * y)$$

$$f_y'\left(net_j^y\right) = \partial b_j^y / \partial\left(net_j^y\right) = \partial\left(\sin^j(j * net_j^y)\right) / \partial\left(net_j^y\right)$$

$$= j\sin^{j-1}(j * net_j^y) * \cos(j * net_j^y) * j = j^2 * \sin^{j-1}(j * net_j^y) * \cos(j * net_j^y)$$

$$= j^2 * \sin^{j-1}(j * c_j^y * y) * \cos(j * c_j^y * y)$$

$$(331)$$

Using the above procedure:

$$c_j^y(t+1) = c_j^y(t) - \eta\left(\partial E_p / \partial c_j^y\right)$$

$$= c_j^y(t) + \eta(d-z)f^{o'}\left(net^o\right)c_{kj}^o * f^{h'}\left(net_{kj}^h\right)c_{kj}^{hx}b_k^x c_{kj}^{hy}f_y'\left(net_j^y\right)y$$

$$= c_j^y(t) + \eta * \delta^{ol} * c_{kj}^o * \delta^{hy} * c_{kj}^{hy} * \left(j^2\right)\sin^{j-1}(j * c_j^y * y)\cos(j * c_j^y * y) * y$$

$$= c_j^y(t) + \eta * \delta^{ol} * c_{kj}^o * \delta^{hy} * c_{kj}^{hy} * \delta^y * y$$

$$(332)$$

where:

$$\delta^{ol} = (d-z)f^{o'}\left(net^o\right) = d - z\left(linear\ neuron\ f^{o'}\left(net^o\right) = 1\right)$$

$$\delta^{hy} = f^{h'}\left(net_{kj}^{hy}\right)c_{kj}^{hx}b_k^x = c_{kj}^{hx}b_k^x\left(linear\ neuron\ f^{h'}\left(net_{kj}^{hy}\right) = 1\right)$$

$$\delta^y = f_y'\left(net_j^y\right) = \left(j^2\right)\sin^{j-1}(j * c_j^y * y)\cos(j * c_j^y * y)$$

UNC-HONN Model First Layer Neuron Weights Learning Formula

Let: $f_k^j\left(c_k^j x\right) = \left(\sin(c_k^x x) / \left(c_k^x x\right)\right)^k$

$$(333)$$

$$f_j^y \left(c_j^k y\right) = \cos^j \left(j * c_j^k y\right) \tag{334}$$

For a SINC function of x input part:

$$b_k^x = f_k^x \left(net_k^x\right) = \left[\sin(net_k^x)/net_k^x\right]^k = \left[\sin(c_k^x x)/c_k^x x\right]^k$$

$$f_x^{'} \left(net_k^x\right) = \partial b_k^x / \partial \left(net_k^x\right)$$

$$= k\left[\sin(net_k^x)/\left(net_k^x\right)\right]^{k-1} * \left[\cos(net_k^x)/\left(net_k^x\right) - \sin(net_k^x)/\left(net_k^x\right)^2\right]$$

$$= k\left[\sin(c_k^x x)/\left(c_k^k x\right)\right]^{k-1} * \left[\cos(c_k^x x)/\left(c_k^x x\right) - \sin(c_k^x x)/\left(c_k^x x\right)^2\right]$$

$$\tag{335}$$

$$c_k^x (t+1) = c_k^x (t) - \eta \left(\partial E_p / \partial c_k^x\right)$$

$$= c_k^x (t) + \eta (d-z) f^{o'} \left(net^o\right) c_{kj}^o * f^{h'} \left(net_{kj}^h\right) c_{kj}^{hy} b_j^y c_{kj}^{hx} f_x^{'} \left(net_k^x\right) x$$

$$= c_k^x (t) + \eta * \delta^{ol} * c_{kj}^o * \delta^{hx} * c_{kj}^{hx} * f_x^{'} \left(net_k^x\right) * x = c_k^x (t) + \eta * \delta^{ol} * c_{kj}^o * \delta^{hx} * c_{kj}^{hx}$$

$$*\left[k\left[\sin(c_k^x x)/\left(c_k^k x\right)\right]^{k-1} * \left[\cos(c_k^x x)/\left(c_k^x x\right) - \sin(c_k^x x)/\left(c_k^x x\right)^2\right]\right] * x$$

$$= c_k^x (t) + \eta * \delta^{ol} * c_{kj}^o * \delta^{hx} * c_{kj}^{hx} * \delta^x * x$$

$$\tag{336}$$

where:

$$\delta^{ol} = (d-z) f^{o'} \left(net^o\right) = (d-z) \qquad \left(\text{linear neuron } f^{o'}\left(net^o\right) = 1\right)$$

$$\delta^{hx} = f^{h'} \left(net_{kj}^h\right) c_{kj}^{hy} b_j^y = c_{kj}^{hy} b_j^y \qquad \left(\text{linear neuron } f^{h'}\left(net_{kj}^h\right) = 1\right)$$

$$\delta^x = f_x^{'} \left(net_k^x\right)$$

$$= k\left[\sin(net_k^x)/\left(net_k^x\right)\right]^{k-1} * \left[\cos(net_k^x)/\left(net_k^x\right) - \sin(net_k^x)/\left(net_k^x\right)^2\right]$$

$$= k\left[\sin(c_k^x x)/\left(c_k^x x\right)\right]^{k-1} * \left[\cos(c_k^x x)/\left(c_k^x x\right) - \sin(c_k^x x)/\left(c_k^x x\right)^2\right]$$

For an ultra-high frequency cosine function of y input part:

$$b_j^{\,y} = f_j^{\,y}\left(net_j^{\,y}\right) = \cos^j(j*net_j^{\,y}) = \cos^j(j*c_j^{\,y}*y)$$

$$f_y^{\,\prime}\left(net_j^{\,y}\right) = \partial b^y_{\,j} / \partial\left(net_j^{\,y}\right)$$

$$= \partial\left(\cos^j(j*net_j^{\,y})\right) / \partial\left(net_j^{\,y}\right) = j\cos^{j-1}(j*net_j^{\,y})*\left(-\sin(j*net_j^{\,y})\right)*j$$

$$= -j^2*\cos^{j-1}(j*net_j^{\,y})*\sin(j*net_j^{\,y}) = -j^2*\cos^{j-1}(j*c_j^{\,y}*y)*\sin(j*c_j^{\,y}*y)$$

$$(337)$$

Using the above procedure:

$$c_j^{\,y}(t+1) = c_j^{\,y}(t) - \eta\left(\partial E_p / \partial c_j^{\,y}\right)$$

$$= c_j^{\,y}(t) + \eta(d-z)f^{o\,\prime}\left(net^o\right)c_{kj}^{\,o}*f^{h\,\prime}\left(net_{kj}^{\,h}\right)c_{kj}^{\,hx}b_k^{\,x}c_{kj}^{\,hy}f_y^{\,\prime}\left(net_j^{\,y}\right)y$$

$$= c_j^{\,y}(t) + \eta*\delta^{ol}*c_{kj}^{\,o}*\delta^{hy}*c_{kj}^{\,hy}*\left(-j^2\right)*\cos^{j-1}(j*c_j^{\,y}*y)*\sin(j*c_j^{\,y}*y)*y$$

$$= c_j^{\,y}(t) + \eta*\delta^{ol}*c_{kj}^{\,o}*\delta^{hy}*c_{kj}^{\,hy}*\delta^y*y$$

$$(338)$$

where:

$$\delta^{ol} = (d-z)f^{o\,\prime}\left(net^o\right) = d - z\left(linear\ neuron\ f^{o\,\prime}\left(net^o\right) = 1\right)$$

$$\delta^{hy} = f^{h\,\prime}\left(net_{kj}^{\,hy}\right)c_{kj}^{\,hx}b_k^{\,x} = c_{kj}^{\,hx}b_k^{\,x} \qquad \left(linear\ neuron\ f^{h\,\prime}\left(net_{kj}^{\,hy}\right) = 1\right)$$

$$\delta^y = f_y^{\,\prime}\left(net_j^{\,y}\right) = \left(-j^2\right)*\cos^{j-1}(j*c_j^{\,y}*y)*\sin(j*c_j^{\,y}*y)$$

FUTURE RESEARCH DIRECTIONS

As the next step of HONN model research, more HONN models for different kinds of data will be built to increase the pool of HONN models. Theoretically, the adaptive HONN models can be built and allow the computer automatically to choose the best model, order, and coefficients. Thus, making the adaptive HONN models easier to use is one of the future research topics.

HONNs can automatically select the initial coefficients for nonlinear data analysis. The next step of this study will also focus on how to allow people working in different areas to understand that HONNs are much easier to use and can have better results. Moreover, further research will develop HONNs software packages for people working in the different area. HONNs will challenge classic procedures and change the research methodology that people are currently using in the prediction areas for nonlinear data application.

CONCLUSION

Twenty-four nonlinear neural network models are listed in the chapter. This chapter introduces the background of HONN models developing history. This chapter also overviews 24 applied artificial higher order neural network models and provides 24 HONN Models learning algorithm and weight update formulae. This chapter uses a single uniform HONN architecture for ALL 24 HONN models and uses a uniform learning algorithm for all 24 HONN models. This chapter provides uniform weight update formulae for all 24 HONN models.

REFERENCES

Crane, J., & Zhang, M. (2005). Data simulation using SINCHONN model. In *Proceedings of 2005 IASTED International Conference on Computational Intelligence* (pp. 50 -55). Calgary, Canada: Academic Press.

Fulcher, J., & Zhang, M. (2005). Higher-order neural networks. In *Proceedings of 2005 International Conference on Advances in the Internet, Processing, Systems, and Interdisciplinary Research* (p.22). Costa Brava, Spain: Academic Press.

Fulcher, J., Zhang, M., & Xu, S. (2006). The application of higher-order neural networks to financial time series prediction. In J. Kamruzzaman, R. K. Begg, & R. A. Aarker (Eds.), *Artificial Neural Networks in Finance and Manufacturing* (pp. 80–108). Hershey, PA: Idea Group Publishing. doi:10.4018/978-1-59140-670-9.ch005

Lu, B., Qi, H., Zhang, M., & Scofield, R. A. (2000). Using PT-HONN models for multi-polynomial function simulation. In *Proceedings of IASTED International Conference on Neural Networks* (pp. 1-5). Academic Press.

Qi, H., Zhang, M., & Scofield, R. A. (2001). Rainfall estimation using M-PHONN model. In *Proceedings of 2001 International Joint Conference on Neural Networks* (pp.1620 - 1624). Washington, DC: Academic Press.

Xu, S., & Zhang, M. (2002). An adaptive activation function for higher order neural networks. In *Proceeding of 15th Australian Joint Conference on Artificial* Intelligence (pp.356-362). Canberra, Australia: Academic Press.

Zhang, J. C., Zhang, M., & Fulcher, J. (1997). Financial prediction using higher order trigonometric polynomial neural network group models. In *Proceedings of ICNN/IEEE International Conference on Neural Networks* (pp. 2231-2234). Houston, TX: IEEE. 10.1109/ICNN.1997.614373

Zhang, M. (2008). SAS and higher order neural network nonlinear model. In *Proceedings of 2008 International Conference on Modeling, Simulation and Visualization Methods* (pp. 32-38). Las Vegas, NV: Academic Press.

Zhang, M. (2001). Financial data simulation using A-PHONN model. In *Proceedings of 2001 International Joint Conference on Neural Networks* (pp.1823 - 1827). Washington, DC: Academic Press.

Zhang, M. (2002a). Rainfall Estimation Using PL-HONN Model. In *Proceedings of 2002 IASTED International Conference on Modeling and Simulation* (pp. 50-53). Marina del Rey, CA: Academic Press.

Zhang, M. (2002b). Financial data simulation using PL-HONN model. In *Proceedings of 2002 IASTED International Conference on Modeling and Simulation* (pp. 229-233). Marina del Rey, CA: Academic Press.

Zhang, M. (2005). A data simulation system using sinc(x)/x and sine polynomial higher order neural networks. In *Proceedings of 2005 IASTED International Conference on Computational Intelligence* (pp.56 – 61). Calgary, Canada: Academic Press.

Zhang, M. (2006). A data simulation system using CSINC polynomial higher order neural networks. In *Proceedings of 2006 International Conference On Artificial Intelligence* (pp. 91-97). Las Vegas, NV: Academic Press.

Zhang, M. (2007). A data simulation system using YSINC polynomial higher order neural networks. In *Proceedings of 2007 IASTED International Conference on Modeling and Simulation* (pp. 465-470). Montreal, Quebec, Canada: Academic Press.

Zhang, M. (Ed.). (2009a). *Artificial higher order neural networks for economics and business*. Hershey, PA: IGI Global. doi:10.4018/978-1-59904-897-0

Zhang, M. (2009b). Artificial higher order neural networks for economics and business – SAS NLIN or HONNs. In M. Zhang (Ed.), *Artificial Higher Order Neural Networks for Economics and Business* (pp. 1–47). Hershey, PA: IGI Global. doi:10.4018/978-1-59904-897-0.ch001

Zhang, M. (2009c). Ultra-high frequency trigonometric higher order neural networks for time series data analysis. In M. Zhang (Ed.), *Artificial Higher Order Neural Networks for Economics and Business* (pp. 133–163). Hershey, PA: IGI Global. doi:10.4018/978-1-59904-897-0.ch007

Zhang, M. (2009d). Time series simulation using ultra high frequency cosine and cosine higher order neural networks. In *Proceedings of International Association of Science and Technology for Development 12th International Conference on Intelligent systems and Control* (pp. 8-15). Cambridge, MA: Academic Press.

Zhang, M. (Ed.). (2010a). *Higher order neural networks for computer science and engineering: trends for emerging applications*. Hershey, PA: IGI-Global. doi:10.4018/978-1-61520-711-4

Zhang, M. (2010b). Higher order neural network group-based adaptive tolerance tree. In M. Zhang (Ed.), *Higher Order Neural Networks for Computer Science and Engineering: Trends for Emerging Applications* (pp. 1–36). Hershey, PA: IGI- Global.

Zhang, M. (2010c). Rainfall estimation using neuron-adaptive higher order neural networks. In M. Zhang (Ed.), *Higher Order Neural Networks for Computer Science and Engineering: Trends for Emerging Applications* (pp. 159–186). Hershey, PA: IGI- Global. doi:10.4018/978-1-61520-711-4.ch007

Zhang, M. (2010d). Time series simulation using ultra high frequency sine and sine higher order neural networks. In *Proceedings of Seventh International Symposium on Neural Networks* (pp. WAD-7). Shanghai, China: Academic Press.

Zhang, M. (2011). Sine and sigmoid higher order neural networks for data simulation. In *proceedings of 2011 International Conference on Software Engineering, Artificial Intelligence, Networking, and Parallel/Distributed Computing (SNPD)* (p.15). Sydney, Australia: Academic Press.

Zhang, M. (2012). Polynomial and sigmoid higher order neural networks for data simulations and prediction. In Proceedings of the 2012 International Journal of Arts & Science Conference (p.16). Florence, Italy: Academic Press.

Zhang, M. (Ed.). (2013a). *Higher order neural networks for modeling and simulation*. Hershey, PA: IGI-Global. doi:10.4018/978-1-4666-2175-6

Zhang, M. (2013b). Artificial multi-polynomial higher order neural network models. In M. Zhang (Ed.), *Higher Order Neural Networks for Modeling and Simulation* (pp. 1–29). Hershey, PA: IGI-Global. doi:10.4018/978-1-4666-2175-6.ch001

Zhang, M. (2013c). Artificial polynomial and trigonometric higher order neural network group models. In M. Zhang (Ed.), *Higher Order Neural Networks for Modeling and Simulation* (pp. 78–102). Hershey, PA: IGI-Global. doi:10.4018/978-1-4666-2175-6.ch005

Zhang, M. (2014a). Sinc and sigmoid higher order neural network for data modeling and simulation. In *Proceedings of Second International Conference on Vulnerability and Risk Analysis* (pp. 2608-2617). 10.1061/9780784413609.262

Zhang, M. (2014b). Ultra-high frequency polynomial and sine artificial higher order neural networks for control signal generator. In *Proceedings of 2014 IEEE Symposium Series on Computational Intelligence* (p.174). 10.1109/CICA.2014.7013235

Zhang, M. (2016a). Ultra-high frequency polynomial and trigonometric higher order neural networks for control signal generator. In M. Zhang (Ed.), *Applied Artificial Higher Order Neural Networks for Control and Recognition* (pp. 1–34). Hershey, PA: IGI Global, Information Science Reference. doi:10.4018/978-1-5225-0063-6.ch001

Zhang, M. (2016b). Ultra-high frequency sigmoid and trigonometric higher order neural networks for data pattern recognition. In M. Zhang (Ed.), *Applied Artificial Higher Order Neural Networks for Control and Recognition* (pp. 80–112). Hershey, PA: IGI Global, Information Science Reference. doi:10.4018/978-1-5225-0063-6.ch004

Zhang, M. (2016c). Artificial sine and cosine trigonometric higher order neural networks for financial data prediction. In M. Zhang (Ed.), *Applied Artificial Higher Order Neural Networks for Control and Recognition. Hershey* (pp. 208–236). IGI Global, Information Science Reference. doi:10.4018/978-1-5225-0063-6.ch009

Zhang, M. (2016d). Ultra-high frequency SINC and trigonometric higher order neural networks for data classification. In M. Zhang (Ed.), *Applied Artificial Higher Order Neural Networks for Control and Recognition* (pp. 113–153). Hershey, PA: IGI Global, Information Science Reference. doi:10.4018/978-1-5225-0063-6.ch005

Zhang, M. (2016e). Cosine and sigmoid higher order neural networks for date simulations. In M. Zhang (Ed.), *Applied Artificial Higher Order Neural Networks for Control and Recognition* (pp. 237–252). Hershey, PA: IGI Global, Information Science Reference. doi:10.4018/978-1-5225-0063-6.ch010

Zhang, M. (2016f). *Applied artificial higher order neural networks for control and recognition*. Hershey, PA: IGI Global, Information Science Reference. doi:10.4018/978-1-5225-0063-6

Zhang, M. (2016g). Artificial Higher Order Neural Network Models. In M. Zhang (Ed.), *Applied Artificial Higher Order Neural Networks for Control and Recognition* (pp. 282–350). Hershey, PA: IGI Global, Information Science Reference. doi:10.4018/978-1-5225-0063-6.ch012

Zhang, M., & Crane, J. (2004). Rainfall estimation using SPHONN model. In *Proceedings of 2004 International Conference on Artificial Intelligence* (pp.695-701). Las Vegas, NV: Academic Press.

Zhang, M., & Fulcher, J. (2004). Higher order neural network for satellite weather predication. In Applied Intelligent Systems (pp. 17-57). Springer-Verlag.

Zhang, M., & Lu, B. (2001). Financial data simulation using M-PHONN model. In *Proceedings of 2001International Joint Conference on Neural Networks* (pp. 1828 - 1832). Washington, DC: Academic Press.

Zhang, M., & Scofield, R. A. (2001). Rainfall estimation using A-PHONN model. In *Proceedings of 2001 International Joint Conference on Neural Networks* (pp. 1583 - 1587), Washington, DC: Academic Press.

Zhang, M., Murugesan, S., & Sadeghi, M. (1995). Polynomial higher order neural network for economic data simulation. In *Proceedings of International Conference on Neural Information Processing* (pp. 493-496). Beijing, China: Academic Press.

Zhang, M., Xu, S., & Fulcher, F. (2002). Neuron-adaptive higher order neural network models for automated financial data modeling. *IEEE Transactions on Neural Networks, 13*(1), 188–204. doi:10.1109/72.977302 PMID:18244418

Zhang, M., Zhang, J. C., & Fulcher, J. (2000). Higher order neural network group models for financial simulation. *International Journal of Neural Systems, 10*(2), 123–142. doi:10.1142/S0129065700000119 PMID:10939345

Zhang, M., Zhang, J. C., & Keen, S. (1999). Using THONN system for higher frequency non-linear data simulation & prediction. In *Proceedings of IASTED International Conference on Artificial Intelligence and Soft Computing* (pp.320-323). Honolulu, HI: Academic Press.

ADDITIONAL READING

Alanis, A. Y., Sanchez, E. N., Loukianov, A. G., & Perez-Cisneros, M. A. (2010). A. G. Real-time discrete neural block control using sliding modes for electric induction motors. *IEEE Transactions on Control Systems Technology, 18*(1), 11–21. doi:10.1109/TCST.2008.2009466

Amartur, S. C., Piraino, D., & Takefuji, Y. (1992). Optimization Neural Networks for the Segmentation of Magnetic Resonance Images. *IEEE Transactions on Medical Imaging, 11*(2), 215–220. doi:10.1109/42.141645 PMID:18218375

Banker, R. D., & Datar, S. M. (1989). Sensitivity, Precision, and Linear Aggregation of Signals for Performance Evaluation. *Journal of Accounting Research, 27*(1), 21–39. doi:10.2307/2491205

Behnke, S., & Karayiannis, N. B. (1998). CNeT: Competitive Neural Trees for Pattern Classifications. *IEEE Transactions on Neural Networks, 9*(6), 1352–1369. doi:10.1109/72.728387 PMID:18255815

Bridgwater, A. V. (2003). Renewable fuels and chemicals by thermal processing of biomass. *Chemical Engineering Journal, 91*(2-3), 87–102. doi:10.1016/S1385-8947(02)00142-0

Charitou, A., & Charalambous, C. (1996). The prediction of earnings using financial statement information: Empirical evidence with logit models and artificial neural networks. *Intelligent Systems in Accounting, Finance & Management, 5*(4), 199–215. doi:10.1002/(SICI)1099-1174(199612)5:4<199::AID-ISAF114>3.0.CO;2-C

Chen, S. M., Shie, J. D. (2008). Fuzzy classification systems based on fuzzy information gain measures. *International Journal of Expert Systems With Applications, 36*(3), 4517-4522.

Cichochi, A., & Unbehauen, R. (1993). *Neural Networks for Optimization and Signal Processing*. Chichester: Wiley.

Crouch, J. R., Pizer, S. M., Chaney, E. L., Hu, Y.-C., Mageras, G. S., & Zaider, M. (2007). Automated Finite-Element Analysis for Deformable Registration of Prostate Images. *IEEE Transactions on Medical Imaging, 26*(10), 1379–1390. doi:10.1109/TMI.2007.898810 PMID:17948728

Dong, G., & Pei, J. (2007). *Sequence Data Mining*. Springer.

Durbin, R., & Rumelhart, D. E. (1989). Product units: A computationally powerful and biologically plausible extension to backpropagation networks. *Neural Computation, 1*(1), 133–142. doi:10.1162/neco.1989.1.1.133

El-Fouly Tarek, H. M., El-Saadany Ehab, F., & Salama Magdy, M. A. (2008). One Day Ahead Prediction of Wind Speed and Direction. *IEEE Transactions on Energy Conversion, 23*(1), 191–201. doi:10.1109/TEC.2007.905069

Fama, E. (1980). Agency problems and the theory of the firm. *Journal of Political Economy, 88*(2), 288–307. doi:10.1086/260866

Foresti, G. L., & Dolso, T. (2004). An adaptive high-order neural tree for pattern recognition. *IEEE Transactions on Systems, Man, and Cybernetics. Part B, Cybernetics, 34*(2), 988–996. doi:10.1109/TSMCB.2003.818538 PMID:15376845

Giltrap, D. L., McKibbin, R., & Barnes, G. R. G. (2003). A steady state model of gas–char reactions in a downdraft gasifier. *Solar Energy, 74*(1), 85–91. doi:10.1016/S0038-092X(03)00091-4

Gore, A., Matsunaga, S. R., & Yeung, E. (2010). The Role of Technical Expertise in Firm Governance Structure: Evidence from Chief Financial Officer Contractual Incentives. *Strategic Management Journal, 32*(7), 771–786. doi:10.1002mj.907

Gupta, M. M., Homma, N., Hou, Z., Solo, A. M. G., & Goto, T. (2009). Fundamental Theory of Artificial Higher Order Neural Networks. In Ming Zhang (Ed.), Artificial Higher Order Neural Networks for Economics and Business (pp.368 - 388). Information Science Reference, Hershey, PA, USA: IGI Global. doi:10.4018/978-1-59904-897-0.ch017

Holubar, P., Zani, L., Hager, M., Froschl, W., Radak, Z., & Braun, R. (2002). Advanced controlling of anaerobic digestion by means of hierarchical neural networks. *Water Research*, *36*(10), 2582–2588. doi:10.1016/S0043-1354(01)00487-0 PMID:12153025

Hornik, K., Stinchombe, M., & White, H. (1989). Multilayer feedforward networks are universal approximations. *Neural Networks*, *2*(5), 359–366. doi:10.1016/0893-6080(89)90020-8

Huang, C. L., & Wang, C. J. (2006). A GA-based feature selection and parameters optimization for support vector machines. *International J Exp. Sys. App*, *31*, 231–240.

Huang, H., Feng, G., & Cao, J. (2008). Robust state estimation for uncertain neural networks with time-varying delay. *IEEE Transactions on Neural Networks*, *19*(8), 1329–1339. doi:10.1109/TNN.2008.2000206 PMID:18701365

Ioannou, P., & Sun, J. (1996). *Robust Adaptive Control*. Prentice Hall.

Jensen, M., & Meckling, W. (1976). Theory of the firm: Managerial behavior, agency costs and ownership structure. *Journal of Financial Economics*, *3*(4), 305–360. doi:10.1016/0304-405X(76)90026-X

Keating, A. (1997). Determinants of divisional performance evaluation practices. *Journal of Accounting and Economics*, *24*(3), 243–273. doi:10.1016/S0165-4101(98)00008-1

Kim, S. H., & Noh, H. J. (1997). Predictability of interest rates using data mining tools: A comparative analysis of Korea and the US. *Expert Systems with Applications*, *13*(2), 85–95. doi:10.1016/S0957-4174(97)00010-9

Leunga, C., & Chan, L. (2003). Dual extended Kalman filtering in recurrent neural networks. *Neural Networks*, *16*(2), 223–239. doi:10.1016/S0893-6080(02)00230-7 PMID:12628608

Li, Y. M. (2008). An Improvement to Ant Colony Optimization Heuristic. *LNCS*, *5263*, 816–825.

Mailleret, L., Bernard, O., & Steyer, J. P. (2004). Nonlinear adaptive control for bioreactors with unknown kinetics. *Automatica, 40*(8), 1379–1385. doi:10.1016/j.automatica.2004.01.030

McCulloch, W. S., & Pitts, W. H. (1943). A logical calculus of the ideas imminent in nervous activity. *The Bulletin of Mathematical Biophysics, 5*(4), 115–133. doi:10.1007/BF02478259

Mitra, S., & Hayashi, Y. (2000). Neuro-fuzzy rule generation: Survey in soft computing framework. *IEEE Transactions on Neural Networks, 11*(3), 748–768. doi:10.1109/72.846746 PMID:18249802

Moreira, J. M., & Auto, D. M. (1993). Intermittency in a neural network with variable threshold. *Europhysics Letters, 21*(6), 639–644. doi:10.1209/0295-5075/21/6/001

Naimark, M. A., & Stern, A. I. (1982). *Theory of Group Representations.* Springer-Verlag. doi:10.1007/978-1-4613-8142-6

Norgaard, M., Ravn, O., Poulsen, N. K., & Hansen, L. K. (2000). *Neural Networks for Modelling and Control of Dynamic Systems: A practitioner's Handbook.* London: Springer-Verlag. doi:10.1007/978-1-4471-0453-7

Palm, G. (1980). On associative memory. *Biological Cybernetics, 36*(1), 19–31. doi:10.1007/BF00337019 PMID:7353062

Pearlmutter, B. A. (1995). Gradient Calculation of Recurrent Neural Networks: A Survey. *IEEE Transactions on Neural Networks, 6*(5), 1212–1228. doi:10.1109/72.410363 PMID:18263409

Poggio, T., & Girosi, F. (1998). A Sparse Representation for Function Approximation. *Neural Computation, 10*(6), 1445–1454. doi:10.1162/089976698300017250 PMID:9698352

Qu, Z. (2009). *Cooperative control of dynamical systems: applications to autonomous vehicles.* New York: Springer-Verlag.

Reeves, J. (1999). An Efficient Implementation of Backward Greedy Algorithm for Sparse Signal Reconstruction. *IEEE Signal Processing Letters, 6*(10), 266–268. doi:10.1109/97.789606

Rizun, P. R. (2004). Robot-assisted neurosurgery. *SeminLaporasc Surgery, 11*, 99–106. PMID:15254648

Rovithakis, G. A., Maniadakis, M., & Zervakis, M. (2004). High-order neural network structure selection for function approximation applications using genetic algorithms. *IEEE Transactions on Systems, Man, and Cybernetics. Part B, Cybernetics, 34*(1), 150–158. doi:10.1109/TSMCB.2003.811767 PMID:15369059

Sanchez Camperos, E. N., & Alanis Garcia, A. Y. (2006). *Redes Neuronales. Conceptos Fundamentales y Aplicaciones a Control Automatico*. Madrid, Spain: Pearson-Prentice Hall.

Shawver, T. (2005). Merger premium predictions using neural network approach. *Journal of Emerging Technologies in Accounting, 1*(1), 61–72. doi:10.2308/jeta.2005.2.1.61

Theilliol, D., Ponsart, J. C., Harmand, J., Join, C., & Gras, P. (2003). On-line estimation of unmeasured inputs for an aerobic wastewater treatment process. *Control Engineering Practice, 11*(9), 1007–1019. doi:10.1016/S0967-0661(02)00230-7

Tiebout, C. M. (1956). A Pure Theory of Local Expenditures. *Journal of Political Economy, 64*(5), 416–424. doi:10.1086/257839

Venzl, G. (1976). Statistical fluctuation of activity in localized neural populations. *Journal of Theoretical Biology, 63*(2), 275–309. doi:10.1016/0022-5193(76)90034-5 PMID:1011845

Wang, L., Weller, C. L., Jones, D. D., & Hanna, M. A. (2008). Contemporary issues in thermal gasification of biomass and its application to electricity and fuel production. *Biomass and Bioenergy, 32*(7), 573–581. doi:10.1016/j.biombioe.2007.12.007

Wang, Y., & Kinoshita, C. M. (1993). Kinetic model of biomass gasification. *Solar Energy, 51*(1), 19–25. doi:10.1016/0038-092X(93)90037-O

Werner, S., & Gemeinhardt, G. (1995). Nonprofit organizations: What factors determine pay levels? *Compensation and Benefits Review, 27*(5), 53–60. doi:10.1177/088636879502700511

Xia, G., Tang, Z., Li, Y., & Wang, J. (2005). A binary Hopfield neural network with hysteresis for large crossbar packet-switches. *Neurocomputing, 67*, 417–425. doi:10.1016/j.neucom.2004.09.004

Xu, S. (2010). Data Mining Using Higher Order Neural Network Models with Adaptive Neuron Activation Functions. *International Journal of Advancements in Computing Technology*, 2(4), 168–177. doi:10.4156/ijact.vol2.issue4.18

Yao, X. (1999). Evolving artificial neural networks. *Proceedings of the IEEE*, 87(9), 1423–1447. doi:10.1109/5.784219

Yousefi, H., Ramezanpour, H., & Rostami, M. (2010). Applications of Needle Insertion with Rotating Capability in Manipulator, *ICBME 17th Iranian Conference on Biomedical Engineering*, 1-4.

Zhang, B. T., Ohm, P., & Mühlenbein, H. (1997). Evolutionary Induction of Sparse Neural Tree. *Evolutionary Computation*, 5(2), 213–236. doi:10.1162/evco.1997.5.2.213 PMID:10021759

Zhu, Q. Y., Qin, A. K., Suganthan, P. N., & Huang, G.-B. (2005). Evolutionary extreme learning machine. *Pattern Recognition, 38*(10), 1759–1763. doi:10.1016/j.patcog.2005.03.028

KEY TERMS AND DEFINITIONS

COS-HONN: Artificial cosine higher order neural network.
CS-HONN: Artificial cosine and sigmoid higher order neural network.
CSINCHONN: Artificial cosine and SINC higher order neural network.
HONN: Artificial higher order neural network.
NS-HONN: Artificial SINC and sigmoid higher order neural network.
PHONN: Artificial polynomial higher order neural network.
PS-HONN: Artificial polynomial and sigmoid higher order neural network.
SIN-HONN: Artificial higher order neural network.
SINCHONN: Artificial SINC higher order neural network.
SPHONN: Artificial sigmoid polynomial higher order neural network.
SS-HONN: Artificial sine and sigmoid higher order neural network.
SSINCHONN: Artificial sine and SINC higher order neural network.
THONN: Artificial trigonometric higher order neural network.
UCCHONN: Artificial ultra-high frequency cosine and cosine higher order neural network.
UCSHONN: Artificial ultra-high frequency trigonometric higher order neural network.

UGC-HONN: Artificial ultra-high frequency sigmoid and cosine higher order neural network.

UGS-HONN: Artificial ultra-high frequency sigmoid and sine higher order neural network.

UNC-HONN: Artificial ultra-high frequency sinc and cosine higher order neural network.

UNS-HONN: Artificial ultra-high frequency sinc and sine higher order neural network.

UPC-HONN: Artificial ultra-high frequency polynomial and cosine higher order neural network.

UPS-HONN: Artificial ultra-high frequency polynomial and sine higher order neural network.

USSHONN: Artificial ultra-high frequency sine and sine higher order neural network.

XCHONN: Artificial polynomial and cosine higher order neural network.

XSHONN: Artificial polynomial and sine higher order neural network.

YSINCHONN: Artificial polynomial and SINC higher order neural network.

Chapter 2
Models of Artificial Multi-Polynomial Higher Order Neural Networks

ABSTRACT

This chapter introduces multi-polynomial higher order neural network models (MPHONN) with higher accuracy. Using Sun workstation, C++, and Motif, a MPHONN simulator has been built. Real-world data cannot always be modeled simply and simulated with high accuracy by a single polynomial function. Thus, ordinary higher order neural networks could fail to simulate complicated real-world data. But MPHONN model can simulate multi-polynomial functions and can produce results with improved accuracy through experiments. By using MPHONN for financial modeling and simulation, experimental results show that MPHONN can always have 0.5051% to 0.8661% more accuracy than ordinary higher order neural network models.

INTRODUCTION

HONN Applications

Artificial Higher Order Neural Network (HONN) has a lot of applications in different areas. Barron, Gilstrap, and Shrier (1987) develop polynomial and neural networks for analogies and engineering applications. An, Mniszewski, Lee, Papcun, and Doolen (1988) test a learning procedure,

DOI: 10.4018/978-1-7998-3563-9.ch002

based on a default hierarchy of high-order neural networks, which exhibited an enhanced capability of generalization and a good efficiency to learn to read English. Mao, Selviah, Tao, and Midwinter (1991) design a holographic high order associative memory system in holographic area. Mendel (1991) study higher-order statistics (spectra) system theory and use it in signal processing. Rovithakis, Kosmatopoulos, and Christodoulou (1993) research robust adaptive control of unknown plants using recurrent high order neural networks for the application of mechanical systems. Miyajima, Yatsuki, and Kubota (1995) build up higher order neural networks with product connections which hold the weighted sum of products of input variables. It is shown that they are more superior in ability than traditional neural networks in applications. Xu, Liu, and Liao (2005) explore global asymptotic stability of high-order Hopfield type neural networks with time delays. There are two major ways of encoding a neural network into a chromosome, as required in design of a genetic algorithm (GA). These are explicit (direct) and implicit (indirect) encoding methods. Siddiqi (2005) genetically evolve higher order neural networks by direct encoding method. Ren and Cao (2006) provide LMI-based criteria for stability of high-order neural networks with time-varying delay for nonlinear analysis. Recently, Selviah (2009) describes the progress in using optical technology to construct high-speed artificial higher order neural network systems. The paper reviews how optical technology can speed up searches within large databases in order to identify relationships and dependencies between individual data records, such as financial or business time-series, as well as trends and relationships within them. Epitropakis, Plagianakos, and Vrahatis (2010) intend evolutionary Algorithm Training of Higher Order Neural Networks, for the aims to further explore the capabilities of the Higher Order Neural Networks class and especially the Pi-Sigma Neural Networks. Selviah and Shawash (2010) celebrate 50 years of first and higher order neural network (HONN) implementations in terms of the physical layout and structure of electronic hardware, which offers high speed, low latency in compact, low cost, low power, mass produced systems. Low latency is essential for practical applications in real time control for which software implementations running on Center Process Units (CPUs) are too slow. Gupta, Homma, Hou, Solo, and Bukovsky (2010) give fundamental principles of higher order neural units (HONUs) and higher order neural networks (HONNs). An essential core of HONNs can be found in higher order weighted combinations or correlations between the input variables. By using some typical examples, this paper describes how and why higher order combinations or correlations can be effective. Das, Lewis, and Subbarao (2010) seek a dynamically tuned higher order like neural network approach; look into the control of quad-rotor. The dynamics of a quad-rotor is a simplified form of helicopter dynamics that exhibit the same basic problems of strong coupling, multi-input/multi-output design, and unknown nonlinearities. Yu (2010) offers a robust adaptive control using higher order neural networks and presents a novel robust adaptive approach for a class of unknown nonlinear systems. The structure is composed by two parts: the neuron-observer and the tracking controller. The simulations of a two-link robot show the effectiveness of the proposed algorithm.

Motivation

For modeling and simulation, there is no single neural network model that could handle the wide variety of complicated data and perform with accuracy. Artificial Intelligent (AI) technique is one way to address this problem. Artificial Neural Network (ANN) computing is an area that is receiving increased research interest, since the classic artificial neural network model is a 'black box'. Artificial neuron network-based models are also not yet sufficiently powerful to characterize complex systems. Thus, a way of solving this problem is to develop new models with higher degree of accuracy for modeling and simulation. Multi-Polynomial Higher Order Neural Network Group (MPHONNG) models are "open box" models with improved accuracy are presented in this chapter.

Contributions

a)   Multi-Polynomial Higher Order Neural Network models are studied.

b)   Multi-Polynomial Higher Neural Network models learning algorithm has been provided.

c)   MPHONN Simulator developed for data modeling has been developed.

d)   MPHONN models have been tested by using data extracted from Reserve Bank.

BACKGROUND

HONN Modeling

Artificial higher order neural networks are used for modeling in a lot of areas. Zhang, Xu, and Fulcher (2002) find that real-world financial data is often nonlinear, comprises high-frequency multi-polynomial components, and is discontinuous (piecewise continuous). Not surprisingly, it is hard to model such data using classical neural networks. But the neuron-adaptive higher order neural-network models can be used for automated financial data modeling. Seiffertt and Wunsch (2009) study the agent-based computational economics and finance grows, so do the need for appropriate techniques for the modeling of complex dynamic systems and the intelligence of the constructive agent. In particular, one area of computational intelligence, approximate dynamic programming, holds much promise for applications in this field and demonstrates the capacity for artificial higher order neural networks to add value in the social sciences and business. Chen, Wu, and Wu (2009) investigate higher order artificial neural networks for stock index modeling problems. New network architectures and their corresponding training algorithms are discussed. These structures demonstrate their processing capabilities over traditional artificial neural network architectures with a reduction in the number of processing elements. Dunis, Laws, and Evans (2009) analysis modeling and trading the soybean-oil crush spread with recurrent higher order networks. A traditional regression analysis is used as a benchmark against more sophisticated models such as a Multi-Layer Perceptron (MLP), Recurrent Neural Networks and Higher Order Neural Networks. These are then used to trade the spread. The implementation of a number of filtering techniques as used in the literature are utilized to further refine the trading statistics of the models. The results show that the best model before transactions costs both in- and out-of-sample is the Recurrent Higher Order Network generating a superior risk adjusted return to all other models investigated. Lu, Shieh, and Chen (2009) develop a systematic approach for optimizing the structure of artificial higher order neural networks for system modeling and function approximation. A new HONN topology, namely polynomial kernel networks, is proposed. Structurally, the polynomial kernel network can be viewed as a three-layer feed-forward neural network with a special polynomial activation function for the nodes in the hidden layer. Both quadratic programming and linear programming based training of the polynomial kernel network are investigated. Zhang (2010) finds that classical neural network models are unable to automatically determine the optimum model and appropriate order for data approximation. In order to solve this problem, Neuron-Adaptive Higher Order Neural Network (NAHONN) Models have been introduced. NAHONN models are shown to be "open box". These models are further shown to be capable of automatically finding not only the optimum model but also the appropriate order for high frequency, multi-polynomial, discontinuous data. Rainfall estimation experimental results confirm model convergence. When the artificial neuron-adaptive higher order neural network model was used for rainfall estimation, the average training error of rainfall estimation and the average test error of rainfall estimation are all better than classic artificial neural network techniques. Karnavas (2010) demonstrates a practical design of an intelligent type of controller using higher order neural network (HONN) concepts, for the excitation control of a practical power generating system. This type of controller is suitable for real time operation, and aims to improve the dynamic characteristics of the generating unit by acting properly on its original excitation system. The modeling of the power system under study consists of a synchronous generator connected via a transformer and a transmission line to an infinite bus. The computer simulation results obtained show clearly that the performance of the developed controllers offers competitive damping effects on the synchronous generator's oscillations.

HONN Models

For better application results, a lot of researchers focus on new HONN model development. Chen, Lee, Maxwell, Sun, Lee, and Giles (1986) build up high order correlation model for associative memory. Machado (1989) gives description of the combinatorial a neural model and a high-order neural network suitable for classification tasks. The model is based on fuzzy set theory, neural sciences studies, and expert knowledge analysis. Horan, Uecker, and Arimoto (1990) expand optical implementation of a second-order neural network discriminator model. Rovithakis, Gaganis, Perrakis, and Christodoulou (1996) learn a recurrent neural network model to describe manufacturing cell dynamics. A neural network approach to the manufacturing cell modeling problem is discussed. A recurrent high-order neural network structure (RHONN) is employed to identify cell dynamics, which is supposed to be unknown. Brucoli, Carnimeo, and Grassi (1997) provide a design method for associative memories using a new model of discrete-time high-order neural networks, which includes local interconnections among neurons. Burshtein (1998) examines long-term attraction in higher order neural networks for the memory storage capacity. Zhang, Xu, and Lu (1999) extend neuron-adaptive higher order neural network group models. Campos, Loukianov, and Sanchez (2003) deliver a nonlinear complete order model of a synchronous motor, which is identified using a dynamic neural network. Based on this model a sliding mode controller is derived. This neural network identifier and the proposed control law allow rejecting external load. Kuroe (2004) supplies recurrent high-order neural network models for learning and identifying deterministic finite state automata. The proposed models are a class of high-order recurrent neural networks. Zhang (2006) widens linear and nonlinear HONN models for the power of chief elected officials and debt. Alanis, Sanchez, and Loukianov (2006) deal with the adaptive tracking problem for discrete time induction motor model in presence of bounded disturbances. A high order neural network structure is developed to identify the plant model. Butt and Shafiq (2006) present higher order neural network, based root-solving controller for adaptive tracking of stable nonlinear plants. Zhang, Simoff, and Zhang (2009) bring trigonometric polynomial higher order neural network group models and weighted kernel models for financial data simulation and prediction. Xu (2010) explores adaptive higher order neural network models for data mining. Zhang (2010) develops higher order neural network group-based adaptive tolerance trees for face recognition. Al-Rawi and Al-Rawi (2010) discuss the equivalence between ordinary neural networks and higher order neural networks. Ricalde, Sanchez, and Alanis (2010) test recurrent higher order neural network control for output trajectory tracking with neural observers and constrained inputs and present the design of an adaptive recurrent neural observer-controller scheme for nonlinear systems whose model is assumed to be unknown and with constrained inputs. Sanchez, Urrego, Alanis, and Carlos-Hernandez (2010) study recurrent higher order neural observers for anaerobic processes and propose the design of a discrete-time neural observer which requires no prior knowledge of the model of an anaerobic process. Najarian, Hosseini, and Fallahnezhad (2010) introduce a new medical instrument, namely, the Tactile Tumor Detector (TTD) able to simulate the sense of touch in clinical and surgical applications. The results show that by having an HONN model of nonlinear input-output mapping, there are many advantages compared with Artificial Neural Network (ANN) model, including faster running for new data, lesser Root Mean Square (RMS) error and better fitting properties.

HONN Theories

To build better HONN models, HONN theories have been studied. Jeffries (1989) presents a specific high-order neural network design that can store, using n neutrons, any number of any of the binomial n-strings. Baldi and Venkatesh (1993) study recurrent networks of polynomial threshold elements with random symmetric interactions. Precise asymptotic estimates are derived for the expected number of fixed points as a function of the margin of stability. Young and Downs (1993) discover that the theory of Pac-learning has provided statements about the generalization capability of linear threshold higher order neural networks. Tseng and Wu (1994) find that high-order neural networks (HONN) are shown to decode some Bose Chaudhuri Hocquenghem (BCH) codes in constant-time with very low hardware complexity. HONN is a direct extension of the linear perceptron: it uses a polynomial consisting of a set of product terms Constant-time neural decoders for some BCH codes. Gupta, Homma, Hou, Solo, and Goto (2009) describe fundamental principles of artificial higher order neural units (AHONUs) and networks (AHONNs). An essential core of AHONNs can be found in higher order weighted combinations or correlations between the input variables.

Cao, Ren, and Liang (2009) concentrate on studying the dynamics of artificial higher order neural networks (HONNs) with delays. Both stability analysis and periodic oscillation are discussed for a class of delayed HONNs with (or without) impulses. Wang, Liu, and Liu (2009) deal with the analysis problem of the global exponential stability for a general class of stochastic artificial higher order neural networks with multiple mixed time delays and Markovian jumping parameters. The mixed time delays under consideration comprise both the discrete time-varying delays and the distributed time-delays. Neto (2010) goes into discrete and recurrent artificial neural networks with a homogenous type of neuron. This paper presents some uses of chaotic computations with the same neurons and synapses, and, thus, creating a hybrid system. Shawash and Selviah (2010) investigate the training of networks using Back Propagation and Levenberg-Marquardt algorithms in limited precision achieving high overall calculation accuracy, using on-line training, a new type of HONN known as the Correlation HONN (CHONN), discrete XOR and continuous optical waveguide sidewall roughness datasets by simulation to find the precision at which the training and operation is feasible. Boutalis, Christodoulou, and Theodoridis (2010) use a new neuron-fuzzy dynamical system definition based on high order neural network function approximators to study the nonlinear systems. Theodoridis, Christodoulou, and Boutalis (2010) deliver neuron–fuzzy control schemes based on high order neural network function approximators to study the control schemes. The indirect or direct adaptive regulation of unknown nonlinear dynamical systems is considered in this research. Dehuri and Chao (2010) present a theoretical and empirical study of functional link neural networks (FLNNs) for classification; focus on theoretical and empirical study of functional link neural networks (FLNNs) for classification. The computational results are then compared with other higher order neural networks (HONNs) like functional link neural network with a generic basis functions, Pi-Sigma neural network (PSNN), radial basis function neural network (RBFNN), and ridge polynomial neural network (RPNN).

HIGHER ORDER NEURAL NETWORKS

Giles & Maxwell (1987) formulate the output from first-order neurons as follows in the equation:

$$y_i(x) = f\left[\sum_j^n W(i,j)x(j)\right] \tag{1}$$

where:

$\{x(j)\}$ = an n-element input vector,
$W(i,j)$=adaptable weights from all other neurons to neuron-i, and
  f   = neuron threshold funciton (e.g. sigmoid).

Such units (neurons or nodes) are said to be linear, since they are only able to capture first-order correlations in the training data. Higher order correlations require more complex units, characterised by Giles & Maxwell (1987) in the following equation:

$$y_i(x) = f[W_0(i) + \sum_j W_1(i,j)x(j) + \sum_j\sum_k W_2(i,j,k)x(j)x(k) + ...] \tag{2}$$

Units which include terms up to and including degree-k are referred to as kth-order nodes. An alternative (simpler) formulaition is equation of Lisboa & Perantonis (1991):

$$y_i = f[W_i^o(i) + \sum_i \sum_k \sum_l \cdots \sum_m W_{i,k,l,\ldots,m} x_i x_k x_l \ldots x_m] \tag{3}$$

where a single weight is applied to all n-tuples $x_{i \ldots} \ x_m$ in order to generate the output y_i from that node. This formulation is reminiscent of the Sigma-Pi units of Rumelhart, Hinton & McClelland (1986):

$$\sum_j W_{ij} \prod a_{i1} a_{i2} \ldots a_{ik}(i,j) \tag{4}$$

and for which they prove that the Generalised Delta Rule can be applied as readily as for simple additive units:

$$\sum_j W_{ij} a_{ij} \tag{5}$$

In summary, HONNs include multiplicative terms in their activation function. Now it is possible to perform these data multiplications within a preprocessing stage; the major computational load then becomes a function of the large number of weights. It should also be pointed out that the output of a kth-order single-layer HONN node is a nonlinear funciton of up to k^{th}-order polynomials. Moreover, since no hidden layers are involved, both Hebbian and Perceptron learning rules can be used (Shin 1991).

Polynomial Higher Order Neural Network (PHONN) model is that to use a combination of linear, power and multiplication neurons for simulation the data. This chapter rewrites the chapter 1 formula (1 - 17) as follows:

PHONN Model 2 (coefficient using a:

$$Z_a = \sum_{k,j=0}^{n} \left(a_{kj}^{\ o}\right)\{a_{kj}^{\ hx}(a_k^{\ x}x)^k\}\{a_{kj}^{\ hy}(a_j^{\ y}y)^j\} \tag{6}$$

Trigonometric polynomial Higher Order Neural Network (THONN) model is an artificial neural network in which every element is a higher order trigonometric neural network. The domain of the neural network inputs is the n-dimensional real number R^n. Likewise; the outputs belong to the m-dimensional real number R^m. The neural network function f is a mapping from the inputs to its outputs. To rewrite the chapter 1 formula (1-42) as follows:

THONN Model 2:

$$Z_c = \sum\nolimits_{k,j=0}^{n} (c_{kj}^{\ o})\{c_{kj}^{\ hx} \sin^k (c_k^{\ x} x)\} \{c_{kj}^{\ hy} \cos^j (c_j^{\ y} y)\} \tag{7}$$

Sigmoid polynomial Higher Order Neural Network (SPHONN) model is that to use a combination of sigmoid, linear, power and multiplication neurons for simulation the data. To rewrite the chapter 1 formula (1-67:) as follows:

SPHONN Model 2 (coefficient using r):

$$Z_r = \sum\nolimits_{k,j=0}^{n} \left(r_{kj}^{\ o}\right) \left\{ r_{kj}^{\ hx} \left[\frac{1}{1+\exp(-r_k^{\ x} x)} \right]^k \right\} \left\{ r_{kj}^{\ hy} \left[\frac{1}{1+\exp(-r_j^{\ y} y)} \right]^j \right\} \tag{8}$$

MULTI-POLYNOMIAL HIGHER ORDER NEURAL NETWORK MODEL (MPHONN)

MPHONN is a multi-layer higher order neural network that consists of an input layer with input-units, and output layer with output-units, and two hidden layers consisting of intermediate processing units. Based on derivatives of MPONNG Model, a Back Propagation leaning algorithm has been developed. It is combined the characteristics of PHONN, THONN, and SPHONN.

MPHONN Model 2:

$$Z = \sum_{k,j=0}^{n} \left(a_{kj}^{\ o}\right)\{a_{kj}^{\ hx}(a_k^{\ x}x)^k\}\{a_{kj}^{\ hy}(a_j^{\ y}y)^j\}$$

$$+\sum_{k,j=0}^{n}(c_{kj}^{\ o})\{c_{kj}^{\ hx}\sin^k(c_k^{\ x}x)\}\{c_{kj}^{\ hy}\cos^j(c_j^{\ y}y)\} \tag{9}$$

$$+\sum_{k,j=0}^{n}\left(r_{kj}^{\ o}\right)\left\{r_{kj}^{\ hx}\left[\frac{1}{1+\exp(-r_k^{\ x}x)}\right]^k\right\}\left\{r_{kj}^{\ hy}\left[\frac{1}{1+\exp(-r_j^{\ y}y)}\right]^j\right\}$$

The derivatives of MPHONN model for polynomial, trigonometric polynomial neuron and sigmoid polynomial are:

Polynomial function

$$\sum_{k,j=0}^{n}\left(a_{kj}^{\ o}\right)\{a_{kj}^{\ hx}(a_k^{\ x}x)^k\}\{a_{kj}^{\ hy}(a_j^{\ y}y)^j\} \tag{10}$$

Trigonometric polynomial function

$$\sum_{k,j=0}^{n}(c_{kj}^{\ o})\{c_{kj}^{\ hx}\cos^k(c_k^{\ x}x)\}\{c_{kj}^{\ hy}\sin^j(c_j^{\ y}y)\} \tag{11}$$

Sigmoid polynomial function

$$\sum_{k,j=0}^{n}\left(r_{kj}^{\ o}\right)\left\{r_{kj}^{\ hx}\left[\frac{1}{1+\exp(-r_k^{\ x}x)}\right]^k\right\}\left\{r_{kj}^{\ hy}\left[\frac{1}{1+\exp(-r_j^{\ y}y)}\right]^j\right\} \tag{12}$$

Let:

$$a_{kj}^{\ hx} = a_{kj}^{\ hy} = 1$$

$$c_{kj}^{\ hx} = c_{kj}^{\ hy} = 1$$

$$r_{kj}^{\ hx} = r_{kj}^{\ hy} = 1$$

MPHONN Model 1:

$$Z = \sum_{k,j=0}^{n} \left(a_{kj}^{\ o}\right)\{(a_k^{\ x}x)^k\}\{(a_j^{\ y}y)^j\}$$

$$+\sum_{k,j=0}^{n}(c_{kj}^{\ o})\{\sin^k(c_k^{\ x}x)\}\{\cos^j(c_j^{\ y}y)\} \tag{13}$$

$$+\sum_{k,j=0}^{n}\left(r_{kj}^{\ o}\right)\left\{\left[\frac{1}{1+\exp(-r_k^{\ x}x)}\right]^k\right\}\left\{\left[\frac{1}{1+\exp(-r_j^{\ y}y)}\right]^j\right\}$$

Let:

$$a_{kj}^{\ hx} = a_k^{\ x} = a_{kj}^{\ hy} = a_j^{\ y} = 1$$

$$c_{kj}^{\ hx} = c_k^{\ x} = c_{kj}^{\ hy} = c_j^{\ y} = 1$$

$$r_{kj}^{\ hx} = r_k^{\ x} = r_{kj}^{\ hy} = r_j^{\ y} = 1$$

MPHONN Model 0:

$$Z = \sum_{k,j=0}^{n} \left(a_{kj}^{\ o}\right)\{(x)^k\}\{(y)^j\}$$

$$+\sum_{k,j=0}^{n}(c_{kj}^{\ o})\{\sin^k(x)\}\{\cos^j(y)\} \tag{14}$$

$$+\sum_{k,j=0}^{n}\left(r_{kj}^{\ o}\right)\left\{\left[\frac{1}{1+\exp(-x)}\right]^k\right\}\left\{\left[\frac{1}{1+\exp(-y)}\right]^j\right\}$$

Let: n = 2
The MPHONN Model 0, Order 2 can be described as:

$$Z = \sum_{k,j=0}^{2} \left(a_{kj}^{\ o}\right)\{(x)^k\}\{(y)^j\}$$

$$+\sum_{k,j=0}^{2}(c_{kj}^{\ o})\{\sin^k(x)\}\{\cos^j(y)\} \tag{15}$$

$$+\sum_{k,j=0}^{2}\left(r_{kj}^{\ o}\right)\left\{\left[\frac{1}{1+\exp(-x)}\right]^k\right\}\left\{\left[\frac{1}{1+\exp(-y)}\right]^j\right\}$$

The MPHONN Model 0, Order 2 can also be described as:

$$Z = a_{00}{}^0 + a_{01}{}^0 y + a_{02}{}^0 y^2 + a_{10}{}^0 x + a_{11}{}^0 xy + a_{12}{}^0 xy^2 + a_{20}{}^0 x^2 + a_{21}{}^0 x^2 y + a_{22}{}^0 x^2 y^2$$

$$+ c_{00}{}^0 + c_{01}{}^0 \cos(y) + c_{02}{}^0 \cos^2(y) + c_{10}{}^0 \sin(x) + c_{11}{}^0 \sin(x)\cos(y) + c_{12}{}^0 \sin(x)\cos^2(y)$$

$$+ b_{20}{}^0 \sin^2(x) + b_{21}{}^0 \sin^2(x)\cos(y) + b_{22}{}^0 \sin^2(x)\cos^2(y) + r_{00}{}^0 + \frac{r_{01}{}^0}{1+e^{-y}} + \frac{r_{02}{}^0}{(1+e^{-y})^2}$$

$$+ \frac{r_{10}{}^0}{1+e^{-x}} + \frac{r_{11}{}^0}{(1+e^{-x})(1+e^{-y})} + \frac{r_{12}{}^0}{(1+e^{-x})(1+e^{-y})^2} + \frac{r_{20}{}^0}{(1+e^{-x})^2}$$

$$+ \frac{r_{21}{}^0}{(1+e^{-x})^2(1+e^{-y})} + \frac{r_{22}{}^0}{(1+e^{-x})^2(1+e^{-y})^2}$$

$$(16)$$

MPHONN STRUCTURE

MPHONN Structure is shown in Figure 1. Details of PHONN, THONN and SPHONN structures are shown in Figure 2, Figure 3, and Figure 4.

All the weights on the layer can be derived directly from the coefficients of the discrete analog form of the Polynomial, Trigonometric polynomial and sigmoid polynomial.

LEARNING ALGORITHM FOR MPHONN MODEL

MPHONN models are the combination of PHONN, THONN, and SPHONN modes. We can simply use the Chapter 1 learning formulae to find out the MPHONN model learning formulae.

All the weights on the layer can be derived directly from the coefficients of the discrete analog form of the Polynomial HONN models, Trigonometric HONN modelsl and sigmoid polynomial HONN models by using the Chapter 1 formulae.

Figure 1. MPHONN Architecture

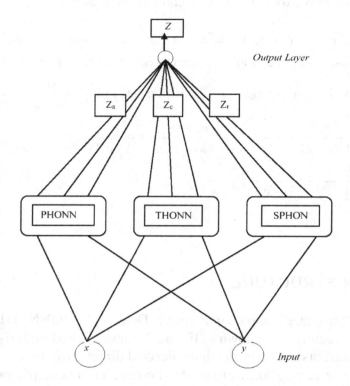

Output Layer Neurons in MPHONN Model (Model 0, 1, and 2)

This chapter rewrites Chapter 1 formulae of (1 - 133), (1 - 144), and (1 - 145) for output layer neurons update as follows:

The output layer weights of THONN part are updated according to:

$$c_{kj}{}^o (t+1) = c_{kj}{}^o (t) - \eta \left(\partial E / \partial c_{kj}{}^o \right) \tag{17}$$

where η = learning rate (positive and usually < 1)

c_{kj} = weight; index k an j = input index
(k, j=0, 1, 2, …, n means one of n*n input neurons from the second hidden layer)
E = error

Figure 2. PHONN Architecture

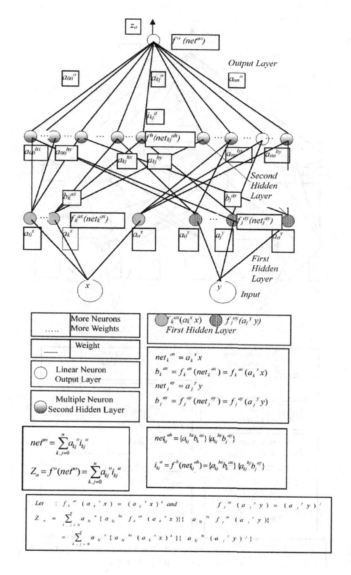

t = training time
o = output layer

The weight update equations are formulated as follows: For linear output neurons, let:

Figure 3. THONN Architecture

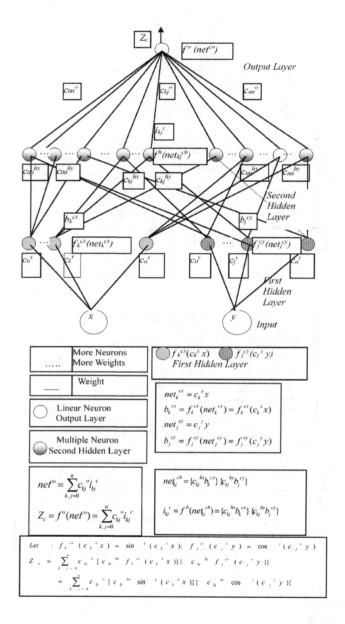

$$\delta o^l = (d - z) \tag{18}$$

Combining Formulae (1 - 133), (1 - 143), and (1 - 144):

Figure 4. SPHONN Architecture

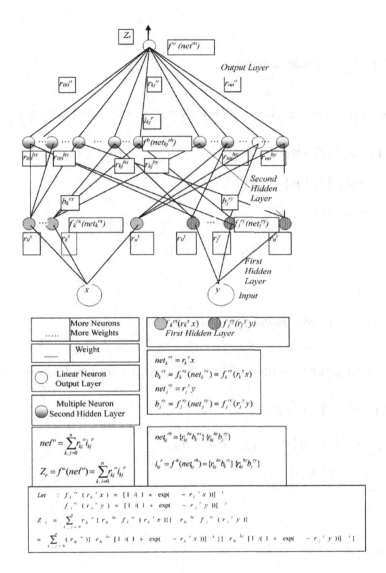

$$c_{kj}{}^{o}(t+1) = c_{kj}{}^{o}(t) - \eta \left(\partial E / \partial a_{kj}{}^{o} \right)$$
$$= c_{kj}{}^{o}(t) + \eta (d-z) f^{o\,\prime}\left(net^{o} \right) i_{kj}$$
$$= c_{kj}{}^{o}(t) + \eta \delta^{ol} i_{kj}$$

where:

$$\delta^{ol} = (d-z)$$
$$f^{o'}(net^o) = 1 \quad (linear\ neuron)$$

(19)

The output layer weights of PHONN part are updated according to:

$$a_{kj}^{\ o}(t+1) = a_{kj}^{\ o}(t) - \eta\left(\partial E / \partial a_{kj}^{\ o}\right)$$
$$= a_{kj}^{\ o}(t) + \eta(d-z) f^{o}{}'(net^o) i_{kj}$$
$$= a_{kj}^{\ o}(t) + \eta\delta^{ol} i_{kj}$$

where:

$$\delta^{ol} = (d-z)$$
$$f^{o'}(net^o) = 1 \quad (linear\ neuron)$$

(20)

The output layer weights of SPHONN part are updated according to:

$$r_{kj}^{\ o}(t+1) = r_{kj}^{\ o}(t) - \eta\left(\partial E / \partial r_{kj}^{\ o}\right)$$
$$= r_{kj}^{\ o}(t) + \eta(d-z) f^{o}{}'(net^o) i_{kj}$$
$$= r_{kj}^{\ o}(t) + \eta\delta^{ol} i_{kj}$$

where:

$$\delta^{ol} = (d-z)$$
$$f^{o'}(net^o) = 1 \quad (linear\ neuron)$$

(21)

Second-Hidden Layer Neurons in MPHONN Model (Model 2)

This chapter rewrites Chapter 1 formulae of (1 - 146), (1 - 158), (1 – 159) and (1 - 160) for the second hidden layer neurons update as follows:

The second hidden layer weights of THONN part are updated according to:

$$c_{kj}^{hx}(t+1) = c_{kj}^{hx}(t) - \eta\left(\partial E / \partial c_{kj}^{hx}\right) \tag{22}$$

where η = learning rate (positive & usually < 1)

k, j = input index
(k, j = 0, 1, 2, …, n means one of $2*n*n$ input combinations from the first hidden layer)
E = error
t = training time
hx = hidden layer, related to x input
c_{kj}^{hx} = hidden layer weight related to x input

The weight update equations are formulated as follows: Let output neuron is a linear neuron:

$$\delta^{ol} = (d-z)f^{o'}_{k}(net^o) = (d-z) \tag{23}$$

Also let the second layer neurons be linear neurons, combining Formulae (1- 146), (1-150), (1-157) and (1-158):

The weight update question for x input neurons is:

$$c_{kj}^{hx}(t+1) = c_{kj}^{hx}(t) - \eta\left(\partial E / \partial c_{kj}^{hx}\right)$$
$$= c_{kj}^{hx}(t) + \eta\left((d-z)f^{o'}(net^o)c_{kj}^{o}f^{h'}(net_{kj}^{hx})c_{kj}^{hy}b_{j}^{y}b_{k}^{x}\right)$$
$$= c_{kj}^{hx}(t) + \eta\left(\delta^{ol}c_{kj}^{o}\delta_{kj}^{hx}b_{k}^{x}\right)$$

where:

$$\delta^{ol} = (d-z) \quad \delta_{kj}^{hx} = c_{kj}^{hy} b_j^{y}$$

$$f^{o'}(net^o) = 1 \qquad\quad (linear\ neuron)$$

$$f^{h'}(net_{kj}^{hx}) = 1 \quad (linear\ neuron)$$

(24)

Use the same rules, the weight update question for y input neurons is:

$$c_{kj}^{hy}(t+1) = c_{kj}^{hy}(t) - \eta\left(\partial E / \partial c_{kj}^{hy}\right)$$

$$= c_{kj}^{hy}(t) + \eta\left((d-z)f^{o'}(net^o)c_{kj}^{o}f^{h'}(net_{kj}^{hy})c_{kj}^{hx}b_k^{x}b_j^{y}\right)$$

$$= c_{kj}^{hy}(t) + \eta\left(\delta^{ol}c_{kj}^{o}\delta_{kj}^{hy}b_j^{y}\right)$$

where:

$$\delta^{ol} = (d-z) \quad \delta_{kj}^{hy} = c_{kj}^{hx}b_k^{x}$$

$$f^{o'}(net^o) = 1 \qquad\quad (linear\ neuron)$$

$$f^{h'}(net_{kj}^{hy}) = 1 \quad (linear\ neuron)$$

(25)

The second hidden layer weights of PHONN part are updated according to: The weight update question for x input neurons is:

$$a_{kj}^{hx}(t+1) = a_{kj}^{hx}(t) - \eta\left(\partial E / \partial a_{kj}^{hx}\right)$$

$$= a_{kj}^{hx}(t) + \eta\left((d-z)f^{o'}(net^o)a_{kj}^{o}f^{h'}(net_{kj}^{hx})a^{hy}b_j^{y}b_k^{x}\right)$$

$$= a_{kj}^{hx}(t) + \eta\left(\delta^{ol}a_{kj}^{o}\delta_{kj}^{hx}b_k^{x}\right)$$

where:

$$\delta^{ol} = (d-z) \quad \delta_{kj}^{hx} = a_{kj}^{hy}b_j^{y}$$

$$f^{o'}(net^o) = 1 \qquad\quad (linear\ neuron)$$

$$f^{h'}(net_{kj}^{hx}) = 1 \quad (linear\ neuron)$$

(26)

Use the same rules, the weight update question for y input neurons is:

$$a_{kj}{}^{hy}(t+1) = a_{kj}{}^{hy}(t) - \eta\left(\partial E / \partial a_{kj}{}^{hy}\right)$$
$$= a_{kj}{}^{hy}(t) + \eta\left((d-z)f^{o}{}'\left(net^{o}\right)a_{kj}{}^{o}f^{h}{}'\left(net_{kj}{}^{hy}\right)a_{kj}{}^{hx}b_{k}{}^{x}b_{j}{}^{y}\right)$$
$$= a_{kj}{}^{hy}(t) + \eta\left(\delta^{ol}a_{kj}{}^{o}\delta_{kj}{}^{hy}b_{j}{}^{y}\right)$$

where:

$$\delta^{ol} = (d-z) \quad \delta_{kj}{}^{hy} = a_{kj}{}^{hx}b_{k}{}^{x}$$
$$f^{o'}\left(net^{o}\right) = 1 \qquad (linear\ neuron) \tag{27}$$
$$f^{h'}\left(net_{kj}{}^{hy}\right) = 1 \quad (linear\ neuron)$$

The second hidden layer weights of SPHONN part are updated according to: The weight update question for x input neurons is:

$$r_{kj}{}^{hx}(t+1) = r_{kj}{}^{hx}(t) - \eta\left(\partial E / \partial r_{kj}{}^{hx}\right)$$
$$= r_{kj}{}^{hx}(t) + \eta\left((d-z)f^{o}{}'\left(net^{o}\right)r_{kj}{}^{o}f^{h}{}'\left(net_{kj}{}^{hx}\right)r_{kj}{}^{hy}b_{j}{}^{y}b_{k}{}^{x}\right)$$
$$= r_{kj}{}^{hx}(t) + \eta\left(\delta^{ol}r_{kj}{}^{o}\delta_{kj}{}^{hx}b_{k}{}^{x}\right)$$

where:

$$\delta^{ol} = (d-z) \quad \delta_{kj}{}^{hx} = r_{kj}{}^{hy}b_{j}{}^{y}$$
$$f^{o'}\left(net^{o}\right) = 1 \qquad (linear\ neuron) \tag{28}$$
$$f^{h'}\left(net_{kj}{}^{hx}\right) = 1 \quad (linear\ neuron)$$

Use the same rules, the weight update question for y input neurons is:

$$r_{kj}^{hy}(t+1) = r_{kj}^{hy}(t) - \eta \left(\partial E / \partial r_{kj}^{hy} \right)$$

$$= r_{kj}^{hy}(t) + \eta \left((d-z) f^{o\,\prime}(net^o) r_{kj}^{o} f^{h\,\prime}(net_{kj}^{hy}) r_{kj}^{hx} b_k^x b_j^y \right)$$

$$= r_{kj}^{hy}(t) + \eta \left(\delta^{ol} r_{kj}^{o} \delta_{kj}^{hy} b_j^y \right)$$

where:

$$\delta^{ol} = (d-z) \quad \delta_{kj}^{hy} = r_{kj}^{hx} b_k^x$$

$$f^{o\,\prime}(net^o) = 1 \qquad (linear\ neuron) \tag{29}$$

$$f^{h\,\prime}(net_{kj}^{hy}) = 1 \qquad (linear\ neuron)$$

First Hidden Layer *x* Neurons in MPHONN (Model 1 and Model 2)

This chapter rewrites Chapter 1 formulae of (1 - 161: C.1), (1 - 176: C.16) and (1 - 177: C.17) for the first hidden layer x neurons update as follows:

The first hidden layer x neuron weights of **THONN** part are updated according to:

$$c_k^x(t+1) = c_k^x(t) - \eta \left(\partial E_p / \partial c_k^x \right) \tag{30}$$

Where:

c_k^x = 1st hidden layer weight for input x; k = kth neuron of first hidden layer

η = learning rate (positive & usually < 1)

E = error

t = training time

By combining Formulae (1-161: C.1), (1-164: C.4), and (1-175:C.15), for a linear the first hidden layer neuron:

For a function of x input side:

$$b_k^x = f_k^x \left(net_k^x \right)$$
$$f_x' \left(net_k^x \right) = \partial b_k^x / \partial \left(net_k^x \right)$$

(31)

$$c_k^x (t+1) = c_k^x (t) - \eta \left(\partial E_p / \partial c_k^x \right)$$
$$= c_k^x (t) + \eta (d-z) f^{o\,'} \left(net^o \right) c_{kj}^{\,o} * f^{h\,'} \left(net_{kj}^{\,h} \right) c_{kj}^{\,hy} b_j^{\,y} c_{kj}^{\,hx} f_x' \left(net_k^x \right) x$$
$$= c_k^x (t) + \eta * \delta^{ol} * c_{kj}^{\,o} * \delta^{hx} * c_{kj}^{\,hx} * \delta^x * x$$

where

$$\delta^x = f_x' \left(net_k^x \right)$$
$$\delta^{ol} = (d-z) f^{o\,'} \left(net^o \right) = d - z \qquad (linear\ neuron)$$

(32)

$$\delta^{hx} = f^{h\,'} \left(net_{kj}^{\,h} \right) c_{kj}^{\,hy} b_j^{\,y} = c_{kj}^{\,hy} b_j^{\,y} \qquad (linear\ neuron)$$

The first hidden layer x neuron weights of PHONN part are updated according to:

By combining Formulae (1-161: C.1), (1-164: C.4), and (1-175:C.15), for a linear the first hidden layer neuron:

For a function of x input side:

$$b_k^x = f_k^x \left(net_k^x \right)$$
$$f_x' \left(net_k^x \right) = \partial b_k^x / \partial \left(net_k^x \right)$$

(33)

$$a_k^x (t+1) = a_k^x (t) - \eta \left(\partial E_p / \partial a_k^x \right)$$
$$= a_k^x (t) + \eta (d-z) f^{o\,'} \left(net^o \right) a_{kj}^{\,o} * f^{h\,'} \left(net_{kj}^{\,h} \right) a_{kj}^{\,hy} b_j^{\,y} a_{kj}^{\,hx} f_x' \left(net_k^x \right) x$$
$$= a_k^x (t) + \eta * \delta^{ol} * a_{kj}^{\,o} * \delta^{hx} * a_{kj}^{\,hx} * \delta^x * x$$

where

$$\delta^x = f_x'\left(net_k^{\ x}\right)$$

$$\delta^{ol} = \left(d-z\right)f^{o'}\left(net^o\right) = d - z \qquad (linear\ neuron) \qquad (34)$$

$$\delta^{hx} = f^{h'}\left(net_{kj}^{\ h}\right)a_{kj}^{\ hy}b_j^{\ y} = a_{kj}^{\ hy}b_j^{\ y} \qquad (linear\ neuron)$$

The first hidden layer x neuron weights of SPHONN part are updated according to:

By combining Formulae (1-161: C.1), (1-164: C.4), and (1-175:C.15), for a linear the first hidden layer neuron:

For a function of x input side:

$$b_k^{\ x} = f_k^{\ x}\left(net_k^{\ x}\right)$$

$$f_x'\left(net_k^{\ x}\right) = \partial b_k^{\ x} / \partial\left(net_k^{\ x}\right) \qquad (35)$$

$$r_k^{\ x}\left(t+1\right) = r_k^{\ x}\left(t\right) - \eta\left(\partial E_p / \partial r_k^{\ x}\right)$$

$$= r_k^{\ x}\left(t\right) + \eta\left(d-z\right)f^{o'}\left(net^o\right)r_{kj}^{\ o} * f^{h'}\left(net_{kj}^{\ h}\right)r_{kj}^{\ hy}b_j^{\ y}r_{kj}^{\ hx}f_x'\left(net_k^{\ x}\right)x$$

$$= r_k^{\ x}\left(t\right) + \eta * \delta^{ol} * r_{kj}^{\ o} * \delta^{hx} * r_{kj}^{\ hx} * \delta^x * x$$

where

$$\delta^x = f_x'\left(net_k^{\ x}\right)$$

$$\delta^{ol} = \left(d-z\right)f^{o'}\left(net^o\right) = d - z \qquad (linear\ neuron) \qquad (36)$$

$$\delta^{hx} = f^{h'}\left(net_{kj}^{\ h}\right)r_{kj}^{\ hy}b_j^{\ y} = r_{kj}^{\ hy}b_j^{\ y} \qquad (linear\ neuron)$$

First Hidden Layer y Neurons in HONN (Model 1 and Model 2)

This chapter rewrites Chapter 1 formulae of (1 - 178: D.1), (1 - 193: D.16) and (1 - 194: D.17) for the first hidden layer y neurons update as follows:

The first hidden layer y neuron weights of THONI N part are updated according to:

$$c_j^{y}(t+1) = c_j^{y}(t) - \eta \left(\partial E_p / \partial c_j^{y} \right) \tag{37}$$

Where:

C_j^{y} = 1st hidden layer weight for input y; $j = j^{th}$ neuron of first hidden layer

η = learning rate (positive & usually < 1)

E = error

t = training time

By combining Formulae (1-178:D.1), (1-181:D.4), and 1-192:D.15), for a linear 1st hidden layer neuron:

For a function of y input part:

$$b_j^{y} = f_j^{y} \left(net_j^{y} \right)$$
$$f_y{}' \left(net_j^{y} \right) = \partial b_j^{y} / \partial \left(net_j^{y} \right) \tag{38}$$

Using the above procedure:

$$c_j^{y}(t+1) = c_j^{y}(t) - \eta \left(\partial E_p / \partial c_j^{y} \right)$$
$$= c_j^{y}(t) + \eta (d-z) f^{o}{}' \left(net^{o} \right) c_{kj}^{o} * f^{h}{}' \left(net_{kj}^{h} \right) c_{kj}^{hx} b_k^{x} c_{kj}^{hy} f_y{}' \left(net_j^{y} \right) y$$
$$= c_j^{y}(t) + \eta * \delta^{ol} * c_{kj}^{o} * \delta^{hy} * c_{kj}^{hy} * \delta^{y} * y$$

where

$$\delta^y = f_y'\left(net_j^{\,y}\right)$$

$$\delta^{ol} = (d-z)f^{o\,\prime}\left(net^o\right) = d-z \qquad \left(linear\;neuron\;\;f^{o\,\prime}\left(net^o\right)=1\right)$$

$$\delta^{hy} = f^{h\prime}\left(net_{kj}^{\,h}\right)c_{kj}^{\;hx}b_k^{\;x} = c_{kj}^{\;hx}b_k^{\;x} \qquad \left(linear\;neuron\;\;f^{h\,\prime}\left(net_{kj}^{\,h}\right)=1\right)$$

$$(39)$$

The first hidden layer y neuron weights of PHONN part are updated according to:

By combining Formulae (1-178:D.1), (1-181:D.4), and 1-192:D.15), for a linear 1st hidden layer neuron: For a function of y input part:

$$b_j^{\,y} = f_j^{\,y}\left(net_j^{\,y}\right)$$

$$f_y'\left(net_j^{\,y}\right) = \partial b_j^{\,y} / \partial\left(net_j^{\,y}\right)$$

$$(40)$$

Using the above procedure:

$$a_j^{\,y}(t+1) = a_j^{\,y}(t) - \eta\left(\partial E_p / \partial a_j^{\,y}\right)$$

$$= a_j^{\,y}(t) + \eta(d-z)f^{o\,\prime}\left(net^o\right)a_{kj}^{\;o} * f^{h\,\prime}\left(net_{kj}^{\,h}\right)a_{kj}^{\;hx}b_k^{\;x}a_{kj}^{\;hy}f_y'\left(net_j^{\,y}\right)y$$

$$= a_j^{\,y}(t) + \eta * \delta^{ol} * a_{kj}^{\;o} * \delta^{hy} * a_{kj}^{\;hy} * \delta^y * y$$

where

$$\delta^y = f_y'\left(net_j^{\,y}\right)$$

$$\delta^{ol} = (d-z)f^{o\,\prime}\left(net^o\right) = d-z \qquad \left(linear\;neuron\;\;f^{o\,\prime}\left(net^o\right)=1\right)$$

$$\delta^{hy} = f^{h\prime}\left(net_{kj}^{\,h}\right)a_{kj}^{\;hx}b_k^{\;x} = a_{kj}^{\;hx}b_k^{\;x} \qquad \left(linear\;neuron\;\;f^{h\,\prime}\left(net_{kj}^{\,h}\right)=1\right)$$

$$(41)$$

The first hidden layer y neuron weights of SPHONN part are updated according to:

122

By combining Formulae (1-178:D.1), (1-181:D.4), and 1-192:D.15), for a linear 1st hidden layer neuron:

For a function of y input part:

$$b_j^{\ y} = f_j^{\ y}\left(net_j^{\ y}\right)$$

$$f_y'\left(net_j^{\ y}\right) = \partial b_j^{\ y} / \partial\left(net_j^{\ y}\right) \tag{42}$$

Using the above procedure:

$$r_j^{\ y}(t+1) = r_j^{\ y}(t) - \eta\left(\partial E_p / \partial r_j^{\ y}\right)$$

$$= r_j^{\ y}(t) + \eta(d-z) f^{o\,\prime}\left(net^o\right) r_{kj}^{\ o} * f^{h\,\prime}\left(net_{kj}^{\ h}\right) r_{kj}^{\ hx} b_k^{\ x} r_{kj}^{\ hy} f_y'\left(net_j^{\ y}\right) y$$

$$= r_j^{\ y}(t) + \eta * \delta^{ol} * r_{kj}^{\ o} * \delta^{hy} * r_{kj}^{\ hy} * \delta^y * y$$

where

$$\delta^y = f_y'\left(net_j^{\ y}\right)$$

$$\delta^{ol} = (d-z) f^{o\,\prime}\left(net^o\right) = d-z \qquad \left(\text{linear neuron } f^{o\,\prime}\left(net^o\right) = 1\right)$$

$$\delta^{hy} = f^{h\,\prime}\left(net_{kj}^{\ h}\right) r_{kj}^{\ hx} b_k^{\ x} = r_{kj}^{\ hx} b_k^{\ x} \qquad \left(\text{linear neuron } f^{h\,\prime}\left(net_{kj}^{\ h}\right) = 1\right)$$

$$\tag{43}$$

APPLICATIONS OF MPHONN

This chapter uses the monthly Canadian dollar and USA dollar exchange rate from November 2009 to December 2010 (See Table 1 and Table 2) as the test data for MPHONN models. Rate and desired output data, R_t are from USA Federal Reserve Bank Data bank. Input1, $R_{t-2,}$ are the data at time t-2. Input 2, R_{t-1} is the data at time t-1. The values of R_{t-2}, R_{t-1}, and R_t are used as inputs and output in the MPHONN model. MPHONN model is used for Table 1 and Table2. The test data of MPHONN orders 6 for using 10,000 epochs are shown on the tables.

In Table 1, CanadianDollar/USDollar Exchange Rate CAD$1.00 = USD$0.9309 on 2-Nov-2009, the average errors of PHONN, THONN, SPHONN, and MPHONN are 2.8037%, 3.8238%, 3.1557%, and 2.3964% respectively. The average error of PHONN, THONN, and SPHONN is 3.2625%. So MPHONN error is 0.8661% better than the average error of PHONN, THONN, and SPHONN models.

Table 1. Canadian dollar/US dollar exchange rate

USA Federal Reserve Bank Data				HONN Output				HONN Error Percentage			
Date	Rate and Desired Output	Input 1 (2 month ago)	Input 2 (1 month ago)	PHONN	THONN	SPHONN	MPHONN	PHONN	THONN	SPHONN	MPHONN
11/2/2009	0.9309										
12/1/2009	0.9588										
1/4/2010	0.9637	0.9309	0.9588	0.9617	0.9243	0.9436	0.9336	0.2075	4.0884	2.0857	3.1234
2/1/2010	0.9389	0.9588	0.9637	0.9346	0.9456	0.9613	0.9524	0.4580	0.7136	2.3858	1.4379
3/1/2010	0.9596	0.9637	0.9389	0.9427	0.9216	0.9472	0.9397	1.7612	3.9600	1.2922	2.0738
4/1/2010	0.9928	0.9389	0.9596	0.9145	0.9337	0.9214	0.9812	7.8868	5.9529	7.1918	1.1684
5/3/2010	0.9869	0.9596	0.9928	0.9949	0.9196	0.9491	0.9631	0.8106	6.8193	3.8302	2.4116
6/1/2010	0.9546	0.9928	0.9869	0.9292	0.9708	0.9732	0.9673	2.6608	1.6970	1.9485	1.3304
7/1/2010	0.9414	0.9869	0.9546	0.9773	0.9069	0.9196	0.9172	3.8135	3.6648	2.3157	2.5706
8/2/2010	0.9778	0.9546	0.9414	0.9494	0.9476	0.9644	0.9585	2.9045	3.0886	1.3704	1.9738
9/1/2010	0.9527	0.9414	0.9778	0.9716	0.9882	0.9223	0.9286	1.9838	3.7263	3.1909	2.5297
10/1/2010	0.9790	0.9778	0.9527	0.9548	0.9644	0.9824	0.9548	2.4719	1.4913	0.3473	2.4719
11/1/2010	0.9869	0.9527	0.9790	0.9284	0.9192	0.9005	0.9349	5.9277	6.8599	8.7547	5.2690
12/1/2010	0.9843	0.9790	0.9869	0.9493	0.9212	0.9028	0.9344	3.5558	6.4106	8.2800	5.0696
Average Error (% Percentage)								2.8078	3.8238	3.1557	2.3964
Average Error pf PHONN, THONN, and SPHONN (% Percentage)								3.2625	MPHONN Better		0.8661

CAD$1.00 = UDS$0.9309 on November 3rd, 2009; USA Federal Reserve Bank Data January 6th, 2011

In Table 2, CanadianDollar/USDollar Exchange Rate CAD$1.00 = USD$0.9430 on 30-Nov-2009, the average errors of PHONN, THONN, SPHONN, and MPHONN are 3.2443%, 3.1593%, 2.9678%, and 2.6187% respectively. The average error of PHONN, THONN, and SPHONN is 3.1238%. So MPHONN error is 0.5051% better than the average error of PHONN, THONN, and SPHONN models.

Table 2. Canadian dollar/ US dollar exchange rate

USA Federal Reserve Bank Data				HONN Output				HONN Error Percentage			
Date	Rate and Desired Output	Input 1 (2 month ago)	Input 2 (1 month ago)	PHONN	THONN	SPHONN	MPHONN	PHONN	THONN	SPHONN	MPHONN
11/30/2009	0.9461										
12/31/2009	0.9559										
1/29/2010	0.9388	0.8091	0.8170	0.9609	0.9366	0.9432	0.9446	2.3541	0.2343	0.4687	0.6178
2/26/2010	0.9506	0.8170	0.8087	0.9608	0.9257	0.9474	0.9055	1.0730	2.6194	0.3366	4.7444
3/31/2010	0.9846	0.8087	0.7868	0.9414	0.9129	0.9365	0.9503	4.3876	7.2821	4.8852	3.4836
4/30/2010	0.9889	0.7868	0.7933	0.9575	0.9484	0.9651	0.9672	3.1752	4.0955	2.4067	2.1944
5/28/2010	0.9527	0.7933	0.8376	0.9785	0.9723	0.9465	0.9544	2.7081	2.0573	0.6508	0.1784
6/30/2010	0.9429	0.8376	0.9127	0.9918	0.9712	0.9833	0.9095	5.1861	3.0014	4.2847	3.5423
7/30/2010	0.9715	0.9127	0.8601	0.9241	0.9782	0.9168	0.9421	4.8791	0.6897	5.6305	3.0262
8/31/2010	0.9398	0.8601	0.9267	0.9036	0.9715	0.9096	0.9275	3.8519	3.3731	3.2134	1.3088
9/30/2010	0.9715	0.9267	0.9118	0.9532	0.9381	0.9301	0.9683	1.8837	3.4380	4.2615	0.3294
10/30/2010	0.9816	0.9118	0.9329	0.9372	0.9279	0.9562	0.9356	4.5232	5.4707	2.5876	4.6862
11/30/2010	0.9741	0.9329	0.9288	0.9642	0.9604	0.9308	0.9598	1.0163	1.4064	4.4451	1.4680
12/30/2010	0.9991	0.9288	0.9461	0.9602	0.9567	0.9747	0.9407	3.8935	4.2438	2.4422	5.8453
Average Error (% Percentage)								3.2443	3.1593	2.9678	2.6187
Average Error of PHONN, THONN, and SPHONN (% Percentage)								3.1238	MPHONN Better		0.5051

CAD$1.00 = UDS$0.9461 on November 30th, 2009; USA Federal Reserve Bank Data January 6th, 2011

FUTURE RESEARCH DIRECTIONS

One of the topics for future research is to continue building models of higher order neural networks for different data series. The coefficients of the higher order models will be studied not only using artificial neural network techniques, but also statistical methods.

CONCLUSION

This chapter develops an open box and nonlinear higher order neural network models of MPHONN. This paper also provides the learning algorithm formulae for MPHONN, based on the structures of MPHONN. This paper uses MPHONN simulator and tests the MPHONN models using high frequency data and the running results are compared with Polynomial Higher Order Neural Network (PHONN), Trigonometric Higher Order Neural Network (THONN), and Sigmoid polynomial Higher Order Neural Network (SPHONN) models. Test results show that average error of MPHONN models are from 2.3964% to 2.6187%, and the average error of Polynomial Higher Order Neural Network

(PHONN), Trigonometric Higher Order Neural Network (THONN), and Sigmoid polynomial Higher Order Neural Network (SPHONN) models are from 2.8078% to 3.8238%. It means that MPHONN models are 0.5051% to 0.8661% better than the average of the PHONN, THONN, and SPHONN models.

REFERENCES

Al-Rawi, M. S., & Al-Rawi, K. R. (2010). On the Equivalence between Ordinary Neural Networks and Higher Order Neural Networks. In Artificial Higher Order Neural Networks for Computer Science and Engineering – Trends for Emerging Application (pp.138 - 158). Hershey, PA: IGI Global. doi:10.4018/978-1-61520-711-4.ch006

Alanis, A. Y., Sanchez, E. N., & Loukianov, A. G. (2006). Discrete- Time Recurrent Neural Induction Motor Control using Kalman Learning. In *Proceedings of International Joint Conference on Neural Networks* (pp.1993 – 2000). Academic Press.

An, Z. G., Mniszewski, S. M., Lee, Y. C., Papcun, G., & Doolen, G. D. (1988). HIERtalker: a default hierarchy of high order neural networks that learns to read English aloud. *Proceedings of the Fourth Conference on Artificial Intelligence Applications.* 10.1109/CAIA.1988.196136

Baldi, P., & Venkatesh, S. S. (1993). Random interactions in higher order neural networks. *IEEE Transactions on Information Theory, 39*(1), 274–283. doi:10.1109/18.179374

Barron, R., Gilstrap, L., & Shrier, S. (1987). Polynomial and Neural Networks: Analogies and Engineering Applications. *Proceedings of International Conference of Neural Networks, 2*, 431-439.

Boutalis, Y. S., Christodoulou, M. A., & Theodoridis, D. C. (2010). Identification of Nonlinear Systems Using a New Neuro-Fuzzy Dynamical System Definition Based on High Order Neural Network Function Approximators. In Artificial Higher Order Neural Networks for Computer Science and Engineering – Trends for Emerging Application (pp.423-449). IGI Global. doi:10.4018/978-1-61520-711-4.ch018

Brucoli, M., Carnimeo, L., & Grassi, G. (1997). Associative memory design using discrete-time second-order neural networks with local interconnections. *IEEE Transactions on Circuits and Systems. I, Fundamental Theory and Applications, 44*(2), 153–158. doi:10.1109/81.554334

Burshtein, D. (1998). Long-term attraction in higher order neural networks. *Neural Networks, 9*(1), 42–50. doi:10.1109/72.655028 PMID:18252428

Butt, N. R., & Shafiq, M. (2006). Higher-Order Neural Network Based Root-Solving Controller for Adaptive Tracking of Stable Nonlinear Plants. *Proceedings of IEEE International Conference on Engineering of Intelligent Systems*. 10.1109/ICEIS.2006.1703175

Campos, J., Loukianov, A. G., & Sanchez, E. N. (2003). Synchronous motor VSS control using recurrent high order neural networks. *Proceedings of 42nd IEEE Conference on Decision and Control*, 4, 3894 – 3899. 10.1109/CDC.2003.1271757

Cao, J., Ren, F., & Liang, J. (2009). Dynamics in Artificial Higher Order Neural Networks with Delays. In Artificial Higher Order Neural Networks for Economics and Business (pp.389 - 429). IGI Global. doi:10.4018/978-1-59904-897-0.ch018

Chen, H. H., Lee, Y. C., Maxwell, T., Sun, G. Z., Lee, H. Y., & Giles, C. L. (1986). High Order Correlation Model for Associative Memory. *AIP Conference Proceedings, 151*, 86–99. doi:10.1063/1.36224

Chen, Y., Wu, P., & Wu, Q. (2009b). Higher Order Neural Networks for Stock Index Modeling. In Artificial Higher Order Neural Networks for Economics and Business (pp.113 - 132). IGI Global. doi:10.4018/978-1-59904-897-0.ch006

Das, A., Lewis, F. L., & Subbarao, K. (2010). Back-Stepping Control of Quadrotor: A Dynamically Tuned Higher Order Like Neural Network Approach. In Artificial Higher Order Neural Networks for Computer Science and Engineering – Trends for Emerging Application (pp.484 - 513). IGI Global. doi:10.4018/978-1-61520-711-4.ch020

Dehuri, S., & Chao, S. (2010). A Theoretical and Empirical Study of Functional Link Neural Networks (FLANNs) for Classification. In Artificial Higher Order Neural Networks for Computer Science and Engineering – Trends for Emerging Application (pp.545- 573). IGI Global.

Dunis, C. L., Laws, J., & Evans, B. (2009). Modeling and Trading the Soybean-Oil Crush Spread with Recurrent and Higher Order Networks: A Comparative Analysis. In Artificial Higher Order Neural Networks for Economics and Business (pp.348 - 367). IGI Global.

Epitropakis, M. G., Plagianakos, V. P., & Vrahatis, M. N. (2010). Evolutionary algorithm Training of Higher Order Neural Networks. In Artificial Higher Order Neural Networks for Computer Science and Engineering – Trends for Emerging Application (pp.57- 85). IGI Global. doi:10.4018/978-1-61520-711-4.ch003

Giles, L., & Maxwell, T. (1987). Learning, invariance and generalization in high-order neural networks. *Applied Optics, 26*(23), 4972–4978. doi:10.1364/AO.26.004972 PMID:20523475

Gupta, M. M., Homma, N., Hou, Z., Solo, A. M. G., & Bukovsky, I. (2010). Higher Order Neural Networks: Fundamental Theory and Applications. In Artificial Higher Order Neural Networks for Computer Science and Engineering – Trends for Emerging Application (pp.397- 422). IGI Global.

Gupta, M. M., Homma, N., Hou, Z., Solo, A. M. G., & Goto, T. (2009). Fundamental Theory of Artificial Higher Order Neural Networks. In Artificial Higher Order Neural Networks for Economics and Business (pp.368 - 388). IGI Global. doi:10.4018/978-1-59904-897-0.ch017

Horan, P., Uecker, D., & Arimoto, A. (1990). Optical implementation of a second-order neural network discriminator model. *Japanese Journal of Applied Physics, 29*(Part 2, No. 7), 361–365. doi:10.1143/JJAP.29.L1328

Jeffries, C. (1989). Dense memory with high order neural networks. *Proceedings of Twenty-First Southeastern Symposium on System Theory,* 436 – 439. 10.1109/SSST.1989.72506

Karnavas, Y. L. (2010). Electrical Machines Excitation Control via Higher Order Neural Networks. In Artificial Higher Order Neural Networks for Computer Science and Engineering – Trends for Emerging Application (pp.366 - 396). IGI Global.

Kuroe, Y. (2004). Learning and identifying finite state automata with recurrent high-order neural networks. *Proceedings of SICE 2004 Annual Conference,* 3, 2241 – 2246.

Lisboa, P., & Perantonis, S. (1991). Invariant pattern recognition usi9ng third-order networks and zernlike moments. *Proceedings of the IEEE International Joint Conference on Neural Networks*, 2, 1421-1425.

Lu, Z., Shieh, L., & Chen, G. (2009). A New Topology for Artificial Higher Order Neural Networks - Polynomial Kernel Networks. In Artificial Higher Order Neural Networks for Economics and Business (pp.430-441). IGI Global.

Machado, R. J. (1989). Handling knowledge in high order neural networks: The combinatorial neural model. *Proceedings of International Joint Conference on Neural Networks*, 2, 582.

Mao, Z. Q., Selviah, D. R., Tao, S., & Midwinter, J. E. (1991). *Holographic high order associative memory system.* Third IEE International Conference on "Holographic Systems, Components and Applications, Heriot Watt University, Edinburgh, UK.

Mendel, J. M. (1991). Tutorial on higher-order statistics (spectra) in signal processing and system theory: Theoretical results and some applications. *Proceedings of the IEEE, 79*(3), 278–305. doi:10.1109/5.75086

Miyajima, H., Yatsuki, S., & Kubota, J. (1995). Dynamical properties of neural networks with product connections. *Proceedings of the IEEE International Conference on Neural Networks*, 6, 3198 – 3203.

Najarian, S., Hosseini, S. M., & Fallahnezhad, M. (2010). Artificial Tactile Sensing and Robotic Surgery Using Higher Order Neural Networks. In Artificial Higher Order Neural Networks for Computer Science and Engineering – Trends for Emerging Application (pp.514- 544). IGI Global. doi:10.4018/978-1-61520-711-4.ch021

Neto, J. P. (2010). Higher Order Neural Networks for Symbolic, Sub-symbolic and Chaotic Computations. In Artificial Higher Order Neural Networks for Computer Science and Engineering – Trends for Emerging Application (pp.37- 56). IGI Global.

Qi, H., Zhang, M., & Scofield, R. (2001). *Rainfall Estimation Using M-PHONN Model.* International Joint Conference on Neural Networks' 2001, Washington, DC.

Ren, F., & Cao, J. (2006). LMI-based criteria for stability of high-order neural networks with time-varying delay. *Nonlinear Analysis Series B: Real World Applications, 7*(5), 967–979. doi:10.1016/j.nonrwa.2005.09.001

Ricalde, L., Sanchez, E., & Alanis, A. Y. (2010). Recurrent Higher Order Neural Network Control for Output Trajectory Tracking with Neural Observers and Constrained Inputs. In Artificial Higher Order Neural Networks for Computer Science and Engineering – Trends for Emerging Application (pp.286 - 311). IGI Global. doi:10.4018/978-1-61520-711-4.ch013

Rovithakis, G., Gaganis, V., Perrakis, S., & Christodoulou, M. (1996). A recurrent neural network model to describe manufacturing cell dynamics. *Proceedings of the 35th IEEE Conference on Decision and Control*, 2, 1728 – 1733. 10.1109/CDC.1996.572808

Rovithakis, G. A., Kosmatopoulos, E. B., & Christodoulou, M. A. (1993). Robust adaptive control of unknown plants using recurrent high order neural networks-application to mechanical systems. *Proceedings of International Conference on Systems, Man and Cybernetics*, 4, 57 – 62. 10.1109/ICSMC.1993.390683

Rumelhart, D., Hinton, G., & McClelland, J. (1986). Learning internal representations by error propagation. In Parallel distributed processing: explorations in the microstructure of cognition, Volume 1: Foundations. Cambridge, MA: MIT Press.

Sanchez, E., Urrego, D. A., Alanis, A. Y., & Carlos-Hernandez, S. (2010). Recurrent Higher Order Neural Observers for Anaerobic Processes. In Artificial Higher Order Neural Networks for Computer Science and Engineering – Trends for Emerging Application (pp.333- 365). IGI Global. doi:10.4018/978-1-61520-711-4.ch015

Seiffertt, J., & Wunsch, D. C., II. (2009). Higher Order Neural Network Architectures for Agent-Based Computational Economics and Finance. In Artificial Higher Order Neural Networks for Economics and Business (pp.79 - 93). IGI Global. doi:10.4018/978-1-59904-897-0.ch004

Selviah, D. (2009). High Speed Optical Higher Order Neural Network for Discovering Data Trends and Patterns in Very Large Databases. In Artificial Higher Order Neural Networks for Economics and Business (pp.442 - 465). IGI Global.

Selviah, D., & Shawash, J. (2010). Fifty Years of Electronic Hardware Implementations of First and Higher Order Neural Networks. In Artificial Higher Order Neural Networks for Computer Science and Engineering – Trends for Emerging Application (pp.269- 285). IGI Global. doi:10.4018/978-1-61520-711-4.ch012

Shawash, J., & Selviah, D. (2010). Artificial Higher Order Neural Network Training on Limited Precision Processors. In Artificial Higher Order Neural Networks for Computer Science and Engineering – Trends for Emerging Application (pp.312-332). IGI Global. doi:10.4018/978-1-61520-711-4.ch014

Shin, Y. (1991). The Pi-Sigma network: An efficient higher-order neural network for pattern classification and function approximation. *Proceedings of International Joint Conference on Neural Networks, I*, 13–18.

Siddiqi, A. A. (2005). Genetically evolving higher order neural networks by direct encoding method. *Proceedings of Sixth International Conference on Computational Intelligence and Multimedia Applications*, 62 – 67. 10.1109/ICCIMA.2005.34

Theodoridis, D. C., Christodoulou, M. A., & Boutalis, Y. S. (2010). Neuro – Fuzzy Control Schemes Based on High Order Neural Network Function Aproximators. In Artificial Higher Order Neural Networks for Computer Science and Engineering – Trends for Emerging Application (pp.450- 483). IGI Global.

Tseng, Y.-H., & Wu, J.-L. (1994). Constant-time neural decoders for some BCH codes. *Proceedings of IEEE International Symposium on Information Theory*, 343.

Wang, Z., Liu, Y., & Liu, X. (2009). On Complex Artificial Higher Order Neural Networks: Dealing with Stochasticity, Jumps and Delays. In Artificial Higher Order Neural Networks for Economics and Business (pp.466 - 483). IGI Global.

Xu, B., Liu, X., & Liao, X. (2005). Global asymptotic stability of high-order Hopfield type neural networks with time delays. *Computers & Mathematics with Applications (Oxford, England), 45*(10-11), 1729–1737. doi:10.1016/S0898-1221(03)00151-2

Xu, S. (2010). Adaptive Higher order Neural Network Models for Data Mining. In Artificial Higher Order Neural Networks for Computer Science and Engineering – Trends for Emerging Application (pp.86- 98). IGI Global. doi:10.4018/978-1-61520-711-4.ch004

Yatsuki, S., & Miyajima, H. (2000). Statistical dynamics of associative memory for higher order neural networks. *Proceedings of the 2000 IEEE International Symposium on Circuits and Systems*, 3, 670 – 673. 10.1109/ISCAS.2000.856149

Young, S., & Downs, T. (1993). Generalisation in higher order neural networks. *Electronics Letters*, 29(16), 1491–1493. doi:10.1049/el:19930996

Yu, W. (2010). Robust Adaptive Control Using Higher Order Neural Networks and Projection. In Artificial Higher Order Neural Networks for Computer Science and Engineering – Trends for Emerging Application (pp.99- 137). IGI Global. doi:10.4018/978-1-61520-711-4.ch005

Zhang, J. (2006). *Linear and nonlinear models for the power of chief elected officials and debt*. Pittsburgh, PA: Mid-Atlantic Region American Accounting Association.

Zhang, L., Simoff, S. J., & Zhang, J. C. (2009). Trigonometric Polynomial Higher Order Neural Network Group Models and Weighted Kernel Models for Financial Data Simulation and Prediction. In Artificial Higher Order Neural Networks for Economics and Business (pp.484 - 503). IGI Global. doi:10.4018/978-1-59904-897-0.ch022

Zhang, M. (2010a). Higher Order Neural Network Group –based Adaptive Trees. In Artificial Higher Order Neural Networks for Computer Science and Engineering – Trends for Emerging Application (pp.1- 36). IGI Global.

Zhang, M. (2010b). Rainfall Estimation Using Neuron-Adaptive Artificial Higher Order Neural Networks. In Artificial Higher Order Neural Networks for Computer Science and Engineering – Trends for Emerging Application (pp.159- 186). IGI Global.

Zhang, M., & Lu, B. (2001). Financial Data Simulation Using M-PHONN Model. *International Joint Conference on Neural Networks' 2001*, 1828 - 1832.

Zhang, M., Xu, S., & Fulcher, J. (2002). Neuron-adaptive higher order neural-network models for automated financial data modeling. *IEEE Transactions on Neural Networks*, 13(1), 188–204. doi:10.1109/72.977302 PMID:18244418

Zhang, M., Xu, S., & Lu, B. (1999). Neuron-adaptive higher order neural network group models. *Proceedings of International Joint Conference on Neural Networks, 1*, 333–336. doi:10.1109/IJCNN.1999.831513

ADDITIONAL READING

Dunis, C. L., Laws, J., & Evans, B. (2006b). Modelling and Trading the Soybean-Oil Crush Spread with Recurrent and Higher Order Networks: A Comparative Analysis. *Neural Network World, 3*(6), 193–213.

Fulcher, G. E., & Brown, D. E. (1994). A polynomial neural network for predicting temperature distributions. *IEEE Transactions on Neural Networks, 5*(3), 372–379. doi:10.1109/72.286909 PMID:18267805

Ghosh, J., & Shin, Y. (1992). Efficient Higher-order Neural Networks for Function Approximation and Classification. *International Journal of Neural Systems, 3*(4), 323–350. doi:10.1142/S0129065792000255

Hornik, K. (1991). Approximation capabilities of multilayer feedforward networks. *Neural Networks, 4*(2), 251–257. doi:10.1016/0893-6080(91)90009-T

Hu, S., & Yan, P. (1992). Level-by-Level learning for artificial neural groups. *Tien Tzu Hsueh Pao, 20*(10), 39–43.

Inui, T., Tanabe, Y., & Onodera, Y. (1978). *Group Theory and Its Application in Physics*. Heidelberg, Germany: Springer-Verlag.

Kariniotakis, G. N., Stavrakakis, G. S., & Nogaret, E. F. (1996). Wind power forecasting using advanced neural networks models. *IEEE Transactions on Energy Conversion, 11*(4), 762–767. doi:10.1109/60.556376

Kosmatopoulos, E. B., Polycarpou, M. M., Christodoulou, M. A., & Ioannou, P. A. (1995). High-order neural network structures for identification of dynamical systems. *Neural Networks, 6*(2), 422–431. doi:10.1109/72.363477 PMID:18263324

Lee, M., Lee, S. Y., & Park, C. H. (1992). Neural controller of nonlinear dynamic systems using higher order neural networks. *Electronics Letters, 28*(3), 276–277. doi:10.1049/el:19920170

Leshno, M., Lin, V., & Ya, P. (1993). Multilayer feedforward networks with a nonpolynomial activation function can approximate any function. *Neural Networks*, *6*(6), 861–867. doi:10.1016/S0893-6080(05)80131-5

Lumer, E. D. (1992). Selective attention to perceptual groups: The phase tracking mechanism. *International Journal of Neural Systems*, *3*(1), 1–17. doi:10.1142/S0129065792000024

Naimark, M. A., & Stern, A. I. (1982). *Theory of Group Representations*. Springer-Verlag. doi:10.1007/978-1-4613-8142-6

Rovithakis, G. A., Chalkiadakis, I., & Zervakis, M. E. (2004). High-order neural network structure selection for function approximation applications using genetic algorithms. *Systems, Man and Cybernetics. Part B*, *34*(1), 150–158. PMID:15369059

Saad, E. W., Prokhorov, D. V., & Wunsch, D. C. II. (1998). Comparative Study of Stock Trend Prediction Using Time Delay Recurrent and Probabilistic Neural Networks. *IEEE Transactions on Neural Networks*, *9*(6), 1456–1470. doi:10.1109/72.728395 PMID:18255823

Tenti, P. (1996). Forecasting Foreign Exchange Rates Using Recurrent Neural Networks. *Applied Artificial Intelligence*, *10*(6), 567–581. doi:10.1080/088395196118434

Willcox, C. R. (1991). Understanding hierarchical neural network behavior: A renormalization group approach. *Journal of Physics. A. Mathematical Nuclear and General*, *24*(11), 2655–2644. doi:10.1088/0305-4470/24/11/030

KEY TERMS AND DEFINITIONS

AHONUs: Artificial higher order neural units.

CHONN: Correlation HONN.

HONN: Artificial higher order neural network.

MPHONN: Multi-polynomial higher order neural network models.

MPONNG: Multi-layer higher order neural network group model. It is combined the characteristics of PHONN, THONN, and SPHONN.

NAHONN: Neuron-adaptive higher order neural network.

PHONN: Polynomial higher order neural network.

RHONN: A recurrent high-order neural network structure.

SPHONN: Sigmoid polynomial higher order neural network.

THONN: Trigonometric polynomial higher order neural network.

Chapter 3
Group Models of Artificial Polynomial and Trigonometric Higher Order Neural Networks

ABSTRACT

Real-world financial data is often discontinuous and non-smooth. Neural network group models can perform this function with more accuracy. Both polynomial higher order neural network group (PHONNG) and trigonometric polynomial higher order neural network group (THONNG) models are studied in this chapter. These PHONNG and THONNG models are open box, convergent models capable of approximating any kind of piecewise continuous function, to any degree of accuracy. Moreover, they are capable of handling higher frequency, higher order nonlinear, and discontinuous data. Results confirm that PHONNG and THONNG group models converge without difficulty and are considerably more accurate (0.7542% - 1.0715%) than neural network models such as using polynomial higher order neural network (PHONN) and trigonometric polynomial higher order neural network (THONN) models.

INTRODUCTION

HONN Models for Simulation

Artificial Higher Order Neural Network (HONN) is powerful technique to simulate data. Ghosh and Shin (1992) develop efficient higher-order neural

DOI: 10.4018/978-1-7998-3563-9.ch003

networks for function approximation and classification. Zhang, Murugesan, and Sadeghi (1995) design polynomial higher order neural network for economic data simulation. Zhang, Fulcher, and Scofield (1996) study neural network group models for estimating rainfall from satellite images. Zhang, Zhang, and Fulcher (1997) explore financial simulation system using a higher order trigonometric polynomial neural network group model. Lu, Qi, Zhang, and Scofield (2000) provide PT-HONN models for multi-polynomial function simulation. Zhang and Lu (2001) research financial data simulation by using Multi-Polynomial Higher Order Neural Network (M-PHONN) model. Zhang (2001) deliver a new model, called Adaptive Multi-Polynomial Higher Order Neural Network (A-PHONN), for financial data simulation. Qi and Zhang (2001) test the rainfall estimation using M-PHONN model and find that the M-PHONN model for estimating heavy convective rainfall from satellite data has 5% to 15% more accuracy than the polynomial higher order neural network. Zhang and Scofield (2001) expand an adaptive multi-polynomial high order neural network (A-PHONN) model for heavy convective rainfall estimation and find that the A-PHONN model has 6% to 16% more accuracy than the polynomial higher order neural network. Zhang (2003) intends PL-HONN model for financial data simulation. Rovithakis, Chalkiadakis, and Zervakis (2004) learn the high-order neural network structure selection for function approximation applications using genetic algorithms. Crane and Zhang (2005) discover the data simulation using SINCHONN Model. Zhang (2005) gives a data simulation system using SINX/X and SINX polynomial higher order neural networks. Zhang (2006) seeks a data simulation system using CSINC polynomial higher order neural networks. Zhang (2009a) delivers general format of Higher Order Neural Networks (HONNs) for nonlinear data analysis and six different HONN models. This paper mathematically proves that HONN models could converge and have mean squared errors close to zero. This paper illustrates the learning algorithm with update formulas. HONN models are compared with SAS Nonlinear (NLIN) models and results show that HONN models are 3 to 12% better than SAS Nonlinear models. Zhang (2009b) develops a new nonlinear model, Ultra high frequency Trigonometric Higher Order Neural Networks (UTHONN), for time series data analysis. Results show that UTHONN models are 3 to 12% better than Equilibrium Real Exchange Rates (ERER) model, and 4 – 9% better than other Polynomial Higher Order Neural Network (PHONN) and Trigonometric Higher Order Neural Network (THONN) models. This study also uses UTHONN models to simulate foreign exchange rates and consumer price index with error approaching 0.0000%. Murata (2010) finds that a Pi-Sigma higher order neural network (Pi-Sigma HONN) is a type of higher order neural network, where, as its name implies, weighted sums of inputs are calculated first and then the sums are multiplied by each other to produce higher order terms that constitute the network outputs. This type of higher order neural networks has accurate function approximation capabilities.

The Motivations of Use of Artificial Higher Order Neural Network Group Theory

Accordingly, artificial higher order neuron network-based models are not yet sufficiently powerful to characterize complex systems. Moreover, a gap exists in the research literature between complex systems and general systems. Using artificial higher order neural network group theory is possible to bridge this gap.

If the function parameters being analyzed vary in a continuous and smooth fashion with respect to variable, then such functions can be effectively simulated by artificial higher order neural network. However, in the real world such variation can be discontinuous and non-smooth. Thus, to use artificial higher order neural network to simulate the functions then accuracy will be a problem. In this case, artificial higher order neural network group can perform much better. Artificial higher order neural network group is possible to simulate discontinuous function to any degree accuracy using neural network group theory, even at the discontinuous points.

Artificial higher order neural networks are massively parallel architectures. Thus, by using parallel artificial higher order neural network-based reasoning network, it can compute all rules, models, knowledge and facts stored in different weights simultaneously. But real-world reasoning is always very complicated, nonlinear, and discontinuous. So simple artificial higher order neural network model cannot always give the correct reasoning, but artificial higher order neural network group potentially could.

The next logical step from artificial neuron-based and artificial neural network-based models is artificial neural network group-based models. Artificial higher order neural network group research is open-ended and holds considerable potential for developing complex systems. In order to develop artificial higher order neural network group-based models, an artificial higher order neural network group theory is required.

The key point of artificial Higher Order Neural Network Group Theory is of using group theory to study the structure of artificial higher order neural network groups. Contributions of the chapter are concerned with the followings:

- To use group theory for building artificial higher order neural network group.
- To give the definitions of artificial higher order neural network groups.
- To describe the artificial higher order neural network group model features.
- To apply artificial higher order neural network group theory to build simulators
- To give the test results of artificial polynomial higher order neural network group models and artificial trigonometric polynomial higher order neural network group models.

BACKGROUND

Dynamic HONN Models for Simulation

Kosmatopoulos, Ioannou, and Christodoulou (1992) study the stability and convergence properties of recurrent high-order neural networks (RHONNs) as models of nonlinear dynamical systems. The overall structure of the RHONN consists of dynamical elements distributed throughout the network for identification of nonlinear systems. Lee, Lee, and Park (1992) bring a neural controller of nonlinear dynamic systems using higher order neural networks. Kosmatopoulos, Polycarpou, Christodoulou, and Ioannou (1995) demonstrate several continuous-time and discrete-time recurrent high-order neural network models and apply these models to various dynamic engineering problems. Draye, Pavisic, Cheron, and Libert (1996) build up dynamic recurrent neural networks for dynamic analysis. Kuroe, Ikeda, and Mori (1997) examine that recently high-order neural networks have been recognized to possess higher capability of nonlinear function representations. This paper presents a method for identification of general nonlinear dynamical systems by recurrent high-order neural network. Ghazali, Hussain, and Nawi (2010) propose a novel Dynamic Ridge Polynomial Higher Order Neural Network (DRPHONN). The architecture of the new DRPHONN incorporates recurrent links into the structure of the ordinary Ridge Polynomial Higher Order Neural Network

(RPHONN). RPHONN is a type of feed-forward Higher Order Neural Network (HONN) which implements a static mapping of the input vectors. In order to model dynamical functions of the brain, it is essential to utilize a system that can store internal states and can implement complex dynamic system. Neural networks with recurrent connections are dynamical systems with temporal state representations. The dynamic structure approach has been successfully used for solving varieties of problems, such as time series forecasting, approximating a dynamical system, forecasting a stream flow, and system control.

HONN for Prediction

Fulcher and Brown (1994) offer a polynomial higher order neural network for predicting temperature distributions. Knowles, Hussain, Deredy, Lisboa, and Dunis (2005) consider higher-order neural network with Bayesian confidence measure for prediction of EUR/USD exchange rate. Saad, Prokhorov, and Wunsch (1998) look at the stock trend prediction using time delay recurrent and probabilistic Neural Networks. Zhang, J. (2005) supplies polynomial full naïve estimated misclassification cost models for financial distress prediction using higher order neural network. Zhang and Fulcher (2004) discuss the higher order neural networks for satellite weather prediction. Christodoulou and Iliopoulos (2006) deal with the MAPK (mitogen-activated protein kinase) which is a three-molecule module. This paper also introduces higher order neural network models for prediction of steady-state and dynamic behavior of MAPK cascade. Sanchez, Alanis, and Rico (2009) propose the use of Higher Order Neural Networks (HONNs) trained with an extended Kalman filter based algorithm to predict the electric load demand as well as the electricity prices, with beyond a horizon of 24 hours. Due to the chaotic behavior of the electrical markets, it is not advisable to apply the traditional forecasting techniques used for time series; the results presented confirm that HONNs can very well capture the complexity underlying electric load demand and electricity prices. The proposed neural network model produces very accurate next day predictions and, prognosticates with very good accuracy, a week-ahead demand and price forecasts.

HONN for Time Series Data Predication

Tenti (1996) investigates forecasting foreign exchange rates using recurrent higher order neural networks. Kariniotakis, Stavrakakis, and Nogaret (1996) present wind power forecasting, the power output profile of a wind park, using advanced recurrent high order neural networks models. Tawfik and Liatsis (1997) go into prediction of non-linear time-series using higher order neural networks. Zhang, Zhang, and Fulcher (1997) build up financial prediction system using higher order trigonometric polynomial neural network group model. Zhang, Zhang, and Keen (1999) extend to use THONN system for higher frequency non-linear data simulation and prediction. Foka (1999) offers time series prediction using evolving polynomial neural networks. Ghazali (2005) develops higher order neural network for financial time series prediction. Hussain, Knowles, Lisboa, El-Deredy, and Al-Jumeily (2006) study pipelined neural network and its application to financial time series prediction. Knowles, ussain, Deredy, Lisboa, and Dunis (2009) present another type of Higher Order Neural Networks (HONN). These can be considered a 'stripped-down' version of MLPs, where joint activation terms are used, relieving the network of the task of learning the relationships between the inputs. The predictive performance of the network is tested with the EUR/USD exchange rate and evaluated using standard financial criteria including the annualized return on investment, showing 8% increase in the return compared with the MLP. Shi, Tan, and Ge (2009) address nonlinear problem by developing a technique consisting of a top-down part using an artificial Higher Order Neural Network (HONN) model and a bottom-up part based on a Bayesian Network (BN) model to automatically identify predictor variables for the stock return prediction from a large financial variable set. Chen, Wu, and Wu (2009) establish that forecasting exchange rates is an important financial problem that is receiving increasing attention especially because of its difficulty and practical applications. This paper applies Higher Order Flexible Neural Trees (HOFNTs), which can design flexible Artificial Neural Network (ANN) architectures automatically, to forecast the foreign exchange rates. Liatsis, Hussain, and Milonidis (2009) concern with the development of novel artificial higher order neural networks architecture called the second-order pipeline recurrent neural network. The proposed artificial neural network consists of a linear and a nonlinear section, extracting relevant features from the input signal. The structuring unit of the proposed neural network is the second-order recurrent neural network. The architecture consists of a series of second-order recurrent neural networks, which are concatenated with each other. Simulation results in one-step ahead predictions of the foreign currency exchange rates demonstrate the superior performance of the proposed pipeline architecture as compared to other feed-forward and recurrent structures. Hussain and Liatsis (2009) introduce the development of novel artificial higher-order neural network architecture, called the recurrent Pi-sigma neural network. The proposed artificial neural network combines the advantages of both higher-order architectures in terms of the multi-linear interactions between inputs, as well as the temporal dynamics of recurrent neural networks, and produces highly accurate one-step ahead predictions of the foreign currency exchange rates, as compared to other feed-forward and recurrent structures. Selviah and Shawash (2009) provide a generalized correlation higher order neural network design. Their performance is compared with that of first order networks, conventional higher order neural network designs, and higher order linear regression networks for financial time series prediction. The correlation higher order neural network design is shown to give the highest accuracy for prediction of stock market share prices and share indices. The simulations compare the performance for three different training algorithms, stationary versus non-stationary input data, different numbers of neurons in the hidden layer and several generalized correlation higher order neural network designs. Onwubolu (2009) describes real world problems of nonlinear and chaotic processes, which make them hard to model and predict. This paper first compares the neural network (NN) and the artificial higher order neural network (HONN) and then presents commonly known neural network architectures and several HONN architectures. The polynomial neural network (PNN) is then chosen as the HONN for application to the time series prediction problem. This research implies that the HONN model can be used as a feasible solution for exchange rate forecasting as well as for interest rate forecasting. Ghazali and Al-Jumeily (2009) discuss the use of two artificial Higher Order Neural Networks (HONNs) models, the Pi-Sigma Neural Networks and the Ridge Polynomial Neural Networks, in financial time series forecasting. From the simulation results, the predictions clearly demonstrated that HONNs models, particularly Ridge Polynomial Neural Networks generate higher profit returns with fast convergence, therefore show considerable promise as a decision-making tool.

Adaptive HONN Adaptive, Group and Other Models

Xu and Zhang (1999a) study approximation to continuous functions and operators using adaptive higher order neural networks. Xu and Zhang (2002) develop adaptive higher order neural networks (AHONN) with a neuron-adaptive activation function (NAF) to any nonlinear continuous functional and any nonlinear continuous operator. Xu (2009) introduces an Adaptive Higher Order Neural Network (HONN) model and applies the adaptive model in business applications such as simulating and forecasting share prices. This adaptive HONN model offers significant advantages over traditional Standard ANN models such as much reduced network size, faster training, as well as much improved simulation and forecasting errors, due to their ability to better approximate complex, non-smooth, often discontinuous training data sets. Zhang, Zhang, and Fulcher (2000) develop higher order neural network group models for data approximation. Jiang, Gielen, and Wang (2010) investigate the combined effects of quantization and clipping on Higher Order Function Neural Networks (HOFNN) and Multi-Layer Feed-forward Neural Networks (MLFNN). Statistical models are used to analyze the effects of quantization in a digital implementation. Lu, song, and Shieh (2010) study the improving sparseness in kernel nonlinear feature extraction algorithms by Polynomial Kernel Higher Order Neural Networks.

Artificial Neural Network Group

Very little artificial neural network research has concentrated on such neuron network-based models as the integrated neural network [Matsuoka *et.al.* 1989] or holistic model [Pentland & Turk, 1989]. Lumer (1992) proposed a new mechanism of selective attention among perceptual groups as part of his computational model of early vision. In this model, perceptual grouping is initially performed in connectionist networks by dynamically binding the neural activities triggered in response to related image features. Lie Groups were used in Tsao's (1989) group theory approach to the computer simulation of 3D rigid motion. More specifically, motion is expressed as an exponential mapping of the linear combination of six infinitesimal generators of the 1-parameter Lie subgroup. Hu (1992) proposed a level-by-level learning scheme for artificial neural groups. The learning process suggested by this method closely resembles the process of knowledge growth for human individuals and/or society and can improve both network generalization and learning efficiency. The neural network hierarchical model devised by Willcox (1991) consists of binary-state neurons grouped into clusters and can be analyzed using a Renormalization Group (RG) approach. Unlike the research previously described, Yang (1990) concerned himself with the activities of neuron *groups*. This work, together with Naimark's (1982) earlier theory of group representations, can be used as the basis for Neural Network Group Theory.

PHONNG GROUP

PHONNG Definition

A *set* (Waerden, 1970) is defined as a collection of *elements* which possess the same properties. The symbol

$a \in A$ (3-1)

means: A is a set, and a is an element of set A.

The *artificial polynomial higher order neural network set* is a set in which every element is a PHONN. The symbol

phonn $\in$ **PHONNS** (where: *phonn* = f:$R^n \rightarrow R^m$) (3-2)

Means:

PHONNS is a PHONN set, and *phonn*, which is one kind of artificial polynomial higher order neural network, is an element of set **PHONNS**. The domain of the artificial polynomial higher order neural network *phonn* inputs is the *n*-dimensional real number R^n. Likewise, the *phonn* outputs belong to the *m*-dimensional real number R^m. The artificial higher order neural network function f is a mapping from the inputs of *phonn* to its outputs.

The artificial polynomial higher order neural network set **PHONNS** is defined as the *union* of the *subsets* of **PHONN (order 2)**, **PHONN (order 3)**, **PHONN (order 4)** ... and so on. In formal notation, we write:

PHONNS

$$= PHONN\ (order\ 2) \cup PHONN\ (order\ 3) \cup PHONN\ (order\ 3) \cup PHONN$$
$$(order\ 4) \cup \ .... \ (3\text{-}3)$$

PHONN Generalized Sets (*PHONNGS*) are defined as the union of additive PHONN sets (*PHONN⁺*) and product PHONN sets (*PHONN**), as detailed, which is written as:

$$PHONNGS = PHONN* \cup PHONN^+ \quad (3\text{-}4)$$

Additive Generalized Artificial Higher Order Neural Network Sets

An *additive generalized PHONN set - PHONN⁺* - is a set, in which element *phonn⁺$_i$* is either an artificial polynomial higher order neural network or an additive generalized polynomial higher order neural network, for which the following conditions hold:

(a) $phonn^+_i \in PHONNS$ (3-5)

or

if an addition $phonn^+_i + phonn^+_j$ is defined every two elements $phonn^+_i$, $phonn^+_j \in PHONNS$,

then $phonn^+_i + phonn^+_j \in PHONN^+, \forall\ phonn^+_i, phonn^+_j \in PHONNS$ (3-6)

   or

if an addition $phonn^+_i + phonn^+_j$ is defined for every two elements $phonn^+_i \in PHONNS$ and $phonn^+_j \in PHONN^+$,

then $phonn^+_i + phonn^+_j \in PHONN^+, \forall\ phonn^+_i \in PHONNS$ and $phonn^+_j \in PHONN^+$ (3-7) or

if an addition $phonn^+_i + phonn^+_j$ is defined every two elements $phonn^+_i$, $phonn^+_j \in PHONN^+$,

then $phonn^+_i + phonn^+_j \in PHONN^+$, $\forall\ phonn^+_i$, $phonn^+_j \in PHONN^+$ (3-8)

(b) $\exists$ an element $phonn^+_{i0}$ in $PHONN^+$ such that

$phonn^+_{i0} + phonn^+_i = phonn^+_i + phonn^+_{i0} = phonn^+_i\ \forall\ phonn^+_i \in PHONN^+$
(3-9)

($phonn^+_{i0}$ is called the *identity* element of the set $PHONN^+$);

(c)   for every element $phonn^+_i \in PHONN^+$,

(c) there exists a unique element, designated $phonn^+_i$,

for which $phonn^+_i + (-phonn^+_i) = (-phonn^+_i) + phonn^+_i = phonn^+_0$ (3-10)

(the element $-phonn^+_i$ is called the *inverse* of $phonn^+_i$);

Product Generalized Artificial Higher Order Neural Network Sets

A *product generalized PHONN set - PHONN** - is a set in which each element $phonn^*_i$ is either an artificial polynomial higher order neural network or a product generalized polynomial higher order neural network, for which the following conditions hold:

(a) $phonn^*_i \in PHONNS$ (3-11)

or

if the product $phonn^* phonn^*_j$ is defined for every two elements $phonn^*_i$, $phonn^*_j \in PHONNS$, then *phonn*$_i$phonn*$_j$* ∈ *PHONN**, ∀ *phonn*$_i$*, *phonn*$_j$* ∈ *PHONNS* (3-12)

or

if a product *phonn*$_i$ phonn*$_j$* is defined for every two elements *phonn*$_i$* ∈ *PHONNS* and *phonn*$_j$* ∈ *PHONN**,

then *phonn*$_i$phonn*$_j$* ∈ *PHONN**, ∀ *phonn*$_i$* ∈ *PHONNS* and *phonn*$_j$* ∈ *PHONN** (3-13)

or

if a product *phonn*$_i$ phonn*$_j$* is defined for every two elements *phonn*$_i$*, *phonn*$_j$* ∈ *PHONN**,

then *phonn*$_i$phonn*$_j$* ∈ *PHONN**, ∀ *phonn*$_i$*, *phonn*$_j$* ∈ *PHONN** (3-14)

(b) ∃ an element *phonn*$_{ie}$* in *PHONN** such that

phonn*$_{ie}$phonn*$_i$ = *phonn*$_i$phonn*$_{ie}$* = *phonn*$_i$* ∀ *phonn*$_i$* ∈ *PHONN** (3-15)

(*phonn*$_{ie}$* is called the *identity* element of the set *PHONN**);

(c) For every element *phonn*$_i$* ∈ *PHONN**, ∃ a unique element, designated *phonn*$^{-1}_i$*,

for which *phonn*$_i$phonn*$^{-1}_i$* = *phonn*$^{-1}_i$phonn*$_i$* = *phonn*$_e$* (3-16)

(the element p*honn*$^{-1}_i$* is called the *inverse* of *phonn*$_i$*);

The elements of set ***PHONNS*** are polynomial higher order neural networks; the elements of set ***PHONNGS***, by contrast, are polynomial higher order neural network *groups*. The difference between a polynomial higher order neural network and a polynomial higher order neural network group was that, in which the polynomial higher order neural network generalized set

HONNGS is a more generalized form of polynomial higher order neural network set ***PHONNS***. Accordingly, polynomial higher order neural network groups should hold more potential for characterizing complex systems.

Following the group definitions by Inui (1978) and Naimark (1982), we have:

a nonempty set ***PHONNG*** is called a *polynomial higher order neural network group*, if ***PHONNG*** ⊂ PHONNGS (the polynomial higher order neural network generalized set), and either the product $h_i h_j$ or the sum $h_i + h_j$ is defined for every two elements h_i, h_j ∈ *PHONNG*.

Inference of Higher Order Neural Network Piecewise Function Groups

Hornik (1991) proved the following general result: "Whenever the activation function is continuous, bounded and non-constant, then for an arbitrary compact subset $X \subseteq R^n$, standard multilayer feed-forward networks can approximate any continuous function on X arbitrarily well with respect to uniform distance, provided that sufficiently many hidden units are available".

A more general result was proved by Leshno (1993): "A standard multilayer feed-forward network with a locally bounded piecewise continuous activation function can approximate *any* continuous function to *any* degree of accuracy if and only if the network's activation function is not a polynomial".

Zhang, Fulcher, & Scofield (1997) provided a general result for neural network group: "Consider a neural network Piecewise Function *Group*, in which each member is a standard multilayer feed-forward neural network, and which has a locally bounded, piecewise continuous (rather than polynomial) activation function and threshold. Each such group can approximate *any* kind of piecewise continuous function, and to *any* degree of accuracy."

An inference is provided as follows: "Consider a higher order neural network Piecewise Function *Group*, in which each member is a standard multilayer feed-forward higher order neural network, and which has a locally bounded, piecewise continuous (rather than polynomial) activation function and threshold. Each such group can approximate *any* kind of piecewise continuous function, and to *any* degree of accuracy."

In the real world, if the function being analyzed varies in a discontinuous and non-smooth fashion with respect to input variables, then such functions cannot be effectively simulated by a higher order neural network. By contrast, if we use higher order neural network *groups* to simulate these functions, it *is* possible to simulate discontinuous functions to any degree accuracy, even at points of discontinuity

HONN Models

Higher Order Neural Network (HONN) models use trigonometric, linear, multiply, power and other neuron functions. This chapter uses the result of Chapter 1 formulae from (1-1) to (1-12) and rewrite formula (1-12) as follows:

HONN general model is:

$$Z = \sum_{k,j=0}^{n} c_{kj}^{\ o} \{c_{kj}^{\ hx} f_k^{\ x}(c_k^{\ x}x)\}\{c_{kj}^{\ hy} f_j^{\ y}(c_j^{\ y}y)\} \text{ (3-17)}$$

where:

x: input variable
y: input variable
$c_k^{\ x}$: The first hidden layer weights
$c_j^{\ y}$: The first hidden layer weights
$c_{kj}^{\ hx}$: The second hidden layer weights
$c_{kj}^{\ hy}$: The second hidden layer weights
$c_{kj}^{\ o}$: The output layer weights
$f_k^{\ x}(c_k^{\ x}x)$: The first hidden layer neuron functions for x input
$f_j^{\ y}(c_j^{\ y}y)$: The first hidden layer neuron functions for y input

PHONN Models

Choosing a different neuron function, results in a different higher order neural network model. This chapter uses the Chapter 1 results of formulae from (1-13) to (1-17), and rewrite formulae (1-13), (1-14) and (1-17: PHONN2) for the PHONN model as follows:

Let

$$f_k^{\ x}(c_k^{\ x}x) = (c_k^{\ x}x)^k \text{ (3-18)}$$

$$f_j^{\ y}\left(c_j^{\ y}y\right) = (c_j^{\ y}y)^j \text{ (3-19)}$$

PHONN Model 2:

$$Z = \sum_{k,j=0}^{n} \left(c_{kj}^{\ o}\right)\{c_{kj}^{\ hx}(c_k^{\ x}x)^k\}\{c_{kj}^{\ hy}(c_j^{\ y}y)^j\} \text{ (3-20)}$$

PHONG Model

The **PHONNG** model is a PHONN model *Group*. It is a piecewise function group of Polynomial Higher Order Neural Networks, and is defined as follows:

$$Z = \{z_1, z_2, z_3, ..., z_i, z_{i+1}, z_{i+2}, ...\} \text{ (3-21)}$$

where: $z_i \in K_i \subset R^n$, K_i is a compact set

$$Z_i = \sum_{k,j=0}^{n} \left(c_{ikj}^{\ o}\right)\{c_{ikj}^{\ hx}(c_{ik}^{\ x}x)^k\}\{c_{ikj}^{\ hy}(c_{ij}^{\ y}y)^j\} \text{ (3-22)}$$

In the **PHONNG** Model (Piecewise Function Group), group *addition* is defined as the *piecewise* function:

$$Z = \begin{cases} z_1, & z_1 \text{ input} \in K_1 \\ z_2, & z_2, \text{ input} \in K_2 \\ ... & \\ z_i, & z_i, \text{ input} \in K_i \\ z_{i+1}, & z_{i+1}, \text{ input} \in K_{i+1} \\ ... & \end{cases} \quad \text{(3-23)}$$

where: z_i inputs $\in K_i \subset R^n$, K_i is a compact set

The **PHONNG** Model is an open and convergent model which can approximate any kind of piecewise continuous function *to any degree of accuracy*, even at discontinuous points (or regions).

An inductive proof of this inference is provided as follows:

Inference:

"Consider an artificial polynomial higher order neural network *group* as Piecewise Function Group, in which each member is a standard multilayer feedforward higher order neural network, and which has a locally bounded, piecewise continuous (rather than polynomial) activation function and threshold. Each such group can approximate *any* kind of piecewise continuous function, and to *any* degree of accuracy."

We use the following definitions in our proof:

H_w: the higher order neural network with n input units, characterized by w;
P: the compact set, $P \subset R^n$;
$C(R^n)$: the family of "real world" functions one may wish to approximate with feedforward higher order neural network architectures of the form H_w;
s: every continuous function, $s \subset C(R^n)$;
G: the family of all functions implied by the network's architecture - namely the family when w runs over all possible values;
g: a good approximation to s on P, $g \subset G$;
$L^\infty(P)$: essentially bounded on P in R^n with respect to Lebesgue measurement;
$L^\infty loc(P)$: locally essentially bounded on P in R^n with respect to Lebesgue measurement;

PHONNG is the higher order neural network group in which each addition $z_i + z_j$ is defined as the *Piecewise Function* for every two elements z_i, $z_j \in$ **PHONNG**.

$$z_i + z_j = \begin{cases} z_i, & I_i = (I \in P_1) \\ z_j, & I_j = (I \in P_2) \end{cases} \text{(3-24)}$$

where I_i, I_j, and I (inputs to the higher order neural networks)

Proof:
Step 1: $P_1 = P$

Based on the Leshno theorem (1993),

$\lim \| s - z_j \| \, L^\infty(P) = 0 \text{ (3-25)}$

$j = \infty$

So, we have

$$\lim \| s - g_j \| L^\infty(\boldsymbol{P}_1) = 0 \ (3\text{-}26)$$

$j = \infty$

Step 2: $\boldsymbol{P}_1 \cup \boldsymbol{P}_2 = \boldsymbol{P}$

$$s = \begin{cases} s_1, & a \ continuous \ function \ on \ \boldsymbol{P}_1 \\ s_2, & a \ continuous \ function \ on \ \boldsymbol{P}_2 \end{cases} \ (3\text{-}27)$$

In $\boldsymbol{P}_1$, we have:

$$\lim \| s_1 - g_j^{(1)} \| L^\infty(\boldsymbol{P}_1) = 0 \ (3\text{-}28)$$

$j = \infty$

There exists a function $g^{(1)}$ which is a good approximation to s_1 on $\boldsymbol{P}_1$.
   In $\boldsymbol{P}_2$, we have:

$$\lim \| s_2 - g_j^{(2)} \| L^\infty(\boldsymbol{P}_2) = 0 \ (3\text{-}29)$$

$j = \infty$

There exists a function $g^{(2)}$ which is a good approximation to s_2 on $\boldsymbol{P}_2$.
   Based on the earlier definition of Neural Network Piecewise Function Groups,

$$z_1 + z_2 = \begin{cases} z_1 = g^{(1)}, & I_1 = (I \in \boldsymbol{P}_1) \\ z_2 = g^{(2)}, & I_2 = (I \in \boldsymbol{P}_2) \end{cases} \ (3\text{-}30)$$

where I_1, I_2, and I (inputs to the higher order neural networks)

Step 3: $P_1 \cup P_2 \cup \ldots\ldots \cup P_m = P,$
m is an any integer and m $\to \infty$.

$$s = \begin{cases} s_1, & a\ continuous\ function\ on\ \boldsymbol{P}_1 \\ s_2, & a\ continuous\ function\ on\ \boldsymbol{P}_2 \\ \ldots \\ s_m, & a\ continuous\ function\ on\ \boldsymbol{P}_m \end{cases} \quad (3\text{-}31)$$

Based on the definition of Neural Network Piecewise Function Group, we have:

$$z_1 + z_2 + \ldots + z_m = \begin{cases} z_1 = g^{(1)}, & I_1 = \left(I \in \boldsymbol{P}_1\right) \\ z_2 = g^{(2)}, & I_2 = \left(I \in \boldsymbol{P}_2\right) \\ \ldots \\ z_m = g^{(m)}, & I_m = \left(I \in \boldsymbol{P}_m\right) \end{cases} \quad (3\text{-}32)$$

Step 4: $P_1 \cup P_2 \cup \ldots\ldots \cup P_m \cup P_{m+1} = P$

$$s = \begin{cases} s_1, & a\ continuous\ function\ on\ \boldsymbol{P}_1 \\ s_2, & a\ continuous\ function\ on\ \boldsymbol{P}_2 \\ \ldots \\ s_m, & a\ continuous\ function\ on\ \boldsymbol{P}_m \\ s_{m+1}, & a\ continuous\ function\ on\ \boldsymbol{P}_{m+1} \end{cases} \quad (3\text{-}33)$$

In $\boldsymbol{P}_{m+1}$, based on Leshno's Theorem (1993), we have:

$$\lim \| s_{m+1} - g_j^{(m+1)} \| \mathbf{L}^\infty(\boldsymbol{P}_{m+1}) = 0 \quad (3\text{-}34)$$

$j = \infty$

There exists a function $g^{(m+1)}$ which is a good approximation to s_{m+1} on P_{m+1}
Based on step 3, we have:

$$z_1 + z_2 + \ldots + z_m + z_{m+1} = \begin{cases} z_1 = g^{(1)}, & I_1 = (I \in P_1) \\ z_2 = g^{(2)}, & I_2 = (I \in P_2) \\ \ldots \\ z_m = g^{(m)}, & I_m = (I \in P_m) \\ z_{m+1} = g^{(m+1)}, & I_{m+1} = (I \in P_{m+1}) \end{cases} \qquad (3\text{-}35)$$

In the real world, if the function being analyzed varies in a discontinuous and non-smooth fashion with respect to input variables, then such functions cannot be effectively simulated by a artificial polynomial higher order neural network. By contrast, if we use artificial polynomial higher order neural network *groups* to simulate these functions, it *is* possible to simulate discontinuous functions to any degree accuracy, even at points of discontinuity

TRIGINIMETRIC POLYNOMIAL HIGHER ORDER NEURAL NETWORK GROUPS

THONNG Definition

A *set* (Waerden, 1970) is defined as a collection of *elements* which possess the same properties. The symbol

$a \in A$ (3-36)

means: A is a set, and a is an element of set A.

The *artificial trigonometric polynomial higher order neural network set* is a set in which every element is a THONN. The symbol

thonn $\in$ *THONNS* (where: *thonn* $= f : R^n \rightarrow R^m$) (3-37)

means:

THONNS is a THONN set, and *thonn*, which is one kind of artificial trigonometric polynomial higher order neural network, is an element of set

THONNS. The domain of the artificial trigonometric polynomial higher order neural network *thonn* inputs is the *n*-dimensional real number R^n. Likewise, the *thonn* outputs belong to the *m*-dimensional real number R^m. The artificial higher order neural network function *f* is a mapping from the inputs of *thonn* to its outputs.

The artificial trigonometric polynomial higher order neural network set *THONNS* is defined as the *union* of the **subsets** of **THONN (order 2)**, **THONN (order 3)**, **THONN (order 4)** ... and so on. In formal notation, we write:

THONNS

$$= THONN\ (order\ 2) \cup THONN\ (order\ 3) \cup THONN\ (order\ 3) \cup THONN\ (order\ 4) \cup \ \text{.......} \ (3\text{-}38)$$

THONN Generalized Sets (*THONNGS*) are defined as the union of additive THONN sets (*THONN⁺*) and product THONN sets (*THONN**), as detailed, which we write as:

$$THONNGS = THONN^* \cup THONN^+ \ (3\text{-}39)$$

Additive Generalized Artificial Higher Order Neural Network Sets

An *additive generalized* **THONN set** - **THONN⁺** - is a set, in which element *thonn⁺$_i$* is either an artificial trigonometric polynomial higher order neural network or an additive generalized trigonometric polynomial higher order neural network, for which the following conditions hold:

(a) *thonn⁺$_i$* $\in$ *THONNS*; (3-40)

or

if an addition *thonn⁺$_i$* + *thonn⁺$_j$* is defined every two elements *thonn⁺$_i$*, *thonn⁺$_j$*
    $\in$ *THONNS*,

then *thonn⁺$_i$+thonn⁺$_j$* $\in$ *THONN⁺*, $\forall$ *thonn⁺$_i$*, *thonn⁺$_j$* $\in$ *THONNS*; (3-41) or

if an addition $thonn^+_i + thonn^+_j$ is defined for every two elements $thonn^+_i \in THONNS$ and $thonn^+_j \in THONN^+$,

then $thonn^+_i + thonn^+_j \in THONN^+$, $\forall \, thonn^+_i \in THONNS$ and $thonn^+_j \in THONN^+$ (3-42)

or

if an addition $thonn^+_i + thonn^+_j$ is defined every two elements $thonn^+_i, thonn^+_j \in THONN^+$,

then $thonn^+_i + thonn^+_j \in THONN^+$, (3-43)

$\forall \, thonn^+_i, thonn^+_j \in THONN^+$;

(b) $\exists$ an element $thonn^+_{i0}$ in $THONN^+$ such that

$thonn^+_{i0} + thonn^+_i = thonn^+_i + thonn^+_{i0} = thonn^+_i \, \forall \, thonn^+_i \in THONN^+$ (3-44)

($thonn^+_{i0}$ is called the *identity* element of the set $THONN^+$);

(c) for every element $thonn^+_i \in THONN^+$ (3-45)

there exists a unique element, designated $thonn^+_i$,

for which $thonn^+_i + (-thonn^+_i) = (-thonn^+_i) + thonn^+_i = thonn^+_0$ (3-46)

(the element $-thonn^+_i$ is called the *inverse* of $thonn^+_i$);

Product Generalized Artificial Higher Order Neural Network Sets

A *product generalized* **THONN** *set* - *THONN** - is a set in which each element *thonn**$_i$ is either an artificial trigonometric polynomial higher order neural network or a product generalized trigonometric polynomial higher order neural network, for which the following conditions hold:

(a) *thonn**$_i$ $\in$ *THONNS* (3-47)

or

if the product *thonn**$_i$*thonn**$_j$ is defined for every two elements *thonn**$_i$, *thonn**$_j$ $\in$ *THONNS*,

then *thonn**$_i$*thonn**$_j$ $\in$ *THONN**, $\forall$ *thonn**$_i$, *thonn**$_j$ $\in$ *THONNS* (3-48)

or

if a product *thonn**$_i$ *thonn**$_j$ is defined for every two elements

thonn*$_i$ $\in$ *THONNS* and *thonn**$_j$ $\in$ *THONN** (3-49)

then *thonn**$_i$*thonn**$_j$ $\in$ *THONN** (3-50)

$\forall$ *thonn**$_i$ $\in$ *THONNS* and *thonn**$_j$ $\in$ *THONN**;

or

if a product *thonn**$_i$ *thonn**$_j$ is defined for every two elements *thonn**$_i$, *thonn**$_j$ $\in$ *THONN**,

then *thonn**$_i$*thonn**$_j$ $\in$ *THONN**, $\forall$ *thonn**$_i$, *thonn**$_j$ $\in$ *THONN** (3-51)

(b) $\exists$ an element *thonn**$_{ie}$ in *THONN** such that

$$thonn^*_{ie}thonn^*_{i} = thonn^*_{i}thonn^*_{ie} = thonn^*_{i} \ \forall \ thonn^*_{i} \in \textbf{\textit{THONN}}^* \ (3\text{-}52)$$

($thonn^*_{ie}$ is called the *identity* element of the set *THONN**);

(c) For every element $thonn^*_{i} \in \textbf{\textit{THONN}}^*$, ∃ a unique element, designated $thonn^{*\text{-}1}_{i}$,

for which $thonn^*_{i}thonn^{*\text{-}1}_{i} = thonn^{*\text{-}1}_{i}thonn^*_{i} = thonn^*_{e} \ (3\text{-}53)$

(the element thonn$^{*\text{-}1}_{i}$ is called the *inverse* of $thonn^*_{i}$);

The elements of set *THONNS* are trigonometric polynomial higher order neural networks; the elements of set *THONNGS*, by contrast, are trigonometric polynomial higher order neural network *groups*. The difference between a trigonometric polynomial higher order neural network and a trigonometric polynomial higher order neural network group was that, in which the trigonometric polynomial higher order neural network generalized set *HONNGS* is a more generalized form of trigonometric polynomial higher order neural network set *THONNS*. Accordingly, trigonometric polynomial higher order neural network groups should hold more potential for characterizing complex systems.

Following the group definitions by Inui (1978) and Naimark (1982), we have:

a nonempty set *THONNG* is called a *trigonometric polynomial higher order neural network group*, if *THONNG* ⊂ THONNGS (the trigonometric polynomial higher order neural network generalized set), and either the product $h_i h_j$ or the sum $h_i + h_j$ is defined for every two elements of $h_i, h_j \in THONNG$.

Trigonometric Polynomial Higher Order Neural Network (Thonn) Model

This chapter uses the Chapter 1 results of formulae from (1-38) to (1-42), and rewrite formulae (1-38), (1-39) and (1-42: THONN2) for the THONN model as follows:

Let:

$$f_k^x\left(c_k^x x\right) = \sin^k(c_k^x x) \ (3\text{-}54)$$

$$f_j^{\,y}\left(c_j^{\,y}y\right) = \cos^j(c_j^{\,y}y) \ (3\text{-}55)$$

THONN Model 2:

$$Z = \sum_{k,j=0}^{n} \left(c_{kj}^{\,o}\right)\{c_{kj}^{\,hx}\sin^k(c_k^{\,x}x)\}\{c_{kj}^{\,hy}\cos^j(c_j^{\,y}y)\} \tag{56}$$

Trigonometric Polynomial Higher Order Neural Network Group (THONG) Model

In order to handle discontinuities in the input training data, the Trigonometric Polynomial Higher Order Neural Network *Group* (*THONNG*) model has also been developed. This is a model in which every element is a *trigonometric polynomial higher order neural network* - THONN (Zhang & Fulcher, 1996b). The domain of the THONN inputs is the *n*-dimensional real number R^n. Likewise, the THONN outputs belong to the *m*-dimensional real number R^m. The artificial trigonometric higher order neural network function *f* constitutes a mapping from the inputs of THONN to its outputs.

The *THONNG* model is a THONN model *Group*. It is a piecewise function group of Trigonometric Polynomial Higher Order Neural Networks, and is defined as follows:

$$\boldsymbol{Z} = \{z_1,\ z_2,\ z_3,\ ...,\ z_i,\ z_{i+1},\ z_{i+2},\ ...\} \ (3\text{-}57)$$

where: $z_i \in \boldsymbol{K}_i \subset \boldsymbol{R}^n$, $\boldsymbol{K}_i$ is a compact set

$$Z_i = \sum_{k,j=0}^{n} \left(c_{ikj}^{\,o}\right)\{c_{ikj}^{\,hx}\sin^k(c_{ik}^{\,x}x)\}\{c_{ikj}^{\,hy}\cos^j(c_{ij}^{\,y}y)\} \tag{58}$$

In the *THONNG* Model (Piecewise Function Group), group *addition* is defined as the *piecewise* function:

$$Z = \begin{cases} z_1, & z_1 \ input \in K_1 \\ z_2, & z_2, \ input \in K_2 \\ \dots \\ z_i, & z_i, \ input \in K_i \\ z_{i+1}, & z_{i+1}, \ input \in K_{i+1} \\ \dots \end{cases} \quad (3\text{-}59)$$

where: $z_i \ inputs \in K_i \subset R^n$, K_i is a compact set

The **THONNG** Model is an open and convergent model which can approximate any kind of piecewise continuous function *to any degree of accuracy*, even at discontinuous points (or regions).

THONN $\in$ **THONNG** (3-60)

where: THONN $= f: R^n \rightarrow R^m$; **THONNG** is the group model

Based on the inference of Zhang, Fulcher & Scofield (1997), each such artificial higher order neural network group can approximate any kind of piecewise continuous function, and to any degree of accuracy. Hence, **THONNG** is also able to simulate discontinuous data.

An inductive proof of this inference is provided as follows:

"Consider an artificial trigonometric polynomial higher order neural network *group* as Piecewise Function Group, in which each member is a standard multilayer feedforward higher order neural network, and which has a locally bounded, piecewise continuous (rather than polynomial) activation function and threshold. Each such group can approximate *any* kind of piecewise continuous function, and to *any* degree of accuracy."

HIGHER ORDER NEURAL NETWORK GROUP FINANCIAL SIMULATION SYSTEM

The above concepts have been incorporated into a Higher Order Neural Network Group financial simulation system. This system comprises two parts, one being a Polynomial Higher Order Neural Network Simulator - **PHONNSim**, and the other a Trigonometric polynomial Higher Order Neural Network

Simulator - *THONNSim*. These *PHONNSim and THONNSim* financial simulation systems were written in the C language, runs under X-Windows on a SUN workstation, and incorporates a user-friendly Graphical User Interface. Any step, data or calculation can be reviewed and modified dynamically in different windows. At the top of the simulator main window, there are three pull-down menus, namely Data, Translators and Neural Network. Each of these offers several options; selecting an option creates another window for further processing. For instance, once we have selected some data via the Data menu, two options are presented for data loading and graphical display.

PRELIMINARY TESTING OF PHONNG AND THONNG SIMULATOR

This paper uses the monthly Australian Dollar and USA dollar exchange rate from November 2009 to December 2010 (See Table 1 and 2) as the test data for PHONNG and THONNG models. Rate and desired output data, R_t, are from USA Federal Reserve Bank Data bank. Input1, R_{t-2}, are the data at time t-2. Input 2, R_{t-1} are the data at time t-1. The values of R_{t-2}, R_{t-1}, and

Table 1. Australian dollar/US dollar exchange rate

USA Federal Reserve Bank Data		Input 1 2 month ago	Input 2 1 month ago	HONN Output				HONN Error Percentage			
Date	Rate desired output			PHONN	THONN	SPHONN	PHONNG	PHONN	THONN	SPHONN	PHONNG
11/2/2009	0.9083										
12/1/2009	0.9249										
1/4/2010	0.9133	0.9083	0.9249	0.9368	0.8708	0.9255	0.9192	2.5731	4.6535	1.3358	0.6460
2/1/2010	0.8877	0.9249	0.9133	0.9112	0.9096	0.9079	0.8758	2.6473	2.4670	2.2755	1.3405
3/1/2010	0.9001	0.9133	0.8877	0.9332	0.9252	0.8713	0.8379	3.6774	2.7886	3.1996	6.9103
4/1/2010	0.9212	0.8877	0.9001	0.8924	0.8876	0.9636	0.8609	3.1264	3.6474	4.6027	6.5458
5/3/2010	0.9255	0.9001	0.9212	0.9424	0.8913	0.9157	0.8739	1.8260	3.6953	1.0589	5.5754
6/1/2010	0.8396	0.9212	0.9255	0.8527	0.8856	0.8759	0.8242	1.5603	5.4788	4.3235	1.8342
7/1/2010	0.8380	0.9255	0.8396	0.8732	0.8632	0.8617	0.8407	4.2005	3.0072	2.8282	0.3222
8/2/2010	0.9135	0.8396	0.8380	0.9264	0.9547	0.9565	0.9366	1.4122	4.5101	4.7072	2.5287
9/1/2010	0.9093	0.8380	0.9135	0.8621	0.9428	0.9567	0.9082	5.1908	3.6842	5.2128	0.1188
10/1/2010	0.9710	0.9135	0.9093	0.8908	0.9541	0.9221	0.9522	8.2595	1.7405	5.0360	1.9361
11/1/2010	0.9878	0.9093	0.9710	0.9708	0.9544	0.9665	0.9681	1.7210	3.3813	2.1563	1.9943
12/1/2010	0.9675	0.9710	0.9878	0.9316	0.9872	0.9441	0.9839	3.7106	2.0362	2.4186	1.6951
Average Error (% Percentage)								3.3254	3.4242	3.2629	2.6206
Average Error of PHONN, THONN, and SPHONN(% percentage)								3.3748	PHONNG Better		0.7542

AUD$1.00 = USD$0.9083 on 2-Nov-2009 , USA Federal Reserve Bank Data January 6th 2011

R_t are used as inputs and output in the PHONNG and THONNG models. PHONNG model is used for Table 1 and THONNG model is used in Table 2. The test data of PHONNG and THONNG orders 6 for using 10,000 epochs are shown on the tables.

Table 2. Australian dollar/ US dollar exchange rate

USA Federal Reserve Bank Data				HONN Output				HONN Error Percentage			
Date	Rate desired output	Input 1 2 month ago	Input 2 1 month ago	PHONN	THONN	SPHONN	THONNG	PHONN	THONN	SPHONN	THONNG
11/30/2009	0.9143										
12/31/2009	0.8978										
1/29/2010	0.8873	0.9143	0.8978	0.8975	0.8675	0.8704	0.8766	1.1496	2.2315	1.9047	1.2059
2/26/2010	0.8961	0.8978	0.8873	0.9254	0.8787	0.8484	0.8886	3.2697	1.9417	5.3231	0.8370
3/31/2010	0.9169	0.8873	0.8961	0.9464	0.8819	0.8629	0.8943	3.2174	3.8172	5.8894	2.4648
4/30/2010	0.9306	0.8961	0.9169	0.8775	0.8755	0.8937	0.9598	5.7060	5.9209	3.9652	3.1378
5/28/2010	0.8491	0.9169	0.9306	0.8621	0.8983	0.8567	0.8215	1.5310	5.7944	0.8951	3.2505
6/30/2010	0.8480	0.9306	0.8491	0.8125	0.8346	0.8226	0.8622	4.1863	1.5802	2.9953	1.6745
7/30/2010	0.9051	0.8491	0.8480	0.8695	0.9195	0.9335	0.9233	3.9333	1.5910	3.1378	2.0108
8/31/2010	0.8910	0.8480	0.9051	0.9405	0.9290	0.8734	0.9173	5.5556	4.2649	1.9753	2.9517
9/30/2010	0.9640	0.9051	0.8910	0.9758	0.9892	0.9075	0.9476	1.2241	2.6141	5.8610	1.7012
10/29/2010	0.9798	0.8910	0.9640	0.9915	0.9205	0.9451	0.9595	1.1941	6.0523	3.5415	2.0719
11/30/2010	0.9607	0.9640	0.9798	0.9806	0.9876	0.9834	0.9755	2.0714	2.8000	2.3629	1.5405
12/30/2010	1.0122	0.9798	0.9607	0.9913	0.9987	0.9616	0.9938	2.0648	1.3337	4.9990	1.8178
Average Error(% Percentage)								2.9253	3.3285	3.5708	2.0554
Average Error of PHONN, THONN, and SPHONN(% percentage)								3.1269	THONNG Better		1.0715

AUD$1.00 = USD$0.9143 on 30-Nov-2009 , USA Federal Reserve Bank Data January 6th 2011

In Table 1, AustralianDollar/USDollar Exchange Rate AUD$1.00 = USD$0.9083 on 2-Nov-2009, the average errors of PHONN, THONN, Sigmoid Polynomial Higher Order Neural Network (SPHONN), and PHONNG are 3.3254%, 3.4242%, 3.2629% and 2.6206% respectively. The average error of PHONN, THONN, and SPHONN is 3.3748%. So PHONNG error is 0.7542% better than the average error of PHONN, THONN, and SPHONN models. In Table 2, AustralianDollar/USDollar Exchange Rate AUD$1.00 = USD$0.9143 on 30-Nov-2009, the average errors of PHONN, THONN, SPHONN, and THONNG are 2.9253%, 3.3085%, 3.5708% and 2.0554% respectively. The average error of PHONN, THONN and SPHONN is 3.1269%. So THONNG error is 1.0715% better than the average error of PHONN, THONN and SPHONN models.

FUTURE RESEARCH DIRECTIONS

One of the topics for future research is to continue building models of higher order neural networks for different data series.

CONCLUSION

The details of open box and nonlinear higher order neural network models of PHONNG and THONNG are developed. The learning algorithm formulae for PHONNG and THONNG are provided based on the structures of PHONNG and THONNG. PHONNG and THONNG simulators are tested for the PHONNG and THONNG models using high frequency data. The running results are compared with Polynomial Higher Order Neural Network (PHONN), Trigonometric Higher Order Neural Network (THONN), and Sigmoid Polynomial Higher Order Neural Network (SPHONN) models. Test results show that errors of PHONNG, THONN, and SPHONNG models are 2.9253% to 3.5708%, and the average error of Polynomial Higher Order Neural Network Group (PHONNG) and Trigonometric Higher Order Neural Network Group (THONNG) models are from 2.0554% to 2.6206%. It means that PHONNG and THONNG models are 0.7542% to 1.0715% better than the average of the PHONN, THONN, and SPHONN models.

REFERENCES

Chen, Y., Wu, P., & Wu, Q. (2009a). Foreign Exchange Rate Forecasting using Higher Order Flexible Neural Tree. In Artificial Higher Order Neural Networks for Economics and Business (pp.94 - 112). IGI Global. doi:10.4018/978-1-59904-897-0.ch005

Christodoulou, M. A., & Iliopoulos, T. N. (2006a). Neural Network Models for Prediction of Steady-State and Dynamic Behavior of MAPK Cascade. *Proceedings of 14th Mediterranean Conference on Control and Automation*, 1 – 9. 10.1109/MED.2006.328820

Crane, J., & Zhang, M. (2005). Data Simulation Using SINCHONN Model. *Proceedings of IASTED International Conference on Computational Intelligence*, 50-55.

Draye, J. S., Pavisic, D. A., Cheron, G. A., & Libert, G. A. (1996), Dynamic recurrent neural networks: a dynamic analysis, *IEEE Transactions SMC- Part B, 26*(5), 692-706.

Dunis, C. L., Laws, J., & Evans, B. (2006b). Modelling and Trading the Soybean-Oil Crush Spread with Recurrent and Higher Order Networks: A Comparative Analysis. *Neural Network World, 3*(6), 193–213.

Foka, A. (1999). *Time Series Prediction using Evolving Polynomial Neural Networks* (MSc Thesis). University of Manchester Institute of Science & Technology.

Fulcher, G. E., & Brown, D. E. (1994). A polynomial neural network for predicting temperature distributions. *IEEE Transactions on Neural Networks, 5*(3), 372–379. doi:10.1109/72.286909 PMID:18267805

Ghazali, R. (2005). *Higher order neural network for financial time series prediction*. Annual Postgraduate Research Conference, School of Computing and Mathematical Sciences, Liverpool John Moores University, UK. http://www.cms.livjm.ac.uk/research/doc/ConfReport2005.doc

Ghazali, R., & Al-Jumeily, D. (2009). Application of Pi-Sigma Neural Networks and Ridge Polynomial Neural Networks to Financial Time Series Prediction. In Artificial Higher Order Neural Networks for Economics and Business (pp.271 - 294). IGI Global. doi:10.4018/978-1-59904-897-0.ch012

Ghazali, R., Hussain, A. J., & Nawi, N. M. (2010). Dynamic Ridge Polynomial Higher Order Neural Network. In Artificial Higher Order Neural Networks for Computer Science and Engineering – Trends for Emerging Application (pp.255- 268). IGI Global. doi:10.4018/978-1-61520-711-4.ch011

Ghosh, J., & Shin, Y. (1992). Efficient Higher-order Neural Networks for Function Approximation and Classification. *International Journal of Neural Systems, 3*(4), 323–350. doi:10.1142/S0129065792000255

Hornik, K. (1991). Approximation capabilities of multilayer feedforward networks. *Neural Networks, 4*(2), 251–257. doi:10.1016/0893-6080(91)90009-T

Hu, S., & Yan, P. (1992). Level-by-Level learning for artificial neural groups. *Tien Tzu Hsueh Pao, 20*(10), 39–43.

Hussain, A., Knowles, A., Lisboa, P., El-Deredy, W., & Al-Jumeily, D. (2006). Polynomial Pipelined Neural Network and Its Application to Financial Time Series Prediction. *Lecture Notes in Artificial Intelligence, 4304*, 597–606.

Hussain, A., & Liatsis, P. (2009). A novel recurrent polynomial neural network for financial time series prediction. In Artificial Higher Order Neural Networks for Economics and Business (pp.190 - 211). IGI Global. doi:10.4018/978-1-59904-897-0.ch009

Inui, T., Tanabe, Y., & Onodera, Y. (1978). *Group Theory and Its Application in Physics*. Heidelberg, Germany: Springer-Verlag.

Jiang, M., Gielen, G., & Wang, L. (2010). Analysis of Quantization Effects on Higher Order Function and Multilayer Feedforward Neural Networks. In Artificial Higher Order Neural Networks for Computer Science and Engineering – Trends for Emerging Application (pp.187- 222). IGI Global. doi:10.4018/978-1-61520-711-4.ch008

Kariniotakis, G. N., Stavrakakis, G. S., & Nogaret, E. F. (1996). Wind power forecasting using advanced neural networks models. *IEEE Transactions on Energy Conversion*, *11*(4), 762–767. doi:10.1109/60.556376

Knowles, A., Hussain, A., Deredy, W. E., Lisboa, P., & Dunis, C. L. (2009). Higher Order Neural Networks with Bayesian Confidence Measure for the Prediction of the EUR/USD Exchange Rate. In Artificial Higher Order Neural Networks for Economics and Business (pp.48- 59). IGI Global.

Knowles, A., Hussain, A., Deredy, W. E., Lisboa, P. G. J., & Dunis, C. (2005). *Higher-Order Neural network with Bayesian Confidence measure for Prediction of EUR/USD Exchange Rate. Forecasting Financial Markets Conference*, Marseilles, France.

Kosmatopoulos, E. B., Ioannou, P. A., & Christodoulou, M. A. (1992). Identification of nonlinear systems using new dynamic neural network structures. *Proceedings of the 31st IEEE Conference on Decision and Control*, *1*, 20 – 25. 10.1109/CDC.1992.371800

Kosmatopoulos, E. B., Polycarpou, M. M., Christodoulou, M. A., & Ioannou, P. A. (1995). High-order neural network structures for identification of dynamical systems. *Neural Networks*, *6*(2), 422–431. doi:10.1109/72.363477 PMID:18263324

Kuroe, Y., Ikeda, H., & Mori, T. (1997). Identification of nonlinear dynamical systems by recurrent high-order neural networks. *Proceedings of IEEE International Conference on Systems, Man, and Cybernetics*, *1*, 70 – 75. 10.1109/ICSMC.1997.625725

Lee, M., Lee, S. Y., & Park, C. H. (1992). Neural controller of nonlinear dynamic systems using higher order neural networks. *Electronics Letters*, *28*(3), 276–277. doi:10.1049/el:19920170

Leshno, M., Lin, V., & Ya, P. (1993). Multilayer feedforward networks with a nonpolynomial activation function can approximate any function. *Neural Networks*, *6*(6), 861–867. doi:10.1016/S0893-6080(05)80131-5

Liatsis, P., Hussain, A., & Milonidis, E. (2009). Artificial higher order pipeline recurrent neural networks for financial time series prediction. In Artificial Higher Order Neural Networks for Economics and Business (pp.164 - 189). IGI Global. doi:10.4018/978-1-59904-897-0.ch008

Lu, B., Qi, H., Zhang, M., & Scofield, R. A. (2000). Using PT-HONN models for multi-polynomial function simulation. *Proceedings of IASTED International Conference on Neural Networks*, 1-5.

Lu, Z., Song, G., & Shieh, L. (2010). Improving Sparsity in Kernel Principal Component Analysis by Polynomial Kernel Higher Order Neural Networks. In Artificial Higher Order Neural Networks for Computer Science and Engineering – Trends for Emerging Application (pp.223- 238). IGI Global.

Lumer, E. D. (1992). Selective attention to perceptual groups: The phase tracking mechanism. *International Journal of Neural Systems*, *3*(1), 1–17. doi:10.1142/S0129065792000024

Matsuoka, T., Hamada, H., & Nakatsu, R. (1989). Syllable Recognition Using Integrated Neural Networks. *Proc. Intl. Joint Conf. Neural Networks*, 251-258. 10.1109/IJCNN.1989.118588

Murata, J. (2010). Analysis and Improvement of Function Approximation Capabilities of Pi-Sigma Higher Order Neural Networks. In Artificial Higher Order Neural Networks for Computer Science and Engineering – Trends for Emerging Application (pp.239- 254). IGI Global. doi:10.4018/978-1-61520-711-4.ch010

Naimark, M. A., & Stern, A. I. (1982). *Theory of Group Representations*. Springer-Verlag. doi:10.1007/978-1-4613-8142-6

Onwubolu, G. C. (2009). Artificial Higher Order Neural Networks in Time Series Prediction. In Artificial Higher Order Neural Networks for Economics and Business (pp.250 - 270). IGI Global. doi:10.4018/978-1-59904-897-0.ch011

Pentland, A., & Turk, M. (1989). Face Processing: Models for Recognition. Proc. SPIE - Intelligent Robots and Computer Vision VIII: Algorithms and Technology, 20-35.

Qi, H., & Zhang, M. (2001). Rainfall estimation using M-THONN model. *Neural Networks*, 1620–1624.

Rovithakis, G. A., Chalkiadakis, I., & Zervakis, M. E. (2004). High-order neural network structure selection for function approximation applications using genetic algorithms. *Systems, Man and Cybernetics. Part B*, *34*(1), 150–158. PMID:15369059

Saad, E. W., Prokhorov, D. V., & Wunsch, D. C. II. (1998). Comparative Study of Stock Trend Prediction Using Time Delay Recurrent and Probabilistic Neural Networks. *IEEE Transactions on Neural Networks*, *9*(6), 1456–1470. doi:10.1109/72.728395 PMID:18255823

Sanchez, E. N., Alanis, A. Y., & Rico, J. (2009). Electric Load Demand and Electricity Prices Forecasting using Higher Order Neural Networks Trained by Kalman Filtering. In Artificial Higher Order Neural Networks for Economics and Business (pp.295 - 313). IGI Global.

Selviah, D. R., & Shawash, J. (2009). Generalized Correlation Higher Order Neural Networks for Financial Time Series Prediction. In Artificial Higher Order Neural Networks for Economics and Business (pp.212 - 249). IGI Global. doi:10.4018/978-1-59904-897-0.ch010

Shi, D., Tan, S., & Ge, S. S. (2009). Automatically Identifying Predictor Variables for Stock Return Prediction. In Artificial Higher Order Neural Networks for Economics and Business (pp.60 - 78). IGI Global. doi:10.4018/978-1-59904-897-0.ch003

Tawfik, H., & Liatsis, P. (1997). Prediction of non-linear time-series using Higher-Order Neural Networks. *Proceeding IWSSIP'97 Conference*.

Tenti, P. (1996). Forecasting Foreign Exchange Rates Using Recurrent Neural Networks. *Applied Artificial Intelligence*, *10*(6), 567–581. doi:10.1080/088395196118434

Tsao, T.-R., Shyu, & Libert. (1989). A group theory approach to neural network computing of 3D rigid motion. *Proceedings of International Joint Conference on Neural Networks*, *2*, 275–280. doi:10.1109/IJCNN.1989.118710

Waerden, B. L. (1970). *Algebra*. New York: Frederick Ungar Publishing Co.

Willcox, C. R. (1991). Understanding hierarchical neural network behavior: A renormalization group approach. *Journal of Physics. A. Mathematical Nuclear and General*, *24*(11), 2655–2644. doi:10.1088/0305-4470/24/11/030

Xu, S. (2009). Adaptive Higher Order Neural Network Models and Their Applications in Business. In Artificial Higher Order Neural Networks for Economics and Business (pp.314 - 329). IGI Global. doi:10.4018/978-1-59904-897-0.ch014

Xu, S., & Zhang, M. (1999). Approximation to continuous functions and operators using adaptive higher order neural networks. *Proceedings of International Joint Conference on Neural Networks'99.*

Xu, S., & Zhang, M. (2002). An adaptive higher-order neural networks (AHONN) and its approximation capabilities. *Proceedings of the 9th International Conference on Neural Information Processing*, *2*, 848 – 852. 10.1109/ICONIP.2002.1198179

Yang, X. (1990). Detection and classification of neural signals and identification of neural networks (synaptic connectivity). *Dissertation Abstracts International - B, 50/12*, 5761.

Zhang, J. (2005). *Polynomial full naïve estimated misclassification cost models for financial distress prediction using higher order neural network. 14th Annual Research Work Shop on: Artificial Intelligence and Emerging Technologies in Accounting.* San Francisco, CA: Auditing, and Ta.

Zhang, J. C., Zhang, M., & Fulcher, J. (1997). Financial simulation system using a higher order trigonometric polynomial neural network group model. In *Proceedings of the IEEE/IAFE 1997 Computational Intelligence for Financial Engineering (CIFEr)* (pp.189 – 194). 10.1109/CIFER.1997.618934

Zhang, M. (2001). Financial data simulation using A-THONN model. *Neural Networks, 3*, 1823–1827.

Zhang, M. (2001). Financial Data Simulation Using A-PHONN Model. In *International Joint Conference on Neural Networks' 2001* (pp.1823 – 1827). Washington, DC: Academic Press.

Zhang, M. (2005). A data simulation System Using sinx/x and sinx Polynomial Higher Order Neural Networks. In *Proceedings of IASTED International Conference on Computational Intelligence* (pp.56 – 61). Calgary, Canada: Academic Press.

Zhang, M. (2006). A Data Simulation System Using CSINC Polynomial Higher Order Neural Networks. In *Proceedings of the 2006 International Conference on Artificial Intelligence* (Vol. I, pp. 91-97). Las Vegas, NV: Academic Press.

Zhang, M. (2009a). Artificial Higher Order Neural Network Nonlinear Model - SAS NLIN or HONNs. In Artificial Higher Order Neural Networks for Economics and Business (pp.1- 47). IGI Global.

Zhang, M. (2009b). Ultra High Frequency Trigonometric Higher Order Neural Networks for Time Series Data Analysis. In Artificial Higher Order Neural Networks for Economics and Business (pp.133 - 163). IGI Global. doi:10.4018/978-1-59904-897-0.ch007

Zhang, M. (2003, May 13-15). Financial data simulation using PL-HONN Model. In *Proceedings IASTED International Conference on Modelling and Simulation* (pp.229-233). Academic Press.

Zhang, M., & Fulcher, J. (2004). Higher Order Neural Networks for Satellite Weather Prediction. In J. Fulcher & L. C. Jain (Eds.), Applied Intelligent Systems (Vol. 153, pp. 17-57). Springer. doi:10.1007/978-3-540-39972-8_2

Zhang, M., Fulcher, J., & Scofield, R. A. (1996) Neural network group models for estimating rainfall from satellite images. In *Proceedings of World Congress on Neural Networks* (pp.897-900). San Diego, CA: Academic Press.

Zhang, M., & Lu, B. (2001). Financial data simulation using M-PHONN model. In Neural Networks (vol. 3, pp. 1828 – 1832). Washington, DC: Academic Press.

Zhang, M., Murugesan, S., & Sadeghi, M. (1995). Polynomial higher order neural network for economic data simulation. In *Proceedings of International Conference on Neural Information Processing* (pp. 493-496). Beijing, China: Academic Press.

Zhang, M., & Scofield, R.A. (2001). Rainfall estimation using A-PHONN model. In *Neural Networks* (Vol. 3, pp.1583 – 1587). Washington, DC: Academic Press.

Zhang, M., Zhang, J. C., & Fulcher, J. (1997). Financial Prediction System Using Higher Order Trigonometric Polynomial Neural Network Group Model. *Proceedings of the IEEE International Conference on Neural Networks*, 2231-2234.

Zhang, M., Zhang, J. C., & Fulcher, J. (2000). Higher order neural network group models for data approximation. *International Journal of Neural Systems, 10*(2), 123–142. doi:10.1142/S0129065700000119 PMID:10939345

Zhang, M., Zhang, J. C., & Keen, S. (1999). Using THONN system for higher frequency non-linear data simulation & prediction. In *Proceedings of IASTED International Conference on Artificial Intelligence and Soft Computing* (pp.320-323). Honolulu, HI: Academic Press.

ADDITIONAL READING

Baldi, P., & Venkatesh, S. S. (1993). Random interactions in higher order neural networks. *IEEE Transactions on Information Theory, 39*(1), 274–283. doi:10.1109/18.179374

Brucoli, M., Carnimeo, L., & Grassi, G. (1997). Associative memory design using discrete-time second-order neural networks with local interconnections. *IEEE Transactions on Circuits and Systems. I, Fundamental Theory and Applications, 44*(2), 153–158. doi:10.1109/81.554334

Burshtein, D. (1998). Long-term attraction in higher order neural networks. *Neural Networks, 9*(1), 42–50. doi:10.1109/72.655028 PMID:18252428

Giles, L., & Maxwell, T. (1987). Learning, invariance and generalization in high-order neural networks. *Applied Optics, 26*(23), 4972–4978. doi:10.1364/AO.26.004972 PMID:20523475

Shin, Y. (1991). The Pi-Sigma network: An efficient higher-order neural network for pattern classification and function approximation. *Proceedings of International Joint Conference on Neural Networks, I*, 13–18.

Xu, B., Liu, X., & Liao, X. (2005). Global asymptotic stability of high-order Hopfield type neural networks with time delays. *Computers & Mathematics with Applications (Oxford, England), 45*(10-11), 1729–1737. doi:10.1016/S0898-1221(03)00151-2

Young, S., & Downs, T. (1993). Generalization in higher order neural networks. *Electronics Letters, 29*(16), 1491–1493. doi:10.1049/el:19930996

Zhang, M., Xu, S., & Fulcher, J. (2002). Neuron-adaptive higher order neural-network models for automated financial data modeling. *IEEE Transactions on Neural Networks, 13*(1), 188–204. doi:10.1109/72.977302 PMID:18244418

KEY TERMS AND DEFINITIONS

AHONUs: Artificial higher order neural units.

HONN: Artificial higher order neural network.

MPHONN: Multi-polynomial higher order neural network models.

MPONNG: Multi-layer higher order neural network group model. It is combined the characteristics of PHONN, THONN, and SPHONN.

NAHONN: Neuron-adaptive higher order neural network.

PHONN: Polynomial higher order neural network.

PHONNG: Polynomial higher order neural network group.

SPHONN: Sigmoid polynomial higher order neural network.

THONN: Trigonometric polynomial higher order neural network.

THONNG: Trigonometric polynomial higher order neural network.

Section 2
Artificial Higher Order Neural Networks for Economics and Business

Chapter 4
SAS Nonlinear Models or Artificial Higher Order Neural Network Nonlinear Models?

ABSTRACT

This chapter delivers general format of higher order neural networks (HONNs) for nonlinear data analysis and six different HONN models. Then, this chapter mathematically proves that HONN models could converge and have mean squared errors close to zero. Moreover, this chapter illustrates the learning algorithm with update formulas. HONN models are compared with SAS nonlinear (NLIN) models, and results show that HONN models are 3 to 12% better than SAS nonlinear models. Finally, this chapter shows how to use HONN models to find the best model, order, and coefficients without writing the regression expression, declaring parameter names, and supplying initial parameter values.

INTRODUCTION

Applications of HONNs in Economics, Finance, and Accounting

Many researchers in the economics, finance, and accounting areas use artificial neural networks in their studies, however, only a few studies use HONN. Lee, Lee, and Park (1992) use HONNs to identify and control the nonlinear

DOI: 10.4018/978-1-7998-3563-9.ch004

dynamic systems. The computer simulation results reveal that HONN models are more effective in controlling nonlinear dynamic systems. Karayiannis and Venetsanopoulos (1995) study the architecture, training, and properties of neural networks of order higher than one. They also study the formulation of the training of HONNs as a nonlinear associative recall problem that provides the basis for their optimal least squares training. Bouzerdoum (1999) presents a class of HONNs, shunting inhibitory artificial neural networks (SIANNs). These HONNs can produce classifiers with complex nonlinear decision boundaries, ranging from simple hyperplanes to very complex nonlinear surfaces. The author also provides a training method for SIANNs. Li, Hirasawa, and Hu (2003) present a constructive method for HONNs with multiplication units. The proposed method provides a flexible mechanism for incremental network growth.

Zhang, Zhang, and Fulcher (1997) develop trigonometric polynomial higher order neural network (THONN) group models for financial data prediction. Results show that THONN group models can handle nonlinear data that has discontinuous points. Xu and Zhang (1999) develop adaptive HONNs with adaptive neuron functions to approximate continuous data. Lu, Zhang, and Scofield (2000) generate Polynomial and Trigonometric Higher Order Neural Network (PTHONN) models for multi-polynomial function simulation. Crane and Zhang (2005) provide a SINC Higher Order Neural Network (SINCHONN) models, which use SINC function as active neurons. These models successfully simulate currency exchange rates.

Ghazali (2005) use HONN for financial time series prediction and find HONN outperforms traditional multilayer neural network models. Knowles, Hussain, Deredy, Lisboa, and Dunis (2005) use HONNs with Bayesian confidence measure for prediction of EUR/USD exchange rates. They show that the simulation results for HONNs are 8% better than multilayer neural network. In the accounting area, Zhang (2005) uses HONN to estimate misclassification cost for different financial distress prediction models. Moreover, HONN has been used to generate nonlinear models for the power of chief elected officials and debt (Zhang, 2006). Dunis, Laws, and Evans (2006) use HONN to build a nonlinear model for modeling and trading the gasoline crack spread. The results show that the spread does indeed exhibit asymmetric adjustment, with movements away from fair value being nearly three times larger on the downside than on the upside.

Zhang, Murugesan and Sadeghi (1995), and Zhang, Zhang and Keen (1999) use both Polynomial and Trigonometric HONNs to simulate and predict financial time series data from the Reserve Bank of Australia Bulletin www.abs.gov.au/ausstats/abs@.nsf/w2.3 to around 90% accuracy. Zhang and Lu (2001) develop the Polynomial and Trigonometric HONN (PTHONN) and Multiple Polynomial functions HONN (MPHONN) models for improved performance. In financial time series prediction, PHONN groups produce around 1.2% error for simulation compared with 11% for HONNs (Zhang, Zhang, and Fulcher, 2000). Improvements in performance are also observed with THONN groups (Zhang, Zhang, and Fulcher, 2000). Currently, multi-PHONN (Zhang 2001, 2002, 2005, and 2006) is capable of simulating not only polynomial and/or trigonometric functions, but also a combination of these and sigmoid and/or logarithmic functions. As a result, they can better approximate real-world economic time series data.

SAS

The overview (http://support.sas.com/documentation/onlinedoc/index.html) of SAS Nonlinear (NLIN) procedure is as follows:

"The NLIN procedure produces least squares or weighted least squares estimates of the parameters of a nonlinear model. Nonlinear models are more difficult to specify and estimates than linear models. Instead of simply listing regression variables, you must write the regression expression, declare parameter names, and supply initial parameter values. Some models are difficult to fit, and there is no guarantee that the procedure can fit the model successfully. For each nonlinear model to be analyzed, you must specify the model (using a single dependent variable) and the names and starting values of the parameters to be estimated."

The first difficulty in using SAS NLIN is that users must provide the correct regression expression. However, this step is troublesome since there are different possible models (polynomial, trigonometric polynomial, etc.) and order that the users can select.

The second difficulty to use SAS NLIN is that you must provide the starting values of the parameters to be estimated. If you give the wrong starting values, SAS NLIN procedure may not converge, and users may waste time in guessing the initial values. The key point is SAS NLIN cannot guarantee that the procedure will fit the model successfully. In most cases, the starting values of the parameters that users provide must be very close to the actual parameters, otherwise SAS NLIN will not converge.

Motivations, Contributions, and Outline of this Chapter

The purpose of this chapter is to develop easy to use and always convergent technique in building nonlinear models. Since HONNs are open-box models and the traditional neural networks are black- box models, people working in economics and business areas may feel more comfortable working with HONN. So the first motivation is to introduce open-box HONN models to people working in economics and business areas. The goal of using SAS NLIN procedure is to find the nonlinear models and the coefficients. However, this goal is difficult to achieve since most of the SAS users cannot provide the expression or the initial values for the coefficients. The second motivation is to develop new nonlinear models, which are easy to use and always convergent, for time series data analysis.

The contributions of this chapter will be:

- Introduce the background of HONNs with the applications of HONNs.
- Introduce 6 different types of HONN models.
- Provide the HONN learning algorithm and weight update formulae.
- Compare HONNs with SAS NLIN and show that HONNs can produce more accurate simulation results than SAS NLIN models.
- Show detailed steps in how to use HONNs to find the best model, order, and coefficients.

Section 1 introduces the background and applications of HONNs and SAS. Section 2 provides the structure of HONN and different types of nonlinear models of HONN. The third section will introduce the convergence theories of HONN and explain why HONNs can outperform SAS NLIN procedure. Section 4 provides the learning formulae for training HONN and the detailed learning algorithm of HONN models and weights update formulae. Section 5 studies six different HONN Nonlinear Models: PHONN (Polynomial Higher Order Neural Network), THONN (Trigonometric Higher Order Neural Network), UCSHONN (Ultra High Frequency Cosine and Sine Trigonometric Higher Order Neural Network), SXSHONN (SINC and Trigonometric Higher Order Neural Network), and SPHONN (Sigmoid Polynomial Higher Order Neural Network). Section 6 shows the HONN simulation system. Section 7 compares SAS nonlinear models with HONN nonlinear models. Section 8 introduces how to find model, order, and coefficients by HONN nonlinear models. Section 9 concludes this paper.

HONN STRUCTURE AND NONLINEAR MODLES

This chapter uses the Chapter 1 results of HONN general models. Based on the formulae of (1-10: HONN 0), (1-11: HONN 1), and (1-12: HONN 2), this chapter rewrite these formulae as follows:

HONN general models are:

HONN General Model 0:

$$Z = \sum_{k,j=0}^{n} c_{kj}{}^{o} \{f_k{}^x(x)\}\{f_j{}^y(y)\}$$
$$where: \left(c_{kj}{}^{hx}\right) = \left(c_{kj}{}^{hy}\right) = 1 \, and \, c_k{}^x = c_j{}^y = 1$$
(4-1)

HONN General Model 1:

$$Z = \sum_{k,j=0}^{n} c_{kj}{}^{o} \{f_k{}^x\left(c_k{}^x x\right)\}\{f_j{}^y\left(c_j{}^y y\right)\} \, where: \left(c_{kj}{}^{hx}\right) = \left(c_{kj}{}^{hy}\right) = 1 \, (4\text{-}2).$$

HONN Model 2:

$$Z = \sum_{k,j=0}^{n} c_{kj}{}^{o} \{c_{kj}{}^{hx} f_k{}^x\left(c_k{}^x x\right)\}\{c_{kj}{}^{hy} f_j{}^y\left(c_j{}^y y\right)\} \, (4\text{-}3)$$

Formula (4-1: HONN 0), (4-2: HONN 1) and (4-3: HONN 2) are the HONN models 0, 1 and 2 respectively. Model 2 has three layers of changeable weights, Model 1 has two layers of changeable weights, and model 0 has one layer of changeable weights. For models 0, 1 and 2, Z is the output while x and y are the inputs of HONN. $c_{kj}{}^o$ is the weight for the output layer, $c_{kj}{}^{hx}$ and $c_{kj}{}^{hy}$ are the weights for the second hidden layer, and $c_k{}^x$ and $c_j{}^y$ are the weights for the first hidden layer. The output layer node of HONN is a linear function of $f^o(net^o) = net^o$, where net^o equals the input of output layer node. The second hidden layer node of HONN is a multiple neuron. The first hidden layer neuron function could be any nonlinear function. HONN is an open neural network model, each weight of HONN has its corresponding coefficient in the model formula, similarly, each node of HONN has its corresponding function in the model formula. The structure of HONN is built by a nonlinear formula. It means, after training, there is rationale for each component of HONN in the nonlinear formula. The values of k and j ranges from 0 to n, where n is an integer. The HONN model can simulate any nonlinear function. This property of the model allows it to easily simulate and predicate any nonlinear functions and ultra-high frequency time series data, since both k and j increase when there is an increase in n.

CONVERGENCE THEORIES OF HONN

How can HONNs outperform SAS NLIN? This chapter proves mathematically that HONNs can always converge and have better accuracy than SAS NLIN. Fortunately, there are a few very good convergences theories proved mathematically in the artificial neural network modeling area.

Hornik (1991) proves the following general result:

"Whenever the activation function is continuous, bounded and nonconstant, then for an arbitrary compact subset $X \subseteq R^n$, standard multilayer feedforward networks can approximate any continuous function on X arbitrarily well with respect to uniform distance, provided that sufficiently many hidden units are available".

Since HONNs are a subset of artificial neural networks, and HONNs are multilayer feedforward networks and the activation functions are continuous, bounded and nonconstant. Therefore, HONNs meet all the requirements of the above result.

Leshno (1993) shows a more general result:

"A standard multilayer feedforward network with a locally bounded piecewise continuous activation function can approximate any continuous function to any degree of accuracy if and only if the network's activation function is not a polynomial".

Since HONNs are standard multiplayer feedforward networks with locally bounded piecewise continuous functions, HONNs can approximate any continuous function to any degree of accuracy. Polynomial Higher Order

Network uses polynomial function as network's activation function on the first hidden layer but use other functions on the second layer and the output layer, so PHONNs still meet the conditions of the above result. Thus, PHONNs can approximate any continue function to any degree of accuracy. Inferring from Hornik (1991) and Leshno (1993), HONNs can simulate any continuous function to any degree of accuracy, since HONNs are a subset of ANN. This is the reason why HONNs can have better results than SAS NLIN.

Given these general results, Zhang and Fulcher (1997) infer the following:

"Consider a neural network Piecewise Function Group, in which each member is a standard multilayer feedforward neural network, and which has a locally bounded, piecewise continuous (rather than polynomial) activation function and threshold. Each such group can approximate any kind of piecewise continuous function, and to any degree of accuracy."

Results from Zhang and Fulcher (1997) show HONN group can simulate any kind of piecewise continuous function and to any degree of accuracy (not discussed in this chapter). To make HONN more powerful, Zhang, Xu, and Fulcher (2002) develop Neuron-Adaptive Higher Order Neural Network (NAHONN). The key point is that the activation functions in the NAHONN are adaptive functions. With the adaptive function as neuron, Zhang, Xu, and Fulcher (2002) generate the following theorem:

"A NAHONN (Neuron-Adaptive Higher Order Neural Network) with a neuron-adaptive activation function can approximate any piecewise continuous function with infinite (countable) discontinuous points to any degree of accuracy."

This theorem shows that one NAHONN can approximate any piecewise continuous function with infinite (countable) discontinuous points to any degree of accuracy. This result is stronger than the results from Hornik (1991), Leshno (1993), and Zhang and Fulcher (1997).

LEARNING ALGORITHM OF HONN MODEL

Chapter 1 already mathematically provide weight update formulae for each weight in different layers. The HONN learning algorithm based on the weight update formulae already be provided in Chapter 1

HONN Learning Algorithm and Update Formulae

We summarize the procedure for performing the learning algorithm:

Step 1: Initialize all weights (coefficients) of the neurons (activation functions).
Step 2: Input a sample from the data pool.
Step 3: Calculate the actual outputs of all neurons using present values of weights (coefficients).
Step 4: Compare the desired output and actual output. If mean squared error reaches to the desired number, stop. Otherwise go to Step 5.
Step 5: Adjust the weights (coefficients) according to the iterative formulae.
Step 6: Input another sample from the data pool, go to step 3.

The above learning algorithm is the back-propagation learning algorithm, the formulae in the above steps are developed in this chapter. The learning formulae of the output layer weight for all HONN models is the same as the learning formula (1-145: A.13) of the output layer weight for HONN in Chapter 1. Similarly, the learning formulae of the second hidden layer weight for all HONN models are the same as learning formula (1-159: B.14) and (1-16-: B.15)) of the second layer weight for HONN in Chapter 1. The first hidden layer weight learning formulae are different for different HONN models and will be rewritten as follows.

HONN NONLINEAR MODELS and Learning Update Formulae

PHONN Model

Polynomial Higher Order Neural Networks (PHONN) are defined when neuron functions ($f_k{}^x$ and $f_j{}^y$) select polynomial functions. Based on Chapter 1 formulae from (1-13) to (1-17: PHONN 2), PHONN models are rewritten as follows:

Let

$$f_k{}^x \left(c_k{}^x x \right) = (c_k{}^x x)^k \ (4\text{-}4)$$

$$f_j^{\,y}\left(c_j^{\,y}y\right) = (c_j^{\,y}y)^j \ (4\text{-}5)$$

PHONN Model 0:

$$z = \sum_{k,j=0}^{n} c_{kj}^{\,o}(x)^k (y)^j$$

$$(4\text{-}6)$$

$$where:\left(c_{kj}^{\,hx}\right) = \left(c_{kj}^{\,hy}\right) = 1\, and\ c_k^{\,x} = c_j^{\,y} = 1$$

PHONN Model 1:

$$z = \sum_{k,j=0}^{n} c_{kj}^{\,o}(c_k^{\,x}x)^k (c_j^{\,y}y)^j \ where:\left(c_{kj}^{\,hx}\right) = \left(c_{kj}^{\,hy}\right) = 1\,(4\text{-}7)$$

PHONN Model 2:

$$Z = \sum_{k,j=0}^{n}\left(c_{kj}^{\,o}\right)\{c_{kj}^{\,hx}(c_k^{\,x}x)^k\}\,\{c_{kj}^{\,hy}(c_j^{\,y}y)^j\}\ (4\text{-}8)$$

The first hidden layer weight learning formulae for PHONN are rewritten as follows, based on the Chapter 1 formulae of (1-98: PHONN C.17) and (1-200: PHONN D.17):

For a polynomial function of x input side:

$$\begin{aligned}
c_k^{\,x}\left(t+1\right) &= c_k^{\,x}\left(t\right) - \eta\left(\partial E_p / \partial c_k^{\,x}\right)\\
&= c_k^{\,x}\left(t\right) + \eta\left(d-z\right)f^{o'}\left(net^o\right)c_{kj}^{\,o} * f^{h'}\left(net_{kj}^{\,h}\right)c_{kj}^{\,hy}b_j^{\,y}c_{kj}^{\,hx}f_x^{\,'}\left(net_k^{\,x}\right)x\\
&= c_k^{\,x}\left(t\right) + \eta * \delta^{ol} * c_{kj}^{\,o} * \delta^{hx} * c_{kj}^{\,hx} * k * (c_k^{\,x} * x)^{k-1} * x\\
&= c_k^{\,x}\left(t\right) + \eta * \delta^{ol} * c_{kj}^{\,o} * \delta^{hx} * c_{kj}^{\,hx} * \delta^{x} * x
\end{aligned}$$

$$(4\text{-}9)$$

where:

$$\delta^{ol} = (d-z)f^{o'}\left(net^o\right) = d-z \qquad \left(linear\ neuron\ f^{o\,'}\left(net^o\right)=1\right)$$

$$\delta^{hx} = f^{h'}\left(net_{kj}^{\ h}\right)c_{kj}^{\ hy}b_j^{\ y} = c_{kj}^{\ hy}b_j^{\ y} \quad \left(linear\ neuron\ f^{h\,'}\left(net_{kj}^{\ h}\right)=1\right)$$

$$\delta^{x} = f_x'\left(net_k^{\ x}\right) = k*\left(net_k^{\ x}\right)^{k-1} = k*(c_k^{\ x}*x)^{k-1}$$

For a polynomial function of *y* input part:

Using the above procedure:

$$c_j^{\ y}(t+1) = c_j^{\ y}(t) - \eta\left(\partial E_p / \partial c_j^{\ y}\right)$$
$$= c_j^{\ y}(t) + \eta(d-z)f^{o\,'}\left(net^o\right)c_{kj}^{\ o}*f^{h\,'}\left(net_{kj}^{\ h}\right)c_{kj}^{\ hx}b_k^{\ x}c_{kj}^{\ hy}f_y'\left(net_j^{\ y}\right)y_4$$
$$= c_j^{\ y}(t) + \eta*\delta^{ol}*c_{kj}^{\ o}*\delta^{hy}*c_{kj}^{\ hy}*j*(c_j^{\ y}*y)^{j-1}*y$$
$$= c_j^{\ y}(t) + \eta*\delta^{ol}*c_{kj}^{\ o}*\delta^{hy}*c_{kj}^{\ hy}*\delta^{y}*y$$

10)

where:

$$\delta^{ol} = (d-z)f^{o'}\left(net^o\right) = d-z \qquad \left(linear\ neuron\ f^{o\,'}\left(net^o\right)=1\right)$$

$$\delta^{hy} = f^{h'}\left(net_{kj}^{\ h}\right)c_{kj}^{\ hx}b_k^{\ x} = c_{kj}^{\ hx}b_k^{\ x} \quad \left(linear\ neuron\ f^{h\,'}\left(net_{kj}^{\ h}\right)=1\right)$$

$$\delta^{y} = f_y\,'\left(net_j^{\ y}\right) = j*(c_j^{\ y}*y)^{j-1}$$

THONN Model

Trigonometric Higher Order Neural Networks (THONN) are defined when neuron functions ($f_k^{\ x}$ and $f_j^{\ y}$) chose trigonometric function. THONN models are defined as follows. Based on Chapter 1 formulae from (1-38) to (1-42: THONN 2), THONN models are rewritten as follows:

Let

$$f_k^x\left(c_k^x x\right)=\sin^k(c_k^x x)\ (4\text{-}11)$$

$$f_j^y\left(c_j^y y\right)=\cos^j(c_j^y y)\ (4\text{-}12)$$

THONN Model 0:

$$z=\sum_{k,j=0}^{n}c_{kj}^{o}\sin^k(x)\cos^j(y)$$

$$(4\text{-}13)$$

$$where:\left(c_{kj}^{hx}\right)=\left(c_{kj}^{hy}\right)=1\ and\ c_k^x=c_j^y=1$$

THONN Model 1:

$$z=\sum_{k,j=0}^{n}c_{kj}^{o}\sin^k(c_k^x x)\cos^j(c_j^y y)\,where:\left(c_{kj}^{hx}\right)=\left(c_{kj}^{hy}\right)=1\,(4\text{-}14)$$

THONN Model 2:

$$Z=\sum_{k,j=0}^{n}\left(c_{kj}^{o}\right)\{c_{kj}^{hx}\sin^k(c_k^x x)\}\,\{c_{kj}^{hy}\cos^j(c_j^y y)\}\ (4\text{-}15)$$

The first hidden layer weight learning formulae for THONN are rewritten as follows, based on the Chapter 1 formulae of (1-228: THONN C.17) and (1-230: THONN D.17):

For a sine function of x input side:

$$c_k^x\left(t+1\right)=c_k^x\left(t\right)-\eta\left(\partial E_p/\partial c_k^x\right)$$
$$=c_k^x\left(t\right)+\eta\left(d-z\right)f^o{}'\left(net^o\right)c_{kj}^{o}*f^h{}'\left(net_{kj}^{h}\right)c_{kj}^{hy}b_j^y c_{kj}^{hx}f_x{}'\left(net_k^x\right)x$$
$$=c_k^x\left(t\right)+\eta*\delta^{ol}*c_{kj}^{o}*\delta^{hx}*c_{kj}^{hx}*k*\sin^{k-1}(c_k^x*x)\cos(c_k^x*x)*x$$
$$=c_k^x\left(t\right)+\eta*\delta^{ol}*c_{kj}^{o}*\delta^{hx}*c_{kj}^{hx}*\delta^x*x$$

16)

where:

$$\delta^{ol} = (d-z) f^{o'}\left(net^o\right) = d-z \quad \left(linear\ neuron\ f^{o'}\left(net^o\right) = 1\right)$$

$$\delta^{hx} = f^{h'}\left(net_{kj}{}^h\right) c_{kj}{}^{hy} b_j{}^y = c_{kj}{}^{hy} b_j{}^y \quad \left(linear\ neuron\ f^{h'}\left(net_{kj}{}^h\right) = 1\right)$$

$$\delta^x = f_x'\left(net_k{}^x\right) = k*\left(net_k{}^x\right)^{k-1} = k*\sin^{k-1}(c_k{}^x * x)*\cos(c_k{}^x * x)$$

For cosine function of y input part:

$$c_j{}^y(t+1) = c_j{}^y(t) - \eta\left(\partial E_p / \partial c_j{}^y\right)$$

$$= c_j{}^y(t) + \eta(d-z) f^{o'}\left(net^o\right) c_{kj}{}^o * f^{h'}\left(net_{kj}{}^h\right) c_{kj}{}^{hx} b_k{}^x c_{kj}{}^{hy} f_y'\left(net_j{}^y\right) y$$

$$= c_j{}^y(t) + \eta * \delta^{ol} * c_{kj}{}^o * \delta^{hy} * c_{kj}{}^{hy} *(-j)*\cos^{j-1}(c_j{}^y * y)*\sin(c_j{}^y * y)*y$$

$$= c_j{}^y(t) + \eta * \delta^{ol} * c_{kj}{}^o * \delta^{hy} * c_{kj}{}^{hy} * \delta^y * y$$

17)

where:

$$\delta^{ol} = (d-z) f^{o'}\left(net^o\right) = d-z \quad \left(linear\ neuron\ f^{o'}\left(net^o\right) = 1\right)$$

$$\delta^{hy} = f^{h'}\left(net_{kj}{}^h\right) c_{kj}{}^{hx} b_k{}^x = c_{kj}{}^{hx} b_k{}^x \quad \left(linear\ neuron\ f^{h'}\left(net_{kj}{}^h\right) = 1\right)$$

$$\delta^y = f_y'\left(net_j{}^y\right) = (-j)*\cos^{j-1}(c_j{}^y * y)*\sin(c_j{}^y * y)$$

SINCHONN

SINC Higher Order Neural Networks (SINCHONN) are defined when neuron functions ($f_k{}^x$ and $f_j{}^y$) all chose SINC functions. Based on Chapter 1 formulae from (1-43) to (1-47: SINCHONN 2), SINCHONN models are rewritten as follows:

Let

$$f_k{}^x\left(c_k{}^x x\right) = \left(\sin(c_k{}^x x)/\left(c_k{}^x x\right)\right)^k \quad (4\text{-}18)$$

$$f_j^y\left(c_j^y y\right) = \left(\sin(c_j^y y)/\left(c_k^x y\right)\right)^j \text{ (4-19)}$$

SINCHONN Model 0:

$$z = \sum_{k,j=0}^{n} c_{kj}^o \left(\sin(x)/x\right)^k \left(\sin(y)/y\right)^j \qquad \text{(4-20)}$$

$$where: \left(c_{kj}^{hx}\right) = \left(c_{kj}^{hy}\right) = 1 \, and \, c_k^x = c_j^y = 1$$

SINCHONN Model 1:

$$z = \sum_{k,j=0}^{n} c_{kj}^o \left(\sin(c_k^x x)/\left(c_k^k x\right)\right)^k \left(\sin(c_j^y y)/\left(c_j^y y\right)\right)^j where: \left(c_{kj}^{hx}\right) = \left(c_{kj}^{hy}\right) = 1 \, \text{(4-21)}$$

SINHONN Model 2:

$$Z = \sum_{k,j=0}^{n} \left(c_{kj}^o\right) \{c_{kj}^{hx} \left(\sin(c_k^x x)/\left(c_k^x x\right)\right)^k\} \{c_{kj}^{hy} \left(\sin(c_j^y y)/\left(c_j^y y\right)\right)^j\} \quad \text{(4-22)}$$

The first hidden layer weight learning formulae for SINCHONN are rewritten as follows, based on the Chapter 1 formulae of (1-234: SINCHONN C.17) and (1-236: SINCHONN D.17):

For a SINC function of x input part:

$$c_k^x(t+1) = c_k^x(t) - \eta\left(\partial E_p / \partial c_k^x\right)$$
$$= c_k^x(t) + \eta(d-z) f^{o'}\left(net^o\right) c_{kj}^o * f^{h'}\left(net_{kj}^h\right) c_{kj}^{hy} b_j^y c_{kj}^{hx} f_x'\left(net_k^x\right) x$$
$$= c_k^x(t) + \eta * \delta^{ol} * c_{kj}^o * \delta^{hx} * c_{kj}^{hx} * f_x'\left(net_k^x\right) * x$$
$$= c_k^x(t) + \eta * \delta^{ol} * c_{kj}^o * \delta^{hx} * c_{kj}^{hx} * [k[\sin(c_k^x x)/\left(c_k^k x\right)]^{k-1}$$
$$*[\cos(c_k^x x)/\left(c_k^x x\right) - \sin(c_k^x x)/\left(c_k^x x\right)^2]] * x = c_k^x(t) + \eta * \delta^{ol} * c_{kj}^o * \delta^{hx} * c_{kj}^{hx} * \delta^x * x \quad \text{(4-23)}$$

where:

$$\delta^{ol} = (d-z) f^{o'}\left(net^o\right) = (d-z) \qquad \left(linear\ neuron\ f^{o'}\left(net^o\right) = 1\right)$$

$$\delta^{hx} = f^{h}\left(net_{kj}^{\ h}\right) c_{kj}^{\ hy} b_j^{\ y} = c_{kj}^{\ hy} b_j^{\ y} \qquad \left(linear\ neuron\ f^{h'}\left(net_{kj}^{\ h}\right) = 1\right)$$

$$\delta^x = f_x{'}\left(net_k^{\ x}\right)$$

$$= k\left[\sin(net_k^{\ x})/\left(net_k^{\ x}\right)\right]^{k-1} * \left[\cos(net_k^{\ x})/\left(net_k^{\ x}\right) - \sin(net_k^{\ x})/\left(net_k^{\ x}\right)^2\right]$$

$$= k\left[\sin(c_k^{\ x}x)/\left(c_k^{\ x}x\right)\right]^{k-1} * \left[\cos(c_k^{\ x}x)/\left(c_k^{\ x}x\right) - \sin(c_k^{\ x}x)/\left(c_k^{\ x}x\right)^2\right]$$

For a SINC function of *y* input part:

$$c_j^{\ y}(t+1) = c_j^{\ y}(t) - \eta\left(\partial E_p / \partial c_j^{\ y}\right)$$

$$= c_j^{\ y}(t) + \eta(d-z) f^{o'}\left(net^o\right) c_{kj}^{\ o} * f^{h'}\left(net_{kj}^{\ h}\right) c_{kj}^{\ hx} b_k^{\ x} c_{kj}^{\ hy} f_y{'}\left(net_j^{\ y}\right) y$$

$$= c_j^{\ y}(t) + \eta * \delta^{ol} * c_{kj}^{\ o} * \delta^{hy} * c_{kj}^{\ hy} * f_y{'}\left(net_j^{\ y}\right) * y$$

$$= c_j^{\ y}(t) + \eta * \delta^{ol} * c_{kj}^{\ o} * \delta^{hy} * c_{kj}^{\ hy} * \left[j\left[\sin(c_j^{\ y}y)/\left(c_j^{\ y}y\right)\right]^{j-1}\right.$$

$$* \left[\cos(c_j^{\ y}y)/\left(c_j^{\ y}y\right) - \sin(c_j^{\ y}y)/\left(c_j^{\ y}y\right)^2\right]\right] * y = c_j^{\ y}(t) + \eta * \delta^{ol} * c_{kj}^{\ o} * \delta^{hy} * c_{kj}^{\ hy} * \delta^y * y$$

24)

where:

$$\delta^{ol} = (d-z) f^{o'}\left(net^o\right) = (d-z) \qquad\qquad \left(linear\ neuron\ f^{o'}\left(net^o\right) = 1\right)$$

$$\delta^{hy} = f^{h}\left(net_{kj}^{\ h}\right) c_{kj}^{\ hx} b_k^{\ x} = c_{kj}^{\ hx} b_k^{\ x} \qquad\qquad \left(linear\ neuron\ f^{h'}\left(net_{kj}^{\ h}\right) = 1\right)$$

$$\delta^y = f_y{'}\left(net_j^{\ y}\right)$$

$$= j\left[\sin(net_j^{\ y})/\left(net_j^{\ y}\right)\right]^{j-1} * \left[\cos(net_j^{\ y})/\left(net_j^{\ y}\right) - \sin(net_j^{\ y})/\left(net_j^{\ y}\right)^2\right]$$

$$= j\left[\sin(c_j^{\ y}y)/\left(c_j^{\ y}y\right)\right]^{j-1} * \left[\cos(c_j^{\ y}y)/\left(c_j^{\ y}y\right) - \sin(c_j^{\ y}y)/\left(c_j^{\ y}y\right)^2\right]$$

SSINCHONN Model

Similarly, Sine and SINC Polynomial Higher Order Neural Networks (SSINCPHONN) are defined when neuron functions ($f_k{}^x$ and $f_j{}^y$) chose SINC and trigonometric functions. Based on Chapter 1 formulae from (1-48) to (1-52: SSINCHONN 2), SSINCHONN models are rewritten as follows:

Let

$$f_k^x\left(c_k{}^x x\right) = \left(\sin(c_k{}^x x)\right)^k \text{ (4-25)}$$

$$f_j^y\left(c_j{}^y y\right) = \left(\sin(c_j{}^y y)/\left(c_k{}^x y\right)\right)^j \text{ (4-26)}$$

SSINCHONN Model 0:

$$z = \sum_{k,j=0}^{n} c_{kj}{}^o \left(\sin(x)\right)^k \left(\sin(y)/y\right)^j \tag{4-27}$$
$$where:\left(c_{kj}{}^{hx}\right) = \left(c_{kj}{}^{hy}\right) = 1\, and\; c_k{}^x = c_j{}^y = 1$$

SSINCHONN Model 1:

$$z = \sum_{k,j=0}^{n} c_{kj}{}^o \left(\sin(c_k{}^x x)\right)^k \left(\sin(c_j{}^y y)/\left(c_j{}^y y\right)\right)^j where:\left(c_{kj}{}^{hx}\right) = \left(c_{kj}{}^{hy}\right) = 1 \text{(4-28)}$$

SSINHONN Model 2:

$$Z = \sum_{k,j=0}^{n}\left(c_{kj}{}^o\right)\{c_{kj}{}^{hx}\left(\sin(c_k{}^x x)\right)^k\}\{c_{kj}{}^{hy}\left(\sin(c_j{}^y y)/\left(c_j{}^y y\right)\right)^j\} \text{(4-29)}$$

The first hidden layer weight learning formulae for SSINCHONN are rewritten as follows, based on the Chapter 1 formulae of (1-240: SSINCHONN C.17) and (1-242: SSINCHONN D.17):

For a sine function of x input side:

$$c_k^{\ x}(t+1) = c_k^{\ x}(t) - \eta\left(\partial E_p / \partial c_k^{\ x}\right)$$

$$= c_k^{\ x}(t) + \eta\left(d-z\right)f^{o\,\prime}\left(net^o\right)c_{kj}^{\ o} * f^{h\,\prime}\left(net_{kj}^{\ h}\right)c_{kj}^{\ hy}b_j^{\ y}c_{kj}^{\ hx}f_x^{\ \prime}\left(net_k^{\ x}\right)x$$

$$= c_k^{\ x}(t) + \eta * \delta^{ol} * c_{kj}^{\ o} * \delta^{hx} * c_{kj}^{\ hx} * k * \sin^{k-1}(c_k^{\ x} * x)\cos(c_k^{\ x} * x) * x$$

$$= c_k^{\ x}(t) + \eta * \delta^{ol} * c_{kj}^{\ o} * \delta^{hx} * c_{kj}^{\ hx} * \delta^x * x$$

(4-30)

where:

$$\delta^{ol} = (d-z)f^{o\,\prime}\left(net^o\right) = d-z \qquad \left(linear\ neuron\ f^{o\,\prime}\left(net^o\right) = 1\right)$$

$$\delta^{hx} = f^{h\,\prime}\left(net_{kj}^{\ h}\right)c_{kj}^{\ hy}b_j^{\ y} = c_{kj}^{\ hy}b_j^{\ y} \qquad \left(linear\ neuron\ f^{h\,\prime}\left(net_{kj}^{\ h}\right) = 1\right)$$

$$\delta^x = f_x^{\ \prime}\left(net_k^{\ x}\right) = k*\left(net_k^{\ x}\right)^{k-1} = k*\sin^{k-1}(c_k^{\ x} * x)*\cos(c_k^{\ x} * x)$$

For a SINC function of *y* input part:

$$c_j^{\ y}(t+1) = c_j^{\ y}(t) - \eta\left(\partial E_p / \partial c_j^{\ y}\right)$$

$$= c_j^{\ y}(t) + \eta\left(d-z\right)f^{o\,\prime}\left(net^o\right)c_{kj}^{\ o} * f^{h\,\prime}\left(net_{kj}^{\ h}\right)c_{kj}^{\ hx}b_k^{\ x}c_{kj}^{\ hy}f_y^{\ \prime}\left(net_j^{\ y}\right)y$$

$$= c_j^{\ y}(t) + \eta * \delta^{ol} * c_{kj}^{\ o} * \delta^{hy} * c_{kj}^{\ hy} * f_y^{\ \prime}\left(net_j^{\ y}\right)*y = c_j^{\ y}(t) + \eta * \delta^{ol} * c_{kj}^{\ o} * \delta^{hy} * c_{kj}^{\ hy}$$

$$*[j[\sin(c_j^{\ y}y)/(c_j^{\ y}y)]^{j-1} * [\cos(c_j^{\ y}y)/(c_j^{\ y}y) - \sin(c_j^{\ y}y)/(c_j^{\ y}y)^2]] * y$$

$$= c_j^{\ y}(t) + \eta * \delta^{ol} * c_{kj}^{\ o} * \delta^{hy} * c_{kj}^{\ hy} * \delta^y * y$$

31)

where:

$$\delta^{ol} = (d-z)f^{o\,\prime}\left(net^o\right) = (d-z) \qquad \left(linear\ neuron\ f^{o\,\prime}\left(net^o\right) = 1\right)$$

$$\delta^{hy} = f^{h\,\prime}\left(net_{kj}^{\ h}\right)c_{kj}^{\ hx}b_k^{\ x} = c_{kj}^{\ hx}b_k^{\ x} \qquad \left(linear\ neuron\ f^{h\,\prime}\left(net_{kj}^{\ h}\right) = 1\right)$$

$$\delta^y = f_y{}'\left(net_j{}^y\right)$$

$$= j\left[\sin(net_j{}^y)/\left(net_j{}^y\right)\right]^{j-1} * \left[\cos(net_j{}^y)/\left(net_j{}^y\right) - \sin(net_j{}^y)/\left(net_j{}^y\right)^2\right]$$

$$= j\left[\sin(c_j{}^y y)/\left(c_j{}^y y\right)\right]^{j-1} * \left[\cos(c_j{}^y y)/\left(c_j{}^y y\right) - \sin(c_j{}^y y)/\left(c_j{}^y y\right)^2\right]$$

SPHONN

The Sigmoid Polynomial Higher Order Neural Networks (SPHONN) are defined when neuron functions ($f_k{}^x$ and $f_j{}^y$) all chose SIGMOID functions. Based on Chapter 1 formulae from (1-63) to (1-67: SPHONN 2), SPHONN models are rewritten as follows:

Let

$$f_k{}^x\left(c_k{}^x x\right) = \left(1/\left(1 + \exp(c_k{}^x(-x))\right)\right)^k \text{ (4-32)}$$

$$f_j{}^y\left(c_j{}^y y\right) = \left(1/\left(1 + \exp(c_j{}^y(-y))\right)\right)^j \text{ (4-33)}$$

SPHONN Model 0:

$$z = \sum_{k,j=0}^{n} c_{kj}{}^o \left(1/\left(1 + \exp(-x)\right)\right)^k \left(1/\left(1 + \exp(-y)\right)\right)^j$$ (4-34)

$$where: \left(c_{kj}{}^{hx}\right) = \left(c_{kj}{}^{hy}\right) = 1 \, and \, c_k{}^x = c_j{}^y = 1$$

SPHONN Model 1:

$$z = \sum_{k,j=0}^{n} c_{kj}{}^o \left(1/\left(1 + \exp(c_k{}^x(-x))\right)\right)^k \left(1/\left(1 + \exp(c_j{}^y(-y))\right)\right)^j \, where: \left(c_{kj}{}^{hx}\right) = \left(c_{kj}{}^{hy}\right) = 1$$

(4-35)

SPHONN Model 2:

$$Z = \sum_{k,j=0}^{n} \left(c_{kj}^{\ o}\right)\{c_{kj}^{\ hx}\left(1/\left(1+\exp(c_k^{\ x}(-x)))\right)\right)^k\}\{c_{kj}^{\ hy}\left(1/\left(1+\exp(c_j^{\ y}(-y)))\right)\right)^j\}$$

36)

The first hidden layer weight learning formulae for SPHONN are rewritten as follows, based on the Chapter 1 formulae of (1-258: SPHONN C.17) and (1-260: SPHONN D.17):

For a sigmoid function of x input side:

$$c_k^{\ x}(t+1) = c_k^{\ x}(t) - \eta\left(\frac{\partial E_p}{\partial c_k^{\ x}}\right) = c_k^{\ x}(t) + \eta(d-z)f^{o'}\left(net^o\right)c_{kj}^{\ o}$$

$$* f^{h'}\left(net_{kj}^{\ h}\right)c_{kj}^{\ hy}b_j^{\ y}c_{kj}^{\ hx}f_x'\left(net_k^{\ x}\right)x = c_k^{\ x}(t) + \eta * \delta^{ol} * c_{kj}^{\ o} * \delta^{hx} * c_{kj}^{\ hx}$$

$$* f_x'\left(net_k^{\ x}\right) * x = c_k^{\ x}(t) + \eta * \delta^{ol} * c_{kj}^{\ o} * \delta^{hx} * c_{kj}^{\ hx} * [k*[1/\left(1+\exp(-c_k^{\ x}*x)\right)]^{k-1}$$

$$* \left(1+\exp(-c_k^{\ x}*x)\right)^{-2} * \exp(-c_k^{\ x}*x)] * x = c_k^{\ x}(t) + \eta * \delta^{ol} * c_{kj}^{\ o} * \delta^{hx} * c_{kj}^{\ hx} * \delta^{x} * x$$

37)

where:

$$\delta^{ol} = (d-z)f^{o'}\left(net^o\right) = d-z \qquad \left(linear\ neuron\ f^{o}{}'\left(net^o\right) = 1\right)$$

$$\delta^{hx} = f^{h'}\left(net_{kj}^{\ h}\right)c_{kj}^{\ hy}b_j^{\ y} = c_{kj}^{\ hy}b_j^{\ y} \qquad \left(linear\ neuron\ f^{h}{}'\left(net_{kj}^{\ h}\right) = 1\right)$$

$$\delta^{x} = f_x'\left(net_k^{\ x}\right) = k*[1/\left(1+\exp(-c_k^{\ x}*x)\right)]^{k-1} * \left(1+\exp(-c_k^{\ x}*x)\right)^{-2} * \exp(-c_k^{\ x}*x)$$

For a sigmoid function of y input side:

$$c_j^{\,y}(t+1) = c_j^{\,y}(t) - \eta\left(\partial E_p / \partial c_j^{\,y}\right)$$

$$= c_j^{\,y}(t) + \eta(d-z) f^{o\,\prime}\left(net^o\right) c_{kj}^{\,o} * f^{h\,\prime}\left(net_{kj}^{\,h}\right) c_{kj}^{\,hx} b_k^{\,x} c_{kj}^{\,hy} f_y^{\,\prime}\left(net_j^{\,y}\right) y$$

$$= c_j^{\,y}(t) + \eta * \delta^{ol} * c_{kj}^{\,o} * \delta^{hy} * c_{kj}^{\,hy} * f_y^{\,\prime}\left(net_j^{\,y}\right) * y = c_j^{\,y}(t) + \eta * \delta^{ol} * c_{kj}^{\,o} * \delta^{hy} * c_{kj}^{\,hy}$$

$$*[j*[1/(1+\exp(-c_j^{\,y}*y))]^{j-1}*(1+\exp(-c_j^{\,y}*y))^{-2}*\exp(-c_j^{\,y}*y)]*y$$

$$= c_j^{\,y}(t) + \eta * \delta^{ol} * c_{kj}^{\,o} * \delta^{hy} * c_{kj}^{\,hy} * \delta^{\,y} * y$$

38)

where:

$$\delta^{ol} = (d-z) f^{o\,\prime}\left(net^o\right) = d-z \qquad \left(linear\ neuron\ f^{o\,\prime}\left(net^o\right) = 1\right)$$

$$\delta^{hy} = f^{h\,\prime}\left(net_{kj}^{\,h}\right) c_{kj}^{\,hx} b_k^{\,x} = c_{kj}^{\,hx} b_k^{\,x} \qquad \left(linear\ neuron\ f^{h\,\prime}\left(net_{kj}^{\,h}\right) = 1\right)$$

$$\delta^{\,y} = f_y^{\,\prime}\left(net_j^{\,y}\right) = j*[1/(1+\exp(-c_j^{\,y}*y))]^{j-1}*(1+\exp(-c_j^{\,y}*y))^{-2}*\exp(-c_j^{\,y}*y)$$

UCSHONN Model

Nyquist Rule says that a sampling rate must be at least twice as fast as the fastest frequency (Synder 2006). In simulating and predicating nonstationary time series data, the new nonlinear models of UCSHONN should have frequency twice as high as the ultra-high frequency of the time series data. To achieve this purpose, Ultra-high frequency Cosine and Sine Trigonometric Higher Order Neural Network (UCSHONN) has neurons with cosine and sine functions. Ultra-high frequency Cosine and Cosine Trigonometric Higher Order Neural Network (UCCHONN) has neurons with cosine functions. Ultra-high frequency Sine and Sine Trigonometric Higher Order Neural Network (USSHONN) has neurons with sine functions. Except for the functions in the neuron all other parts of these three models are the same. The Ultra High Frequency Cosine and Sine Higher Order Neural Networks (UCSHONN) are defined when neuron functions $(f_k^{\,x}$ and $f_j^{\,y})$ chose trigonometric functions with k times x and j times y. Based on Chapter 1 formulae from (1-88) to (1-92: UCSHONN 2), UCSHONN models are rewritten as follows:

Let

$$f_k^x\left(c_k^x x\right) = \cos^k(k * c_k^x x)\,(4\text{-}39)$$

$$f_j^y\left(c_j^y y\right) = \sin^j(j * c_j^y y)\,(4\text{-}40)$$

UCSHONN Model 0:

$$z = \sum_{k,j=0}^{n} c_{kj}^{\ o} \cos^k(k * x)\sin^j(j * y)$$

$$(4\text{-}41)$$

$$where:\left(c_{kj}^{\ hx}\right) = \left(c_{kj}^{\ hy}\right) = 1\,and\ c_k^{\ x} = c_j^{\ y} = 1$$

UCSHONN Model 1:

$$z = \sum_{k,j=0}^{n} c_{kj}^{\ o} \cos^k(k * c_k^x x)\sin^j(j * c_j^y y)\,where:\left(c_{kj}^{\ hx}\right) = \left(c_{kj}^{\ hy}\right) = 1\,(4\text{-}42)$$

UCSHONN Model 2:

$$Z = \sum_{k,j=0}^{n}\left(c_{kj}^{\ o}\right)\{c_{kj}^{\ hx} \cos^k(k * c_k^x x)\}\,\{c_{kj}^{\ hy} \sin^j(j * c_j^y y)\}\,(4\text{-}43)$$

The first hidden layer weight learning formulae for UCSHONN are rewritten as follows, based on the Chapter 1 formulae of (1-288: UCSHONN C.17) and (1-290: UCSHONN D.17):

For an ultra-high frequency cosine function of *x* input part:

$$c_k{}^x(t+1) = c_k{}^x(t) - \eta\left(\partial E_p / \partial c_k{}^x\right)$$
$$= c_k{}^x(t) + \eta(d-z)f^{o\,\prime}\left(net^o\right)c_{kj}{}^o * f^{h\,\prime}\left(net_{kj}{}^h\right)c_{kj}{}^{hy}b^y{}_j c_{kj}{}^{hx} f_x{}^\prime\left(net_k{}^x\right)x \quad 4$$
$$= c_k{}^x(t) + \eta * \delta^{ol} * c_{kj}{}^o * \delta^{hx} * c_{kj}{}^{hx} * \left(-k^2\right)\cos^{k-1}(k*c_k{}^x*x)\sin(k*c_k{}^x*x)*x$$
$$= c_k{}^x(t) + \eta * \delta^{ol} * c_{kj}{}^o * \delta^{hx} * c_{kj}{}^{hx} * \delta^x * x$$

44)

where:

$$\delta^{ol} = (d-z)f^{o\prime}\left(net^o\right) = d-z \qquad\qquad \left(linear\ neuron\ f^{o\,\prime}\left(net^o\right)=1\right)$$

$$\delta^{hx} = f^{h\,\prime}\left(net_{kj}{}^h\right)c_{kj}{}^{hy}b^y{}_j = a_{kj}{}^{hy}b_j \qquad \left(linear\ neuron\ f^{h\,\prime}\left(net_{kj}{}^h\right)=1\right)$$

$$\delta^x = f_x{}^\prime\left(net_k{}^x\right) = \left(-k^2\right)\cos^{k-1}(k*c_k{}^x*x)\sin(k*c_k{}^x*x)$$

For an ultra-high frequency sine function of *y* input part:

$$c_j{}^y(t+1) = c_j{}^y(t) - \eta\left(\partial E_p / \partial c_j{}^y\right)$$
$$= c_j{}^y(t) + \eta(d-z)f^{o\,\prime}\left(net^o\right)c_{kj}{}^o * f^{h\,\prime}\left(net_{kj}{}^h\right)c_{kj}{}^{hx}b_k{}^x c_{kj}{}^{hy} f_y{}^\prime\left(net_j{}^y\right)y \quad 4$$
$$= c_j{}^y(t) + \eta * \delta^{ol} * c_{kj}{}^o * \delta^{hy} * c_{kj}{}^{hy} * \left(j^2\right)\sin^{j-1}(j*c_j{}^y*y)\cos(j*c_j{}^y*y)*y$$
$$= c_j{}^y(t) + \eta * \delta^{ol} * c_{kj}{}^o * \delta^{hy} * c_{kj}{}^{hy} * \delta^y * y$$

45)

where:

$$\delta^{ol} = (d-z)f^{o\prime}\left(net^o\right) = d-z \qquad\qquad \left(linear\ neuron\ f^{o\,\prime}\left(net^o\right)=1\right)$$

$$\delta^{hy} = f^{h\prime}\left(net_{kj}{}^{hy}\right)c_{kj}{}^{hx}b_k{}^x = c_{kj}{}^{hx}b_k{}^x \qquad \left(linear\ neuron\ f^{h\,\prime}\left(net_{kj}{}^{hy}\right)=1\right)$$

$$\delta^y = f_y{}^\prime\left(net_j{}^y\right) = \left(j^2\right)\sin^{j-1}(j*c_j{}^y*y)\cos(j*c_j{}^y*y)$$

COMPARISONS OF SAS NONLINEAR MODELS AND HONN NOLINEAR MODELS

This section compares SAS NLIN and HONN nonlinear models by using the data provided by the SAS NLIN manual. Two examples (45.1 and 45.2) are chosen from the SAS NLIN manual.

Comparison Using Quadratic With Plateau Data (45.1)

In Tale 1, the Quadratic with Plateau data has 16 inputs. The desired output numbers are from 0.46 to 0.80, with the last three outputs 0.80, 0.80, and 0.78. SAS uses two functions to simulate these data, Quadratic function and Plateau function. SAS provide 0.0101 as the sum of squared error and 0.000774 as the residual mean squared error (MSE). Table 1 uses HONN nonlinear models to simulate the data from SAS NLIN document, and list both HONN and SAS simulating results. Six HONN models have smaller residual mean squared error than that of SAS NLIN model. UCSHONN model 0 Order 4 produces the smallest residual mean squared error (0.0007096). Comparing the residual mean squared error (0.000774) from SAS NLIN, HONN model is 8.32% more accurate using the formula below:

(SAS MSE - HONN MSE)/(SAS MSE) *100%.

The key point is when using HONN, the initial coefficients are automatically selected by the HONN system, while SAS NLIN procedure requires the user to input the initial coefficients. Moreover, the simulations can always converge using HONN, but may not converge under SAS NLIN. The reason is that in SAS NLIN, the convergence range for the initial coefficient is small and sensitive. It is very hard for the user to guess the initial coefficients in the convergence range.

In Table 2, data shows the coefficient for the minimum convergence range. SAS provides the initial coefficients a, b, and c. The coefficients are increased or decreased to test whether SAS can still converge using the new coefficients. When changing these coefficients by +0.002 or -0.015, SAS NLIN still can converge. However, when changing these coefficients to +0.003 or -0.02, SAS NLIN provides the same output values for different inputs. The residual mean squared error increases from 0.000774 to 0.0125. For the Quadratic with Plateau data, the convergence range for the coefficient is less than 0.023. There are two problems in using SAS NLIN. First, users might accept the wrong results where sum of squared error equals to 0.1869. Second, users might discontinue guessing for the correct initial coefficients after a couple trial and errors. Users have less chance to guess correct initial coefficients, since the convergence range is small.

Comparison Using US Population Growth Data

In Table 3, the US population growth data has a total of 21 inputs from 1790 to 1990. The desired output numbers are population amounts from 3.929

Table 1. Quadratic with Plateau Data Modeling Accuracy - SAS NLIN or HONNs?

Input and desired output data are chosen from SAS NLIN Document Example 45.1, page 30 6 HONN models have better modeling accuracy than SAS NLIN modeling result UCSHONN Model 0 Order 4 has the best accuracy which is 8.32% better than SAS NLIN model					
Input*	**Desired Output***	**SAS NLIN Output**	**PHONN MOO5 Output**	**UCSHONN MOO3 Output**	**UCSHONN MOO4 Output**
1	0.46	0.450207	0.447760	0.461038	0.459786
2	0.47	0.503556	0.502626	0.493809	0.494116
3	0.57	0.552161	0.552784	0.541046	0.541922
4	0.61	0.596023	0.597898	0.593829	0.593482
5	0.62	0.635143	0.637699	0.643296	0.641043
6	0.68	0.669519	0.672012	0.682927	0.680231
7	0.69	0.699152	0.700779	0.710014	0.709530
8	0.78	0.724042	0.724084	0.725899	0.729204
9	0.70	0.744189	0.742177	0.734944	0.740915
10	0.74	0.759593	0.755500	0.742575	0.747891
11	0.77	0.770254	0.764709	0.753038	0.754511
12	0.78	0.776172	0.770699	0.767594	0.764455
13	0.74	0.777497	0.774632	0.783726	0.778102
13**	0.80	0.777497	0.774632	0.783726	0.778102
15	0.80	0.777497	0.782433	0.795838	0.795214
16	0.78	0.777497	0.790162	0.777513	0.782444
Sum of Squared Error	0.0101*	0.009665	0.009416	**0.009225**
Residual Mean Squared Error	0.000774*	0.0007435	0.0007243	**0.0007096**
HONN better than SAS***		3.94%	6.42%	*8.32%*

*: These numbers are published in the SAS NLIN manual.
**: This is 13, based on SAS NLIN manual.
***: HONN better than SAS (%) = (SAS MSE - HONN MSE) /(SAS MSE)*100%

Table 2. Quadratic with Plateau Data Modeling Convergence – SAS NLIN or HONNs?

Input and desired output data are chosen from SAS NLIN Document Example 45.1, page 30 SAS coefficient global minimum convergence range < |0.003-(-0.02)| = 0.023						
Coefficient	SAS value *	HONN initial Coefficient value	SAS initial Coefficient value (SAS value -0.1)	SAS initial Coefficient value (SAS value -0.02)	SAS initial Coefficient value (SAS Value +0.003)	SAS initial Coefficient value (SAS value +0.1)
a	0.3029	HONN automatically chose coefficients	0.2029	0.2829	0.3059	0.4029
b	0.0605		-0.0395	0.0405	0.0635	0.1605
c	-0.0024		-0.10237	-0.02237	0.00063	0.09763
Input*	Desired Output*	UCSHONN MOO4 Output	SAS NLIN Output	SAS NLIN Output	SAS NLIN Output	SAS NLIN Output
1	0.46	0.459786	0.686880	0.686880	0.686880	0.686880
2	0.47	0.494116	0.686880	0.686880	0.686880	0.686880
3	0.57	0.541922	0.686880	0.686880	0.686880	0.686880
4	0.61	0.593482	0.686880	0.686880	0.686880	0.686880
5	0.62	0.641043	0.686880	0.686880	0.686880	0.686880
6	0.68	0.680231	0.686880	0.686880	0.686880	0.686880
7	0.69	0.709530	0.686880	0.686880	0.686880	0.686880
8	0.78	0.729204	0.686880	0.686880	0.686880	0.686880
9	0.70	0.740915	0.686880	0.686880	0.686880	0.686880
10	0.74	0.747891	0.686880	0.686880	0.686880	0.686880
11	0.77	0.754511	0.686880	0.686880	0.686880	0.686880
12	0.78	0.764455	0.686880	0.686880	0.686880	0.686880
13	0.74	0.778102	0.686880	0.686880	0.686880	0.686880
13**	0.80	0.778102	0.686880	0.686880	0.686880	0.686880
15	0.80	0.795214	0.686880	0.686880	0.686880	0.686880
16	0.78	0.782444	0.686880	0.686880	0.686880	0.686880
Sum of Squared Error	0.009225	0.186900	0.186900	0.186900	0.186900
Residual Mean Squared Error	0.0007096	0.0125	0.0125	0.0125	0.0125

*: These numbers are published in the SAS NLIN manual.
**: This is 13, based on SAS NLIN manual.

to 248.710 million. SAS NLIN uses a polynomial function with order 2 to model these data. Using the NLIN procedure, the sum of squared error is 159.9628 and the residual mean squared error equals to 8.8868. Table 3 shows the actual data and the results generated from both SAS NLIN and HONN. This table lists 4 HONN models that have a smaller residual mean squared error than that of SAS NLIN model. The smallest residual mean squared error from UCSHONN model 0 Order 5 is 4.8792, while SAS NLIN has a residual mean squared error of 8.8868. This shows HONN is 45.10% better (SAS MSE - HONN MSE)/(SAS MSE) *100%.

In Table 4, data shows the convergence range for the coefficients. The coefficients for b0, b1, and b2, are modified and these new values are used as the initial coefficient in SAS NLIN. When modifying these coefficients by +0.0000051 or -0.000001, SAS can still converge. However, when changing these coefficients by +0.0000052 or -0.000002, SAS cannot converge or provides no observation. The residual mean squared error of 8.8868 is increased to 527.7947. For the US population growth data, the convergence range for the coefficients is less than 0.0000072.

Comparison Using Japanese vs. US Dollar Exchange Data

In Table 5, the monthly Japanese vs. US dollar exchange rate from November 1999 to December 2000 is shown. The input R_{t-2} uses exchange rates from November 1999 to October 2000. The input R_{t-1} uses exchange rates from December 1999 to November 2000. The desired output R_t numbers are exchange rates from January 2000 to December 2000. UCSHONN simulator with Model 0 and Order 5 is used to simulate these data. The simulation results and coefficients are shown in Table 5. Sum of squared error for UCSHONN is 9.04E-08 and the mean squared error is 7.53E-09. Using the same data, SAS also converges with sum of squared error of 6.04E-05 and mean squared error of 5.05E-06. Clearly, HONN model is more accurate than SAS NLIN. The Japanese vs. US dollar exchange rate data has been tested using different order.

In Table 6, data uses UCSHONN Model 0 Order 4 in SAS, SAS system converges with sum of squared error of 4.7E-05 and mean squared error of 3.92E-06. When using UCSHONN Model 0 Order 3 in SAS, SAS system converges with a sum of squared error of 1.25E-05 and mean squared error of 1.052E-06. This shows that HONN model is still more accurate than the SAS model. When using UCSHONN Model 0 Order 2 in SAS, SAS system converges with a sum of squared error of 8.986128 and mean squared error of 0.748844 (not shown in Table 6). This means Order 2 is not suitable for simulating the year 2000 Japanese vs. US dollar exchange rate.

Table 3. US Population Growth Modeling Accuracy – SAS NLIN or HONNs?

input* (Year)	Desired Output * (Population Million)	SAS NLIN Output Error (pop-model. Pop)*	UCS HONN M0O4 Output Error	UCS HONN M0O5 Output Error	THONN M0O2 Output Error
	Input and desired output data are chosen from SAS NLIN Document Example 45.2, page 33 HONN models have better modeling accuracy than SAS NLIN modeling result UCSHONN M0O5 has the best accuracy which is 45.10% better than SAS NLIN model				
1790	3.929	-0.93711	0.35839	0.28030	-0.22135
1800	5.308	0.46091	0.92843	0.88043	0.59541
1810	7.239	1.11853	0.61332	0.62924	0.83865
1820	9.638	0.95176	-0.25145	-0.18753	0.41783
1830	12.866	0.32159	-0.93167	-0.85929	-0.31611
1840	17.069	-0.62597	-1.22365	-1.16794	-1.23087
1850	23.191	-0.94692	-0.52154	-0.48896	-1.39974
1860	31.443	-0.43027	0.82224	0.82224	-0.63197
1870	39.818	-1.08302	0.33476	0.28726	-0.95803
1880	50.155	-1.06615	-0.22558	-0.31661	-0.56407
1890	62.947	0.11332	0.00771	-0.08406	1.01573
1900	75.994	0.25539	-0.52975	-0.56805	1.55319
1910	91.972	2.03607	1.37711	1.40919	3.69558
1920	105.710	0.28436	0.69017	0.75608	2.24361
1930	122.775	0.56725	2.60822	2.65523	2.73656
1940	131.669	-8.61325	-5.05453	-5.04682	-6.34957
1950	151.325	-8.32415	-4.02885	-4.04303	-6.10558
1960	179.323	-0.98543	2.93528	2.92383	1.02742
1970	203.211	0.95088	3.49835	3.49562	2.58186
1980	226.542	1.03780	1.62358	1.62557	2.09787
1990	248.710	-1.33067	-2.86763	-2.85942	-1.03737
Sum of Squared Error		159.9628**	87.85605	**87.82611**	126.9089
Residual Mean Squared Error		8.8868**	4.8809	**4.8792**	7.0505
HONN better than SAS***			45.08%	**45.10%**	20.66%

*: These numbers are published in the SAS NLIN manual.

**: These numbers are calculated based on the data in the SAS NLIN manual.

***: HONN better than SAS (%) = (SAS MSE - HONN MSE) /(SAS MSE)*100%

Table 4. US Population Growth Modeling Convergence- SAS NLIN or HONNs?

Coefficient	SAS value *	HONN initial Coefficient value	SAS initial Coefficient value (SAS Value -0.000002)	SAS initial Coefficient (SAS Value -0.000001)	SAS initial Coefficient (SAS Value +0.0000052)
	Input and desired output data are chosen from SAS NLIN Document Example 45.2, page 33 SAS coefficient global minimum convergence range <|0.0064625-0.006458|=0.0000072				
b0	20828.7	HONN automatically chose coefficients	20828.699998	20828.699999	20828.7000052
b1	-23.2004		-23.200402	-23.200401	-23.2003949
b2	0.00646		0.006458	0.006459	0.0064652
Input* (Year)	Desired Output* (Population Million)	UCSHONN M0O5 Output	SAS NLIN Output	SAS NLIN Output	SAS NLIN Output
1790	3.929	3.649	-8.29042	4.866109	
1800	5.308	4.428	-8.00767	4.847093	
1810	7.239	6.610	-6.43241	6.120471	
1820	9.638	9.826	-3.56462	8.686243	
1830	12.866	13.725	0.595686	12.54441	
1840	17.069	18.237	6.04851	17.69497	
1850	23.191	23.680	12.79385	24.13792	
1860	31.443	30.621	20.83172	31.87327	
1870	39.818	39.531	30.1621	40.90101	
1880	50.155	50.472	40.785	51.22115	
1890	62.947	63.031	52.70042	62.83368	
1900	75.994	76.562	65.90836	75.73861	
1910	91.972	90.563	80.40882	89.93593	
1920	105.710	104.954	96.2018	105.4256	
1930	122.775	120.120	113.2873	122.2077	
1940	131.669	136.716	131.6653	140.2822	
1950	151.325	155.368	151.3358	159.6491	
1960	179.323	176.399	172.2989	180.3084	
1970	203.211	199.715	194.5545	202.2601	
1980	226.542	224.916	218.1026	225.5042	
1990	248.710	251.569	242.9432	250.0407	
Sum of Squared Error		87.82611	2111.17886	159.962906	
Residual Mean Squared Error		4.8792	527.7947	8.8868277	
Convergence		Yes	No	yes	No

*: These numbers are published in the SAS NLIN manual.

Comparison Using US Consumer Price Index 1992-2004 Data

Table 5. Japanese vs. US Dollar Exchange Rate 2000 Simulation Accuracy - SAS NLIN or HONNs?

Original Data		Input		Desired Output R_t	UCS HONN M0O5 Output	SAS NLIN UCS M0O5 Output
Date	JA/US Exchange Rate 2000	R_{t-2}	R_{t-1}			
11/99	104.65					
12/99	102.58					
01/00	105.30	104.65	102.58	105.30	105.29995	105.30189
02/00	109.39	102.58	105.30	109.39	109.38980	109.39005
03/00	106.31	105.30	109.39	106.31	106.31003	106.31270
04/00	105.63	109.39	106.31	105.63	105.62997	105.63321
05/00	108.32	106.31	105.63	108.32	108.31998	108.32189
06/00	106.13	105.63	108.32	106.13	106.13000	106.13061
07/00	108.21	108.32	106.13	108.21	108.20997	108.21188
08/00	108.08	106.13	108.21	108.08	108.07998	108.08179
09/00	106.84	108.21	108.08	106.84	106.83992	106.84377
10/00	108.44	108.08	106.84	108.44	108.43997	108.44230
11/00	109.01	106.84	108.44	109.01	109.00993	109.01237
12/00	112.21	108.44	109.01	112.21	112.20982	112.21186
Sum of Squared Error					**9.04E-08**	6.04E-05
Mean Squared Error					**7.53E-09**	5.04E-06
Convergence					Yes	Yes

Table 6. UCSHONN Model 0 Order 5 Coefficient Values

c_{kj}	k=0	k=1	k=2	k=3	k=4	k=5
j=0	0.593760	-0.535650	-0.338650	0.654490	-0.322780	-0.219680
j=1	0.638860	1.258700	-0.423250	-0.433140	-0.572700	-0.292430
j=2	-0.681450	-0.603180	0.080626	-0.494270	0.161860	-0.376570
j=3	-0.818090	0.973730	0.447020	-0.237580	0.903690	-0.335620
j=4	-0.462390	-0.067789	0.230140	-0.182000	0.385220	0.076637
j=5	-0.495590	0.679350	-0.458800	1.935000	0.301420	-0.458880

In Table 7, the yearly US Consumer Price Index 1992-2004 is shown. The input C_{t-2} uses Consumer Price Index data from November 1990 to October 2002. The input C_{t-1} uses Consumer Price Index data from 1991 to November 2003. The desired output, R_t, is the Consumer Price Index from 1992 to December 2004.

In Table 8, UCSHONN simulator with Model 0 and Order 5 has been used for simulating these data. The simulation results and coefficients are shown in Table 8. UCSHONN has a sum of squared error of 2.1E-05 and a mean squared error of 1.61E-06. Using the same data, SAS converges with sum of squared error of 7.93-04 and mean squared error of 6.1E-05. Clearly, HONN model is still more accurate than SAS model. SAS is also tested by using different models with the same order. When using the THONN Model 0 Order 5 in SAS NLIN, the procedure converges with a sum of squared error of 2.647E-02 and mean squared error of 2.036E-03. When using PHONN Model 0 Order 5, SAS procedure also converges with sum of squared error of 1.41E04 and mean squared error of 1.08E-05. This table shows HONN model is more accurate than SAS NLIN.

FININDING MODEL, ORDER, & COEFFICIENT BY HONN NONLINEAR MODELS

To find the model, order, and coefficients of HONN, the following functions and data are used.

- a linear function: $z = 0.402x + 0.598y$
- a nonlinear function with order 1: $z = 0.2815682 - 0.2815682\cos(x) + 1.0376218*\sin(y)$
- Japanese Yen vs. US Dollars (2000 and 2004)
- US Consumer Price Index (1992-2004)
- Japanese Consumer Price Index (1992-2004).

There are two reasons why these examples have been selected. First, some simple and easy to understand functions are chosen, i.e. $z = 0.402x + 0.598y$ and $z = 0.2815682 - 0.2815682\cos(x) + 1.0376218*\sin(y)$, for testing HONN nonlinear models. The second reason is that these data are used as examples for the Nobel Prize in Economics in 2003 (Vetenskapsakademien, 2003).

Table 7. US Consumer Price Index 1992-2004 Simulation Accuracy -SAS NLIN or HONNs?

Original Data		Input		Desired Output C_t	UCS HONN M0O5 Output	SAS NLIN UCS M0O5 Output
Year	US CPI 1992-2004	C_{t-2}	C_{t-1}			
1990	130.7					
1991	136.2					
1992	140.3	130.70	136.20	140.30	140.29781	140.29514
1993	144.5	136.20	140.30	144.50	144.49874	144.49474
1994	148.2	140.30	144.50	148.20	148.19833	148.20409
1995	152.4	144.50	148.20	152.40	152.40005	152.41332
1996	156.9	148.20	152.40	156.90	156.89931	156.90537
1997	160.5	152.40	156.90	160.50	160.50033	160.49693
1998	163.0	156.90	160.50	163.00	162.99956	163.01259
1999	166.6	160.50	163.00	166.60	166.60021	166.60187
2000	172.2	163.00	166.60	172.20	172.19995	172.19802
2001	177.1	166.60	172.20	177.10	177.10061	177.1059
2002	179.9	172.20	177.10	179.90	179.90124	179.91536
2003	184.0	177.10	179.90	184.00	184.00205	184.00772
2004	188.9	179.90	184.00	188.90	188.90221	188.89646
Sum of Squared Error					2.1E-05	7.93E-04
Mean Squared Error					1.61E-06	6.1E-05
Convergence					Yes	Yes

Table 8. UCSHONN Model 0 Order 5 Coefficients

c_{kj}	k=0	k=1	k=2	k=3	k=4	k=5
j=0	0.040466	0.282650	0.332090	-1.023600	0.320600	0.047749
j=1	0.692880	-0.414550	0.352800	0.160460	-0.407040	0.469310
j=2	0.786420	-0.515200	0.654160	0.271940	-0.458820	-0.187380
j=3	0.199470	-0.786580	0.454880	0.241370	1.055600	0.161010
j=4	0.041666	-0.340980	-0.124510	0.546370	0.122520	-0.443290
j=5	-0.027490	0.216360	-0.305750	-0.714690	-0.203870	-0.809710

The test time will depend on the computer system used. The computer system for the test has the following properties:

Computer Model: Personal computer, DELL OPTIPLEX GX260, made by 2003;
Central Process Unit: Pentium 4CPU, 2.66GHz;
Random Access Memory: 512 MB;
Operation System: Microsoft Window XP, Professional, Version 2002;
VNC Viewer: Version 3.3.3.2, for running UNIX on the PC
SUN Operation System: Solaris 9;
Common Desktop Environment: Version 1.5.7;
Computer Language: c;
Test time unit: second.

HONN Can Choose the Best Model in a Pool of HONN Nonlinear Models for Different Data

The first question a user might ask is what model the best nonlinear model for the data is. Should a polynomial model or a trigonometric polynomial model be used for simulating data? Or should a sigmoid polynomial model or a SINC (sin(x)/x) polynomial model be used?

From SAS manual, "The (SAS) NLIN procedure produces least squares or weighted least squares estimates of the parameters of a nonlinear model. . . For each nonlinear model to be analyzed, you must specify the model (using a single dependent variable) . . .." Users may feel that this is a complicated task since they do not know which model is the best model for their data. This section shows that users can select the best model in a pool of HONN nonlinear models for different data.

In Table 9, Data shows that in 530 seconds HONN selects the best model for $z = 0.402x + 0.598y$ as PHONN order 1 model. The mean squared error for PHONN order 1 model is only 7.371E-13, while the mean squared errors for PHONN nonlinear models are more than 2.30E-6. The mean squared errors of all other models (THONN, UCSHONN, SXSPHONN, SINCHONN, and SPHONN) are more than 1.33E-6.

Table 9 also shows that in around 502 seconds, HONN can recognize the best model for $z = 0.2815682 - 0.2815682\cos(x) + 1.0376218*\sin(y)$ which is THONN or UCSHONN order 1. Since the mean squared error for THONN order 1 is only 2.965E-8 and 2.841E-8 for UCSHONN order 1. THONN order 1 and UCSHONN order 1 have the same expression. The mean squared error for THONN order 2 or more is above is more than 3.27E-6. The mean squared error of UCSHONN order 2 or more is above 2.21E-6. The mean squared error for all other models (PHONN, SXSPHONN, SINCHONN, and SPHONN) are more than 3.27E-6.

In Table 10, data shows that the best model for the Yen vs. US dollar exchange rate (year 2000) is UCSHONN order 5, with the mean squared error of 8.999E-10. The mean squared error of all other models (PHONN, THONN, UCSHONN order 1 to 4, SXSPHONN, SINCHONN, and SPHONN) is more than 4.9E-5. This means HONN can recognize the year 2000 Yen vs. US dollar exchange rate in around 2241 seconds. Moreover, Table 10 also shows that the best model for the year 2004 Yen vs. US dollar exchange rate is UCSHONN order 5 with the mean squared error of 3.604E-21. The mean squared error of all other models (PHONN, THONN, UCSHONN order 1 to 4, SXSPHONN, SINCHONN, and SPHONN) is more than 5.185E-3. That means HONN can recognize 2004 Yen vs. US dollar exchange rate in about 2170 seconds.

In Table 11, data shows that in about 2360 seconds HONN can select the best model for US Consumer Price Index (1992-2004), which is UCSHONN order 5 with the mean squared error of 4.910E-7. The mean squared errors for all other models (PHONN, THONN, UCSHONN order 1 to 4, SXSPHONN, SINCHONN, and SPHONN) are more than 9.0E-6. Moreover, the best model for Japan Consumer Price Index (1992- 2004) is UCSHONN order 5 with the mean squared error of 2.360E-5. The mean squared errors of all other models (PHONN, THONN, UCSHONN order 1 to 4, SXSPHONN, SINCHONN, and SPHONN) are more than 6.024E-3. This means HONN can recognize Japan Consumer Price Index (1992- 2004) in around 2364 seconds.

The above tests show that the average time to select the best model for linear or simple nonlinear data is about 516 seconds (8.6 minutes). The above tests also show that the average time to decide on the best model for nonlinear data is about 2284 seconds (38 minutes) under the computer environment given above. The computer speed could be 10 times quicker than the computer used today within several years. If the computer speed increases 10 times, only 0.86 minutes are needed to find the best model for linear or simple nonlinear data, and 3.8 minutes for more complicated data, which will make HONN more acceptable for nonlinear data modeling.

Table 9. Linear and Nonlinear Function Simulation Analysis – 20,000 Epochs

		Z=0.402*x + 0.598*y Mean Squared Error	Running Time Seconds	Z = 0.2815682 - 0.2815682*COS(x) + 1.0376218*SIN(y) -0.0056414*COS(x)*SIN(y) Mean Squared Error	Running Time Seconds
PHONN (Model 0)	Order 1	0.0000000000007371	7	0.00001616	6
	Order 2	0.00006853	10	0.00002722	10
	Order 3	0.00000230	16	0.00010718	14
	Order 4	0.00000320	18	0.00009285	19
	Order 5	0.00000866	27	0.00006714	28
THONN (Model 0)	Order 1	0.00001351	8	0.00000002965	7
	Order 2	0.00002849	12	0.00000983	10
	Order 3	0.00000241	17	0.00000327	14
	Order 4	0.00005881	22	0.00000437	19
	Order 5	0.00001503	28	0.00000851	25
UCSHONN (Model 0)	Order 1	0.00000309	8	0.00000002841	6
	Order 2	0.00000133	14	0.00001162	11
	Order 3	0.00004071	18	0.00012063	14
	Order 4	0.00009228	24	0.00000221	19
	Order 5	0.00004116	30	0.00001962	27
SSINCHONN (Model 0)	Order 1	0.00063820	9	0.00014997	10
	Order 2	0.00022918	12	0.00014330	12
	Order 3	0.00003515	16	0.00001520	15
	Order 4	0.00000392	22	0.00003035	22
	Order 5	0.00002715	28	0.00002728	30
SINCHONN (Model 0)	Order 1	0.00556992	8	0.00747188	7
	Order 2	0.00430713	14	0.00470922	13
	Order 3	0.00266424	17	0.00345466	17
	Order 4	0.00163071	25	0.00199684	24
	Order 5	0.00172761	32	0.00192670	34
SPHONN (M0del 0)	Order 1	0.00001199	9	0.00013751	8
	Order 2	0.00001996	12	0.000120826	12
	Order 3	0.00040773	17	0.00053905	16
	Order 4	0.00029652	21	0.000151535	23
	Order 5	0.00008046	29	0.00016194	30
Total Time			530		502

HONN Can Select the Best Order for the Data Simulation

Table 10. Japanese Yen vs. US Dollar Exchange Rate Analysis – 100,000 Epochs

		Year 2000, Mean Squared Error	Running Time Seconds	Year 2004, Mean Squared Error	Running Time Seconds
PHONN (Model 0)	Order 1	0.044682	29	0.046985	28
	Order 2	0.021795	36	0.042055	34
	Order 3	0.005409	61	0.028939	54
	Order 4	0.003894	84	0.021681	79
	Order 5	0.002886	119	0.018649	116
THONN (Model 0)	Order 1	0.047336	28	0.047920	21
	Order 2	0.023417	36	0.041571	35
	Order 3	0.017139	63	0.041396	60
	Order 4	0.013265	92	0.040135	88
	Order 5	0.011807	125	0.037297	124
UCSHONN (Model 0)	Order 1	0.047322	23	0.047635	20
	Order 2	0.038550	42	0.043269	40
	Order 3	0.002560	66	0.005185	65
	Order 4	0.000049	99	0.00000025	98
	Order 5	0.0000000008999	135	3.604E-21	141
SSINCHONN (Model 0)	Order 1	0.057007	34	0.053115	32
	Order 2	0.026508	46	0.046244	43
	Order 3	0.020817	67	0.042628	66
	Order 4	0.018062	101	0.041210	99
	Order 5	0.015119	138	0.040873	136
SINCHONN (Model 0)	Order 1	0.067045	31	0.063458	27
	Order 2	0.060276	48	0.062408	45
	Order 3	0.045554	76	0.059483	72
	Order 4	0.040522	112	0.051622	108
	Order 5	0.038970	157	0.049495	152
SPHONN (Model 0)	Order 1	0.062906	33	0.053220	26
	Order 2	0.052687	45	0.051223	43
	Order 3	0.043711	70	0.048336	72
	Order 4	0.038198	100	0.046790	103
	Order 5	0.035725	145	0.046638	143
Total Time			2241		2170

Table 11. Consumer Price Index Analysis (1992-2004) – 100,000 Epochs

		US, Mean Squared Error	Running time Seconds	Japan, Mean Squared Error	Running Time Seconds
PHONN (Model 0)	Order 1	0.000268	23	0.018847	18
	Order 2	0.000272	38	0.018221	33
	Order 3	0.000249	64	0.017771	56
	Order 4	0.000238	95	0.017517	87
	Order 5	0.000220	125	0.016992	122
THONN (Model 0)	Order 1	0.000293	22	0.019113	24
	Order 2	0.000277	34	0.019016	40
	Order 3	0.000283	68	0.018384	62
	Order 4	0.000271	97	0.018370	102
	Order 5	0.000250	137	0.018030	142
UCSHONN (Model 0)	Order 1	0.000295	24	0.019113	23
	Order 2	0.000271	43	0.019113	42
	Order 3	0.000080	72	0.013411	71
	Order 4	0.000009	108	0.006024	107
	Order 5	0.0000004910	148	0.00002360	149
SSINCHONN (Model 0)	Order 1	0.000295	28	0.0022522	29
	Order 2	0.000272	46	0.018958	47
	Order 3	0.000289	71	0.018711	72
	Order 4	0.000279	102	0.018793	109
	Order 5	0.000285	151	0.018868	156
SINCHONN (Model 0)	Order 1	0.004945	29	0.028309	30
	Order 2	0.002652	51	0.025280	52
	Order 3	0.001572	80	0.020918	83
	Order 4	0.001492	119	0.020263	118
	Order 5	0.001480	167	0.020081	166
SPHONN (M0del 0)	Order 1	0.000442	27	0.022215	27
	Order 2	0.000355	47	0.019550	47
	Order 3	0.000295	77	0.018764	78
	Order 4	0.000300	110	0.018735	114
	Order 5	0.000287	157	0.018643	158
Total Time			2360		2364

Knowing which model is the best for the data, the second question should be asked is what order is the best order for these specific data? In some cases, the higher order model might give you better simulation result, but it does not mean the higher the better. For different data, to find the best order is one of the important steps to build a good model. Since SAS can never guarantee to converge in finding the order, user cannot be sure if the order selected yields the optimal solution. The following results show that HONN can easily find the best order in a pool of potential orders for different data.

In Table 12, data shows HONN can find the best order for different data. When simulating data, it does not always mean that higher order yield better results. To simulate linear data, $Z = 0.402x+0.598y$, the best orders are order 1, 3, 2, 4, and 2 for models PHONN, THONN, UCSHONN, SXSPHONN, and SPHONN, respectively. To simulate simple nonlinear data, $Z = 0.2815682-0.2815682*\cos(x) +1.0376216\sin(y)$, the best orders are order 1, 1, 3, and 2 for models THONN, UCSHONN, SXSPHONN, and SPHONN, respectively. To simulate US consumer price index (1992-2004), the best orders are order 5 for model UCSHONN, and order 2 for SXSPHONN model. To simulate data for Japanese consumer price index (1992-2004), the best orders are order 5 for model UCSHONN and order 1 for SXSPHONN model. Table 12 clearly shows that HONN can find the best order.

In Table 13, data shows the average convergence time for each model and order. Based on the average convergence time, Table 13 calculates the average time for finding the order that produces the best results. If you know the model for the data, time to find order are 325, 350, 379, 393, 431, and 406 seconds for model PHONN, THON, UCSHONN, SXSPHON, SINCHONN, and SPHONN respectively. As a result, in only 5 to 7 minutes, users can find the order that produce the best result for different data. Another key point is that users do not need to guess what coefficients they should provide. HONN will select the coefficients to make the simulation converge.

HONN Can Find the Coefficients for Data Simulation

After finding the best model and the order for the data, the third question is how to find the coefficients for the data? SAS requires the users to supply the initial parameter values. The problem is that the users cannot guess the correct initial parameter values, given that these values are what the users are trying to obtain. In most cases, SAS NLIN does not converge when the initial parameter values are not in the convergence range. In this section, this

Table 12. Finding the Best Order for different Models (Best Order Mean Squared Error Numbers Are Align Left)

		Z=0.402X+0.598 Mean Squared Error	Z=0.2815682 -0.2815682*cos(x) + 1.0376216*sin(y) Mean Square Error	US Consumer Price Index (1992-2004) Mean Squared Error	Japan Consumer Price Index (1992-2004) Mean Squared Error
PHONN	Order 1	7.371E-13	0.00001616	0.000268	0.018847
(Model 0)	Order 2	0.00006853	0.00002722	0.000272	0.018221
	Order 3	0.00000230	0.00010718	0.000249	0.017771
	Order 4	0.00000320	0.00009285	0.000238	0.017517
	Order 5	0.00000866	0.00006714	0.000220	0.016992
THONN	Order 1	0.00001351	2.965E-08	0.000293	0.019113
(Model 0)	Order 2	0.00002849	0.00000983	0.000277	0.019016
	Order 3	0.00000241	0.00000327	0.000283	0.018384
	Order 4	0.00005881	0.00000437	0.000271	0.018370
	Order 5	0.00001503	0.00000851	0.000250	0.018030
UCSHONN	Order 1	0.00000309	2.841E-08	0.000295	0.019113
(Model 0)	Order 2	0.00000133	0.00001162	0.000271	0.019113
	Order 3	0.00004071	0.00012063	0.000080	0.013411
	Order 4	0.00009228	0.00000221	0.000009	0.006024
	Order 5	0.00004116	0.00001962	0.000000491	0.000024
SSINCHONN	Order 1	0.00063820	0.00014997	0.000295	0.002252
(Model 0)	Order 2	0.00022918	0.00014330	0.000272	0.018958
	Order 3	0.00003515	0.00001520	0.000289	0.018711
	Order 4	0.00000392	0.00003035	0.000279	0.018793
	Order 5	0.00002715	0.00002728	0.000285	0.018868
SINCHONN	Order 1	0.00556992	0.00747188	0.004945	0.028309
(Model 0)	Order 2	0.00430713	0.00470922	0.002652	0.025280
	Order 3	0.00266424	0.00345466	0.001572	0.020918
	Order 4	0.00163071	0.00199684	0.001492	0.020263
	Order 5	0.00172761	0.00192670	0.001480	0.020081
SPHONN	Order 1	0.00001199	0.00013751	0.000442	0.022215
(Model 0)	Order 2	0.00001996	0.00012083	0.000355	0.019550
	Order 3	0.00040773	0.00053905	0.000295	0.018764
	Order 4	0.00029652	0.00015154	0.000300	0.018735
	Order 5	0.00008046	0.00016194	0.000287	0.018643

chapter demonstrates that HONN can easily find the coefficients for different models and orders and converge all the time.

Table 13 illustrates the average time to find the coefficients, after providing the model and order. Average time for finding the coefficients are 27, 42, 69, 101, and 142 seconds for orders 1, 2, 3, 4, and 5 of HONN model 0. HONN can automatically choose the initial coefficients for simulation and can always converge.

Table 13. Average Convergence Time*(100,000 Epochs, Nonstationary Data, Model 0, Time Unit: second)

	PHONN	THONN	UCS HONN	SSINC HONN	SINC HONN	SP HONN	Average Time for Finding Coefficients (seconds)
Order 1	25	24	23	31	29	28	27
Order 2	35	36	42	46	49	46	42
Order 3	59	63	69	69	78	74	69
Order 4	86	95	103	103	114	107	101
Order 5	121	132	143	145	161	151	142
Average Convergence Time	325	350	379	393	431	406	

* Under the computer environment as follows:
Computer Model: Personal computer, DELL OPTIPLEX GX260, made by 2003;
Central Process Unit: Pentium 4CPU, 2.66GHz;
Random Access Memory: 512 MB;
Operation System: Microsoft Window XP, Professional, Version 2002;
VNC Viewer: Version 3.3.3.2, for running UNIX on the PC
SUN Operation System: Solaris 9;
Common Desktop Environment: Version 1.5.7;
Computer Language: c;

CONCLUSION

The chapter presents HONN models (PHONN, THONN, UCSHONN, SINCHONN, SXSPHONN, and SHONN). This chapter mathematically proves that HONN models can have mean squared error close to zero and provide the learning algorithm with update formulas. HONN models are compared with SAS NLIN procedures. How to use HONN models to find the best model, order and coefficients are shown.

In Table 14, this chapter finds:

Table 14. Difference between SAS NLIN and HONN Models

	SAS NLIN	**HONN Models**
Easy to use	No Users should provide the model, order, and initial coefficients.	Yes Users select a model and order. The system will automatically choose initial coefficients.
Finding the best model	Users find the best model by trial and error.	Users run existing models and select the best model.
Finding the best order	Users find the best order by trial and error.	Users run existing orders and decide on the best order.
Providing the initial coefficients	Users find the initial coefficients by trial and error.	The HONN system, rather than the users, chooses the initial coefficients.
Convergence	SAS cannot guarantee convergence. If the user gives the wrong model, wrong order, or/ and wrong initial coefficient, SAS NLIN will not converge.	Always converge.
Accuracy	If converges, SAS NLIN may use the average value for the outputs and the mean squared error could be very big.	Theoretically, mean squared error is close to zero.
Market	SAS NLIN not free.	As of May 2006, the authors cannot find HONN commercial software in the market.

As the next step of HONN model research, more HONN models for different data simulations will be built for increasing the pool of HONN models. Theoretically, the adaptive HONN models can be built and allow the computer automatically to choose the best model, order, and coefficients. Making the adaptive HONN models easier to use can be one of the research topics.

FUTHER RESEARCH DIRECTIONS

As the next step of HONN model research, more HONN models for different data simulations will be built to increase the pool of HONN models. Theoretically, the adaptive HONN models can be built and allow the computer automatically to choose the best model, order, and coefficients. Making the adaptive HONN models easier to use is one of the future research topics.

SAS Nonlinear (NLIN) procedure produces least squares or weighted least squares estimates of the parameters of a nonlinear model. SAS Nonlinear models are more difficult to specify and estimate than linear models. Instead of simply generating the parameter estimates, users must write the regression expression, declare parameter names, and supply initial parameter values. Some models are difficult to fit, and there is no guarantee that the procedure can fit the model successfully. For each nonlinear model to be analyzed, users must specify the model (using a single dependent variable) and the names and starting values of the parameters to be estimated. Therefore, SAS NLIN method is not user-friendly in finding nonlinear models using economics and business data.

HONNs can automatically select the initial coefficients for nonlinear data analysis.

The next step of this study is to allow people working in economics and business areas to understand that HONNs are much easier to use and can have better simulation results than SAS NLIN. Moreover, further research will develop HONNs software packages for people working in nonlinear data simulation and prediction area. HONNs will challenge SAS NLIN procedures and change the research methodology that people are currently using in economics and business areas for the nonlinear data simulation and prediction. Some detail steps are to:

- Introduce HONNs to people working in the fields of economics and business.
- Tell all SAS users that HONNs are much better tools than SAS NLIN models.
- Develop HONN software packages, and let more people use HONNs software packages.
- Write a good HONNs user manual, which provides the detailed information for people working in the economics and business areas to successfully use these HONNs software packages.
- Explain why HONNs can approximate any nonlinear data to any degree of accuracy, and make sure people working in economics and business areas can understand why HONNs are much easier to use, and HONNs can have better nonlinear data simulation accuracy than SAS nonlinear (NLIN) procedures.
- Introduce the HONN group models and adaptive HONNs, and make sure people working in economics and business areas can understand HONN group models and adaptive HONN models, which can simulate not only nonlinear data, but also discontinuous and unsmooth nonlinear data.

REFERENCES

Bouzerdoum, A. (1999). A new class of high-order neural networks with nonlinear decision boundaries. *Proceedings of ICONIP'99 6th International Conference on Neural Information Processing, 3,* 1004-1009. 10.1109/ICONIP.1999.844673

Crane, J., & Zhang, M. (2005). Data Simulation Using SINCHONN Model. In *Proceedings of IASTED International Conference on Computational Intelligence* (pp. 50-55). Calgary, Canada: Academic Press.

Dunis, C. L., Laws, J., & Evans, B. (2006). *Modeling and trading the gasoline crack spread: A Non-linear story, working paper.* http://www.ljmu.ac.uk/AFE/CIBEF/67756.htm

Ghazali, R. (2005). Higher order neural network for financial time series prediction. In *Annual Postgraduate Research Conference.* School of Computing and Mathematical Sciences, Liverpool John Moores University. http://www.cms.livjm.ac.uk/research/doc/ConfReport2005.doc

Hu, S., & Yan, P. (1992). Level-by-Level Learning for Artificial Neural Groups. *Electronica Sinica, 20*(10), 39–43.

Karayiannis, N. B., & Venetsanopoulos, A. N. (1995). On the training and performance of High-order neural networks. *Mathematical Biosciences, 129*(2), 143–168. doi:10.1016/0025-5564(94)00057-7 PMID:7549218

Knowles, A., Hussain, A., Deredy, W. E., Lisboa, P. G. J., & Dunis, C. (2005). Higher-Order Neural network with Bayesian Confidence measure for Prediction of EUR/USD Exchange Rate. *Forecasting Financial Markets Conference.*

Lee, M., Lee, S. Y., & Park, C. H. (1992). Neural controller of nonlinear dynamic systems using higher order neural networks. *Electronics Letters, 28*(3), 276–277. doi:10.1049/el:19920170

Leshno, M., Lin, V., Pinkus, A., & Schoken, S. (1993). Multi-Layer Feedforward Networks with a Non-Polynomial Activation Can Approximate Any Function. *Neural Networks, 6*(6), 861–867. doi:10.1016/S0893-6080(05)80131-5

Li, D., Hirasawa, K., & Hu, J. (2003). A new strategy for constructing higher order neural networks with multiplication units. *SICS 2003 Annual Conference.*

Lu, B., Qi, H., Zhang, M., & Scofield, R. A. (2000). Using PT-HONN models for multi-polynomial function simulation. *Proceedings of IASTED International Conference on Neural Networks*, 1-5.

Shin, Y. (1991). The Pi-Sigma Network: An Efficient Higher-Order Neural Network for Pattern Classification and Function Approximation. *Proceedings of International Joint Conference on Neural Networks*, *1*, 13–18.

Synder, L. (2006). *Fluency with Information Technology*. Boston, MA: Addison Wesley.

Venkatesh, S. S., & Baldi, P. (1991, September). Programmed interactions in higher-order neural networks: Maximal capacity. *Journal of Complexity*, *7*(3), 316–337. doi:10.1016/0885-064X(91)90040-5

Xu, S., & Zhang, M. (1999). Approximation to continuous functions and operators using adaptive higher order neural networks. *Proceedings of International Joint Conference on Neural Networks'99*.

Zhang, J. (2005). *Polynomial full naïve estimated misclassification cost models for financial distress prediction using higher order neural network. In 14th Annual Research Work Shop on: Artificial Intelligence and Emerging Technologies in Accounting*. San Francisco, CA: Auditing, and Ta.

Zhang, J. (2006). *Linear and nonlinear models for the power of chief elected officials and debt*. Pittsburgh, PA: Mid-Atlantic Region American Accounting Association.

Zhang, J. C., Zhang, M., & Fulcher, J. (1997). Financial prediction using higher order trigonometric polynomial neural network group models. In *Proceedings of ICNN/IEEE International Conference on Neural Networks* (pp. 2231-2234). Houston, TX: IEEE. 10.1109/ICNN.1997.614373

Zhang, M. (2001). Financial Data Simulation Using A-PHONN Model. In *International Joint Conference on Neural Networks' 2001* (pp.1823 – 1827). Washington, DC: Academic Press.

Zhang, M. (2002). Financial Data Simulation Using PL-HONN Model. In *Proceeding of IASTED International Conference on Modeling and Simulation (NS2002)*. Marina del Rey, CA: Academic Press.

Zhang, M. (2005). A data simulation System Using sinx/x and sinx Polynomial Higher Order Neural Networks. In *Proceedings of IASTED International Conference on Computational Intelligence* (pp.56 – 61). Calgary, Canada: Academic Press.

Zhang, M. (2006). A Data Simulation System Using CSINC Polynomial Higher Order Neural Networks. In *Proceedings of the 2006 International Conference on Artificial Intelligence* (Vol. 1, pp. 91-97). Las Vegas, NV: Academic Press.

Zhang, M., & Lu, B. (2001). Financial Data Simulation Using M-PHONN Model. In *International Joint Conference on Neural Networks'* 2001 (pp. 1828 – 1832). Washington, DC: Academic Press..

Zhang, M., Murugesan, S., & Sadeghi, M. (1995). Polynomial higher order neural network for economic data simulation. In *Proceedings of International Conference on Neural Information Processing* (pp. 493-496). Beijing, China: Academic Press.

Zhang, M., Zhang, J. C., & Fulcher, J. (2000, April). Higher Order Neural network group models for Financial Simulation. *International Journal of Neural Systems*, *10*(2), 123–142. doi:10.1142/S0129065700000119 PMID:10939345

Zhang, M., Zhang, J. C., & Keen, S. (1999). Using THONN system for higher frequency non-linear data simulation & prediction. In *Proceedings of IASTED International Conference on Artificial Intelligence and Soft Computing* (pp.320-323). Honolulu, HI: Academic Press.

ADDITIONAL READING

Azoff, E. (1994). *Neural Network Time Series Forecasting of Financial Markets*. New York: Wiley.

Balke, N. S., & Fomby, T. B. (1997). Threshold cointegration. *International Economic Review*, *38*(3), 627–645. doi:10.2307/2527284

Chang, Y., & Park, J. Y. (2003). Index models with integrated time series. *Journal of Econometrics*, *114*(1), 73–106. doi:10.1016/S0304-4076(02)00220-8

Gardeazabal, J., & Regulez, M. (1992). *The monetary model of exchange rates and cointegration*. New York: Springer-Verlag. doi:10.1007/978-3-642-48858-0

Hornik, K. (1993). Some new results on neural network approximation. *Neural Networks*, *6*(8), 1069–1072. doi:10.1016/S0893-6080(09)80018-X

Meese, R., & Rogoff, K. (1983A). Empirical exchange rate models of the seventies: Do they fit out of sample. *Journal of International Economics*, *14*(1-2), 3–24. doi:10.1016/0022-1996(83)90017-X

Taylor, M. P., & Peel, D. A. (2000). Nonlinear adjustment, long run equilibrium and exchange rate fundamentals. *Journal of International Money and Finance*, *19*(1), 33–53. doi:10.1016/S0261-5606(99)00044-3

Werbos, P. (1994). *The Roots of Backpropagation: from Ordered Derivatives to Neural Networks and Political Forecasting*. New York: Wiley.

KEY TERMS AND DEFINITIONS

ANN: Artificial neural network.
HONN: Artificial higher order neural network.
NLIN: Nonlinear.
PHONN: Artificial polynomial higher order neural network.
SAS: Statistical analysis system.
SINCHONN: Artificial SINC higher order neural network.
SPHONN: Artificial sigmoid polynomial higher order neural network.
SSINCHONN: Artificial sine and SINC higher order neural network.
THONN: Artificial trigonometric higher order neural network.
UCSHONN: Artificial ultra-high frequency trigonometric higher order neural network.

Chapter 5
Time Series Data Analysis by Ultra–High Frequency Trigonometric Higher Order Neural Networks

ABSTRACT

This chapter develops a new nonlinear model, ultra high frequency trigonometric higher order neural networks (UTHONN) for time series data analysis. UTHONN includes three models: UCSHONN (ultra high frequency sine and cosine higher order neural networks) models, UCCHONN (ultra high frequency cosine and cosine higher order neural networks) models, and USSHONN (ultra high frequency sine and sine higher order neural networks) models. Results show that UTHONN models are 3 to 12% better than equilibrium real exchange rates (ERER) model, and 4–9% better than other polynomial higher order neural network (PHONN) and trigonometric higher order neural network (THONN) models. This study also uses UTHONN models to simulate foreign exchange rates and consumer price index with error approaching 10-6.

DOI: 10.4018/978-1-7998-3563-9.ch005

INTRODUCTION

Conventional ANN models are incapable of handling discontinuities in the input training data. ANNs do not always perform well because of the complexity of the patterns. Artificial neural networks function as "black boxes", and thus are unable to provide explanations for their behavior. The "black boxes" characteristic is seen as a disadvantage by users, who prefer to be presented with a rationale for the recognition being generated. To overcome these limitations, interest has recently been expressed in using Higher Order Neural Network (HONN) models for data simulation and pattern recognition. Such models can provide information concerning the basis of the data they are recognition, and hence can be considered as 'open box' rather than 'black box' models. Furthermore, HONN models are also capable of simulating higher frequency and higher order nonlinear data, thus producing superior data recognition, compared with those derived from ANN-based models. This is the motivation therefore for developing the Polynomial Higher Order Neural Network (PHONN) model for data simulation and recognition (Zhang, Murugesan, and Sadeghi, 1995). Zhang & Fulcher (1996b) extend this idea to group PHONN models for data simulation. Zhang, Zhang and Fulcher (2000) develop higher order neural network group models for data approximation. The problem we need to address is to devise a neural network structure that will not only act as an open box to simulate modeling and recognition functions, but which will also facilitate learning algorithm convergence. We would like todemonstrate how it is possible to simulate discontinuous functions, to any degree accuracy, using higher orderneural network group theory, even at points of discontinuity.

Time series models are the most studied models in macroeconomics as well as in financial economics. Nobel Prize in Economics in 2003 rewards two contributions: nonstationarity and time-varying volatility. These contributions have greatly deepened our understanding of two central properties of many economic time series (Vetenskapsakademien, 2003). Nonstationarity is a property common to many macroeconomic and financial time series models. It means that a variable has no clear tendency to return to a constant value or a linear trend. Examples include the value of the US dollar expressed in Japanese yen and consumer price indices of the US and Japan. Granger (1981) changes the way of empirical models in macroeconomic relationships by introducing the concept of cointegrated variables. Granger and Bates (1969) research the combination of forecasts. Granger and Weiss (1983) show the importance of cointegration in the modeling of nonstationary economic series. Granger and Lee (1990) studied multicointegration. Granger and Swanson (1996) further develop multicointegration in studying of cointegrated variables. The first motivation of this chapter is to develop a new nonstationary data analysis system by using new generation computer techniques that will improve the accuracy of the analysis.

After Meese and Rogof's (1983A, and 1983B) pioneering study on exchange rate predictability, the goal of using economic models to beat naïve random walk forecasts is remaining questionable (Taylor, 1995). One possibility is that the standard economic models of exchange rate determination are inadequate, which is a common response of many professional exchange rate forecasters (Kiliam and Taylor, 2003; Cheung and Chinn, 1999). Another possibility is that linear forecasting models fail to consider important nonlinear properties in the data. Recent studies document various nonlinearities in deviations of the spot exchange rate from economic fundamentals (Balke and Fomby, 1997; Taylor and Peel, 2000; Taylor et al., 2001). Gardeazabal and Regulez (1992) study monetary model of exchange rates and cointegration for estimating, testing and predicting long run and short run nominal exchange rates. MacDonald and Marsh (1999) provide a cointegration and VAR (Vector Autoregressive) modeling for high frequency exchange rates. Estimating the equilibrium exchange rates has been rigorously studied (Williamson 1994). Ibrahima A. Elbradawi (1994) provided a model for estimating long-run equilibrium real exchange rates. Based on Elbradawi's study, the average error percentage (error percentage = |error|/rate; average error percentage = total error percentage/n years) of long-run equilibrium real exchange rate is 14.22% for Chile (1968-1990), 20.06% for Ghana (1967-1990) and 4.73% for India (1967-1988). The second motivation for this chapter is to simulate actual exchange rate by developing new neural network models for improving prediction accuracy.

Barron, Gilstrap, and Shrier (1987) use polynomial neural networks for the analogies and engineering applications. Blum and Li (1991) and Hornik (1993) study approximation by feed-forward networks. Chakraborty et. al. (1992), and Gorr (1994) study the forecasting behavior of multivariate time series using neural networks. Azoff (1994) presents neural network time series forecasting of financial markets. Chen and Chen, (1993, 1995) provide the results of approximations of continuous functions by neural networks with application to dynamic systems. Chen and Chang (1996) study feedforward neural network with function shape auto-tuning. Scarselli and Tsoi (1998) conduct a survey of the existing methods for universal approximation using feed-forward neural networks. Granger (1995) studies modeling nonlinear relationships between extended-memory variables and briefly considered neural networks for building nonlinear models. Bierens and Ploberger (1997) derive the asymptotic distribution of the test statistic of a generalized version of the integrated conditional moment (ICM) test, which includes neural network tests. Chen and Shen (1998) give convergence rates for nonparametric regression via neural networks, splines, and wavelets. Hans and Draisma (1997) study a graphical method based on the artificial neural network model to investigate how and when seasonal patterns in macroeconomic time series change over time. Chang and Park (2003) use a simple neural network model to analyze index models with integrated time series. Shintani and Linton (2004) derive the asymptotic distribution of the nonparametric neural network estimation of Lyapunov exponents in a noisy system. However, all the studies mentioned above use traditional artificial neural network models - black box models that do not provide users with a function that describes the relationship between the input and output. The third motivation of this chapter is to develop nonlinear "open box" neural network models that will provide rationale for network's decisions, also provide better results.

Traditional Artificial Neural Networks (ANNs) by default, employ the Standard BackPropagation (SBP) learning algorithm (Rumelhart, Hinton, and Williams,1986; Werbos, 1994), which despite being guaranteed to converge, can take a long time to converge to a solution. In the recent years, numerous modifications to SBP have been proposed in order to speed up the convergence process. Fahlman (1988) assumes the error surface is locally quadratic in order to approximate second order (i.e. gradient) changes. Zell (1995) uses only the sign of the derivative to affect weight changes. In addition to long convergence time, ANNs also suffer from several other well-known limitations. First, ANNs can often become stuck in local, rather than global minima. Second, ANNs are unable to handle high frequency, non-linear, discontinuous data. Third, since ANNs function as "black boxes", they are incapable of providing explanations for their behavior. Researchers working in the economics and business area would rather have a rationale for the network's decisions. To overcome these limitations, research has focused on using Higher Order Neural Network (HONN) models for simulation and modeling (Redding, Kowalczyk, and Downs, 1993). HONN models can provide information concerning the basis of the data they are simulating and prediction, and therefore can be considered as 'open box' rather than 'black box' solutions. The fourth motivation of this chapter is to develop new HONN models for nonstationary time series data analysis with more accuracy.

Psaltis, Park, and Hong (1988) study higher order associative memories and their optical implementations. Redding, Kowalczyk, Downs (1993) develop constructive high-order network algorithm. Zhang, Murugesan, and Sadeghi (1995) develop a Polynomial Higher Order Neural Network (PHONN) model for data simulation. The idea first extends to PHONN Group models for data simulation (Zhang, Fulcher, and Scofield, 1996), then to Trigonometric Higher Order Neural Network (THONN) models for data simulation and prediction (Zhang, Zhang, and Keen, 1999). Zhang, Zhang, and Fulcher (2000) study HONN group model for data simulation. By utilizing adaptive neuron activation functions, Zhang, Xu, and Fulcher (2002) develop a new HONN neural network model. Furthermore, HONN models are also capable of simulating higher frequency and higher order nonlinear data, thus producing superior data simulations, compared with those derived from ANN-based models. Zhang and Fulcher (2004) publish a book chapter to provided detail mathematics for THONN models, which are used for high frequency, nonlinear data simulation. However, THONN models may have around 10% simulation error if the data are ultra-high frequency. The fifth motivation of this chapter is to develop new HONN models, which are suitable for ultra-high frequency data simulation but with more accuracy.

The contributions of this chapter will be:

- Introduce the background of HONNs with the applications of HONNs.
- Develop a new HONN model called UTHONN for ultra-high frequency data simulation.
- Provide the UTHOHH learning algorithm and weight update formulae.
- Compare UTHONN with SAS NLIN, prove HONNs are better than SAS NLIN models.
- Applications of UTHONN model for data simulation.

This chapter is organized as follows: Section 1 gives the background knowledge of HONNs. Section 2 introduces UTHONN structure and different modes of the UTHONN model. Section 3 provides the UTHONN model update formula, learning algorithms, and convergence theories of HONN. Section 4 describes UTHONN computer software system and testing results. Section 5 compares UTHONN with other HONN models. Section 6 shows the results for UTHONN and equilibrium real exchange rates (ERER). Section

7 includes three applications of UTHONN in the time series analysis area. Conclusions are presented in Section 8.

UTHONN MODELS

Nyquist Rule says that a sampling rate must be at least twice as fast as the fastest frequency (Synder 2006). In simulating and predicting time series data, the new nonlinear models of UTHONN should have twice as high frequency as that of the ultra-high frequency of the time series data. To achieve this purpose, a new model should be developed to enforce high frequency of HONN in order to make the simulation and prediction error close to zero. The new HONN model, Ultra High Frequency Trigonometric Higher Order Neural Network (UTHONN), includes three different models base on the different neuron functions. Ultra-high frequency Cosine and Sine Trigonometric Higher Order Neural Network (UCSHONN) has neurons with cosine and sine functions. Ultra-high frequency Cosine and Cosine Trigonometric Higher Order Neural Network (UCCHONN) has neurons with cosine functions. Similarly, ultra-high frequency Sine and Sine Trigonometric Higher Order Neural Network (USSHONN) has neurons with sine functions. Except for the functions in the neuron all other parts of these three models are the same. The following section will discuss the UCSHONN in detail.

UCSHONN Model

UCSHONN Model Structure can be seen as in Figure 1:

The different types of UCSHONN models are shown as follows. Formula (1) (2) and (3) are for UCSHONN model 2, 1 and 0 respectively. Model 1b has three layers of weights changeable, Model 1 has two layers of weights changeable, and model 0 has one layer of weights changeable. For models 2, 1 and 0, Z is the output while x and y are the inputs of UCSHONN. $c_{kj}{}^o$ is the weight for the output layer, $c_{kj}{}^{hx}$ and $c_{kj}{}^{hy}$ are the weights for the second hidden layer, and $c_k{}^x$ and $c_j{}^y$ are the weights for the first hidden layer. Functions cosine and sine are the first and second hidden layer nodes of UCSHONN. The output layer node of UCSHONN is a linear function of $f^o(net^o) = net^o$, where net^o equals the input of output layer node. UCSHONN is an open neural network model, each weight of HONN has its corresponding coefficient in the model formula, and each node of UCSHONN has its corresponding function

223

Figure 1. HONN Architecture

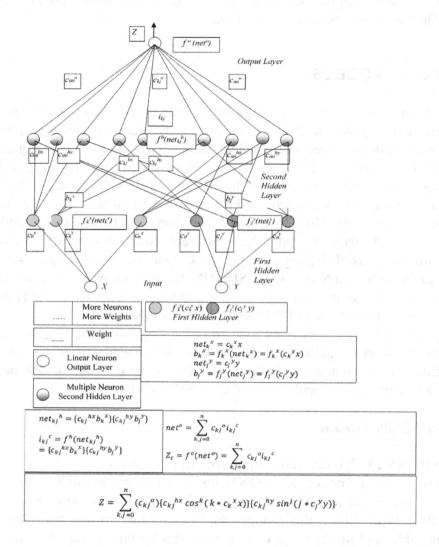

in the model formula. The structure of UCSHONN is built by a nonlinear formula. It means, after training, there is rationale for each component of UCSHONN in the nonlinear formula.

Based on Chapter 1 formulae from (1-88) to (1-92: UCSHONN 2), UCSHONN models are rewritten as follows:

Let

$$f_k^x \left(c_k^x x \right) = \cos^k (k * c_k^x x) \ (5\text{-}1)$$

$$f_j^y \left(c_j^y y \right) = \sin^j (j * c_j^y y) \ (5\text{-}2)$$

UCSHONN Model 0:

$$z = \sum_{k,j=0}^{n} c_{kj}^{\ o} \cos^k (k * x) \sin^j (j * y)$$

$$(5\text{-}3)$$

$$where: \left(c_{kj}^{hx} \right) = \left(c_{kj}^{hy} \right) = 1 \ and \ c_k^x = c_j^y = 1$$

UCSHONN Model 1:

$$z = \sum_{k,j=0}^{n} c_{kj}^{\ o} \cos^k (k * c_k^x x) \sin^j (j * c_j^y y) where : \left(c_{kj}^{hx} \right) = \left(c_{kj}^{hy} \right) = 1 \ (5\text{-}4)$$

UCSHONN Model 2:

$$Z = \sum_{k,j=0}^{n} \left(c_{kj}^{\ o} \right) \{ c_{kj}^{hx} \cos^k (k * c_k^x x) \} \{ c_{kj}^{hy} \sin^j (j * c_j^y y) \} \ (5\text{-}5)$$

For equations (5-3: UCSHONN 0), (5-4: UCSHONN 1) and (5-5: UCSHONN 2), values of k and j ranges from 0 to n, where n is an integer. The UCSHONN model can simulate ultra-high frequency time series data, when n increases to a big number. This property of the model allows it to easily simulate and predicate ultra-high frequency time series data, since both k and j increase when there is an increase in n.

The following is an expansion of model UCSHONN order two. This model is used in later sections to predict the exchange rates.

$$Z = c_{00}{}^{o}c_{00}{}^{hx}c_{00}{}^{hy} + c_{01}{}^{o}c_{01}{}^{hx}c_{01}{}^{hy}\sin\left(c_1{}^y y\right) + c_{02}{}^{o}c_{02}{}^{hx}c_{02}{}^{hy}\sin^2\left(2c_2{}^y y\right)$$

$$+c_{10}{}^{o}c_{10}{}^{hx}c_{10}{}^{hy}\cos\left(c_1{}^x x\right) + c_{11}{}^{o}c_{11}{}^{hx}c_{11}{}^{hy}\cos\left(c_1{}^x x\right)\sin\left(c_1{}^y y\right)$$

$$+c_{12}{}^{o}c_{12}{}^{hx}c_{12}{}^{hy}\cos\left(c_1{}^x x\right)\sin^2\left(2c_2{}^y y\right) + c_{20}{}^{o}c_{20}{}^{hx}c_{20}{}^{hy}\cos^2\left(2c_2{}^x x\right)$$

$$+c_{21}{}^{o}c_{21}{}^{hx}c_{21}{}^{hy}\cos^2\left(2c_2{}^x x\right)\sin\left(c_1{}^y y\right) + c_{22}{}^{o}c_{22}{}^{hx}c_{22}{}^{hy}\cos^2\left(2c_2{}^x x\right)\sin^2\left(2c_2{}^y y\right)$$

(5-6)

The "UCSHONN Architecture is used to develop the model learning algorithm, which make sure the convergence of learning. This allows the deference between desired output and real output of UCSHONN close to zero.

UCCHONN Model

The UCCHONN models replace the sine functions from UCSHONN with cosine functions models. Based on Chapter 1 formulae from (1-93) to (1-97: UCCHONN 2), UCCHONN models are rewritten as follows:
    Let

$$f_k{}^x\left(c_k{}^x x\right) = \cos^k(k * c_k{}^x x)\ (5\text{-}7)$$

$$f_j{}^y\left(c_j{}^y y\right) = \cos^j(j * c_j{}^y y)\ (5\text{-}8)$$

UCCHONN Model 0:

$$z = \sum_{k,j=0}^{n} c_{kj}{}^{o}\cos^k(k * x)\cos^j(j * y)$$

(5-9)

$$where : \left(c_{kj}{}^{hx}\right) = \left(c_{kj}{}^{hy}\right) = 1\ and\ c_k{}^x = c_j{}^y = 1$$

UCCHONN Model 1:

$$z = \sum_{k,j=0}^{n} c_{kj}{}^{o} \cos^k (k * c_k{}^x x) \cos^j (j * c_j{}^y y) where : \left(c_{kj}{}^{hx} \right) = \left(c_{kj}{}^{hy} \right) = 1 (5\text{-}10)$$

UCCHONN Model 2:

$$Z = \sum_{k,j=0}^{n} \left(c_{kj}{}^{o} \right) \{ c_{kj}{}^{hx} \cos^k (k * c_k{}^x x) \} \{ c_{kj}{}^{hy} \cos^j (j * c_j{}^y y) \} (5\text{-}11)$$

USSHONN Model

The USSHONN models use sine functions instead of the cosine functions in the UCSHONN models. Based on Chapter 1 formulae from (1-98) to (1-102: USSHONN 2), USSHONN models are rewritten as follows:
Let

$$f_k{}^x \left(c_k{}^x x \right) = \sin^k (k * c_k{}^x x) (5\text{-}12)$$

$$f_j{}^y \left(c_j{}^y y \right) = \sin^j (j * c_j{}^y y) (5\text{-}13)$$

USSHONN Model 0:

$$z = \sum_{k,j=0}^{n} c_{kj}{}^{o} \sin^k (k * x) \sin^j (j * y)$$

$$(5\text{-}14)$$

$$where : \left(c_{kj}{}^{hx} \right) = \left(c_{kj}{}^{hy} \right) = 1 \ and \ c_k{}^x = c_j{}^y = 1$$

USSHONN Model 1:

$$z = \sum_{k,j=0}^{n} c_{kj}{}^{o} \sin^k (k * c_k{}^x x) \sin^j (j * c_j{}^y y) where : \left(c_{kj}{}^{hx} \right) = \left(c_{kj}{}^{hy} \right) = 1 (5\text{-}15)$$

USSHONN Model 2:

$$Z = \sum_{k,j=0}^{n} \left(c_{kj}{}^{o} \right) \{ c_{kj}{}^{hx} \sin^k (k * c_k{}^x x) \} \{ c_{kj}{}^{hy} \sin^j (j * c_j{}^y y) \} (5\text{-}16)$$

LEARNING ALGORITHM OF UTHONN MODELS

The learning formula for the output layer weights in UTHONN models (UCSHONN, UCCHONN, USSHONN model 0, 1, and 2) are the same. The learning formula for the second-hidden layer weights in the UTHONN models (UCSHONN, UCCHONN, USSHONN Model 2) are the same. The learning formula for the first-hidden layer weights in the UTHONN models (UCSHONN, UCCHONN, USSHONN Model 2) are different. Details are listed here.

Learning Formulae of Output Neurons in UTHONN Model (model 0, 1, and 2)

Based on Chapter 1 formulae from (1-133: A.1) to (1-145: A.13), UTHONN models (model 0, 1, and 2) are rewritten as follows:

$$c_{kj}{}^o(t+1) = c_{kj}{}^o(t) - \eta\left(\partial E / \partial c_{kj}{}^o\right)$$

$$= c_{kj}{}^o(t) + \eta(d-z)f^o{}'\left(net^o\right)i_{kj} = c_{kj}{}^o(t) + \eta\delta^{ol}i_{kj}$$

where

$$\delta^{ol} = (d-z)$$

$$f^{o'}\left(net^o\right) = 1 \quad (linear\ neuron) \quad (5\text{-}17)$$

Learning Formulae of Second-Hidden Layer Neurons in UTHONN Model (Model 2)

Based on Chapter 1 formulae from (1-146: B.1) to (1-160: B.15), UTHONN models (model 2) are rewritten as follows:

The weight update question for x input neurons is:

$$c_{kj}{}^{hx}(t+1) = c_{kj}{}^{hx}(t) - \eta \left(\partial E / \partial c_{kj}{}^{hx} \right)$$

$$= c_{kj}{}^{hx}(t) + \eta \left((d-z) f^{o}{}'\left(net^{o}\right) c_{kj}{}^{o} f^{h}{}'\left(net_{kj}{}^{hx}\right) c_{kj}{}^{hy} b_{j}{}^{y} b_{k}{}^{x} \right)$$

$$= c_{kj}{}^{hx}(t) + \eta \left(\delta^{ol} c_{kj}{}^{o} \delta_{kj}{}^{hx} b_{k}{}^{x} \right)$$

where

$$\delta^{ol} = (d-z) \quad \delta_{kj}{}^{hx} = c_{kj}{}^{hy} b_{j}{}^{y}$$

$$f^{o'}\left(net^{o}\right) = 1 \qquad (linear\ neuron)\,(5\text{-}18)$$

$$f^{h'}\left(net_{kj}{}^{hx}\right) = 1 \quad (linear\ neuron)$$

The weight update question for y input neurons is:

$$c_{kj}{}^{hy}(t+1) = c_{kj}{}^{hy}(t) - \eta \left(\partial E / \partial c_{kj}{}^{hy} \right)$$

$$= c_{kj}{}^{hy}(t) + \eta \left((d-z) f^{o}{}'\left(net^{o}\right) c_{kj}{}^{o} f^{h}{}'\left(net_{kj}{}^{hy}\right) c_{kj}{}^{hx} b_{k}{}^{x} b_{j}{}^{y} \right)$$

$$= c_{kj}{}^{hy}(t) + \eta \left(\delta^{ol} c_{kj}{}^{o} \delta_{kj}{}^{hy} b_{j}{}^{y} \right)$$

where

$$\delta^{ol} = (d-z) \quad \delta_{kj}{}^{hy} = c_{kj}{}^{hx} b_{k}{}^{x}$$

$$f^{o'}\left(net^{o}\right) = 1 \qquad (linear\ neuron)\,(5\text{-}19)$$

$$f^{h'}\left(net_{kj}{}^{hy}\right) = 1 \quad (linear\ neuron)$$

General Learning Formulae of First Hidden Layer x Neurons in UTHONN (Model 1 and Model 2)

Based on Chapter 1 formulae from (1-161: C.1) to (1-177: C.17), UTHONN models (model 1 and 2) are rewritten as follows:

For a function of *x* input side:

$$b_k^{\ x} = f_k^{\ x}\left(net_k^{\ x}\right)$$

$$f_x{}'\left(net_k^{\ x}\right) = \partial b_k^{\ x} / \partial\left(net_k^{\ x}\right) \qquad (5\text{-}20)$$

$$
\begin{aligned}
c_k^{\ x}\left(t+1\right) &= c_k^{\ x}\left(t\right) - \eta\left(\partial E_p / \partial c_k^{\ x}\right) \\
&= c_k^{\ x}\left(t\right) + \eta\left(d-z\right) f^o{}'\left(net^o\right) c_{kj}^{\ o} * f^h{}'\left(net_{kj}^{\ h}\right) c_{kj}^{\ hy} b_j^{\ y} c_{kj}^{\ hx} f_x{}'\left(net_k^{\ x}\right) x \\
&= c_k^{\ x}\left(t\right) + \eta * \delta^{ol} * c_{kj}^{\ o} * \delta^{hx} * c_{kj}^{\ hx} * \delta^x * x
\end{aligned}
$$

where

$$\delta^{ol} = \left(d-z\right) f^o{}'\left(net^o\right) = d-z \qquad (linear\ neuron)$$

$$\delta^{hx} = f^h{}'\left(net_{kj}^{\ h}\right) c_{kj}^{\ hy} b_j^{\ y} = c_{kj}^{\ hy} b_j^{\ y} \qquad (linear\ neuron) \qquad (5\text{-}21)$$

$$\delta^x = f_x{}'\left(net_k^{\ x}\right)$$

General Learning Formulae of First Hidden Layer y Neurons in UTHONN (Model 1 and Model 2)

Based on Chapter 1 formulae from (1-178: D.1) to (1-194: D.17), UTHONN models (model 1 and 2) are rewritten as follows:

For a function of *y* input part:

$$b_j^{\ y} = f_j^{\ y}\left(net_j^{\ y}\right)$$

$$f_y{}'\left(net_j^{\ y}\right) = \partial b_j^{\ y} / \partial\left(net_j^{\ y}\right) \qquad (5\text{-}22)$$

Using the above procedure:

$$c_j^y(t+1) = c_j^y(t) - \eta\left(\frac{\partial E_p}{\partial c_j^y}\right)$$

$$= c_j^y(t) + \eta(d-z) f^{o'}\left(net^o\right)c_{kj}^o * f^{h'}\left(net_{kj}^h\right)c_{kj}^{hx}b_k^x c_{kj}^{hy} f_y'\left(net_j^y\right)y$$

$$= c_j^y(t) + \eta * \delta^{ol} * c_{kj}^o * \delta^{hy} * c_{kj}^{hy} * \delta^y * y$$

where

$$\delta^{ol} = (d-z) f^{o'}\left(net^o\right) = d-z \qquad \left(\text{linear neuron } f^{o'}\left(net^o\right) = 1\right)$$

$$\delta^{hy} = f^{h'}\left(net_{kj}^h\right)c_{kj}^{hx}b_k^x = c_{kj}^{hx}b_k^x \qquad \left(\text{linear neuron } f^{h'}\left(net_{kj}^h\right) = 1\right)$$

$$\delta^y = f_y'\left(net_j^y\right)$$

Learning Formulae of UCSHONN Model for the First Hidden Layer

The first hidden layer neurons in UCSHONN (Model 1 and Model 2) use sine and cosine functions. Based on Chapter 1 formulae from (1-285) to (1-290: UCSHONN D.17), update learning formulae of UCSHONN models (model 1 and 2) are rewritten as follows:

Let:

$$f_k^x\left(c_k^x x\right) = \cos^k(k * c_k^x x) \text{ (5-24)}$$

$$f_j^y\left(c_j^y y\right) = \sin^j(j * c_j^y y) \text{ (5-25)}$$

For an ultra-high frequency cosine function of x input part:

$$b_k^x = f_k^x\left(net_k^x\right) = \cos^k(k * net_k^x)$$

$$f_x{}'\left(net_k{}^x\right)=\partial b^x{}_k\,/\,\partial\left(net_k{}^x\right)=\partial\left(\cos^k\left(k*net_k{}^x\right)\right)/\,\partial\left(net_k{}^x\right)$$

$$=k\cos^{k-1}\left(k*net_k{}^x\right)*\left(-\sin(k*net_k{}^x)\right)*k$$

$$=-k^2\cos^{k-1}\left(k*net_k{}^x\right)\sin(k*net_k{}^x)$$

$$=-k^2\cos^{k-1}\left(k*c_k{}^x*x\right)\sin(k*c_k{}^x*x)$$

(5-26)

$$c_k{}^x\left(t+1\right)=c_k{}^x\left(t\right)-\eta\left(\partial E_p\,/\,\partial c_k{}^x\right)$$

$$=c_k{}^x\left(t\right)+\eta\left(d-z\right)f^o{}'\left(net^o\right)c_{kj}{}^o*f^h{}'\left(net_{kj}{}^h\right)c_{kj}{}^{hy}b^y{}_j c_{kj}{}^{hx}f_x{}'\left(net_k{}^x\right)x$$

$$=c_k{}^x\left(t\right)+\eta*\delta^{ol}*c_{kj}{}^o*\delta^{hx}*c_{kj}{}^{hx}*\left(-k^2\right)\cos^{k-1}(k*c_k{}^x*x)\sin(k*c_k{}^x*x)*x$$

$$=c_k{}^x\left(t\right)+\eta*\delta^{ol}*c_{kj}{}^o*\delta^{hx}*c_{kj}{}^{hx}*\delta^x*x$$

where

$$\delta^{ol}=\left(d-z\right)f^o{}'\left(net^o\right)=d-z\qquad\left(linear\ neuron\ f^o{}'\left(net^o\right)=1\right)$$

$$\delta^{hx}=f^h{}'\left(net_{kj}{}^h\right)c_{kj}{}^{hy}b^y{}_j=a_{kj}{}^{hy}b_j\qquad\left(linear\ neuron\ f^h{}'\left(net_{kj}{}^h\right)=1\right)$$ (5-27)

$$\delta^x=f_x{}'\left(net_k{}^x\right)=\left(-k^2\right)\cos^{k-1}(k*c_k{}^x*x)\sin(k*c_k{}^x*x)$$

For an ultra-high frequency sine function of y input part:

$$b_j{}^y=f_j{}^y\left(net_j{}^y\right)=\sin^j(j*net_j{}^y)=\sin^j(j*c_j{}^y*y)$$

$$f_y{}'\left(net_j{}^y\right)=\partial b_j{}^y\,/\,\partial\left(net_j{}^y\right)$$

$$=\partial\left(\sin^j(j*net_j{}^y)\right)/\,\partial\left(net_j{}^y\right)=j\sin^{j-1}(j*net_j{}^y)*\cos(j*net_j{}^y)*j$$

$$=j^2*\sin^{j-1}(j*net_j{}^y)*\cos(j*net_j{}^y)=j^2*\sin^{j-1}(j*c_j{}^y*y)*\cos(j*c_j{}^y*y)$$

(5-28)

Using the above procedure:

$$c_j^y(t+1) = c_j^y(t) - \eta\left(\partial E_p / \partial c_j^y\right)$$

$$= c_j^y(t) + \eta(d-z)f^o{}'\left(net^o\right)c_{kj}^o * f^h{}'\left(net_{kj}^h\right)c_{kj}^{hx}b_k^x c_{kj}^{hy}f_y{}'\left(net_j^y\right)y$$

$$= c_j^y(t) + \eta * \delta^{ol} * c_{kj}^o * \delta^{hy} * c_{kj}^{hy} * \left(j^2\right)\sin^{j-1}(j*c_j^y*y)\cos(j*c_j^y*y)*y$$

$$= c_j^y(t) + \eta * \delta^{ol} * c_{kj}^o * \delta^{hy} * c_{kj}^{hy} * \delta^y * y$$

where

$$\delta^{ol} = (d-z)f^o{}'\left(net^o\right) = d-z \qquad \left(linear\ neuron\ f^o{}'\left(net^o\right) = 1\right)$$

$$\delta^{hy} = f^h{}'\left(net_{kj}^{hy}\right)c_{kj}^{hx}b_k^x = c_{kj}^{hx}b_k^x \qquad \left(linear\ neuron\ f^h{}'\left(net_{kj}^{hy}\right) = 1\right) \quad \text{(5-}$$

$$\delta^y = f_y{}'\left(net_j^y\right) = \left(j^2\right)\sin^{j-1}(j*c_j^y*y)\cos(j*c_j^y*y)$$

29)

Learning Formulae of UCCHONN Model for the First Hidden Layer

The first hidden layer neurons in UCCHONN (Model 1 and Model 2) use cosine functions. Based on Chapter 1 formulae from (1-291) to (1-296: UCCHONN D.17), update learning formulae of UCCHONN models (model 1 and 2) are rewritten as follows:

Let

$$f_k^x\left(c_k^x x\right) = \cos^k(k*c_k^x x)\ (5\text{-}30)$$

$$f_j^y\left(c_j^y y\right) = \cos^j(j*c_j^y y)\ (5\text{-}31)$$

For an ultra-high frequency cosine function of x input part:

$$b_k^x = f_k^x\left(net_k^x\right) = \cos^k(k*net_k^x)$$

$$f_x'\left(net_k^x\right) = \partial b_k^x / \partial\left(net_k^x\right)$$
$$= \partial\left(\cos^k(k*net_k^x)\right) / \partial\left(net_k^x\right) = k\cos^{k-1}(k*net_k^x)*\left(-\sin(k*net_k^x)\right)*k \quad \text{(5-}$$
$$= -k^2\cos^{k-1}(k*net_k^x)\sin(k*net_k^x) = -k^2\cos^{k-1}(k*c_k^x*x)\sin(k*c_k^x*x)$$
32)

$$c_k^x(t+1) = c_k^x(t) - \eta\left(\partial E_p / \partial c_k^x\right)$$
$$= c_k^x(t) + \eta(d-z)f^{o'}\left(net^o\right)c_{kj}^o * f^h\left(net_{kj}^h\right)c_{kj}^{hy}b_j^y{}_j c_{kj}^{hx} f_x'\left(net_k^x\right)x$$
$$= c_k^x(t) + \eta * \delta^{ol} * c_{kj}^o * \delta^{hx} * c_{kj}^{hx} *\left(-k^2\right)\cos^{k-1}(k*c_k^x*x)\sin(k*c_k^x*x)*x$$
$$= c_k^x(t) + \eta * \delta^{ol} * c_{kj}^o * \delta^{hx} * c_{kj}^{hx} * \delta^x * x$$

where

$$\delta^{ol} = (d-z)f^{o'}\left(net^o\right) = d-z \qquad \left(linear\ neuron\ f^{o'}\left(net^o\right) = 1\right)$$
$$\delta^{hx} = f^h\left(net_{kj}^h\right)c_{kj}^{hy}b_j^y{}_j = a_{kj}^{hy}b_j \qquad \left(linear\ neuron\ f^{h'}\left(net_{kj}^h\right) = 1\right) \quad \text{(5-}$$
$$\delta^x = f_x'\left(net_k^x\right) = \left(-k^2\right)\cos^{k-1}(k*c_k^x*x)\sin(k*c_k^x*x)$$
33)

For an ultra-high frequency cosine function of *y* input part:

$$b_j^y = f_j^y\left(net_j^y\right) = \cos^j(j*net_j^y) = \cos^j(j*c_j^y*y)$$

$$f_y'\left(net_j^y\right) = \partial b_j^y / \partial\left(net_j^y\right)$$
$$= \partial\left(\cos^j(j*net_j^y)\right) / \partial\left(net_j^y\right) = j\cos^{j-1}(j*net_j^y)*\left(-\sin(j*net_j^y)\right)*j \qquad \text{(5-}$$
$$= -j^2*\cos^{j-1}(j*net_j^y)*\sin(j*net_j^y) = -j^2*\cos^{j-1}(j*c_j^y*y)*\sin(j*c_j^y*y)$$
34)

Using the above procedure:

$$c_j^{y}(t+1) = c_j^{y}(t) - \eta\left(\partial E_p / \partial c_j^{y}\right)$$

$$= c_j^{y}(t) + \eta(d-z) f^{o\,\prime}\left(net^o\right) c_{kj}^{o} * f^{h\,\prime}\left(net_{kj}^{h}\right) c_{kj}^{hx} b_k^{x} c_{kj}^{hy} f_y^{\,\prime}\left(net_j^{y}\right) y$$

$$= c_j^{y}(t) + \eta * \delta^{ol} * c_{kj}^{o} * \delta^{hy} * c_{kj}^{hy} * \left(-j^2\right) * \cos^{j-1}(j * c_j^{y} * y) * \sin(j * c_j^{y} * y) * y$$

$$= c_j^{y}(t) + \eta * \delta^{ol} * c_{kj}^{o} * \delta^{hy} * c_{kj}^{hy} * \delta^{y} * y$$

where

$$\delta^{ol} = (d-z) f^{o\,\prime}\left(net^o\right) = d - z \qquad \left(linear\ neuron\ f^{o\,\prime}\left(net^o\right) = 1\right)$$

$$\delta^{hy} = f^{h\,\prime}\left(net_{kj}^{hy}\right) c_{kj}^{hx} b_k^{x} = c_{kj}^{hx} b_k^{x} \qquad \left(linear\ neuron\ f^{h\,\prime}\left(net_{kj}^{hy}\right) = 1\right) \quad (5-$$

$$\delta^{y} = f_y^{\,\prime}\left(net_j^{y}\right) = \left(-j^2\right) * \cos^{j-1}(j * c_j^{y} * y) * \sin(j * c_j^{y} * y)$$

35)

Learning Formulae of USSHONN Model for the First Hidden Layer

The first hidden layer neurons in USSHONN (Model 1 and Model 2) use sine functions. Based on Chapter 1 formulae from (1-297) to (1-302: USSHONN D.17), update learning formulae of USSHONN models (model 1 and 2) are rewritten as follows:

Let

$$f_k^{x}\left(c_k^{x} x\right) = \sin^k(k * c_k^{x} x) \text{ (5-36)}$$

$$f_j^{y}\left(c_j^{y} y\right) = \sin^j(j * c_j^{y} y) \text{ (5-37)}$$

For an ultra-high frequency sine function of x input part:

$$b^x{}_k = f_k{}^x\left(net_k{}^x\right) = \sin^k(k*net_k{}^x)$$

$$f_x{}'\left(net_k{}^x\right) = \partial b^x{}_k / \partial\left(net_k{}^x\right)$$

$$= \partial\left(\sin^k(k*net_k{}^x)\right)/\partial\left(net_k{}^x\right) = k\sin^{k-1}(k*net_k{}^x)*\cos(k*net_k{}^x)*k \qquad (5-$$

$$= k^2\sin^{k-1}(k*net_k{}^x)\cos(k*net_k{}^x) = k^2\sin^{k-1}(k*c_k{}^x*x)\cos(k*c_k{}^x*x)$$

38)

$$c_k{}^x\left(t+1\right) = c_k{}^x\left(t\right) - \eta\left(\partial E_p / \partial c_k{}^x\right)$$

$$= c_k{}^x\left(t\right) + \eta\left(d-z\right)f^o{}'\left(net^o\right)c_{kj}{}^o * f^h{}'\left(net_{kj}{}^h\right)c_{kj}{}^{hy}b^y{}_j c_{kj}{}^{hx} f_x{}'\left(net_k{}^x\right)x$$

$$= c_k{}^x\left(t\right) + \eta*\delta^{ol}*c_{kj}{}^o*\delta^{hx}*c_{kj}{}^{hx}*\left(k^2\right)\sin^{k-1}(k*c_k{}^x*x)\cos(k*c_k{}^x*x)*x$$

$$= c_k{}^x\left(t\right) + \eta*\delta^{ol}*c_{kj}{}^o*\delta^{hx}*c_{kj}{}^{hx}*\delta^x*x$$

where

$$\delta^{ol} = \left(d-z\right)f^o{}'\left(net^o\right) = d-z \qquad \left(\text{linear neuron } f^o{}'\left(net^o\right) = 1\right)$$

$$\delta^{hx} = f^h{}'\left(net_{kj}{}^h\right)c_{kj}{}^{hy}b^y{}_j = a_{kj}{}^{hy}b_j \qquad \left(\text{linear neuron } f^h{}'\left(net_{kj}{}^h\right) = 1\right) \qquad (5-$$

$$\delta^x = f_x{}'\left(net_k{}^x\right) = \left(k^2\right)\sin^{k-1}(k*c_k{}^x*x)\cos(k*c_k{}^x*x)$$

39)

For an ultra-high frequency sine function of *y* input part:

$$b_j{}^y = f_j{}^y\left(net_j{}^y\right) = \sin^j(j*net_j{}^y) = \sin^j(j*c_j{}^y*y)$$

$$f_y{}'\left(net_j{}^y\right) = \partial b_j{}^y / \partial\left(net_j{}^y\right)$$

$$= \partial\left(\sin^j(j*net_j{}^y)\right)/\partial\left(net_j{}^y\right) = j\sin^{j-1}(j*net_j{}^y)*\cos(j*net_j{}^y)*j \qquad 5$$

$$= j^2*\sin^{j-1}(j*net_j{}^y)*\cos(j*net_j{}^y) = j^2*\sin^{j-1}(j*c_j{}^y*y)*\cos(j*c_j{}^y*y)$$

40)

Using the above procedure:

$$c_j^{y}(t+1) = c_j^{y}(t) - \eta\left(\partial E_p / \partial c_j^{y}\right)$$

$$= c_j^{y}(t) + \eta(d-z)f^{o\,\prime}\left(net^{o}\right)c_{kj}^{o} * f^{h\,\prime}\left(net_{kj}^{h}\right)c_{kj}^{hx}b_{k}^{x}c_{kj}^{hy}f_{y}^{\prime}\left(net_{j}^{y}\right)y$$

$$= c_j^{y}(t) + \eta * \delta^{ol} * c_{kj}^{o} * \delta^{hy} * c_{kj}^{hy} * \left(j^2\right)\sin^{j-1}(j*c_j^{y}*y)\cos(j*c_j^{y}*y)*y$$

$$= c_j^{y}(t) + \eta * \delta^{ol} * c_{kj}^{o} * \delta^{hy} * c_{kj}^{hy} * \delta^{y} * y$$

where

$$\delta^{ol} = (d-z)f^{o\,\prime}\left(net^{o}\right) = d-z \qquad\qquad \left(linear\ neuron\ f^{o\,\prime}\left(net^{o}\right) = 1\right)$$

$$\delta^{hy} = f^{h\,\prime}\left(net_{kj}^{hy}\right)c_{kj}^{hx}b_{k}^{x} = c_{kj}^{hx}b_{k}^{x} \qquad \left(linear\ neuron\ f^{h\,\prime}\left(net_{kj}^{hy}\right) = 1\right) \quad 5$$

$$\delta^{y} = f_{y}^{\prime}\left(net_{j}^{y}\right) = \left(j^2\right)\sin^{j-1}(j*c_j^{y}*y)\cos(j*c_j^{y}*y)$$

41)

UTHONN TESTING

This chapter uses the monthly Australian and USA dollar exchange rate from Nov. 2003 to Dec. 2004.

In Table 1, as the test data for UCSHONN models. Input 1, R_{t-2} is the data at time t-2. Input 2, R_{t-1} is data at time t-1. While, the output, R_t is the data for the current month. The values of R_{t-2}, R_{t-1}, and R_t are converted to a range from 0 to 1 and then used as inputs and output in the UCSHONN model. Using data from Table 1, the error of UCSHONN model 1b, order 2, epochs 100 is 9.4596%, (not shown in table) while the error is only 1.9457% (not shown in table) for model UCSHONN 1b Order 6 Epochs 100. This shows a decrease in error when there is increase in the order of the model.

In Table 2, data uses the Australian and USA dollar Exchange rate as the test data for UCSHONN model 0, model 1, and model 1b. The orders from 2

Table 1. Testing UCSHONN System - Australia Dollars Vs US Dollars and Data for UTHONN Simulator

Date	Rate 1 AU$ = ? US$	Two monthes before input 1	One month before input 2	Prediction Simulation output	UTHONN input 1	UTHONN input 2	UTHONN Desired Output
11/28/2003	0.7236						
12/31/2003	0.7520						
1/30/2004	0.7625	0.7236	0.7520	0.7625	0.3712	0.7367	0.7890
2/27/2004	0.7717	0.7520	0.7625	0.7717	0.7425	0.8729	0.8968
3/31/2004	0.7620	0.7625	0.7717	0.7620	0.8797	0.9922	0.7831
4/30/2004	0.7210	0.7717	0.7620	0.7210	1.0000	0.8664	0.3025
5/28/2004	0.7138	0.7620	0.7210	0.7138	0.8732	0.3346	0.2181
6/30/2004	0.6952	0.7210	0.7138	0.6952	0.3373	0.2412	0.0000
7/30/2004	0.7035	0.7138	0.6952	0.7035	0.2431	0.0000	0.0973
8/31/2004	0.7071	0.6952	0.7035	0.7071	0.0000	0.1077	0.1395
9/30/2004	0.7244	0.7035	0.7071	0.7244	0.1085	0.1543	0.3423
10/29/2004	0.7468	0.7071	0.7244	0.7468	0.1556	0.3787	0.6049
11/30/2004	0.7723	0.7244	0.7468	0.7723	0.3817	0.6693	0.9039
12/31/2004	0.7805	0.7468	0.7723	0.7805	0.6745	1.0000	1.0000

Table 2. 2004 AU$/US$ Exchange Rate Prediction Simulation Error (Epochs: 10,000)

Error	Order 2	Order 3	Order 4	Order 5	Order 6
UCS Model 0	8.5493%	6.3269%	2.4368%	0.4486%	0.0197%
UCS Model 1	9.3254%	8.5509%	5.0727%	1.7119%	3.2635%
UCS Model 1b	12.5573%	8.8673%	8.5555%	4.9947%	4.1619%

Table 3. 2004 AU$/US$ Exchange Rate Prediction Simulation Error (Epochs: 100,000)

Error	Order 2	Order 3	Order 4	Order 5	Order 6
UCS Model 0	6.2852%	4.1944%	0.0781%	0.0000%	0.0000%
UCS Model 1	11.3713%	6.2309%	0.0409%	1.8470%	0.0000%
UCS Model 1b	15.5525%	4.0699%	4.8051%	0.0000%	0.0000%

to 6 for using epochs are shown. The errors are 0.0197% (model 0), 3.2635% (Model 1), and 4.1619% (Model 1b).

In Table 3, data shows the results for 100,000 epochs using the same test data. From Table 2 with order 6, all UCSHONN models have reached an error percentage of 0.0000%. This shows that UCSHONN models can successfully simulate Table 3 data with 0.000% error.

COMPARISON OF THONN WITH OTHER HIGHER ORDER NEURAL NETWORKS

Currency Exchange Rate model by using THONN model 0 (Zhang and Fulcher, 2004) is as follows:

$$R_t = a_{00} + a_{01} \sin\left(R_{t-1}\right) + a_{10} \cos\left(R_{t-2}\right) + \sum_{j=2}^{n} a_{0j} sin^j\left(R_{t-1}\right)$$

$$+ \sum_{k=2}^{n} a_{k0} cos^k\left(R_{t-2}\right) + \sum_{k=1, j=1}^{n} a_{kj} cos^k\left(R_{t-2}\right) sin^j\left(R_{t-1}\right) \tag{5-42}$$

Currency Exchange Rate model by using PHONN model 0 (Zhang and Fulcher, 2004) is as follows:

$$R_t = a_{00} + a_{01} R_{t-1} + a_{10} R_{t-2} + \sum_{j=2}^{n} a_{0j} R_{t-1}^{\ j}$$

$$+ \sum_{k=2}^{n} a_{k0}\left(R_{t-2}\right)^k + \sum_{k=1, j=1}^{n} a_{kj}\left(R_{t-2}\right)^k\left(R_{t-1}\right)^j \tag{5-43}$$

In Table 4, data shows the results for Model 0 of UCSHONN, PHONN and THONN. After 1000 epochs, the three models UCSHONN, PHONN, and THONN have reached errors of 2.3485%, 8.7080% and 10.0366%. This shows that UCSHONN can reach a smaller error in the same time frame. After 100,000 epochs, error for UCSHONN error is close to 0.0000%, but error for PHONN and THONN are still 4.4457% and 4.5712%, respectively. This result shows that UCSHONN can simulate ultra-high frequency data. UCSHONN is more accurate than PHONN and THONN.

Table 4. Comparison of HTHONN with PHONN and THONN: 2004 AU$/US$ Exchange Rate Prediction Simulation Error – Model 0 and Order 6

Error	1,000 Epochs	10,000 Epochs	100,000 Epochs
UCSHONN Model 0	2.3485%	0.0197%	0.0000%
PHONN Model 0	8.7080%	7.1142%	4.4457%
THONN Model 0	10.0366%	9.2834%	4.5712%

Table 5. 2004 AU$/US$ Exchange Rate Prediction Simulation Error - Model 1 and Order 6

Error	1,000 Epochs	10,000 Epochs	100,000 Epochs
UCSHONN Model 1	4.0094%	3.2635%	0.0000%
PHONN Model 1	9.5274%	8.3484%	7.8234%
THONN Model 1	10.8966%	7.3811%	7.3468%

In Table 5, data compare the results for Model 1 of UCSHONN, PHONN and THONN. After 100,000 epochs, all the UCSHONN models have reached an error close to 0.000%, while errors for PHONN and THONN are still around

Table 6: 2004 AU$/US$ Dollar Exchange Rate Prediction Simulation Error – Model 1B and Order 6

Error	1,000 Epochs	10,000 Epochs	100,000 Epochs
UCSHONN Model 1b	5.0633%	4.1619%	0.0000%
PHONH Model 1b	14.8800%	9.1474%	9.0276%
THONN Model 1b	10.560%	10.1914%	6.7119%

6% to 9% (similar results are generated for 1,000,000 epochs for PHONN and THONN models) Therefore, the UCSHONN model is more superior for data analysis than any other HONN models.

In Table 6, data compare the results for Model 1B of UCSHONN, PHONN and THONN. After 100,000 epochs, all the UCSHONN models have reached an error close to 0.000%, while errors for PHONN and THONN are still around 6% to 9% (similar results are generated for 1,000,000 epochs for PHONN and THONN models) Therefore, the UCSHONN model is more superior for data analysis than any other HONN models.

COMPARISONS WITH UTHONN AND EQUILIBRIUM REAL EXCHANGE RATES

Chile Exchange Rate Estimation

One of the central issues in the international monetary debate is the feasibility of calculating the fundamental equilibrium exchange rates (John Williamson, 1994). Elbradawi (1994) provides a formula to calculate Equilibrium Real Exchange Rates (ERER) as follows:

$$\log \tilde{e}_t = \frac{1}{1-\lambda} \delta ' \tilde{\mathbf{F}}_t + \eta_{t'} \ (5\text{-}44)$$

Where:

$\tilde{e}_t$: Equilibrium Real Exchange Rate

$\dfrac{1}{1-\lambda}$: the co-integration vectors

$\delta '$: Parameter vector

$\tilde{\mathbf{F}}_t$: Vector pf fundamentals

$\eta_{t'}$: Stationary disturbance term

In Table 7, data compares the UCSHONN with ERER. It shows the actual real exchange rates for Chile, misalignment from equilibrium rate (actual 1980 = 100), and estimations from the UCSHONN model. The average absolute difference of Elbradawi's ERER is 20.5%. Using the actual real exchange rates, UCSHONN predicts the next period actual real exchange rates by using the rates from t − 1 to t − 2. The average absolute difference of UCSHONN is 3.8% and the absolute error of UCSHONN is only 4.24%. However, the absolute average error of Elbradawi's ERER is 14.22%, using the formula of (absolute difference)/(current rate)*100. From Table 7, the results show that UCSHONN model can reach a smaller error percentage than Elbradawi's ERER model.

Table 7. Comparison of UCSHONN and ERER – Chile

Year	Rate	Elbradawi ERRA			UCSHONN		
		Equilibrium (Elbradawi)	Absolute Difference	Absolute percentage	UCSHONN Estimation	Absolute Difference	Absolute Percentage
1965	294.3						
1966	275.4						
1967	261.7						
1968	244	238.8	5.2	2.13	245.8875	1.9	0.77
1969	234.1	239	4.9	2.09	231.7034	2.4	1.02
1970	223.2	236.4	13.2	5.91	226.8309	3.6	1.63
1971	242.7	261.1	18.4	7.58	241.2088	1.5	0.61
1972	254.2	285.7	31.5	12.39	254.8970	0.7	0.27
1973	398.2	259.4	138.8	34.86	396.8596	1.3	0.34
1974	136.1	196.8	60.7	44.60	136.0834	0.0	0.01
1975	103.7	172.7	69.0	66.54	103.7502	0.1	0.05
1976	99	115.7	16.7	16.87	98.3935	0.6	0.61
1977	106.4	109.7	3.3	3.10	93.8473	12.6	11.80
1978	88.4	100.3	11.9	13.46	97.4030	9.0	10.18
1979	87.4	105.9	18.5	21.17	88.9480	1.5	1.77
1980	100	104.5	4.5	4.50	88.1116	11.9	11.89
1981	118.1	96.5	21.6	18.29	111.5722	6.5	5.53
1982	109.5	98.5	11.0	10.05	108.3879	1.1	1.02
1983	87.7	96.9	9.2	10.49	86.8537	0.8	0.96
1984	87	87	0.0	0.00	90.9335	3.9	4.52
1985	70.4	81.7	11.3	16.05	88.0505	17.7	25.07
1986	63.3	73	9.7	15.32	59.7513	3.5	5.61
1987	60.2	65.4	5.2	8.64	59.4128	0.8	1.31
1988	54.7	56.8	2.1	3.84	58.8049	4.1	7.50
1989	52.8	57.5	4.7	8.90	51.6882	1.1	2.11
1990	51.4	51.6	0.2	0.39	49.9417	1.5	2.84
Average			20.5	14.22		3.8	4.24

Ghana Exchange Rate

In Table 8, data shows the actual real exchange rates for Ghana and the misalignment from equilibrium. The average absolute difference of Elbradawi's ERER model is 35.25%. Using data from Table 8, the average absolute difference for UCSHONN is 5.6, and the absolute error of UCSHONN is 8.89%, while the absolute average error for Elbradawi's ERER is 20.08%. Clearly, UCSHONN model can reach a smaller error percentage than Elbradawi's ERER model.

Table 8. Comparison of UCSHONN and ERER – Ghana

Year	Rate	Elbradawi's ERER			UCSHONN		
		Equilibrium (Elbradawi)	Absolute Difference	Absolute percentage	UCSHONN Estimation	Absolute Difference	Absolute Percentage
1965	72.8						
1966	79.9						
1967	60.4	65.8	5.4	8.94	90.1	29.7	49.16
1968	56.8	62.1	5.3	9.33	44.1	12.7	22.30
1969	59.2	59.1	0.1	0.17	57.8	1.4	2.36
1970	57.8	57.4	0.4	0.69	65.1	7.3	12.67
1971	57.6	60.1	2.5	4.34	60.5	2.9	5.01
1972	44.4	55.5	11.1	25.00	61.3	16.9	38.16
1973	50.8	55.6	4.8	9.45	47.2	3.6	7.17
1974	51.3	60.2	8.9	17.35	56.2	4.9	9.62
1975	58.9	68.3	9.4	15.96	55.8	3.1	5.26
1976	90.7	91.6	0.9	0.99	68.3	22.4	24.71
1977	177.2	112.4	64.8	36.57	162.9	14.3	8.06
1978	167.9	138.3	29.6	17.63	167.6	0.3	0.18
1979	144.7	186.2	41.5	28.68	144.8	0.1	0.05
1980	189.3	261.4	72.1	38.09	188.8	0.5	0.27
1981	432.3	292.7	139.6	32.29	431.5	0.8	0.19
1982	549	316.4	232.6	42.37	548.6	0.4	0.08
1983	388.8	308.7	80.1	20.60	388.5	0.3	0.07
1984	134.6	202	67.4	50.07	134.4	0.2	0.12
1985	100.1	117.1	17	16.98	99.9	0.2	0.17
1986	67.4	78.5	11.1	16.47	68.5	1.1	1.63
1987	49.3	55.4	6.1	12.37	44.4	4.9	9.85
1988	45.6	13.6	32	70.18	45.2	0.4	0.98
1989	44.2	44.4	0.2	0.45	45.2	1.0	2.16
1990	44	47.1	3.1	7.05	49.8	5.8	13.08
Average			35.25	20.08		5.6	8.89

Table 9. Comparison of UCSHONN and ERER – India

Year	Rate	Elbradawi's ERER			USCHONN		
		Equilibrium (Elbradawi)	Absolute Difference	Absolute percentage	USCHONN Estimation	Absolute Difference	Absolute Percentage
1965	275.5	236.9					
1966	239.6	222.7					
1967	212.8	215.8	3.00	1.41	212.8	0.00	0.00
1968	218.8	206.3	12.50	5.71	218.8	0.02	0.01
1969	215	205.5	9.50	4.42	214.6	0.38	0.17
1970	218.2	205.8	12.40	5.68	217.9	0.30	0.14
1971	206.7	200.5	6.20	3.00	207.2	0.50	0.24
1972	197	187.8	9.20	4.67	197.1	0.10	0.05
1973	180	170.9	9.10	5.06	180.0	0.02	0.01
1974	149.6	152.5	2.90	1.94	149.6	0.00	0.00
1975	143.2	136.7	6.50	4.54	143.2	0.02	0.01
1976	119.5	127	7.50	6.28	119.5	0.01	0.01
1977	121.2	119.1	2.10	1.73	121.3	0.14	0.11
1978	118.9	113.7	5.20	4.37	119.2	0.32	0.27
1979	106.8	110.2	3.40	3.18	106.0	0.75	0.71
1980	100	106.7	6.70	6.70	100.0	0.02	0.02
1981	99.6	103.2	3.60	3.61	101.7	2.05	2.06
1982	101.1	100.7	0.40	0.40	103.2	2.12	2.09
1983	109.5	100.8	8.70	7.95	105.9	3.59	3.28
1984	107.9	101.8	6.10	5.65	108.4	0.46	0.43
1985	105.4	101.6	3.80	3.61	105.2	0.18	0.17
1986	110.2	99.6	10.60	9.62	106.9	3.30	3.00
1987	104.5	98.4	6.10	5.84	106.0	1.55	1.48
1988	103.6	94.7	8.90	8.59	104.9	1.31	1.27
Average			6.56	4.73		0.78	0.71

India Exchange Rate

In Table 9, data compares the UCSHONN with ERER model using the exchange rates for India. Table 9 shows the actual real exchange rates for India, misalignment from equilibrium rate (actual 1980 = 100), and estimations from the UCSHONN model. The average absolute difference of Elbradawi's ERER is 6.56, and the average absolute difference of UCSHONN is only 0.78.

Also, Table 9 shows that the absolute average error of Elbradawi's ERER is 4.73%, while the absolute error of UCSHONN is 0.71%. Again, UCSHONN outperforms the Elbradawi's ERER model.

APPLICATIONS

Exchange rates for Japanese Yen vs. US Dollars (2000 and 2004), US Consumer Price Index (1992-2004), and Japan Consumer Price Index (1992-2004) are selected as applications for UTHONN models. There are two reasons why these applications have been selected. The first reason is that all selected applications are high frequency data. The second reason is that these applications are used as contributing examples for the Nobel Prize in Economics in 2003. (Vetenskapsakademien, 2003).

Exchange Rate Predication Simulation

Currency Exchange Rate Models
   Let:

$$z = R_t; \; x = R_{t-2}; \; y = R_{t-1}; \; a_{kj}^{\,0} = a_{kj}; \; n = 6$$

   Currency Exchange Rate Model using UCSHONN Model 0:

$$R_t = \sum_{k,j=0}^{n} a_{kj} cos^k \left(k * R_{t-2} \right) sin^j \left(j * R_{t-1} \right)$$

$$(5\text{-}45)$$

$$where \left(a_{kj}^{\,hx} \right) = \left(a_{kj}^{\,hy} \right) = 1 \, and \, a_k^{\,x} = a_j^{\,y} = 1$$

   Since:

$$cos^0 \left(0 * R_{t-2} \right) = sin^0 \left(0 * R_{t-1} \right) = 1 \, (5\text{-}46)$$

   Currency Exchange Rate model by using UCSHONN model 0:

$$R_t = a_{00} + a_{01} \sin\left(R_{t-1}\right) + a_{10} \cos\left(R_{t-2}\right)$$
$$+ \sum_{j=2}^{6} a_{0j} \sin^j \left(j * R_{t-1}\right) + \sum_{j=2}^{6} a_{k0} \cos^k \left(k * R_{t-2}\right) + \sum_{j=2}^{6} a_{kj} \cos^k \left(k * R_{t-2}\right) \sin^j \left(j * R_{t-1}\right)$$

47)

Before using UCSHONN models, the raw data are converted by the following formula to scale the data to range from 0 to 1 in order to meet constraints:

$$individual\_data - lowest\_data \Big/ (highest\_data - lowest\_data) \quad (5\text{-}48)$$

This formula is applied to each separate entry of a given set of data. Each entry serves as the individual data in the formula. The lowest entry of the data set serves as the lowest data and the highest entry is the highest data in the formula. The converted data are shown as R_{t-2}, R_{t-1}, and R_t (see Table 6 and 7). The values of R_{t-2}, R_{t-1}, and R_t are used as UCSHONN input and desired output.

In Table 10, the exchange rates for Japanese Yen vs. US Dollars in both 2000 and 2004 are used as test data for UCSHONN. After 20,000 epochs, the simulation error reaches 0.0000% for the Yen/Dollars exchange rate in 2000. Details are in Table 10.

In Table 11, data shows that after 60,000 epochs, the simulation error is 0.0000% for the Yen/Dollars exchange rate in 2004. Also, both Table10 and 11, show the coefficients for the exchange rate models. Based on the output from UCSHONN, the exchange rate model for Japanese Yen Vs US dollars in 2000 can be written as follows:

$$R_t = 0.6971 + 0.2311 * \sin\left(R_{t-1}\right) - 0.3790 * \cos\left(R_{t-2}\right) + 0.1096 * sin^2\left(2R_{t-1}\right)$$
$$-0.5196 * sin^3\left(3R_{t-1}\right) - 0.5659 * sin^4\left(4R_{t-1}\right) - 0.3698 * sin^5\left(5R_{t-1}\right) + 0.3440 * sin^6\left(6R_{t-1}\right)$$
$$-0.4455 * cos^2\left(2R_{t-2}\right) - 0.1089 * cos^3\left(3R_{t-2}\right) - 0.7142 * cos^4\left(4R_{t-2}\right) - 0.1167 * cos^5\left(5R_{t-2}\right)$$
$$+0.3644 * cos^6\left(6R_{t-2}\right) + \sum_{k=1, j=1}^{6} a_{kj} cos^k\left(k * R_{t-2}\right) sin^j\left(j * R_{t-1}\right)$$

49)

246

Table 10. Japanese Yen vs. US Dollar Exchange Rate Analysis (2000)

Date	Japanese Yen/ US Dollars	Data before convert to R_{t-2}	R_{t-2}	Data before convert to R_{t-1}	R_{t-1}	Data before convert to R_t	R_t
Nov-99	104.65						
Dec-99	102.58						
Jan-00	105.30	104.65	0.3040	102.58	0.0000	105.30	0.0000
Feb-00	109.39	102.58	0.0000	105.30	0.3994	109.39	0.5919
Mar-00	106.31	105.30	0.3994	109.39	1.0000	106.31	0.1462
Apr-00	105.63	109.39	1.0000	106.31	0.5477	105.63	0.0478
May-00	108.32	106.31	0.5477	105.63	0.4479	108.32	0.4370
Jun-00	106.13	105.63	0.4479	108.32	0.8429	106.13	0.1201
Jul-00	108.21	108.32	0.8429	106.13	0.5213	108.21	0.4211
Aug-00	108.08	106.13	0.5213	108.21	0.8267	108.08	0.4023
Sep-00	106.84	108.21	0.8267	108.08	0.8076	106.84	0.2229
Oct-00	108.44	108.08	0.8076	106.84	0.6256	108.44	0.4544
Nov-00	109.01	106.84	0.6256	108.44	0.8605	109.01	0.5369
Dec-00	112.21	108.44	0.8605	109.01	0.9442	112.21	1.0000

R_{t-2}	R_{t-1}	R_t					
x=input 0	y=input 1	Z=output		$R_t = \sum_{k=0,j=0}^{6} a_{kj} \cos^k(k * R_{t-2}) \sin^j(j * R_{t-1})$			
0.4479	0.8429	0.1201					

a_{kj}	k=0	k=1	k=2	k=3	k=4	k=5	k=6
j=0	0.6971	-0.3790	-0.4455	-0.1089	-0.7142	-0.1167	0.3644
j=1	0.2311	0.3925	-0.6079	-0.5677	0.6576	0.0344	-1.0445
j=2	0.1096	0.0486	-0.0078	-0.1606	-0.2579	0.0833	-0.4352
j=3	-0.5196	-0.1491	-0.5827	0.1983	0.5528	-0.4081	0.0343
j=4	-0.5659	1.4019	-0.4672	0.2546	-0.0376	0.6464	0.5250
j=5	-0.3698	0.4701	0.8380	0.7653	0.6454	-0.3509	-0.3028
j=6	0.3440	-0.2593	0.0850	-0.1246	-0.8161	-1.0314	0.3107
Sub $\sum$	1.3099	-0.4406	-0.5463	-0.0130	-0.0029	0.0566	-0.2436

US Consumer Price Index Analysis

Let:

$$z = C_t; \ x = C_{t-2}; \ y = C_{t-1}; \ a_{kj}^{\ 0} = a_{kj}$$

Table 11. Japanese Yen vs. US Dollar Exchange Rate Analysis (2004)

Date	Japanese Yen/ US Dollars	Data before convert to R_{t-2}	R_{t-2}	Data before convert to R_{t-1}	R_{t-1}	Data before convert to R_t	R_t
Nov-03	109.18						
Dec-03	107.74						
Jan-04	106.27	109.18	0.4907	107.74	0.4053	106.27	0.2932
Feb-04	106.71	107.74	0.2479	106.27	0.2093	106.71	0.3456
Mar-04	108.52	106.27	0.0000	106.71	0.2680	108.52	0.5614
Apr-04	107.66	106.71	0.0742	108.52	0.5093	107.66	0.4589
May-04	112.20	108.52	0.3794	107.66	0.3947	112.20	1.0000
Jun-04	109.43	107.66	0.2344	112.20	1.0000	109.43	0.6698
Jul-04	109.49	112.20	1.0000	109.43	0.6307	109.49	0.6770
Aug-04	110.23	109.43	0.5329	109.49	0.6387	110.23	0.7652
Sep-04	110.09	109.49	0.5430	110.23	0.7373	110.09	0.7485
Oct-04	108.78	110.23	0.6678	110.09	0.7187	108.78	0.5924
Nov-04	104.70	110.09	0.6442	108.78	0.5440	104.70	0.1061
Dec-04	103.81	108.78	0.4233	104.70	0.0000	103.81	0.0000

R_{t-2}	R_{t-1}	R_t	
x=input 0	y=input 1	Z=output	$$R_t = \sum_{k=0, j=0}^{6} a_{kj} \cos^k(k * R_{t-2}) \sin^j(j * R_{t-1})$$
0.0000	0.2680	0.5614	

a_{kj}	k=0	k=1	k=2	k=3	k=4	k=5	k=6
j=0	0.0005	0.4346	-0.5648	0.6230	0.5479	0.7872	-0.4324
j=1	0.5773	0.7995	0.8272	-0.4217	-0.0067	-0.5834	0.0070
j=2	-0.5283	0.4781	0.3663	-0.2656	-1.1565	-0.8809	0.6540
j=3	0.4060	-0.2691	-0.6332	-0.2581	0.0737	0.4867	-0.4085
j=4	-0.4227	-0.0263	0.3667	-0.9254	0.3035	0.7627	-0.0051
j=5	0.2559	0.9138	0.0368	0.2523	-0.6093	-0.2594	-0.1121
j=6	-0.3610	-0.5928	0.2382	-0.4285	0.2153	-0.1543	0.0497
Sub $\sum$	-0.2199	0.8634	0.0008	-0.4108	0.1342	0.6579	-0.4641

USA Consumer Price Index model by using UCSHONN model 0 is defined as follows:

$$C_t = a_{00} + a_{01} \sin(C_{t-1}) + a_{10} \cos(C_{t-2})$$

$$+ \sum_{j=2}^{n} a_{0j} \sin^j (j*C_{t-1}) + \sum_{j=2}^{n} a_{k0} \cos^k (k*C_{t-2}) + \sum_{j=2}^{6} a_{kj} \cos^k (k*C_{t-2}) \sin^j (j*C_{t-1})$$

50)

In Table 12, US Consumer Price Index (1992-2004) is the test data in this section. After 100,000 epochs, the simulation error reaches 0.0000% for the 1992-2004 US Consumer Price Index. Table 12 provides the coefficients for US consumer Price Index (1992-2004) model. The model can be written as follows.

$$C_t = 1.0579 + 0.2936 * \sin(C_{t-1}) - 0.8893 * \cos(C_{t-2}) - 0.6608 * \sin^2(2C_{t-1})$$

$$+ 0.2960 * \sin^3(3C_{t-1}) - 0.5318 * \sin^4(4C_{t-1}) - 0.5792 * \sin^5(5C_{t-1})$$

$$- 0.3132 * \sin^6(6C_{t-1}) + 0.5705 * \cos^2(2C_{t-2}) - 0.7094 * \cos^3(3C_{t-2}) - 0.2269 * \cos^4(4C_{t-2})$$

$$+ 0.1620 * \cos^5(5C_{t-2}) + 0.0307 * \cos^6(6C_{t-2}) + \sum_{k=1, j=1}^{6} a_{kj} \cos^k (k*C_{t-2}) \sin^j (j*C_{t-1})$$

51)

Japan Consumer Price Index Prediction Simulation

Let:

$$z = J_t; \quad x = J_{t-2}; \quad y = J_{t-1}; \quad a_{kj}{}^0 = a_{kj}$$

Japan Consumer Price Index model by using UCSHOON model 0 is:

$$J_t = a_{00} + a_{01} \sin(J_{t-1}) + a_{10} \cos(J_{t-2})$$

$$+ \sum_{j=2}^{n} a_{0j} \sin^j (j*J_{t-1}) + \sum_{j=2}^{n} a_{k0} \cos^k (k*J_{t-2}) + \sum_{j=2}^{6} a_{kj} \cos^k (k*J_{t-2}) \sin^j (j*J_{t-1})$$

52)

In Table 13, Japan Consumer Price Index (1992-2004) is the test data for USCHONN. After 200,000 epochs, the simulation error is 0.0000% for the 1992-2004 Japan Consumer Price Index. Table 13 shows the coefficients for

Table 12. US Consumer Price Index Analysis (1992-2004)

Date	US CPI	Data before convert to C_{t-2}	C_{t-2}	Data before convert to C_{t-1}	C_{t-1}	Data before convert to C_t	C_t
1990	130.7						
1991	136.2						
1992	140.3	130.7	0.0000	136.2	0.0000	140.3	0.0000
1993	144.5	136.2	0.1118	140.3	0.0858	144.5	0.0864
1994	148.2	140.3	0.1951	144.5	0.1736	148.2	0.1626
1995	152.4	144.5	0.2805	148.2	0.2510	152.4	0.2490
1996	156.9	148.2	0.3557	152.4	0.3389	156.9	0.3416
1997	160.5	152.4	0.4411	156.9	0.4331	160.5	0.4156
1998	163.0	156.9	0.5325	160.5	0.5084	163.0	0.4671
1999	166.6	160.5	0.6057	163.0	0.5607	166.6	0.5412
2000	172.2	163.0	0.6565	166.6	0.6360	172.2	0.6564
2001	177.1	166.6	0.7297	172.2	0.7531	177.1	0.7572
2002	179.9	172.2	0.8435	177.1	0.8556	179.9	0.8148
2003	184.0	177.1	0.9431	179.9	0.9142	184.0	0.8992
2004	188.9	179.9	1.0000	184.0	1.0000	188.9	1.0000

C_{t-2}	C_{t-1}	C_t					
x=input 0	y=input 1	Z=output		$C_t = \sum\limits_{k=0, j=0}^{6} a_{kj} \cos^k(k * C_{t-2}) \sin^j(j * C_{t-1})$			
0.0000	0.0000	0.0000					
a_{kj}	k=0	k=1	k=2	k=3	k=4	k=5	k=6
j=0	1.0579	-0.8893	0.5705	-0.7049	-0.2269	0.1620	0.0307
j=1	0.2936	0.7221	-0.3522	-0.0652	0.7003	-1.2471	-0.1326
j=2	-0.6608	-0.9835	0.8478	0.3926	0.2648	0.4667	-0.3908
j=3	0.2960	0.6595	-0.1415	0.8827	-0.0713	-0.1142	0.3791
j=4	-0.5318	0.4256	0.2436	-0.4823	-0.5585	0.4195	-0.2299
j=5	-0.5792	-0.4201	0.8837	-0.5358	0.1797	-0.9943	-0.6201
j=6	-0.3132	0.4875	-0.0767	-0.4164	-0.1399	-0.5029	0.1857
Sub$\sum$	1.0579	-0.8893	0.5705	-0.7049	-0.2269	0.1620	0.0307

Japan Consumer Price Index (1992-2004). The1992-2004 Japan Consumer Price Index model can be written as follows.

Table 13. Japan Consumer Price Index Analysis (1992-2004)

Date	Japan CPI	Data before convert to J_{t-2}	J_{t-2}	Data before convert to J_{t-1}	J_{t-1}	Data before convert to J_t	J_t
1990	93.10						
1991	96.10						
1992	97.70	93.10	0.0000	96.10	0.0000	97.70	0.0000
1993	98.80	96.10	0.3659	97.70	0.3077	98.80	0.3056
1994	99.30	97.70	0.5610	98.80	0.5192	99.30	0.4444
1995	99.00	98.80	0.6951	99.30	0.6154	99.00	0.3611
1996	99.00	99.30	0.7561	99.00	0.5577	99.00	0.3611
1997	100.60	99.00	0.7195	99.00	0.5577	100.60	0.8056
1998	101.30	99.00	0.7195	100.60	0.8654	101.30	1.0000
1999	100.90	100.60	0.9146	101.30	1.0000	100.90	0.8889
2000	100.00	101.30	1.0000	100.90	0.9231	100.00	0.6389
2001	99.10	100.90	0.9512	100.00	0.7500	99.10	0.3889
2002	98.00	100.00	0.8415	99.10	0.5769	98.00	0.0833
2003	97.70	99.10	0.7317	98.00	0.3654	97.70	0.0000
2004	97.70	98.00	0.5976	97.70	0.3077	97.70	0.0000
J_{t-2}	J_{t-1}	J_t					
x=input 0	y=input 1	Z=output					
0.9146	1.0000	0.8889					

$$J_t = \sum_{k=0,j=0}^{6} a_{kj} \cos^k(k * J_{t-2}) \sin^j(j * J_{t-1})$$

a_{kj}	k=0	k=1	k=2	k=3	k=4	k=5	k=6
j=0	-0.1275	0.6917	1.3996	0.4697	-0.2287	-1.0493	-1.1555
j=1	-0.9274	0.6106	0.6374	0.0933	0.3337	0.3734	0.1258
j=2	-0.8318	0.3397	0.0496	-1.2872	-1.3823	0.3479	0.1871
j=3	0.9529	-0.7762	0.7556	-0.8851	0.2710	-0.3120	-0.7980
j=4	0.1854	0.7115	-0.6467	0.6516	0.1924	-2.0840	-0.9574
j=5	-0.8606	-1.3979	0.4677	0.5297	-0.2723	0.8944	0.8357
j=6	0.7071	-0.2297	-0.0614	-0.0172	0.0925	0.2005	-0.3268
Sub$\sum$	-0.8340	1.7394	0.0906	0.5754	-0.4605	0.0001	-0.2220

$$J_t = -0.1275 - 0.9274 * \sin\left(J_{t-1}\right) + 0.6917 * \cos\left(J_{t-2}\right) - 0.8318 * \sin^2\left(2J_{t-1}\right)$$
$$+0.9529 * \sin^3\left(3J_{t-1}\right) + 0.1854 * \sin^4\left(4J_{t-1}\right) - 0.8606 * \sin^5\left(5J_{t-1}\right)$$
$$+0.7017 * \sin^6\left(6J_{t-1}\right) + 1.3996 * \cos^2\left(2J_{t-2}\right) + 0.4697 * \cos^3\left(3J_{t-2}\right) - 0.2287 * \cos^4\left(4J_{t-2}\right)$$
$$-1.0493 * \cos^5\left(5J_{t-2}\right) - 1.1555 * \cos^6\left(6J_{t-2}\right) + \sum_{k=1, j=1}^{6} a_{kj} \cos^k\left(k * J_{t-2}\right) \sin^j\left(j * J_{t-1}\right)$$

53)

CONCLUSION

Three nonlinear neural network models, UCSHONN, UCCHONN, and USSHONN, that are part of the Ultra High Frequency Trigonometric Higher Order Neural Networks (UTHONN), are developed. Based on the structures of UTHONN, this provides three model learning algorithm formulae. This chapter tests the UCSHONN model using ultra high frequency data and the running results are compared with THONN, PHONN, and ERER models. Experimental results show that UTHONN models are 4 – 9% better than other Polynomial Higher Order Neural Network (PHONN) and Trigonometric Higher Order Neural Network (THONN) models. The results also show that the UTHONN model is 3 - 12% better than exchange equilibrium (ERER) models. Using the UTHONN models, models are developed for Yan vs. US dollar exchange rate, US consumer price index, and Japan consumer price index with an error reaching 0.0000%.

One of the topics for future research is to continue building models using UTHONN for different data series. The coefficients of the higher order models will be studied not only using artificial neural network techniques, but also statistical methods. Using nonlinear functions to model and analyze time series data will be a major goal in the future.

FUTHER RESEARCH DIRECTIONS

One of the topics for future research is to continue building models using Higher Order artificial Neural Networks (HONNs) for different data series. The coefficients of the higher order models will be studied not only using artificial neural network techniques, but also statistical methods. Using nonlinear functions to model and analyze time series data will be a major goal in the future. The future research direction aims at the construction of an automatic model selection simulation and prediction systems based on HONNs. There are many kinds of data, for example nonlinear, discontinuous, unsmooth, which are difficult to simulate and predict. One unsolved issue in HONNs is that there is no single higher order neural network, which can accurately simulate piecewise and discontinuous functions. Future research in this area can develop new functional-neuron multi-layer feed-forward HONN models to approximate any continuous, unsmooth, piecewise continuous, and discontinuous special functions to any degree of accuracy. Traditional methods of forecasting are highly inaccurate. Artificial HONNs have strong pattern finding ability and better accuracy in nonlinear simulation and prediction. However, currently the solution to automate the choice of the optimal HONN models for simulation and prediction is still not available. A model auto-selection prediction system will be studied in the future based on the adaptive HONNs. This study has a good chance of finding the solutions to automate the choice of the optimal HONN models for simulation and prediction.

Benefits of this study will be:

- This study draws together the skills and expertise of researchers from disciplines including information science, computer science, business, and economics.
- This study can be further developed for other financial simulation and prediction such as forecasting stock market and currency futures.

Immediate outcomes will be the construction of new higher order neural network models, and the construction of innovative forecasting techniques which will be able to manipulate both normal situations and changing situations. Long term outcomes will be the development of a practical simulation and prediction system in real world conditions based on new HONN models and techniques.

REFERENCES

Azoff, E. (1994). *Neural Network Time Series Forecasting of Financial Markets*. New York: Wiley.

Balke, N. S., & Fomby, T. B. (1997). Threshold cointegration. *International Economic Review, 38*(3), 627–645. doi:10.2307/2527284

Barron, R., Gilstrap, L., & Shrier, S. (1987). Polynomial and Neural Networks: Analogies and Engineering Applications. In *Proceedings of International Conference of Neural Networks* (vol. 2, pp. 431-439). New York: Academic Press.

Bierens, H. J., & Ploberger, W. (1997). Asymptotic theory of integrated conditional moment tests. *Econometrica, 65*(5), 1129–1151. doi:10.2307/2171881

Blum, E., & Li, K. (1991). Approximation theory and feed-forward networks. *Neural Networks, 4*(4), 511–515. doi:10.1016/0893-6080(91)90047-9

Box, G. E. P., & Jenkins, G. M. (1976). *Time Series Analysis: Forecasting and Control. San Francisco*. Holden-Day.

Chakraborty, K., Mehrotra, K., Mohan, C., & Ranka, S. (1992). Forecasting the behavior of multivariate time series using neural networks. *Neural Networks, 5*(6), 961–970. doi:10.1016/S0893-6080(05)80092-9

Chang, Y., & Park, J. Y. (2003). Index models with integrated time series. *Journal of Econometrics, 114*(1), 73–106. doi:10.1016/S0304-4076(02)00220-8

Chen, C. T., & Chang, W. D. (1996). A feed-forward neural network with function shape autotuning. *Neural Networks, 9*(4), 627–641. doi:10.1016/0893-6080(96)00006-8

Chen, T., & Chen, H. (1993). Approximations of continuous functional by neural networks with application to dynamic systems. *IEEE Transactions on Neural Networks, 4*(6), 910–918. doi:10.1109/72.286886 PMID:18276521

Chen, T., & Chen, H. (1995). Approximation capability to functions of several variables, nonlinear functionals, and operators by radial basis function neural networks. *IEEE Transactions on Neural Networks, 6*(4), 904–910. doi:10.1109/72.392252 PMID:18263378

Chen, X., & Shen, X. (1998). Sieve extremum estimates for weakly dependent data. *Econometrica, 66*(2), 289–314. doi:10.2307/2998559

Chenug, Y. W., & Chinn, M. D. (1999). *Macroeconomic implications of the Beliefs and Behavior of Foreign exchange Traders.* NBER, Working paper no. 7414.

Elbradawi, I. A. (1994). Estimating Long-Run Equilibrium Real Exchange Rates. In J. Williamson (Ed.), *Estimating Equilibrium Exchange Rates* (pp. 93–131). Institute for International Economics.

Fahlman, S. (1988). Faster-learning Variations on Back-Propagation: An Empirical Study. *Proceedings of 1988 Connectionist Models Summer School.*

Gardeazabal, J., & Regulez, M. (1992). *The monetary model of exchange rates and cointegration.* New York: Springer-Verlag. doi:10.1007/978-3-642-48858-0

Gorr, W. L. (1994). Research prospective on neural network forecasting. *International Journal of Forecasting, 10*(1), 1–4. doi:10.1016/0169-2070(94)90044-2

Granger, C. W. J. (1981). Some properties of time series data and their use in econometric model specification. *Journal of Econometrics, 16*(1), 121–130. doi:10.1016/0304-4076(81)90079-8

Granger, C. W. J. (1995). Modeling nonlinear relationships between extended-memory variables. *Econometrica, 63*(2), 265–279. doi:10.2307/2951626

Granger, C. W. J. (2001). Spurious regressions in econometrics. In B. H. Baltagi (Ed.), *A Companion to Theoretical Econometrics* (pp. 557–561). Oxford: Blackwell.

Granger, C. W. J., & Bates, J. (1969). The combination of forecasts. *Operational Research Quarterly, 20*(4), 451–468. doi:10.1057/jors.1969.103

Granger, C. W. J., & Lee, T. H. (1990). Multicointegration. In G. F. Rhodes Jr & T. B. Fomby (Eds.), *Advances in Econometrics: Cointegration, Spurious Regressions and Unit Roots* (pp. 17–84). New York: JAI Press.

Granger, C. W. J., & Newbold, P. (1974). Spurious regressions in econometrics. *Journal of Econometrics, 2*(2), 111–120. doi:10.1016/0304-4076(74)90034-7

Granger, C. W. J., & Swanson, N. R. (1996). Further developments in study of cointegrated variables. *Oxford Bulletin of Economics and Statistics*, *58*, 374–386.

Granger, C. W. J., & Weiss, A. A. (1983). Time series analysis of error-correction models. In S. Karlin, T. Amemiya, & L. A. Goodman (Eds.), Studies in Econometrics, Time Series and Multivariate Statistics (pp. 255-278). Academic Press. doi:10.1016/B978-0-12-398750-1.50018-8

Hans, P., & Draisma, G. (1997). Recognizing changing seasonal patterns using artificial neural networks. *Journal of Econometrics*, *81*(1), 273–280. doi:10.1016/S0304-4076(97)00047-X

Hornik, K. (1993). Some new results on neural network approximation. *Neural Networks*, *6*(8), 1069–1072. doi:10.1016/S0893-6080(09)80018-X

Kilian, L., & Taylor, M. P. (2003). Why is it so difficult to beat the random walk forecast of exchange rate? *Journal of International Economics*, *60*(1), 85–107. doi:10.1016/S0022-1996(02)00060-0

MacDonald, R., & Marsh, I. (1999). *Exchange Rate Modeling*. Boston: Kluwer Academic Publishers. doi:10.1007/978-1-4757-2997-9_6

Meese, R., & Rogoff, K. (1983A). Empirical exchange rate models of the seventies: Do they fit out of sample. *Journal of International Economics*, *14*(1-2), 3–24. doi:10.1016/0022-1996(83)90017-X

Meese, R., & Rogoff, K. (1983B). The out-of-samples failure of empirical exchange rate models: sampling error or misspecification. In J. A. Frenkel (Ed.), *Exchange rate and International macroeconomics*. Chicago: Chicago University Press and National Bureau of Economic Research.

Psaltis, D., Park, C., & Hong, J. (1988). Higher Order Associative Memories and their Optical Implementations. *Neural Networks*, *1*(2), 149–163. doi:10.1016/0893-6080(88)90017-2

Redding, N., Kowalczyk, A., & Downs, T. (1993). Constructive high-order network algorithm that is polynomial time. *Neural Networks*, *6*(7), 997–1010. doi:10.1016/S0893-6080(09)80009-9

Rumelhart, D. G., Hinton, G., & Williams, R. (1986). Learning Representations by Back-Propagating Errors. In D. Rumelhart & J. McClelland (Eds.), *Parallel Distributed Processing: Explorations in the Microstructure of Cognition* (Vol. 1). Cambridge, MA: MIT Press.

Scarselli, F., & Tsoi, A. C. (1998). Universal approximation using feed-forward neural networks: A survey of some existing methods, and some new results. *Neural Networks, 11*(1), 15–37. doi:10.1016/S0893-6080(97)00097-X PMID:12662846

Shintani, M., & Linton, O. (2004). Nonparametric neural network estimation of Lyapunov exponents and direct test for chaos. *Journal of Econometrics, 120*(1), 1–33. doi:10.1016/S0304-4076(03)00205-7

Synder, L. (2006). *Fluency with Information Technology*. Boston, MA: Addison Wesley.

Taylor, M. P. (1995). The economics of exchange rates. *Journal of Economic Literature, 33*, 13–47.

Taylor, M. P., & Peel, D. A. (2000). Nonlinear adjustment, long run equilibrium and exchange rate fundamentals. *Journal of International Money and Finance, 19*(1), 33–53. doi:10.1016/S0261-5606(99)00044-3

Taylor, M. P., Peel, D. A., & Sarno, L. (2001). Nonlinear adjustments in real exchange rate: Towards a solution to the purchasing power parity puzzles. *International Economic Review, 42*(4), 1015–1042. doi:10.1111/1468-2354.00144

Vetenskapsakademien, K. (2003). Time-series econometrics: Co-integration and Autoregressive Conditional Heteroskedasticity. *Advanced information on the Bank of Sweden Prize in Economic Sciences in Memory of Alfred Nobel.*

Werbos, P. (1994). *The Roots of Backpropagation: from Ordered Derivatives to Neural Networks and Political Forecasting*. New York: Wiley.

Williamson, J. (1994). *Estimating Equilibrium Exchange Rates*. Institute for International Economics.

Zell, A. (1995). *Stuttgart Neural Network Simulator V4.1*. University of Stuttgart, Institute for Parallel & Distributed High-Performance Systems. ftp.informatik.uni-stuttgart.de

Zhang, M., & Fulcher, J. (2004). Higher Order Neural Networks for Satellite Weather Prediction. In J. Fulcher & L. C. Jain (Eds.), Applied Intelligent Systems (Vol. 153, pp. 17-57). Springer. doi:10.1007/978-3-540-39972-8_2

Zhang, M., Fulcher, J., & Scofield, R. A. (1996) Neural network group models for estimating rainfall from satellite images. In *Proceedings of World Congress on Neural Networks* (pp.897-900). San Diego, CA: Academic Press.

Zhang, M., Murugesan, S., & Sadeghi, M. (1995). Polynomial higher order neural network for economic data simulation. In *Proceedings of International Conference on Neural Information Processing* (pp. 493-496). Beijing, China: Academic Press.

Zhang, M., Xu, S., & Fulcher, J. (2002). Neuron-Adaptive Higher Order Neural Network Models for Automated Financial Data Modeling. *IEEE Transactions on Neural Networks*, *13*(1), 188–204. doi:10.1109/72.977302 PMID:18244418

Zhang, M., Zhang, J. C., & Fulcher, J. (2000). Higher order neural network group models for data approximation. *International Journal of Neural Systems*, *10*(2), 123–142. doi:10.1142/S0129065700000119 PMID:10939345

Zhang, M., Zhang, J. C., & Keen, S. (1999). Using THONN system for higher frequency non-linear data simulation & prediction. In *Proceedings of IASTED International Conference on Artificial Intelligence and Soft Computing* (pp. 320-323). Honolulu, HI: Academic Press.

ADDITIONAL READING

Bengtsson, M. (1990). *Higher Order Artificial Neural Networks*. Diano Pub Co.

Chen, Y., Jiang, Y., & Xu, J. (2003). Dynamic properties and a new learning mechanism in higher order neural networks. *Neurocomputing*, *50*(January), 17–30.

Crane, J., & Zhang, M. (2005). Data Simulation Using SINCHONN Model, *Proceedings of IASTED International Conference on Computational Intelligence* (pp. 50-55).Calgary, Canada.

Fulcher, J., Zhang, M., & Xu, S. (2006). The Application of Higher-Order Neural Networks to Financial Time Series. In J. Kamruzzaman (Ed.), *Artificial Neural Networks in Finance, Health and Manufacturing: Potential and Challenges* (pp. 80–108). IGI. doi:10.4018/978-1-59140-670-9.ch005

Giles, L., Griffin, R., & Maxwell, T. (1988). Encoding Geometric Invariances in High-Order Neural Networks. *Proceedings Neural Information Processing Systems*, 301-309.

Giles, L., & Maxwell, T. (1987). Learning, Invariance and Generalization in High-Order Neural Networks. *Applied Optics*, *26*(23), 4972–4978. doi:10.1364/AO.26.004972 PMID:20523475

He, Z., & Siyal, M. Y. (1999, August). Improvement on higher-order neural networks for invariant object recognition. *Neural Processing Letters*, *10*(1), 49–55. doi:10.1023/A:1018610829733

Hornik, K. (1991). Approximation Capabilities of Multilayer Feedforward Networks. *Neural Networks*, *4*(2), 251–257. doi:10.1016/0893-6080(91)90009-T

Hu, S., & Yan, P. (1992). Level-by-Level Learning for Artificial Neural Groups. *Electronica Sinica*, *20*(10), 39–43.

Kanaoka, T., Chellappa, R., Yoshitaka, M., & Tomita, S. (1992). A Higher-order neural network for distortion unvariant pattern recognition. *Pattern Recognition Letters*, *13*(12), 837–841. doi:10.1016/0167-8655(92)90082-B

Karayiannis, N., & Venetsanopoulos, A. (1993). *Artificial Neural Networks: Learning Algorithms, Performance Evaluation and Applications*. Boston, MA: Kluwer. doi:10.1007/978-1-4757-4547-4

Karayiannis, N. B., & Venetsanopoulos, A. N. (1995). On the training and performance of High-order neural networks. *Mathematical Biosciences*, *129*(2), 143–168. doi:10.1016/0025-5564(94)00057-7 PMID:7549218

Lee, M., Lee, S. Y., & Park, C. H. (1992). Neural controller of nonlinear dynamic systems using higher order neural networks. *Electronics Letters*, *28*(3), 276–277. doi:10.1049/el:19920170

Leshno, M., Lin, V., Pinkus, A., & Schoken, S. (1993). Multi-Layer Feedforward Networks with a Non-Polynomial Activation Can Approximate Any Function. *Neural Networks*, *6*(6), 861–867. doi:10.1016/S0893-6080(05)80131-5

Manykin, E. A., & Belov, M. N. (1991). Higher-order neural networks and photo-echo effect. *Neural Networks*, *4*(3), 417–420. doi:10.1016/0893-6080(91)90079-K

Park, S., Smith, M. J. T., & Mersereau, R. M. (2000, October). Target Recognition Based on Directional Filter Banks and higher-order neural network. *Digital Signal Processing, 10*(4), 297–308. doi:10.1006/dspr.2000.0376

Shin, Y. (1991). The Pi-Sigma Network: An Efficient Higher-Order Neural Network for Pattern Classification and Function Approximation. *Proceedings of International Joint Conference on Neural Networks, I,* 13–18.

Spirkovska, L., & Reid, M. B. (1992, September). Robust position, scale, and rotation invariant object recognition using higher-order neural networks. *Pattern Recognition, 25*(9), 975–985. doi:10.1016/0031-3203(92)90062-N

Tai, H., & Jong, T. (1990). Information storage in high-order neural networks with unequal neural activity. *Journal of the Franklin Institute, 327*(1), 129–141. doi:10.1016/0016-0032(90)90061-M

Venkatesh, S. S., & Baldi, P. (1991, September). Programmed interactions in higher-order neural networks: Maximal capacity. *Journal of Complexity, 7*(3), 316–337. doi:10.1016/0885-064X(91)90040-5

Wilcox, C. (1991). Understanding Hierarchical Neural Network Behavior: A Renormalization Group Approach. *Journal of Physics. A. Mathematical Nuclear and General, 24,* 2644–2655.

Zhang, J. (2005). *Polynomial full naïve estimated misclassification cost models for financial distress prediction using higher order neural network. 14th Annual Research Work Shop on: Artificial Intelligence and Emerging Technologies in Accounting.* San Francisco, CA: Auditing, and Ta.

Zhang, J. (2006). *Linear and nonlinear models for the power of chief elected officials and debt.* Pittsburgh, PA: Mid-Atlantic Region American Accounting Association.

Zhang, M., Fulcher, J., & Scofield, R. (1997). Rainfalll estimation using artificial neural network group. *International Journal of Neurlcomputing, 16*(2), 97–115. doi:10.1016/S0925-2312(96)00022-7

Zhang, M., Zhang, J. C., & Fulcher, J. (2000, April). Higher order neural network group models for data approximation. *International Journal of Neural Systems, 10*(2), 123–142. doi:10.1142/S0129065700000119 PMID:10939345

KEY TERMS AND DEFINITIONS

ERER: Real exchange rates.

HONN: Artificial higher order neural network.

PHONN: Artificial polynomial higher order neural network.

THONN: Artificial trigonometric higher order neural network.

UCCHONN: Artificial ultra-high frequency cosine and cosine higher order neural network.

USSHONN: Artificial ultra-high frequency sine and sine higher order neural network.

UTHONN: Artificial ultra-high frequency trigonometric higher order neural network.

Chapter 6
Financial Data Prediction by Artificial Sine and Cosine Trigonometric Higher Order Neural Networks

ABSTRACT

This chapter develops two new nonlinear artificial higher order neural network models. They are sine and sine higher order neural networks (SIN-HONN) and cosine and cosine higher order neural networks (COS-HONN). Financial data prediction using SIN-HONN and COS-HONN models are tested. Results show that SIN-HONN and COS-HONN models are good models for some sine feature only or cosine feature only financial data simulation and prediction compared with polynomial higher order neural network (PHONN) and trigonometric higher order neural network (THONN) models.

INTRODUCTION

The contributions of this chapter will be:

- Introduce the background of HONNs with the applications of HONNs in prediction area.
- Develop new HONN models called SIN-HONN and COS-HONN for financial data prediction.

DOI: 10.4018/978-1-7998-3563-9.ch006

- Provide the SIN-HONN and COS-HONN learning algorithm and weight update formulae.
- Compare SIN-HONN and COS-HONN with PHONN and THONN for data prediction.

This chapter is organized as follows: Section BACKGROUND gives the background knowledge of HONNs and introduction to applications using HONN in the data prediction area. Section SIN-HONN AND COS-HONN MODELS introduces both SIN-HONN structure and COS-HONN structure. Section LEARNING ALGORITHM OF SIN-HONN and COS-HONN MODELS provides the SIN-HONN model and COS-HONN model update formula, learning algorithms, and convergence theories. Section FINANCIAL DATA PREDICTION USING HONN MODELS compares SIN-HONN and COS-HONN models with other HONN models and shows the results for data prediction using SIN-HONN and COS-HONN models.

BACKGROUND

Background of Higher-Order Neural Networks (HONNs)

Although traditional Artificial Neural Network (ANN) models are recognized for their great performance in pattern matching, pattern recognition, and mathematical function approximation, they are often stuck in local, rather than global minima. In addition, ANNs take unacceptably long time to converge in practice (Fulcher, Zhang, and Xu 2006). Moreover, ANNs are unable to manage non-smooth, discontinuous training data, and complex mappings in financial time series simulation and prediction. ANNs are 'black box' in nature, which means the explanations for their output are not obvious. This leads to the motivation for studies on Higher Order Neural Networks (HONNs).

HONN includes the neuron activation functions, preprocessing of the neuron inputs, and connections to more than one layer (Bengtsson, 1990). In this chapter, HONN refers to the neuron type, which can be linear, power, multiplicative, sigmoid, logarithmic, etc. The first-order neural networks can be formulated by using linear neurons that are only capable of capturing first-order correlations in the training data (Giles & Maxwell, 1987). The second order or above HONNs involve higher-order correlations in the training data that require more complex neuron activation functions (Barron, Gilstrap & Shrier, 1987; Giles & Maxwell, 1987; Psaltis, Park & Hong, 1988). Neurons which include terms up to and including degree-k are referred to as k*th*-order neurons (Lisboa and Perantonis, 1991).

Rumelhart, Hinton, and McClelland (1986) develop 'sigma-pi' neurons where they show that the generalized standard Backpropagation algorithm can be applied to simple additive neurons. Both Hebbian and Perceptron learning rules can be employed when no hidden layers are involved (Shin 1991). The performance of first order ANNs can be improved by utilizing sophisticated learning algorithms (Karayiannis and Venetsanopoulos, 1993). Redding, Kowalczy and Downs (1993) develop a constructive HONN algorithm. Zhang and Fulcher (2004) develop Polynomial, Trigonometric and other HONN models. Giles, Griffin and Maxwell (1988) and Lisboa and Pentonis (1991) show that the multiplicative interconnections within ANNs have been used in many applications, including invariant pattern recognition.

Others suggest groups of individual neurons (Willcox, 1991; Hu and Pan, 1992). ANNs can simulate any nonlinear functions to any degree of accuracy (Hornik, 1991; and Leshno, 1993). Zhang, Fulcher, and Scofield (1997) show that ANN groups offer superior performance compared with ANNs when dealing with discontinuous and non-smooth piecewise nonlinear functions. Compared with Polynomial Higher Order Neural Network (PHONN) and Trigonometric Higher Order Neural Network (THONN), Neural Adaptive Higher Order Neural Network (NAHONN) offers more flexibility and more accurate approximation capability. Since using NAHONN the hidden layer variables are adjustable (Zhang, Xu, and Fulcher, 2002). In addition, Zhang, Xu, and Fulcher (2002) proves that NAHONN groups can approximate any kinds of piecewise continuous function, to any degree of accuracy. In addition, these models are capable of automatically selecting both the optimum model for a time series and the appropriate model order.

Jeffries (1989) presents a specific HONN design which can store any of the binomial n-strings for error-correcting decoding of any binary string code. Tai and Jong (1990) show why the probability of the states of neurons being active and passive can always be chosen equally. Manykin and Belov (1991) propose an optical scheme of the second order HONN and show the importance of an additional time coordinate inherent in the photo-echo effect.

Venkatesh and Baldi (1991) study the estimation of the maximum number of states that can be stable in higher order extensions of the HONN models. Estevez and Okabe (1991) provide a piecewise linear HONN with the structure consisting of two layers of modifiable weights. HONN is seven times faster than that of standard feedforward neural networks when simulating the XOR/ parity problem.

Spirkovska and Reid (1992) find that HONNs can reduce the training time significantly, since distortion invariance can be built into the architecture of the HONNs. Kanaoka, Chellappa, Yoshitaka, and Tomita (1992) show that a single layer of HONN is effective for scale, rotation, and shift invariance recognition. Chang, Lin, and Cheung (1993) generalize back propagation algorithm for multi-layer HONNs, and discuss the two basic structures, the standard form and the polynomial form. Based on their simulation results, both standard and polynomial HONNs can recognize noisy data under rotation up to 70% and noisy irrational data up to 94%. Spirkovska and Reid (1994) point out that invariances can be built directly into the architecture of a HONN. Thus, for 2D object recognition, the HONN needs to be trained on just one view of each object class and HONNs have distinct advantages for position, scale, and rotation-invariant object recognition. By modifying the constraints imposed on the weights in HONNs (He and Siyal, 1999) the performance of a HONN with respect to distortion can be improved. Park, Smith, and Mersereau (2000) combine maximally decimated directional filter banks with HONNs. The new approach is effective in enhancing the discrimination power of the HONN inputs. Chen, Jiang, and Xu (2003) deduce a higher order projection learning mechanism. Numerical simulations to clarify the merits of the HONN associative memory and the potential applications of the new learning rule are presented.

Artificial Neural Network (ANN) has been widely used in prediction area. Durbin and Rumelhart (1989) study a computationally powerful and biologically plausible extension to backpropagation networks. Yapo, Embrechets, and Cathey (1992) analyze prediction of critical heat using a hybrid kohon-backpropagation neural network intelligent. Moon and Chang (1994) experiment classification and prediction of the critical heat flux using fuzzy clustering and artificial neural networks. Charitou and Charalambous (1996) show the prediction of earnings using financial statement information with logic models and artificial neural networks. Doulamis, Doulamis, and Kollias (2000) research recursive nonlinear models for online traffic prediction of VBR MPEG Coded video sources. Atiya (2001) seeks bankruptcy prediction for credit risk using neural networks. Su, Fukuda, Jia, and Morita (2002) look into application of an artificial neural network in reactor thermo hydraulic problem which related to prediction of critical heat flux. Doulamis, Doulamis, and Kollias, (2003) revise an adaptable neural network model for recursive nonlinear traffic prediction and modeling of MPEG video sources. Sanchez,

Alanis, and Rico (2004) expose electric load demand prediction using neural networks trained by Kalman filtering. Shawver (2005) scrutinize merger premium predictions using neural network approach.

Vaziri, Hojabri, Erfani, Monsey, and Nilforooshan (2007) disclose critical heat flux prediction by using radial basis function and multilayer perceptron neural networks. Welch, Ruffing, and Venayagamoorthy (2009) display comparison of feed-forward and feedback neural network architectures for short term wind speed prediction.

Artificial Higher Order Neural Network (HONN) has been widely used in the prediction areas as well. Saad, Prokhorov, and Wunsch (1998) provide comparative study of stock trend prediction using time delay recurrent and probabilistic neural networks. Zhang and Fulcher (2004) grant higher order neural networks for satellite weather prediction. Fulcher, Zhang, and Xu (2006) demonstrate an application of higher-order neural networks to financial time series prediction.

Knowles, Hussain, Dereby, Lisboa, and Dunis (2009) develop higher order neural networks with Bayesian confidence measure for the prediction of the EUR/USD exchange rate. The higher order neural networks can be considered a 'stripped-down' version of MLPs, where joint activation terms are used, relieving the network of the task of learning the relationships between the inputs. The predictive performance of the network is tested with the EUR/USD exchange rate and evaluated using standard financial criteria including the annualized return on investment, showing an 8% increase in the return compared with the MLP. The output of the networks that give the highest annualized return in each category was subjected to a Bayesian based confidence measure.

Shi, Tan, and Ge (2009) expand automatically identifying predictor variables for stock return prediction and address nonlinear problem by developing a technique consisting of a top-down part using an artificial Higher Order Neural Network (HONN) model and a bottom-up part based on a Bayesian Network (BN) model to automatically identify predictor variables for the stock return prediction from a large financial variable set. Our study provides an operational guidance for using HONN and BN in selecting predictor variables from many financial variables to support the prediction of the stock return, including the prediction of future stock return value and future stock return movement trends.

Chen, Wu, and Wu (2009) focus foreign exchange rate forecasting using higher order flexible neural tree and establish that forecasting exchange rates is an important financial problem that is receiving increasing attention especially because of its difficulty and practical applications. In this chapter, we apply Higher Order Flexible Neural Trees (HOFNTs), which can design flexible Artificial Neural Network (ANN) architectures automatically, to forecast the foreign exchange rates. To demonstrate the efficiency of HOFNTs, we consider three different datasets in our forecast performance analysis. The data sets used are daily foreign exchange rates obtained from the Pacific Exchange Rate Service. The data comprises of the US dollar exchange rate against Euro, Great Britain Pound (GBP) and Japanese Yen (JPY). Under the HOFNT framework, we consider the Gene Expression Programming (GEP) approach and the Grammar Guided Genetic Programming (GGGP) approach to evolve the structure of HOFNT. The particle swarm optimization algorithm is employed to optimize the free parameters of the two different HOFNT models. This chapter briefly explains how the two different learning paradigms could be formulated using various methods and then investigates whether they can provide a reliable forecast model for foreign exchange rates. Simulation results are shown the effectiveness of the proposed methods.

Hussain, and Liatsis (2009) learn a novel recurrent polynomial neural network for financial time series prediction and this research is concerned with the development of a novel artificial higher-order neural networks architecture called the recurrent Pi-sigma neural network. The proposed artificial neural network combines the advantages of both higher-order architectures in terms of the multi-linear interactions between inputs, as well as the temporal dynamics of recurrent neural networks, and produces highly accurate one-step ahead of predictions of the foreign currency exchange rates, as compared to other feed-forward and recurrent structures.

Selviah, and Shawash (2009) generalize correlation higher order neural networks for financial time series prediction and develop a generalized correlation higher order neural network design. Their performance is compared with that of first order networks, conventional higher order neural network designs, and higher order linear regression networks for financial time series prediction. The correlation higher order neural network design is shown to give the highest accuracy for prediction of stock market share prices and share indices. The simulations compare the performance for three different training algorithms, stationary versus non-stationary input data, different numbers of neurons in the hidden layer and several generalized correlation higher order neural network designs. Generalized correlation higher order linear regression networks are also introduced, and two designs are shown by simulation to give good correct direction prediction and higher prediction accuracies, particularly for long-term predictions, than other linear regression networks for the prediction of inter-bank lending risk Libor and Swap interest rate yield curves. The simulations compare the performance for different input data sample lag lengths.

Onwubolu (2009) tests the artificial higher order neural networks in time series prediction and describes real world problems of nonlinear and chaotic processes, which make them hard to model and predict. This chapter first compares the neural network (NN) and the artificial higher order neural network (HONN) and then presents commonly known neural network architectures and several HONN architectures. The time series prediction problem is formulated as a system identification problem, where the input to the system is the past values of a time series, and its desired output is the future values of a time series. The polynomial neural network (PNN) is then chosen as the HONN for application to the time series prediction problem. This chapter presents the application of HONN model to the nonlinear time series prediction problems of three major international currency exchange rates, as well as two key U.S. interest rates—the Federal funds rate and the yield on the 5-year U.S. Treasury note. Empirical results indicate that the proposed method is competitive with other approaches for the exchange rate problem and can be used as a feasible solution for interest rate forecasting problem. This implies that the HONN model can be used as a feasible solution for exchange rate forecasting as well as for interest rate forecasting.

Ghazali, and Al-Jumeily (2009) offer the application of Pi-Sigma neural networks and ridge polynomial neural networks to financial time series prediction and discuss the use of two artificial Higher Order Neural Networks (HONNs) models; the Pi-Sigma Neural Networks and the Ridge Polynomial Neural Networks, in financial time series forecasting. The networks were used to forecast the upcoming trends of three noisy financial signals; the exchange rate between the US Dollar and the Euro, the exchange rate between the Japanese Yen and the Euro, and the United States 10-year government bond. The authors systematically investigate a method of pre-processing the signals in order to reduce the trends in them. The performance of the networks is benchmarked against the performance of Multilayer Perceptron. From the simulation results, the predictions clearly demonstrated that HONNs models, particularly Ridge Polynomial Neural Networks generate higher profit returns with fast convergence, therefore show considerable promise as a decision-making tool. It is hoped that individual investor could benefit from the use of this forecasting tool.

Sanchez, Alanis, and Rico (2009) intent the electric load demand and electricity prices forecasting using higher order neural networks Trained by

Kalman Filtering and proposes the use of *Higher Order Neural Networks* (HONNs) trained with an *extended Kalman filter* based algorithm to predict the electric load demand as well as the electricity prices, with beyond a horizon of 24 hours. Due to the *chaotic behavior* of the electrical markets, it is not advisable to apply the traditional forecasting techniques used for time series; the results presented here confirm that HONNs can very well capture the complexity underlying electric load demand and electricity prices. The proposed neural network model produces very accurate next day predictions and, prognosticates with very good accuracy, a week-ahead demand and price forecasts.

Eskander, and Atiya (2013) derive symbolic function network for the application to telecommunication networks prediction and introduce that Quality of Service (QoS) of telecommunication networks could be enhanced by applying predictive control methods. Such controllers rely on utilizing good and fast (real-time) predictions of the network traffic and quality parameters. Accuracy and recall speed of the traditional Neural Network models are not satisfactory to support such critical real-time applications. The Symbolic Function Network (SFN) is a HONN-like model that was originally motivated by the current needs of developing more enhanced and fast predictors for such applications. In this chapter, authors use the SFN model to design fast and accurate predictors for the telecommunication networks quality control applications. Three predictors are designed and tested for the network traffic, packet loss, and round-trip delay. This chapter aims to open a door for researchers to investigate the applicability of SFN in other prediction tasks and to develop more accurate and faster predictors.

Ricalde, Catzin, Alanis, and Sanchez (2013) investigate time series forecasting via. higher order neural network trained with the extended Kalman filter for smart grid applications and present the design of a neural network which combines higher order terms in its input layer and an Extended Kalman Filter (EKF) based algorithm for its training. The neural network-based scheme is defined as a Higher Order Neural Network (HONN) and its applicability is illustrated by means of time series forecasting for three important variables present in smart grids: Electric Load Demand (ELD), Wind Speed (WS) and Wind Energy Generation (WEG). The proposed model is trained and tested using real data values taken from a microgrid system in the UADY School of Engineering. The length of the regression vector is determined via the Lipschitz quotient's methodology.

SIN-HONN AND COS-HONN MODELS

Figure 1. SIN-HONN Architecture

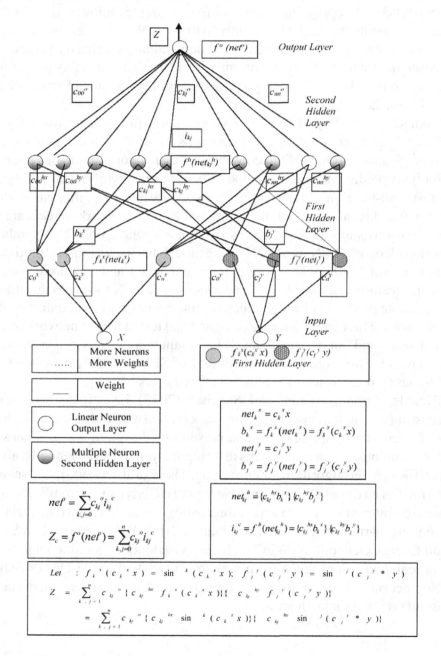

Figure 2. COS-HONN Architecture

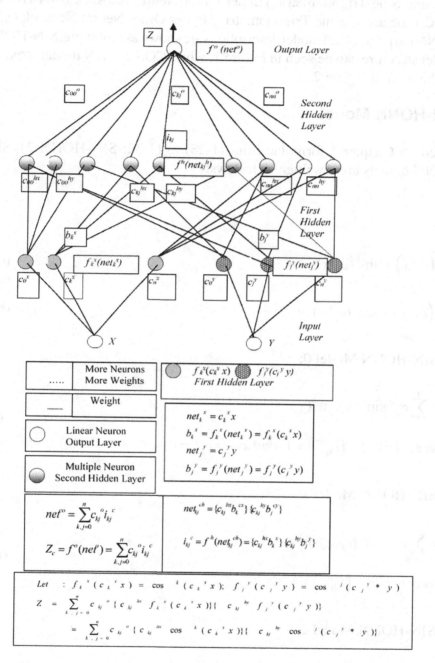

Sine and Sine Trigonometric Higher Order Neural Network (SIN-HONN) and Cosine and Cosine Trigonometric Higher Order Neural Network (SIN-HONN) structures and model descriptions are shown as following. SIN-HONN model structure can be seen in Figure 1, while COS-HONN model structure can be seen in Figure 2.

SIN-HONN Model

Based on Chapter 1 formulae from (1-28) to (1-32: SIN-HONN 2), SIN-HONN models are rewritten as follows:

Let

$$f_k^x \left(c_k^{\ x} x \right) = \sin^k \left(c_k^{\ x} x \right) \tag{6-1}$$

$$f_j^y \left(c_j^{\ y} y \right) = \sin^j \left(c_j^{\ y} y \right) \tag{6-2}$$

SIN-HONN Model 0:

$$z = \sum_{k,j=0}^{n} c_{kj}^{\ o} \sin^k (x) \sin^j (y) \tag{6-3}$$

$$where: \left(c_{kj}^{\ hx} \right) = \left(c_{kj}^{\ hy} \right) = 1 \ and \ c_k^{\ x} = c_j^{\ y} = 1$$

SIN-HONN Model 1:

$$z = \sum_{k,j=0}^{n} c_{kj}^{\ o} \sin^k \left(c_k^{\ x} x \right) \sin^j \left(c_j^{\ y} y \right) \tag{6-4}$$

$$where: \left(c_{kj}^{\ hx} \right) = \left(c_{kj}^{\ hy} \right) = 1$$

SIN-HONN Model 2:

$$Z = \sum_{k,j=0}^{n} \left(c_{kj}^{\ o} \right) \{ c_{kj}^{\ hx} \sin^k \left(c_k^{\ x} x \right) \} \{ c_{kj}^{\ hy} \sin^j \left(c_j^{\ y} y \right) \} \tag{6-5}$$

COS-HONN Model

Based on Chapter 1 formulae from (1-33) to (1-37: COS-HONN 2), COS-HONN models are rewritten as follows:

Let

$$f_k^x\left(c_k^x x\right) = \cos^k\left(c_k^x x\right) \tag{6-6}$$

$$f_j^y\left(c_j^y y\right) = \cos^j\left(c_j^y y\right) \tag{6-7}$$

COS-HONN Model 0:

$$z = \sum_{k,j=0}^n c_{kj}^{\ o} \cos^k(x)\cos^j(y)$$

$$\tag{6-8}$$

$$where: \left(c_{kj}^{\ hx}\right) = \left(c_{kj}^{\ hy}\right) = 1 \ \ and \ \ c_k^x = c_j^y = 1$$

COS-HONN Model 1:

$$z = \sum_{k,j=0}^n c_{kj}^{\ o} \cos^k\left(c_k^x x\right)\cos^j\left(c_j^y y\right)$$

$$\tag{6-9}$$

$$where: \left(c_{kj}^{\ hx}\right) = \left(c_{kj}^{\ hy}\right) = 1$$

COS-HONN Model 2:

$$Z = \sum_{k,j=0}^n \left(c_{kj}^{\ o}\right)\{c_{kj}^{\ hx}\cos^k\left(c_k^x x\right)\}\{c_{kj}^{\ hy}con^j\left(c_j^y y\right)\} \tag{6-10}$$

LEARNING ALGORITHM OF SIN-HONN Model and COS-HONN MODEL

The learning formula for the output layer weights in SIN-HONN models and COS-HONN models are the same. The learning formula for the second-hidden layer weights in the SIN-HONN modes and COS-HONN models are the same. The learning formula for the first-hidden layer weights in the SIN-HONN models and COS-HONN models are different. Details are listed here.

Learning Formulae of Output Neurons in SIN-HONN Model and COS-HONN Model (Model 0, 1, and 2)

Based on Chapter 1 formulae from (1-133: A.1) to (1-145: A.13), SIN-HONN models and COS-HONN models (model 0, 1, and 2) are rewritten as follows:

$$c_{kj}^{\,o}(t+1) = c_{kj}^{\,o}(t) - \eta\left(\partial E / \partial c_{kj}^{\,o}\right) = c_{kj}^{\,o}(t) + \eta(d-z)f^{o\,\prime}\left(net^o\right)i_{kj} = c_{kj}^{\,o}(t) + \eta\delta^{ol}i_{kj}$$

where

$$\delta^{ol} = (d-z)f^{o\prime}\left(net^o\right) = 1 \;\;(linear\,neuron)\,(6\text{-}11)$$

Learning Formulae of Second-Hidden Layer Neurons in SIN-HONN Model and COS-HONN Model (Model 2)

Based on Chapter 1 formulae from (1-146: B.1) to (1-160: B.15), SIN-HONN and COS-HONN models (model 2) are rewritten as follows:

The weight update question for x input neurons is:

$$c_{kj}^{\,hx}(t+1) = c_{kj}^{\,hx}(t) - \eta\left(\partial E / \partial c_{kj}^{\,hx}\right)$$
$$= c_{kj}^{\,hx}(t) + \eta\left((d-z)f^{o\,\prime}\left(net^o\right)c_{kj}^{\,o}f^{h\,\prime}\left(net_{kj}^{\,hx}\right)c_{kj}^{\,hy}b_j^{\,y}b_k^{\,x}\right) = c_{kj}^{\,hx}(t) + \eta\left(\delta^{ol}c_{kj}^{\,o}\delta_{kj}^{\,hx}b_k^{\,x}\right)$$

where:

274

$$\delta^{ol} = (d-z)\delta_{kj}^{\ hx} = c_{kj}^{\ hy}b_j^{\ y}f^{o'}(net^o) = 1 \qquad (linear\ neuron)$$

$$f^{h'}(net_{kj}^{\ hx}) = 1 \qquad (linear\ neuron) \tag{6-12}$$

The weight update question for y input neurons is:

$$c_{kj}^{\ hy}(t+1) = c_{kj}^{\ hy}(t) - \eta(\partial E / \partial c_{kj}^{\ hy})$$

$$= c_{kj}^{\ hy}(t) + \eta\left((d-z)f^{o'}(net^o)c_{kj}^{\ o}f^{h'}(net_{kj}^{\ hy})c_{kj}^{\ hx}b_k^{\ x}b_j^{\ y}\right) = c_{kj}^{\ hy}(t) + \eta\left(\delta^{ol}c_{kj}^{\ o}\delta_{kj}^{\ hy}b_j^{\ y}\right)$$

where:

$$\delta^{ol} = (d-z)\delta_{kj}^{\ hy} = c_{kj}^{\ hx}b_k^{\ x}f^{o'}(net^o) = 1 \qquad (linear\ neuron)$$

$$f^{h'}(net_{kj}^{\ hy}) = 1 \qquad (linear\ neuron) \tag{6-13}$$

General Learning Formulae of First Hidden Layer x Neurons in SIN-HONN Model and COS-HONN Model (Model 1 and Model 2)

Based on Chapter 1 formulae from (1-161: C.1) to (1-177: C.17), SIN-HONN and COS-HONN models (model 1 and 2) are rewritten as follows:

For a function of x input side:

$$b_k^{\ x} = f_k^{\ x}(net_k^{\ x})$$

$$f_x'(net_k^{\ x}) = \partial b_k^{\ x} / \partial(net_k^{\ x}) \tag{6-14}$$

$$c_k^{\ x}(t+1) = c_k^{\ x}(t) - \eta\left(\frac{\partial E_p}{\partial c_k^{\ x}}\right)$$

$$= c_k^{\ x}(t) + \eta(d-z)f^{o'}(net^o)c_{kj}^{\ o} * f^{h'}(net_{kj}^{\ h})c_{kj}^{\ hy}b_j^{\ y}c_{kj}^{\ hx}f_x'(net_k^{\ x})x$$

$$= c_k^{\ x}(t) + \eta * \delta^{ol} * c_{kj}^{\ o} * \delta^{hx} * c_{kj}^{\ hx} * \delta^x * x$$

where:

$$\delta^{ol} = (d-z) f^{o'}(net^o) = d-z \qquad (linear\ neuron)$$

$$\delta^{hx} = f^{h'}(net_{kj}{}^h) c_{kj}{}^{hy} b_j{}^y = c_{kj}{}^{hy} b_j{}^y \qquad (linear\ neuron) \qquad (6\text{-}15)$$

$$\delta^x = f_x'(net_k{}^x)$$

General Learning Formulae of First Hidden Layer y Neurons in SIN-HONN Model and COS-HONN Model (Model 1 and Model 2)

Based on Chapter 1 formulae from (1-178: D.1) to (1-194: D.17), SIN-HONN and COS-HONN models (model 1 and 2) are rewritten as follows:

For a function of y input part:

$$b_j{}^y = f_j{}^y(net_j{}^y)$$

$$f_y'(net_j{}^y) = \partial b_j{}^y / \partial(net_j{}^y) \qquad (6\text{-}16)$$

Using the above procedure:

$$c_j{}^y(t+1) = c_j{}^y(t) - \eta \left(\frac{\partial E_p}{\partial c_j{}^y}\right)$$

$$= c_j{}^y(t) + \eta (d-z) f^{o'}(net^o) c_{kj}{}^o * f^{h'}(net_{kj}{}^h) c_{kj}{}^{hx} b_k{}^x c_{kj}{}^{hy} f_y'(net_j{}^y) y$$

$$= c_j{}^y(t) + \eta * \delta^{ol} * c_{kj}{}^o * \delta^{hy} * c_{kj}{}^{hy} * \delta^y * y$$

where:

$$\delta^{ol} = (d-z) f^{o'}\left(net^o\right) = d - z \qquad \left(linear\ neuron\ \ f^{o'}\left(net^o\right) = 1\right)$$

$$\delta^{hy} = f^{h'}\left(net_{kj}{}^h\right) c_{kj}{}^{hx} b_k{}^x = c_{kj}{}^{hx} b_k{}^x \qquad \left(linear\ neuron\ f^{h'}\left(net_{kj}{}^h\right) = 1\right)$$

$$\delta^y = f_y'\left(net_j{}^y\right)$$

$$(6\text{-}17)$$

Learning formulae of SIN-HONN Model for the First Hidden Layer

The first hidden layer neurons in SIN-HONN (Model 1 and Model 2) use sine functions. Based on Chapter 1 formulae from (1-213) to (1-218: SIN-HONN D.17), update learning formulae of SIN-HONN models (model 1 and 2) are rewritten as follows:

Let

$$f_k{}^x\left(c_k{}^x x\right) = \sin^k(c_k{}^x x) \tag{6-18}$$

$$f_j{}^y\left(c_j{}^y y\right) = \sin^j(c_j{}^y y) \tag{6-19}$$

For a sine function of x input side:

$$b_k{}^x = f_k{}^x\left(net_k{}^x\right) = \sin^k(net_k{}^x) = \sin^k(c_k{}^x * x) f_x'\left(net_k{}^x\right) = \frac{\partial b_k{}^x}{\partial\left(net_k{}^x\right)}$$

$$= \partial\left(\sin^k(net_k{}^x)\right)/\partial\left(net_k{}^x\right) = k*\sin^{k-1}(net_k{}^x)*\cos(net_k{}^x) = k*\sin^{k-1}(c_k{}^x * x)*\cos(c_k{}^x * x)$$

$$(6\text{-}20)$$

$$c_k{}^x(t+1) = c_k{}^x(t) - \eta\left(\frac{\partial E_p}{\partial c_k{}^x}\right)$$

$$= c_k{}^x(t) + \eta(d-z)f^{o'}(net^o)c_{kj}{}^o * f^{h'}(net_{kj}{}^h)c_{kj}{}^{hy}b_j{}^y c_{kj}{}^{hx}f_x'(net_k{}^x)x \quad (6\text{-}21)$$

$$= c_k{}^x(t) + \eta * \delta^{ol} * c_{kj}{}^o * \delta^{hx} * c_{kj}{}^{hx} * k * \sin^{k-1}(c_k{}^x * x)\cos(c_k{}^x * x) * x$$

$$= c_k{}^x(t) + \eta * \delta^{ol} * c_{kj}{}^o * \delta^{hx} * c_{kj}{}^{hx} * \delta^x * x$$

where:

$$\delta^{ol} = (d-z)f^{o'}(net^o) = d-z \qquad \left(\text{linear neuron } f^{o'}(net^o) = 1\right)$$

$$\delta^{hx} = f^{h'}(net_{kj}{}^h)c_{kj}{}^{hy}b_j{}^y = c_{kj}{}^{hy}b_j{}^y \qquad \left(\text{linear neuron } f^{h'}(net_{kj}{}^h) = 1\right)$$

$$\delta^x = f_x'(net_k{}^x) = k*(net_k{}^x)^{k-1} = k*\sin^{k-1}(c_k{}^x * x)*\cos(c_k{}^x * x)$$

For a sine function of y input part:

$$f_j{}^y(net_j{}^y) = \sin^j(net_j{}^y) = \sin^j(c_j{}^y * y)f_y'(net_j{}^y) = \frac{\partial b_j{}^y}{\partial(net_j{}^y)}$$

$$= \partial(\sin^j(net_j{}^y))/\partial(net_j{}^y) = j*\sin^{j-1}(net_j{}^y)*\cos(net_j{}^y) = j*\sin^{j-1}(c_j{}^y * y)*\cos(c_j{}^y * y)$$

$$(6\text{-}22)$$

Using the above procedure:

$$c_j{}^y(t+1) = c_j{}^y(t) - \eta\left(\frac{\partial E_p}{\partial c_j{}^y}\right)$$

$$= c_j{}^y(t) + \eta(d-z)f^{o'}(net^o)c_{kj}{}^o * f^{h'}(net_{kj}{}^h)c_{kj}{}^{hx}b_k{}^x c_{kj}{}^{hy}f_y'(net_j{}^y)y$$

$$= c_j{}^y(t) + \eta * \delta^{ol} * c_{kj}{}^o * \delta^{hy} * c_{kj}{}^{hy} * j*\sin^{j-1}(c_j{}^y * y)\cos(c_j{}^y * y)*y \quad (6\text{-}23)$$

$$= c_j{}^y(t) + \eta * \delta^{ol} * c_{kj}{}^o * \delta^{hy} * c_{kj}{}^{hy} * \delta^y * y$$

where:

$$\delta^{ol} = (d-z) f^{o'}(net^o) = d-z \qquad \left(linear\ neuron\ f^{o'}(net^o) = 1\right)$$

$$\delta^{hy} = f^{h'}\left(net_{kj}^{\ h}\right) c_{kj}^{\ hx} b_k^{\ x} = c_{kj}^{\ hx} b_k^{\ x} \qquad \left(linear\ neuron\ f^{h'}\left(net_{kj}^{\ h}\right) = 1\right)$$

$$\delta^{y} = f_y'\left(net_j^{\ y}\right) = j * \sin^{j-1}(c_j^{\ y} * y) * \cos(c_j^{\ y} * y)$$

Learning Formulae of COS-HONN Model for the First Hidden Layer

The first hidden layer neurons in COS-HONN (Model 1 and Model 2) use cosine functions. Based on Chapter 1 formulae from (1-219) to (1-224: COS-HONN D.17), update learning formulae of COS-HONN models (model 1 and 2) are rewritten as follows:

Let

$$f_k^{\ x}\left(c_k^{\ x} x\right) = \cos^k (c_k^{\ x} x) \tag{6-24}$$

$$f_j^{\ y}\left(c_j^{\ y} y\right) = \cos^j (c_j^{\ y} y) \tag{6-25}$$

For a cosine function of x input side:

$$b_k^{\ x} = f_k^{\ x}\left(net_k^{\ x}\right) = \cos^k(net_k^{\ x}) = \cos^k (c_k^{\ x} * x) f_x'\left(net_k^{\ x}\right) = \frac{\partial b_k^{\ x}}{\partial\left(net_k^{\ x}\right)}$$

$$= \partial\left(\cos^k(net_k^{\ x})\right)/\partial\left(net_k^{\ x}\right) = k * \cos^{k-1}(net_k^{\ x}) * \left(-\sin(net_k^{\ x})\right) = (-k) * \cos^{k-1}(c_k^{\ x} * x) * \sin(c_k^{\ x} * x) \tag{6-26}$$

$$c_k^x(t+1) = c_k^x(t) - \eta\left(\frac{\partial E_p}{\partial c_k^x}\right)$$

$$= c_k^x(t) + \eta(d-z) f^{o'}\left(net^o\right) c_{kj}^o * f^{h'}\left(net_{kj}^h\right) c_{kj}^{hy} b_j^y c_{kj}^{hx} f_x'\left(net_k^x\right) x$$

$$= c_k^x(t) + \eta * \delta^{ol} * c_{kj}^o * \delta^{hx} * c_{kj}^{hx} * (-k) * \cos^{k-1}(c_k^x * x) * \sin(c_k^x * x) * x$$

$$= c_k^x(t) + \eta * \delta^{ol} * c_{kj}^o * \delta^{hx} * c_{kj}^{hx} * \delta^x * x$$

$$(6\text{-}27)$$

where:

$$\delta^{ol} = (d-z) f^{o'}\left(net^o\right) = d-z \qquad \left(\text{linear neuron } f^{o'}\left(net^o\right) = 1\right)$$

$$\delta^{hx} = f^{h'}\left(net_{kj}^h\right) c_{kj}^{hy} b_j^y = c_{kj}^{hy} b_j^y \qquad \left(\text{linear neuron } f^{h'}\left(net_{kj}^h\right) = 1\right)$$

$$\delta^x = f_x'\left(net_k^x\right) = (-k) * \cos^{k-1}\left(net_k^x\right) * \sin\left(net_k^x\right) = (-k) * \cos^{k-1}(c_k^x * x) * \sin(c_k^x * x)$$

For cosine function of *y* input part:

$$b_j^y = f_y\left(net_j^y\right) = \cos^j(net_j^y) = \cos^j(c_j^y * y) f_y'\left(net_j^y\right) = \frac{\partial b_j^y}{\partial\left(net_j^y\right)}$$

$$= \partial\left(\cos^j(net_j^y)\right) / \partial\left(net_j^y\right) = j\cos^{j-1}(net_j^y) * \left(-\sin(net_j^y)\right)$$

$$= (-j) * \cos^{j-1}(net_j^y) * \sin(net_j^y) = (-j) * \cos^{j-1}(c_j^y * y) * \sin(c_j^y * y) \qquad (6\text{-}28)$$

Using the above procedure:

$$c_j^y(t+1) = c_j^y(t) - \eta\left(\frac{\partial E_p}{\partial c_j^y}\right)$$

$$= c_j^y(t) + \eta(d-z)f^{o'}(net^o)c_{kj}^o * f^{h'}(net_{kj}^h)c_{kj}^{hx}b_k^x c_{kj}^{hy}f_y'(net_j^y)y$$

$$= c_j^y(t) + \eta*\delta^{ol}*c_{kj}^o*\delta^{hy}*c_{kj}^{hy}*(-j)*\cos^{j-1}(c_j^y*y)*\sin(c_j^y*y)*y$$

$$= c_j^y(t) + \eta*\delta^{ol}*c_{kj}^o*\delta^{hy}*c_{kj}^{hy}*\delta^y*y$$

$$(6\text{-}29)$$

where:

$$\delta^{ol} = (d-z)f^{o'}(net^o) = d-z \qquad \left(linear\ neuron\ f^{o'}(net^o) = 1\right)$$

$$\delta^{hy} = f^{h'}(net_{kj}^h)c_{kj}^{hx}b_k^x = c_{kj}^{hx}b_k^x \qquad \left(linear\ neuron\ f^{h'}(net_{kj}^h) = 1\right)$$

$$\delta^y = f_y'(net_j^y) = (-j)*\cos^{j-1}(c_j^y*y)*\sin(c_j^y*y)$$

FINANCIAL DATA PREDICTION USING HONN MODELS

Time Series Data Prediction Simulation Test Using SIN-HONN

This test uses the monthly Australian dollar and USA dollar exchange rate from November 2003 to November 2004 as the test data for SIN-HONN models. In Table 1, the "Exchange Rates" are chosen from USA Federal Reserve Bank Data bank. The "Input1"data are the exchange rates for two months prior to the prediction date. The "Input 2" data are the exchange rates for one month before the prediction date. The "Output Data" are chosen from USA Federal Reserve Bank Data bank for prediction simulating. The values of "Exchange Rates", "Input 1 Data", "Input 2 Data", and "Output Data" are converted to a range from 0 to 1 and then used as inputs and output in the SIN-HONN model. SIN-HONN model 0, 1, and 2 are tested. The order number for SIN-HONN model is 6. The epochs numbers for the tests are 1000, 10000, and 100000. Table 2 shows the test results for exchange rate prediction simulation errors by using SIN-HONN models, PHONN models, and THONN models.

For example, in Table 1 of "AustralianDollar/USDollar Exchange Rate" and based on "Exchange Rates" column, AUD$1.00 = USD$0.7236 on 28-Nov-2003, and AUD$1.00 = USD$0.7520 on 31-Dec-2003. The value 0.7236 (AUD$1.00 = USD$0.7236 on 28-Nov-2003) has been used as Input 1 Data for 30-January-2004 row in the Column of "Two months before Input 1 Data". The value 0.7520 (AUD$1.00 = USD$0.7520 on 31-Dec-2003) has been used as Input 1 Data for 27-February-2004 row in the Column of "Two months before Input 1 Data" and has been used as Input 2 Data for 30-january-2004 row in the column of "One month before Input 2 Data".

In Table 2 of "2004 AU$/US$ Exchange Rate Prediction Simulation Error", The average errors of SIN-HONN Model 0, PHONN Model 0, and THONN Model 0 with Epochs 1000 are 7.3674%, 8.7080%, and 10.0366% respectively. The average errors of SIN-HONN Model 0, PHONN Model 0, and THONN Model 0 with Epochs 10000 are 6.0274%, 7.1142%, and 9.2834% respectively. The average errors of SIN-HONN Model 0, PHONN Model 0, and THONN Model 0 with Epochs 100000 are 4.4401%, 4.4457%, and 4.5712% respectively.

In Table 2 of "2004 AU$/US$ Exchange Rate Prediction Simulation Error", The average errors of SIN-HONN Model 1, PHONN Model 1, and THONN Model 1 with Epochs 1000 are 8.0236%, 9.5274%, and 10.8966% respectively. The average errors of SIN-HONN Model 1, PHONN Model 1, and THONN Model 1 with Epochs 10000 are 7.1892%, 8.3484%, and 7.3811% respectively. The average errors of SIN-HONN Model 1, PHONN Model 1, and THONN Model 1 with Epochs 100000 are 7.3012%, 7.8234%, and 7.3468% respectively.

In Table 2 of "2004 AU$/US$ Exchange Rate Prediction Simulation Error", The average errors of SIN-HONN Model 2, PHONN Model 2, and THONN Model 2 with Epochs 1000 are 14.2982%, 14.8800%, and 10.5600% respectively. The average errors of SIN-HONN Model 2, PHONN Model 2, and THONN Model 2 with Epochs 10000 are 9.0278%, 9.1474%, and 10.1914% respectively. The average errors of SIN-HONN Model 2, PHONN Model 2, and THONN Model 2 with Epochs 100000 are 6.6030%, 9.0276%, and 6.7119% respectively.

The 2004 AU$/US$ exchange rate prediction simulation errors by chart is shown in Figure 3. Test results tell that SIN-HONN models are better when using these data shown in Table 1. SIN-HONN Models should have similar test results compared with PHONN and THONN models.

Table 1. Australia Dollars Vs US Dollars for SIN-HONN Models

Date	Exchange Rates 1AU$ = ? US$	Two months before Input 1Data	One month before Input 2 Data	Prediction Simulating Output Data
11/28/2003	0.7236			
12/31/2003	0.7520			
1/30/2004	0.7625	0.7236	0.7520	0.7625
2/27/2004	0.7717	0.7520	0.7625	0.7717
3/31/2004	0.7620	0.7625	0.7717	0.7620
4/30/2004	0.7210	0.7717	0.7620	0.7210
5/28/2004	0.7138	0.7620	0.7210	0.7138
6/30/2004	0.6952	0.7210	0.7138	0.6952
7/30/2004	0.7035	0.7138	0.6952	0.7035
8/31/2004	0.7071	0.6952	0.7035	0.7071
9/30/2004	0.7244	0.7035	0.7071	0.7244
10/29/2004	0.7468	0.7071	0.7244	0.7468
11/30/2004	0.7723	0.7244	0.7468	0.7723

Table 2. 2004 AU$ /US$ Exchange Rate Prediction Simulation Average Error

Models	Order 6 Epochs 1,000	Order 6 Epochs 10,000	Order 6 Epochs 100,000
SIN-HONN Model 0	7.3674%	6.0274%	4.4401%
PHONN Model 0	8.7080%	7.1142%	4.4457%
THONN Model 0	10.0366%	9.2834%	4.5712%
SIN-HONN Model 1	8.0236%	7.1892%	7.3012%
PHONN Model 1	9.5274%	8.3484%	7.8234%
THONN Model 1	10.8966%	7.3811%	7.3468%
SIN-HONN Model 2	14.2982%	9.0278%	6.6030%
PHONN Model 2	14.8800%	9.1474%	9.0276%
THONN Model 2	10.5600%	10.1914%	6.7119%

Figure 3. 2004 AU$/US$ exchange rate prediction simulation errors

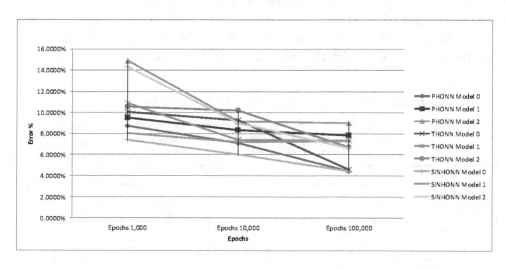

COS-HONN Model Prediction for All Banks Deposits Repayable in Australia

The *COS-HONN* model (Model 2, Order 6) has been used to predict All Banks

Table 3. All Banks Deposits Repayable in Australia ($Million) - Reserve Bank of Australia Bulletin (August 1996, page s5)

Month/Year	Total Deposit Certificates	COS-HONN |Error|%	Case
11/1994	53011	12.85%	Training
12/1994	55867	12.81%	Training
01/1995	55449	6.83%	Training
02/1995	55594	19.45%	Training
03/1995	57366	6.74%	Training
04/1995	57548	0.73%	Training
05/1995	56798	19.19%	Training
06/1995	58197	12.65%	Training
07/1995 (Prediction)	59472	19.61%	Prediction Testing
08/1995 (Prediction)	59045	8.63%	Prediction Testing
Average Prediction |Error|		14.12%	

Figure 4. All banks deposits repayable in Austrailia ($ million) training and prediction (error %)

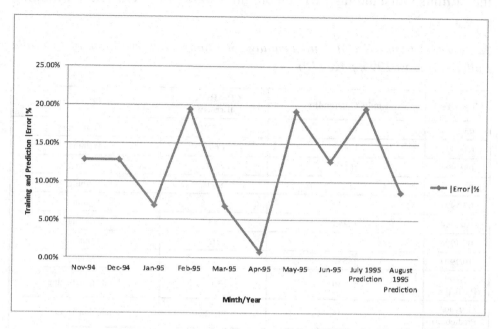

Deposits Repayable in Australia. In Table 3 of "All Banks Deposits Repayable in Australia ($Million)", Column 1 shows the "Month/Year". Column 2 shows "Total Deposit Certificates". Column 3 shows the COS-HONN training or prediction testing absolute error values. Column 4 of "Case" shows which data have been used for training the COS-HONN model, and which data have been used for prediction testing the COS-HONN model.

In Table 3, the data from 11/1994 to 06/1995 are used as training data. The data of 07/1995 and 08/1995 are used as testing cases for prediction. Prediction results shows that the average error of *COS-HONN* model is about 14.12%. Figure 4 of "All Banks Deposits Repayable in Australia ($Million) Training and Prediction |Error|%" shows the absolute error of training and prediction test for COS-HONN model (Model 2, Order 6).

COS-HONN Model Prediction for All Banks Credit Card Lending in Australia

The *COS-HONN* model (Model 2, Order 6) has been used to predict All Banks Credit Lending in Australia. In Table 4 of "All Banks Credit Card in

Australia ($Million)", Column 1 shows the "Month/Year". Column 2 shows the "Limits Outstanding", while column 3 shows the COS-HONN training

Table 4. All Banks Credit Card Lending ($million) - Reserve Bank of Australia Bulletin (August 1996, page s18)

Month/Year	Limits Outstanding	COS-HONN |Error|%	Case
03/1994	18274	11.52%	Training
04/1994	18432	7.69%	Training
05/1994	18268	0.11%	Training
06/1994	18357	18.71%	Training
07/1994	18427	0.72%	Training
08/1994	18343	6.43%	Training
09/1994	18423	1.92%	Training
10/1994	18556	3.46%	Training
11/1994 (Prediction)	18450	13.13%	Prediction Testing
12/1994 (Prediction)	18925	12.72%	Prediction Testing
Average Prediction |Error|		12.93%	

Figure 5. All Banks credit lending in Austrailia ($million) training and prediction (Error%)

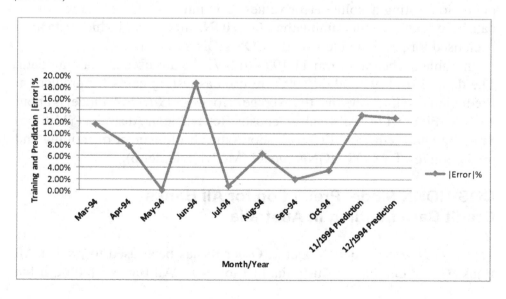

or prediction testing absolute error values. Column 4 of "Case" shows which data have been used for training the COS-HONN model, and which data have been used for prediction testing the COS-HONN model.

In Table 4, the data from 03/1994 to 11/1994 are used as training data. The data of 11/1994 and 12/1994 are used as testing cases for prediction. Prediction results showed that the average error of *COS-HONN* model is about 12.93%. Figure 5 of "All Banks Credit Lending in Australia ($Million) Training and Prediction |Error|%" shows the absolute error of training and prediction test for COS-HONN model (Model 2, Order 6).

FUTURE RESEARCH DIRECTIONS

As the next step of HONN model research, more HONN models for different data control will be built to increase the pool of HONN models. Theoretically, the adaptive HONN models can be built and allow the computer automatically to choose the best model, order, and coefficients. Thus, making the adaptive HONN models easier to use is one of the future research topics.

HONNs can automatically select the initial coefficients for nonlinear data analysis. The next step of this study will also focus on how to allow people working in the prediction area to understand that HONNs are much easier to use and can have better results. Moreover, further research will develop HONNs software packages for people working in the prediction area. HONNs will challenge classic procedures and change the research methodology that people are currently using in the prediction areas for the nonlinear data control application.

CONCLUSION

Two nonlinear neural network models, SIN-HONN, and COS-HONN models are developed. Based on the structures of SIN-HONN and COS-HONN models, this chapter provides model learning algorithm formulae. This chapter tests the SIN-HONN modes using nonlinear data for prediction simulation and the running results are compared with PHONN and PHONN models. This chapter also tests the COS-HONN models using nonlinear data for prediction tests. Test results tell that, SIN-HONN models can do prediction simulation with similar or better results than PHONN and THONN models, if the data has sine or cosine feature only. Test results also tell that COS-HONN model can do nonlinear data prediction with around 10% error.

One of the topics for future research is to continue building HONN models for different data series. The coefficients of the higher order models will be studied not only using artificial neural network techniques, but also statistical methods. Using nonlinear functions to predict and analyze time series data will be a major goal in the future.

REFERENCES

Atiya, A.F. (2001). Bankruptcy prediction for credit risk using neural networks: A survey and new results. *IEEE Transactions on Neural Networks*, *12*(4), 929-935.

Barron, R., Gilstrap, L., & Shrier, S. (1987). Polynomial and Neural Networks: Analogies and Engineering Applications. In *Proceedings of the International Conference on Neural Networks*, (Vol. 2, pp. 431-439). New York, NY: Academic Press.

Bengtsson, M. (1990). *Higher Order Artificial Neural Networks*. Diano Pub Co.

Chang, C. H., Lin, J. L., & Cheung, J. Y. (1993). Polynomial and Standard higher order neural network. In *Proceedings of IEEE International Conference on Neural Networks* (Vol. 2, pp. 989 – 994). San Francisco, CA: IEEE. 10.1109/ICNN.1993.298692

Charitou, A., & Charalambous, C. (1996). The prediction of earnings using financial statement information: Empirical evidence with logit models and artificial neural networks. *Intelligent Systems in Accounting, Finance & Management*, *5*(4), 199–215. doi:10.1002/(SICI)1099-1174(199612)5:4<199::AID-ISAF114>3.0.CO;2-C

Chen, Y., Jiang, Y., & Xu, J. (2003). Dynamic properties and a new learning mechanism in higher order neural networks. *Neurocomputing*, *50*(January), 17–30.

Chen, Y., Wu, P., & Wu, Q. (2009). Foreign Exchange Rate Forecasting Using Higher Order Flexible Neural Tree. In Artificial Higher Order Neural Networks for Economics and Business (pp. 94-112). IGI Global.

Doulamis, A. D., Doulamis, N. D., & Kollias, S. D. (2000). Recursive nonlinear models for online traffic prediction of VBR MPEG Coded video sources. In Proceedings of IEEE-INNS-ENNS international joint conference on neural networks IJCNN (pp. 114-119). Como, Italy: IEEE.

Doulamis, A. D., Doulamis, N. D., & Kollias, S. D. (2003). An adaptable neural network model for recursive nonlinear traffic prediction and modeling of MPEG video sources. *IEEE Transactions on Neural Networks*, *14*(1), 150–166. doi:10.1109/TNN.2002.806645 PMID:18237998

Durbin, R., & Rumelhart, D. E. (1989). Product units: A computationally powerful and biologically plausible extension to backpropagation networks. *Neural Computation*, *1*(1), 133–142. doi:10.1162/neco.1989.1.1.133

Eskander, G. S., & Atiya, A. (2013). Symbolic Function Netwers: Application to Telecommunication Networks Prediction. In Artificial Higher Order Neural Networks for Modeling and Simulation (pp. 237-253). IGI Global.

Estevez, P. A., & Okabe, Y. (1991). Training the piecewise linear-high order neural network through error back propagation. *Proceedings of IEEE International Joint Conference on Neural Networks*. 10.1109/IJCNN.1991.170483

Fulcher, J., Zhang, M., & Shuxiang, Xu. (2006). Application of higher-order neural networks to financial time series prediction. In J. B. Kamruzzaman (Eds.), Artificial neural networks in finance and manufacturing (pp. 80-108). New York: Idea Group Inc (IGI). doi:10.4018/978-1-59140-670-9.ch005

Fulcher, J., Zhang, M., & Xu, S. (2006). The Application of Higher-Order Neural Networks to Financial Time Series. In J. Kamruzzaman (Ed.), *Artificial Neural Networks in Finance, Health and Manufacturing: Potential and Challenges* (pp. 80–108). IGI. doi:10.4018/978-1-59140-670-9.ch005

Ghazali, R., & Al-Jumeily, D. (2009). Application of Pi-Sigma Neural Networks and Ridge Polynomial Neural Networks to Financial Time Series Prediction. In Artificial Higher Order Neural Networks for Economics and Business (pp. 271-294). IGI Global.

Giles, L., Griffin, R., & Maxwell, T. (1988). Encoding Geometric Invariances in High-Order Neural Networks. *Proceedings Neural Information Processing Systems*, 301-309.

Giles, L., & Maxwell, T. (1987). Learning, Invariance and Generalization in High-Order Neural Networks. *Applied Optics*, *26*(23), 4972–4978. doi:10.1364/AO.26.004972 PMID:20523475

He, Z., & Siyal, M. Y. (1999, August). Improvement on higher-order neural networks for invariant object recognition. *Neural Processing Letters*, *10*(1), 49–55. doi:10.1023/A:1018610829733

Hornik, K. (1991). Approximation Capabilities of Multilayer Feedforward Networks. *Neural Networks*, *4*(2), 251–257. doi:10.1016/0893-6080(91)90009-T

Hussain, A., & Liatsis, P. (2009). A Novel Recurrent Polynomial Neural Network for Financial Time Series Prediction. In Artificial Higher Order Neural Networks for Economics and Business (pp. 190-211). IGI Global.

Jeffries, C. (1989). High Order Neural Networks. In *Proceedings of IJCNN International Joint Conference on Neural Networks* (*Vol. 2*, p. 59). Academic Press.

Kanaoka, T., Chellappa, R., Yoshitaka, M., & Tomita, S. (1992). A Higher-order neural network for distortion unvariant pattern recognition. *Pattern Recognition Letters*, *13*(12), 837–841. doi:10.1016/0167-8655(92)90082-B

Karayiannis, N., & Venetsanopoulos, A. (1993). *Artificial Neural Networks: Learning Algorithms, Performance Evaluation and Applications*. Boston, MA: Kluwer. doi:10.1007/978-1-4757-4547-4

Knowles, A., Hussain, A., Dereby, W. E., Lisboa, P. G. J., & Dunis, C. L. (2009). Higher Order Neural Networks with Bayesian Confidence Measure for the Prediction of the EUR/USD Exchange Rate. In Artificial Higher Order Neural Networks for Economics and Business (pp. 48-59). IGI Global.

Lisboa, P., & Perantonis, S. (1991). Invariant Pattern Recognition Using Third-Order Networks and Zernlike Moments. In *Proceedings of the IEEE International Joint Conference on Neural Networks* (Vol. 2, pp. 1421-1425). Singapore: IEEE.

Manykin, E. A., & Belov, M. N. (1991). Higher-order neural networks and photo-echo effect. *Neural Networks*, *4*(3), 417–420. doi:10.1016/0893-6080(91)90079-K

Moon, S., & Chang, S. H. (1994). Classification and prediction of the critical heat flux using fuzzy clustering and artificial neural networks. *Nuclear Engineering and Design, 150*(1), 151–161. doi:10.1016/0029-5493(94)90059-0

Onwubolu, G. C. (2009). Artificial Higher Order Neural Networks in Time Series Prediction. In Artificial Higher Order Neural Networks for Economics and Business (pp. 250-270). IGI Global.

Park, S., Smith, M. J. T., & Mersereau, R. M. (2000, October). Target Recognition Based on Directional Filter Banks and higher-order neural network. *Digital Signal Processing, 10*(4), 297–308. doi:10.1006/dspr.2000.0376

Psaltis, D., Park, C., & Hong, J. (1988). Higher Order Associative Memories and their Optical Implementations. *Neural Networks, 1*(2), 149–163. doi:10.1016/0893-6080(88)90017-2

Redding, N., Kowalczyk, A., & Downs, T. (1993). Constructive Higher-Order Network Algorithm that is Polynomial Time. *Neural Networks, 6*(7), 997–1010. doi:10.1016/S0893-6080(09)80009-9

Ricalde, L. J., Catzin, G. A., Alanis, A. Y., & Sanchez, E. N. (2013). Time Series Forecasting via a Higher Order Neural Network trained with the Extended Kalman Filter for Smart Grid Applications. In Artificial Higher Order Neural Networks for Modeling and Simulation (pp. 254-275). IGI Global.

Rumelhart, D., Hinton, G., & McClelland, J. (1986). Learning Internal Representations by Error Propagation. In Parallel Distributed Processing: Explorations in the Microstructure of Cognition, Volume 1 – Foundations. Cambridge, MA: MIT Press.

Saad, E. W., Prokhorov, D. V., & Wunsch, D. C. II. (1998). Comparative Study of Stock Trend Prediction Using Time Delay Recurrent and Probabilistic Neural Networks. *IEEE Transactions on Neural Networks, 9*(6), 1456–1470. doi:10.1109/72.728395 PMID:18255823

Sanchez, E. N., Alanis, A. Y., & Rico, J. (2004). Electric Load Demand Prediction Using Neural Networks Trained by Kalman Filtering. In *Proceedings of the IEEE International Joint Conference on Neural Networks* (pp. 2771-2775). Budapest, Hungary: IEEE. 10.1109/IJCNN.2004.1381093

Sanchez, E. N., Alanis, A. Y., & Rico, J. (2009). Electric Load Demand and Electricity Prices Forecasting Using Higher Order Networks Trained by Kalman Filtering. In Artificial Higher Order Neural Networks for Economics and Business (pp. 295-313). IGI Global.

Selviah, D. R., & Shawash, J. (2009). Generalized Correlation Higher Order Neural Networks for Financial Time Series Prediction. In Artificial Higher Order Neural Networks for Economics and Business (pp. 212-249). IGI Global.

Shawver, T. (2005). Merger premium predictions using neural network approach. *Journal of Emerging Technologies in Accounting*, *1*(1), 61–72. doi:10.2308/jeta.2005.2.1.61

Shi, Da, Tan, Shaohua, & Sam. (2009). Automatically Identifying Predictor Variables for Stock Return Prediction. In *Artificial Higher Order Neural Networks for Economics and Business* (pp. 60-78). IGI Global.

Spirkovska, L., & Reid, M. B. (1992, September). Robust position, scale, and rotation invariant object recognition using higher-order neural networks. *Pattern Recognition*, *25*(9), 975–985. doi:10.1016/0031-3203(92)90062-N

Spirkovska, L., & Reid, M. B. (1994). Higher-order neural networks applied to 2D and 3D object recognition. *Machine Learning*, *15*(2), 169-199.

Su, G., Fukuda, K., Jia, D., & Morita, K. (2002). Application of an artificial neural network in reactor thermo hydraulic problem: Prediction of critical heat flux. *Journal of Nuclear Science and Technology*, *39*(5), 564–571. doi:10.1080/18811248.2002.9715235

Tai, H., & Jong, T. (1990). Information storage in high-order neural networks with unequal neural activity. *Journal of the Franklin Institute*, *327*(1), 129–141. doi:10.1016/0016-0032(90)90061-M

Vaziri, N., Hojabri, A., Erfani, A., Monsey, M., & Nilforooshan, N. (2007). Critical heat flux prediction by using radial basis function and multilayer perceptron neural networks: A comparison study. *Nuclear Engineering and Design*, *237*(4), 377–385. doi:10.1016/j.nucengdes.2006.05.005

Welch, R. L., Ruffing, S. M., & Venayagamoorthy, G. K. (2009). *Comparison of Feedforward and Feedback Neural Network Architectures for Short Term Wind Speed Prediction*. Paper presented at the IEEE International Joint Conference on Neural Networks, Atlanta, GA. 10.1109/IJCNN.2009.5179034

Wilcox, C. (1991). Understanding Hierarchical Neural Network Behavior: A Renormalization Group Approach. *Journal of Physics. A. Mathematical Nuclear and General*, *24*, 2644–2655.

Yapo, T., Embrechets, S. T., & Cathey, S. T. (1992). Prediction of critical heat using a hybrid kohon-backpropagation neural network intelligent. Eng. *Systems through Artificial Neural Networks-Proc. Artificial Neural Networks in Eng.*, *2*, 853–858.

Zhang, M., & Fulcher, J. (2004). Higher Order Neural Networks for Satellite Weather Prediction. In J. Fulcher & L. C. Jain (Eds.), *Applied Intelligent Systems* (Vol. 153, pp. 17–57). Springer. doi:10.1007/978-3-540-39972-8_2

Zhang, M., & Fulcher, J. (2004). Higher Order Neural Networks for Satellite Weather Prediction. In Applied Intelligent Systems (pp. 17-57). Springer-Verlag Publisher.

Zhang, M., Fulcher, J., & Scofield, R. (1997). Rainfalll estimation using artificial neural network group. *International Journal of Neurlcomputing*, *16*(2), 97–115. doi:10.1016/S0925-2312(96)00022-7

Zhang, M., Xu, S., & Fulcher, J. (2002). Neuron-Adaptive Higher Order Neural Network Models for Automated Financial Data Modeling. *IEEE Transactions on Neural Networks*, *13*(1), 188–204. doi:10.1109/72.977302 PMID:18244418

ADDITIONAL READING

Adas, A. N. (1998). Using adaptive Linear Prediction to Support Real – Time VBR Video under RCBR Network Service Model. *IEEE/ACM Transactions on Networking*, *6*(5), 635–644. doi:10.1109/90.731200

Amari, S. (1971). Characteristics of randomly connected threshold element networks and network systems. *Proceedings of the IEEE*, *59*(1), 35–47. doi:10.1109/PROC.1971.8087

Baber, W., Kang, S., & Kumar, K. (1998). Accounting Earnings and Executive Compensation: The Role of Earnings Persistence. *Journal of Accounting and Economics*, *25*(2), 169–193. doi:10.1016/S0165-4101(98)00021-4

Bierens, H. J., & Ploberger, W. (1997). Asymptotic theory of integrated conditional moment tests. *Econometrica, 65*(5), 1129–1151. doi:10.2307/2171881

Blum, E., & Li, K. (1991). Approximation theory and feed-forward networks. *Neural Networks, 4*(4), 511–515. doi:10.1016/0893-6080(91)90047-9

Brucoli, M., Carnimeo, L., & Grassi, G. (1997). Associative memory design using discrete-time second-order neural networks with local interconnections. *IEEE Transactions on Circuits and Systems. I, Fundamental Theory and Applications, 44*(2), 153–158. doi:10.1109/81.554334

Butt, N. R., & Shafiq, M. (2006). Higher-Order Neural Network Based Root-Solving Controller for Adaptive Tracking of Stable Nonlinear Plants. *Proceedings of IEEE International Conference on Engineering of Intelligent Systems* (pp.1 – 6). 10.1109/ICEIS.2006.1703175

Chakraborty, K., Mehrotra, K., Mohan, C., & Ranka, S. (1992). Forecasting the behavior of multivariate time series using neural networks. *Neural Networks, 5*(6), 961–970. doi:10.1016/S0893-6080(05)80092-9

Chen, C. T., & Chang, W. D. (1996). A feed-forward neural network with function shape autotuning. *Neural Networks, 9*(4), 627–641. doi:10.1016/0893-6080(96)00006-8

Chen, T., & Chen, H. (1993). Approximations of continuous functional by neural networks with application to dynamic systems. *IEEE Transactions on Neural Networks, 4*(6), 910–918. doi:10.1109/72.286886 PMID:18276521

Chen, T., & Chen, H. (1995). Approximation capability to functions of several variables, nonlinear functionals, and operators by radial basis function neural networks. *IEEE Transactions on Neural Networks, 6*(4), 904–910. doi:10.1109/72.392252 PMID:18263378

Chen, X., & Shen, X. (1998). Sieve extremum estimates for weakly dependent data. *Econometrica, 66*(2), 289–314. doi:10.2307/2998559

Chen, Y., Cheng, J. J., & Creamer, K. S. (2007). Inhibition of anaerobic digestion process: A review. *Bioresource Technology, 99*(10), 4044–4064. doi:10.1016/j.biortech.2007.01.057 PMID:17399981

Chenug, Y. W., & Chinn, M. D. (1999). *Macroeconomic implications of the Beliefs and Behavior of Foreign exchange Traders.* NBER, Working paper no. 7414.

Cho, K. B., & Wang, B. H. (1996). Radial basis function based adaptive fuzzy systems and their applications to system identification and prediction. *Fuzzy Sets and Systems, 83*(3), 325–339. doi:10.1016/0165-0114(95)00322-3

Core, J., Guay, W., & Larcker, D. (2008). The Power of the Pen and Executive Compensation. *Journal of Financial Economics, 88*(1), 1–25. doi:10.1016/j.jfineco.2007.05.001

Daey-Ouwens, W. T. (1997). Gasification of biomass wastes and residues for electricity production. *Biomass and Bioenergy, 12*(6), 387–407. doi:10.1016/S0961-9534(97)00010-X

Das, T., & Kar, I. N. (2006). Design and implementation of an adaptive fuzzy logic-based controller for wheeled mobile robots. *IEEE Transactions on Control Systems Technology, 14*(3), 501–510. doi:10.1109/TCST.2006.872536

Draye, J. S., Pavisic, D. A., Cheron, G. A., & Libert, G. A. (1996), Dynamic recurrent neural networks: a dynamic analysis, *IEEE Transactions SMC- Part B, 26*(5), 692-706.

Elbradawi, I. A. (1994). Estimating Long-Run Equilibrium Real Exchange Rates. In J. Williamson (Ed.), *Estimating Equilibrium Exchange Rates* (pp. 93–131). Institute for International Economics.

Fahlman, S. (1988). *Faster-learning Variations on Back-Propagation: An Empirical Study*, Proceedings of 1988 Connectionist Models Summer School.

Feng, G., Huang, G.-B., Lin, Q., & Gay, R. (2009). Error minimized extreme learning machine with growth of hidden nodes and incremental learning. *IEEE Transactions on Neural Networks, 20*(8), 1352–1357. doi:10.1109/TNN.2009.2024147 PMID:19596632

Fulcher, G. E., & Brown, D. E. (1994). A polynomial neural network for predicting temperature distributions. *IEEE Transactions on Neural Networks, 5*(3), 372–379. doi:10.1109/72.286909 PMID:18267805

Giles, C. L., & Maxwell, T. (1987). Learning invariance, and generalization in higher-order networks. *Applied Optics, 26*(23), 4972–4978. doi:10.1364/AO.26.004972 PMID:20523475

Gopalsamy, K. (2007). Learning dynamics in second order networks. *Nonlinear Analysis Real World Applications, 8*(9), 688–698. doi:10.1016/j.nonrwa.2006.02.007

Gorr, W. L. (1994). Research prospective on neural network forecasting. *International Journal of Forecasting, 10*(1), 1–4. doi:10.1016/0169-2070(94)90044-2

Granger, C. W. J. (1981). Some properties of time series data and their use in econometric model specification. *Journal of Econometrics, 16*(1), 121–130. doi:10.1016/0304-4076(81)90079-8

Granger, C. W. J. (1995). Modeling nonlinear relationships between extended-memory variables. *Econometrica, 63*(2), 265–279. doi:10.2307/2951626

Granger, C. W. J. (2001). Spurious regressions in econometrics. In B. H. Baltagi (Ed.), *A Companion to Theoretical Econometrics* (pp. 557–561). Oxford: Blackwell.

Granger, C. W. J., & Bates, J. (1969). The combination of forecasts. *Operational Research Quarterly, 20*(4), 451–468. doi:10.1057/jors.1969.103

Granger, C. W. J., & Lee, T. H. (1990). Multicointegration. In G. F. Rhodes Jr & T. B. Fomby (Eds.), *Advances in Econometrics: Cointegration, Spurious Regressions and Unit Roots* (pp. 17–84). New York: JAI Press.

Granger, C. W. J., & Newbold, P. (1974). Spurious regressions in econometrics. *Journal of Econometrics, 2*(2), 111–120. doi:10.1016/0304-4076(74)90034-7

Granger, C. W. J., & Swanson, N. R. (1996). Further developments in study of cointegrated variables. *Oxford Bulletin of Economics and Statistics, 58,* 374–386.

Granger, C. W. J., & Weiss, A. A. (1983). Time series analysis of error-correction models. In S. Karlin, T. Amemiya and L. A. Goodman (Eds), Studies in Econometrics, Time Series and Multivariate Statistics (pp. 255–278). San Diego: Academic Press. doi:10.1016/B978-0-12-398750-1.50018-8

Güler, M. (1999). Neural Classifiers for Learning Higher-Order Correlations. *Transactions Journal of Physics, 23,* 39–46.

Hans, P., & Draisma, G. (1997). Recognizing changing seasonal patterns using artificial neural networks. *Journal of Econometrics, 81*(1), 273–280. doi:10.1016/S0304-4076(97)00047-X

Ho, D. W. C., Liang, J. L., & Lam, J. (2006). Global exponential stability of impulsive high-order BAM neural networks with time-varying delays. *Neural Networks, Volume, 19*(10), 1581–1590. doi:10.1016/j.neunet.2006.02.006 PMID:16580174

Hopfield, J. J., & Tank, D. W. (1985). Neural computation of decisions in optimization problems. *Biological Cybernetics, 52*(1), 141–152. PMID:4027280

Huang, G. B., Li, M. B., Chen, L., & Siew, C. K. (2008). Incremental Extreme Learning Machine with Fully Complex Hidden Nodes. *Neurocomputing, 71*(4-6), 576–583. doi:10.1016/j.neucom.2007.07.025

Hwang, B., & Kim, S. (2009, July). It pays to have friends. *Journal of Financial Economics, 93*(1), 138–158. doi:10.1016/j.jfineco.2008.07.005

Jarungthammachote, S., & Dutta, A. (2007). Thermodynamic equilibrium model and second law analysis of a downdraft waste gasifier. *Energy, 32*(9), 1660–1669. doi:10.1016/j.energy.2007.01.010

Khalil, H. K. (2002). *Nonlinear Systems*. Upper Saddle River, NJ: Prentice-Hall.

Kilian, L., & Taylor, M. P. (2003). Why is it so difficult to beat the random walk forecast of exchange rate? *Journal of International Economics, 60*(1), 85–107. doi:10.1016/S0022-1996(02)00060-0

Kohonen, T., Kaski, S., Lagus, K., Salojarvi, J., Honkela, J., Paatero, V., & Saarela, A. (2000). Self-organization of a massive document collection. *IEEE Transactions on Neural Networks, 11*(3), 574–585. doi:10.1109/72.846729 PMID:18249786

Lee, M., Lee, S. Y., & Park, C. H. (1992). Neural controller of nonlinear dynamic systems using higher order neural networks. *Electronics Letters, 28*(3), 276–277. doi:10.1049/el:19920170

Li, R. P., & Mukaidono, M. (1995). A new approach to rule learning based on fusion of fuzzy logic and neural networks. *IEICE Transactions on Information and Systems, E78-D*(11), 1509–1514.

Little, R. J., & Rubin, D. B. (1987). *Statistical Analysis with Missing Data*. New York: John Wiley and Sons.

Lumer, E. D. (1992). Selective attention to perceptual groups: the phase tracking mechanism. *Intl. J.* Machado, R.J. (1989). Handling knowledge in high order neural networks: the combinatorial neural model. *Proceedings of International Joint Conference on Neural Networks, 2,* 582.

MacDonald, R., & Marsh, I. (1999). *Exchange Rate Modeling* (pp. 145–171). Boston: Kluwer Academic Publishers. doi:10.1007/978-1-4757-2997-9_6

Meese, R., & Rogoff, K. (1983B). The out-of-samples failure of empirical exchange rate models: sampling error or misspecification. In J. A. Frenkel (Ed.), *Exchange rate and International macroeconomics.* Chicago, Boston: Chicago University Press and National Bureau of Economic Research.

Mendel, J. M. (1991). Tutorial on higher-order statistics (spectra) in signal processing and system theory: Theoretical results and some applications. *Proceedings of the IEEE, 79*(3), 278–305. doi:10.1109/5.75086

Miyajima, H., Yatsuki, S., & Maeda, M. (1996). Some characteristics of higher order neural networks with decreasing energy functions. *IEICE Trans. Fundamentals, E99-A*(10), 1624–1629.

Moylan, P. J., & Anderson, B. D. O. (1973). Nonlinear regulator theory and an inverse optimal control problem. *IEEE Transactions on Automatic Control, 18*(5), 460–465. doi:10.1109/TAC.1973.1100365

Natarjan, B. K. (1995). Sparse Approximate Solutions to Linear System. *SIAM Journal on Computing, 24*(2), 227–234. doi:10.1137/S0097539792240406

Olfati-Saber, R., Fax, A. J., & Murray, R. M. (2007). Consensus and cooperation in networked multi-agent systems. *Proceedings of the IEEE, 95*(1), 215–233. doi:10.1109/JPROC.2006.887293

Passino, K. M., & Yurkovich, S. (1998). *Fuzzy Control.* Menlo Park, CA: Addison Wesley Longman.

Picton, P. (2000). *Neural Networks.* Basingstoke: Palsgrave.

Rashid, T., Huang, B. Q., & Kechadi, T. (2007). Auto Regressive Recurrent Neural Network Approach for Electricity Load Forecasting. *International Journal of Computational Intelligence, 3*(1), 66–71.

Ren, W., & Beard, R. W. (2005). Consensus seeking in multiagent systems under dynamically changing interaction topologies. *IEEE Transactions on Automatic Control, 50*(5), 655–661. doi:10.1109/TAC.2005.846556

Rodriguez-Angeles, A., & Nijmeijer, H. (2004). Mutual synchronization of robots via estimated state feedback: A cooperative approach. *IEEE Transactions on Control Systems Technology, 12*(4), 542–554. doi:10.1109/TCST.2004.825065

Rovithakis, G. A., Kosmatopoulos, E. B., & Christodoulou, M. A. (1993). Robust adaptive control of unknown plants using recurrent high order neural networks-application to mechanical systems. *Proceedings of International Conference on Systems, Man and Cybernetics* (vol.4, pp. 57 – 62). 10.1109/ICSMC.1993.390683

Rumelhart, D. E., & McClelland, J. L. (1986). *Parallel distributed computing: exploration in the microstructure of cognition.* Cambridge, MA: MIT Press.

Sanchez, E. N., Alanis, A. Y., & Chen, G. (2006). Recurrent Neural Networks Trained with Kalman Filtering for Discrete Chaos Reconstruction. *Dynamics of Continuous. Discrete and Impulsive Systems Series B: Applications and Algorithms, 6*(13), 1–17.

Scarselli, F., & Tsoi, A. C. (1998). Universal approximation using feed-forward neural networks: A survey of some existing methods, and some new results. *Neural Networks, 11*(1), 15–37. doi:10.1016/S0893-6080(97)00097-X PMID:12662846

Schuster, G., Löffler, G., Weigl, K., & Hofbauer, H. (2001). Biomass steam gasification--an extensive parametric modeling study. *Bioresource Technology, 77*(1), 71–79. doi:10.1016/S0960-8524(00)00115-2 PMID:11211078

Sethi, I. K. (1990). Entropy Nets: From Decision Trees to Neural Networks. *Proceedings of the IEEE, 78*(10), 1605–1613. doi:10.1109/5.58346

Shintani, M., & Linton, O. (2004). Nonparametric neural network estimation of Lyapunov exponents and direct test for chaos. *Journal of Econometrics, 120*(1), 1–33. doi:10.1016/S0304-4076(03)00205-7

Simeonov, I., & Queinnec, I. (2006). Linearizing control of the anaerobic digestion with addition of acetate (control of the anaerobic digestion). *Control Engineering Practice, 14*(7), 799–810. doi:10.1016/j.conengprac.2005.04.011

Sloan, R. (1993). Accounting earnings and top executive compensation. *Journal of Accounting and Economics, 16*(1-3), 55–100. doi:10.1016/0165-4101(93)90005-Z

Taylor, M. P. (1995). The economics of exchange rates. *Journal of Economic Literature*, *33*, 13–47.

Taylor, M. P., Peel, D. A., & Sarno, L. (2001). Nonlinear adjustments in real exchange rate: Towards a solution to the purchasing power parity puzzles. *International Economic Review*, *42*(4), 1015–1042. doi:10.1111/1468-2354.00144

Taylor, R. H., & Kazanzides, P. (2007). Medical robotics and computer-integrated interventional medicine. *International Journal of Advance in Computers*, *73*, 219–260. doi:10.1016/S0065-2458(08)00405-1

Theodoridis, D. C., Christodoulou, M. A., & Boutalis, Y. S. (2010). Neuro – Fuzzy Control Schemes Based on High Order Neural Network Function Approximators. In M. Zhang (Ed.), *Artificial Higher Order Neural Networks for Computer Science and Engineering: Trends for Emerging Applications* (pp. 450–483). Hershey, PA: IGI Global. doi:10.4018/978-1-61520-711-4.ch019

Van Impe, J. F., & Bastin, G. (1995). Optimal adaptive control of fed-batch fermentation processes. *Control Engineering Practice*, *3*(7), 939–954. doi:10.1016/0967-0661(95)00077-8

Wang, L. (1994). *Adaptive Fuzzy Systems and Control*. Englewood Cliffs, NJ: Prentice Hall.

Williamson, J. (1994). *Estimating Equilibrium Exchange Rates*. Institute for International Economics.

Wolfram, S. (1984). Universality and complexity in cellular automata. *Physical*, *10*(1-2), 1–35.

Xu, B., Liu, X., & Liao, X. (2005). Global asymptotic stability of high-order Hopfield type neural networks with time delays. *Computers & Mathematics with Applications (Oxford, England)*, *45*(10-11), 1729–1737. doi:10.1016/S0898-1221(03)00151-2

KEY TERMS AND DEFINITIONS

ANN: Artificial neural network.

COS-HONN: Artificial cosine higher order neural network.

HONN: Artificial higher order neural network.

PHONN: Artificial polynomial higher order neural network.

SIN-HONN: Artificial higher order neural network.

THONN: Artificial trigonometric higher order neural network.

Section 3
Artificial Higher Order Neural Networks for Modeling and Simulation

Chapter 7
Data Classification Using Ultra–High Frequency SINC and Trigonometric Higher Order Neural Networks

ABSTRACT

This chapter develops a new nonlinear model, ultra high frequency sinc and trigonometric higher order neural networks (UNT-HONN), for data classification. UNT-HONN includes ultra high frequency sinc and sine higher order neural networks (UNS-HONN) and ultra high frequency sinc and cosine higher order neural networks (UNC-HONN). Data classification using UNS-HONN and UNC-HONN models are tested. Results show that UNS-HONN and UNC-HONN models are more accurate than other polynomial higher order neural network (PHONN) and trigonometric higher order neural network (THONN) models, since UNS-HONN and UNC-HONN models can classify data with error approaching 10-6.

INTRODUCTION

The contributions of this chapter will be:

- Introduce the background of HONNs with the applications of HONNs in classification area.

DOI: 10.4018/978-1-7998-3563-9.ch007

- Develop a new HONN models called UNS-HONN and UNC-HONN
- Provide the UNS-HONN and UNC-HONN learning algorithm and weight update formulae.
- Compare UNS-HONN and UNC-HONN models with other HONN models.
- Applications of UNS-HONN and UNC-HONN models for ultra-high frequency data.

This chapter is organized as follows: the background section gives the background knowledge of HONN and HONN applications in classification area. Section HONN models introduces UNS-HONN and UNC-HONN structures. Section update formula provides the UNS-HONN and UNC-HONN model update formulae, learning algorithms, and convergence theories of HONN. Section test describes UNS-HONN and UNC-HONN testing results in the data classification area. Conclusions are presented in last section.

BACKGROUND

Artificial Neural Network (ANN) has been widely used in the classification areas. Lippman (1989) studies pattern classification using neural networks. Moon and Chang (1994) learn classification and prediction of the critical heat flux using fuzzy clustering and artificial neural networks. Lin and Cunningham (1995) develop a new approach to fuzzy-neural system modelling. Behnke and Karayiannis (1998) present a competitive Neural Trees for pattern classifications. Bukovsky, Bila, Gupta, Hou, and Homma (2010) provide foundation and classification of nonconventional neural units and paradigm of non-synaptic neural interaction.

Artificial higher order neural network models have been widely used for pattern recognition with the benefit of HONNs being open box models (Bishop (1995); Park, Smith, & Mersereau (2000); Spirkovska, & Reid (1992, and 1994); and Zhang, Xu, & Fulcher (2007)). Shin and Ghosh (1991) introduce a novel feedforward network called the pi-sigma network. This network utilizes product cells as the output units to indirectly incorporate the capabilities of higher order networks while using a fewer number of weights and processing units. The pi-sigma network is an efficient higher order neural network for pattern classification and function approximation. Linhart and Dorffner (1992) present a self-learning visual pattern explorer and recognizer using a higher order neural network, which could improve the efficiency of higher order neural networks, is built into a pattern recognition system that autonomously learns to categorize and recognize patterns independently of their position in an input image. Schmidt and Davis (1993) explore alternatives that reduce the number of network weights while pattern recognition properties of various feature spaces for higher order neural networks. Spirkovska and Reid (1993) describe coarse-coded higher order neural networks for PSRI object recognition. The authors describe a coarse coding technique and present simulation results illustrating its usefulness and its limitations. Simulations show that a third-order neural network can be trained to distinguish between two objects of 4096×4096 pixels. Wan and Sun (1996) show that the higher order neural networks (HONN) have numerous advantages over other translational rotational scaling invariant (TRSI) pattern recognition techniques for automatic target recognition. Morad and Yuan (1998) present a method for automatic model building from multiple images of an object to be recognized. The model contains knowledge which has been computed during the learning phase from large 2D images of an object for automatic model building and 3D object recognition. A neuro-based adaptive higher order neural network model has been developed by Zhang, Xu, and Fulcher (2002) for data model recognition. Voutriaridis, Boutalis, and Mertzios (2003) propose ridge polynomial networks in pattern recognition. Ridge polynomial networks (RPNs) are special class of high order neural networks with the ability of high order neural networks for perform shift and rotation.

Artificial Higher Order Neural Network (HONN) has been widely used in the classification area too. Reid, Spirkovska, and Ochoa (1989) research simultaneous position, scale, rotation invariant pattern classification using third-order neural networks. Shin (1991) investigate tThe Pi-Sigma network: an Efficient Higher-Order Neural Network for Pattern Classification and Function Approximation. Ghosh and Shin (1992) show efficient higher order neural networks for function approximation and classification. Shin, Ghosh, and Samani (1992) analyze computationally efficient invariant pattern classification with higher order Pi-Sigma networks. Husken and Stagge (2003) expand recurrent neural networks for time series classification. Fallahnezhad, Moradi, and Zaferanlouei (2011) contribute a hybrid higher order neural classifier for handling classification problems.

Shawash and Selviah (2010) test artificial higher order neural network training on limited precision processors, and investigate the training of networks using Back Propagation and Levenberg-Marquardt algorithms in limited precision achieving high overall calculation accuracy, using on-line training, a new type of HONN known as the Correlation HONN (CHONN), discrete XOR and continuous optical waveguide sidewall roughness datasets by simulation to find the precision at which the training and operation is feasible. The BP algorithm converged to a precision beyond which the performance did not improve. The results support previous findings in literature for Artificial Neural Network operation that discrete datasets require lower precision than continuous datasets. The importance of the chapter findings is that they demonstrate the feasibility of on-line, real-time, low-latency training on limited precision electronic hardware.

Sanchez, Urrego, Alanis, and Carlos-Hernandez (2010) focus on recurrent higher order neural observers for anaerobic processes, and propose the design of a discrete-time neural observer which requires no prior knowledge of the model of an anaerobic process, for estimate biomass, substrate and inorganic carbon which are variables difficult to measure and very important for anaerobic process control in a completely stirred tank reactor (CSTR) with biomass filter; this observer is based on a recurrent higher order neural network, trained with an extended Kalman filter based algorithm.

Boutalis, Christodoulou, and Theodoridis (2010) provide identification of nonlinear systems using a new neuro-fuzzy dynamical system definition based on high order neural network function approximators and study the nonlinear systems. A new definition of Adaptive Dynamic Fuzzy Systems (ADFS) is presented in this chapter for the identification of unknown nonlinear dynamical systems. The proposed scheme uses the concept of Adaptive Fuzzy Systems operating in conjunction with High Order Neural Network Functions (HONNFs). Since the plant is considered unknown, this chapter first proposes its approximation by a special form of an adaptive fuzzy system and in the sequel the fuzzy rules are approximated by appropriate HONNFs. Thus, the identification scheme leads up to a Recurrent High Order Neural Network, which however takes into account the fuzzy output partitions of the initial ADFS. Weight updating laws, for the involved HONNFs, are provided, which guarantee that the identification error reaches zero exponentially fast. Simulations illustrate the potency of the method and comparisons on well-known benchmarks are given.

Najarian, Hosseini, and Fallahnezhad (2010) explore artificial tactile sensing and robotic surgery using higher order neural networks, and introduce a new medical instrument, namely, the Tactile Tumor Detector (TTD) able to simulate the sense of touch in clinical and surgical applications. All theoretical and experimental attempts for its construction are presented. Theoretical analyses are mostly based on finite element method (FEM), artificial neural networks (ANN), and higher order neural networks (HONN). The TTD is used for detecting abnormal masses in biological tissue, specifically for breast examinations. This chapter presents a research work on ANN and HONN done on the theoretical results of the TTD to reduce the subjectivity of estimation in diagnosing tumor characteristics. This chapter uses HONN as a stronger open box intelligent unit than traditional black box neural networks (NN) for estimating the characteristics of tumor and tissue. The results show that by having an HONN model of our nonlinear input-output mapping, there are many advantages compared with ANN model, including faster running for new data, lesser RMS error and better fitting properties.

ULTRA-HIGH FREQUENCY SINC AND TRIGONOMETRIC HIGHER ORDER NEURAL NETWORKS (UNT-HONN)

Nyquist Rule says that a sampling rate must be at least twice as fast as the fastest frequency (Shannon 1998). In classification, simulating and predicting data, the new nonlinear models of UNT-HONN should have twice as high frequency as that of the ultra-high frequency of data. To achieve this purpose, a new model should be developed to enforce high frequency of HONN in order to make the classification, simulation, and prediction error close to zero. The new HONN model, Ultra High Frequency SINC and Trigonometric Higher Order Neural Network (UNT-HONN), includes two different models base on the different neuron functions. Ultra-high frequency siNc and Sine Trigonometric Higher Order Neural Network (UNS-HONN) has neurons with SINC and sine functions. Ultra-high frequency siNc and Cosine Trigonometric Higher Order Neural Network (UNC-HONN) has neurons with SINC and cosine functions. Except for the functions in the neuron all other parts of these two models are the same. The following section will discuss the UNS-HONN and UNC models in detail.

UNS-HONN Model Structure can be seen in Figure 1. UNC-HONN Model Structure can be seen in Figure 2.

The Nyquist–Shannon sampling theorem, after Harry Nyquist and Claude Shannon, in the literature more commonly referred to as the Nyquist sampling theorem or simply as the sampling theorem, is a fundamental result in the field of information theory, in particular telecommunications and signal processing. Shannon's version of the theorem states:[Shannon 1998]

Figure 1. UNS-HON Architecture

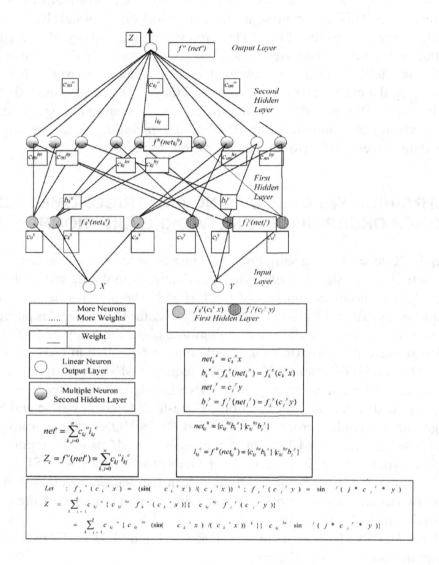

If a function x(t) contains no frequencies higher than B hertz, it is completely determined by giving its ordinates at a series of points spaced 1/(2B) seconds apart.

In other words, a band limited function can be perfectly reconstructed from a countable sequence of samples if the band limit, B, is no greater than ½ the sampling rate (samples per second).

Figure 2. UNC-HONN Architecture

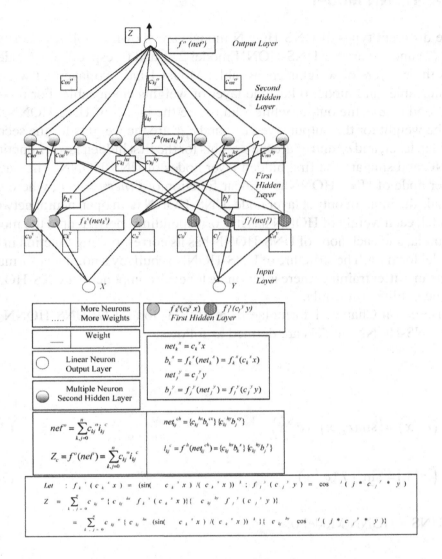

In classification, simulating and predicting data, the new nonlinear models of UNS-HONN and UNC-HONN models should have twice as high frequency as that of the ultra-high frequency of the data. To achieve this purpose, a new model should be developed to enforce high frequency of HONN in order to make the simulation and prediction error close to zero.

UNS-HONN Model

The different types of UNS-HONN models are shown as follows. Formula (1) (2) and (3) are for UNS-HONN model 2, 1 and 0 respectively. Model 2 has three layers of weights changeable; Model 1 has two layers of weights changeable, and model 0 has one layer of weights changeable. For models 2, 1 and 0, Z is the output while x and y are the inputs of UNS-HONN. c_{kj}^{o} is the weight for the output layer, c_{kj}^{hx} and c_{kj}^{hy} are the weights for the second hidden layer, and c_{k}^{x} and c_{j}^{y} are the weights for the first hidden layer. Functions SINC and sine are the first hidden layer nodes of UNS-HONN. The output layer node of UNS-HONN is a linear function of $f^{o}(net^{o}) = net^{o}$, where net^{o} equals the input of output layer node. UNS-HONN is an open neural network model, each weight of HONN has its corresponding coefficient in the model formula, and each node of UNS-HONN has its corresponding function in the model formula. The structure of UNS-HONN is built by a nonlinear formula. It means, after training, there is rationale for each component of UNS-HONN in the nonlinear formula.

Based on Chapter 1 formulae from (1-123) to (1-127: UNS-HONN 2), the UNS-HONN models are defined as follows:

Let

$$f_k^{j}\left(c_k^{j}x\right)=\left(\sin(c_k^{x}x)/\left(c_k^{x}x\right)\right)^{k} \tag{7-1}$$

$$f_j^{y}\left(c_j^{k}y\right)=\sin^{j}(j*c_j^{k}y) \tag{7-2}$$

UNS – HONN Model 0:

$$z=\sum_{k,j=0}^{n}c_{kj}^{o}\left(\sin(x)/(x)\right)^{k}\left(\sin^{j}(j*y)\right)) \tag{7-3}$$

$$where: \left(c_{kj}^{hx}\right)=\left(c_{kj}^{hy}\right)=1 \ and \ c_{k}^{x}=c_{j}^{y}=1$$

UNS – HONN Model 1:

$$z = \sum_{k,j=0}^{n} c_{kj}{}^{o}\left(\sin(c_k{}^x * x)/\left(c_k{}^x * x\right)\right)^k \left(\sin^j\left(j * c_j{}^y y\right)\right)$$

(7-4)

$$where: \left(c_{kj}{}^{hx}\right) = \left(c_{kj}{}^{hy}\right) = 1$$

UNS – Honn Model 2:

$$Z = \sum_{k,j=0}^{n}\left(c_{kj}{}^{o}\right)\{c_{kj}{}^{hx}\left(\sin(c_k{}^x * x)/\left(c_k{}^x * x\right)\right)^k\}\{c_{kj}{}^{hy}\left(\sin^j\left(j * c_j{}^y y\right)\right)\}$$

(7-5)

For equations (7-3: UNS-HONN 0), (7-2: UNS-HONN 1), and (7-3: UNS-HONN2), values of k and j ranges from 0 to n, where n is an integer. The UNS-HONN model can classify ultra-high frequency data, when n increases to a big number. This property of the model allows it to easily classify, simulate and predicate ultra-high frequency data, since both k and j increase when there is an increase in n.

The following is an expansion of model UNS-HONN order two.

$$
\begin{aligned}
z = &\ c_{00}{}^{o}\, c_{00}{}^{hx}\, c_{00}{}^{hy}\, (\sin(c_0{}^x\, x)/\, c_0{}^x\, x)^0 \sin^0(0*c_0{}^y y)\\
&+ c_{01}{}^{o}\, c_{01}{}^{hx}\, c_{01}{}^{hy}\, (\sin(c_0{}^x\, x)/\, c_0{}^x\, x)^0 \sin^1(1*c_1{}^y\, y)\\
&+ c_{02}{}^{o}\, c_{02}{}^{hx}\, c_{02}{}^{hy}\, (\sin(c_0{}^x\, x)/\, c_0{}^x\, x)^0 \sin^2(2*c_2{}^y\, y)\\
&+ c_{10}{}^{o}\, c_{10}{}^{hx}\, c_{10}{}^{hy}\, (\sin(c_1{}^x\, x)/\, c_1{}^x\, x)^1 \sin^0(0*c_0{}^y y)\\
&+ c_{11}{}^{o}\, c_{11}{}^{hx}\, c_{11}{}^{hy}\, (\sin(c_1{}^x\, x)/\, c_1{}^x\, x)^1 \sin^1(1*c_1{}^y\, y)\\
&+ c_{12}{}^{o}\, c_{12}{}^{hx}\, c_{12}{}^{hy}\, (\sin(c_1{}^x\, x)/\, c_1{}^x\, x)^1 \sin^2(2*c_2{}^y\, y)\\
&+ c_{20}{}^{o}\, c_{20}{}^{hx}\, c_{20}{}^{hy}\, (\sin(c_2{}^x\, x)/\, c_2{}^x\, x)^2 \sin^0(0*c_0{}^y y)\\
&+ c_{21}{}^{o}\, c_{21}{}^{hx}\, c_{21}{}^{hy}\, (\sin(c_2{}^x\, x)/\, c_2{}^x\, x)^2 \sin^1(1*c_1{}^y\, y)\\
&+ c_{22}{}^{o}\, c_{22}{}^{hx}\, c_{22}{}^{hy}\, (\sin(c_2{}^x\, x)/\, c_2{}^x\, x)^2 \sin^2(2*c_2{}^y\, y)
\end{aligned}
$$

(7-6)

The UNS-HONN Architecture is shown in Figure 1 and 1B. This model structure is used to develop the model learning algorithm, which make sure the convergence of learning. This allows the deference between desired output and real output of UNS-HONN close to zero.

UNC-HONN Model

The UNC-HONN models replace the sine functions from UNS-HONN with cosine functions. Based on Chapter 1 formulae from (1-128) to (1-132: UNC-HONN 2), the UNC-HONN models are defined as follows:

311

Let

$$f_k^j\left(c_k^{\,j}x\right) = \left(\sin(c_k^{\,x}x) / \left(c_k^{\,x}x\right)\right)^k \tag{7-7}$$

$$f_j^y\left(c_j^{\,k}y\right) = \cos^j\left(j * c_j^{\,k}y\right) \tag{7-8}$$

UNC – HONN Model 0:

$$z = \sum_{k,j=0}^{n} c_{kj}^{\,o}\left(\sin(x)/(x)\right)^k \left(\cos^j\left(j * y\right)\right)$$

$$where: \left(c_{kj}^{\,hx}\right) = \left(c_{kj}^{\,hy}\right) = 1 \ \ and \ \ c_k^{\,x} = c_j^{\,y} = 1 \tag{7-9}$$

UNC – HONN Model 1:

$$z = \sum_{k,j=0}^{n} c_{kj}^{\,o}\left(\sin(c_k^{\,x} * x)/\left(c_k^{\,x} * x\right)\right)^k \left(\cos^j\left(j * c_j^{\,y} y\right)\right)$$

$$where: \left(c_{kj}^{\,hx}\right) = \left(c_{kj}^{\,hy}\right) = 1 \tag{7-10}$$

UNC – HONN Model 2:

$$Z = \sum_{k,j=0}^{n} \left(c_{kj}^{\,o}\right)\{c_{kj}^{\,hx}\left(\sin(c_k^{\,x} * x)/\left(c_k^{\,x} * x\right)\right)^k\}\{c_{kj}^{\,hy}\left(\cos^j\left(j * c_j^{\,y} y\right)\right)\} \tag{7-11}$$

LEARNING ALGORITHM OF UNS-HONN Model and UNC-HONN MODEL

The learning formula for the output layer weights in UNS-HONN models and UNC-HONN models are the same. The learning formula for the second-hidden layer weights in the UNS-HONN modes and UNC-HONN models are the same. The learning formula for the first-hidden layer weights in the

UNS-HONN models and UNC-HONN models are different. Details are listed here.

Learning Formulae of Output Neurons in UNS-HONN Model and UNC-HONN Model (model 0, 1, and 2)

Based on Chapter 1 formulae from (1-133: A.1) to (1-145: A.13), UNS-HONN models and UNC-HONN models (model 0, 1, and 2) are rewritten as follows:

$$c_{kj}^{\ o}(t+1) = c_{kj}^{\ o}(t) - \eta\left(\frac{\partial E}{\partial c_{kj}^{\ o}}\right) = c_{kj}^{\ o}(t) + \eta(d-z)f^{o'}(net^o)i_{kj} = c_{kj}^{\ o}(t) + \eta\delta^{ol}i_{kj}$$

where: $\delta o^{l=}(d-z)$

$$f^{o'}(net^o) = 1 \quad (linear\ neuron) \tag{7-12}$$

Learning Formulae of Second-Hidden Layer Neurons in UNS-HONN Model and UNC-HONN Model (Model 2)

Based on Chapter 1 formulae from (1-146: B.1) to (1-160: B.15), UNS-HONN and UNC-HONN models (model 2) are rewritten as follows:

The weight update question for x input neurons is:

$$c_{kj}^{\ hx}(t+1) = c_{kj}^{\ hx}(t) - \eta\left(\partial E / \partial c_{kj}^{\ hx}\right)$$
$$= c_{kj}^{\ hx}(t) + \eta\left((d-z)f^{o'}(net^o)c_{kj}^{\ o}f^{h'}(net_{kj}^{\ hx})c_{kj}^{\ hy}b_j^{\ y}b_k^{\ x}\right) = c_{kj}^{\ hx}(t) + \eta\left(\delta^{ol}c_{kj}^{\ o}\delta_{kj}^{\ hx}b_k^{\ x}\right)$$

where: $\delta o^{l=}(d-z)$

$$\delta_{kj}^{\ hx} = c_{kj}^{\ hy}b_j^{\ y}f^{o'}(net^o) = 1 \quad (linear\ neuron)$$

$$f^{h'}\left(net_{kj}^{hx}\right)=1 \qquad \left(linear\ neuron\right) \qquad (7\text{-}13)$$

The weight update question for y input neurons is:

$$c_{kj}^{hy}\left(t+1\right)=c_{kj}^{hy}\left(t\right)-\eta\left(\frac{\partial E}{\partial c_{kj}^{hy}}\right)$$

$$=c_{kj}^{hy}\left(t\right)+\eta\left(\left(d-z\right)f^{o'}\left(net^{o}\right)c_{kj}^{o}f^{h'}\left(net_{kj}^{hy}\right)c_{kj}^{hx}b_{k}^{x}b_{j}^{y}\right)=c_{kj}^{hy}\left(t\right)+\eta\left(\delta^{ol}c_{kj}^{o}\delta_{kj}^{hy}b_{j}^{y}\right)$$

where: $\delta o^{l=}(d-z)$

$$\delta_{kj}^{hy}=c_{kj}^{hx}b_{k}^{x}f^{o'}\left(net^{o}\right)=1 \qquad \left(linear\ neuron\right)$$

$$f^{h'}\left(net_{kj}^{hy}\right)=1 \qquad \left(linear\ neuron\right) \qquad (7\text{-}14)$$

General Learning Formulae of First Hidden Layer x Neurons in UNS-HONN Model and UNC-HONN Model (Model 1 and Model 2)

Based on Chapter 1 formulae from (1-161: C.1) to (1-177: C.17), UNS-HONN and UNC-HONN models (model 1 and 2) are rewritten as follows:

For a function of x input side:

$$b_{k}^{x}=f_{k}^{x}\left(net_{k}^{x}\right)$$

$$f_{x}'\left(net_{k}^{x}\right)=\partial b_{k}^{x}/\partial\left(net_{k}^{x}\right) \qquad (7\text{-}15)$$

$$c_{k}^{x}\left(t+1\right)=c_{k}^{x}\left(t\right)-\eta\left(\frac{\partial E_{p}}{\partial c_{k}^{x}}\right)$$

$$=c_{k}^{x}\left(t\right)+\eta\left(d-z\right)f^{o'}\left(net^{o}\right)c_{kj}^{o}*f^{h'}\left(net_{kj}^{h}\right)c_{kj}^{hy}b_{j}^{y}c_{kj}^{hx}f_{x}'\left(net_{k}^{x}\right)x$$

$$=c_{k}^{x}\left(t\right)+\eta*\delta^{ol}*c_{kj}^{o}*\delta^{hx}*c_{kj}^{hx}*\delta^{x}*x$$

where:

$$\delta^{ol} = (d-z)f^{o'}\left(net^{o}\right) = d-z \qquad (linear\ neuron)$$

$$\delta^{hx} = f^{h'}\left(net_{kj}{}^{h}\right)c_{kj}{}^{hy}b_{j}{}^{y} = c_{kj}{}^{hy}b_{j}{}^{y} \qquad (linear\ neuron)$$

$$\delta^{x} = f_{x}'\left(net_{k}{}^{x}\right) \qquad\qquad\qquad (7\text{-}16)$$

General Learning Formulae of First Hidden Layer y Neurons in UNS-HONN Model and UNC-HONN Model (Model 1 and Model 2)

Based on Chapter 1 formulae from (1-178: D.1) to (1-194: D.17), UNS-HONN and UNC-HONN models (model 1 and 2) are rewritten as follows:

For a function of *y* input part:

$$b_{j}{}^{y} = f_{j}{}^{y}\left(net_{j}{}^{y}\right)$$
$$f_{y}'\left(net_{j}{}^{y}\right) = \partial b_{j}{}^{y} / \partial\left(net_{j}{}^{y}\right) \qquad (7\text{-}17)$$

Using the above procedure:

$$c_{j}{}^{y}\left(t+1\right) = c_{j}{}^{y}\left(t\right) - \eta\left(\partial E_{p} / \partial c_{j}{}^{y}\right)$$
$$= c_{j}{}^{y}\left(t\right) + \eta\left(d-z\right)f^{o\,'}\left(net^{o}\right)c_{kj}{}^{o} * f^{h\,'}\left(net_{kj}{}^{h}\right)c_{kj}{}^{hx}b_{k}{}^{x}c_{kj}{}^{hy}f_{y}'\left(net_{j}{}^{y}\right)y$$
$$= c_{j}{}^{y}\left(t\right) + \eta * \delta^{ol} * c_{kj}{}^{o} * \delta^{hy} * c_{kj}{}^{hy} * \delta^{y} * y$$

where:

$$\delta^{ol} = (d-z)f^{o'}\left(net^{o}\right) = d-z \qquad \left(linear\ neuron\ \ f^{o\,'}\left(net^{o}\right) = 1\right)$$

$$\delta^{hy} = f^{h'}\left(net_{kj}^{\ h}\right)c_{kj}^{\ hx}b_k^{\ x} = c_{kj}^{\ hx}b_k^{\ x} \qquad \left(linear\ neuron\ f^{h\ '}\left(net_{kj}^{\ h}\right)=1\right)$$

$$\delta^y = f_y'\left(net_j^{\ y}\right) \qquad\qquad (7\text{-}18)$$

Learning formulae of UNS-HONN Model for the First Hidden Layer

The first hidden layer neurons in UNS-HONN (Model 1 and Model 2) use sinc and sine functions. Based on Chapter 1 formulae from (1-327) to (1-332: UNS-HONN D.17), update learning formulae of UNS-HONN models (model 1 and 2) are rewritten as follows:

Let

$$f_k^{\ j}\left(c_k^{\ j}x\right)=\left(\sin(c_k^{\ x}x)/\left(c_k^{\ x}x\right)\right)^k \qquad\qquad (7\text{-}19)$$

$$f_j^{\ y}\left(c_j^{\ k}y\right)=\sin^j(j*c_j^{\ k}y) \qquad\qquad (7\text{-}20)$$

For a SINC function of x input part:

$$b_k^{\ x} = f_k^{\ x}\left(net_k^{\ x}\right)=\left[\sin(net_k^{\ x})/net_k^{\ x}\right]^k =\left[\sin(c_k^{\ x}x)/c_k^{\ x}x\right]^k$$

$$f_x'\left(net_k^{\ x}\right)=\partial b_k^{\ x}/\partial\left(net_k^{\ x}\right)$$
$$=k\left[\sin(net_k^{\ x})/\left(net_k^{\ x}\right)\right]^{k-1}*\left[\cos(net_k^{\ x})/\left(net_k^{\ x}\right)-\sin(net_k^{\ x})/\left(net_k^{\ x}\right)^2\right]$$
$$=k\left[\sin(c_k^{\ x}x)/\left(c_k^{\ k}x\right)\right]^{k-1}*\left[\cos(c_k^{\ x}x)/\left(c_k^{\ x}x\right)-\sin(c_k^{\ x}x)/\left(c_k^{\ x}x\right)^2\right]$$

$$(7\text{-}21)$$

316

$$c_k^{\ x}(t+1) = c_k^{\ x}(t) - \eta \left(\partial E_p / \partial c_k^{\ x} \right)$$

$$= c_k^{\ x}(t) + \eta (d-z) f^{o\,\prime}\left(net^o\right) c_{kj}^{\ o} * f^{h\,\prime}\left(net_{kj}^{\ h}\right) c_{kj}^{\ hy} b_j^{\ y} c_{kj}^{\ hx} f_x^{\ \prime}\left(net_k^{\ x}\right) x$$

$$= c_k^{\ x}(t) + \eta * \delta^{ol} * c_{kj}^{\ o} * \delta^{hx} * c_{kj}^{\ hx} * f_x^{\ \prime}\left(net_k^{\ x}\right) * x = c_k^{\ x}(t) + \eta * \delta^{ol} * c_{kj}^{\ o} * \delta^{hx} * c_{kj}^{\ hx}$$

$$* \left[k \left[\sin(c_k^{\ x}x) / \left(c_k^{\ k}x\right) \right]^{k-1} * \left[\cos(c_k^{\ x}x) / \left(c_k^{\ x}x\right) - \sin(c_k^{\ x}x) / \left(c_k^{\ k}x\right)^2 \right] \right] * x$$

$$= c_k^{\ x}(t) + \eta * \delta^{ol} * c_{kj}^{\ o} * \delta^{hx} * c_{kj}^{\ hx} * \delta^x * x$$

$$(7\text{-}22)$$

where:

$$\delta^{ol} = (d-z) f^{o\,\prime}\left(net^o\right) = (d-z) \qquad \left(linear\ neuron\ f^{o\,\prime}\left(net^o\right) = 1\right)$$

$$\delta^{hx} = f^{h\,\prime}\left(net_{kj}^{\ h}\right) c_{kj}^{\ hy} b_j^{\ y} = c_{kj}^{\ hy} b_j^{\ y} \qquad \left(linear\ neuron\ f^{h\,\prime}\left(net_{kj}^{\ h}\right) = 1\right)$$

$$\delta^x = f_x^{\ \prime}\left(net_k^{\ x}\right)$$

$$= k \left[\sin(net_k^{\ x}) / \left(net_k^{\ x}\right) \right]^{k-1} * \left[\cos\left(net_k^{\ x}\right) / \left(net_k^{\ x}\right) - \sin(net_k^{\ x}) / \left(net_k^{\ x}\right)^2 \right]$$

$$= k \left[\sin(c_k^{\ x}x) / \left(c_k^{\ x}x\right) \right]^{k-1} * \left[\cos(c_k^{\ x}x) / \left(c_k^{\ x}x\right) - \sin(c_k^{\ x}x) / \left(c_k^{\ x}x\right)^2 \right]$$

For an ultra-high frequency sine function of *y* input part:

$$b_j^{\ y} = f_j^{\ y}\left(net_j^{\ y}\right) = \sin^j(j * net_j^{\ y}) = \sin^j(j * c_j^{\ y} * y)$$

$$f_y^{\ \prime}\left(net_j^{\ y}\right) = \partial b_j^{\ y} / \partial\left(net_j^{\ y}\right)$$

$$= \partial\left(\sin^j(j * net_j^{\ y})\right) / \partial\left(net_j^{\ y}\right) = j \sin^{j-1}(j * net_j^{\ y}) * \cos(j * net_j^{\ y}) * j$$

$$= j^2 * \sin^{j-1}(j * net_j^{\ y}) * \cos(j * net_j^{\ y}) = j^2 * \sin^{j-1}(j * c_j^{\ y} * y) * \cos(j * c_j^{\ y} * y)$$

$$(7\text{-}23)$$

Using the above procedure:

$$c_j^y(t+1) = c_j^y(t) - \eta\left(\partial E_p / \partial c_j^y\right)$$

$$= c_j^y(t) + \eta(d-z)f^{o\,\prime}\left(net^o\right)c_{kj}^{\,o} * f^{h\,\prime}\left(net_{kj}^{\,h}\right)c_{kj}^{\,hx}b_k^{\,x}c_{kj}^{\,hy}f_y^{\,\prime}\left(net_j^{\,y}\right)y$$

$$= c_j^y(t) + \eta * \delta^{ol} * c_{kj}^{\,o} * \delta^{hy} * c_{kj}^{\,hy} * \left(j^2\right)\sin^{j-1}(j*c_j^y*y)\cos(j*c_j^y*y)*y$$

$$= c_j^y(t) + \eta * \delta^{ol} * c_{kj}^{\,o} * \delta^{hy} * c_{kj}^{\,hy} * \delta^y * y$$

$$(7\text{-}24)$$

where:

$$\delta^{ol} = (d-z)f^{o\prime}\left(net^o\right) = d-z \qquad\qquad \left(linear\ neuron\ f^{o\,\prime}\left(net^o\right) = 1\right)$$

$$\delta^{hy} = f^{h\prime}\left(net_{kj}^{\,hy}\right)c_{kj}^{\,hx}b_k^{\,x} = c_{kj}^{\,hx}b_k^{\,x} \qquad\qquad \left(linear\ neuron\ f^{h\,\prime}\left(net_{kj}^{\,hy}\right) = 1\right)$$

$$\delta^y = f_y^{\,\prime}\left(net_j^{\,y}\right) = \left(j^2\right)\sin^{j-1}(j*c_j^y*y)\cos(j*c_j^y*y)$$

Learning Formulae of UNC-HONN Model for the First Hidden Layer

The first hidden layer neurons in UNC-HONN (Model 1 and Model 2) use sinc and cosine functions. Based on Chapter 1 formulae from (1-333) to (1.338: UNC-HONN D.17), update learning formulae of UNC-HONN models (model 1 and 2) are rewritten as follows:

Let

$$f_k^{\,j}\left(c_k^{\,j}x\right) = \left(\sin(c_k^{\,x}x)/\left(c_k^{\,x}x\right)\right)^k \qquad\qquad (7\text{-}25)$$

$$f_j^{\,y}\left(c_j^{\,k}y\right) = \cos^j(j*c_j^{\,k}y) \qquad\qquad (7\text{-}26)$$

For a SINC function of x input part:

$$b_k^{\ x} = f_k^{\ x}\left(net_k^{\ x}\right) = \left[\sin(net_k^{\ x})/net_k^{\ x}\right]^k = \left[\sin(c_k^{\ x}x)/c_k^{\ x}x\right]^k$$

$$f_x'\left(net_k^{\ x}\right) = \partial b_k^{\ x}/\partial\left(net_k^{\ x}\right)$$

$$= k\left[\sin(net_k^{\ x})/\left(net_k^{\ x}\right)\right]^{k-1} * \left[\cos(net_k^{\ x})/\left(net_k^{\ x}\right) - \sin(net_k^{\ x})/\left(net_k^{\ x}\right)^2\right]$$

$$= k\left[\sin(c_k^{\ x}x)/\left(c_k^{\ k}x\right)\right]^{k-1} * \left[\cos(c_k^{\ x}x)/\left(c_k^{\ x}x\right) - \sin(c_k^{\ x}x)/\left(c_k^{\ x}x\right)^2\right]$$

$$(7-27)$$

$$c_k^{\ x}\left(t+1\right) = c_k^{\ x}\left(t\right) - \eta\left(\partial E_p/\partial c_k^{\ x}\right)$$

$$= c_k^{\ x}\left(t\right) + \eta\left(d-z\right)f^{o\,\prime}\left(net^o\right)c_{kj}^{\ o} * f^{h\,\prime}\left(net_{kj}^{\ h}\right)c_{kj}^{\ hy}b_j^{\ y}c_{kj}^{\ hx}f_x'\left(net_k^{\ x}\right)x$$

$$= c_k^{\ x}\left(t\right) + \eta * \delta^{ol} * c_{kj}^{\ o} * \delta^{hx} * c_{kj}^{\ hx} * f_x'\left(net_k^{\ x}\right) * x = c_k^{\ x}\left(t\right) + \eta * \delta^{ol} * c_{kj}^{\ o} * \delta^{hx} * c_{kj}^{\ hx}$$

$$*[k[\sin(c_k^{\ x}x)/\left(c_k^{\ k}x\right)]^{k-1} * \left[\cos(c_k^{\ x}x)/\left(c_k^{\ x}x\right) - \sin(c_k^{\ x}x)/\left(c_k^{\ x}x\right)^2\right]] * x$$

$$= c_k^{\ x}\left(t\right) + \eta * \delta^{ol} * c_{kj}^{\ o} * \delta^{hx} * c_{kj}^{\ hx} * \delta^x * x$$

$$(7-28)$$

where:

$$\delta^{ol} = \left(d-z\right)f^{o\,\prime}\left(net^o\right) = \left(d-z\right) \qquad \left(linear\ neuron\ f^{o\,\prime}\left(net^o\right) = 1\right)$$

$$\delta^{hx} = f^{h\,\prime}\left(net_{kj}^{\ h}\right)c_{kj}^{\ hy}b_j^{\ y} = c_{kj}^{\ hy}b_j^{\ y} \qquad \left(linear\ neuron\ f^{h\,\prime}\left(net_{kj}^{\ h}\right) = 1\right)$$

$$\delta^x = f_x'\left(net_k^{\ x}\right)$$

$$= k\left[\sin(net_k^{\ x})/\left(net_k^{\ x}\right)\right]^{k-1} * \left[\cos(net_k^{\ x})/\left(net_k^{\ x}\right) - \sin(net_k^{\ x})/\left(net_k^{\ x}\right)^2\right]$$

$$= k\left[\sin(c_k^{\ x}x)/\left(c_k^{\ k}x\right)\right]^{k-1} * \left[\cos(c_k^{\ x}x)/\left(c_k^{\ x}x\right) - \sin(c_k^{\ x}x)/\left(c_k^{\ x}x\right)^2\right]$$

For an ultra-high frequency cosine function of y input part:

$$b_j^{\ y} = f_j^{\ y}\left(net_j^{\ y}\right) = \cos^j\left(j * net_j^{\ y}\right) = \cos^j\left(j * c_j^{\ y} * y\right)$$

$$f_y'\left(net_j^y\right) = \partial b_j^y / \partial\left(net_j^y\right)$$

$$= \partial\left(\cos^j(j*net_j^y)\right)/\partial\left(net_j^y\right) = j\cos^{j-1}(j*net_j^y)*\left(-\sin(j*net_j^y)\right)*j$$

$$= -j^2*\cos^{j-1}(j*net_j^y)*\sin(j*net_j^y) = -j^2*\cos^{j-1}(j*c_j^y*y)*\sin(j*c_j^y*y)$$

$$(7\text{-}29)$$

Using the above procedure:

$$c_j^y(t+1) = c_j^y(t) - \eta\left(\partial E_p / \partial c_j^y\right)$$

$$= c_j^y(t) + \eta(d-z)f^{o\,\prime}\left(net^o\right)c_{kj}^o * f^{h\,\prime}\left(net_{kj}^h\right)c_{kj}^{hx}b_k^x c_{kj}^{hy}f_y'\left(net_j^y\right)y$$

$$= c_j^y(t) + \eta * \delta^{ol} * c_{kj}^o * \delta^{hy} * c_{kj}^{hy} * \left(-j^2\right)*\cos^{j-1}(j*c_j^y*y)*\sin(j*c_j^y*y)*y$$

$$= c_j^y(t) + \eta * \delta^{ol} * c_{kj}^o * \delta^{hy} * c_{kj}^{hy} * \delta^y * y$$

$$(7\text{-}30)$$

where:

$$\delta^{ol} = (d-z)f^{o\,\prime}\left(net^o\right) = d-z \qquad\qquad \left(linear\ neuron\ f^{o\,\prime}\left(net^o\right) = 1\right)$$

$$\delta^{hy} = f^{h\,\prime}\left(net_{kj}^{hy}\right)c_{kj}^{hx}b_k^x = c_{kj}^{hx}b_k^x \qquad\qquad \left(linear\ neuron\ f^{h\,\prime}\left(net_{kj}^{hy}\right) = 1\right)$$

$$\delta^y = f_y'\left(net_j^y\right) = \left(-j^2\right)*\cos^{j-1}(j*c_j^y*y)*\sin(j*c_j^y*y)$$

UNS-HONN AND UNC-HONN MODELTESTING

This chapter uses UNS-HONN model to classify data. Test results are shown in Tables 1 and 2 and Figures 3A and 3B. Next, the UNC-HONN model is used to classify data. Results are provided in Tables 3 and 4 and Figures 4A and 4B.

The UNS-HONN model 0 is used in Table 1 of "UNS-HONN Data Classification 1",. The order number for UNS-HONN model is 6. In the first table of Table 1, the "No." column shows that a total of 19 points are chosen. The "UNS-HONN x" column displays the input x values, which are all "1"s. The "UNS-HONN y" column displays the input y values, which are 0, 0.1, 0.2, 0.3, 0.4, 05, 0.7, 0.8, 0.9, 1, 2, 3, 4, 5, 6, 7 and 8. The "UNS-HONN z" column displays the output z values. The "Original Data" column displays the original data values. The "Absolute Original Data" column displays the absolute values for original data. The "Difference" column shows the difference between UNS-HONN output z and the original data (UNS-HONN z – Original Data). The "Absolute Difference" column shows the absolute difference between UNS-HONN output z and the original data (|UNS-HONN z – Original Data|). The "UNS-HONN Error %" column gives the error percentage for UNS-HONN Model (UNS-HONN error % = absolute difference / Absolute original Data * 100%). The average UNS-HONN error is 0.00002926%, which is close to zero. After training UNS-HONN model by using original data values, the UNS-HONN all coefficients are displayed in the second table of Table 1. For examples, $c_{00}{}^o$= 0.3884, $c_{01}{}^o$ = 0.9624, and $c_{10}{}^o$= -0.1712. In the third table of Table 1, the values for $c_{kj}{}^o*(sin(x)/x)^k*sin^j(j*y)$ *are provided* when $x=1$, $y=0.1$, $k=0,1,2,3,4,5,6$, and $j=0,1,2,3,4,5,6$. For examples, $c_{01}{}^o*(sin(x)/x)^0*sin^1(1*0.1)=0.09607968$, $c_{02}{}^o*(sin(x)/x)^0*sin^2(2*0.1)=0.03910638$, and $c_{03}{}^o*(sin(x)/x)^0*sin^3(3*0.1)=-0.01388493$.

$And z = å c_{kj}{}^o*(sin(x)/x)^k*sin^j(j*y) = å c_{kj}{}^o*(sin(1)/1)^k*sin^j(j*0.1)=0.13133595$.

In Table 2 of "UNS-HONN Data Classification 2", the UNS-HONN model 0 is used. The order number for UNS-HONN model is 6. In the first table of Table 2, the "No." column shows that a total of 19 points are chosen. The "UNS-HONN x" column displays the input x values, which are all "1"s . The "UNS-HONN y" column displays the input y values, which are 0, 0.1, 0.2, 0.3, 0.4, 05, 0.7, 0.8, 0.9, 1, 2, 3, 4, 5, 6, 7 and 8. The "UNS-HONN z" column displays the output z values. The "Original Data" column displays the original data values. The "Absolute Original Data" column displays the absolute values for the original data. The "Difference" column shows the difference between UNS-HONN output z and the original data (UNS-HONN z – Original Data). The "Absolute Difference" column shows the absolute difference between UNS-HONN output z and the original data (|UNS-HONN z – Original Data|). The "UNS-HONN Error %" column gives the error percentage for UNS-HONN Model (UNS-HONN error % = absolute difference / Absolute original Data * 100%). The average UNS-HONN error is 0.00002926%, which is close to zero. The UNS-HONN all coefficients are displayed in the second table of Table 2 after training UNS-HONN model by using original data values. For examples, $c_{00}{}^o$= 0.2896, $c_{01}{}^o$= 0.9747, and $c_{10}{}^o$= -0.0624. In the third table of Table 2, gives the values for $c_{kj}{}^o*(sin(x)/x)^k*sin^j(j*y)$, when $x=1$, $y=0.1$, $k=0,1,2,3,4,5,6$, and $j=0,1,2,3,4,5,6$. For examples, $c_{01}{}^o*(sin(x)/x)^0*sin^1(1*0.1)=0.09730763$, $c_{02}{}^o*(sin(x)/x)^0*sin^2(2*0.1)=0.00491395$, and $c_{03}{}^o*(sin(x)/x)^0*sin^3(3*0.1)=-0.02231139$.

And $z = å\ c_{kj}{}^o*(sin(x)/x)^k*sin^j(j*y) = å\ c_{kj}{}^o*(sin(1)/1)^k*sin^j(j*0.1)=0.106026689$.

In Figure 3, UNS-HONN data classification results are shown. Original Data are shown by Figure 3. And UNS-HONN data classification results are shown by Figure 3B. In Figure 3, the data have been divided into two classifications. The Figure 4 also tells us the UNS-HONN model can classify data very well, since the average error percentage is close to 10^{-6}.

Based on the training of UNS-HONN model, UNS-HONN has the following formula (see Table 1) to describe the data classification 1:

$z=å\ c_{kj}{}^o*(sin(x)/x)^k*sin^j(j*y)\ (k, j = 0,1,2,3,4,5,6,)$
$= c_{00}{}^o*(sin(x)/x)^0*sin^0(0*y)+ c_{10}{}^o*(sin(x)/x)^1*sin^0(0*y)$
$+ c_{20}{}^o*(sin(x)/x)^2*sin^0(0*y)+ c_{30}{}^o*(sin(x)/x)^3*sin^0(0*y)$
$+ c_{40}{}^o*(sin(x)/x)^4*sin^0(0*y)+ c_{50}{}^o*(sin(x)/x)^5*sin^0(0*y)$
$+ c_{60}{}^o*(sin(x)/x)^6*sin^0(0*y)$
$+c_{01}{}^o*(sin(x)/x)^0*sin^1(1*y)+ c_{11}{}^o*(sin(x)/x)^1*sin^1(1*y)$
$+ c_{21}{}^o*(sin(x)/x)^2*sin^1(1*y)+ c_{31}{}^o*(sin(x)/x)^3*sin^1(1*y)$
$+ c_{41}{}^o*(sin(x)/x)^4*sin^1(1*y)+ c_{51}{}^o*(sin(x)/x)^5*sin^1(1*y)$
$+ c_{61}{}^o*(sin(x)/x)^6*sin^1(1*y)$
$+c_{02}{}^o*(sin(x)/x)^0*sin^2(2*y)+ c_{12}{}^o*(sin(x)/x)^1*sin^2(2*y)$
$+ c_{22}{}^o*(sin(x)/x)^2*sin^2(2*y)+ c_{32}{}^o*(sin(x)/x)^3*sin^2(2*y)$
$+ c_{42}{}^o*(sin(x)/x)^4*sin^2(2*y)+ c_{52}{}^o*(sin(x)/x)^5*sin^2(2*y)$
$+ c_{62}{}^o*(sin(x)/x)^6*sin^2(2*y)$
$+c_{03}{}^o*(sin(x)/x)^0*sin^3(3*y)+ c_{13}{}^o*(sin(x)/x)^1*sin^3(3*y)$
$+ c_{23}{}^o*(sin(x)/x)^2*sin^3(3*y)+ c_{33}{}^o*(sin(x)/x)^3*sin^3(3*y)$
$+ c_{43}{}^o*(sin(x)/x)^4*sin^3(3*y)+ c_{53}{}^o*(sin(x)/x)^5*sin^3(3*y)$
$+ c_{63}{}^o*(sin(x)/x)^6*sin^3(3*y)$
$+c_{04}{}^o*(sin(x)/x)^0*sin^4(4*y)+ c_{14}{}^o*(sin(x)/x)^1*sin^4(4*y)$
$+ c_{24}{}^o*(sin(x)/x)^2*sin^4(4*y)+ c_{34}{}^o*(sin(x)/x)^3*sin^4(4*y)$
$+ c_{44}{}^o*(sin(x)/x)^4*sin^4(4*y)+ c_{54}{}^o*(sin(x)/x)^5*sin^4(4*y)$
$+ c_{64}{}^o*(sin(x)/x)^6*sin^4(4*y)$
$+c_{05}{}^o*(sin(x)/x)^0*sin^5(5*y)+ c_{15}{}^o*(sin(x)/x)^1*sin^5(5*y)$
$+ c_{25}{}^o*(sin(x)/x)^2*sin^5(4*y)+ c_{35}{}^o*(sin(x)/x)^3*sin^5(5*y)$
$+ c_{45}{}^o*(sin(x)/x)^4*sin^5(5*y)+ c_{55}{}^o*(sin(x)/x)^5*sin^5(5*y)$
$+ c_{65}{}^o*(sin(x)/x)^6*sin^5(5*y)$

$+c_{06}{}^{o}*(\sin(x)/x)^{0}*\sin^{6}(6*y)+ c_{16}{}^{o}*(\sin(x)/x)^{1}*\sin^{6}(6*y)$

$+ c_{26}{}^{o}*(\sin(x)/x)^{2}*\sin^{6}(6*y)+ c_{36}{}^{o}*(\sin(x)/x)^{3}*\sin^{6}(6*y)$

$+ c_{46}{}^{o}*(\sin(x)/x)^{4}*\sin^{6}(6*y)+ c_{56}{}^{o}*(\sin(x)/x)^{5}*\sin^{6}(6*y)$

$+ c_{66}{}^{o}*(\sin(x)/x)^{6}*\sin^{6}(6*y)$

$= 0.3884*(\sin(x)/x)^{0}*\sin^{0}(0*y)+ (-0.1712)*(\sin(x)/x)^{1}*\sin^{0}(0*y)$

$+ (-0.3580)*(\sin(x)/x)^{2}*\sin^{0}(0*y)+ (-0.2535)*(\sin(x)/x)^{3}*\sin^{0}(0*y)$

$+ (-0.9590)*(\sin(x)/x)^{4}*\sin^{0}(0*y)+ (-0.2524)*(\sin(x)/x)^{5}*\sin^{0}(0*y)$

$+ 0.8223*(\sin(x)/x)^{6}*\sin^{0}(0*y)$

$+0.9624*(\sin(x)/x)^{0}*\sin^{1}(1*y)+ 0.0838*(\sin(x)/x)^{1}*\sin^{1}(1*y)$

$+ (-0.0760)*(\sin(x)/x)^{2}*\sin^{1}(1*y)+ (-0.9257)*(\sin(x)/x)^{3}*\sin^{1}(1*y)$

$+ 0.9045*(\sin(x)/x)^{4}*\sin^{1}(1*y)+ 0.2691*(\sin(x)/x)^{5}*\sin^{1}(1*y)$

$+ (-0.0672)*(\sin(x)/x)^{6}*\sin^{1}(1*y)$

$+0.9908*(\sin(x)/x)^{0}*\sin^{2}(2*y)+ 0.0399*(\sin(x)/x)^{1}*\sin^{2}(2*y)$

$+ (-0.0250)*(\sin(x)/x)^{2}*\sin^{2}(2*y)+ (-0.3347)*(\sin(x)/x)^{3}*\sin^{2}(2*y)$

$+(-0.1048)*(\sin(x)/x)^{4}*\sin^{2}(2*y)+ 0.0837*(\sin(x)/x)^{5}*\sin^{2}(2*y)$

$+ (-0.3587)*(\sin(x)/x)^{6}*\sin^{2}(2*y)$

$+(-0.5380)*(\sin(x)/x)^{0}*\sin^{3}(3*y)+ (-0.2394)*(\sin(x)/x)^{1}*\sin^{3}(3*y)$

$+ (-0.0419)*(\sin(x)/x)^{2}*\sin^{3}(3*y)+ 0.2238*(\sin(x)/x)^{3}*\sin^{3}(3*y)$

$+ 0.5765*(\sin(x)/x)^{4}*\sin^{3}(3*y)+ (-0.3017)*(\sin(x)/x)^{5}*\sin^{3}(3*y)$

$+ 0.2658*(\sin(x)/x)^{6}*\sin^{3}(3*y)$

$+(-0.1784)*(\sin(x)/x)^{0}*\sin^{4}(4*y)+ 0.4013*(\sin(x)/x)^{1}*\sin^{4}(4*y)$

$+ (-0.7152)*(\sin(x)/x)^{2}*\sin^{4}(4*y)+ 0.4915*(\sin(x)/x)^{3}*\sin^{4}(4*y)$

$+ (-0.5638)*(\sin(x)/x)^{4}*\sin^{4}(4*y)+ 0.6601*(\sin(x)/x)^{5}*\sin^{4}(4*y)$

$+ 0.0392*(\sin(x)/x)^{6}*\sin^{4}(4*y)$

$+(-0.1825)*(\sin(x)/x)^{0}*\sin^{5}(5*y)+ 0.9703*(\sin(x)/x)^{1}*\sin^{5}(5*y)$

$+ 0.2072*(\sin(x)/x)^{2}*\sin^{5}(4*y)+ 0.2234*(\sin(x)/x)^{3}*\sin^{5}(5*y)$

$+ 0.7835*(\sin(x)/x)^{4}*\sin^{5}(5*y)+ (-0.3868)*(\sin(x)/x)^{5}*\sin^{5}(5*y)$

$+ (-0.3376)*(\sin(x)/x)^{6}*\sin^{5}(5*y)$

$+0.3604*(\sin(x)/x)^{0}*\sin^{6}(6*y)+ (-0.9528)*(\sin(x)/x)^{1}*\sin^{6}(6*y)$

$+ 0.6653*(\sin(x)/x)^{2}*\sin^{6}(6*y)+ (-0.2069)*(\sin(x)/x)^{3}*\sin^{6}(6*y)$

$+ (-0.2853)*(\sin(x)/x)^{4}*\sin^{6}(6*y)+ (-0.3984)*(\sin(x)/x)^{5}*\sin^{6}(6*y)$

$+ 0.5546*(\sin(x)/x)^{6}*\sin^{6}(6*y)$ (7-31)

Based on the training of UNS-HONN model, UNS-HONN has the following formula (see Table 2) to describe the data classification 2:

$z=\text{å } c_{kj}{}^{o}*(sin(x)/x)^{k}*sin^{j}(j*y)\ (k, j = 0,1,2,3,4,5,6,)$

$= c_{00}{}^{o}*(\sin(x)/x)^{0}*\sin^{0}(0*y)+ c_{10}{}^{o}*(\sin(x)/x)^{1}*\sin^{0}(0*y)$

$+ c_{20}{}^{o}*(\sin(x)/x)^{2}*\sin^{0}(0*y)+ c_{30}{}^{o}*(\sin(x)/x)^{3}*\sin^{0}(0*y)$

$+ c_{40}{}^{o}*(\sin(x)/x)^4*\sin^0(0*y)+ c_{50}{}^{o}*(\sin(x)/x)^5*\sin^0(0*y)$

$+ c_{60}{}^{o}*(\sin(x)/x)^6*\sin^0(0*y)$

$+c_{01}{}^{o}*(\sin(x)/x)^0*\sin^1(1*y)+ c_{11}{}^{o}*(\sin(x)/x)^1*\sin^1(1*y)$

$+ c_{21}{}^{o}*(\sin(x)/x)^2*\sin^1(1*y)+ c_{31}{}^{o}*(\sin(x)/x)^3*\sin^1(1*y)$

$+ c_{41}{}^{o}*(\sin(x)/x)^4*\sin^1(1*y)+ c_{51}{}^{o}*(\sin(x)/x)^5*\sin^1(1*y)$

$+ c_{61}{}^{o}*(\sin(x)/x)^6*\sin^1(1*y)$

$+c_{02}{}^{o}*(\sin(x)/x)^0*\sin^2(2*y)+ c_{12}{}^{o}*(\sin(x)/x)^1*\sin^2(2*y)$

$+ c_{22}{}^{o}*(\sin(x)/x)^2*\sin^2(2*y)+ c_{32}{}^{o}*(\sin(x)/x)^3*\sin^2(2*y)$

$+ c_{42}{}^{o}*(\sin(x)/x)^4*\sin^2(2*y)+ c_{52}{}^{o}*(\sin(x)/x)^5*\sin^2(2*y)$

$+ c_{62}{}^{o}*(\sin(x)/x)^6*\sin^2(2*y)$

$+c_{03}{}^{o}*(\sin(x)/x)^0*\sin^3(3*y)+ c_{13}{}^{o}*(\sin(x)/x)^1*\sin^3(3*y)$

$+ c_{23}{}^{o}*(\sin(x)/x)^2*\sin^3(3*y)+ c_{33}{}^{o}*(\sin(x)/x)^3*\sin^3(3*y)$

$+ c_{43}{}^{o}*(\sin(x)/x)^4*\sin^3(3*y)+ c_{53}{}^{o}*(\sin(x)/x)^5*\sin^3(3*y)$

$+ c_{63}{}^{o}*(\sin(x)/x)^6*\sin^3(3*y)$

$+c_{04}{}^{o}*(\sin(x)/x)^0*\sin^4(4*y)+ c_{14}{}^{o}*(\sin(x)/x)^1*\sin^4(4*y)$

$+ c_{24}{}^{o}*(\sin(x)/x)^2*\sin^4(4*y)+ c_{34}{}^{o}*(\sin(x)/x)^3*\sin^4(4*y)$

$+ c_{44}{}^{o}*(\sin(x)/x)^4*\sin^4(4*y)+ c_{54}{}^{o}*(\sin(x)/x)^5*\sin^4(4*y)$

$+ c_{64}{}^{o}*(\sin(x)/x)^6*\sin^4(4*y)$

$+c_{05}{}^{o}*(\sin(x)/x)^0*\sin^5(5*y)+ c_{15}{}^{o}*(\sin(x)/x)^1*\sin^5(5*y)$

$+ c_{25}{}^{o}*(\sin(x)/x)^2*\sin^5(4*y)+ c_{35}{}^{o}*(\sin(x)/x)^3*\sin^5(5*y)$

$+ c_{45}{}^{o}*(\sin(x)/x)^4*\sin^5(5*y)+ c_{55}{}^{o}*(\sin(x)/x)^5*\sin^5(5*y)$

$+ c_{65}{}^{o}*(\sin(x)/x)^6*\sin^5(5*y)$

$+c_{06}{}^{o}*(\sin(x)/x)^0*\sin^6(6*y)+ c_{16}{}^{o}*(\sin(x)/x)^1*\sin^6(6*y)$

$+ c_{26}{}^{o}*(\sin(x)/x)^2*\sin^6(6*y)+ c_{36}{}^{o}*(\sin(x)/x)^3*\sin^6(6*y)$

$+ c_{46}{}^{o}*(\sin(x)/x)^4*\sin^6(6*y)+ c_{56}{}^{o}*(\sin(x)/x)^5*\sin^6(6*y)$

$+ c_{66}{}^{o}*(\sin(x)/x)^6*\sin^6(6*y)$

$= 0.2896*(\sin(x)/x)^0*\sin^0(0*y)+ (-0.0624)*(\sin(x)/x)^1*\sin^0(0*y)$

$+ (-0.2592)*(\sin(x)/x)^2*\sin^0(0*y)+ (-0.1347)*(\sin(x)/x)^3*\sin^0(0*y)$

$+ (-0.8502)*(\sin(x)/x)^4*\sin^0(0*y)+ (-0.1496)*(\sin(x)/x)^5*\sin^0(0*y)$

$+ 0.7235*(\sin(x)/x)^6*\sin^0(0*y)$

$+0.9747*(\sin(x)/x)^0*\sin^1(1*y)+ 0.0951*(\sin(x)/x)^1*\sin^1(1*y)$

$+ (-0.0883)*(\sin(x)/x)^2*\sin^1(1*y)+ (-0.9370)*(\sin(x)/x)^3*\sin^1(1*y)$

$+ 0.9148*(\sin(x)/x)^4*\sin^1(1*y)+ 0.2784*(\sin(x)/x)^5*\sin^1(1*y)$

$+ (-0.0795)*(\sin(x)/x)^6*\sin^1(1*y)$

$+0.1245*(\sin(x)/x)^0*\sin^2(2*y)+ 0.1525*(\sin(x)/x)^1*\sin^2(2*y)$

$+ (-0.1486)*(\sin(x)/x)^2*\sin^2(2*y)+ (-0.4573)*(\sin(x)/x)^3*\sin^2(2*y)$

$+(-0.2274)*(\sin(x)/x)^4*\sin^2(2*y)+ 0.1063*(\sin(x)/x)^5*\sin^2(2*y)$

$+ (-0.4713)*(\sin(x)/x)^6*\sin^2(2*y)$

$+(-0.8645)*(\sin(x)/x)^0*\sin^3(3*y)+ (-0.4651)*(\sin(x)/x)^1*\sin^3(3*y)$

$+ (-0.2776)*(\sin(x)/x)^{2}*\sin^{3}(3*y)+ 0.4598*(\sin(x)/x)^{3}*\sin^{3}(3*y)$
$+ 0.7022*(\sin(x)/x)^{4}*\sin^{3}(3*y)+ (-0.5463)*(\sin(x)/x)^{5}*\sin^{3}(3*y)$
$+ 0.4915*(\sin(x)/x)^{6}*\sin^{3}(3*y)$
$+(-0.4352)*(\sin(x)/x)^{0}*\sin^{4}(4*y)+ 0.7681*(\sin(x)/x)^{1}*\sin^{4}(4*y)$
$+ (-0.0720)*(\sin(x)/x)^{2}*\sin^{4}(4*y)+ 0.7583*(\sin(x)/x)^{3}*\sin^{4}(4*y)$
$+ (-0.8246)*(\sin(x)/x)^{4}*\sin^{4}(4*y)+ 0.9273*(\sin(x)/x)^{5}*\sin^{4}(4*y)$
$+ 0.3969*(\sin(x)/x)^{6}*\sin^{4}(4*y)$
$+(-0.7514)*(\sin(x)/x)^{0}*\sin^{5}(5*y)+ 0.5173*(\sin(x)/x)^{1}*\sin^{5}(5*y)$
$+ 0.8751*(\sin(x)/x)^{2}*\sin^{5}(4*y)+ 0.8913*(\sin(x)/x)^{3}*\sin^{5}(5*y)$
$+ 0.3492*(\sin(x)/x)^{4}*\sin^{5}(5*y)+ (-0.9547)*(\sin(x)/x)^{5}*\sin^{5}(5*y)$
$+ (-0.0855)*(\sin(x)/x)^{6}*\sin^{5}(5*y)$
$+0.0493*(\sin(x)/x)^{0}*\sin^{6}(6*y)+ (-0.6317)*(\sin(x)/x)^{1}*\sin^{6}(6*y)$
$+ 0.3442*(\sin(x)/x)^{2}*\sin^{6}(6*y)+ (-0.9858)*(\sin(x)/x)^{3}*\sin^{6}(6*y)$
$+ (-0.2642)*(\sin(x)/x)^{4}*\sin^{6}(6*y)+ (-0.2773)*(\sin(x)/x)^{5}*\sin^{6}(6*y)$
$+ 0.2373*(\sin(x)/x))^{6}*\sin^{6}(6*y)$ (7-32)

In Table 3 of "UNC-HONN Data Classification 1", UNC-HONN model 0 has been used. The order number for UNC-HONN model is 6. In the first table of Table 3, the "No." column shows a total of 19 points. The "UNC-HONN x" column displays the input x values, which are all "1"s. The "UNC-HONN y" column displays the input y values, which are 0, 0.1, 0.2, 0.3, 0.4, 05, 0.7, 0.8, 0.9, 1, 2, 3, 4, 5, 6, 7 and 8. The "UNC-HONN z" column displays the output z values. The "Original Data" column displays the original data values. The "Absolute Original Data" column displays the absolute values for original data. The "Difference" column shows the difference between UNC-HONN output z and the original data (UNC-HONN z – Original Data). The "Absolute Difference" column shows the absolute difference between UNC-HONN output z and the original data (|UNC-HONN z – Original Data|). The "UNC-HONN Error %" column gives the error percentage for UNC-HONN Model (UNC-HONN error % = absolute difference / Absolute original Data * 100%). The average UNC-HONN error is 0.00002394%, which is close to zero. All of the coefficients for the UNC-HONN model are displayed in the second table of Table 3 after training UNC-HONN model by using original data values. For examples, $c_{00}{}^{o}= 0.2650$, $c_{01}{}^{o}= 0.7389$, and $c_{10}{}^{o}= -0.0588$. The third table of Table 3 provides the values for $c_{kj}{}^{o}*(\sin(x)/x)^{k}*\cos^{j}(j*y)$, when $x=1$, $y=0.1$, $k=0,1,2,3,4,5,6$, and $j=0,1,2,3,4,5,6$. For examples, $c_{01}{}^{o}*(\sin(x)/x)^{0}*\cos^{1}(1*0.1)=0.73520858$, $c_{02}{}^{o}*(\sin(x)/x)^{0}*\cos^{2}(2*0.1)=0.73605452$, and $c_{03}{}^{o}*(\sin(x)/x)^{0}*\cos^{3}(3*0.1)=-0.15894826$.

$And z = \mathring{a}c_{kj}{}^{o}*(\sin(x)/x)^{k}*\cos^{j}(j*y)=\mathring{a}c_{kj}{}^{o}*(\sin(1)/1)^{k}*\cos^{j}(j*0.1)=093927060$.

In Table 4 of "UNC-HONN Data Classification 2", UNC-HONN model 0 has been used. The order number for UNC-HONN model is 6. In the first table of Table 4, the "No." column shows total 19 points are chosen. The "UNC-HONN x" column displays the input x values, which are all "1"s. The "UNC-HONN y" column displays the input y values, which are 0, 0.1, 0.2, 0.3, 0.4, 05, 0.7, 0.8, 0.9, 1, 2, 3, 4, 5, 6, 7 and 8 are used. The "UNC-HONN z" column displays the output z values. The "Original Data" column displays the original data values. The "Absolute Original Data" column displays the absolute values for original data. The "Difference" column shows the difference between UNC-HONN output z and the original data (UNC-HONN z – Original Data). The "Absolute Difference" column shows the absolute difference between UNC-HONN output z and the original data (|UNC-HONN z – Original Data|). The "UNC-HONN Error %" column gives the error percentage for UNC-HONN Model (UNC-HONN error % = absolute difference / Absolute original Data * 100%). The average UNC-HONN error is 0.00005338%, which is much closed to zero. All the coefficients for UNC-HONN model are displayed in the second table of Table 4 after training UNC-HONN model by using original data values. For examples, $c_{00}{}^o = 0.7228$, $c_{01}{}^o = 0.3068$, and $c_{10}{}^o = -0.5156$. In the third table of Table 4, gives the values for $c_{kj}{}^o*(sin(x)/x)^k*cos^j(j*y)$, when $x=1$, $y=0.1$, $k=0,1,2,3,4,5,6$, and $j=0,1,2,3,4,5,6$. For examples, $c_{01}{}^o*(sin(x)/x)^0*cos^1(1*0.1)=0.30526728$, $c_{02}{}^o*(sin(x)/x)^0*cos^2(2*0.1)=0.42782028$, and $c_{03}{}^o*(sin(x)/x)^0*cos^3(3*0.1)=-0.84871219$.

And $z = å\ c_{kj}{}^o*(sin(x)/x)^k*cos^j(j*y) = å\ c_{kj}{}^o*(sin(1)/1)^k*cos^j(j*0.1)=-1.78433940$.

In Figure 4, UNC-HONN data classification results are shown. Original Data are shown in Figure 5. UNC-HONN data classification results are shown in Figure 4B. In Figure 4, the data have been divided into two classifications. The Figure 6 presents the evidence that the UNC-HONN model can classify data very well, since the average error percentage is close to 10^{-6}.

Based on the training of UNC-HONN model, UNC-HONN has the following formula (see Table 3) to describe the data classification 1:

$z = å\ c_{kj}{}^o*(sin(x)/x)^k*cos^j(j*y)$ (k, j = 0,1,2,3,4,5,6,)
$= c_{00}{}^o*(sin(x)/x)^0*cos^0(0*y) + c_{10}{}^o*(sin(x)/x)^1*cos^0(0*y)$
$+ c_{20}{}^o*(sin(x)/x)^2*cos^0(0*y) + c_{30}{}^o*(sin(x)/x)^3*cos^0(0*y)$
$+ c_{40}{}^o*(sin(x)/x)^4*cos^0(0*y) + c_{50}{}^o*(sin(x)/x)^5*cos^0(0*y)$
$+ c_{60}{}^o*(sin(x)/x)^6*cos^0(0*y)$
$+ c_{01}{}^o*(sin(x)/x)^0*cos^1(1*y) + c_{11}{}^o*(sin(x)/x)^1*cos^1(1*y)$
$+ c_{21}{}^o*(sin(x)/x)^2*cos^1(1*y) + c_{31}{}^o*(sin(x)/x)^3*cos^1(1*y)$

$+ c_{41}{}^{o}*(sin(x)/x)^4*cos^1(1*y)+ c_{51}{}^{o}*(sin(x)/x)^5*cos^1(1*y)$

$+ c_{61}{}^{o}*(sin(x)/x)^6*cos^1(1*y)$

$+c_{02}{}^{o}*(sin(x)/x)^0*cos^2(2*y)+ c_{12}{}^{o}*(sin(x)/x)^1*cos^2(2*y)$

$+ c_{22}{}^{o}*(sin(x)/x)^2*cos^2(2*y)+ c_{32}{}^{o}*(sin(x)/x)^3*cos^2(2*y)$

$+ c_{42}{}^{o}*(sin(x)/x)^4*cos^2(2*y)+ c_{52}{}^{o}*(sin(x)/x)^5*cos^2(2*y)$

$+ c_{62}{}^{o}*(sin(x)/x)^6*cos^2(2*y)$

$+c_{03}{}^{o}*(sin(x)/x)^0*cos^3(3*y)+ c_{13}{}^{o}*(sin(x)/x)^1*cos^3(3*y)$

$+ c_{23}{}^{o}*(sin(x)/x)^2*cos^3(3*y)+ c_{33}{}^{o}*(sin(x)/x)^3*cos^3(3*y)$

$+ c_{43}{}^{o}*(sin(x)/x)^4*cos^3(3*y)+ c_{53}{}^{o}*(sin(x)/x)^5*cos^3(3*y)$

$+ c_{63}{}^{o}*(sin(x)/x)^6*cos^3(3*y)$

$+c_{04}{}^{o}*(sin(x)/x)^0*cos^4(4*y)+ c_{14}{}^{o}*(sin(x)/x)^1*cos^4(4*y)$

$+ c_{24}{}^{o}*(sin(x)/x)^2*cos^4(4*y)+ c_{34}{}^{o}*(sin(x)/x)^3*cos^4(4*y)$

$+ c_{44}{}^{o}*(sin(x)/x)^4*cos^4(4*y)+ c_{54}{}^{o}*(sin(x)/x)^5*cos^4(4*y)$

$+ c_{64}{}^{o}*(sin(x)/x)^6*cos^4(4*y)$

$+c_{05}{}^{o}*(sin(x)/x)^0*cos^5(5*y)+ c_{15}{}^{o}*(sin(x)/x)^1*cos^5(5*y)$

$+ c_{25}{}^{o}*(sin(x)/x)^2*cos^5(4*y)+ c_{35}{}^{o}*(sin(x)/x)^3*cos^5(5*y)$

$+ c_{45}{}^{o}*(sin(x)/x)^4*cos^5(5*y)+ c_{55}{}^{o}*(sin(x)/x)^5*cos^5(5*y)$

$+ c_{65}{}^{o}*(sin(x)/x)^6*cos^5(5*y)$

$+c_{06}{}^{o}*(sin(x)/x)^0*cos^6(6*y)+ c_{16}{}^{o}*(sin(x)/x)^1*cos^6(6*y)$

$+ c_{26}{}^{o}*(sin(x)/x)^2*cos^6(6*y)+ c_{36}{}^{o}*(sin(x)/x)^3*cos^6(6*y)$

$+ c_{46}{}^{o}*(sin(x)/x)^4*cos^6(6*y)+ c_{56}{}^{o}*(sin(x)/x)^5*cos^6(6*y)$

$+ c_{66}{}^{o}*(sin(x)/x)^6*cos^6(6*y)$

$= 0.2650*(sin(x)/x)^0*cos^0(0*y)+ (-0.0588)*(sin(x)/x)^1*cos^0(0*y)$

$+ (-0.2356)*(sin(x)/x)^2*cos^0(0*y)+ (-0.1101)*(sin(x)/x)^3*cos^0(0*y)$

$+ (-0.8366)*(sin(x)/x)^4*cos^0(0*y)+ (-0.1290)*(sin(x)/x)^5*cos^0(0*y)$

$+ 0.7099*(sin(x)/x)^6*cos^0(0*y)$

$+0.7389*(sin(x)/x)^0*cos^1(1*y)+ 0.8593*(sin(x)/x)^1*cos^1(1*y)$

$+ (-0.8425)*(sin(x)/x)^2*cos^1(1*y)+ (-0.7912)*(sin(x)/x)^3*cos^1(1*y)$

$+ 0.7700*(sin(x)/x)^4*cos^1(1*y)+ 0.0356*(sin(x)/x)^5*cos^1(1*y)$

$+ (-0.8337)*(sin(x)/x)^6*cos^1(1*y)$

$+0.7663*(sin(x)/x)^0*cos^2(2*y)+ 0.7943*(sin(x)/x)^1*cos^2(2*y)$

$+ (-0.7804)*(sin(x)/x)^2*cos^2(2*y)+ (-0.0991)*(sin(x)/x)^3*cos^2(2*y)$

$+(-0.8692)*(sin(x)/x)^4*cos^2(2*y)+ 0.7481*(sin(x)/x)^5*cos^2(2*y)$

$+ (-0.0131)*(sin(x)/x)^6*cos^2(2*y)$

$+(-0.1823)*(sin(x)/x)^0*cos^3(3*y)+ (-0.8837)*(sin(x)/-x)^1*cos^3(3*y)$

$+ (-0.6952)*(sin(x)/x)^2*cos^3(3*y)+ 0.8774*(sin(x)/x)^3*cos^3(3*y)$

$+ 0.1208*(sin(x)/x)^4*cos^3(3*y)+ (-0.9640)*(sin(x)/x)^5*cos^3(3*y)$

$+ 0.8191*(sin(x)/x)^6*cos^3(3*y)$

$+(-0.6116)*(sin(x)/x)^0*cos^4(4*y)+ 0.9445*(sin(x)/x)^1*cos^4(4*y)$

$$+ (-0.2584)*(\sin(x)/x)^2*\cos^4(4*y)+ 0.9347*(\sin(x)/x)^3*\cos^4(4*y)$$
$$+ (-0.0066)*(\sin(x)/x)^4*\cos^4(4*y)+ 0.1033*(\sin(x)/x)^5*\cos^4(4*y)$$
$$+ 0.5724*(\sin(x)/x)^6*\cos^4(4*y)$$
$$+(-0.5156)*(\sin(x)/x)^0*\cos^5(5*y)+ 0.3725*(\sin(x)/x)^1*\cos^5(5*y)$$
$$+ 0.6393*(\sin(x)/x)^2*\cos^5(4*y)+ 0.6555*(\sin(x)/x)^3*\cos^5(5*y)$$
$$+ 0.1156*(\sin(x)/x)^4*\cos^5(5*y)+ (-0.7189)*(\sin(x)/x)^5*\cos^5(5*y)$$
$$+ (-0.7697)*(\sin(x)/x)^6*\cos^5(5*y)$$
$$+0.6813*(\sin(x)/x)^0*\cos^6(6*y)+ (-0.2737)*(\sin(x)/x)^1*\cos^6(6*y)$$
$$+ 0.9862*(\sin(x)/x)^2*\cos^6(6*y)+ (-0.5278)*(\sin(x)/x)^3*\cos^6(6*y)$$
$$+ (-0.5062)*(\sin(x)/x)^4*\cos^6(6*y)+ (-0.6193)*(\sin(x)/x)^5*\cos^6(6*y)$$
$$+ 0.8795*(\sin(x)/-x)^6*\cos^6(6*y) \tag{7-33}$$

Based on the training of UNC-HONN model, UNC-HONN has the following formula (see Table 4) to describe the data classification 2:

$$z=\text{å } c_{kj}{}^o*(\sin(x)/x)^k*\cos^j(j*y) \ (k, j = 0,1,2,3,4,5,6,)$$
$$= c_{00}{}^o*(\sin(x)/x)^0*\cos^0(0*y)+ c_{10}{}^o*(\sin(x)/x)^1*\cos^0(0*y)$$
$$+ c_{20}{}^o*(\sin(x)/x)^2*\cos^0(0*y)+ c_{30}{}^o*(\sin(x)/x)^3*\cos^0(0*y)$$
$$+ c_{40}{}^o*(\sin(x)/x)^4*\cos^0(0*y)+ c_{50}{}^o*(\sin(x)/x)^5*\cos^0(0*y)$$
$$+ c_{60}{}^o*(\sin(x)/x)^6*\cos^0(0*y)$$
$$+c_{01}{}^o*(\sin(x)/x)^0*\cos^1(1*y)+ c_{11}{}^o*(\sin(x)/x)^1*\cos^1(1*y)$$
$$+ c_{21}{}^o*(\sin(x)/x)^2*\cos^1(1*y)+ c_{31}{}^o*(\sin(x)/x)^3*\cos^1(1*y)$$
$$+ c_{41}{}^o*(\sin(x)/x)^4*\cos^1(1*y)+ c_{51}{}^o*(\sin(x)/x)^5*\cos^1(1*y)$$
$$+ c_{61}{}^o*(\sin(x)/x)^6*\cos^1(1*y)$$
$$+c_{02}{}^o*(\sin(x)/x)^0*\cos^2(2*y)+ c_{12}{}^o*(\sin(x)/x)^1*\cos^2(2*y)$$
$$+ c_{22}{}^o*(\sin(x)/x)^2*\cos^2(2*y)+ c_{32}{}^o*(\sin(x)/x)^3*\cos^2(2*y)$$
$$+ c_{42}{}^o*(\sin(x)/x)^4*\cos^2(2*y)+ c_{52}{}^o*(\sin(x)/x)^5*\cos^2(2*y)$$
$$+ c_{62}{}^o*(\sin(x)/x)^6*\cos^2(2*y)$$
$$+c_{03}{}^o*(\sin(x)/x)^0*\cos^3(3*y)+ c_{13}{}^o*(\sin(x)/x)^1*\cos^3(3*y)$$
$$+ c_{23}{}^o*(\sin(x)/x)^2*\cos^3(3*y)+ c_{33}{}^o*(\sin(x)/x)^3*\cos^3(3*y)$$
$$+ c_{43}{}^o*(\sin(x)/x)^4*\cos^3(3*y)+ c_{53}{}^o*(\sin(x)/x)^5*\cos^3(3*y)$$
$$+ c_{63}{}^o*(\sin(x)/x)^6*\cos^3(3*y)$$
$$+c_{04}{}^o*(\sin(x)/x)^0*\cos^4(4*y)+ c_{14}{}^o*(\sin(x)/x)^1*\cos^4(4*y)$$
$$+ c_{24}{}^o*(\sin(x)/x)^2*\cos^4(4*y)+ c_{34}{}^o*(\sin(x)/x)^3*\cos^4(4*y)$$
$$+ c_{44}{}^o*(\sin(x)/x)^4*\cos^4(4*y)+ c_{54}{}^o*(\sin(x)/x)^5*\cos^4(4*y)$$
$$+ c_{64}{}^o*(\sin(x)/x)^6*\cos^4(4*y)$$
$$+c_{05}{}^o*(\sin(x)/x)^0*\cos^5(5*y)+ c_{15}{}^o*(\sin(x)/x)^1*\cos^5(5*y)$$
$$+ c_{25}{}^o*(\sin(x)/x)^2*\cos^5(4*y)+ c_{35}{}^o*(\sin(x)/x)^3*\cos^5(5*y)$$
$$+ c_{45}{}^o*(\sin(x)/x)^4*\cos^5(5*y)+ c_{55}{}^o*(\sin(x)/x)^5*\cos^5(5*y)$$

$+ c_{65}{}^o*(\sin(x)/x)^6*\cos^5(5*y)$

$+c_{06}{}^o*(\sin(x)/x)^0*\cos^6(6*y)+ c_{16}{}^o*(\sin(x)/x)^1*\cos^6(6*y)$

$+ c_{26}{}^o*(\sin(x)/x)^2*\cos^6(6*y)+ c_{36}{}^o*(\sin(x)/x)^3*\cos^6(6*y)$

$+ c_{46}{}^o*(\sin(x)/x)^4*\cos^6(6*y)+ c_{56}{}^o*(\sin(x)/x)^5*\cos^6(6*y)$

$+ c_{66}{}^o*(\sin(x)/x)^6*\cos^6(6*y)$

$= 0.7228*(\sin(x)/x)^0*\cos^0(0*y)+ (-0.5156)*(\sin(x)/x)^1*\cos^0(0*y)$

$+ (-0.7924)*(\sin(x)/x)^2*\cos^0(0*y)+ (-0.6779)*(\sin(x)/x)^3*\cos^0(0*y)$

$+ (-0.3934)*(\sin(x)/x)^4*\cos^0(0*y)+ (-0.6828)*(\sin(x)/x)^5*\cos^0(0*y)$

$+ 0.2667*(\sin(x)/x)^6*\cos^0(0*y)$

$+0.3068*(\sin(x)/x)^0*\cos^1(1*y)+ 0.4272*(\sin(x)/x)^1*\cos^1(1*y)$

$+ (-0.4104)*(\sin(x)/x)^2*\cos^1(1*y)+ (-0.3691)*(\sin(x)/x)^3*\cos^1(1*y)$

$+ 0.3489*(\sin(x)/x)^4*\cos^1(1*y)+ 0.6035*(\sin(x)/x)^5*\cos^1(1*y)$

$+ (-0.4016)*(\sin(x)/x)^6*\cos^1(1*y)$

$+0.4454*(\sin(x)/x)^0*\cos^2(2*y)+ 0.4734*(\sin(x)/x)^1*\cos^2(2*y)$

$+ (-0.4695)*(\sin(x)/x)^2*\cos^2(2*y)+ (-0.7782)*(\sin(x)/x)^3*\cos^2(2*y)$

$+(-0.5483)*(\sin(x)/x)^4*\cos^2(2*y)+ 0.4272*(\sin(x)/x)^5*\cos^2(2*y)$

$+ (-0.7922)*(\sin(x)/x)^6*\cos^2(2*y)$

$+(-0.9734)*(\sin(x)/x)^0*\cos^3(3*y)+ (-0.6749)*(\sin(x)/x)^1*\cos^3(3*y)$

$+ (-0.4864)*(\sin(x)/x)^2*\cos^3(3*y)+ 0.6686*(\sin(x)/x)^3*\cos^3(3*y)$

$+ 0.9110*(\sin(x)/x)^4*\cos^3(3*y)+ (-0.7552)*(\sin(x)/x)^5*\cos^3(3*y)$

$+ 0.6003*(\sin(x)/x)^6*\cos^3(3*y)$

$+(-0.5239)*(\sin(x)/x)^0*\cos^4(4*y)+ 0.8568*(\sin(x)/x)^1*\cos^4(4*y)$

$+ (-0.1607)*(\sin(x)/x)^2*\cos^4(4*y)+ 0.8460*(\sin(x)/x)^3*\cos^4(4*y)$

$+ (-0.9123)*(\sin(x)/x)^4*\cos^4(4*y)+ 0.0156*(\sin(x)/x)^5*\cos^4(4*y)$

$+ 0.4846*(\sin(x)/x)^6*\cos^4(4*y)$

$+(-0.6380)*(\sin(x)/x)^0*\cos^5(5*y)+ 0.4959*(\sin(x)/x)^1*\cos^5(5*y)$

$+ 0.7527*(\sin(x)/x)^2*\cos^5(4*y)+ 0.7789*(\sin(x)/x)^3*\cos^5(5*y)$

$+ 0.2380*(\sin(x)/x)^4*\cos^5(5*y)+ (-0.8313)*(\sin(x)/x)^5*\cos^5(5*y)$

$+ (-0.8821)*(\sin(x)/x)^6*\cos^5(5*y)$

$+0.8158*(\sin(x)/x)^0*\cos^6(6*y)+ (-0.4072)*(\sin(x)/x)^1*\cos^6(6*y)$

$+ 0.1107*(\sin(x)/x)^2*\cos^6(6*y)+ (-0.7513)*(\sin(x)/x)^3*\cos^6(6*y)$

$+ (-0.7307)*(\sin(x)/x)^4*\cos^6(6*y)+ (-0.8438)*(\sin(x)/x)^5*\cos^6(6*y)$

$+ 0.0038*(\mathrm{Sin}(x)/x)^6*\cos^6(6*y)$ (7-34)

329

FUTURE RESEARCH DIRECTIONS

As the next step of HONN model research, more HONN models for different data control will be built to increase the pool of HONN models. Theoretically, the adaptive HONN models can be built and allow the computer automatically to choose the best model, order, and coefficients. Thus, making the adaptive HONN models easier to use is one of the future research topics.

HONNs can automatically select the initial coefficients for nonlinear data analysis. The next step of this study will also focus on how to allow people working in the prediction area to understand that HONNs are much easier to use and can have better results. Moreover, further research will develop HONNs software packages for people working in the prediction area. HONNs will challenge classic procedures and change the research methodology that people are currently using in the prediction areas for the nonlinear data control application.

Table 1. UNS-HONN data classification 1 (n=6, model 0)

No.	UNS-HONN x	UNS-HONN y	UNS-HONN z	Original Data	Absolute Original Data	Difference	Absolute Difference	UNS-HONN Error %	No.	UNS-HONN x	UNS-HONN y	UNS-HONN z	Original Data	Absolute Original Data	Difference	Absolute Difference	UNS-HONN Error %
1	1	0	0.00000000	0.000000	0.000000	0.00000000	0.00000000	0.000000%	1	1	0	0.00000000	0.000000	0.000000	0.00000000	0.00000000	0.000000%
2	1	0.1	0.13133895	0.131336	0.131336	-0.00000005	0.00000005	0.000006%	2	1	0.1	0.06026689	0.060267	0.060267	-0.00000011	0.00000011	0.000015%
3	1	0.2	0.50814169	0.508142	0.508142	-0.00000031	0.00000031	0.000042%	3	1	0.2	-0.23159418	-0.231594	0.231594	-0.00000018	0.00000018	0.000024%
4	1	0.3	1.11380489	1.113805	1.113805	-0.00000011	0.00000011	0.000015%	4	1	0.3	0.02612711	0.026127	0.026127	0.00000011	0.00000011	0.000016%
5	1	0.4	0.98063803	0.980638	0.980638	0.00000003	0.00000003	0.000004%	5	1	0.4	0.47560577	0.475606	0.475606	-0.00000023	0.00000023	0.000031%
6	1	0.5	0.60215662	0.602157	0.602157	-0.00000038	0.00000038	0.000051%	6	1	0.5	-0.11718982	-0.11719	0.117190	0.00000018	0.00000018	0.000025%
7	1	0.6	0.75884561	0.758846	0.758846	-0.00000039	0.00000039	0.000052%	7	1	0.6	-0.42981304	-0.429813	0.429813	-0.00000024	0.00000024	0.000033%
8	1	0.7	0.92516394	0.925164	0.925164	-0.00000006	0.00000006	0.000008%	8	1	0.7	-0.71430141	-0.714301	0.714301	-0.00000041	0.00000041	0.000056%
9	1	0.8	0.78311983	0.78312	0.783120	-0.00000017	0.00000017	0.000023%	9	1	0.8	-1.04031943	-1.040319	1.040319	-0.00000043	0.00000043	0.000058%
10	1	0.9	0.39932453	0.399325	0.399325	-0.00000047	0.00000047	0.000064%	10	1	0.9	-0.34015426	-0.340154	0.340154	-0.00000026	0.00000026	0.000035%
11	1	1	0.51901116	0.519011	0.519011	0.00000016	0.00000016	0.000022%	11	1	1	0.29665747	0.296657	0.296657	0.00000047	0.00000047	0.000063%
13	1	2	1.17415686	1.174157	1.174157	-0.00000014	0.00000014	0.000020%	13	1	2	1.35395383	1.353954	1.353954	-0.00000017	0.00000017	0.000023%
14	1	3	0.23994608	0.239946	0.239946	0.00000008	0.00000008	0.000011%	14	1	3	-0.00160868	-0.001609	0.001609	0.00000032	0.00000032	0.000044%
15	1	4	0.50750588	0.507506	0.507506	-0.00000012	0.00000012	0.000016%	15	1	4	-1.13635617	-1.136356	1.136356	-0.00000017	0.00000017	0.000031%
16	1	5	-1.06444736	-1.064447	1.064447	-0.00000036	0.00000036	0.000049%	16	1	5	-1.70555477	-1.705555	1.705555	0.00000023	0.00000023	0.000058%
17	1	6	-1.10951452	-1.109515	1.109515	0.00000048	0.00000048	0.000066%	17	1	6	-0.99931470	-0.999315	0.999315	0.00000030	0.00000030	0.000040%
18	1	7	0.92533087	0.925331	0.925331	-0.00000013	0.00000013	0.000018%	18	1	7	-0.81816258	-0.818163	0.818163	0.00000042	0.00000042	0.000058%
19	1	8	1.48832443	1.488324	1.488324	0.00000043	0.00000043	0.000019%	19	1	8	1.59289786	1.592898	1.592898	-0.00000014	0.00000014	0.000019%
	Average			0.7350428			0.0000002151	0.0000002926%		Average			0.6299932			0.0000002425	0.0000003299%

c_{ij}^{x}	k=0	k=1	k=2	k=3	k=4	k=5	k=6	c_{ij}^{y}	k=0	k=1	k=2	k=3	k=4	k=5	k=6
j=0	0.3884	-0.1712	-0.3580	-0.2535	-0.9590	-0.2524	0.8223	j=0	0.2896	-0.0624	-0.2592	-0.1347	-0.8502	-0.1496	0.7235
j=1	0.9624	0.0838	-0.0760	-0.9257	0.9045	0.2691	-0.0672	j=1	0.9747	0.0951	-0.0883	-0.9370	0.9148	0.2784	-0.0795
j=2	0.9908	0.0399	-0.0250	-0.3347	-0.1048	0.0837	-0.3587	j=2	0.1245	0.1525	-0.1486	-0.4573	-0.2274	0.1063	-0.4713
j=3	-0.5380	-0.2394	-0.0419	0.2238	0.5765	-0.3107	0.2658	j=3	-0.8645	-0.4651	-0.2776	0.4598	0.7022	-0.5463	0.4915
j=4	-0.1784	0.4013	-0.7152	0.4915	-0.5638	0.6601	0.0392	j=4	-0.4352	0.7681	-0.0720	0.7583	-0.8246	0.9273	0.3969
j=5	-0.1825	0.9703	0.2072	0.2234	0.7835	-0.3868	-0.3376	j=5	-0.7514	0.5173	0.8751	0.8913	0.3492	-0.9547	-0.0855
j=6	0.3604	-0.9528	0.6653	-0.2069	-0.2853	-0.3984	0.5546	j=6	0.0493	-0.6317	0.3442	-0.9858	-0.2642	-0.2773	0.2373

x=1, y=0.1	k=0	k=1	k=2	k=3	k=4	k=5	k=6	x=1, y=0.1	k=0	k=1	k=2	k=3	k=4	k=5	k=6
j=1	0.09607968	0.00703978	-0.00537239	-0.05506348	0.04527319	0.01133406	-0.00238166	j=1	0.09730763	0.00798906	-0.00624187	-0.05573564	0.04578874	0.01172576	-0.00281759
j=2	0.03910638	0.00132518	-0.00069868	-0.00787109	-0.00207386	0.00139374	-0.00502606	j=2	0.00491395	0.00506490	-0.00415207	-0.01075425	-0.00449996	0.00177007	-0.00660380
j=3	-0.01388493	-0.00519006	-0.00076569	0.00344143	0.00745963	-0.00338297	0.00243529	j=3	-0.02231139	-0.01010060	-0.00507294	0.00707046	0.00908613	-0.00594824	0.00450319
j=4	-0.00410261	0.00776558	-0.01164586	0.00673452	-0.00650051	0.00640429	0.00032003	j=4	-0.01000817	0.01486355	-0.00117240	0.01039020	-0.00950748	0.00899667	0.00324027
j=5	-0.00462241	0.02068002	0.00371598	0.00337137	0.00994950	-0.00413322	0.00603559	j=5	-0.01903168	0.01102522	0.01569429	0.01345077	0.00443442	-0.01020160	-0.00076879
j=6	0.01167955	-0.02598257	0.01526642	-0.00399502	-0.00463553	-0.00544699	0.00638052	j=6	0.00159767	-0.01722627	0.00789824	-0.01903476	-0.00429270	-0.00379129	0.00273007
Subtotal	0.12425565	0.00562893	0.00049978	-0.05338227	0.04947242	0.00616892	-0.00130747	Subtotal	0.05246803	0.01161586	0.00695236	-0.05461321	0.04100914	0.00255136	0.00028335
$z = \Sigma c_{ij}^{x}*(sin(x)/x)^k*sin(j*y)$		(k= 0, 1, 2, 3, 4, 5, 6			j=1, 2, 3, 4, 5, 6) =		0.13133595	$z = \Sigma c_{ij}^{y}*(sin(x)/x)^k*sin(j*y)$		(k= 0, 1, 2, 3, 4, 5, 6			j=1, 2, 3, 4, 5, 6) =		0.06026689

Table 2. UNS-HONN data classification 2 (n=6, Model 0)

No.	UNS-HONN x	UNS-HONN y	UNS-HONN z	Original Data	Absolute Original Data	Difference	Absolute Difference	UNS-HONN Error %	No.	UNS-HONN x	UNS-HONN y	UNS-HONN z	Original Data	Absolute Original Data	Difference	Absolute Difference	UNS-HONN Error %
1	1	0	0.00000000	0.000000	0.000000	0.00000000	0.00000000	0.000000%	1	1	0	0.00000000	0.000000	0.000000	0.00000000	0.00000000	0.000000%
2	1	0.1	0.13133595	0.131336	0.131336	-0.00000005	0.00000005	0.000006%	2	1	0.1	0.06026689	0.060267	0.060267	-0.00000011	0.00000011	0.000015%
3	1	0.2	0.50814169	0.508142	0.508142	-0.00000031	0.00000031	0.000042%	3	1	0.2	-0.23159418	-0.231594	0.231594	-0.00000018	0.00000018	0.000024%
4	1	0.3	1.11380489	1.113805	1.113805	-0.00000011	0.00000011	0.000015%	4	1	0.3	0.02612711	0.026127	0.026127	0.00000011	0.00000011	0.000016%
5	1	0.4	0.98065803	0.980638	0.980638	0.00000003	0.00000003	0.000004%	5	1	0.4	0.47560577	0.475606	0.475606	-0.00000023	0.00000023	0.000031%
6	1	0.5	0.60215662	0.602157	0.602157	-0.00000038	0.00000038	0.000051%	6	1	0.5	-0.11718982	-0.11719	0.117190	0.00000018	0.00000018	0.000025%
7	1	0.6	0.75884561	0.758846	0.758846	-0.00000039	0.00000039	0.000052%	7	1	0.6	-0.42981324	-0.429813	0.429813	-0.00000024	0.00000024	0.000033%
8	1	0.7	0.92516394	0.925164	0.925164	-0.00000006	0.00000006	0.000008%	8	1	0.7	-0.71430141	-0.714301	0.714301	-0.00000041	0.00000041	0.000056%
9	1	0.8	0.78311983	0.78312	0.783120	-0.00000017	0.00000017	0.000023%	9	1	0.8	-1.04031943	-1.040319	1.040319	-0.00000043	0.00000043	0.000058%
10	1	0.9	0.39932453	0.399325	0.399325	-0.00000047	0.00000047	0.000064%	10	1	0.9	-0.34015426	-0.340154	0.340154	-0.00000026	0.00000026	0.000035%
11	1	1	0.51901116	0.519011	0.519011	0.00000016	0.00000016	0.000022%	11	1	1	0.29665747	0.296657	0.296657	0.00000047	0.00000047	0.000063%
13	1	2	1.17415686	1.174157	1.174157	-0.00000014	0.00000014	0.000020%	13	1	2	1.35395383	1.353954	1.353954	-0.00000017	0.00000017	0.000023%
14	1	3	0.23994608	0.239946	0.239946	0.00000008	0.00000008	0.000011%	14	1	3	-0.00160868	-0.001609	0.001609	0.00000032	0.00000032	0.000044%
15	1	4	0.50750588	0.507506	0.507506	-0.00000012	0.00000012	0.000016%	15	1	4	-1.13635617	-1.136356	1.136356	-0.00000017	0.00000017	0.000023%
16	1	5	-1.06444736	-1.064447	1.064447	-0.00000036	0.00000036	0.000049%	16	1	5	-1.70555477	-1.705555	1.705555	0.00000023	0.00000023	0.000031%
17	1	6	-1.10951452	-1.109515	1.109515	0.00000048	0.00000048	0.000066%	17	1	6	-0.99931470	-0.999315	0.999315	0.00000030	0.00000030	0.000040%
18	1	7	0.92533087	0.925331	0.925331	-0.00000013	0.00000013	0.000018%	18	1	7	-0.81816258	-0.818163	0.818163	0.00000042	0.00000042	0.000058%
19	1	8	1.48832443	1.488324	1.488324	0.00000043	0.00000043	0.000058%	19	1	8	1.59289786	1.592898	1.592898	-0.00000014	0.00000014	0.000019%
Average				0.7350428			0.000002151	0.0000292616%	Average				0.6299932			0.0000002425	0.0000003299%

$c_o^?$	k=0	k=1	k=2	k=3	k=4	k=5	k=6	$c_o^?$	j=0	k=1	k=2	k=3	k=4	k=5	k=6
j=0	0.3884	-0.1712	-0.3580	-0.2535	-0.9590	-0.2524	0.8223	j=0	0.2896	-0.0624	-0.2592	-0.1347	-0.8502	-0.1496	0.7235
j=1	0.9624	0.0838	-0.0760	-0.9257	0.9045	0.2691	-0.0672	j=1	0.9747	0.0951	-0.0883	-0.9370	0.9148	0.2784	-0.0795
j=2	0.9908	0.0399	-0.0250	-0.3347	-0.1048	0.0837	-0.3887	j=2	0.1245	0.1525	-0.1486	-0.4573	-0.2274	0.1063	-0.4713
j=3	-0.5380	-0.2394	-0.0419	0.2238	0.5765	-0.3107	0.2658	j=3	-0.8645	-0.4651	-0.2776	0.4598	0.7022	-0.5463	0.4915
j=4	-0.1784	0.4013	-0.7152	0.4915	-0.5638	0.6601	0.0392	j=4	-0.4352	0.7681	-0.0720	0.7583	-0.8246	0.9273	0.3969
j=5	-0.1825	0.9703	0.2072	0.2234	0.7835	-0.3868	-0.3376	j=5	-0.7514	0.5173	0.8751	0.8913	0.3492	-0.9547	-0.0855
j=6	0.3604	-0.9528	0.6653	-0.2069	-0.2853	-0.3984	0.5546	j=6	0.0493	-0.6317	0.3442	-0.9858	-0.2642	-0.2773	0.2373

x=1, y=0.1	k=0	k=1	k=2	k=3	k=4	k=5	k=6	x=1, y=0.1	k=0	k=1	k=2	k=3	k=4	k=5	k=6
j=1	0.09607968	0.00703978	-0.00537239	-0.05506348	0.04527319	0.01133406	-0.00238166	j=1	0.09730763	0.00798906	-0.00624187	-0.05573564	0.04578874	0.01172576	-0.00281759
j=2	0.03910638	0.00132518	-0.00069868	-0.00787109	-0.00207386	0.00139374	-0.00502606	j=2	0.00491395	0.00506490	-0.00415297	-0.01075425	-0.00449996	0.00177007	-0.00660380
j=3	-0.01388493	-0.00519906	-0.00076569	0.00344143	0.00745963	-0.00338297	0.00243529	j=3	-0.02231139	-0.01010060	-0.00507294	0.00770046	0.00908613	-0.00594824	0.00450319
j=4	-0.00410261	0.00776558	-0.01164586	0.00673452	-0.00650051	0.00640429	0.00032003	j=4	-0.01000817	0.01486355	-0.00117240	0.01039020	-0.00950748	0.00899667	0.00324027
j=5	-0.00462241	0.02068002	0.00371598	0.00337137	0.00994950	-0.00413322	-0.00303559	j=5	-0.01903168	0.01102522	0.01569429	0.01345077	0.00443442	-0.01020160	-0.00076879
j=6	0.01167955	-0.02598257	0.01526642	-0.00399502	-0.00463553	-0.00544699	0.00638052	j=6	0.00159767	-0.01722627	0.00789824	-0.01903476	-0.00492970	-0.00379129	0.00273307
Subtotal	0.12425565	0.00562093	0.00049978	-0.05338227	0.04947242	0.00616892	-0.00130747	Subtotal	0.05246803	0.01161586	0.00695236	-0.05461321	0.04100914	0.00255136	0.00028335
$z = \Sigma c_o^?*(\sin(x)/x)^j*\sin(j*y)$	(k=0, 1, 2, 3, 4, 5, 6)			j = 1, 2, 3, 4, 5, 6) =			0.11333595	$z = \Sigma c_o^?*(\sin(x)/x)^j*\sin(j*y)$	(k=0, 1, 2, 3, 4, 5, 6)		j = 1, 2, 3, 4, 5, 6) =			0.06026689	

CONCLUSION

Two nonlinear higher order neural network models, UNS-HONN and UNC-HONN, that are part of the Ultra High Frequency SINC and Trigonometric Higher Order Neural Networks (UNT-HONN), are developed. Based on the structures of UNS-HONN and UNC-HONN, this paper provides two model learning algorithm formulae. This chapter tests the UNS-HONN and UNC-HONN models for ultra-high frequency data classifications. The running results show that UNS-HONN and UNC-HONN models are better than other Polynomial Higher Order Neural Network (PHONN) and Trigonometric Higher Order Neural Network (THONN) models, since UNS-HONN and UNC-HONN models can classify the data with error approaching 10^{-6}.

One of the topics for future research is to continue building models using HONN for different data series. The coefficients of the higher order models will be studied not only using artificial neural network techniques, but also statistical methods. Using nonlinear functions to model and analyze time series data will be a major goal in the future.

Figure 3. a) UNS-HONN data classification; b) UNS-HONN data classification

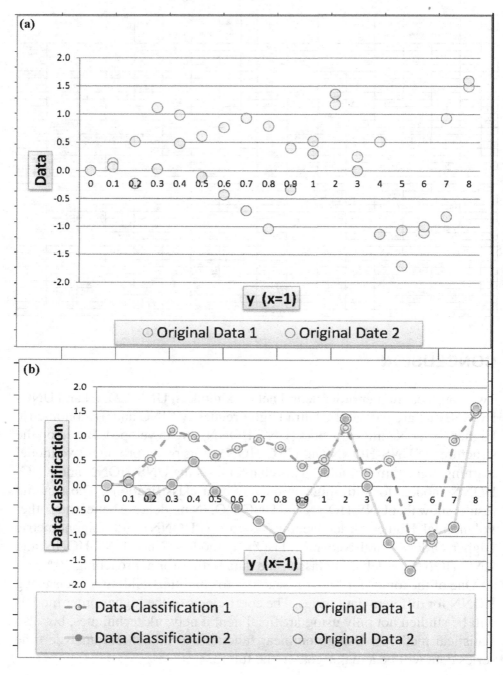

Table 3. UNC-HONN data classification 1 (n=6, Model 0)

No.	UNC-HONN x	UNC-HONN y	UNC-HONN z	Original Data	Absolute Original Data	Difference	Absolute Difference	UNC-HONN Error %	No.	UNC-HONN x	UNC-HONN y	UNC-HONN z	Original Data	Absolute Original Data	Difference	Absolute Difference	UNC-HONN Error %
1	1	0	1.56288479	1.562885	1.562885	-0.00000021	0.00000021	0.000023%	1	1	0	-2.16502776	-2.165028	2.165028	0.00000000	0.00000000	0.000000%
2	1	0.1	0.93927060	0.939271	0.939271	-0.00000040	0.00000040	0.000044%	2	1	0.1	-1.78433940	-1.78434	1.784340	0.00000060	0.00000060	0.000006%
3	1	0.2	0.50395438	0.503954	0.503954	0.00000038	0.00000038	0.000042%	3	1	0.2	-1.46798691	-1.46799	1.467990	0.00000369	0.00000369	0.000406%
4	1	0.3	0.49922245	0.499222	0.499222	0.00000045	0.00000045	0.000050%	4	1	0.3	-1.13496419	-1.134964	1.134964	-0.00000019	0.00000019	0.000021%
5	1	0.4	0.61472187	0.614722	0.614722	0.00000013	0.00000013	0.000014%	5	1	0.4	-0.97438327	-0.974383	0.974383	-0.00000027	0.00000027	0.000030%
6	1	0.5	0.98132019	0.981320	0.981320	0.00000019	0.00000019	0.000021%	6	1	0.5	-1.42257068	-1.422571	1.422571	0.00000032	0.00000032	0.000030%
7	1	0.6	0.72493825	0.724938	0.724938	0.00000025	0.00000025	0.000027%	7	1	0.6	-1.18117045	-1.181170	1.181170	0.00000045	0.00000045	0.000050%
8	1	0.7	0.83707694	0.837077	0.837077	-0.00000006	0.00000006	0.000006%	8	1	0.7	-0.52365606	-0.523656	0.523656	-0.00000006	0.00000006	0.000005%
9	1	0.8	1.27132289	1.271323	1.271323	-0.00000011	0.00000011	0.000012%	9	1	0.8	-0.02415629	-0.024156	0.024156	-0.00000029	0.00000029	0.000032%
10	1	0.9	1.36908792	1.369088	1.369088	-0.00000008	0.00000008	0.000009%	10	1	0.9	0.19021619	0.190216	0.190216	0.00000019	0.00000019	0.000021%
11	1	1	1.71589352	1.715894	1.715894	-0.00000048	0.00000048	0.000053%	11	1	1	-0.20877411	-0.208774	0.208774	-0.00000011	0.00000011	0.000013%
13	1	2	-0.81211013	-0.812110	0.812110	-0.00000013	0.00000013	0.000014%	13	1	2	-2.71593563	-2.715936	2.715936	0.00000037	0.00000037	0.000040%
14	1	3	1.05732450	1.057325	1.057325	-0.00000050	0.00000050	0.000055%	14	1	3	-0.90161623	-0.901616	0.901616	-0.00000023	0.00000023	0.000025%
15	1	4	-0.44306287	-0.443063	0.443063	0.00000013	0.00000013	0.000015%	15	1	4	-1.78712533	-1.787125	1.787125	-0.00000033	0.00000033	0.000036%
16	1	5	0.95061990	0.950620	0.950620	-0.00000010	0.00000010	0.000011%	16	1	5	-0.44375750	-0.443758	0.443758	0.00000050	0.00000050	0.000055%
17	1	6	0.48989025	0.489890	0.489890	0.00000025	0.00000025	0.000027%	17	1	6	-1.19241464	-1.192415	1.192415	0.00000036	0.00000036	0.000040%
18	1	7	0.92299498	0.922995	0.922995	-0.00000002	0.00000002	0.000002%	18	1	7	-0.42963855	-0.429639	0.429639	0.00000045	0.00000045	0.000049%
19	1	8	0.67149105	0.671491	0.671491	0.00000005	0.00000005	0.000005%	19	1	8	-1.44245633	-1.442456	1.442456	-0.00000033	0.00000033	0.000036%
Average				0.9092882		0.0000002176		0.000023945%	Average				1.1105663		0.0000048854		0.00005338%

c_{kj}^{o}	k=0	k=1	k=2	k=3	k=4	k=5	k=6	c_{kj}^{o}	k=0	k=1	k=2	k=3	k=4	k=5	k=6
j=0	0.2650	-0.0588	-0.2356	-0.1101	-0.8366	-0.1290	0.7099	j=0	0.7228	-0.5156	-0.7924	-0.6779	-0.3934	-0.5828	0.2607
j=1	0.7389	0.8593	-0.8425	-0.7912	0.7700	0.0356	-0.8337	j=1	0.3068	0.4272	-0.0404	-0.3691	0.3489	0.6035	-0.4016
j=2	0.7663	0.7943	-0.7804	-0.0991	-0.8692	0.7481	-0.0131	j=2	0.4454	0.4734	-0.4695	-0.7782	-0.5483	0.4272	-0.7922
j=3	-0.1823	-0.8837	-0.6952	0.8774	0.1208	-0.9640	0.8191	j=3	-0.9734	-0.6749	-0.4864	0.6686	0.9110	-0.7552	0.6003
j=4	-0.6116	0.9445	-0.2584	0.9347	-0.0066	0.1033	0.5724	j=4	-0.5239	0.8568	-0.1607	0.8460	-0.9123	0.0156	0.4846
j=5	-0.5156	0.3725	0.6393	0.6555	0.1156	-0.7189	-0.7697	j=5	-0.6380	0.4959	0.7527	0.7789	0.2380	-0.8313	-0.8821
j=6	0.6813	-0.2737	0.9862	-0.5278	-0.5062	-0.6193	0.8795	j=6	0.8158	-0.4072	0.1107	-0.7513	-0.7307	-0.8438	0.0038

x=1, y=0.1	k=0	k=1	k=2	k=3	k=4	k=5	k=6	x=1, y=0.1	k=0	k=1	k=2	k=3	k=4	k=5	k=6
j=0	0.26500000	-0.04947849	-0.16682210	-0.06560014	-0.41944444	-0.05442337	0.23201828	j=0	0.72280000	-0.43386244	-0.56107738	-0.40390857	-0.19723816	-0.28806417	0.09467992
j=1	0.73520858	0.71946365	-0.59357158	-0.46906023	0.38412467	0.01494413	-0.29448934	j=1	0.30526728	0.35768052	-0.28914157	-0.21881968	0.17405338	0.25333658	-0.14185788
j=2	0.73605452	0.64199976	-0.53077042	-0.05071556	-0.41858866	0.30315626	-0.00446701	j=2	0.42782028	0.38262959	-0.31931921	-0.44536683	-0.26404989	0.17311637	-0.27013501
j=3	-0.15894826	-0.64835535	-0.42919747	0.45581033	0.05280714	-0.35460255	0.25353674	j=3	-0.84871219	-0.49516241	-0.30029006	0.34733849	0.39823925	-0.27779652	0.18581138
j=4	-0.44017061	0.57199821	-0.13168138	0.40081433	-0.00238152	0.09136531	0.14624737	j=4	-0.37705262	0.51888025	-0.08189318	0.36277835	-0.32919090	0.00473668	0.12381460
j=5	-0.26838166	0.16313495	0.23562584	0.20329657	0.03016854	-0.15787165	-0.14223166	j=5	-0.33209367	0.21720668	0.27742151	0.24156781	0.06211171	-0.18255487	-0.16300188
j=6	0.21533861	-0.07294431	0.22071244	-0.09939633	-0.08021623	-0.08258104	0.00868570	j=6	0.25785005	-0.10830049	0.02477476	-0.14148628	-0.11579217	-0.11251716	0.00042639
Subtotal	1.08410118	1.32590843	-1.39570466	0.36914897	-0.45353049	-0.30001290	0.30930008	Subtotal	0.15587913	0.43997770	-1.24952513	-0.25789972	-0.27186679	-0.42974310	-0.17026249
$z = \Sigma c_{kj}^{o}*(\sin(x)/x)^{k}*\cos(j*y)$	(k=0, 1, 2, 3, 4, 5, 6)	j=0, 1, 2, 3, 4, 5, 6) =					0.93927060	$z = \Sigma c_{kj}^{o}*(\sin(x)/x)^{k}*\cos(j*y)$	(k=0, 1, 2, 3, 4, 5, 6)	j=0, 1, 2, 3, 4, 5, 6) =					-1.78433940

Table 4. UNC-HONN data classification 2 (n=6, Model 0)

No.	UNC-HONN x	UNC-HONN y	UNC-HONN z	Original Data	Absolute Original Data	Difference	Absolute Difference	UNC-HONN Error %
1	1	0	-2.16502776	-2.165028	2.165028	0.00000000	0.00000000	0.000000%
2	1	**0.1**	**-1.78433940**	-1.78434	1.784340	0.00000060	0.00000060	0.000066%
3	1	0.2	-1.46798631	-1.46799	1.467990	0.00000369	0.00000369	0.000406%
4	1	0.3	-1.13496419	-1.134964	1.134964	-0.00000019	0.00000019	0.000021%
5	1	0.4	-0.97438327	-0.974383	0.974383	-0.00000027	0.00000027	0.000030%
6	1	0.5	-1.42257068	-1.422571	1.422571	0.00000032	0.00000032	0.000036%
7	1	0.6	-1.18117045	-1.181170	1.181170	-0.00000045	0.00000045	0.000050%
8	1	0.7	-0.52365606	-0.523656	0.523656	-0.00000006	0.00000006	0.000006%
9	1	0.8	-0.02415629	-0.024156	0.024156	-0.00000029	0.00000029	0.000032%
10	1	0.9	0.19021619	0.190216	0.190216	0.00000019	0.00000019	0.000021%
11	1	1	-0.20877411	-0.208774	0.208774	-0.00000011	0.00000011	0.000013%
13	1	2	-2.71593563	-2.715936	2.715936	0.00000037	0.00000037	0.000040%
14	1	3	-0.90161623	-0.901616	0.901616	-0.00000023	0.00000023	0.000025%
15	1	4	-1.78712533	-1.787125	1.787125	-0.00000033	0.00000033	0.000036%
16	1	5	-0.44375750	-0.443758	0.443758	0.00000050	0.00000050	0.000055%
17	1	6	-1.19241464	-1.192415	1.192415	0.00000036	0.00000036	0.000040%
18	1	7	-0.42963855	-0.429639	0.429639	0.00000045	0.00000045	0.000049%
19	1	8	-1.44245633	-1.442456	1.442456	-0.00000033	0.00000033	0.000036%
Average					1.1105663		0.0000004854	0.00005338%

$c_{kj}{}^{o}$	k=0	k=1	k=2	k=3	k=4	k=5	k=6
j=0	0.7228	-0.5156	-0.7924	-0.6779	-0.3934	-0.6828	0.2667
j=1	0.3068	0.4272	-0.4104	-0.3691	0.3489	0.6035	-0.4016
j=2	0.4454	0.4734	-0.4695	-0.7782	-0.5483	0.4272	-0.7922
j=3	-0.9734	-0.6749	-0.4864	0.6686	0.9110	-0.7552	0.6003
j=4	-0.5239	0.8568	-0.1607	0.8460	-0.9123	0.0156	0.4846
j=5	-0.6380	0.4959	0.7527	0.7789	0.2380	-0.8313	-0.8821
j=6	0.8158	-0.4072	0.1107	-0.7513	-0.7307	-0.8438	0.0038

x=1, y=0.1	k = 0	k = 1	k = 2	k = 3	k = 4	k = 5	k = 6
j = 0	0.72280000	-0.43386244	-0.56107738	-0.40390857	-0.19723816	-0.28806417	0.09467992
j = 1	0.30526728	0.35768052	-0.28914157	-0.21881968	0.17405338	0.25333658	-0.14185788
j = 2	0.42782028	0.38262959	-0.31931921	-0.44536883	-0.26404989	0.17311637	-0.27013501
j = 3	-0.84871219	-0.49516241	-0.30029006	0.34733849	0.39823925	-0.27779652	0.18581138
j = 4	-0.37705262	0.51888625	-0.08189318	0.36277835	-0.32919090	0.00473668	0.12381460
j = 5	-0.33209367	0.21720668	0.27742151	0.24156781	0.06211171	-0.18255487	-0.16300188
j = 6	0.25785005	-0.10830049	0.02477476	-0.14148628	-0.11579217	-0.11251716	0.00042639
Subtotal	0.15587913	0.43907770	-1.24952513	-0.25789872	-0.27186679	-0.42974310	-0.17026249
$z = \Sigma c_{kj}{}^{o} * (\sin(x)/x)^{k} * \cos^{j}(j*y)$		(k= 0, 1, 2, 3, 4, 5, 6		j = 0, 1, 2, 3, 4, 5, 6) =				-1.78433940

Figure 4. a) UNC-HONN data classification; b) UNC-HONN data classification

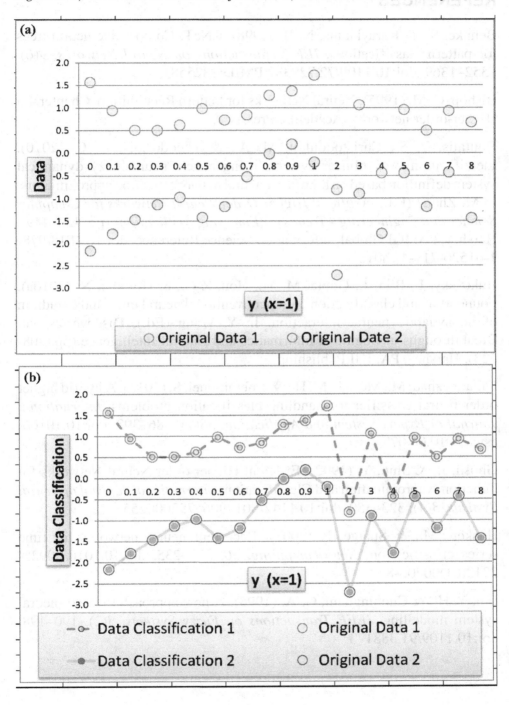

REFERENCES

Behnke, S., & Karayiannis, N. B. (1998). CNeT: Competitive neural trees for pattern classifications. *IEEE Transactions on Neural Networks*, 9(6), 1352–1369. doi:10.1109/72.728387 PMID:18255815

Bishop, C. M. (1995). Neural Networks for Pattern Recognition, Chapter 4.5 Higher-order networks. Academic Press.

Boutalis, Y. S., Christodoulou, M. A., & Theodoridis, D. C. (2010). Identification of nonlinear systems using a new neuro-fuzzy dynamical system definition based on high order neural network function approximators. In M. Zhang (Ed.), *Artificial Higher Order Neural Networks for Computer Science and Engineering – Trends for Emerging Applications* (pp. 423–449). Hershey, PA: IGI Global, Information Science Reference. doi:10.4018/978-1-61520-711-4.ch018

Bukovsky, I., Bila, J., Gupta, M. M., Hou, Z-G., & Homma, N. (2010a). Foundation and classification of nonconventional neural units and paradigm of nonsynaptic neural interaction. In Y. Wang (Ed.), Discoveries and Breakthroughs in Cognitive Informatics and Natural Intelligence (pp. 508-523). Hershey, PA: IGI Publishing.

Fallahnezhad, M., Moradi, M. H., & Zaferanlouei, S. (2011). A hybrid higher order neural classifier for handling classification problems. *International Journal of Expert System and Application*, 38(1), 386–393. doi:10.1016/j.eswa.2010.06.077

Ghosh, J., & Shin, Y. (1992). Efficient Higher-order Neural Networks for Function Approximation and Classification. *International Journal of Neural Systems*, 3(4), 323–350. doi:10.1142/S0129065792000255

Husken, M., & Stagge, P. (2003). Recurrent neural networks for time series classification. *Neurocomputing*, 50, 223–235. doi:10.1016/S0925-2312(01)00706-8

Lin, Y. H., & Cunningham, G. A. (1995). A new approach to fuzzy-neural system modelling. *IEEE Transactions on Fuzzy Systems*, 3(2), 190–198. doi:10.1109/91.388173

Linhart, G., & Dorffner, G. (1992). A self-learning visual pattern explorer and recognizer using a higher order neural network. In *Proceedings of International Joint Conference on Neural Networks* (vol.3, pp.705 – 710). 10.1109/IJCNN.1992.227069

Lippman, R. P. (1989). Pattern classification using neural networks. *IEEE Communications Magazine, 27*(11), 47–64. doi:10.1109/35.41401

Moon, S., & Chang, S. H. (1994). Classification and prediction of the critical heat flux using fuzzy clustering and artificial neural networks. *Nuclear Engineering and Design, 150*(1), 151–161. doi:10.1016/0029-5493(94)90059-0

Morad, A. H., & Yuan, B. Z. (1998). HONN approach for automatic model building and 3D object recognition. In *Proceedings of 1998 Fourth International Conference on Signal Processing* (vol.2, pp. 881 – 884). 10.1109/ICOSP.1998.770752

Najarian, S., Hosseini, S. M., & Fallahnezhad, M. (2010). Artificial tactile sensing and robotic surgery using higher order neural networks. In M. Zhang (Ed.), *Artificial Higher Order Neural Networks for Computer Science and Engineering – Trends for Emerging Applications* (pp. 514–544). Hershey, PA: IGI Global, Information Science Reference. doi:10.4018/978-1-61520-711-4.ch021

Park, S., Smith, M. J. T., & Mersereau, R. M. (2000, October). Target Recognition Based on Directional Filter Banks and higher-order neural network. *Digital Signal Processing, 10*(4), 297–308. doi:10.1006/dspr.2000.0376

Reid, M. B., Spirkovska, L., & Ochoa, E. (1989). Simultaneous position, scale, rotation invariant pattern classification using third-order neural networks. *Int. J. Neural Networks, 1*, 154–159.

Sanchez, E. N., Urrego, D. A., Alanis, A. Y., & Carlos-Hernandez, S. (2010). Recurrent higher order neural observers for anaerobic processes. In M. Zhang (Ed.), *Artificial Higher Order Neural Networks for Computer Science and Engineering – Trends for Emerging Applications* (pp. 333–365). Hershey, PA: IGI Global, Information Science Reference. doi:10.4018/978-1-61520-711-4.ch015

Schmidt, W. A. C., & Davis, J. P. (1993). Pattern recognition properties of various feature spaces for higher order neural networks. *Pattern Analysis and Machine Intelligence, 15*(8), 795–801. doi:10.1109/34.236250

Shannon, C. E. (1998, February). Communication in the presence of noise. *Proceedings of the IEEE, 86*(2).

Shawash, J., & Selviah, D. R. (2010). Artificial higher order neural network training on limited precision processors. In M. Zhang (Ed.), *Artificial Higher Order Neural Networks for Computer Science and Engineering – Trends for Emerging Applications* (pp. 312–332). Hershey, PA: IGI Global, Information Science Reference. doi:10.4018/978-1-61520-711-4.ch014

Shin, Y. (1991). The pi-sigma network: An efficient higher-order neural network for pattern classification and function approximation. *Proceedings of International Joint Conference on Neural Networks, I,* 13–18.

Shin, Y., & Ghosh, J. (1991). The pi-sigma network: an efficient higher-order neural network for pattern classification and function approximation. *Proceedings of the International Joint Conference on Neural Networks* (vol. 1, pp. 13 – 18). 10.1109/IJCNN.1991.155142

Shin, Y., Ghosh, J., & Samani, D. (1992). Computationally efficient invariant pattern classification with higher-order pi-sigma networks. In Intelligent Engineering Systems through Artificial Neural Networks (vol 2, pp. 379-384). ASME Press.

Spirkovska, L., & Reid, M. B. (1992). Robust position, scale, and rotation invariant object recognition using higher-order neural networks. *Pattern Recognition, 25*(9), 975–985. doi:10.1016/0031-3203(92)90062-N

Spirkovska, L., & Reid, M. B. (1993). Coarse-coded higher-order neural networks for PSRI object recognition. *IEEE Transactions on Neural Networks, 4*(2), 276–283. doi:10.1109/72.207615 PMID:18267727

Spirkovska, L., & Reid, M. B. (1994). Higher-order neural networks applied to 2D and 3D object recognition. *Machine Learning, 15*(2), 169–199. doi:10.1007/BF00993276

Voutriaridis, C., Boutalis, Y. S., & Mertzios, B. G. (2003). Ridge polynomial networks in pattern recognition. In *Proceedings of 4th EURASIP Conference on Video/Image Processing and Multimedia Communications* (*vol.2,* pp.519 – 524). Academic Press.

Wan L., & Sun L. (1996). Automatic target recognition using higher order neural network. In *Proceedings of the IEEE 1996 National Aerospace and Electronics Conference* (Vol. 1, pp. 221 – 226). IEEE.

Zhang, M., Xu, S., & Fulcher, J. (2002). Neuron-Adaptive Higher Order Neural Network Models for Automated Financial Data Modeling, IEEE Transactions on Neural Networks, 13(1), 188-204.

ADDITIONAL READING

Al-Rawi, M. S., & Al-Rawi, K. R. (2010). On the Equivalence between Ordinary Neural Networks and Higher Order Neural Networks. In M. Zhang (Ed.), *Artificial Higher Order Neural Networks for Computer Science and Engineering – Trends for Emerging Application* (pp. 138–158). Information Science. doi:10.4018/978-1-61520-711-4.ch006

Alanis, A. Y., Sanchez, E. N., Loukianov, A. G., & Perez-Cisneros, M. A. (2010). Real-Time Discrete Neural Block Control Using Sliding Modes for Electric Induction Motors. *IEEE Transactions on Control Systems Technology, 18*(1), 11–21. doi:10.1109/TCST.2008.2009466

Amari, S. (1974). A Method of Statistical Neurodynamics. *Kybernetik, 14,* 201–215. PMID:4850221

Artyomov, E., & Yadid-Pecht, O. (2005). Modified High-Order Neural Network for Invariant Pattern Recognition. *Pattern Recognition Letters, 26*(6), 843–851. doi:10.1016/j.patrec.2004.09.029

Babu, B. V., & Sheth, P. N. (2006). Modeling and simulation of reduction zone of downdraft biomass gasifier: Effect of char reactivity factor. *Energy Conversion and Management, 47*(15–16), 2602–2611. doi:10.1016/j.enconman.2005.10.032

Bastin, G., & Dochain, D. (1990). *On-line estimation and adaptive control of bioreactors.* Amsterdam: Elsevier Science Publications.

Boutalis, Y. S., Christodoulou, M. A., & Theodoridis, D. C. (2010). Identification of Nonlinear Systems Using a New Neuro-Fuzzy Dynamical System Definition Based on High Order Neural Network Function Approximators. In M. Zhang (Ed.), *Artificial Higher Order Neural Networks for Computer Science and Engineering: Trends for Emerging Applications* (pp. 423–449). Hershey, PA: IGI Global. doi:10.4018/978-1-61520-711-4.ch018

Bukovsky, I., Bila, J., & Gupta, M. M. (2006). Stable Neural Architecture of Dynamic Neural Units with Adaptive Time Delays. In *7th International FLINS Conference on Applied Artificial Intelligence.* ISBN 981-256-690-2. pp. 215-222. 10.1142/9789812774118_0033

Cao, J., Ren, F., & Liang, J. (2009). Dynamics in Artificial Higher Order Neural Networks with Delays. In Ming Zhang (Ed.), Artificial Higher Order Neural Networks for Economics and Business (pp.389 - 429). Information Science Reference, Hershey, PA, USA: IGI Global. doi:10.4018/978-1-59904-897-0.ch018

Chen, Y., Abraham, A., & Yang, J. (2005). Feature Selection, and Intrusion Detection using Hybrid Flexible Neural Trees. *Lecture Notes in Computer Science, 3498,* 439–444. doi:10.1007/11427469_71

Chen, Y., Zhang, Y., Dong, J., & Yang, J. (2004). System Identification by Evolved Flexible Neural Tree, *proceeding of the 5th Congress of Intelligent Control and Automation.*

Chung, S., & Slotine, J. J. E. (2009). Cooperative robot control and concurrent synchronization of Lagrangian systems. *IEEE Transactions on Robotics, 25*(3), 686–700. doi:10.1109/TRO.2009.2014125

Cotter, N. (1990). The Stone-Weierstrass Theorem and Its Application to Neural Networks. *IEEE Transactions on Neural Networks, 1*(4), 290–295. doi:10.1109/72.80265 PMID:18282849

De Baere, L. (2000). Anaerobic digestion of solid waste: State-of-the-art. *Water Science and Technology, 41*(3), 283–290. doi:10.2166/wst.2000.0082 PMID:11382003

Dochain, D. M., & Perrier, M. (1997). Dynamical modelling, analysis, monitoring and control design for nonlinear bioprocesses. *Advances in Biochemical Engineering/Biotechnology, 56,* 147–197. doi:10.1007/BFb0103032

Dunis, C. L., Laws, J., & Evans, B. (2009). Modeling and Trading the Soybean-Oil Crush Spread with Recurrent and Higher Order Networks: A Comparative Analysis. In Ming Zhang (Ed.), Artificial Higher Order Neural Networks for Economics and Business (pp.348 - 367). Information Science Reference, Hershey, PA, USA: IGI Global.

Fallahnezhad, M., Moradi, M. H., & Zaferanlouei, S. (2011). A Hybrid Higher Order Neural Classifier for handling classification problems. *Expert Systems with Applications, 38*(1), 386–393. doi:10.1016/j.eswa.2010.06.077

Fisher, J., & Govindarajan, V. (1992). Profit Center Manager Compensation: An Examination of Market, Political and Human Capital Factors. *Strategic Management Journal, 13*(3), 205–217. doi:10.1002mj.4250130304

Freeman, R., & Tse, S. (1992). A non-linear model of security price responses to unexpected earnings. *Journal of Accounting Research, 30*(2), 85–109. doi:10.2307/2491123

Garcia, C., Molina, F., Roca, E., & Lema, J. M. (2007). Fuzzy-based control of an anaerobic reactor treating wastewaters containing ethanol and carbohydrates. *Industrial & Engineering Chemistry Research, 46*(21), 6707–6715. doi:10.1021/ie0617001

Ghosh, J., & Shin, Y. (1992). Efficient Higher-order Neural Networks for Function Approximation and Classification. *International Journal of Neural Systems, 3*(4), 323–350. doi:10.1142/S0129065792000255

Gupta, M. M., Jin, L., & Homma, N. (2003). *Static and Dynamic Neural Networks: From Fundamentals to Advanced Theory*. Hoboken, NJ: IEEE & Wiley. doi:10.1002/0471427950

Harston, C. T. (1990). The Neurological Basis for Neural Computation. In A. J. Maren, C. T. Harston, & R. M. Pap (Eds.), *Handbook of Neural Computing Applications* (Vol. 1, pp. 29–44). New York: Academic. doi:10.1016/B978-0-12-546090-3.50007-3

Homma, N., & Gupta, M. M. (2002). A general second order neural unit. *Bull. Coll. Med. Sci. Tohoku Univ., 11*(1), 1–6.

Hornik, K., Stinchcombe, M., & White, H. (1989). Multilayer Feedforward Networks Are Universal Approximators. *Neural Networks, 2*(5), 359–366. doi:10.1016/0893-6080(89)90020-8

Huang, G. B., Chen, L., & Siew, C. K. (2006). Universal approximation using incremental constructive feedforward networks with random hidden nodes. *IEEE Transactions on Neural Networks, 17*(4), 879–892. doi:10.1109/TNN.2006.875977 PMID:16856652

Hussain, A., & Liatsis, P. (2008). A Novel Recurrent Polynomial Neural Network for Financial Time Series Prediction. In Z. M., Higher Order Neural Networks for Economics and Business.(pp. 190- 211). Idea Group Inc (IGI).

Jagannathan, S., & Lewis, F. L. (1996). Identification of nonlinear dynamical systems using multilayered neural networks. *Automatica, 32*(12), 1707–1712. doi:10.1016/S0005-1098(96)80007-0

Jiang, M., Gielen, G., & Wang, L. (2010). Analysis of Quantization Effects on Higher Order Function and Multilayer Feedforward Neural Networks. In Ming Zhang (Ed.), Artificial Higher Order Neural Networks for Computer Science and Engineering – Trends for Emerging Application (pp.187-222). Information Science Reference, Hershey, PA, USA: IGI Global. doi:10.4018/978-1-61520-711-4.ch008

Karayiannis, N. B., & Venetsanopoulos, A. N. (1995). On the Training and Performance of High-Order Neural Networks. *Mathematical Biosciences, 129*(2), 143–168. doi:10.1016/0025-5564(94)00057-7 PMID:7549218

Kesavadas, T., Srimathveeravalli, G., Arulesan, V., (2005). Parametric Modeling and Simulation of Trocar Insertion. Journal of studies in health technologies and informatics, 119, 252-254.

Knowles, A., Hussain, A., Deredy, W. E., Lisboa, P., & Dunis, C. L. (2009). Higher Order Neural Networks with Bayesian Confidence Measure for the Prediction of the EUR/USD Exchange Rate. In Ming Zhang (Ed.), Artificial Higher Order Neural Networks for Economics and Business (pp.48- 59). Information Science Reference, Hershey, PA, USA: IGI Global.

Kumar, N., Panwar, V., Sukavanam, N., Sharma, S. P., & Borm, J. H. (2011). Neural Network-Based Nonlinear Tracking Control of Kinematically Redundant Robot Manipulators. *Mathematical and Computer Modelling, 53*(9), 1889–1901. doi:10.1016/j.mcm.2011.01.014

Lee, Y. C., Doolen, G., Chen, H., Sun, G., Maxwell, T., Lee, H., & Giles, C. L. (1986). Machine learning using a higher order correlation network. *Physica D. Nonlinear Phenomena, 22*(1-3), 276–306. doi:10.1016/0167-2789(86)90300-6

Li, X., Chen, Z. Q., & Yuan, Z. Z. (2002). Simple Recurrent Neural Network-Based Adaptive Predictive Control for Nonlinear Systems. *Asian Journal of Control, 4*(2), 31–239.

Lu, Y., Guo, L., Zhang, X., & Yan, Q. (2007). Thermodynamic modeling and analysis of biomass gasification for hydrogen production in supercritical water. *Chemical Engineering Journal, 131*(1-3), 233–244. doi:10.1016/j.cej.2006.11.016

Mahvash, M., & Dupont, P. E. (2009). Fast Needle Insertion to Minimize Tissue Deformation and Damage, *ICRA '09. IEEE International Conference on Robotics and Automation,* 3097-3102.

Meiqin, M., Ming, D., Jianhui, S., Chang, L., Min, S., & Guorong, Z. (2008). *Testbed for Microgrid with Multi-Energy Generators.* Paper presented at the Canadian Conference on Electrical and Computer Engineering CCECE, pp. 637-640.

Mishra, S. (2006). Neural-network-based adaptive UPFC for improving transient stability performance of power system. *IEEE Transactions on Neural Networks, Volume, 17*(Issue: 2), 461–470. doi:10.1109/TNN.2006.871706 PMID:16566472

Moon, S., Baek, W. P., & Chang, S. H. (1996). Parametric trends analysis of the critical heat flux based on artificial neural networks. *Nuclear Engineering and Design, 163*(1-2), 29–49. doi:10.1016/0029-5493(95)01178-1

Ou, C. (2008). Anti-periodic solutions for high-order Hopfield neural networks. *Computers & Mathematics with Applications (Oxford, England), 56*(3), 1838–1844. doi:10.1016/j.camwa.2008.04.029

Peng, H., & Zhu, S. (2007). Handling of incomplete data sets using ICA and SOM in data mining. *Neural Computing & Applications, Volume, 16*(2), 167–172. doi:10.100700521-006-0058-6

Polycarpou, M. M., & Ioannou, P. A. (1996). A robust adaptive nonlinear control design. *Automatica, 32*(3), 423–427. doi:10.1016/0005-1098(95)00147-6

Ren, F., & Cao, J. (2006). LMI-based criteria for stability of high-order neural networks with time-varying delay. *Nonlinear Analysis Series B: Real World Applications, 7*(5), 967–979. doi:10.1016/j.nonrwa.2005.09.001

Ross, S. M. (1970). Applied Probability Models with Optimization Applications, Dover Publications, INC. Propagation. In D. E. Rumelhart & J. L. McClelland (Eds.), *Parallel Distributed Processing: Explorations in the Microstructure of Cognition* (Vol. 1, pp. 318–362). Cambridge, MA: MIT Press.

Schwartz, J. M., Denninger, M., & vRancourt, D. (2005). Modeling liver tissue properties using a non-linear visco-elastic model for surgery simulation. *Medical Image Analysis*, *9*(2), 103–112. doi:10.1016/j.media.2004.11.002 PMID:15721226

Shafie-khah, M., Parsa Moghaddam, M., & Sheikh-El-Eslami, M. K. (2011). Price Forecasting of Day-Ahead Electricity Markets Using a Hybrid Forecast Method. *Energy Conversion and Management*, *52*(5), 2165–2169. doi:10.1016/j.enconman.2010.10.047

Talebi, H., Abdollahi, F., Patel, R., & Khorasani, K. (2010). *Neural Network-Based State Estimation of Nonlinear Systems* (3rd ed.). Springer. doi:10.1007/978-1-4419-1438-5

Tseng, Y.-H., & Wu, J.-L. (1994). Constant-time neural decoders for some BCH codes. *Proceedings of IEEE International Symposium on Information Theory*, 343.

Villalobos, L., & Merat, F. (1995). Learning capability assessment and feature space optimization for higher-order neural networks. *IEEE Transactions on Neural Networks*, *6*(1), 267–272. doi:10.1109/72.363427 PMID:18263308

Wang, L. P., Li, S., Tian, F. Y., & Fu, X. J. (2004). A Noisy Chaotic Neural Network for Solving Combinatorial Optimization Problems: Stochastic Chaotic Simulated Annealing. *IEEE Trans. on Sys. Man, Cybern., Part B - Cybern.*, *34*(5), 2119–2125. doi:10.1109/TSMCB.2004.829778 PMID:15503507

Werbos, P. J. (1990). Backpropagation through time: What it is and how to do it. *Proceedings of the IEEE*, *78*(10), 1550–1560. doi:10.1109/5.58337

Wu, C. W. (2007). *Synchronization in Complex Networks of Nonlinear Dynamical Systems*. Singapore: World Scientific. doi:10.1142/6570

Yao, Y., Freeman, W. J., Burke, B., & Yang, Q. (1991). Pattern recognition by a distributed neural network: An industrial application. *Neural Networks*, *4*(1), 103–121. doi:10.1016/0893-6080(91)90036-5

Yih, G. L., Wei, Y. W., & Tsu, T. L. (2005). Observer-based direct adaptive fuzzy-neural control for nonaffine nonlinear systems. *IEEE Transactions on Neural Networks*, *16*(4), 853–861. doi:10.1109/TNN.2005.849824 PMID:16121727

KEY TERMS AND DEFINITIONS

HONN: Artificial higher order neural network.

PHONN: Artificial polynomial higher order neural network.

SPHONN: Artificial sigmoid polynomial higher order neural network.

SSINCHONN: Artificial sine and sinc higher order neural network.

THONN: Artificial trigonometric higher order neural network.

UCSHONN: Artificial ultra-high frequency trigonometric higher order neural network.

UNC-HONN: Ultra high frequency sinc and cosine higher order neural networks.

UNS-HONN: Ultra high frequency sinc and sine higher order neural networks.

UNT-HONN: Ultra high frequency sinc and trigonometric higher order neural networks.

Chapter 8

Data Simulations Using Cosine and Sigmoid Higher Order Neural Networks

ABSTRACT

A new open box and nonlinear model of cosine and sigmoid higher order neural network (CS-HONN) is presented in this chapter. A new learning algorithm for CS-HONN is also developed in this chapter. In addition, a time series data simulation and analysis system, CS-HONN simulator, is built based on the CS-HONN models. Test results show that the average error of CS-HONN models are from 2.3436% to 4.6857%, and the average error of polynomial higher order neural network (PHONN), trigonometric higher order neural network (THONN), and sigmoid polynomial higher order neural network (SPHONN) models range from 2.8128% to 4.9077%. This suggests that CS-HONN models are 0.1174% to 0.4917% better than PHONN, THONN, and SPHONN models.

INTRODUCTION

This chapter introduces a new Higher Order Neural Network (HONN) model. This new model is tested in the data simulation areas. The contributions of this chapter are:

• Present a new model – CS-HONN.

DOI: 10.4018/978-1-7998-3563-9.ch008

- Based on the CS-HONN models, build a time series simulation system – CS-HONN simulator.
- Develop the CS-HONN learning algorithm and weight update formulae.
- Shows that CS-HONN can do better than Polynomial Higher Order Neural Network (PHONN), Trigonometric Higher Order Neural Network (THONN), and Sigmoid Polynomial Higher Order Neural Network (SPHONN) models in the data simulation examples.

BACKGROUND

Many studies use traditional artificial neural network models. Blum and Li (1991) studied approximation by feed-forward networks. Gorr (1994) studied the forecasting behavior of multivariate time series using neural networks. Barron, Gilstrap, and Shrier (1987) used polynomial neural networks for the analogies and engineering applications. However, all the studies above use traditional artificial neural network models - black box models that did not provide users with a function that describe the relationship between the input and output. The first motivation of this paper is to develop nonlinear "open box" neural network models that will provide rationale for network's decisions, also provide better results.

Jiang, Gielen, and Wang (2010) investigated the combined effects of quantization and clipping on Higher Order function neural networks (HOFNN) and multilayer feedforward neural networks (MLFNN). Statistical models were used to analyze the effects of quantization in a digital implementation This study established and analyzed the relationships for a true nonlinear neuron between inputs and outputs bit resolution, training and quantization methods, the number of network layers, network order and performance degradation, all based on statistical models, and for on-chip and off-chip training. The experimental simulation results verify the presented theoretical analysis.

Randolph and Smith (2000) have a **new approach to object classification in binary images.** In this paper, Randolph and Smith address the problem of classifying binary objects using a cascade of a binary directional filter bank (DFB) and a higher order neural network (HONN). Rovithakis, Maniadakis, and Zervakis (2000) present a **genetically optimized artificial neural network structure for feature extraction and classification of vascular tissue fluorescence spectrums.** The optimization of artificial neural network structures for feature extraction and classification by employing Genetic Algorithms is addressed here. More precisely, a non-linear filter based on High Order Neural Networks whose weights are updated is used. Zhang, Liu, Li, Liu, and Ouyang (2002) discuss the problems of the translation and rotation invariance of a physiological signal in long-term clinical custody. This paper presents a solution using high order neural networks with the advantage of large sample size. Rovithakis, Chalkiadakis, and Zervakis (2004) design a **high order neural network structure for function approximation applications with using genetic algorithms, which** entails both parametric (weights determination) and structural learning (structure selection). Siddiqi (2005) proposed direct encoding method to design higher **order neural networks, since t**here are two major ways of encoding a higher order neural network into a chromosome, as required in design of a genetic algorithm (GA). These are explicit (direct) and implicit (indirect) encoding methods. The first motivation of this chapter is to use artificial HONN models for applications in the computer science and engineering areas.

Lu, Song, and Shieh (2010) studied the polynomial kernel higher order neural networks. As a general framework to represent data, the kernel method can be used if the interactions between elements of the domain occur only through inner product. As a major stride towards the nonlinear feature extraction and dimension reduction, two important kernel-based feature extraction algorithms, kernel principal component analysis and kernel Fisher discriminant, have been proposed. In an attempt to mitigate these drawbacks, this study focused on the application of the newly developed polynomial kernel higher order neural networks in improving the sparsity and thereby obtaining a succinct representation for kernel-based nonlinear feature extraction algorithms. Particularly, the learning algorithm is based on linear programming support vector regression, which outperforms the conventional quadratic programming support vector regression in model sparsity and computational efficiency.

Murata (2010) found that A Pi-Sigma higher order neural network (Pi-Sigma HONN) is a type of higher order neural network, where, as its name implies, weighted sums of inputs are calculated first and then the sums are multiplied by each other to produce higher order terms that constitute the network outputs. This type of higher order neural networks has good function approximation capabilities. In this study, the structural feature of Pi-Sigma HONNs is discussed in contrast to other types of neural networks. The reason for their good function approximation capabilities is given based on pseudo-theoretical analysis together with empirical illustrations.

Ghazali, Hussain, and Nawi (2010) proposed a novel Dynamic Ridge Polynomial Higher Order Neural Network (DRPHONN). The architecture of the new DRPHONN incorporates recurrent links into the structure of the ordinary Ridge Polynomial Higher Order Neural Network (RPHONN). RPHONN is a type of feed-forward Higher Order Neural Network (HONN) which implements a static mapping of the input vectors. In order to model dynamical functions of the brain, it is essential to utilize a system that is capable of storing internal states and can implement complex dynamic system. Neural networks with recurrent connections are dynamical systems with temporal state representations. The dynamic structure approach has been successfully used for solving varieties of problems, such as time series forecasting, approximating a dynamical system, forecasting a stream flow, and system control.

Granger and Bates (1981) researched the combination of forecasts. Granger and Weiss (1983) showed the importance of cointegration in the modeling of nonstationary economic series. Granger and Lee (1990) studied multicointegration. Granger and Swanson (1996) further developed multicointegration in studying of cointegrated variables. The second motivation of this paper is to develop a new nonstationary data analysis system by using new generation computer techniques that will improve the accuracy of the data simulation.

Psaltis, Park, and Hong (1988) studied higher order associative memories and their optical implementations. Redding, Kowalczyk, Downs (1993) developed constructive high-order network algorithm. Zhang, Murugesan, and Sadeghi (1995) developed a Polynomial Higher Order Neural Network (PHONN) model for data simulation. The idea first extended to PHONN Group models (Zhang, Fulcher, and Scofield, (1996)), then to Trigonometric Higher Order Neural Network (THONN) models for data simulation (Zhang, Zhang, and Keen, (1999)). Zhang, Zhang, and Fulcher (2000) studied HONN group model for data simulation. By utilizing adaptive neuron activation functions, Zhang, Xu, and Fulcher (2002) developed a neuron adaptive HONN. Zhang and Fulcher (2004) provide detail mathematics for THONN models. Zhang (2009A) published a HONN book, where all 22 chapters focused on artificial higher order neural networks for economics and business. Zhang (2009B) found that HONN can simulate non-continuous data with better accuracy than SAS NLIN (non-linear) models. Zhang (2009C) also developed Ultra High Frequency Trigonometric Higher Order Neural Networks, in which model details of UCSHONN (Ultra High Frequency Cosine and Sine Higher Order Neural Network) was given.

MODELS OF CS-HONN

CS-HONN model structure can be seen in Figure 1. Formula (1) (2) and (3) are for CS-HONN models 1b, 1 and 0 respectively. Model 1b has three layers of weights changeable, Model 1 has two layers of weights changeable, and model 0 has one layer of weights changeable. For models 1b, 1 and 0, Z is the output while x and y are the inputs of CS-HONN. $a_{kj}{}^{o}$ is the weight for the output layer, $a_{kj}{}^{hx}$ and $a_{kj}{}^{hy}$ are the weights for the second hidden layer, and $a_{k}{}^{x}$ and $a_{j}{}^{y}$ are the weights for the first hidden layer. Functions polynomial and sigmoid are the first hidden layer nodes of CS-HONN. The nodes of the second hidden layer are multiplication neurons. The output layer node of CS-HONN is a linear function of $f^{o}(net^{o}) = net^{o}$, where net^{o} equals the input of output layer node. CS-HONN is an open neural network model, each weight of HONN has its corresponding coefficient in the model formula, and each node of CS-HONN has its corresponding function in the model formula. The structure of CS-HONN is built by a nonlinear formula. It means, after training, there is rationale for each component of CS-HONC in the nonlinear formula.

For formula 1, 2, and 3, values of k and j ranges from 0 to n, where n is an integer. The CS-HONN model can simulate high frequency time series data, when n increases to a big number. This property of the model allows it to easily simulate and predicate high frequency time series data, since both k and j increase when there is an increase in n.

The CS-HONN Architecture was shown in Figure 1. This model structure is used to develop the model learning algorithm, which make sure the convergence of learning. This allows the deference between desired output and real output of CS-HONN close to zero.

Based on Chapter 1 formulae from (1-78) to (1-82: CS-HONN 2), the CS-HONN models are defined as follows:

Let

$$f_k{}^x \left(c_k{}^x x \right) = \cos^k (c_k{}^x x) \tag{8-1}$$

$$f_j{}^y \left(c_j{}^y y \right) = \left(1 / \left(1 + \exp(c_j{}^y (-y)) \right) \right)^j \tag{8-2}$$

CS – HONN Model 0:

$$z = \sum_{k,j=0}^{n} c_{kj}{}^{o} \cos^{k}(x)\left(1/\left(1+\exp(-y)\right)\right)^{j}$$

$$where: \left(c_{kj}{}^{hx}\right) = \left(c_{kj}{}^{hy}\right) = 1 \ \ and \ \ c_{k}{}^{x} = c_{j}{}^{y} = 1$$

(8-3)

CS – HONN Model 1:

$$z = \sum_{k,j=0}^{n} c_{kj}{}^{o} \cos^{k}(c_{k}{}^{x}x)\left(1/\left(1+\exp(c_{j}{}^{y}(-y))\right)\right)^{j}$$

$$where: \left(c_{kj}{}^{hx}\right) = \left(c_{kj}{}^{hy}\right) = 1$$

(8-4)

CS – HONN Model 2:

$$Z = \sum_{k,j=0}^{n} \left(c_{kj}{}^{o}\right)\{c_{kj}{}^{hx}\cos^{k}\left(c_{k}{}^{x}x\right)\}\{c_{kj}{}^{hy}\left(1/\left(1+\exp(c_{j}{}^{y}(-y))\right)\right)^{j}\}$$

(8-5)

CS-HONN TIME SERIES ANALYSIS SYSTEM

The CS-HONN simulator is written in C language, runs under X window on Sun workstation, based on previous work by Zhang, Fulcher, Scofield (1996). A user-friendly *GUI* (Graphical User Interface) system has also been incorporated. When you run the system, any step, data or calculation can be reviewed and modified from different windows during processing. Hence, changing data, network models and comparing results can be done very easily and efficiently.

LEARNING ALGORITHM OF CS-HONN

The learning formula for the output layer weights in CS-HONN models are the same as other HONN models. The learning formula for the second-hidden layer weights in the CS-HONN modes are the same as other HONN models. The learning formula for the first-hidden layer weights in the CS-HONN models are different. Details are listed here.

Figure 1. CS-HONN Architecture

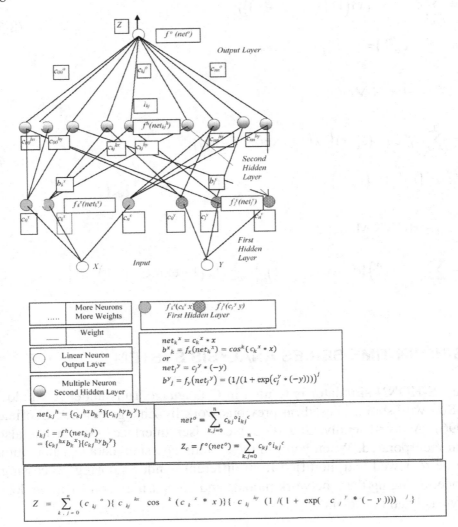

Learning Formulae of Output Neurons in CS-HONN Models (model 0, 1, and 2)

Based on Chapter 1 formulae from (1-133: A.1) to (1-145: A.13), CS-HONN models (model 0, 1, and 2) are rewritten as follows:

$$c_{kj}^{\,o}\left(t+1\right)=c_{kj}^{\,o}\left(t\right)-\eta\left(\partial E\,/\,\partial c_{kj}^{\,o}\right)=c_{kj}^{\,o}\left(t\right)+\eta\left(d-z\right)f^{o\,\prime}\left(net^{o}\right)i_{kj}=c_{kj}^{\,o}\left(t\right)+\eta\delta^{ol}i_{kj}$$

where: $\delta o^{l=}(d-z)$

$$f^{o\prime}\left(net^{o}\right)=1 \quad (linear\ neuron)$$

(8-6)

Learning Formulae of Second-Hidden Layer Neurons in CS-HONN Models (Model 2)

Based on Chapter 1 formulae from (1-146: B.1) to (1-160: B.15), CS-HONN models (model 2) are rewritten as follows:

The weight update question for x input neurons is:

$$c_{kj}^{\,hx}\left(t+1\right)=c_{kj}^{\,hx}\left(t\right)-\eta\left(\partial E\,/\,\partial c_{kj}^{\,hx}\right)$$

$$=c_{kj}^{\,hx}\left(t\right)+\eta\left(\left(d-z\right)f^{o\prime}\left(net^{o}\right)c_{kj}^{\,o}f^{h\prime}\left(net_{kj}^{\,hx}\right)c_{kj}^{\,hy}b_{j}^{\,y}b_{k}^{\,x}\right)=c_{kj}^{\,hx}\left(t\right)+\eta\left(\delta^{ol}c_{kj}^{\,o}\delta_{kj}^{\,hx}b_{k}^{\,x}\right)$$

where: $\delta o^{l=}(d-z)$

$$\delta_{kj}^{\,hx}=c_{kj}^{\,hy}b_{j}^{\,y}$$

$$f^{o\prime}\left(net^{o}\right)=1 \quad (linear\ neuron)$$

$$f^{h\prime}\left(net_{kj}^{\,hx}\right)=1 \quad (linear\ neuron)$$

(8-7)

The weight update question for y input neurons is:

$$c_{kj}^{\,hy}\left(t+1\right)=c_{kj}^{\,hy}\left(t\right)-\eta\left(\partial E\,/\,\partial c_{kj}^{\,hy}\right)$$

$$=c_{kj}^{\,hy}\left(t\right)+\eta\left(\left(d-z\right)f^{o\prime}\left(net^{o}\right)c_{kj}^{\,o}f^{h\prime}\left(net_{kj}^{\,hy}\right)c_{kj}^{\,hx}b_{k}^{\,x}b_{j}^{\,y}\right)=c_{kj}^{\,hy}\left(t\right)+\eta\left(\delta^{ol}c_{kj}^{\,o}\delta_{kj}^{\,hy}b_{j}^{\,y}\right)$$

where: $\delta o^{l=}(d-z)$

$$\delta_{kj}{}^{hy} = c_{kj}{}^{hx} b_k{}^x$$

$$f^{o'}\left(net^o\right) = 1 \qquad (linear\ neuron)$$

$$f^{h'}\left(net_{kj}{}^{hy}\right) = 1 \qquad (linear\ neuron) \qquad (8\text{-}8)$$

General Learning Formulae of First Hidden Layer x Neurons in CS-HONN Models (Model 1 and Model 2)

Based on Chapter 1 formulae from (1-161: C.1) to (1-177: C.17), CS-HONN models (model 1 and 2) are rewritten as follows:

For a function of x input side:

$$b_k{}^x = f_k{}^x\left(net_k{}^x\right)$$
$$f_x{}'\left(net_k{}^x\right) = \partial b_k{}^x / \partial\left(net_k{}^x\right) \qquad (8\text{-}9)$$

$$c_k{}^x(t+1) = c_k{}^x(t) - \eta\left(\partial E_p / \partial c_k{}^x\right)$$
$$= c_k{}^x(t) + \eta(d-z)f^{o'}\left(net^o\right)c_{kj}{}^o * f^{h'}\left(net_{kj}{}^h\right)c_{kj}{}^{hy}b_j{}^y c_{kj}{}^{hx} f_x{}'\left(net_k{}^x\right)x$$
$$= c_k{}^x(t) + \eta * \delta^{ol} * c_{kj}{}^o * \delta^{hx} * c_{kj}{}^{hx} * \delta^x * x$$

where:

$$\delta^{ol} = (d-z)f^{o'}\left(net^o\right) = d-z \qquad (linear\ neuron)$$

$$\delta^{hx} = f^{h'}\left(net_{kj}{}^h\right)c_{kj}{}^{hy}b_j{}^y = c_{kj}{}^{hy}b_j{}^y \qquad (linear\ neuron)$$

$$\delta^x = f_x'\left(net_k{}^x\right) \tag{8-10}$$

General Learning Formulae of First Hidden Layer y Neurons in CS-HONN Models (Model 1 and Model 2)

Based on Chapter 1 formulae from (1-178: D.1) to (1-194: D.17), CS-HONN models (model 1 and 2) are rewritten as follows:

For a function of y input part:

$$b_j{}^y = f_j{}^y\left(net_j{}^y\right)$$
$$f_y'\left(net_j{}^y\right) = \partial b_j{}^y / \partial\left(net_j{}^y\right) \tag{8-11}$$

Using the above procedure:

$$c_j{}^y(t+1) = c_j{}^y(t) - \eta\left(\partial E_p / \partial c_j{}^y\right)$$
$$= c_j{}^y(t) + \eta(d-z)f^o{}'\left(net^o\right)c_{kj}{}^o * f^h{}'\left(net_{kj}{}^h\right)c_{kj}{}^{hx}b_k{}^x c_{kj}{}^{hy} f_y'\left(net_j{}^y\right)y$$
$$= c_j{}^y(t) + \eta * \delta^{ol} * c_{kj}{}^o * \delta^{hy} * c_{kj}{}^{hy} * \delta^y * y$$

where:

$$\delta^{ol} = (d-z)f^o{}'\left(net^o\right) = d - z \qquad \left(linear\ neuron\ f^o{}'\left(net^o\right) = 1\right)$$

$$\delta^{hy} = f^h{}'\left(net_{kj}{}^h\right)c_{kj}{}^{hx}b_k{}^x = c_{kj}{}^{hx}b_k{}^x \qquad \left(linear\ neuron\ f^h{}'\left(net_{kj}{}^h\right) = 1\right)$$

$$\delta^y = f_y'\left(net_j{}^y\right) \tag{8-12}$$

Learning Formulae of CS-HONN Model
for the First Hidden Layer

The first hidden layer neurons in CS-HONN (Model 1 and Model 2) use Cosine and Sigmoid functions. Based on Chapter 1 formulae from (1-273) to (1-278: CS-HONN D.17), update learning formulae of CS-HONN models (model 1 and 2) are rewritten as follows:

Let

$$f_k^{\ x}\left(c_k^{\ x}x\right) = \cos^k(c_k^{\ x}x) \tag{8-13}$$

$$f_j^{\ y}\left(c_j^{\ y}y\right) = \left(1/\left(1+\exp(c_j^{\ y}(-y))\right)\right)^j \tag{8-14}$$

For a cosine function of x input side:

$$b_k^{\ x} = f_k^{\ x}\left(net_k^{\ x}\right) = \cos^k(net_k^{\ x}) = \cos^k(c_k^{\ x}*x)$$

$$f_x{}'\left(net_k^{\ x}\right) = \partial b_k^{\ x}/\partial\left(net_k^{\ x}\right) = \partial\left(\cos^k(net_k^{\ x})\right)/\partial\left(net_k^{\ x}\right)$$
$$= k*\cos^{k-1}(net_k^{\ x})*\left(-\sin(net_k^{\ x})\right) = (-k)*\cos^{k-1}(c_k^{\ x}*x)*\sin(c_k^{\ x}*x) \tag{8-15}$$

$$c_k^{\ x}\left(t+1\right) = c_k^{\ x}\left(t\right)-\eta\left(\frac{\partial E_p}{\partial c_k^{\ x}}\right)$$
$$= c_k^{\ x}\left(t\right)+\eta\left(d-z\right)f^{o'}\left(net^o\right)c_{kj}^{\ o}*f^{h'}\left(net_{kj}^{\ h}\right)c_{kj}^{\ hy}b_j^{\ y}c_{kj}^{\ hx}f_x'\left(net_k^{\ x}\right)x$$
$$= c_k^{\ x}\left(t\right)+\eta*\delta^{ol}*c_{kj}^{\ o}*\delta^{hx}*c_{kj}^{\ hx}*(-k)*\cos^{k-1}(c_k^{\ x}*x)*\sin(c_k^{\ x}*x)*x$$
$$= c_k^{\ x}\left(t\right)+\eta*\delta^{ol}*c_{kj}^{\ o}*\delta^{hx}*c_{kj}^{\ hx}*\delta^{x}*x$$

$$\tag{8-16}$$

where:

$$\delta^{ol} = (d-z)f^{o'}(net^{o}) = d-z \qquad \left(linear\ neuron\ f^{o}{}'(net^{o}) = 1 \right)$$

$$\delta^{hx} = f^{h'}\left(net_{kj}{}^{h}\right)c_{kj}{}^{hy}b_{j}{}^{y} = c_{kj}{}^{hy}b_{j}{}^{y} \qquad \left(linear\ neuron\ f^{h}{}'\left(net_{kj}{}^{h}\right) = 1 \right)$$

$$\delta^{x} = f_{x}'\left(net_{k}{}^{x}\right) = (-k)*\cos^{k-1}\left(net_{k}{}^{x}\right)*\sin\left(net_{k}{}^{x}\right) = (-k)*\cos^{k-1}(c_{k}{}^{x}*x)*\sin(c_{k}{}^{x}*x)$$

For a sigmoid function of *y* input side:

$$b_{j}{}^{y} = f_{j}{}^{y}\left(net_{j}{}^{y}\right) = \left[1/\left(1+\exp(-net_{j}{}^{y})\right)\right]^{j} = \left[1/\left(1+\exp(c_{j}{}^{y}*(-y))\right)\right]^{j}$$

$$
\begin{aligned}
f_{y}{}'\left(net_{j}{}^{y}\right) &= \partial b_{j}{}^{y}/\partial\left(net_{j}{}^{y}\right) \\
&= \partial\left[1/\left(1+\exp(-net_{j}{}^{y})\right)\right]^{k}/\partial\left(net_{j}{}^{y}\right) \\
&= j*\left[1/\left(1+\exp(-net_{j}{}^{y})\right)\right]^{j-1}*\left(1+\exp(-net_{j}{}^{y})\right)^{-2}*\exp(-net_{j}{}^{y}) \\
&= j*\left[1/\left(1+\exp(-c_{j}{}^{y}*y)\right)\right]^{j-1}*\left(1+\exp(-c_{j}{}^{y}*y)\right)^{-2}*\exp(-c_{j}{}^{y}*y)
\end{aligned}
$$

$$(8\text{-}17)$$

$$
\begin{aligned}
c_{j}{}^{y}(t+1) &= c_{j}{}^{y}(t)-\eta\left(\partial E_{p}/\partial c_{j}{}^{y}\right) \\
&= c_{j}{}^{y}(t)+\eta(d-z)f^{o}{}'(net^{o})c_{kj}{}^{o}*f^{h}{}'(net_{kj}{}^{h})c_{kj}{}^{hx}b_{k}{}^{x}c_{kj}{}^{hy}f_{y}{}'(net_{j}{}^{y})y \\
&= c_{j}{}^{y}(t)+\eta*\delta^{ol}*c_{kj}{}^{o}*\delta^{hy}*c_{kj}{}^{hy}*f_{y}{}'(net_{j}{}^{y})*y = c_{j}{}^{y}(t)+\eta*\delta^{ol}*c_{kj}{}^{o}*\delta^{hy}*c_{kj}{}^{hy} \\
&*[j*[1/(1+\exp(-c_{j}{}^{y}*y))]^{j-1}*(1+\exp(-c_{j}{}^{y}*y))^{-2}*\exp(-c_{j}{}^{y}*y)]*y \\
&= c_{j}{}^{y}(t)+\eta*\delta^{ol}*c_{kj}{}^{o}*\delta^{hy}*c_{kj}{}^{hy}*\delta^{y}*y
\end{aligned}
$$

$$(8\text{-}18)$$

where:

$$\delta^{ol} = (d-z)f^{o'}(net^{o}) = d-z \qquad \left(linear\ neuron\ f^{o}{}'(net^{o}) = 1 \right)$$

$$\delta^{hy} = f^{h'}\left(net_{kj}{}^{h}\right)c_{kj}{}^{hx}b_{k}{}^{x} = c_{kj}{}^{hx}b_{k}{}^{x} \qquad \left(linear\ neuron\ f^{h}{}'\left(net_{kj}{}^{h}\right) = 1 \right)$$

$$\delta^y = f_y{'}\left(net_j{}^y\right) = j*\left[1/\left(1+\exp(-c_j{}^y*y)\right)\right]^{j-1}*\left(1+\exp(-c_j{}^y*y)\right)^{-2}*\exp(-c_j{}^y*y)$$

TIME SERIES DATA TEST USING CS-HONN

This paper uses the monthly Switzerland Franc and USA dollar exchange rate from November 2008 to December 2009 (See Table 1 and 2) as the test data for CS-HONN models. This paper also uses the monthly New Zealand dollar and USA dollar exchange rate from November 2008 to December 2009 (See Table 3 and 4) as the test data for CS-HONN models. The rate and desired output data, R_t are from USA Federal Reserve Bank Data bank. Input1, R_{t-2}, are the data at time t-2. Input 2, R_{t-1} are the data at time t-1. The values of R_{t-2}, R_{t-1}, and R_t are converted to a range from 0 to 1 and then used as inputs and output in the CS-HONN model. CS-HONN model 1b is used for Table 1, 2, 3 and 4. The test data of CS-HONN orders 6 for using 10,000 epochs are shown on the tables.

In Table 1, "SwitzelandFranc/USDollar Exchange Rate CHF$1.00 = USD$0.8561 on 3-Nov-08", the average errors of PHONN, THONN, SPHONN, and CS-HONN are 2.7552%, 2.8547%, 2.8286%, and 2.6954% respectively. The average error of PHONN, THONN, and SPHONN is 2.8128%. So CS-HONN error is 0.1174% better than the average error of PHONN, THONN, and SPHONN models.

In Table 2, "SwitzelandFranc/USDollar Exchange Rate CHF$1.00 = USD$0.8220 on 28-Nov-08", the average errors of PHONN, THONN, SPHONN, and CS-HONN are 2.1962%, 3.5549%, 2.7549%, and 2.3436% respectively. The average error of PHONN, THONN, and SPHONN is 2.8353%. So CS-HONN error is 0.4917% better than the average error of PHONN, THONN, and SPHONN models.

In Table 3, "NewZealandDollar/USDollar Exchange Rate NZD$1.00 = USD$0.5975 on 3-Nov-09", the average errors of PHONN, THONN, SPHONN, and CS-HONN are 4.3653%, 5.6771%, 4.6806%, and 4.6857% respectively. The average error of PHONN, THONN, and SPHONN is 4.9077%. So CS-HONN error is 0.2220% better than the average error of PHONN, THONN, and SPHONN models.

In Table 4, "NewZealandDollar/USDollar Exchange RateNZD$1.00 = USD$0.5500 on 28-Nov-08", the average errors of PHONN, THONN,

SPHONN, and CS-HONN are 4.2512%, 4.6730%, 5.1945%, and 4.3306%

Table 1. Switzerland Franc/US Dollar Exchange Rate

	Original Data			HONN Output				HONN Error (% Percentage)			
Date	Rate Desired Output	Input1 2 month ago data	Input2 1 month ago data	PHONN	THONN	SPHONN	CS-HONN	PHONN	THONN	SPHONN	CS-HONN
11/3/08	0.8561										
12/1/08	0.8281										
1/2/09	0.9359	0.8561	0.8281	0.8812	0.8769	0.8755	0.8677	5.8430	6.3031	6.4530	7.2911
2/2/09	0.8591	0.8281	0.9359	0.8946	0.9074	0.8690	0.9267	4.1348	5.6271	1.1502	7.8697
3/2/09	0.8530	0.9359	0.8591	0.9317	0.9262	0.9475	0.8827	9.2218	8.5760	11.0770	3.4834
4/1/09	0.8722	0.8591	0.8530	0.8904	0.8874	0.8818	0.8510	2.0869	1.7424	1.0994	2.4305
5/1/09	0.8800	0.8530	0.8722	0.8928	0.8921	0.8797	0.8674	1.4608	1.3811	0.0303	1.4298
6/1/09	0.9356	0.8722	0.8800	0.9062	0.9030	0.8967	0.9187	3.1402	3.4828	4.1572	1.8121
7/1/09	0.9328	0.8800	0.9356	0.9292	0.9269	0.9115	0.9270	0.3914	0.6384	2.2919	0.6289
8/3/09	0.9454	0.9356	0.9328	0.9619	0.9518	0.9581	0.9361	1.7537	0.6836	1.3511	0.9771
9/1/09	0.9387	0.9328	0.9454	0.9659	0.9548	0.9576	0.9539	2.9019	1.7175	2.0163	1.6171
10/1/09	0.9593	0.9454	0.9387	0.9704	0.9593	0.9678	0.9532	1.1493	0.0008	0.8883	0.6373
11/2/09	0.9826	0.9387	0.9593	0.9754	0.9624	0.9645	0.9585	0.7378	2.0527	1.8387	2.4571
12/1/09	1.0016	0.9593	0.9826	0.9992	0.9811	0.9857	0.9845	0.2403	2.0503	1.5903	1.7111
Average Error (% Percentage)								2.7552	2.8547	2.8286	2.6954
Average Error pf PHONN, THONN, and SPHONN(% Percentage)								2.8128	CS-HONN Better		0.1174

CHF$1.00 = USD$0.8561 on 3-Nov-08, USA Federal Reserve Bank Data (CHF-USD2009-1.dat)

respectively. The average error of PHONN, THONN, and SPHONN is 4.7062%. So CS-HONN error is 0.3756% better than the average error of PHONN, THONN, and SPHONN models.

FUTURE RESEARCH DIRECTIONS

As the next step of HONN model research, more HONN models for different data control will be built to increase the pool of HONN models. Theoretically, the adaptive HONN models can be built and allow the computer automatically choose the best model, order, and coefficients. Thus, making the adaptive HONN models easier to use is one of the future research topics.

HONNs can automatically select the initial coefficients for nonlinear data analysis. The next step of this study will also focus on how to allow people working in the prediction area to understand that HONNs are much easier to use and can have better results. Moreover, further research will develop

Table 2. Switzerland Franc/US Dollar Exchange Rate

	Original Data			HONN Output				HONN Error (% Percentage)			
Date	Rate Desired Output	Input1 2 month ago data	Input2 1 month ago data	PHONN	THONN	SPHONN	CS-HONN	PHONN	THONN	SPHONN	CS-HONN
11/28/08	0.8220										
12/31/08	0.9369										
1/30/09	0.8612	0.8220	0.9369	0.8811	0.9418	0.9446	0.9153	2.3101	9.3580	9.6816	6.2900
2/27/09	0.8568	0.9369	0.8612	0.9445	0.9396	0.8796	0.8853	10.237	9.6676	2.6646	3.3379
3/31/09	0.8776	0.8612	0.8568	0.8629	0.8718	0.8822	0.8604	1.6766	0.6562	0.5229	1.9525
4/30/09	0.8770	0.8568	0.8776	0.8701	0.8805	0.8978	0.8523	0.7881	0.3918	2.3658	2.8196
5/29/09	0.9353	0.8776	0.8770	0.8913	0.8790	0.8958	0.8912	4.7000	6.0191	4.2212	4.7106
6/30/09	0.9202	0.8770	0.9353	0.9249	0.9035	0.9390	0.9255	0.5037	1.8210	2.0391	0.5754
7/31/09	0.9374	0.9353	0.9202	0.9553	0.9314	0.9224	0.9287	1.9114	0.6362	1.6021	0.9228
8/31/09	0.9462	0.9202	0.9374	0.9531	0.9173	0.9365	0.9529	0.7342	3.0516	1.0219	0.7091
9/30/09	0.9639	0.9374	0.9462	0.9636	0.9369	0.9412	0.9525	0.0309	2.7975	2.3536	1.1806
10/30/09	0.9768	0.9462	0.9639	0.9708	0.9511	0.9532	0.9876	0.6073	2.6243	2.4104	1.1100
11/30/09	0.9950	0.9639	0.9768	0.9739	0.9799	0.9607	0.9562	2.1224	1.5225	3.4524	3.9009
12/31/09	0.9654	0.9768	0.9950	0.9725	1.0051	0.9724	0.9595	0.7329	4.1133	0.7226	0.6136
Average Error (% Percentage)								2.1962	3.5549	2.7549	2.3436
Average Error pf PHONN, THONN, and SPHONN(% Percentage)								2.8353	CS-HONN Better		0.4917

CHF$1.00 = USD$0.8220 on 28-Nov-08, USA Federal Reserve Bank Data (CHF-USD2009-2.dat)

HONNs software packages for people working in the prediction area. HONNs will challenge classic procedures and change the research methodology that people are currently using in the prediction areas for the nonlinear data control application

CONCLUSION

This paper develops the details of a open box and nonlinear higher order neural network models of CS-HONN. This paper also provides the learning algorithm formulae for CS-HONN, based on the structures of CS-HONN. This paper uses CS-HONN simulator and tests the CS-HONN models using high frequency data and the running results are compared with Polynomial Higher Order Neural Network (PHONN), Trigonometric Higher Order Neural Network (THONN), and Sigmoid Polynomial Higher Order Neural Network

Table 3. New Zealand Dollar/US Dollar Exchange Rate

	Original Data			HONN Output				HONN Error (% Percentage)			
Date	Rate Desired Output	Input1 2 month ago data	Input2 1 month ago data	PHONN	THONN	SPHONN	CS-HONN	PHONN	THONN	SPHONN	CS-HONN
11/3/08	0.5975										
12/1/08	0.5355										
1/2/09	0.5850	0.5975	0.5355	0.5706	0.5599	0.5914	0.5904	2.4682	4.2988	1.0934	0.9242
2/2/09	0.5026	0.5355	0.5850	0.5883	0.5867	0.5934	0.5516	17.0441	16.7252	18.0587	9.7552
3/2/09	0.4926	0.5850	0.5026	0.5486	0.5413	0.5668	0.5698	11.3602	9.8961	15.0575	15.6726
4/1/09	0.5635	0.5026	0.4926	0.5310	0.5474	0.5290	0.5245	5.7669	2.8580	6.1159	6.9175
5/1/09	0.5687	0.4926	0.5635	0.5629	0.5906	0.5649	0.5552	1.0178	3.8500	0.6719	2.3739
6/1/09	0.6509	0.5635	0.5687	0.5856	0.5745	0.5964	0.6119	10.0259	11.7383	8.3807	5.9887
7/1/09	0.6452	0.5687	0.6509	0.6449	0.6281	0.6377	0.6564	0.0401	2.6484	1.1580	1.7328
8/3/09	0.6683	0.6509	0.6452	0.6648	0.6484	0.6703	0.6591	0.5194	2.9829	0.2982	1.3775
9/1/09	0.6794	0.6452	0.6683	0.6825	0.6652	0.6780	0.6672	0.4502	2.0911	0.2039	1.7942
10/1/09	0.7168	0.6683	0.6794	0.6954	0.6877	0.6917	0.6578	2.9920	4.0592	3.5002	8.2364
11/2/09	0.7225	0.6794	0.7168	0.7271	0.7343	0.7110	0.7154	0.6389	1.6371	1.5895	0.9824
12/1/09	0.7285	0.7168	0.7225	0.7289	0.7674	0.7288	0.7251	0.0600	5.3400	0.0400	0.4726
Average Error (% Percentage)								4.3653	5.6771	4.6806	4.6857
Average Error pf PHONN, THONN, and SPHONN(% Percentage)								4.9077	CS-HONN Better		0.2220

NZD$1.00 = USD$0.5975 on 3-Nov-09, USA Federal Reserve Bank Data (NZD-USD2009-1.dat)

Table 4. New Zealand Dollar/US Dollar Exchange Rate

	Original Data			HONN Output				HONN Error (% Percentage)			
Date	Rate Desired Output	Input1 2 month ago data	Input2 1 month ago	PHONN	THONN	SPHONN	CS-HONN	PHONN	THONN	SPHONN	CS-HONN
11/28/08	0.5500										
12/31/08	0.5815										
1/30/09	0.5084	0.5500	0.5815	0.5911	0.5974	0.5882	0.5453	16.2598	17.5013	15.6890	7.2636
2/27/09	0.5030	0.5815	0.5084	0.5390	0.5318	0.5655	0.5354	7.1663	5.7240	12.4309	6.4485
3/31/09	0.5692	0.5084	0.5030	0.5293	0.5269	0.5376	0.5307	7.0055	7.4388	5.5524	6.7720
4/30/09	0.5695	0.5030	0.5692	0.5758	0.5858	0.5638	0.5565	1.1114	2.8694	1.0033	2.2788
5/29/09	0.6370	0.5692	0.5695	0.5851	0.5860	0.5903	0.6690	8.1451	8.0084	7.3365	5.0224
6/30/09	0.6447	0.5695	0.6370	0.6400	0.6509	0.6221	0.6536	0.7347	0.9646	3.5030	1.3809
7/31/09	0.6605	0.6370	0.6447	0.6646	0.6572	0.6565	0.6536	0.6254	0.4950	0.6049	1.0476
8/31/09	0.6856	0.6447	0.6605	0.6792	0.6722	0.6681	0.6530	0.9316	1.9474	2.5506	4.7550
9/30/09	0.7233	0.6605	0.6856	0.7016	0.6958	0.6886	0.6823	3.0059	3.7983	4.8013	5.6676
10/30/09	0.7230	0.6856	0.7233	0.7265	0.7297	0.7206	0.7388	0.4863	0.9278	0.3366	2.1913
11/30/09	0.7151	0.7233	0.7230	0.7243	0.7275	0.7389	0.7495	1.2920	1.7283	3.3312	4.8089
12/31/09	0.7255	0.7230	0.7151	0.7227	0.7203	0.7349	0.7271	0.3900	0.7100	1.2900	0.2236
Average Error (% Percentage)								4.2513	4.6730	5.1945	4.3306
Average Error pf PHONN, THONN, and SPHONN(% Percentage)								4.7062	CS-HONN Better		0.3756

NZD$1.00 = USD$0.5500 on 28-Nov-08, USA Federal Reserve Bank Data (NZD-USD2009-2.dat)

(SPHONN) models. Test results show that average error of CS-HONN models are from 2.3436% to 4.6857%, and the average error of Polynomial Higher Order Neural Network (PHONN), Trigonometric Higher Order Neural Network (THONN), and Sigmoid polynomial Higher Order Neural Network (SPHONN) models are from 2.8128% to 4.9077%. It means that CS-HONN models are 0.1174% to 0.4917% better than PHONN, THONN, and SPHONN models.

One of the topics for future research is to continue building models of higher order neural networks for different data series. The coefficients of the higher order models will be studied not only using artificial neural network techniques, but also statistical methods.

REFERENCES

Barron, R., Gilstrap, L., & Shrier, S. (1987). Polynomial and neural networks: analogies and engineering applications. In *Proceedings of International Conference of Neural Networks* (Vol. 2, pp. 431-439) New York: Academic Press.

Blum, E., & Li, K. (1991). Approximation theory and feed-forward networks. *Neural Networks*, 4(4), 511–515. doi:10.1016/0893-6080(91)90047-9

Ghazali, R., Hussain, A., & Nawi, N. (2010). Dynamic ridge polynomial higher order neural network. In M. Zhang (Ed.), *Artificial Higher Order Neural Networks for Computer Science and Engineering* (pp. 255–268). Information Science Reference.

Gorr, W. L. (1994). Research prospective on neural network forecasting. *International Journal of Forecasting*, 10(1), 1–4. doi:10.4018/978-1-61520-711-4.ch011

Granger, C. W. J. (1981). Some properties of time series data and their use in econometric model specification. *Journal of Econometrics*, 16(1), 121–130. doi:10.1016/0304-4076(81)90079-8

Granger, C. W. J., & Lee, T. H. (1990). Multicointegration. In G. F. Rhodes, Jr & T. B. Fomby (Eds.), Advances in Econometrics: Cointegration, Spurious Regressions and Unit Roots (pp. 17-84). New York: JAI Press.

Granger, C. W. J., & Swanson, N. R. (1996). Further developments in study of cointegrated variables. *Oxford Bulletin of Economics and Statistics, 58,* 374–386.

Granger, C. W. J., & Weiss, A. A. (1983). Time series analysis of error-correction models. In S. Karlin, T. Amemiya & L. A. Goodman (Eds), Studies in Econometrics, Time Series and Multivariate Statistics (pp. 255-278). San Diego, CA: Academic Press. doi:10.1016/B978-0-12-398750-1.50018-8

Jiang, M., Gielen, G., & Wang, L. (2010). Analysis of quantization effects of higher order function and multilayer feedforward neural networks. In M. Zhang (Ed.), *Artificial Higher Order Neural Networks for Computer Science and Engineering* (pp. 187–222). Hershey, PA: Information Science Reference (an imprint of IGI Global). doi:10.4018/978-1-61520-711-4.ch008

Lu, Z., Song, G., & Shieh, L. (2010). Improving sparsity in kernelized nonlinear feature extraction algorithms by polynomial kernel higher order neural networks. In M. Zhang (Ed.), *Artificial Higher Order Neural Networks for Computer Science and Engineering* (pp. 223–238). Hershey, PA: Information Science Reference (an imprint of IGI Global). doi:10.4018/978-1-61520-711-4.ch009

Murata, J. (2010). Analysis and improvement of function approximation capabilities of pi-sigma higher order neural networks. In M. Zhang (Ed.), *Artificial Higher Order Neural Networks for Computer Science and Engineering* (pp. 239–254). Hershey, PA: Information Science Reference (an imprint of IGI Global). doi:10.4018/978-1-61520-711-4.ch010

Psaltis, D., Park, C., & Hong, J. (1988). Higher order associative memories and their optical implementations. *Neural Networks, 1*(2), 149–163. doi:10.1016/0893-6080(88)90017-2

Randolph, T. R., & Smith, M. J. T. (2000). A new approach to object classification in binary images. In *Proceeding of the 7th IEEE International Conference on Electronics, Circuits and Systems* (vol.1, pp.307 – 310). IEEE. 10.1109/ICECS.2000.911543

Redding, N., Kowalczyk, A., & Downs, T. (1993). Constructive high-order network algorithm that is polynomial time. *Neural Networks, 6*(7), 997–1010. doi:10.1016/S0893-6080(09)80009-9

Rovithakis, G., Maniadakis, M., & Zervakis, M. (2000). A genetically optimized artificial neural network structure for feature extraction and classification of vascular tissue fluorescence spectrums. In *Proceedings. Fifth IEEE International Workshop on Computer Architectures for Machine Perception* (pp.107 – 111). IEEE. 10.1109/CAMP.2000.875964

Rovithakis, G. A., Chalkiadakis, I., & Zervakis, M. E. (2004). High-order neural network structure selection for function approximation applications using genetic algorithms. *Systems, Man and Cybernetics. Part B, 34*(1), 150–158. PMID:15369059

Siddiqi, A. A. (2005, August). Genetically evolving higher order neural networks by direct encoding method. *Proceedings of Computational Intelligence and Multimedia Applications, 16-18,* 62–67. doi:10.1109/ICCIMA.2005.34

Zhang, M. (2009A). *Artificial higher order neural networks for economics and business.* Hershey, PA: IGI-Global Publisher. doi:10.4018/978-1-59904-897-0

Zhang, M. (2009B). Artificial higher order neural network nonlinear models: SAS NLIN or HONNs. In M. Zhang (Ed.), *Artificial higher order neural networks for economics and business* (pp. 1–47). Hershey, PA: IGI-Global Publisher. doi:10.4018/978-1-59904-897-0.ch001

Zhang, M. (2009C). Ultra high frequency trigonometric higher order neural networks. In M. Zhang (Ed.), *Artificial higher order neural networks for economics and business* (pp. 133–163). Hershey, PA: IGI-Global Publisher. doi:10.4018/978-1-59904-897-0.ch007

Zhang, M., & Fulcher, J. (2004). Higher order neural networks for satellite weather prediction. In J. Fulcher & L. C. Jain (Eds.), *Applied Intelligent Systems* (Vol. 153, pp. 17–57). New York: Springer. doi:10.1007/978-3-540-39972-8_2

Zhang, M., Fulcher, J., & Scofield, R. A. (1996). Neural network group models for estimating rainfall from satellite images. In *Proceedings of World Congress on Neural Networks* (pp. 897-900). San Diego, CA: Academic Press.

Zhang, M., Murugesan, S., & Sadeghi, M. (1995). Polynomial higher order neural network for economic data simulation. In *Proceedings of International Conference on Neural Information Processing* (pp. 493-496). Beijing, China: Academic Press.

Zhang, M., Xu, S., & Fulcher, J. (2002). Neuron-adaptive higher order neural network models for automated financial data modeling. *IEEE Transactions on Neural Networks, 13*(1), 188–204. doi:10.1109/72.977302 PMID:18244418

Zhang, M., Xu, S., & Fulcher, J. (2002). Neuron-adaptive higher order neural-network models for automated financial data modeling. *Neural Networks, 13*(1), 188–204. doi:10.1109/72.977302 PMID:18244418

Zhang, M., Zhang, J. C., & Fulcher, J. (2000). Higher order neural network group models for data approximation. *International Journal of Neural Systems, 10*(2), 123–142. doi:10.1142/S0129065700000119 PMID:10939345

Zhang, M., Zhang, J. C., & Keen, S. (1999). Using THONN system for higher frequency non-linear data simulation & prediction. In *Proceedings of IASTED, International Conference on Artificial Intelligence and Soft Computing* (pp. 320-323). Honolulu, HI: Academic Press.

ADDITIONAL READING

Abdelbar, A. M. (1998). Achieving superior generalisation with a high order neural network. *Neural Computing & Applications, Volume, 7*(2), 141–146. doi:10.1007/BF01414166

Alanis, A., Sanchez, E., & Ricalde, L. (2010). Discrete Time Reduced Order Neural Observers for Uncertain Nonlinear Systems. *International Journal of Neural Systems, 20*(1), 29–38. doi:10.1142/S0129065710002218 PMID:20180251

Alanis, A. Y., Sanchez, E. N., Loukianov, A. G., & Hernandez, E. A. (2010). Discrete-Time Recurrent High Order Neural Networks for Nonlinear Identification. *Journal of the Franklin Institute, 347*(7), 1253–1265. doi:10.1016/j.jfranklin.2010.05.018

Angeline, P. J., Sunders, G. M., & Pollack, J. B. (1994). An Evolutionary Algorithm that Constructs Recurrent Artificial Neural Networks. *IEEE Transactions on Neural Networks, 5*(1), 54–65. doi:10.1109/72.265960 PMID:18267779

Azoff, E. M. (1994). *Neural Network Time Series Forecasting of Financial Markets*. New York: John Wiley & Sons.

Baber, W., Daniel, P., & Roberts, A. (2002). Compensation to managers of charitable organizations: An empirical study of the role of accounting measures of program activities. *The Accounting Review, 77*(3), 679–693. doi:10.2308/accr.2002.77.3.679

Barbe, L., Bayle, B., de Mathelin, M., & Gangi, A. (2007). Needle insertions modeling: Identiðability and limitations. *International Journal of Biomedical Signal Processing and Control, 2*(3), 191–198. doi:10.1016/j.bspc.2007.06.003

Barbounis, T. G., Theocaris, J. B., Alexiadis, M. C., & Dokoupoulos, P. S. (2006). Long-Term Wind Speed and Power Forecasting Using Local Recurrent Neural Network Models. *IEEE Transactions on Energy Conversion, 21*(1), 273–284. doi:10.1109/TEC.2005.847954

Belmonte-Izquierdo, R., Carlos-Hernandez, S., & Sanchez, E. N. (2010). A new neural observer for an anaerobic bioreactor. *International Journal of Neural Systems, 20*(1), 75–86. doi:10.1142/S0129065710002267 PMID:20180255

Bigus, J. P. (1996). *Data Mining with Neural Networks.* McGraw-Hill.

Burshtein, D. (1998). Long-term attraction in higher order neural networks. *Neural Networks, 9*(1), 42–50. doi:10.1109/72.655028 PMID:18252428

Chen, F. C., & Khalil, H. K. (1992). Adaptive control of nonlinear systems using neural networks. *International Journal of Control, 55*(6), 1299–1317. doi:10.1080/00207179208934286

Chen, H. H., Lee, Y. C., Maxwell, T., Sun, G. Z., Lee, H. Y., & Giles, C. L. (1986). High Order Correlation Model for Associative Memory. *AIP Conference Proceedings, 151*, 86–99. doi:10.1063/1.36224

Chen, S. S., Donoho, D. L., & Saunders, M. A. (1998). Atomic Decomposition by Basis Pursuit. *SIAM Journal on Scientific Computing, 20*(1), 33–61. doi:10.1137/S1064827596304010

Cios, K. J., Pedrycz, W., Swiniarski, R. W., & Kurgan, L. A. (2007). *Data Mining: A Knowledge Discovery Approach.* Springer.

Dantigny, P., Ninow, J. L., & Lakrori, M. (1989). A new control strategy for yeast production based on the L/A approach. *Applied Microbiology and Biotechnology, 36*(3), 352–357.

Detournay, M., Hemati, M., & Andreux, R. (2011). Biomass steam gasification in fluidized bed of inert or catalytic particles: Comparison between experimental results and thermodynamic equilibrium predictions. *Powder Technology, 208*(2), 558–567. doi:10.1016/j.powtec.2010.08.059

Eskander, G., & Atiya, A. (2009). Symbolic function network. *Neural Networks, 22*(4), 395–404. doi:10.1016/j.neunet.2009.02.003 PMID:19342195

Farret, F., & Simoes, G. (2006). *Integration of alternative sources of energy.* John Wiley.

Feldkamp, L. A., Prokhorov, D. V., & Feldkamp, T. M. (2003). Simple and conditioned adaptive behavior from Kalman filter trained recurrent networks. *Neural Networks, 16*(5-6), 683–689. doi:10.1016/S0893-6080(03)00127-8 PMID:12850023

Fitzek, F., & Reisslein, M. (1998). *MPEG-4 and h.236 video traces for network performance evaluation.* Technical University of Berlin.

Frost, V. S., & Melamed, B. (1994). Traffic modeling for telecommunications networks. *IEEE Communications Magazine, 32*(3), 70–81. doi:10.1109/35.267444

Ge, S. S., Zhang, J., & Lee, T. H. (2004). Adaptive neural network control for a class of MIMO nonlinear systems with disturbances in discrete-time. *IEEE Transactions on Systems, Man, and Cybernetics, 34*, 1–4. PMID:15462431

Gellings, C. W. (2009). *The Smart Grid: Enabling Energy Efficiency and Demand Response.* Boca Raton, FL: CRC Press Taylor & Francis Group.

Giles, C. L., & Maxwell, T. (1988). Learning, invariance and generalization high-order neural networks. *Applied Optics, 26*(23), 4972–4978. doi:10.1364/AO.26.004972 PMID:20523475

Gordillo, E. D., & Belghit, A. (2011). A two-phase model of high temperature steam-only gasification of biomass char in bubbling fluidized bed reactors using nuclear heat. *International Journal of Hydrogen Energy, 36*(1), 374–381. doi:10.1016/j.ijhydene.2010.09.088

Gore, A. (2009). Why do Cities Hoard Cash? Determinants and Implications of Municipal Cash Holdings. *The Accounting Review, 84*(1), 183–207. doi:10.2308/accr.2009.84.1.183

Guo, B., Li, D., Cheng, C., Lu, Z. A., & Shen, Y. (2001). Simulation of biomass gasification with a hybrid neural network model. *Bioresource Technology,* *76*(2), 77–83. doi:10.1016/S0960-8524(00)00106-1 PMID:11131803

Haidar, A. M. A., Mohamed, A., Al-Dabbagh, M., Hussain, A., & Masoum, M. (2009). *An* intelligent load shedding scheme using neural networks and neuro-fuzzy. *International Journal of Neural Systems, 19*(6), 473–479. doi:10.1142/S0129065709002178 PMID:20039470

Hensen, R. H. A., Angelis, G. Z., van de Molengraft, M. J. G., de Jager, A. G., & Kok, J. J. (2000). Grey-box modeling of friction: An experimental case-study. *European Journal of Control, 6*(3), 258–267. doi:10.1016/S0947-3580(00)71134-4

Horan, P., Uecker, D., & Arimoto, A. (1990). Optical implementation of a second-order neural network discriminator model. *Japanese Journal of Applied Physics, 29*(Part 2, No. 7), 361–365. doi:10.1143/JJAP.29.L1328Horn, R. A., & Johnson, C. R. (1987). *Matrix Analysis.* Cambridge, UK: Cambridge Univ. Press.

Hu, X., & Balasubramaniam, P. (2008). *Recurrent Neural Networks.* In-Tech. doi:10.5772/68

Huang, G. B., & Siew, C. K. (2005). Extreme Learning Machine with Randomly Assigned RBF Kernels. *International Journal of Information Technology, 11*(1), 16–24.

Huang, G. B., Zhu, Q. Y., & Siew, C. K. (2006). Extreme Learning Machine: Theory and Applications. *Neurocomputing, 70*(1-3), 489–501. doi:10.1016/j.neucom.2005.12.126

Inui, T., Tanabe, Y., & Onodera, Y. (1978). Group Theory and Its Application in Physics. Heidelberg, Germany: Springer-Verlag.

Jadbabaie, A., Lin, J., & Morse, A. S. (2003). Coordination of groups of mobile autonomous agents using nearest neighbor rules. *IEEE Transactions on Automatic Control, 48*(6), 988–1001. doi:10.1109/TAC.2003.812781

Jayanti, S., & Valette, M. (2004). Prediction of dry-out and postdry-out heat transfer at high pressures using a one dimensional three-fluid model. *International Journal of Heat and Mass Transfer, 47*(22), 4895–4910. doi:10.1016/j.ijheatmasstransfer.2004.03.028

Kariniotakis, G. N., Stavrakakis, G. S., & Nogaret, E. F. (1996). Wind Power Forecasting Using Advanced Neural Networks Models. *IEEE Transactions on Energy Conversion*, *11*(4), 762–767. doi:10.1109/60.556376

Kaushal, P., Abedi, J., & Mahinpey, N. (2010). A comprehensive mathematical model for biomass gasification in a bubbling fluidized bed reactor. *Fuel*, *89*(12), 3650–3661. doi:10.1016/j.fuel.2010.07.036

Kim, O., & Suh, Y. (1993). Incentive efficiency of compensation based on accounting and market performance. *Journal of Accounting and Economics*, *16*(1-3), 25–53. doi:10.1016/0165-4101(93)90004-Y

Kohonen, T. (1988). *Self-Organization and Associative Memory* (2nd ed.). New York: Springer-Verlag. doi:10.1007/978-3-662-00784-6

Kosmatopoulos, E. B., Christodoulou, M. A., & Ioannou, A. P. (1997). Dynamic Neural Networks that Ensure Exponential Identification Error Convergence. *Neural Networks*, *10*(2), 299–314. doi:10.1016/S0893-6080(96)00060-3 PMID:12662528

Lange, M. (2003). *Analysis of the Uncertainty of Wind Power Predictions* (Unpublished doctoral dissertation). Carl von Ossietzky Universität Oldenburg, Oldenburg, Germany.

Leshno, M., Lin, V., & Ya, P. (1993). Multilayer feedforward networks with a nonpolynomial activation function can approximate any function. *Neural Networks*, *6*(6), 861–867. doi:10.1016/S0893-6080(05)80131-5

Lewis, F. L., Yesildirek, A., & Liu, K. (1996). Multilayer neural-net robot controller with guaranteed tracking performance. *IEEE Transactions on Neural Networks*, *7*(2), 388–399. doi:10.1109/72.485674 PMID:18255592

Liatsis, P., Hussain, A., & Milonidis, E. (2009). Artificial higher order pipeline recurrent neural networks for financial time series prediction. In Artificial Higher Order Neural Networks for Economics and Business (pp.164 - 189). IGI Global. doi:10.4018/978-1-59904-897-0.ch008

Lin, Y. H., & Cunningham, G. A. (1995). A new approach to fuzzy-neural system modelling. *IEEE Transactions on Fuzzy Systems*, *3*(2), 190–198. doi:10.1109/91.388173

Lippman, R. P. (1989). Pattern classification using neural networks. *IEEE Communications Magazine*, *27*(11), 47–64. doi:10.1109/35.41401

Lu, Z., Shieh, L., & Chen, G. (2009). A New Topology for Artificial Higher Order Neural Networks - Polynomial Kernel Networks. In Artificial Higher Order Neural Networks for Economics and Business (pp.430 - 441). IGI Global.

Malone, J., McGarry, K., Wermter, S., & Bowerman, C. (2006). Data mining using rule extraction from Kohonen self-organising maps. *Neural Computing & Applications, Volume, 15*(1), 9–17. doi:10.100700521-005-0002-1

Mandal, P., Senjyu, T., & Funabashi, T. (2006). Neural Networks Approach to Forecast Several Hour Ahead Electricity Prices and Loads in Deregulated Market. *Energy Conversion and Management, 47*(15-16), 2128–2142. doi:10.1016/j.enconman.2005.12.008

Masamune, K., Kobayashi, E., Masutani, Y., Suzuki, M., Dohi, T., Iseki, H., & Takakura, K. (1995). Development of an MRI-Compatible Needle Insertion Manipulator for Stereotactic Neurosurgery. *Computer Aided Surgery, 1*(4), 242–248. doi:10.3109/10929089509106330 PMID:9079451

Morita, M., Yoshizawa S., & Nakano K. (1990). Analysis and improvement of the dynamics of autocorrelation associative memory. *Trans. Inst. Electronics, Information, Communication Engineers Japan*, J73-D-II, 232-242.

Narendra, P. M., & Fuknaga, K. (1997). A Branch and Bound Algorithm for Feature Subset Selection. *IEEE Transactions on Computers, 26*(9), 917–922. doi:10.1109/TC.1977.1674939

Olfati-Saber, R., & Murray, R. M. (2004). Consensus problems in networks of agents with switching topology and time-delays. *IEEE Transactions on Automatic Control, 49*(9), 1520–1533. doi:10.1109/TAC.2004.834113

Pao, Y. H. (1989). *Adaptive Pattern Recognition and Neural Networks.* Reading, MA: Addison-Wesley.

Park, B. S., Yoo, S. J., Park, J. B., & Choi, Y. H. (2010). A simple adaptive control approach for trajectory tracking of electrically driven nonholonomic mobile robots. *IEEE Transactions on Control Systems Technology, 18*(5), 1199–1206. doi:10.1109/TCST.2009.2034639

Perantonis, S. J., & Lisboa, P. J. G. (1992). Translation, rotation and scale invariant pattern recognition by high-order neural networks and moment classifiers. *IEEE Transactions on Neural Networks, 3*(2), 241–251. doi:10.1109/72.125865 PMID:18276425

Poznyak, A. S., Sanchez, E. N., & Yu, W. (2000). *Differential Neural Networks for Robust Nonlinear Control.* World Scientific.

Puig-Arnavat, M., Carles Bruno, J., & Coronas, A. (2010). Review and analysis of biomass gasification models. *Renewable & Sustainable Energy Reviews, 14*(9), 2481–2851. doi:10.1016/j.rser.2010.07.030

Ragothaman, S., & Lavin, A. (2008). Restatements Due to Improper Revenue Recognition: A Neural Networks Perspective. *Journal of Emerging Technologies in Accounting, 5*(1), 129–142. doi:10.2308/jeta.2008.5.1.129

Ramanathan, K., & Guan, S. U. (2007). Multiorder neurons for evolutionary higher-order clustering and growth. *Neural Computation, Volume, 19*(12), 3369–3391. doi:10.1162/neco.2007.19.12.3369 PMID:17970658

Reed, T. B. (1981). *Biomass Gasification principle and technology.* Noyes Data Corporation.

Reed T. B., B. Levie and M. S Graboski (1988). *Fundamentals, development and scaleup of the air-oxygen stratified downdraft gasifier,* SERI, PNL-6600.

Ren, W., Beard, R. W., & Atkins, E. M. (2007). Information consensus in multivehicle cooperative control. *IEEE Control Systems Magazine, 27*(2), 71–82. doi:10.1109/MCS.2007.338264

Ricalde, L., Sanchez, E., & Alanis, A. Y. (2010). Recurrent Higher Order Neural Network Control for Output Trajectory Tracking with Neural Observers and Constrained Inputs. In Artificial Higher Order Neural Networks for Computer Science and Engineering – Trends for Emerging Application (pp.286 - 311). IGI Global. doi:10.4018/978-1-61520-711-4.ch013

Rovithakis, G. A., Chalkiadakis, I., & Zervakis, M. E. (2004). High-order neural network structure selection for function approximation applications using genetic algorithms. *Systems, Man and Cybernetics. Part B, 34*(1), 150–158. PMID:15369059

Rumelhart, D. E., & McClelland, J. L. (1986). *Parallel Distributed Processing.* Cambridge: The MIT Press.

Sanchez, E., Urrego, D. A., Alanis, A. Y., & Carlos-Hernandez, S. (2010). Recurrent Higher Order Neural Observers for Anaerobic Processes. In Artificial Higher Order Neural Networks for Computer Science and Engineering – Trends for Emerging Application (pp.333- 365). IGI Global. doi:10.4018/978-1-61520-711-4.ch015

Sanchez, E. N., Alanis, A. Y., & Chen, G. R. (2006). Recurrent neural networks trained with the Kalman filtering for discrete chaos reconstruction. Dyn. *Continuous Discrete Impulsive Syst. B, 13c,* 1–18.

Sankar, A., & Mammone, R. J. (1993). Growing and Pruning Neural Tree Networks, IEEE Trans. *Computers, 42,* 291–299.

Selviah, D., & Shawash, J. (2010). Fifty Years of Electronic Hardware Implementations of First and Higher Order Neural Networks. In Artificial Higher Order Neural Networks for Computer Science and Engineering – Trends for Emerging Application (pp.269- 285). IGI Global. doi:10.4018/978-1-61520-711-4.ch012

Shin, Y., & Ghosh, J. (1995). Ridge Polynomial Networks. *IEEE Transactions on Neural Networks, 6*(3), 610–622. doi:10.1109/72.377967 PMID:18263347

Sinha, N., Gupta, M. M., & Zadeh, L. (1999). *Soft Computing and Intelligent Control Systems: Theory and Applications.* New York: Academic.

Su, G., Morita, K., Fukuda, K., Pidduck, M., Dounan, J., & Miettinen, J. (2003). Analysis of the critical heat flux in round vertical tubes under low pressure and flow oscillation conditions. Applications of artificial neural network. *Nuclear Engineering and Design, 220*(1), 17–35. doi:10.1016/S0029-5493(02)00304-7

Taylor, J. G., & Commbes, S. (1993). Learning higher order correlations. *Neural Networks, 6*(3), 423–428. doi:10.1016/0893-6080(93)90009-L

Thammano, A., & Ruxpakawong, P. (2010). Nonlinear dynamic System Identification Using Recurrent Neural Network with Multi-Segment Piecewise-Linear Connection Weight. *Memetic Computing, 2*(4), 273–282. doi:10.100712293-010-0042-7

Theodoridis, D. C., Boutalis, Y. S., & Christodoulou, M. A. (2010). A new adaptive Neuro-Fuzzy controller for trajectory tracking of robot manipulators. *International Journal of Robotics and Automation, 26*(1), 1–12.

Thimm, G., & Fiesler, E. (1997). High-order and multilayer perceptron initialization. *IEEE Transactions on Neural Networks, 8*(2), 349–359. doi:10.1109/72.557673 PMID:18255638

Tsoi, A. C., & Back, A. D. (1994). Locally Recurrent Feed Forward Networks: A Critical Review of Architectures. *IEEE Transactions on Neural Networks, 5*(2), 229–239. doi:10.1109/72.279187 PMID:18267793

Vaziri, N., Hojabri, A., Erfani, A., Monsey, M., & Nilforooshan, N. (2007). Critical heat flux prediction by using radial basis function and multilayer perceptron neural networks: A comparison study. *Nuclear Engineering and Design*, *237*(4), 377–385. doi:10.1016/j.nucengdes.2006.05.005

Vijayarangan, B. R., Jayanti, S., & Balakrishnan, A. R. (2006). Studies on critical heat flux in flow boiling at near critical pressures. *International Journal of Heat and Mass Transfer*, *49*(1-2), 259–268. doi:10.1016/j.ijheatmasstransfer.2005.06.029

Wang, J., & Tang, Z. (2004). An improved optimal competitive Hopfield network for bipartite subgraph problems. *Neurocomputing*, *61*(5), 413–419. doi:10.1016/j.neucom.2004.03.012

Willcox, C. R. (1991). Understanding hierarchical neural network behavior: A renormalization group approach. *Journal of Physics. A. Mathematical Nuclear and General*, *24*(11), 2655–2644. doi:10.1088/0305-4470/24/11/030

Willems, J. L., & Voorde, H. V. D. (1977). Inverse optimal control problem for linear discrete-time systems. *Electronics Letters*, *13*(17), 493. doi:10.1049/el:19770361

Xiao, G., Ni, M. J., Chi, Y., Jin, B. S., Xiao, R., Zhong, Z. P., & Huang, Y. J. (2008). Gasification characteristics of MSW and an ANN prediction model. *Waste Management (New York, N.Y.)*, *29*(1), 240–244. doi:10.1016/j.wasman.2008.02.022 PMID:18420400

Xu, S. (2008). Adaptive Higher Order Neural Network Models and Their Applications in Business. In M. Zhang, Artificial Higher Order Neural Networks for Economics and Business (pp. 314-329). IGI Global.

Xu, S. (2009). Adaptive Higher Order Neural Network Models and Their Applications in Business. In Ming Zhang (Ed.), Artificial Higher Order Neural Networks for Economics and Business (pp.314 - 329). Information Science Reference, Hershey, PA, USA: IGI Global. doi:10.4018/978-1-59904-897-0.ch014

Yao, X., Lin, Y., & Lin, G. (1999). Evolutionary programming made faster. *IEEE Transactions on Evolutionary Computation*, *3*(2), 82–122. doi:10.1109/4235.771163

Yu, W., & Li, X. (2004). Nonlinear system identification using discrete-time recurrent neural networks with stable learning algorithms. *Information Sciences, 158*, 131–147. doi:10.1016/j.ins.2003.08.002

Zhang, B. T. (2002). A Bayesian Evolutionary Approach to the Design and Learning of Heterogeneous Neural Trees. *Integrated Computer-Aided Engineering, 9*(1), 73–86. doi:10.3233/ICA-2002-9105

Zivanovic, A., & Davies, B. L. (2000). A robotic system for blood sampling. *IEEE Transaction in Information Technology Biomedical Engineering, 4*(1), 8–14. doi:10.1109/4233.826854 PMID:10761769

Zurada, J. M. (1992). *Introduction to Artificial Neural Systems*. St. Paul: West Publishing Company.

KEY TERMS AND DEFINITIONS

ANN: Artificial neural network.
CS-HONN: Artificial cosine and sigmoid higher order neural network.
HONN: Artificial higher order neural network.
PHONN: Artificial polynomial higher order neural network.
SPHONN: Artificial sigmoid polynomial higher order neural network.
THONN: Artificial trigonometric higher order neural network.

Chapter 9
Rainfall Estimation Using Neuron–Adaptive Higher Order Neural Networks

ABSTRACT

Real-world data is often nonlinear, discontinuous, and may comprise high frequency, multi-polynomial components. Not surprisingly, it is hard to find the best models for modeling such data. Classical neural network models are unable to automatically determine the optimum model and appropriate order for data approximation. In order to solve this problem, neuron-adaptive higher order neural network (NAHONN) models have been introduced. Definitions of one-dimensional, two-dimensional, and n-dimensional NAHONN models are studied. Specialized NAHONN models are also described. NAHONN models are shown to be "open box." These models are further shown to be capable of automatically finding not only the optimum model but also the appropriate order for high frequency, multi-polynomial, discontinuous data. Rainfall estimation experimental results confirm model convergence. The authors further demonstrate that NAHONN models are capable of modeling satellite data.

DOI: 10.4018/978-1-7998-3563-9.ch009

INTRODUCTION

Artificial Higher Order Neural Network (HONN) models are the trends for emerging applications in the computer science and engineering areas. An, Mniszewski, Lee, Papcun, and Doolen (1988A and 1988B) test a learning procedure (HIERtalker), based on a default hierarchy of high order neural networks, which exhibited an enhanced capability of generalization and a good efficiency to learn to read English aloud. HIERtalker learns the `building blocks' or clusters of symbols in a stream that appear repeatedly. Salem and Young (1991) study the interpreting line drawings with higher order neural networks. A higher order neural network solution to line labeling is presented. Line labeling constraints in trihedral scenes are designed into a Hopfield-type network. The labeling constraints require a higher order of interaction than that of Hopfield-type network. Liou and Azimi-Sadjadi (1993) present a dim target detection using high order correlation method. This work presents a method for clutter rejection and dim target track detection from infrared (IR) satellite data using neural networks. A high-order correlation method which recursively computes the spatio-temporal cross-correlations is used. Liatsis, Wellstead, Zarrop, and Prendergast (1994) propose a versatile visual inspection tool for the manufacturing process. The dynamically changing nature and the complex behavior of processes in manufacturing cells dictate the need for lean, agile and flexible manufacturing systems. Tseng and Wu (1994) post Constant-time neural decoders for some BCH codes. High order neural networks are shown to decode some BCH codes in constanttime with very low hardware complexity. HONN is a direct extension of the linear perceptron: it uses a polynomial consisting of a set of product terms as its discriminant. Zardoshti-Kermani and Afshordi (1995) try classification of chromosomes by using higher-order neural networks. In this paper, the application of a higher-order neural network for the classification of human chromosomes is described. The higher order neural network's inputs are 30-dimensional feature space extracted from chromosome images. Starke, Kubota, and Fukuda (1995) research combinatorial optimization with higher order neural networks-cost oriented competing processes in flexible manufacturing systems. Higher order neural networks are applied to handle combinatorial optimization problems by using cost oriented competing processes (COCP). This method has a high adaptability to complicated problems. Miyajima, Yatsuki, and Kubota (1995) study the dynamical properties of neural networks with product connections. Higher order neural networks with product connections which hold the weighted sum of products of input variables have been proposed as a new concept. In some applications, it is shown that they are more superior in ability than traditional neural networks. Wang (1996) researches the suppressing chaos with hysteresis in a higher order neural network. Artificial higher order neural networks attempt to mimic various features of a most powerful computational system-the human brain.

HONN models have been widely researched. Jeffries (1989) presents a specific high order neural network design that can store, using n neutrons, any of the binomial n-strings. Machado (1989) gives a description of the combinatorial high order neural network model which is suitable for classification tasks. The model is based on fuzzy set theory, neural sciences studies, and expert knowledge analysis, which can handle knowledge in high order neural networks. Kosmatopoulos, Ioannou, and Christodoulou (1992) present the identification of nonlinear systems using new dynamic higher order neural network structures. The authors study the stability and convergence properties of recurrent higher order neural networks (RHONNs) as models of nonlinear dynamical systems. The overall structure of the RHONN consists of dynamical elements distributed throughout the higher order neural network. Kosmatopoulos, Polycarpou, Christodoulou, and Ioannou (1995) design the high order neural network structures for identification of dynamical systems. Several continuous-time and discrete-time recurrent higher order neural network models have been developed and applied to various engineering problems. Kariniotakis, Stavrakakis, and Nogaret (1996) try the wind power forecasting using advanced higher order neural networks models. In this paper, an advanced model, based on recurrent high order neural networks, is developed for the prediction of the power output profile of a wind park. This model outperforms simple methods like persistence, as well as classical methods. Rovithakis, Gaganis, Perrakis, and Christodoulou (1996) design a recurrent higher order neural network model to describe manufacturing cell dynamics. A recurrent higher order neural network structure (RHONN) is employed to identify cell dynamics, which is supposed to be unknown. Brucoli, Carnimeo, and Grassi (1997) provide a design method for associative memories using a new model of discrete-time second-order higher order neural networks which includes local interconnections among neurons. Zhang, Zhang, and Fulcher (1997) present a financial simulation system using a higher order trigonometric polynomial neural network group model. *The model of* trigonometric polynomial high order neural network (THONN) is presented. The financial system was written in C, incorporates a user-friendly graphical user interface (GUI), and runs under X-Windows on a Sun workstation.

Burshtein (1998) believes that recent results on the memory storage capacity of higher order neural networks indicate a significant improvement compared to the limited capacity of the Hopfield model. However, such results have so far been obtained. Zhang and Lu (2001) simulate financial data by using Multi-Polynomial Higher Order Neural Network (M-PHONN) model. A new model, called (M-PHONN), has been developed. Using Sun workstation, C++, and Motif, a M-PHONN simulator has been built as well. Qi and Zhang (2001) estimate rainfall using M-PHONN model. The M-PHONN model for estimating heavy convective rainfall from satellite data was tested. The M-PHONN model has 5% to 15% more accuracy than other existing higher order neural models. Campos, Loukianov, and Sanchez (2003) use recurrent high order neural networks to control motor synchronously. A nonlinear complete order model of a synchronous motor is identified using a dynamic higher order neural network. Based on this model a sliding mode controller is derived. This neural network identifier and the proposed control law allow rejecting external load. Kuroe (2004) presents higher order neural network models for learning and identifying deterministic finite state automata (FSA). The proposed models are a class of high order recurrent neural networks. The models can represent FSA with the network size. Christodoulou, and Iliopoulos (2006) study higher order neural network models for prediction of steady-state and dynamic behavior, A three molecule module present, which has a wide range of functions in signal transduction, such as stress-response, cell-cycle-control, and cell-wall-construction. The second motivation of this chapter is to present new artificial HONN models for applications in the computer science and engineering areas.

A lot of design issues of artificial higher order neural network structures, algorithms and models have been studied recently. Jeffries (1989) presents a specific high order neural network design which can store, using n neurons, any number of any of the binomial n-strings. Yang and Guest (1990) design the high order neural networks with reduced numbers of interconnection weights. A multilayered network with the first layer consisting of parabolic neurons (constrained second-order neurons) is proposed. Each parabolic neuron requires only N+2 interconnections (where N is the number of inputs). Chang and Cheung (1992) study backpropagation algorithm in higher order neural network. By restructuring the basic HONN architecture, the traditional backpropagation algorithm can be extended to the supervised backpropagation learning scheme, which is used to develop a training algorithm for multilayer higher order neural networks. Chang, Lin, and Cheung (1993) provide polynomial and standard higher order neural network. The generalized back propagation algorithm is extended to multi-layer higher order neural networks. Two basic structures, the standard form and the polynomial form, are discussed. Heywood and Noakes (1993) contribute a simple addition to backpropagation learning for dynamic weight pruning, sparse higher order network extraction and faster learning. The enhancement to the backpropagation algorithm presented results from the need to extract sparsely connected networks from networks employing product terms. Young and Downs (1993) generalize the higher order neural networks. The theory of Pac-learning has provided statements about the generalization capability of linear threshold networks. The authors present an extension of this work to higher order threshold neural networks and shows that the generalization ability of the higher order neural network. Cooper (1995) investigates higher order neural networks for combinatorial optimization improving the scaling properties of the Hopfield network. The dynamics of the Hopfield network are investigated too to determine why the network does not scale well to large problem sizes. It is seen that the Hopfield network encourages the formation of locally optimal segments, resulting in multiple seed points. Villalobos and Merat (1995) present a technique for evaluating the learning capability and optimizing the feature space of a class of higher-order neural networks. It is shown that supervised learning can be posed as an optimization problem in which inequality constraints. Yatsuki and Miyajima (1997) show associative ability of higher order neural networks. Higher order neural networks have been proposed as new systems. The authors also show some theoretical results on the associative ability of HONNs. Abdelbar and Tagliarini (1998) present a method that combines Bayesian learning, a statistical technique, a high order neural network with the property that the mapping embodied by the network can always be described by a polynomial-like equation. Li, Wang, Li, Zhang, and Li (1998) introduce the fullyconnected higher order neuron and sparselized higher-order neuron. The mapping capabilities of the fullyconnected higher order neural networks are investigated by authors. Gulez, Mutoh, Harashima, Ohnishi, and Pastaci (2000) design a high order neural network for the performance increasing of an induction motor under changeable load. Motor drives are traditionally designed with relatively inexpensive analog components. The weaknesses of analog systems are their susceptibility to temperature variations and the component aging. A higher order neural network has benefit to balance the load. Yamashita, Hirasawa, Hu, and Murata (2002) study multi-branch structure of layered higher order neural networks to make their size compact. The multi-branch structure has shown improved performance against conventional neural networks. Li,

Hirasawa, and Hu (2003) research a new strategy for constructing higher order neural networks with multiplication units. The proposed method provides a flexible mechanism for incremental higher order neural network growth where higher order terms can be naturally generated. Wang, Wu, and Chang (2004) present a novel approach, called scale equalization (SE), to implement higher-order neural networks. SE is particularly useful in eliminating the scale divergence problem commonly encountered in higher order networks. Lin, Wu, and Wang (2005) also show that, by using scale equalization (SE) technique, scale equalized higher order neural network (SEHNN) is particularly useful in alleviating the scale divergence problem that plagues higher order neural network. The third motivation of this chapter is to provide new design of artificial HONN for applications in the computer science and engineering areas.

Recurrent higher order neural networks are researched a lot in the recent years. Baldi and Venkatesh (1993) examine the recurrent higher order neural networks of polynomial threshold elements with random symmetric interactions. Precise asymptotic estimates are derived for the expected number of fixed points as a function of the margin of stability. Kosmatopoulos and Christodoulou (1994) study the capabilities of recurrent high order neural networks (RHONNs), whose synapses are adjusted according to the learning law. Kosmatopoulos and Christodoulou (1995) investigate the structural properties of Recurrent High Order Neural Networks (RHONN) whose weights are restricted to satisfy the symmetry property. Tanaka and Kumazawa (1996) use recurrent higher order neural networks to learn regular languages. Kuroe, Ikeda, and Mori (1997) study a method for identification of nonlinear dynamical systems by recurrent high order neural networks. Rovithakis, Malamos, Varvarigon, and Christodoulou (1998) employ recurrent high order neural networks (RHONNs) to determine the unknown values of media characteristics that lead to user satisfaction without violating network limitations. Rovithakis (2000) discusses the tracking problem in the presence of additive and multiplicative external disturbances, for affine in the control nonlinear dynamical systems, whose nonlinearities are assumed unknown. A robustness of a neural controller in the presence of additive and multiplicative external perturbations based on recurrent high order neural networks has been provided. Christodoulou and Zarkogianni (2006) use recurrent High Order Neural Networks for identification of the Epidermal Growth Factor Receptor (EGFR) Signaling Pathway. The present work deals with a specific signaling pathway called EGFR PATHWAY which is composed of twenty-three proteins and their interactions. The fourth motivation of this chapter is to provide new HONN for applications in the computer science and engineering areas.

Artificial higher order neural networks are good at simulating nonlinear models. Estevez and Okabe (1991) introduce a piecewise linear-high order neural network through error back propagation, which has a structure consisting of two layers of modifiable weights. The hidden units implement a piecewise linear function in the augmented input space, which includes high-order terms. Lee, Lee, and Park (1992) develop a neural controller of nonlinear dynamic systems using higher order neural networks. Higher order multilayer neural networks are used for identification and control of nonlinear dynamic systems, and their performance is compared with the performance of conventional linear multilayer neural networks. Vidyasagar studies the convergence of higher order neural networks with modified updating. The problem of maximizing a general objective function over the hypercube $\{-1, 1\}^n$ is formulated as that of maximizing a multi-linear polynomial over $\{-1, 1\}^n$. Kosmatopoulos and Christodoulou (1997) use higher order neural networks for the learning of robot contact surface shape. The problem of learning the shape parameters of unknown surfaces that are in contact with a robot end-effector can be formulated as a nonlinear parameter estimation problem. Rovithakis (1998) reinforces robustness using higher order neural network controllers for affine in the control nonlinear dynamical systems. A correction control signal is added to a nominal controller to guarantee a desired performance for the corresponding nominal system. Bouzerdoum (1999) present a new class of higher order neural networks with nonlinear decision boundaries.

This new class of HONN called shunting inhibitory artificial neural networks (SIANNs) for classification and function approximation tasks. In these networks, the basic synaptic interaction is of the shunting inhibitory type. Rovithakis (1999) tries robustifying nonlinear systems using higher order neural network controllers. A robust control methodology for affine control of nonlinear dynamical systems is developed. A correction control signal is added to a nominal controller to guarantee a desired performance for the corresponding nominal system. Zhang, Peng, and Rovithakis (2000) indicates that Rovithakis (1999) overlooked some essential assumptions regarding "robustifying nonlinear systems using high-order neural network controllers" (Rovithakis 1999). The authors consider a nonlinear dynamical system in their study. Rovithakis, Maniadakis, and Zervakis (2000) study artificial neural networks for feature extraction and classification of vascular tissue fluorescence spectrums. The use of neural network structures for feature extraction and classification is addressed here. More precisely, a nonlinear filter based on higher order neural networks (HONN) whose weights are updated by stable learning laws is used to extract the features. More than 10 chapters in Zhang (2009A) looks at nonlinear data simulations and predictions. Zhang (2009B) finds HONN nonlinear models can simulate nonlinear data better than SAS nonlinear method. Zhang (2009C) develops ultra-high frequency trigonometric higher order neural networks. The author finds the error to simulate economics and business data by using ultra high frequency trigonometric HONN can be close to zero. The fifth motivation of this chapter is to provide new HONN for nonlinear model simulation in the computer science and engineering areas.

Adaptive higher order neural network models have been rigorously studied. Rovithakis, Kosmatopoulos, and Christodoulou (1993) use recurrent high order neural networks for robust adaptive control of unknown plants to mechanical systems. The proposed algorithm employs a recurrent higher order neural network (RHONN) identifier. Yu and Liang (1995) propose a higher order new neural network approach for eigenstructure extraction. It is based on the constraint optimal problem. It can be used to estimate the largest eigenvector of the covariance matrix adaptively and efficiently. Rovithakis, Gaganis, Perrakis, and Christodoulou (1998) use higher order neural networks to control manufacturing systems. Authors evaluate a neuron adaptive scheduling methodology by comparing its performance with conventional schedulers. Zhang, Xu, and Lu (1999) develop neuron-adaptive higher order neural network group models with neuron-adaptive activation functions. A learning algorithm is derived to adjust free parameters in the neuron-adaptive activation function as well as coefficients of the higher order neural networks. Rovithakis (2000) perform a neural adaptive tracking controller for multi-input nonlinear dynamical systems in the presence of additive and multiplicative external disturbances. Author discusses the tracking problem in the presence of additive and multiplicative external disturbances, for affine in the control nonlinear dynamical systems, whose nonlinearities are assumed unknown based on a recurrent higher order neural network. Zhang (2001) presents a new model, called Adaptive Multi-Polynomial Higher Order Neural Network (A-PHONN). Using Sun workstation, C++, and Motif, an A-PHONN simulator has been built as well. Real world financial data simulations are presented by using A-PHONN model.

Zhang and Scofield (2001) test the A-PHONN model for estimating heavy convective rainfall from satellite data. The A-PHONN model has 6% to 16% more accuracy than the polynomial HONN and Trigonometric HONN.

Zhang, Xu, and Fulcher (2002) point out that real-world financial data is often nonlinear, comprises high frequency multipolynomial components, and is discontinuous (piecewise continuous). Not surprisingly, it is hard to model such data. Classical neural networks are unable to automatically model these data. The authors design neuron-adaptive higher order neural network models for automated financial data modeling. Xu and Zhang (2002) study adaptive higher order neural networks (AHONN) and its approximation capabilities. Authors also study the approximation capabilities of an adaptive higher-order neural network (AHONN) with a neuron-adaptive activation function (NAF) to any nonlinear continuous functional and any nonlinear continuous operator. Ge, Zhang, and Lee (2004) investigate adaptive higher order neural network control for a class of nonlinear systems with disturbances in discrete time. Ricalde and Sanchez (2005) present the design of an adaptive recurrent neural observer for nonlinear systems which model is assumed to be unknown. The neural observer is composed of a recurrent higher order neural network which builds an online model. Zhang, Ge, and Lee (2005) study adaptive higher order neural network control for a class of discrete-time multi-input-multi-output (MIMO) nonlinear systems with triangular form inputs. Each subsystem of the MIMO system is in strict feedback form. Alanis, Sanchez, and Loukianov (2006) study discrete-time recurrent neural induction motor control using Kalman learning. This paper deals with the adaptive tracking problem for discrete-time induction motor model in presence of bounded disturbances. In this paper, a high order neural network structure is used to identify the plant model. Butt and Shafiq (2006) present a higher order neural network-based root-solving controller for adaptive tracking of stable nonlinear plants. The use of intelligent control schemes in Nonlinear Model Based Control (NMBC) has gained widespread popularity. The higher order neural networks have been used extensively to model the dynamics of nonlinear plants. The sixth motivation of this chapter is to provide adaptive HONN for applications in the computer science and engineering areas.

In this chapter, Neuron-Adaptive Higher Order Neural Network (*NAHONN*) Models with neuron-adaptive activation functions are introduced. How to use NAHONN to estimate rainfall will be discussed. Experimental results obtained by using NAHONNs for rainfall estimating are presented in this chapter.

NEURON-ADAPTIVE HIGHER ORDER NEURAL NETWORK (NAHONN)

Based on Zhang, Xu, and Fulcher (2002), followings are the definitions for neuron-adaptive higher order neural networks (NAHONNs).

Let:

h: the hth term in the *NAF* (Neural network Activation Function)

i: the ith neuron in layer-k

k: the kth layer of the neural network (k will be used later in the learning algorithm proof)

w: the maximum number of terms in the *NAF*

x: first neural network input

y: second neural network input

Z_1: one output of neuron for one, two, ... m dimensional NAHONNs

$net_{i,k}$: the input or internal state of the ith neuron in the kth layer

$a_{i,j,k}$: the weight that connects the jth neuron in layer $k-1$ with the ith neuron in layer k

j will be used in the two-dimensional NAHONN formula

$o_{i,k}$: the value of the output from the ith neuron in layer k $\hspace{2cm}$ (9-1)

For one-dimensional Neuron-Adaptive Higher Order Neural Networks:

$$net_{i,k} = a_{i,x,k} \cdot x \hspace{4cm} (9\text{-}2)$$

For two-dimensional Neuron-adaptive higher order neural networks:

$net_{i,x,k}$: the input of the x neuron in the input layer

$net_{i,y,k}$: the input of the y neuron in the input layer

$$net_{i,x,k} = a_{i,x,k} \cdot x$$

$$net_{i,y,k} = a_{i,y,k} \cdot y \hspace{4cm} (9\text{--}3)$$

For m-dimensional Neuron-Adaptive Higher Order Neural Networks:

$$net_{i,1,k} = a_{i,1,k} \cdot x_1$$

$$net_{i,2,k} = a_{i,2,k} \cdot x_2$$

$$net_{i,m,k} = a_{i,m,k} \cdot x_m \tag{9-4}$$

For multi m-dimensional Neuron-Adaptive Higher Order Neural Networks:

z: The zth output neuron in the output layer $\tag{9-5}$

Z_z: The zth output of the multi m dimensional *NAHONN*. $\tag{9-6}$

Multi m Dimensional *NAHONN* Definition

The multi m-dimensional Neuron-adaptive higher order neural network Activation Function (*NAF*) is:

$$\Phi_{i,k}\left(net_{i,1,k}, net_{i,2,k}, \ldots\ldots net_{i,m,k}\right) = \sum_{h=1}^{w} f_{i,k,h}\left(net_{i,1,k}, net_{i,2,k}, \ldots\ldots, net_{i,m,k}\right) \tag{9-7}$$

The *multi* m dimensional NAHONN is defined as follows:

$$
\begin{aligned}
Z_z &= \sum_{i=0}^{n} a_{z,i,k+1} \cdot \Phi_{i,k}\left(net_{i,1,k}, net_{i,2,k}, \ldots\ldots, net_{i,m,k}\right) \\
&= \sum_{i=0}^{n} a_{z,i,k+1} \cdot \sum_{h=1}^{w} f_{i,k,h}(net_{i,1,k}, net_{i,2,k}, \ldots\ldots, net_{i,m,k}) \\
&= \sum_{i=0}^{n} a_{z,i,k+1} \cdot \sum_{h=1}^{w} f_{i,k,h}\left(a_{i,1,k} \cdot x_1, a_{i,2,k} \cdot x_2 \ldots\ldots, a_{i,m,k} \cdot x_m\right)
\end{aligned} \tag{9-8}
$$

The structure of the multi m dimensional *NAHONN* is shown in Figure 1.

m Dimensional NAHONN Definition

The m-dimensional Neuron-adaptive higher order neural network Activation Function (*NAF*) is:

Figure 1. Multi m-dimensional NAHONN structure

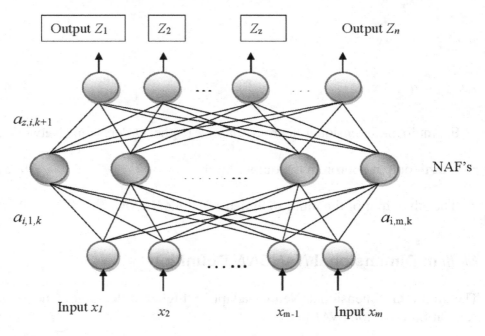

$$\Phi_{i,k}\left(net_{i,1,k}, net_{i,2,k}, \ldots\ldots net_{i,m,k}\right) = \sum_{h=1}^{w} f_{i,k,h}\left(net_{i,1,k}, net_{i,2,k}, \ldots\ldots, net_{i,m,k}\right)$$

(9-9)

The m-dimensional Neuron-Adaptive Higher Order Neural Network is defined as:

NAHONN (m-Dimensional):

$$
\begin{aligned}
Z_1 &= \sum_{i=0}^{n} a_{1,i,k+1} \cdot \Phi_{i,k}\left(net_{i,1,k}, net_{i,2,k}, \ldots\ldots, net_{i,m,k}\right) \\
&= \sum_{i=0}^{n} a_{1,i,k+1} \cdot \sum_{h=1}^{w} f_{i,k,h}\left(a_{i,1,k} \cdot x_1, a_{i,2,k} \cdot x_2 \ldots\ldots, a_{i,m,k} \cdot x_m\right)
\end{aligned}
$$

(9-10)

The network structure of an m dimensional *NAHONN* is the same as that of a multi-layer *FNN*. That is, it consists of an input layer with *m* input-units, an output layer with one output-unit, and one hidden layer consisting of intermediate processing units. A typical two-dimensional *NAHONN* architecture is depicted in Figure 2. Again, while there is no activation function in the input layer and the output neuron is a summing unit (linear activation), the activation function for the hidden units is the m-dimensional

Figure 2. m dimensional NAHONN structure

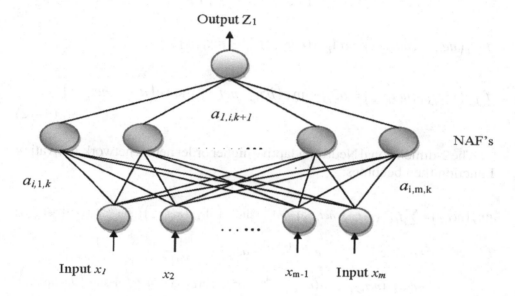

neuron-adaptive higher order neural network NAF.

Two-Dimensional *NAHONN* Definition

The two-dimensional Neuron-adaptive higher order neural network Activation Function (*NAF*) is defined as:

$$NAF : \Phi_{i,k}\left(net_{i,x,k}, net_{i,y,k}\right) = O_{i,k}\left(net_{i,x,k}, net_{i,y,k}\right) = \sum_{h=1}^{w} f_{i,k,h}\left(net_{i,x,k}, net_{i,y,k}\right)$$

$$(9\text{--}11)$$

Suppose: $w=5$

$$f_{i,k,1}\left(net_{i,x,k}, net_{i,y,k}\right) = a1_{i,k} \cdot \sin^{c1_{i,k}}\left(b1_{i,k} \cdot \left(net_{i,x,k}\right)\right) \cdot \sin^{e1_{i,k}}\left(d1_{i,k} \cdot \left(net_{i,y,k}\right)\right)$$

$$f_{i,k,2}\left(net_{i,x,k}, net_{i,y,k}\right) = a2_{i,k} \cdot e^{-b2_{i,k} \cdot \left(net_{i,x,k}\right)} \cdot e^{-d2_{i,k} \cdot \left(net_{i,x,k}\right)}$$

$$f_{i,k,3}\left(net_{i,x,k}, net_{i,y,k}\right) = a3_{i,k} \cdot \frac{1}{1+e^{-b3_{i,k} \cdot \left(net_{i,x,k}\right)}} \cdot \frac{1}{1+e^{-d3_{i,k} \cdot \left(net_{i,y,k}\right)}}$$

$$f_{i,k,4}\left(net_{i,x,k}, net_{i,y,k}\right) = a4_{i,k} \cdot \left(net_{i,x,k}\right)^{b4_{i,k}} \cdot \left(net_{i,y,k}\right)^{d4_{i,k}}$$

$$f_{i,k,5}\left(net_{i,x,k}, net_{i,y,k}\right) = a5_{i,k} \cdot \sin c\left(b5_{i,k} \cdot net_{i,x,k}\right) \cdot \sin c\left(d5_{i,k} \cdot net_{i,y,k}\right)$$

$$(9\text{--}12)$$

The 2-dimensional Neuron-adaptive higher order neural network Activation Function then becomes:

$$\Phi_{i,k}\left(net_{i,k}\right) = \sum_{h=1}^{5} f_{i,k,h}\left(net_{i,x,k}, net_{i,y,k}\right) = a1_{i,k} \cdot \sin^{c1_{i,k}}\left(b1_{i,k} \cdot \left(net_{i,x,k}\right)\right) \cdot \sin^{e1_{i,k}}\left(d1_{i,k} \cdot \left(net_{i,y,k}\right)\right)$$

$$+ a2_{i,k} \cdot e^{-b2_{i,k} \cdot \left(net_{i,x,k}\right)} \cdot e^{-d2_{i,k} \cdot \left(net_{i,y,k}\right)} + a3_{i,k} \cdot \frac{1}{1+e^{-b3_{i,k} \cdot \left(net_{i,x,k}\right)}} \cdot \frac{1}{1+e^{-d3_{i,k} \cdot \left(net_{i,y,k}\right)}}$$

$$+ a4_{i,k} \cdot \left(net_{i,x,k}\right)^{b4_{i,k}} \cdot \left(net_{i,y,k}\right)^{d4_{i,k}} + a5_{i,k} \cdot \sin c\left(b5_{i,k} \cdot net_{i,x,k}\right) \cdot \sin c\left(d5 \cdot net_{i,y,k}\right)$$

$$(9\text{--}13)$$

where:

$$a1_{i,k}, b1_{i,k}, c1_{i,k}, d1_{i,k}, e1_{i,k}, a2_{i,k}, b2_{i,k}, d2_{i,k}, a3_{i,k}, b3_{i,k}, d3_{i,k}, a4_{i,k}, b4_{i,k}, d4_{i,k}, a5_{i,k}, b5_{i,k}, d5_{i,k}$$

are free parameters which can be adjusted (as well as weights) during training.

The two-dimensional Neuron-Adaptive Higher Order Neural Network is defined as:

NAHONN (2-dimensional)

$$Z_1 = \sum_{i=0}^{n} a_{1,i,k+1} \cdot \Phi_{i,k}\left(net_{i,x,k}, net_{i,y,k}\right) = \sum_{i=0}^{n} a_{1,i,k+1} \cdot \sum_{h=1}^{w} f_{i,k,h}\left(a_{i,x,k} \cdot x, a_{i,y,k} \cdot y\right)$$

$$(9\text{--}14)$$

Let: $w=5$, NAHONN (2-dimensional)

$$Z_1 = \sum_{i=0}^{n} a_{1,i,k+1} \cdot \Phi_{i,k}\left(net_{i,x,k}, net_{i,y,k}\right)$$

$$= \sum_{i=0}^{n} a_{1,i,k+1} \cdot \sum_{h=1}^{5} f_{i,k,h}\left(a_{i,x,k} \cdot x, a_{i,y,k} \cdot y\right)$$

$$= \sum_{i=0}^{n} a_{1,i,k+1} \cdot ((a1_{i,k} \cdot \sin^{c1_{i,k}}\left(b1_{i,k} \cdot \left(a_{i,x,k} \cdot x\right)\right) \cdot \sin^{e1_{i,k}}\left(d1_{i,k} \cdot \left(a_{i,y,k} \cdot y\right)\right)$$

$$+a2_{i,k} \cdot e^{-b2_{i,k} \cdot \left(a_{i,x,k} \cdot x\right)} \cdot e^{-d2_{i,k} \cdot \left(a_{i,y,k} \cdot y\right)} + a3_{i,k} \cdot \frac{1}{1+e^{-b3_{i,k} \cdot \left(a_{i,x,k} \cdot x\right)}} \cdot \frac{1}{1+e^{-d3_{i,k} \cdot \left(a_{i,y,k} \cdot y\right)}})$$

$$+a4_{i,k} \cdot \left(a_{i,x,k} \cdot x\right)^{b4_{i,k}} \cdot \left(a_{i,y,k} \cdot y\right)^{d4_{i,k}} + a5_{i,k} \cdot \sin c\left(a_{i,x,k} \cdot x\right) \cdot \sin c\left(a_{i,y,k} \cdot y\right))$$

$$(9\text{--}15)$$

Where:

$$a1_{i,k}, b1_{i,k}, c1_{i,k}, d1_{i,k}, e1_{i,k}, a2_{i,k}, b2_{i,k}, d2_{i,k}, a3_{i,k}, b3_{i,k}, d3_{i,k}, a4_{i,k}, b4_{i,k}, d4_{i,k}, a5_{i,k}, b5_{i,k}, d5_{i,k}$$

are free parameters which can be adjusted (as well as weights) during training.

The network structure of the two-dimensional *NAHONN* is the same as that of a multi-layer *FNN*. That is, it consists of an input layer with *two* input-units, an output layer with one output-unit, and one hidden layer consisting of intermediate processing units. A typical two-dimensional *NAHONN* architecture is depicted in Figure 3. Again, while there is no activation function in the input layer and the output neuron is a summing unit (linear activation), the activation function for the hidden units is the two-dimensional neuron-adaptive higher order neural network NAF.

One-Dimensional NAHONN Definition

The one-dimension Neuron-adaptive higher order neural network Activation Function (*NAF*) is defined as:

Figure 3. 2-dimensional NAHONN structure

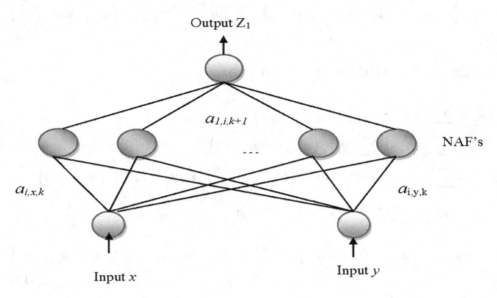

$$NAF: \ \Phi_{i,k}\left(net_{i,k}\right) = O_{i,k}\left(net_{i,k}\right) = \sum_{h=1}^{w} f_{i,k,h}\left(net_{i,k}\right) \qquad (9-16)$$

Let: $w=5$

$$f_{i,k,1}\left(net_{i,k}\right) = a1_{i,k} \cdot \sin^{c1_{i,k}}\left(b1_{i,k} \cdot \left(net_{i,k}\right)\right)$$

$$f_{i,k,2}\left(net_{i,k}\right) = a2_{i,k} \cdot e^{-b2_{i,k} \cdot \left(net_{i,k}\right)}$$

$$f_{i,k,3}\left(net_{i,k}\right) = a3_{i,k} \cdot \frac{1}{1+e^{-b3_{i,k} \cdot \left(net_{i,k}\right)}}$$

$$f_{i,k,4}\left(net_{i,k}\right) = a4_{i,k} \cdot (net_{i,k})^{b4_{i,k}}$$

$$f_{i,k,5}\left(net_{i,k}\right) = a5_{i,k} \cdot \sin c\left(b5_{i,k} \cdot net_{i,k}\right)$$

The one-dimensional Neuron-adaptive higher order neural network Activation Function (*NAF*) then becomes:

$$\Phi_{i,k}\left(net_{i,k}\right) = \sum_{h=1}^{5} f_{i,k,h}\left(net_{i,k}\right) = a1_{i,k} \cdot \sin^{c1_{i,k}}\left(b1_{i,k} \cdot \left(net_{i,k}\right)\right)$$

$$+a2_{i,k} \cdot e^{-b2_{i,k} \cdot \left(net_{i,k}\right)} + a3_{i,k} \cdot \frac{1}{1+e^{-b3_{i,k} \cdot \left(net_{i,k}\right)}} + a4_{i,k} \cdot \left(net_{i,k}\right)^{b4_{i,k}} + a5_{i,k} \cdot \sin c\left(b5_{i,k} \cdot net_{i,k}\right)$$

$$(9\text{-}17)$$

Where:

$$a1_{i,k}, b1_{i,k}, c1_{i,k}, a2_{i,k}, b2_{i,k}, a3_{i,k}, b3_{i,k}, a4_{i,k}, b4_{i,k}, a5_{i,k}, b5_{i,k}$$

are free parameters which can be adjusted (as well as weights) during training.
The one-dimensional Neuron-Adaptive Higher Order Neural Network is defined as:

NAHONN (1-dimensional)

$$Z_1 = \sum_{i=0}^{n} a_{1,i,k+1} \cdot \Phi_{i,k}\left(net_{i,k}\right)$$

$$= \sum_{i=0}^{n} a_{1,i,k+1} \cdot \sum_{h=1}^{w} f_{i,k,h}\left(a_{i,x,k} \cdot x\right)$$

Let *w*=5, NAHONN (1-dimensional)

$$Z_1 = \sum_{i=0}^{n} a_{1,i,k+1} \cdot \Phi_{i,k}\left(net_{i,k}\right) = \sum_{i=0}^{n} a_{1,i,k+1} \cdot \sum_{h=1}^{5} f_{i,k,h}\left(a_{i,x,k} \cdot x\right)$$

$$= \sum_{i=0}^{n} a_{1,i,k+1} \cdot \left(a1_{i,k} \cdot \sin^{c1_{i,k}}\left(b1_{i,k} \cdot \left(a_{i,x,k} \cdot x\right)\right)\right) + a2_{i,k} \cdot e^{-b2_{i,k} \cdot \left(a_{i,x,k} \cdot x\right)}$$

$$+a3_{i,k} \cdot \frac{1}{1+e^{-b3_{i,k} \cdot \left(a_{i,x,k} \cdot x\right)}} + a4_{i,k} \cdot \left(a_{i,x,k} \cdot x\right)^{b4_{i,k}} + a5_{i,k} \cdot \sin c\left(b5_{i,k} \cdot a_{i,x,k} \cdot x\right)$$

$$(9\text{--}18)$$

where:

$$a1_{i,k}, b1_{i,k}, c1_{i,k}, a2_{i,k}, b2_{i,k}, a3_{i,k}, b3_{i,k}, a4_{i,k}, b4_{i,k}, a5_{i,k}, b5_{i,k}$$

are free parameters which can be adjusted (as well as weights) during training.

The network structure of a one-dimensional *NAHONN* is the same as that of a multi-layer Feed-forward Neural Network (*FNN*). That is, it consists of an input layer with *one* input-unit, an output layer with one output-unit, and one hidden layer consisting of intermediate processing units. A typical one-dimensional *NAHONN* architecture is depicted in Figure 4. Now while there is no activation function in the input layer and the output neuron is a summing unit only (linear activation), the activation function in the hidden units is the one-dimensional neuron-adaptive higher order neural network NAF defined by equation (9-17). The one-dimensional *NANONN* is described by equation (9-18).

Figure 4. 1-dimesnional NAHONN structure

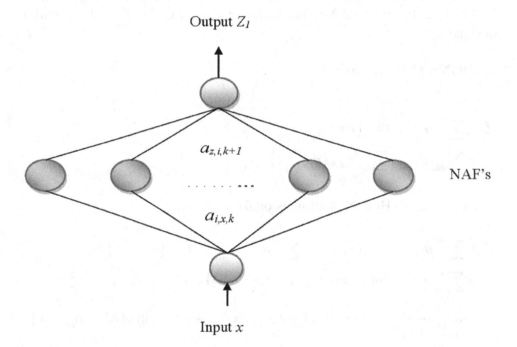

Output Z_1

$a_{z,i,k+1}$

. . . .

$a_{i,x,k}$

NAF's

Input x

Learning Algorithm and Universal Approximation Capability of NAHONN

NAHONN learning algorithm is based on the steepest descent gradient rule (Zhang, Xu, and Fulcher, 2002). However, as the variables in the hidden layer activation function can be adjusted, NAHONN provides more flexibility and more accurate approximation than traditional higher order (and indeed NAHONN includes traditional higher order FNN (fixed activation function) FNNs as a special case).

A NAHONN with a neuron-adaptive activation function can approximate any piecewise continuous function with infinite (countable) discontinuous points to any degree of accuracy (Zhang, Xu, and Fulcher, 2002)

HEAVY RAINFALL ESTIMATION USING NAHONN MODELS

So far, no model can work well if the weather forecasting must use non-continuous and unsmooth data as input. A challenge in this area is to build a new model for weather forecasting that uses non-continuous and unsmooth data is. An artificial neuron-Adaptive higher order Neural network expert System for Estimating Rainfall using satellite data (ANSER) has been developed for estimating rainfall within NOAA (the National Oceanic and Atmospheric Administration, US Department of Commerce). Artificial neuron-adaptive higher order neural network (NAHONN) models were used in this ANSER system.

Rainfall estimation systems are complex. The fixed-neuron ANN models or HONN models are not sufficiently powerful to characterize such complex systems. Using neuron-adaptive NAHONN models enabled us to build a very powerful rainfall estimation system. In the ANSER system, cloud features and nonlinear functions vary in a discontinuous and unsmooth fashion with respect to input variables. Such features and functions cannot be effectively simulated using fixed-neuron ANNs or HONNs, since accuracy will be necessarily limited. Neuron-adaptive NAHONN models were instead used in the ANSER system to determine cloud features and nonlinear functions, for subsequent use in rainfall estimation. Rainfall estimation is a complicated, nonlinear, discontinuous process. Even using parallel and ANN-based reasoning networks leads to poor results. In other words, feed-forward neural networks with fixed activation function neural models could not provide correct reasoning in ANSER. Artificial neuron-adaptive higher order neural network models, on the other hand, can successfully perform this task.

ANSER Architecture

The architecture of the ANSER system can be seen in Figure 5. Output of ANSER is displayed in following Figure 6 and Figure 7. ANSER system uses satellite data as input. Satellite data have been pre-processed and then ANSER uses all image processing methods and pattern recognition techniques to extract the feature, rule, model, and knowledge of rainfall. Seven features are extracted from the satellite data. They are cloud top temperature (CT), cloud top growth factor (CG), rain-burst factor (RB), overshooting top factor (OS), cloud merger factor (M), saturated environment factor (SE), and storm speed factor(S). The cloud top temperature (CT) and cloud top growth factor (CG) are used as input for half an hour rainfall factor (G) predication using NAHONN model. Then half an hour rainfall factor (G), with rain-burst factor (RB), overshooting top factor (OS), cloud merger factor (M), saturated environment factor (SE), storm speed factor (S), and moisture correction data (MC) are used as input for Neuron–Adaptive Higher Order Neural Network Reasoning Subsystem. The output of Neuron–Adaptive Higher Order Neural Network Reasoning Subsystem is the rainfall estimation.

The Structures of NAHONNs for ANSER System

The two-dimensional Neuron-Adaptive Higher Order Neural Network is used for rainfall estimate factor G. Details are:

Let:

$Z_1 = G$ (Rainfall estimate factor)
$x =$ cloud top temperature
$y =$ cloud growth

Figure 5. ANSER structure with using neuron adaptive higher order neural networks

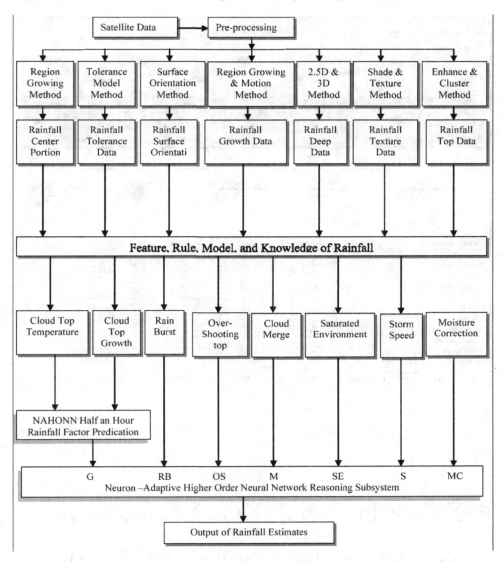

Figure 6. The interface of the ANSER system

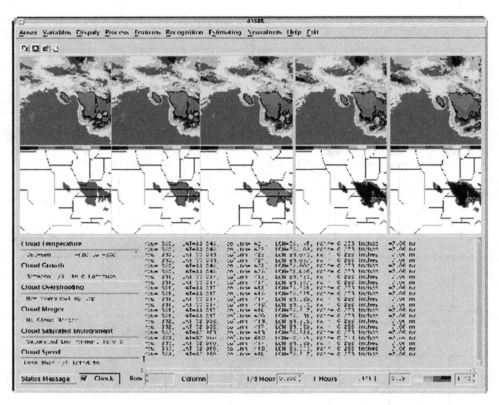

$$G = \sum_{i=0}^{3} a_{1,i,k+1} \cdot \Phi_{i,k}\left(net_{i,x,k}, net_{i,y,k}\right) = \sum_{i=0}^{3} a_{1,i,k+1} \cdot \sum_{h=1,3} f_{i,k,h}\left(a_{i,x,k} \cdot x, a_{i,y,k} \cdot y\right)$$

$$= \sum_{i=0}^{3} a_{1,i,k+1} \cdot ((a1_{i,k} \cdot \sin^{c1_{i,k}}\left(b1_{i,k} \cdot \left(a_{i,x,k} \cdot x\right)\right)) \cdot \sin^{e1_{i,k}}\left(d1_{i,k} \cdot \left(a_{i,y,k} \cdot y\right)\right)$$

$$+ a3_{i,k} \cdot \frac{1}{1 + e^{-b3_{i,k} \cdot \left(a_{i,x,k} \cdot x\right)}} \cdot \frac{1}{1 + e^{-d3_{i,k} \cdot \left(a_{i,y,k} \cdot y\right)}}))$$

$$(9\text{–}19)$$

Where:

Figure 7. Output of rainfall estimate

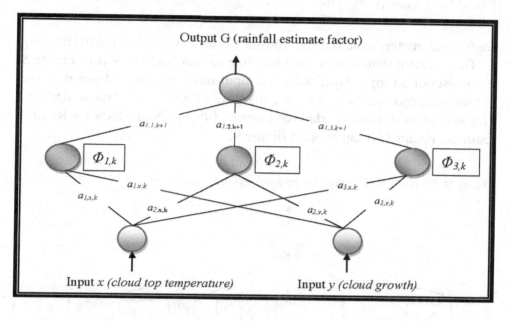

Figure 8. NAHONN for rainfall estimate factor

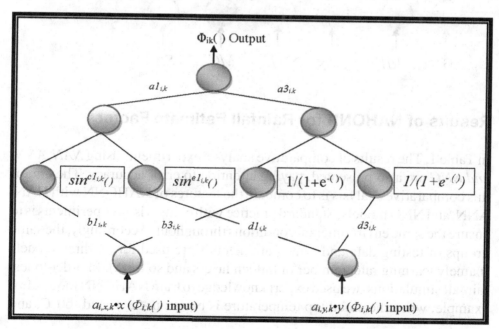

$$a1_{i,k}, b1_{i,k}, c1_{i,k}, d1_{i,k}, e1_{i,k}, a3_{i,k}, b3_{i,k}, d3_{i,k}$$

are free parameters which can be adjusted (as well as weights) during training.

The network structure of the two-dimensional *NAHONN* is in Figure 8. It consists of an input layer with *two* input-units, an output layer with one output-unit, and one hidden layer consisting of 3 neuron-adaptive neurons. The structures of neuron-adaptive neurons ($\Phi_{i,k}$) in NAHONN for Rainfall Estimate Factor G is depicted in Figure 9.

Figure 9. NAHONN structure for rainfall estimate factor g

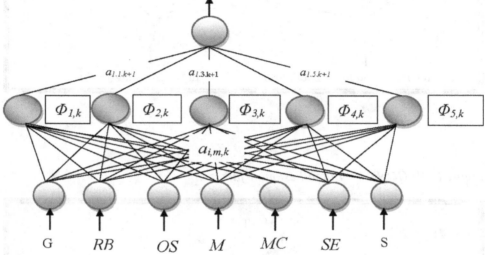

Results of NAHONN for Rainfall Estimate Factor

In Table 1, The results of comparative analysis experiments using *NAN, ANN, and NNG* are also presented, paying attention to error accuracy. The aim of this comparative analysis is to compare the features of NAHONN with NAN, ANN, and NNG models. Standard practice with comparison experiments is to ensure the same environmental conditions throughout. Accordingly, the same groups of testing data and same parameters were used for all three models (namely learning rate, number of hidden layers and so forth). In order to test rainfall simulations, we used expert knowledge to train NAHONN model. For example, when the cloud top temperature is between -58°C and -60°C, and

Table 1. Rainfall data simulation using ANN, NNG, NAN, and NAHONN models

Cloud Top Temperature	Cloud Growth Latitude Degree	Half Hour Rainfall inches	ANN |Error|%	NNG |Error| %	NAN |Error|%	NAHONN |Error|%
> -32° C	2/3	0.05	3.22	8.78	7.89	4.69
-36° C	2/3	0.20	9.92	6.52	6.97	5.34
-46° C	2/3	0.48	25.19	22.58	21.43	9.65
-55° C	2/3	0.79	14.63	14.21	15.32	8.32
-60° C	2/3	0.94	3.66	0.12	1.13	2.53
> - 32° C	1/3	0.05	10.47	8.03	7.56	6.34
- 36° C	1/3	0.13	3.50	4.18	4.09	5.63
- 46° C	1/3	0.24	3.52	4.24	4.21	5.12
- 55° C	1/3	0.43	0.22	1.89	1.84	3.21
- 60° C	1/3	0.65	3.21	0.65	0.75	2.14
- 70° C	1/3	0.85	9.01	5.12	4.56	3.24
< - 80° C	1/3	0.95	3.89	1.32	1.24	2.21
> -32° C	0	0.03	9.81	7.24	6.54	5.84
- 36° C	0	0.06	2.98	3.25	3.45	4.25
- 46° C	0	0.11	5.69	5.67	5.76	5.23
- 55° C	0	0.22	5.28	4.03	4.21	5.22
- 60° C	0	0.36	3.32	1.43	1.26	2.17
-70° C	0	0.49	0.77	2.78	1.76	1.52
< -80° C	0	0.55	2.50	1.12	1.08	1.23
Average			6.36	5.42	5.32	4.41

the cloud growth is more than 2/3 latitude, the half hour rainfall estimate is 0.94 inch, according to experts from the Scofield (1987) of NOAA. Details of this expert knowledge are listed in the Table 1. The values in the table 1 are ground truth based on the Scofield (1987) of NOAA. Table 1 presents the rainfall data estimation results using *ANN* (Artificial Neural Network), *NNG* (artificial Neural Network Group), *NAN*(artificial Neuron-Adaptive Neural network), and NAHONN(artificial Neuron-Adaptive Higher Order Neural Network) models. The average errors of *ANN, NNG, NAN,* and NAHONN are 6.32%, 5.42%, 5.32%, and 4.41% respectively. This means the *NAHONNN* model is about 17.1% better than the *NAN* model when using the rainfall estimate experimental database of Table 1; likewise, *NAHONN* is around 18.6% better than NNG and 30.6% better than ANN model.

Figure 10. NAHONN for rainfall estimate

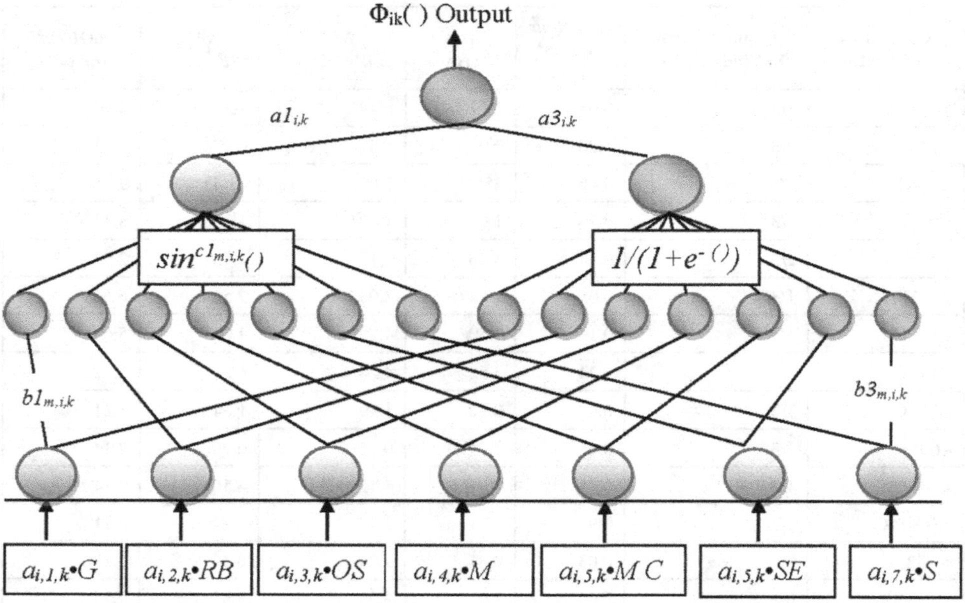

NAHONN Reasoning Network Structure

The basic architecture of the reasoning network for half-hourly satellite-derived rainfall estimation is a 3-layer 7-dimensional NAHONN model, comprising 7 input neurons, 5 adaptive neurons and 1 output neuron. The structure of the NAHONN mode for reasoning is shown in Figure 10. The structures of neuron-adaptive neurons ($\Phi_{i,k}$) in NAHONN for Rainfall Estimate is depicted in Figure 11.

Let: Z_l = Half Hour Rainfall Estimates (inches)

x_1: G;
x_2: RB;
x_3: OS;
x_4: M;
x_5: MC;
x_6: SE;
x_7: S

Figure 11. NAHONN structure for half hour rainfall estimates

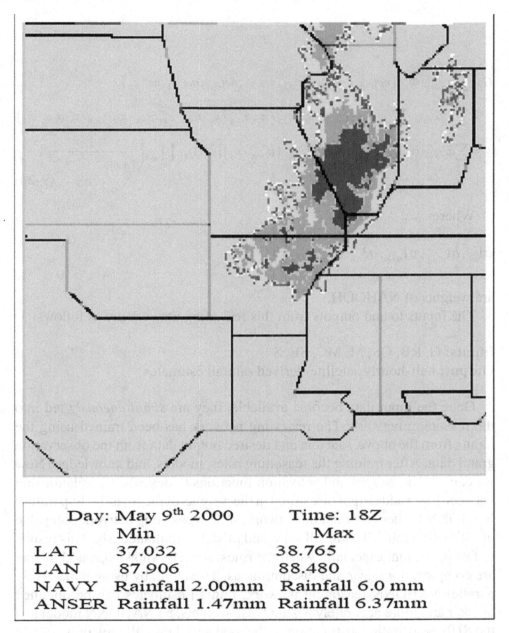

Day: May 9th 2000		Time: 18Z
	Min	Max
LAT	37.032	38.765
LAN	87.906	88.480
NAVY	Rainfall 2.00mm	Rainfall 6.0 mm
ANSER	Rainfall 1.47mm	Rainfall 6.37mm

$$G = \sum_{i=0}^{5} a_{1,i,k+1} \cdot \Phi_{i,k} \left(net_{i,1,k}, net_{i,2,k}, net_{i,3,k}, net_{i,4,k}, net_{i,5,k}, net_{i,6,k}, net_{i,7,k} \right)$$

$$= \sum_{i=0}^{5} a_{1,i,k+1} \cdot \sum_{h=1,3} f_{i,k,h} \left(a_{i,1,k} \cdot x_1, a_{i,2,k} \cdot x_2, a_{i,3,k} \cdot x_3, a_{i,4,k} \cdot x_4, a_{i,5,k} \cdot x_5, a_{i,6,k} \cdot x_6, a_{i,7,k} \cdot x_7 \right)$$

$$= \sum_{i=0}^{5} a_{1,i,k+1} \cdot \left((a1_{i,k} \cdot \prod_{m=1}^{7} \sin^{c1_{m,i,k}} \left(b1_{m,i,k} \cdot \left(a_{i,m,k} \cdot x_m \right) \right) + a3_{i,k} \cdot \prod_{m=1}^{7} \left(\frac{1}{1 + e^{-b3_{m,i,k} \cdot \left(a_{i,m,k} \cdot x_m \right)}} \right) \right)$$

$$(9\text{-}20)$$

Where:

$$a1_{i,k}, b1_{m,i,k}, c1_{mi,k}, a3_{i,k}, b3_{m,i,k}$$

are weights of NAHOOH.

The inputs to and outputs from this reasoning network are as follows:

Inputs: G, RB, OS, M, MC, SE, S
Output: half-hourly satellite-derived rainfall estimates

Once the input data become available, they are *simultaneously* fed into the reasoning network. The reasoning network has been trained using the inputs from the above 7 factors and desired output data from the observation grand data. After training the reasoning rules, models, and knowledge (Now we can use the weighs and activation functions to describe the relationship between input and output) are stored in the weights of the (massively-parallel) NAHONN higher order neural network, so the reasoning network is capable of estimating rainfall using all rules and models simultaneously. This results in fast operation, especially when the rules, models, knowledge and factors are complex, nonlinear and discontinuous. Therefore, by using a massively parallel NAHONN reasoning network, rainfall estimates can be obtained quicker and more accurately. Using these weights, an NAHONN model and the SUN workstation, estimation of the total aerial rainfall took only several seconds, once all the input data were fed into the reasoning network.

Rainfall Estimation Results Using NAHONN Model

A comparison of the results of statistics method (Xie and Scofield, 1989), an ANN reasoning network (Zhang and Scofield, 1994), a neural network group (Zhang, Fulcher, and Scofield, 1997), the NAN model Zhang, Xu, and Fulcher, 2007), and the NAHONN model of the present study is presented in Table 2. When the Xie & Scofield technique was used, the average error of the operator-computed IFFA rainfall estimates was 30.41%. For the ANN reasoning network, the training error was 6.55% and the test error 16.91%, respectively. When the neural network group was used on these same fifteen cases, the average training error of rainfall estimation was 1.43%, and the average test error of rainfall estimation was 3.89%. When the neuron-adaptive

Table 2. Satellite-derived precipitation estimates

No.	Date	Location	Observation (Inch)	X/S Error %	ANN Error %	NNG Error %	NAN Error %	NAHONN Error %
1 #	07/19/85	NY	6.0	+0.83	+14.0	+6.28	+4.36	3.56
2 *	05/16/86	IL/ MO	7.0	+10.0	-5.52	-3.37	-2.57	-2.32
3 *	08/04/82	WI	5.3	+62.08	-8.30	-1.64	-1.72	-1.83
4 *	05/03/87	MO	7.0	+47.86	-10.39	-0.94	-1.12	-0.93
5 *	05/26/87	IA	5.8	-18.62	-7.08	-1.64	-1.38	-1.27
6 #	08/13/87	KS	12.2	+16.62	+15.25	+1.59	+1.61	1.89
7 #	08/12/87	KS	8.7	-30.57	-21.0	-1.92	-1.74	-1.83
8 #	07/19/85	IA	9.5	+96.21	+18.2	-0.74	-0.72	-0.67
9 #	08/22/85	KS	4.2	-22.86	-13.3	+4.12	+3.83	+3.42
10 #	07/02/83	IL	5.2	+13.65	+18.1	+8.71	+7.65	+7.33
11 *	05/01/83	MO	6.0	-31.17	+4.0	+0.72	+0.65	+0.45
12 #	05/27/85	MO	4.2	+2.62	+18.5	-3.88	-3.84	-3.82
13 *	09/05/85	KS	6.2	-5.16	-1.90	-0.90	-0.87	-0.76
14 *	07/15/84	IA	5.0	+78.4	+8.80	+1.20	+1.18	+1.21
15 *	07/16/84	TN	4.2	+19.52	+6.43	-1.00	-0.98	-0.81
			Average |Error| %	30.41	6.55 * 16.91 #	1.43 * 3.89 #	1.31* 3.40 #	1.20* 3.12 #

X/S: Xie/Scofield's study
ANN: Artificial Neural Network multi-layer perceptron as basic reasoning network
NNG: Neural Network Group used as reasoning network
NAN: Neuron-Adaptive artificial neural network as reasoning network in ANSER
NAHONN: artificial Neuron-Adaptive Higher Order Neural Network as reasoning network
*: Training cases for training neural network(s)
#: Test cases

artificial neural network group models was used on these same fifteen cases, the average training error of rainfall estimation was 1.31%, and the average test error of rainfall estimation was 3.40%.

When the artificial neuron-adaptive higher order neural network model was used on these same fifteen cases, the average training error of rainfall estimation was 1.20%, and the average test error of rainfall estimation was 3.12%.

In Table 2, let us now consider a specific example of case 08. The rainfall estimation error resulting from Xie & Scofield's study is +96.21%, which falls to 18.2% with the ANN reasoning network. When the neural network group is used, the rainfall estimation test error is only -0.74%. However, when the NAN model is used, the rainfall estimation test error falls to -0.72%. When NAHONN model is used, the rainfall estimation test error is -0.67%. The *largest* observed error using the ANSER technique (incorporating a neuron adaptive HONN model) is only +7.33% (case 10 of Table 2). By contrast, the largest error reported by Xie & Scofield was 96.21% (case 8 of Table 2).

CONCLUSION

In this chapter, we have presented *NAHONN* models with neuron-adaptive activation functions to automatically model any continuous function. Experiments with rainfall estimate data simulation indicate that the proposed *NAHONN* models offer significant advantages over traditional neural networks, which including much reduced network size, faster learning, and smaller simulation error.

Definitions of one-dimensional, two-dimensional, n-dimensional, and multi n-dimensional *NAHONN* models are studied. Specialized NAHONN models are also described. *NAHONN* models are shown to be "open box". These models are further shown to be capable of automatically finding not only the optimum model but also the appropriate order for high frequency, multi-polynomial, discontinuous data. Rainfall estimation experimental results confirm model convergence. We further demonstrate that *NAHONN* models are capable of modeling satellite data. When the Xie and Scofield (1989) technique was used, the average error of the operator-computed IFFA rainfall estimates was 30.41%. For the Artificial Neural Network (ANN) reasoning network, the training error was 6.55% and the test error 16.91%, respectively. When the neural network group was used on these same fifteen cases, the average training error of rainfall estimation was 1.43%, and the average test error of rainfall estimation was 3.89%. When the neuron-adaptive artificial neural network group models was used on these same fifteen cases, the average training error of rainfall estimation was 1.31%, and the average test error of rainfall estimation was 3.40%. When the artificial neuron-adaptive higher order neural network model was used on these same fifteen cases, the average training error of rainfall estimation was 1.20%, and the average test error of rainfall estimation was 3.12%. Neuron-adaptive higher order neural network models hold considerable promise for both the understanding and development of complex systems. Neuron-adaptive higher order neural network research remains open-ended, and holds considerable potential for developing complex systems.

REFERENCES

Abdelbar, A. M., & Tagliarini, G. A. (1998). A hybrid Bayesian neural learning strategy applied to CONNECT-4. In *Proceeding of the IEEE World Congress on Computational Intelligence* (vol. 1, pp.402–407). IEEE. 10.1109/ IJCNN.1998.682300

Alanis, A. Y., Sanchez, E. N., & Loukianov, A. G. (2006). Discrete- Time Recurrent Neural Induction Motor Control using Kalman Learning. In *Proceedings of International Joint Conference on Neural Networks* (pp.1993 – 2000). Academic Press.

An, Z. G., Mniszewski, S. M., Lee, Y. C., Papcun, G., & Doolen, G. D. (1988A). HIERtalker: a default hierarchy of high order neural networks that learns to read English aloud. In *Proceedings of the Fourth Conference on Artificial Intelligence Applications* (p. 388). Academic Press. 10.1109/ CAIA.1988.196136

An, Z. G., Mniszewski, S. M., Lee, Y. C., Papcun, G., & Doolen, G. D. (1988B). HIERtalker: a default hierarchy of high order neural networks that learns to read English aloud. In *Proceedings of IEEE International Conference on Neural Networks* (vol. 2, pp.221 - 228). IEEE. 10.1109/ICNN.1988.23932

Baldi, P., & Venkatesh, S. S. (1993). Random interactions in higher order neural networks. *Information Theory, 39*(1), 274–283. doi:10.1109/18.179374

Bouzerdoum, A. (1999). A new class of high-order neural networks with nonlinear decision boundaries. *Proceedings of International Conference on, 3*, 1004 – 1009. 10.1109/ICONIP.1999.844673

Brucoli, M., Carnimeo, L., & Grassi, G. (1997). Associative memory design using discrete-time second-order neural networks with local interconnections. *IEEE Transactions on Circuits and Systems. I, Fundamental Theory and Applications, 44*(2), 153–158. doi:10.1109/81.554334

Burshtein, D. (1998). Long-term attraction in higher order neural networks. *IEEE Transactions on Neural Networks, 9*(1), 42–50. doi:10.1109/72.655028 PMID:18252428

Butt, N. R., & Shafiq, M. (2006). Higher-Order Neural Network Based Root-Solving Controller for Adaptive Tracking of Stable Nonlinear Plants. In *Proceedings of IEEE International Conference on Engineering of Intelligent Systems* (pp.1 – 6). IEEE. 10.1109/ICEIS.2006.1703175

Campos, J., Loukianov, A. G., & Sanchez, E. N. (2003). Synchronous motor VSS control using recurrent high order neural networks. In *Proceedings of 42nd IEEE Conference on Decision and Control* (vol. 4, pp.3894 – 3899). IEEE. 10.1109/CDC.2003.1271757

Chang, C., & Cheung, J. Y. (1992). Backpropagation algorithm in higher order neural network. In *Proceedings of International Joint Conference on Neural Networks* (*vol. 3*, pp.511 – 516). Academic Press. 10.1109/IJCNN.1992.227123

Chang, C.-H., Lin, J.-L., & Cheung, J.-Y. (1993). Polynomial and standard higher order neural network. In *Proceedings of IEEE International Conference on Neural Networks* (vol.2, pp.989 – 994). IEEE. 10.1109/ICNN.1993.298692

Christodoulou, M., & Zarkogianni, D. (2006). Recurrent High Order Neural Networks for Identification of the EGFR Signaling Pathway. In Proceedings of Control and Automation (pp.1 – 6). doi:10.1109/MED.2006.328819

Christodoulou, M. A., & Iliopoulos, T. N. (2006). Neural Network Models for Prediction of Steady-State and Dynamic Behavior of MAPK Cascade. In *Proceedings of 14th Mediterranean Conference on Control and Automation* (pp.1 – 9). 10.1109/MED.2006.328820

Cooper, B. S. (1995). Higher order neural networks for combinatorial optimisation improving the scaling properties of the Hopfield network. *Proceedings of IEEE International Conference on, 4*, 1855 – 1860. 10.1109/ICNN.1995.488904

Estevez, P. A., & Okabe, Y. (1991). Training the piecewise linear-high order neural network through error back propagation. *Proceedings of IEEE International Joint Conference on Neural Networks, 1*, 711 – 716. 10.1109/IJCNN.1991.170483

Ge, S. S., Zhang, J., & Lee, T. H. (2004). Adaptive neural network control for a class of MIMO nonlinear systems with disturbances in discrete-time. *IEEE Transactions on, 34*(4), 1630–1645. PMID:15462431

Gulez, K., Mutoh, N., Harashima, F., Ohnishi, K., & Pastaci, H. (2000). Design of a HONN (high order neural network) by using a DSP based system for the performance increasing of an induction motor under changeable load. *Proceedings of 26th Annual Conference of the IEEE on, 4*, 2315 – 2320.

Heywood, M., & Noakes, P. (1993). Simple addition to back-propagation learning for dynamic weight pruning, sparse network extraction and faster learning. In *Proceedings of the IEEE International Conference on Neural Networks* (vol.2, pp. 620 – 625). 10.1109/ICNN.1993.298546

Jeffries, C. (1989). Dense memory with high order neural networks. In *Proceedings of Twenty-First Southeastern Symposium on System Theory* (pp.436 – 439). 10.1109/SSST.1989.72506

Jeffries, C. (1989). High order neural networks. In *Proceedings of International Joint Conference on Neural Networks* (*vol. 2*, pp. 594). Academic Press.

Kariniotakis, G. N., Stavrakakis, G. S., & Nogaret, E. F. (1996). Wind power forecasting using advanced neural networks models. *IEEE Transactions on Energy Conversion, 11*(4), 762–767. doi:10.1109/60.556376

Kosmatopoulos, E. B., & Christodoulou, M. A. (1994). Filtering, prediction, and learning properties of ECE neural networks. *IEEE Transactions on Systems, Man, and Cybernetics, 24*(7), 971–981. doi:10.1109/21.297787

Kosmatopoulos, E. B., & Christodoulou, M. A. (1995). Structural properties of gradient recurrent high-order neural networks. *IEEE Transactions on, 42*(9), 592–603.

Kosmatopoulos, E. B., & Christodoulou, M. A. (1997). High-order neural networks for the learning of robot contact surface shape. *IEEE Transactions on Robotics and Automation*, *13*(3), 451–455. doi:10.1109/70.585906

Kosmatopoulos, E. B., Ioannou, P. A., & Christodoulou, M. A. (1992). Identification of nonlinear systems using new dynamic neural network structures. In *Proceedings of the 31st IEEE Conference on Decision and Control* (vol. 1, pp. 20 – 25). 10.1109/CDC.1992.371800

Kosmatopoulos, E. B., Polycarpou, M. M., Christodoulou, M. A., & Ioannou, P. A. (1995). High-order neural network structures for identification of dynamical systems. *Neural Networks*, *6*(2), 422–431. doi:10.1109/72.363477 PMID:18263324

Kuroe, Y. (2004). Learning and identifying finite state automata with recurrent high-order neural networks. In *Proceedings of SICE 2004 Annual Conference* (*vol. 3*, pp.2241 – 2246). Academic Press.

Kuroe, Y., Ikeda, H., & Mori, T. (1997). Identification of nonlinear dynamical systems by recurrent high-order neural networks. In *Proceedings of IEEE International Conference on Systems, Man, and Cybernetics* (Vol. 1, pp. 70 – 75). IEEE. 10.1109/ICSMC.1997.625725

Lee, M., Lee, S. Y., & Park, C. H. (1992). Neural controller of nonlinear dynamic systems using higher order neural networks. *Electronics Letters*, *28*(3), 276–277. doi:10.1049/el:19920170

Li, D., Hirasawa, K., & Hu, J. (2003). A new strategy for constructing higher order neural networks with multiplication units. *Proceedings of*, *3*, 2342–2347.

Li, W., Wang, Y., Li, W., Zhang, J., & Li J. (1998). *Sparselized higher-order neural network and its pruning algorithm*. Academic Press.

Liatsis, P., Wellstead, P. E., Zarrop, M. B., & Prendergast, T. (1994). A versatile visual inspection tool for the manufacturing process. In *Proceedings of the Third IEEE Conference on Control Applications* (vol.3, pp. 1505 – 1510). IEEE. 10.1109/CCA.1994.381492

Lin, C., Wu, K., & Wang, J. (2005). Scale equalized higher-order neural networks. In *Proceedings of Systems, Man and Cybernetics* (Vol. 1, pp. 816 – 821). Academic Press.

Liou, R.-J., & Azimi-Sadjadi, M. R. (1993). Dim target detection using high order correlation method. *IEEE Transactions on Aerospace and Electronic Systems*, 29(3), 841–856. doi:10.1109/7.220935

Machado, R. J. (1989). Handling knowledge in high order neural networks: the combinatorial neural model. In *Proceedings of the International Joint Conference on Neural Networks* (*vol.2*, pp.582). Academic Press. 10.1109/IJCNN.1989.118339

Miyajima, H., Yatsuki, S., & Kubota, J. (1995). Dynamical properties of neural networks with product connections. In *Proceedings of the IEEE International Conference on Neural Networks* (vol. 6, pp. 3198 – 3203). IEEE.

Qi, H., & Zhang, M. (2001). Rainfall estimation using M-PHONN model. In Neural Networks (Vol., pp.1620 – 1624). Academic Press.

Ricalde, L. J., & Sanchez, E. N. (2005). Inverse optimal nonlinear recurrent high order neural observer. In *Proceedings. IEEE International Joint Conference on Neural Networks* (Vol. 1, pp.361 – 365). IEEE. 10.1109/IJCNN.2005.1555857

Rovithakis, G., Gaganis, V., Perrakis, S., & Christodoulou, M. (1996). A recurrent neural network model to describe manufacturing cell dynamics. In *Proceedings of the 35th IEEE Conference on Decision and Control* (vol.2, pp.1728 – 1733). 10.1109/CDC.1996.572808

Rovithakis, G. A. (1998). Reinforcing robustness using high order neural network controllers. In *Proceedings of the 37th IEEE Conference on Decision and Control* (vol.1, pp.1052 – 1057). IEEE. 10.1109/CDC.1998.760836

Rovithakis, G. A. (1999). Robustifying nonlinear systems using high-order neural network controllers. *IEEE Transactions on Automatic Control*, 44(1), 102–108. doi:10.1109/9.739082

Rovithakis, G. A. (2000). Performance of a neural adaptive tracking controller for multi-input nonlinear dynamical systems in the presence of additive and multiplicative external disturbances. *Systems, Man and Cybernetics. Part A*, 30(6), 720–730.

Rovithakis, G. A. (2000, July). Robustness of a neural controller in the presence of additive and multiplicative external perturbations. *Intelligent Control*, 17-19, 7–12.

Rovithakis, G. A., Gaganis, V. I., Perrakis, S. E., & Christodoulou, M. A. (1998). High order neural networks to control manufacturing systems-a comparison study. In *Proceedings of the 37th IEEE Conference on Decision and Control* (vol.3, pp.2736 – 2737). IEEE. 10.1109/CDC.1998.757868

Rovithakis, G. A., Kosmatopoulos, E. B., & Christodoulou, M. A. (1993). Robust adaptive control of unknown plants using recurrent high order neural networks-application to mechanical systems. In *Proceedings of International Conference on Systems, Man and Cybernetics* (*vol.4*, pp. 57 – 62). Academic Press. 10.1109/ICSMC.1993.390683

Rovithakis, G. A., Malamos, A. G., Varvarigon, T., & Christodoulou, M. A. (1998). Quality assurance in networks-a high order neural net approach. In *Proceedings of the 37th IEEE Conference on Decision and Control* (vol.2, pp.1599 – 1604). 10.1109/CDC.1998.758521

Rovithakis, G. A., Maniadakis, M., & Zervakis, M. (2000). Artificial neural networks for feature extraction and classification of vascular tissue fluorescence spectrums. In *Proceedings. 2000 IEEE International Conference on Acoustics, Speech, and Signal Processing* (vol.6, pp.3454 – 3457). 10.1109/ICASSP.2000.860144

Salem, G. J., & Young, T. Y. (1991). Interpreting line drawings with higher order neural networks. In *Proceedings of the International Joint Conference on Neural Networks* (vol.1, pp. 713 – 721). 10.1109/IJCNN.1991.155268

Scofield, R. A. (1987). The NESDIS operational convective precipitation estimation technique. *Monthly Weather Review*, *115*(8), 1773–1792. doi:10.1175/1520-0493(1987)115<1773:TNOCPE>2.0.CO;2

Starke, J., Kubota, N., & Fukuda, T. (1995). Combinatorial optimization with higher order neural networks-cost oriented competing processes in flexible manufacturing systems. In *Proceedings of IEEE International Conference on Neural Networks* (Vol. 5, pp. 2658 – 2663). 10.1109/ICNN.1995.487830

Tanaka, K., & Kumazawa, I. (1996). Learning regular languages via recurrent higher-order neural networks. In *Proceedings of IEEE International Conference on Neural Networks* (Vol. 2, pp. 1378 – 1383). 10.1109/ICNN.1996.549100

Tseng, Y.-H., & Wu, J.-L. (1994). Constant-time neural decoders for some BCH codes. *Proceedings of IEEE International Symposium on*.

Vidyasagar, M. (1993). Convergence of higher-order neural networks with modified updating. In *Proceedings of the IEEE International Conference on Neural Networks* (vol.3, pp. 1379 – 1384). 10.1109/ICNN.1993.298758

Villalobos, L., & Merat, F. L. (1995). Learning capability assessment and feature space optimization for higher-order neural networks. *Neural Networks*, 6(1), 267–272. doi:10.1109/72.363427 PMID:18263308

Wang, J., Wu K., & Chang F. (2004). Scale equalization higher-order neural networks. In *Information Reuse and Integration* (pp. 612 – 617). Academic Press.

Wang, L. (1996). Suppressing chaos with hysteresis in a higher order neural network. *IEEE Transactions on Circuits and Systems. 2, Analog and Digital Signal Processing*, 43(12), 845–846. doi:10.1109/82.553405

Xie, J., & Scofield, R. A. (1989). Satellite-derived rainfall estimates and propagation characteristics associated with mesoscal convective system (MCSs). *NAOO Technical Memorandum NESDIS, 25*.

Xu, S., & Zhang, M. (2002). An adaptive higher-order neural networks (AHONN) and its approximation capabilities. In *Proceedings of the 9th International Conference on Neural Information Processing* (Vol. 2, pp. 848 – 852). 10.1109/ICONIP.2002.1198179

Yamashita, T., Hirasawa, K., Hu, J., & Murata, J. (2002). Multi-branch structure of layered neural networks. In *Proceedings of the 9th International Conference on Neural Information Processing* (vol.1, pp.243 – 247). 10.1109/ICONIP.2002.1202170

Yang, H., & Guest, C. C. (1990). High order neural networks with reduced numbers of interconnection weights. In *Proceedings of the International Joint Conference on Neural Networks* (vol.3, pp. 281 – 286). 10.1109/IJCNN.1990.137857

Yatsuki, S., & Miyajima, H. (1997). Associative ability of higher order neural networks. In *Proceedings of International Conference on Neural Networks* (Vol. 2, pp. 1299 – 1304). 10.1109/ICNN.1997.616222

Young, S., & Downs, T. (1993). Generalization in higher order neural networks. *Electronics Letters*, 29(16), 1491–1493. doi:10.1049/el:19930996

Yu, S. J., & Liang, D. N. (1995). Neural network-based approach for eigen-structure extraction. In *Proceedings of the IEEE 1995 National Aerospace and Electronics Conference* (vol.1, pp. 102 – 105). IEEE.

Zardoshti-Kermani, M., & Afshordi, A. (1995). Classification of chromosomes using higher-order neural networks. In *Proceedings of IEEE International Conference on* (Vol. 5, pp. 2587 – 2591). IEEE. 10.1109/ICNN.1995.487816

Zhang, J., Ge, S. S., & Lee, T. H. (2005). Output feedback control of a class of discrete MIMO nonlinear systems with triangular form inputs. *IEEE Transactions on Neural Networks*, *16*(6), 1491–1503. doi:10.1109/TNN.2005.852242 PMID:16342490

Zhang, J. C., Zhang, M., & Fulcher, J. (1997). Financial simulation system using a higher order trigonometric polynomial neural network group model. In *Proceedings of the IEEE/IAFE 1997 Computational Intelligence for Financial Engineering (CIFEr)* (pp.189 – 194). IEEE. 10.1109/CIFER.1997.618934

Zhang, M. (2001). Financial data simulation using A-PHONN model. Neural Networks, 3, 1823 – 1827.

Zhang, M. (2009C). Ultra-High Frequency Trigonometric Higher Order Neural Networks. In Artificial Higher Order Neural Networks for Economics and Business. IGI-Global Publisher.

Zhang, M. (2009a). Artificial Higher Order Neural Networks for Economics and Business. IGI-Global Publisher. doi:10.4018/978-1-59904-897-0

Zhang, M. (2009b). Artificial Higher Order Neural Network Nonlinear Models: SAS NLIN or HONNs? In Artificial Higher Order Neural Networks for Economics and Business. IGI-Global Publisher.

Zhang, M., Fulcher, J., & Scofield, R. (1997). Rainfall estimation using artificial neural network group. *Neurocomputing*, *16*(2), 97–115. doi:10.1016/S0925-2312(96)00022-7

Zhang, M., & Scofield, R. A. (1994). Artificial neural network techniques for estimating heavy convective rainfall and recognition cloud mergers from satellite data. *International Journal of Remote Sensing*, *15*(16), 3241–3262. doi:10.1080/01431169408954324

Zhang, M., & Scofield, R.A. (2001). Rainfall estimation using A-PHONN model. *Neural Networks*, *3*, 1583 – 1587.

Zhang, M., Xu, S., & Fulcher, J. (2007). ANSER: Adaptive neuron artificial neural network system for estimating rainfall. *International Journal of Computers and Applications, 29*(3), 215–222. doi:10.1080/120621 2X.2007.11441850

Zhang, M., Xu, S., & Lu, B. (1999). Neuron-adaptive higher order neural network group models. In *Proceedings of International Joint Conference on Neural Networks* (Vol. 1, pp. 333 - 336). 10.1109/IJCNN.1999.831513

Zhang, Y., Liu, W. F., Li, Y., Liu, X. L., & Ouyang, K. (2002). Translation and rotation invariance of physiological signal in long-term custody. *Proceedings of 24th Annual Conference and the Annual Fall Meeting of the Biomedical Engineering Society* (vol.1, pp. 250 – 251). 10.1109/IEMBS.2002.1134477

Zhang, Y., Peng, P. Y., & Rovithakis, G. A. (2000). Comments on "Robustifying nonlinear systems using high-order neural network controllers". *IEEE Transactions on Automatic Control, 45*(5), 1033–1036. doi:10.1109/9.855579

ADDITIONAL READING

An, Z. G., Mniszewski, S. M., Lee, Y. C., Papcun, G., & Doolen, G. D. (1988). HIERtalker: a default hierarchy of high order neural networks that learns to read English aloud. *Proceedings of the Fourth Conference on Artificial Intelligence Applications.* pp.388. 10.1109/CAIA.1988.196136

Brock, W., & Sayers, C. (1988). Is the business cycle characterized by deterministic chaos? *Journal of Monetary Economics, 22*(1), 71–91. doi:10.1016/0304-3932(88)90170-5

Chen, Y., Yang, B., Dong, J., & Abraham, A. (2004). Time Series Forecasting using Flexible Neural Tree Model. *Information Science, 174*(3-4), 219–235. doi:10.1016/j.ins.2004.10.005

Doulamis, A. D., Doulamis, N. D., & Kollias, S. D. (2003). An adaptable neural network model for recursive nonlinear traffic prediction and modeling of MPEG video sources, IEEE Transactions on neural networks, vol.14, Gunaseelan, V.N. (1997). Anaerobic digestion of biomass for methane production: A review. *Biomass and Bioenergy, 13*(1), 83–114.

Khalil, H. (1996). *Nonlinear Systems* (3rd ed.). Upper Saddle River: Pearson Education.

Lewis, F. L., Jagannathan, S., & Yesildirek, A. (1998). *Neural Network Control of Robot Manipulators and Non-Linear Systems*. New York: Taylor & Francis.

Murphy, K. (1985). Corporate performance and managerial remuneration. *Journal of Accounting and Economics*, *7*(1-3), 11–42. doi:10.1016/0165-4101(85)90026-6

Young, S., & Downs, T. (1993). Generalization in higher order neural networks. *Electronics Letters*, *29*(16), 1491–1493. doi:10.1049/el:19930996

KEY TERMS AND DEFINITIONS

ANSER: An artificial neuron-adaptive higher order neural network expert system for estimating rainfall using satellite data.

CG: Cloud top growth factor.

CT: Cloud top temperature.

HONN: Artificial higher order neural network.

M: Cloud merger factor.

NAHONN: Artificial neuron-adaptive higher order neural network.

OS: Overshooting top factor.

RB: Rain-burst factor.

S: Storm speed factor.

SE: Saturated environment factor.

Section 4
Artificial Higher Order Neural Networks for Control and Recognition

Chapter 10

Control Signal Generator Based on Ultra–High Frequency Polynomial and Trigonometric Higher Order Neural Networks

ABSTRACT

This chapter develops a new nonlinear model, ultra high frequency polynomial and trigonometric higher order neural networks (UPT-HONN) for control signal generator. UPT-HONN includes UPS-HONN (ultra high frequency polynomial and sine function higher order neural networks) and UPC-HONN (ultra high frequency polynomial and cosine function higher order neural networks). UPS-HONN and UPC-HONN model learning algorithms are developed in this chapter. UPS-HONN and UPC-HONN models are used to build nonlinear control signal generator. Test results show that UPS-HONN and UPC-HONN models are better than other polynomial higher order neural network (PHONN) and trigonometric higher order neural network (THONN) models, since UPS-HONN and UPC-HONN models can generate control signals with error approaching 10-6.

DOI: 10.4018/978-1-7998-3563-9.ch010

INTRODUCTION

The perspective of this chapter will be: introduce the background of HONNs with the applications of HONNs in control area; develop a new HONN model called UPT-HONN for ultra-high frequency control signal generator; provide the UPT-HONN learning algorithm and weight update formulae; applications of UPT-HONN model for control signals.

This chapter is organized as follows: Section background gives the background knowledge of HONNs in control area. Section UPT-HONN models introduces UPT-HONN structure and different modes of the UPT-HONN model. Section learning algorithm of UPT-HONN models provides the UPT-HONN model update formula, learning algorithms, and convergence theories of HONN. Section UPT-HONN testing describes UPT-HONN computer software system and testing results.

BACKGROUND

Neural Networks for Control Signals and Control Systems

Artificial Neural Networks have been widely used in the control area. Studies found that artificial neural networks are good tools for system control and control signal generating. Narendra and Parthasarathy (1990) develop identification and control techniques of dynamical systems using artificial neural networks. Arai, Kohon, and Imai (1991) study an adaptive control of neural network with variable function of a unit and its application. Chen and Khalil (1992) develop an adaptive control of nonlinear systems using neural networks. Hu and Shao (1992) show the neural network adaptive control systems. Yamada and Yabuta (1992) investigate a neural network controller which uses an auto-tuning method for nonlinear functions. Campolucci, Capparelli, Guarnieri, Piazza, & Uncini (1996) learn neural networks with adaptive spline activation function. Lewis, Yesildirek, & Liu, (1996) design Multilayer neural-net robot controller with guaranteed tracking performance. Polycarpou (1996) applies stable adaptive neural control scheme for nonlinear systems. Lewis, Jagannathan, & Yesildirek (1998) build neural network control for robot manipulators and non-linear systems.

Norgaard, Ravn, Poulsen, & Hansen (2000) generate neural networks for modelling and control of dynamic systems. Poznyak, Sanchez, & Yu (2000) investigate differential neural networks for robust nonlinear control. Chen & Narendra (2002) present nonlinear adaptive control using neural networks and multiple models. Diao & Passino (2002) examine adaptive neural/fuzzy control for interpolated nonlinear systems. Holubar, Zani, Hager, Froschl, Radak, Braun (2002) explore advanced controlling of anaerobic digestion by means of hierarchical neural networks. Plett (2003) inspects adaptive inverse control of linear and nonlinear systems using dynamic neural networks. Ge, Zhang, & Lee (2004) probe adaptive neural network control for a class of MIMO nonlinear systems with disturbances in discrete-time. Shi & Li (2004) contribute a novel control of a small wind turbine driven generator based on neural networks. Bukovsky, Bila, & Gupta (2005) analyze linear dynamic neural units with time delay for identification and control. Yih, Wei, & Tsu (2005) experiment observer-based direct adaptive fuzzy-neural control for nonffine nonlinear systems. Farrell & Polycarpou (2006) indicate adaptive approximation-based control by unifying neural, fuzzy and traditional adaptive approximation approaches. Boutalis, Theodoridis, & Christodoulou (2009) suppose a new neuro FDS definition for indirect adaptive control of unknown nonlinear systems using a method of parameter hopping. Hou, Cheng, & Tan (2009) supply decentralized robust adaptive control for the multiagent system consensus problem using neural networks. Alanis, Sanchez, Loukianov, & Perez-Cisneros (2010) seek real-time discrete neural block control using sliding modes for electric induction motors. Weidong, Yubing, & Xingpei (2010) offer short-term forecasting of wind turbine power generation based on genetic neural network. Kumar, Panwar, Sukavanam, Sharma, & Borm (2011) run neural network-based nonlinear tracking control of kinematically redundant robot manipulators. Pedro, & Dahunsi (2011) grant neural network-based feedback linearization control of a servo-hydraulic vehicle suspension system. All the studies above suggest that artificial neural networks are powerful tools for control signals and control systems

Higher Order Neural Networks for Control Signals and Control Systems

Artificial Higher Order Neural Networks (HONNs) have been widely used in the control area too. Studies also found that artificial higher order neural networks are good tools for system control and generating control signal Lee,

Lee, & Park (1992) pilot neural controller of nonlinear dynamic systems using higher order neural networks. Rovithakis, Kosmatopoulos, & Christodoulou (1993) look at robust adaptive control of unknown plants using recurrent high order neural networks-application to mechanical systems. Rovithakis, Gaganis, Perrakis, & Christodoulou (1996) obtain a recurrent neural network model to describe manufacturing cell dynamics. Rovithakis & Chistodoulou (2000) disclose adaptive control with recurrent high-order neural networks. Li, Chen, & Yuan (2002) create simple recurrent neural network-based adaptive predictive control for nonlinear systems. Campos, Loukianov, & Sanchez (2003) deliver synchronous motor VSS control using recurrent high order neural networks. Alanis, Sanchez, & Loukianov (2006) test discrete-time recurrent neural induction motor control using Kalman learning. Butt & Shafiq (2006) examine higher-order neural network-based root-solving controller for adaptive tracking of stable nonlinear plants. Sanchez, Alanis, & Loukianov (2008) produce discrete time high order neural control trained with Kalman filtering. Baruch, Galvan-Guerra, Nenkova (2008) achieve centralized indirect control of an anaerobic digestion bioprocess using recurrent neural identifier. Theodoridis, Boutalis, & Christodoulou (2009) expand a new neuro-fuzzy dynamical system definition based on high order neural network function approximators. All the researches above indicate that artificial higher order neural networks are useful tools for control signals and control systems.

Detail Examples of Artificial Higher Order Neural Networks for Control

Yu (2010) scans robust adaptive control using higher order neural networks and projection and presents a novel robust adaptive approach for a class of unknown nonlinear systems. Firstly, the neural networks are designed to identify the nonlinear systems. Dead-zone and projection techniques are applied to weights training, in order to avoid singular cases. Secondly, a linearization controller is proposed based on the neuro identifier. Since the approximation capability of the neural networks is limited, four types of compensators are addressed. This chapter also proposes a robust neuro-observer, which has an extended Luenberger structure. Its weights are learned on-line by a new adaptive gradient-like technique. The control scheme is based on the proposed neuro-observer. The final structure is composed by two parts: the neuro-observer and the tracking controller. The simulations of a two-link robot show the effectiveness of the proposed algorithm.

Karnavas (2010) values electric machines excitation control via higher order neural networks and is demonstrating a practical design of an intelligent type of controller using higher order neural network (HONN) concepts, for the excitation control of a practical power generating system. This type of controller is suitable for real time operation and aims to improve the dynamic characteristics of the generating unit by acting properly on its original excitation system. The modeling of the power system under study consists of a synchronous generator connected via a transformer and a transmission line to an infinite bus. For comparison purposes and also for producing useful data in order for the demonstrating neural network controllers to be trained, digital simulations of the above system are performed using fuzzy logic control (FLC) techniques, which are based on previous work. Then, two neural network controllers are designed and applied by adopting the HONN architectures. The first one utilizes a single pi-sigma neural network (PSNN) and the significant advantages over the standard multi layered perceptron (MLP) are discussed. Secondly, an enhanced controller is designed, leading to a ridge polynomial neural network (RPNN) by combining multiple PSNNs if needed. Both controllers used, can be pre-trained rapidly from the corresponding FLC output signal and act as model dynamics capturers. The dynamic performances of the fuzzy logic controller (FLC) along with those of the two demonstrated controllers are presented by comparison using the well-known integral square error criterion (ISE). The latter controllers show excellent convergence properties and accuracy for function approximation. Typical transient responses of the system are shown for comparison in order to demonstrate the effectiveness of the designed controllers. The computer simulation results obtained show clearly that the performance of the developed controllers offers competitive damping effects on the synchronous generator's oscillations, with respect to the associated ones of the FLC, over a wider range of operating conditions, while their hardware implementation is apparently much easier and the computational time needed for real-time applications is drastically reduced.

Theodoridis, Christodoulou, and Boutalis (2010) inspect neuro–fuzzy Control schemes based on high order neural network function approximators and study the control schemes. The indirect or direct adaptive regulation of unknown nonlinear dynamical systems is considered in this chapter. Since the plant is considered unknown, this chapter first proposes its approximation by a special form of a fuzzy dynamical system (FDS) and in the sequel the fuzzy rules are approximated by the appropriate HONNFs. The system is regulated to zero adaptivity by providing weight updating laws for the involved HONNFs, which guarantee that both the identification error and the system states reach zero exponentially fast. At the same time, all signals in the closed loop are kept bounded. The existence of the control signal is always assured by introducing a novel method of parameter hopping, which is incorporated in the weight updating laws. The indirect control scheme is developed for square systems (number of inputs equal to the number of states) as well as for systems in Brunovsky canonical form. The direct control scheme is developed for systems in square form. Simulations illustrate the potency of the method and comparisons with conventional approaches on benchmarking systems are given.

Das, Lewis, and Subbarao (2010) discover back-stepping control of quadrotor by a dynamically tuned higher order like neural network approach and revise the control of quadrotor. The dynamics of a quadrotor is a simplified form of helicopter dynamics that exhibit the same basic problems of strong coupling, multi-input/multi-output design, and unknown nonlinearities. The Lagrangian model of a typical quadrotor that involves four inputs and six outputs results in an underactuated system. There are several design techniques are available for nonlinear control of mechanical underactuated system. One of the most popular among them is backstepping. Backstepping is a well-known recursive procedure where underactuation characteristic of the system is resolved by defining 'desired' virtual control and virtual state variables. Virtual control variables is determined in each recursive step assuming the corresponding subsystem is Lyapunov stable and virtual states are typically the errors of actual and desired virtual control variables. The application of the backstepping even more interesting when a virtual control law is applied to a Lagrangian subsystem. The necessary information to select virtual control and state variables for these systems can be obtained through model identification methods. One of these methods includes Neural Network approximation to identify the unknown parameters of the system. The unknown parameters may include uncertain aerodynamic force and moment coefficients or unmodeled dynamics. These aerodynamic coefficients generally are the functions of higher order state polynomials. This chapter discusses how can implement linear in parameter first order neural network approximation methods to identify these unknown higher order state polynomials in every recursive step of the backstepping. Thus, the first order neural network eventually estimates the higher order state polynomials which is in fact a higher order like neural net (HOLNN). Moreover, when these artificial Neural Networks placed into a control loop, they become dynamic artificial Neural Network whose weights are tuned only. Due to the inherent characteristics of the quadrotor, the Lagrangian form for the position dynamics is bilinear in the controls, which is confronted using a bilinear inverse kinematics solution. The result is a controller of intuitively appealing structure having an outer kinematics loop for position control and an inner dynamic loop for attitude control. The stability of the control law is guaranteed by a Lyapunov proof. The control approach described in this chapter is robust since it explicitly deals with un-modeled state dependent disturbances without needing any prior knowledge of the same. A simulation study validates the results such as decoupling, tracking etc. obtained in the paper.

Das and Lewis (2013) bestow distributed adaptive control for multi-agent systems with pseudo higher order neural net and suggest that the idea of using multi-agent systems is getting popular every day. It not only saves time and resource but also eliminates the requirement of large human coordination. These ideas are especially effective in combating zone where multiple unmanned aerial vehicles are required to control for achieving multiple simultaneous objectives or targets. The evolution of distributed control has started with simple integrator systems and then gradually different control methodologies have been adopted for more and more complex nonlinear systems. Also, from practical standpoint, the dynamics of the agents involved in networked control architecture might not be identical. Therefore, an ideal distributed control should accommodate multiple agents which are nonlinear systems associated with unknown dynamics. In this chapter, a distributed control methodology has been presented, where nonidentical nonlinear agents communicate among themselves following directed graph topology. In addition, the nonlinear dynamics are considered unknown. While the pinning control strategy has been adopted to distribute the input command among the agents, a Pseudo Higher Order Neural Net (PHONN) based identification strategy is introduced for identifying the unknown dynamics. These two strategies are combined beautifully such that the stability of the system is assured even with minimum interaction among the agents. A detailed stability analysis is presented based on Lyapunov theory and a simulation study is performed to verify the theoretical claims.

Chen and Lewis (2013) afford cooperative control of unknown networked Lagrange systems using higher order neural networks and explore the cooperative control problem for a group of Lagrange systems with a target system to be tracked. The development is suitable for the case that the desired trajectory of the target node is only available to a portion of the networked systems. All the networked systems can have different dynamics. The dynamics of the networked systems, as well as the target system, are all assumed unknown. A higher-order neural network is used at each node to approximate the distributed unknown dynamics. A distributed adaptive neural network control protocol is proposed so that the networked systems synchronize to the motion of the target node. The theoretical analysis shows that the synchronization error can be made arbitrarily small by appropriately tuning the design parameters.

UPT-HONN MODELS

Nyquist Rule says that a sampling rate must be at least twice as fast as the fastest frequency (Synder 2006). In simulating and predicting time series data, the new nonlinear models of UPT-HONN should have twice as high frequency as that of the ultra-high frequency of the time series data. To achieve this purpose, a new model should be developed to enforce high frequency of HONN in order to make the simulation and prediction error close to zero. The new HONN model, Ultra High Frequency Polynomial and Trigonometric Higher Order Neural Network (UPT-HONN), includes two different models base on the different neuron functions. Ultra-high frequency Polynomial and Sine Trigonometric Higher Order Neural Network (UPS-HONN) has neurons with polynomial and sine functions. Ultra-high frequency Polynomial and Cosine Trigonometric Higher Order Neural Network (UPC-HONN) has neurons with polynomial and cosine functions. Except for the functions in the neuron all other parts of these two models are the same.

UPS-HONN Model and UPC-HONN Model

UPS-HONN Model Structure can be seen in Figure 1. UPC-HONN Model Structure can be seen in Figure 2.

The Nyquist–Shannon sampling theorem, after Harry Nyquist and Claude Shannon, in the literature more commonly referred to as the Nyquist sampling theorem or simply as the sampling theorem, is a fundamental result in the field of information theory, telecommunications and signal processing. Shannon's version of the theorem states: [Shannon, 1998]

If a function x(t) contains no frequencies higher than B hertz, it is completely determined by giving its ordinates at a series of points spaced 1/(2B) seconds apart.

In other words, a band limited function can be perfectly reconstructed from a countable sequence of samples if the band limit, B, is no greater than ½ the sampling rate (samples per second).

In simulating and predicting time series data, the new nonlinear models of UPT-HONN should have twice as high frequency as that of the ultra-high frequency of the time series data. To achieve this purpose, a new model should be developed to enforce high frequency of HONN in order to make the simulation and prediction error close to zero.

The different types of UPS-HONN models are shown as follows. Formula (1) (2) and (3) are for UPS-HONN model 2, 1 and 0 respectively. Model 2 has three layers of weights changeable; Model 1 has two layers of weights changeable, and model 0 has one layer of weights changeable. For models 2, 1 and 0, Z is the output while x and y are the inputs of UPS-HONN. $c_{kj}{}^{o}$ is the weight for the output layer, $c_{kj}{}^{hx}$ and $c_{kj}{}^{hy}$ are the weights for the second hidden layer, and $c_k{}^{x}$ and $a_j{}^{y}$ are the weights for the first hidden layer. Functions cosine and sine are the first and second hidden layer nodes of UPS-HONN. The output layer node of UPS-HONN is a linear function of $f^o(net^o) = net^o$, where net^o equals the input of output layer node. UPS-HONN is an open neural network model, each weight of HONN has its corresponding coefficient in the model formula, and each node of UPS-HONN has its corresponding function in the model formula. The structure of UPS-HONN is built by a nonlinear formula. It means, after training, there is rationale for each component of UPS-HONN in the nonlinear formula.

Based on Chapter 1 formulae from (1-103) to (1-107: UPS-HONN 2), the UPS-HONN models are defined as follows:

Let

$$f_k{}^{x}\left(c_k{}^{x}x\right) = (c_k{}^{x}x)^k \tag{10-1}$$

$$f_j{}^{y}\left(c_j{}^{y}y\right) = \sin^{j}(j*c_j{}^{y}y) \tag{10-2}$$

UPS - HONN Model 0:

Figure 1. UPS-HONN architecture

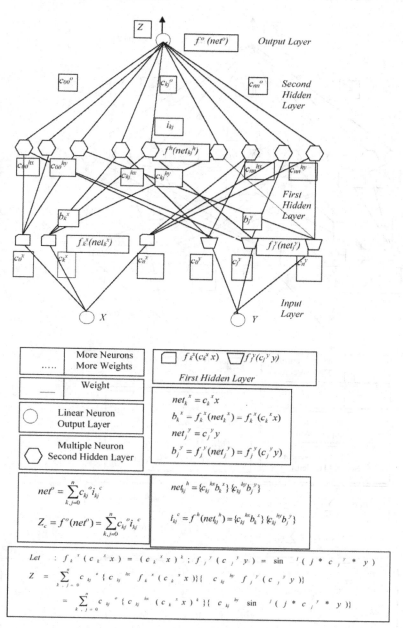

Figure 2. UPS-HONN architecture

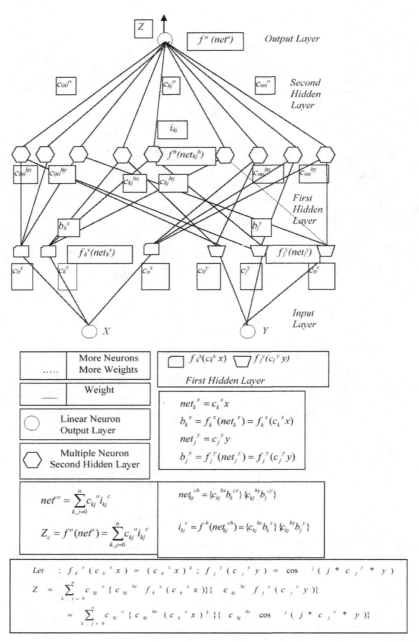

$$z = \sum_{k,j=0}^{n} c_{kj}{}^{o} \left(x \right)^{k} \left(\sin^{j}(j*y) \right)$$

$$\text{where}: \left(c_{kj}{}^{hx} \right) = \left(c_{kj}{}^{hy} \right) = 1 \ \text{and} \ c_{k}{}^{x} = c_{j}{}^{y} = 1 \tag{10-3}$$

UPS - HONN Model 1:

$$z = \sum_{k,j=0}^{n} c_{kj}{}^{o} \left(c_{k}{}^{x} * x \right)^{k} \left(\sin^{j}(j*c_{j}{}^{y}y) \right)$$

$$\text{where}: \left(c_{kj}{}^{hx} \right) = \left(c_{kj}{}^{hy} \right) = 1 \tag{10-4}$$

UPS - HONN Model 2:

$$Z = \sum_{k,j=0}^{n} \left(c_{kj}{}^{o} \right) \{ c_{kj}{}^{hx} (c_{k}{}^{x} * x)^{k} \} \{ c_{kj}{}^{hy} \left(\sin^{j}(j*c_{j}{}^{y}y) \right) \} \tag{10-5}$$

For formula (10-3: UPS-HONN 0), (10-4: UPS-HONN 1), and (10-3: UPS-HONN 2), values of k and j ranges from 0 to n, where n is an integer. The UPS-HONN model can simulate ultra-high frequency time series data, when n increases to a big number. This property of the model allows it to easily simulate and predicate ultra-high frequency time series data, since both k and j increase when there is an increase in n.

The following is an expansion of model UPS-HONN order two. This model is used in later sections to predict the exchange rates.

$$\begin{aligned}
z = {} & c_{00}{}^{o} \ c_{00}{}^{hx} \ c_{00}{}^{hy} \sin^{0}(0*c_{0}{}^{y}y) \\
& + c_{01}{}^{o} \ c_{01}{}^{hx} \ c_{01}{}^{hy} \ \sin(1*c_{1}{}^{y} \ y) \\
& + c_{02}{}^{o} \ c_{02}{}^{hx} \ c_{02}{}^{hy} \ \sin^{2}(2*c_{2}{}^{y} \ y) \\
& + c_{10}{}^{o} \ c_{10}{}^{hx} \ c_{10}{}^{hy} \ (c_{1}{}^{x} \ x) \sin^{0}(0*c_{0}{}^{y}y) \\
& + c_{11}{}^{o} \ c_{11}{}^{hx} \ c_{11}{}^{hy} \ (c_{1}{}^{x} \ x) \sin(1*c_{1}{}^{y} \ y) \\
& + c_{12}{}^{o} \ c_{12}{}^{hx} \ c_{12}{}^{hy} \ (c_{1}{}^{x} \ x) \sin^{2}(2*c_{2}{}^{y} \ y) \\
& + c_{20}{}^{o} \ c_{20}{}^{hx} \ c_{20}{}^{hy} \ (c_{2}{}^{x} \ x)^{2} \sin^{0}(0*c_{0}{}^{y}y) \\
& + c_{21}{}^{o} \ c_{21}{}^{hx} \ c_{21}{}^{hy} \ (c_{2}{}^{x} \ x)^{2} \sin(1*c_{1}{}^{y} \ y) \\
& + c_{22}{}^{o} \ c_{22}{}^{hx} \ c_{22}{}^{hy} \ (c_{2}{}^{x} \ x)^{2} \sin^{2}(2*c_{2}{}^{y} \ y)
\end{aligned} \tag{10–6}$$

The "UPS-HONN Architecture" is shown. This model structure is used to develop the model learning algorithm, which make sure the convergence of learning. This allows the deference between desired output and real output of UPS-HONN close to zero.

UPC-HONN Model

The UPC-HONN models replace the sine functions from UPS-HONN with cosine functions models. Based on Chapter 1 formulae from (1-108) to (1-112: UPC-HONN 2), the UPC-HONN models are defined as follows:

Let

$$f_k^x\left(c_k{}^x x\right) = (c_k{}^x x)^k \tag{10-7}$$

$$f_j^y\left(c_j{}^y y\right) = \cos^j (j * c_j{}^y y) \tag{10-8}$$

UPC – HONN Model 0:

$$z = \sum_{k,j=0}^{n} c_{kj}{}^o \left(x \right)^k \left(\cos^j (j * y) \right) \tag{10-9}$$

$$where : \left(c_{kj}{}^{hx} \right) = \left(c_{kj}{}^{hy} \right) = 1 \ \ and \ c_k{}^x = c_j{}^y = 1$$

UPC – HONN Model 1:

$$z = \sum_{k,j=0}^{n} c_{kj}{}^o \left(c_k{}^x * x \right)^k \left(\cos^j (j * c_j{}^y y) \right) \tag{10-10}$$

$$where : \left(c_{kj}{}^{hx} \right) = \left(c_{kj}{}^{hy} \right) = 1$$

UPC – HONN Model 2:

$$Z = \sum_{k,j=0}^{n} \left(c_{kj}{}^o \right) \{ c_{kj}{}^{hx} (c_k{}^x * x)^k \} \{ c_{kj}{}^{hy} \left(\cos^j (j * c_j{}^y y) \right) \} \tag{10-11}$$

LEARNING ALGORITHM OF UPT-HONN MODELS

The learning formula for the output layer weights in UPS-HONN models and UPC-HONN models are the same. The learning formula for the second-hidden layer weights in the UPS-HONN modes and UPC-HONN models are the same. The learning formula for the first-hidden layer weights in the UPS-HONN models and UPC-HONN models are different. Details are listed here.

Learning Formulae of Output Neurons in UPS-HONN Model and UPC-HONN Model (model 0, 1, and 2)

Based on Chapter 1 formulae from (1-133: A.1) to (1-145: A.13), UPS-HONN models and UPC-HONN models (model 0, 1, and 2) are rewritten as follows:

$$c_{kj}{}^o(t+1) = c_{kj}{}^o(t) - \eta\left(\partial E / \partial c_{kj}{}^o\right) = c_{kj}{}^o(t) + \eta(d-z)f^{o\,\prime}\left(net^o\right)i_{kj} = c_{kj}{}^o(t) + \eta\delta^{ol}i_{kj}$$

where: $\delta o^{l} = (d - z)$

$$f^{o\,\prime}\left(net^o\right) = 1 \quad (\text{linear neuron}) \tag{10-12}$$

Learning Formulae of Second-Hidden Layer Neurons in UPS-HONN Model and UPC-HONN Model (Model 2)

Based on Chapter 1 formulae from (1-146: B.1) to (1-160: B.15), UPS-HONN and UPC-HONN models (model 2) are rewritten as follows:

The weight update question for x input neurons is:

$$
\begin{aligned}
c_{kj}{}^{hx}(t+1) &= c_{kj}{}^{hx}(t) - \eta\left(\partial E / \partial c_{kj}{}^{hx}\right) \\
&= c_{kj}{}^{hx}(t) + \eta\left((d-z)f^{o\,\prime}\left(net^o\right)c_{kj}{}^o f^{h\,\prime}\left(net_{kj}{}^{hx}\right)c_{kj}{}^{hy}b_j{}^y b_k{}^x\right) \\
&= c_{kj}{}^{hx}(t) + \eta\left(\delta^{ol}c_{kj}{}^o\delta_{kj}{}^{hx}b_k{}^x\right)
\end{aligned}
$$

where: $\delta o^{l=} (d - z)$

$$\delta_{kj}^{hx} = c_{kj}^{hy} b_j^{y}$$

$$f^{o'}\left(net^o\right) = 1 \qquad (linear\ neuron)$$

$$f^{h'}\left(net_{kj}^{hx}\right) = 1 \qquad (linear\ neuron) \qquad (10\text{-}13)$$

The weight update question for y input neurons is:

$$c_{kj}^{hy}\left(t+1\right) = c_{kj}^{hy}\left(t\right) - \eta\left(\partial E / \partial c_{kj}^{hy}\right)$$

$$= c_{kj}^{hy}\left(t\right) + \eta\left((d-z) f^{o'}\left(net^o\right) c_{kj}^{o} f^{h'}\left(net_{kj}^{hy}\right) c_{kj}^{hx} b_k^{x} b_j^{y}\right)$$

$$= c_{kj}^{hy}\left(t\right) + \eta\left(\delta^{ol} c_{kj}^{o} \delta_{kj}^{hy} b_j^{y}\right)$$

where: $\delta o^{l=} (d - z)$

$$\delta_{kj}^{hy} = c_{kj}^{hx} b_k^{x}$$

$$f^{o'}\left(net^o\right) = 1 \qquad (linear\ neuron)$$

$$f^{h'}\left(net_{kj}^{hy}\right) = 1 \qquad (linear\ neuron) \qquad (10\text{-}14)$$

General Learning Formulae of First Hidden Layer x Neurons in UPS-HONN Model and UPC-HONN Model (Model 1 and Model 2)

Based on Chapter 1 formulae from (1-161: C.1) to (1-177: C.17), UPS-HONN and UPC-HONN models (model 1 and 2) are rewritten as follows:

For a function of x input side:

$$b_k^{\ x} = f_k^{\ x}\left(net_k^{\ x}\right)$$

$$f_x{}'\left(net_k^{\ x}\right) = \partial b_k^{\ x} / \partial\left(net_k^{\ x}\right) \tag{10-15}$$

$$c_k^{\ x}\left(t+1\right) = c_k^{\ x}\left(t\right) - \eta\left(\partial E_p / \partial c_k^{\ x}\right)$$

$$= c_k^{\ x}\left(t\right) + \eta\left(d-z\right)f^{o\,\prime}\left(net^o\right)c_{kj}^{\ o} * f^{h\,\prime}\left(net_{kj}^{\ h}\right)c_{kj}^{\ hy}b_j^{\ y}c_{kj}^{\ hx}f_x{}'\left(net_k^{\ x}\right)x$$

$$= c_k^{\ x}\left(t\right) + \eta * \delta^{ol} * c_{kj}^{\ o} * \delta^{hx} * c_{kj}^{\ hx} * \delta^x * x$$

where

$$\delta^{ol} = \left(d-z\right)f^{o\,\prime}\left(net^o\right) = d-z \qquad (linear\ neuron)$$

$$\delta^{hx} = f^{h\,\prime}\left(net_{kj}^{\ h}\right)c_{kj}^{\ hy}b_j^{\ y} = c_{kj}^{\ hy}b_j^{\ y} \qquad (linear\ neuron)$$

$$\delta^x = f_x'\left(net_k^{\ x}\right) \tag{10-16}$$

General Learning Formulae of First Hidden Layer y Neurons in UPS-HONN Model and UPC-HONN Model (Model 1 and Model 2)

Based on Chapter 1 formulae from (1-178: D.1) to (1-194: D.17), UPS-HONN and UPC-HONN models (model 1 and 2) are rewritten as follows:

For a function of y input part:

$$b_j^{\ y} = f_j^{\ y}\left(net_j^{\ y}\right)$$

$$f_y{}'\left(net_j^{\ y}\right) = \partial b_j^{\ y} / \partial\left(net_j^{\ y}\right) \tag{10-17}$$

Using the above procedure:

$$c_j^{y}(t+1) = c_j^{y}(t) - \eta\left(\partial E_p / \partial c_j^{y}\right)$$

$$= c_j^{y}(t) + \eta(d-z) f^{o}{}'(net^{o}) c_{kj}^{o} * f^{h}{}'(net_{kj}^{h}) c_{kj}^{hx} b_k^{x} c_{kj}^{hy} f_y{}'(net_j^{y}) y$$

$$= c_j^{y}(t) + \eta * \delta^{ol} * c_{kj}^{o} * \delta^{hy} * c_{kj}^{hy} * \delta^{y} * y$$

where

$$\delta^{ol} = (d-z) f^{o}{}'(net^{o}) = d - z \qquad \left(linear\ neuron\ f^{o}{}'(net^{o}) = 1\right)$$

$$\delta^{hy} = f^{h}{}'(net_{kj}^{h}) c_{kj}^{hx} b_k^{x} = c_{kj}^{hx} b_k^{x} \qquad \left(linear\ neuron\ f^{h}{}'(net_{kj}^{h}) = 1\right)$$

$$\delta^{y} = f_y'(net_j^{y}) \qquad\qquad\qquad\qquad\qquad (10\text{-}18)$$

Learning Formulae of UPS-HONN Model for the First Hidden Layer

The first hidden layer neurons in UPS-HONN (Model 1 and Model 2) use SINC and sine functions. Based on Chapter 1 formulae from (1-303) to (1-308: UPS-HONN D.17), update learning formulae of UPS-HONN models (model 1 and 2) are rewritten as follows:

Let

$$f_k^{x}(c_k^{x}x) = (c_k^{x}x)^k \qquad\qquad\qquad\qquad (10\text{-}19)$$

$$f_j^{y}(c_j^{y}y) = \sin^{j}(j * c_j^{y}y) \qquad\qquad\qquad (10\text{-}20)$$

For a polynomial function of x input side:

$$b_k^{x} = f_k^{x}(net_k^{x}) = (net_k^{x})^k = (c_k^{x} * x)^k$$

$$f_x'\left(net_k{}^x\right) = \partial b_k{}^x / \partial\left(net_k{}^x\right) = \partial\left(net_k{}^x\right)^k\right) / \partial\left(net_k{}^x\right) = k(net_k{}^x)^{k-1} = k*(c_k{}^x * x)^{k-1}$$

$$(10\text{-}21)$$

$$c_k{}^x\left(t+1\right) = c_k{}^x\left(t\right) - \eta\left(\partial E_p / \partial c_k{}^x\right)$$

$$= c_k{}^x\left(t\right) + \eta\left(d-z\right) f^{o'}\left(net^o\right) c_{kj}{}^o * f^{h'}\left(net_{kj}{}^h\right) c_{kj}{}^{hy} b_j{}^y c_{kj}{}^{hx} f_x'\left(net_k{}^x\right) x$$

$$= c_k{}^x\left(t\right) + \eta * \delta^{ol} * c_{kj}{}^o * \delta^{hx} * c_{kj}{}^{hx} * k*(c_k{}^x * x)^{k-1} * x$$

$$= c_k{}^x\left(t\right) + \eta * \delta^{ol} * c_{kj}{}^o * \delta^{hx} * c_{kj}{}^{hx} * \delta^x * x$$

$$(10\text{-}22)$$

where

$$\delta^{ol} = \left(d-z\right) f^{o'}\left(net^o\right) = d-z \qquad \left(linear\ neuron\ f^{o\,'}\left(net^o\right) = 1\right)$$

$$\delta^{hx} = f^{h'}\left(net_{kj}{}^h\right) c_{kj}{}^{hy} b_j{}^y = c_{kj}{}^{hy} b_j{}^y \qquad \left(linear\ neuron\ f^{h\,'}\left(net_{kj}{}^h\right) = 1\right)$$

$$\delta^x = f_x'\left(net_k{}^x\right) = k*\left(net_k{}^x\right)^{k-1} = k*(c_k{}^x * x)^{k-1}$$

For an ultra-high frequency sine function of *y* input part:

$$b_j{}^y = f_j{}^y\left(net_j{}^y\right) = \sin^j(j*net_j{}^y) = \sin^j(j*c_j{}^y * y)$$

$$f_y'\left(net_j{}^y\right) = \partial b_j{}^y / \partial\left(net_j{}^y\right)$$

$$= \partial\left(\sin^j(j*net_j{}^y)\right) / \partial\left(net_j{}^y\right) = j\sin^{j-1}(j*net_j{}^y)*\cos(j*net_j{}^y)*j$$

$$= j^2 * \sin^{j-1}(j*net_j{}^y)*\cos(j*net_j{}^y) = j^2 * \sin^{j-1}(j*c_j{}^y * y)*\cos(j*c_j{}^y * y)$$

$$(10\text{-}23)$$

Using the above procedure:

$$c_j^{\ y}(t+1) = c_j^{\ y}(t) - \eta\left(\partial E_p / \partial c_j^{\ y}\right)$$

$$= c_j^{\ y}(t) + \eta(d-z)f^{o\,\prime}\left(net^o\right)c_{kj}^{\ o} * f^{h\,\prime}\left(net_{kj}^{\ h}\right)c_{kj}^{\ hx}b_k^{\ x}c_{kj}^{\ hy}f_y^{\ \prime}\left(net_j^{\ y}\right)y$$

$$= c_j^{\ y}(t) + \eta * \delta^{ol} * c_{kj}^{\ o} * \delta^{hy} * c_{kj}^{\ hy} * \left(j^2\right)\sin^{j-1}(j*c_j^{\ y}*y)\cos(j*c_j^{\ y}*y)*y$$

$$= c_j^{\ y}(t) + \eta * \delta^{ol} * c_{kj}^{\ o} * \delta^{hy} * c_{kj}^{\ hy} * \delta^y * y$$

$$(10\text{-}24)$$

where

$$\delta^{ol} = (d-z)f^{o\,\prime}\left(net^o\right) = d-z \qquad\qquad \left(linear\ neuron\ f^{o\,\prime}\left(net^o\right) = 1\right)$$

$$\delta^{hy} = f^{h\,\prime}\left(net_{kj}^{\ hy}\right)c_{kj}^{\ hx}b_k^{\ x} = c_{kj}^{\ hx}b_k^{\ x} \qquad\qquad \left(linear\ neuron\ f^{h\,\prime}\left(net_{kj}^{\ hy}\right) = 1\right)$$

$$\delta^y = f_y^{\ \prime}\left(net_j^{\ y}\right) = \left(j^2\right)\sin^{j-1}(j*c_j^{\ y}*y)\cos(j*c_j^{\ y}*y)$$

Learning Formulae of UPC-HONN Model for the First Hidden Layer

The first hidden layer neurons in UPC-HONN (Model 1 and Model 2) use SINC and cosine functions. Based on Chapter 1 formulae from (1-309) to (1-314: UPC-HONN D.17), update learning formulae of UPC-HONN models (model 1 and 2) are rewritten as follows:

Let

$$f_k^{\ x}\left(c_k^{\ x}x\right) = (c_k^{\ x}x)^k \qquad\qquad\qquad (10\text{-}25)$$

$$f_j^y\left(c_j^y y\right) = \cos^j(j * c_j^y y) \tag{10-26}$$

For a polynomial function of x input side:

$$b_k^x = f_k^x\left(net_k^x\right) = (net_k^x)^k = (c_k^x * x)^k$$

$$f_x'\left(net_k^x\right) = \partial b_k^x / \partial\left(net_k^x\right) = \partial\left(net_k^x)^k\right) / \partial\left(net_k^x\right) = k(net_k^x)^{k-1} = k * (c_k^x * x)^{k-1} \tag{10-27}$$

$$c_k^x\left(t+1\right) = c_k^x\left(t\right) - \eta\left(\frac{\partial E_p}{\partial c_k^x}\right)$$

$$= c_k^x\left(t\right) + \eta\left(d-z\right) f^{o'}\left(net^o\right) c_{kj}^o * f^{h'}\left(net_{kj}^h\right) c_{kj}^{hy} b_j^y c_{kj}^{hx} f_x'\left(net_k^x\right) x$$

$$= c_k^x\left(t\right) + \eta * \delta^{ol} * c_{kj}^o * \delta^{hx} * c_{kj}^{hx} * k * (c_k^x * x)^{k-1} * x$$

$$= c_k^x\left(t\right) + \eta * \delta^{ol} * c_{kj}^o * \delta^{hx} * c_{kj}^{hx} * \delta^x * x \tag{10-28}$$

where

$$\delta^{ol} = \left(d-z\right) f^{o'}\left(net^o\right) = d-z \qquad \left(\text{linear neuron } f^{o\,'}\left(net^o\right) = 1\right)$$

$$\delta^{hx} = f^{h'}\left(net_{kj}^h\right) c_{kj}^{hy} b_j^y = c_{kj}^{hy} b_j^y \quad \left(\text{linear neuron } f^{h\,'}\left(net_{kj}^h\right) = 1\right)$$

$$\delta^x = f_x'\left(net_k^x\right) = k * \left(net_k^x\right)^{k-1} = k * (c_k^x * x)^{k-1}$$

For an ultra-high frequency cosine function of y input part:

$$b_j^y = f_j^y\left(net_j^y\right) = \cos^j(j * net_j^y) = \cos^j(j * c_j^y * y)$$

$$f_y{}'\left(net_j{}^y\right) = \partial b^y{}_j \,/\, \partial\left(net_j{}^y\right)$$

$$= \partial\left(\cos^j(j*net_j{}^y)\right)/\partial\left(net_j{}^y\right) = j\cos^{j-1}(j*net_j{}^y)*\left(-\sin(j*net_j{}^y)\right)*j$$

$$= -j^2*\cos^{j-1}(j*net_j{}^y)*\sin(j*net_j{}^y) = -j^2*\cos^{j-1}(j*c_j{}^y*y)*\sin(j*c_j{}^y*y)$$

$$(10\text{-}29)$$

Using the above procedure:

$$c_j{}^y(t+1) = c_j{}^y(t) - \eta\left(\partial E_p \,/\, \partial c_j{}^y\right)$$

$$= c_j{}^y(t) + \eta(d-z)f^o{}'\left(net^o\right)c_{kj}{}^o*f^h{}'\left(net_{kj}{}^h\right)c_{kj}{}^{hx}b_k{}^x c_{kj}{}^{hy}f_y{}'\left(net_j{}^y\right)y$$

$$= c_j{}^y(t) + \eta*\delta^{ol}*c_{kj}{}^o*\delta^{hy}*c_{kj}{}^{hy}*\left(-j^2\right)*\cos^{j-1}(j*c_j{}^y*y)*\sin(j*c_j{}^y*y)*y$$

$$= c_j{}^y(t) + \eta*\delta^{ol}*c_{kj}{}^o*\delta^{hy}*c_{kj}{}^{hy}*\delta^y*y$$

$$(10\text{-}30)$$

where

$$\delta^{ol} = (d-z)f^o{}'\left(net^o\right) = d-z \qquad\qquad \left(linear\ neuron\ f^o{}'\left(net^o\right)=1\right)$$

$$\delta^{hy} = f^h{}'\left(net_{kj}{}^{hy}\right)c_{kj}{}^{hx}b_k{}^x = c_{kj}{}^{hx}b_k{}^x \qquad \left(linear\ neuron\ f^h{}'\left(net_{kj}{}^{hy}\right)=1\right)$$

$$\delta^y = f_y{}'\left(net_j{}^y\right) = \left(-j^2\right)*\cos^{j-1}(j*c_j{}^y*y)*\sin(j*c_j{}^y*y)$$

UPT-HONN TESTING

UPS-HONN model is used to generate the control signals. The test results are shown in Table 1 and Figure 3. Next, test results for the control signals generated by UPC-HONN model are shown in Table 2 and Figure 4.

In Table 1, UPS-HONN model 0 has been used. The order number for UPS-HONN model is 6. In the first table of Table 1, the "No." column shows a total of 19 points are chosen. The "UPS-HONN x" column displays the input x values, which are all "1" s. The "UPS-HONN y" column displays the input y values, which are 0, 0.1, 0.2, 0.3, 0.4, 05, 0.7, 0.8, 0.9, 1, 2, 3, 4, 5, 6, 7 and 8. The "UPS-HONN z" column displays the output z values. The "Desired Signal" column displays the desired signal values. The "Absolute Desired Signal" column displays the absolute values for desired signal. The "Difference" column shows the difference between UPS-HONN output z and the desired signal (UPS-HONN z - Desired Signal). The "Absolute Difference" column shows the absolute difference between UPS-HONN output z and the desired signal (|UPS-HONN z - Desired Signal|). The "UPS-HONN Error %" column gives the error percentage for UPS-HONN Model (UPS-HONN error % = absolute difference / Absolute Desired Signal * 100%). The average UPS-HONN error is 0.00002383%, which is much closer to zero. After training UPS-HONN model by using desired signal values, in the second table of Table 1, the coefficients for UPS-HONN are displayed. For examples, $c_{00}{}^o= 0.7082$, $c_{01}{}^o= 0.1200$, and $c_{10}{}^o= -0.5910$. In the third table of Table 1, gives the values for $c_{kj}{}^o*(x)^k*sin^j(j*y)$, when $x=1, y=0.1, k=0,1,2,3,4,5,6$, and $j=0,1,2,3,4,5,6$. For example, $c_{01}{}^o*(1)^0*sin^1(1*0.1)=0.01198001$, $c_{02}{}^o*(1)^0*sin^2(2*0.1)=0.01736370$, and $c_{03}{}^o*(1)^0*sin^3(3*0.1)=-0.11646451$. And $z=å$ $c_{kj}{}^o*(x)^k*sin^j(j*y) =å$ $c_{kj}{}^o*(1)^k*sin^j(j*0.1) =-0.43642320$.

In Figure 3, UPS-HONN signal generator results are shown. Designed signals are shown by solid line. And UPS-HONN generated signals are shown by using dashed line. Evidence from Figure 3 suggests that UPS-HONN signal generator can match the desired signals well, since the average error percentage is close to 10^{-6}.

Based on the training of UPS-HONN model, UPS-HONN signal generator has the following formula:

$$z=å\ c_{kj}{}^o*(x)^k*sin^j(j*y)\ (k, j = 0,1,2,3,4,5,6,)$$
$$= c_{00}{}^o*(x)^0*sin^0(0*y) + c_{10}{}^o*(x)^1*sin^0(0*y) + c_{20}{}^o*(x)^2*sin^0(0*y) + c_{30}{}^o*(x)^3*sin^0(0*y)$$
$$+ c_{40}{}^o*(x)^4*sin^0(0*y) + c_{50}{}^o*(x)^5*sin^0(0*y) + c_{60}{}^o*(x)^6*sin^0(0*y)$$
$$+c_{01}{}^o*(x)^0*sin^1(1*y) + c_{11}{}^o*(x)^1*sin^1(1*y) + c_{21}{}^o*(x)^2*sin^1(1*y) + c_{31}{}^o*(x)^3*sin^1(1*y)$$
$$+ c_{41}{}^o*(x)^4*sin^1(1*y) + c_{51}{}^o*(x)^5*sin^1(1*y) + c_{61}{}^o*(x)^6*sin^1(1*y)$$
$$+c_{02}{}^o*(x)^0*sin^2(2*y) + c_{12}{}^o*(x)^1*sin^2(2*y) + c_{22}{}^o*(x)^2*sin^2(2*y) + c_{32}{}^o*(x)^3*sin^2(2*y)$$
$$+ c_{42}{}^o*(x)^4*sin^2(2*y) + c_{52}{}^o*(x)^5*sin^2(2*y) + c_{62}{}^o*(x)^6*sin^2(2*y)$$
$$+c_{03}{}^o*(x)^0*sin^3(3*y) + c_{13}{}^o*(x)^1*sin^3(3*y) + c_{23}{}^o*(x)^2*sin^3(3*y) + c_{33}{}^o*(x)^3*sin^3(3*y)$$

$+ c_{43}{}^{o}*(x)^4*\sin^3(3*y) + c_{53}{}^{o}*(x)^5*\sin^3(3*y) + c_{63}{}^{o}*(x)^6*\sin^3(3*y)$

$+c_{04}{}^{o}*(x)^0*\sin^4(4*y) + c_{14}{}^{o}*(x)^1*\sin^4(4*y) + c_{24}{}^{o}*(x)^2*\sin^4(4*y) + c_{34}{}^{o}*(x)^3*\sin^4(4*y)$

$+ c_{44}{}^{o}*(x)^4*\sin^4(4*y) + c_{54}{}^{o}*(x)^5*\sin^4(4*y) + c_{64}{}^{o}*(x)^6*\sin^4(4*y)$

$+c_{05}{}^{o}*(x)^0*\sin^5(5*y) + c_{15}{}^{o}*(x)^1*\sin^5(5*y) + c_{25}{}^{o}*(x)^2*\sin^5(4*y) + c_{35}{}^{o}*(x)^3*\sin^5(5*y)$

$+ c_{45}{}^{o}*(x)^4*\sin^5(5*y) + c_{55}{}^{o}*(x)^5*\sin^5(5*y) + c_{65}{}^{o}*(x)^6*\sin^5(5*y)$

$+c_{06}{}^{o}*(x)^0*\sin^6(6*y) + c_{16}{}^{o}*(x)^1*\sin^6(6*y) + c_{26}{}^{o}*(x)^2*\sin^6(6*y) + c_{36}{}^{o}*(x)^3*\sin^6(6*y)$

$+ c_{46}{}^{o}*(x)^4*\sin^6(6*y) + c_{56}{}^{o}*(x)^5*\sin^6(6*y) + c_{66}{}^{o}*(x)^6*\sin^6(6*y)$

$= 0.7082*(x)^0*\sin^0(0*y) +(-0.5910)*(x)^1*\sin^0(0*y) +(-0.7788)*(x)^2*\sin^0(0*y)$

$+ (-0.6533)*(x)^3*\sin^0(0*y) +(-1.3808)*(x)^4*\sin^0(0*y)$

$+ (-0.6622)*(x)^5*\sin^0(0*y) + 1.2421*(x)^6*\sin^0(0*y)$

$+0.1200*(x)^0*\sin^1(1*y)+0.2814*(x)^1*\sin^1(1*y)+(-0.2746)*(x)^2*\sin^1(1*y)$

$+ (-0.1233)*(x)^3*\sin^1(1*y) + 0.1021*(x)^4*\sin^1(1*y)$

$+ 0.4677*(x)^5*\sin^1(1*y) + (-0.2658)*(x)^6*\sin^1(1*y)$

$+0.0874*(x)^0*\sin^2(2*y)+0.0153*(x)^1*\sin^2(2*y)+(-0.0034)*(x)^2*\sin^2(2*y)$

$+ (-0.6101)*(x)^3*\sin^2(2*y) + (-0.1802)*(x)^4*\sin^2(2*y)$

$+ 0.0611*(x)^5*\sin^2(2*y) + (-0.3341)*(x)^6*\sin^2(2*y)$

$+ (-0.3941)*(x)^0*\sin^3(3*y) + (-0.0935)*(x)^1*\sin^3(3*y) + (-0.8050)*(x)^2*\sin^3(3*y)$

$+ 0.0872*(x)^3*\sin^3(3*y) + 0.3306*(x)^4*\sin^3(3*y)$

$+ (-0.1748)*(x)^5*\sin^3(3*y) + 0.0299*(x)^6*\sin^3(3*y)$

$+(-0.9193)*(x)^0*\sin^4(4*y) + 0.7422*(x)^1*\sin^4(4*y) + (-0.3561)*(x)^2*\sin^4(4*y)$

$+ 0.0324*(x)^3*\sin^4(4*y) + (-0.0043)*(x)^4*\sin^4(4*y)$

$+ 0.2020*(x)^5*\sin^4(4*y) + 0.9701*(x)^6*\sin^4(4*y)$

$+(-0.5921)*(x)^0*\sin^5(5*y)+0.3590*(x)^1*\sin^5(5*y)+0.6168*(x)^2*\sin^5(4*y)$

$+ 0.4320*(x)^3*\sin^5(5*y) + 0.1921*(x)^4*\sin^5(5*y)$

$+ (-0.7954)*(x)^5*\sin^5(5*y) + (-0.6462)*(x)^6*\sin^5(5*y)$

$+0.4562*(x)^0*\sin^6(6*y)+(-0.1482)*(x)^1*\sin^6(6*y)+0.7517*(x)^2*\sin^6(6*y)$

$+ (-0.8923)*(x)^3*\sin^6(6*y) + (-0.3717)*(x)^4*\sin^6(6*y)$

$+ (-0.4859)*(x)^5*\sin^6(6*y) + 0.6441*(x)^6*\sin^6(6*y)$

In Table 2, UPC-HONN model 0 has been used. The order number for UPC-HONN model is 6. In the first table of Table 1, the "No." column shows total 19 points are chosen. The "UPC-HONN x" column displays the input x values, which are all "1" has been used. The "UPC-HONN y" column displays the input y values, which are 0, 0.1, 0.2, 0.3, 0.4, 05, 0.7, 0.8, 0.9, 1, 2, 3, 4, 5, 6, 7 and 8. The "UPC-HONN z" column displays the output z values. The "Desired Signal" column displays the desired signal values. The "Absolute Desired Signal" column displays the absolute values for desired signal. The "Difference" column shows the difference between UPC-HONN output z and the desired signal (UPC-HONN z - Desired Signal). The "Absolute Difference" column shows the absolute difference between UPC-HONN output z and the desired signal (|UPC-HONN z - Desired Signal|). The "UPC-HONN Error %" column gives the error percentage for UPC-HONN Model (UPC-HONN error % = absolute difference / Absolute Desired Signal * 100%). The average UPC-HONN error is 0.00001231%, which is very close to zero. After training UPC-HONN model by using desired signal values, in the second table of Table 2, the UPC-HONN all coefficients are displayed. For examples, $c_{00}{}^o =$ 1.4159, $c_{01}{}^o = 0.9866$, and $c_{10}{}^o = -1.6558$. In the third table of Table 2, gives the values for $c_{kj}{}^o*(x)^k*cos^j(j*y)$, when $x=1$, $y=0.1$, $k=0,1,2,3,4,5,6$, and $j=0,1,2,3,4,5,6$. For examples, $c_{01}{}^o*(1)^0*cos^1(1*0.1)=0.98167111$, $c_{02}{}^o*(1)^0*cos^2(2*0.1)=0.14005151$, and $c_{03}{}^o*(1)^0*cos^3(3*0.1)=-0.80104965$.

And $z = å\, c_{kj}{}^o*(x)^k*cos^j(j*y) = å\, c_{kj}{}^o*(1)^k*cos^j(j*0.1) = -1.65434689$.

In Figure 4, UPC-HONN signal generator results are shown. Designed signals are shown by solid line. And UPC-HONN generated signals are shown by using dashed line. Figure 4 presents the results that UPC-HONN signal generator can match the desired signals well, since the average error percentage is close to 10^{-6}.

Based on the training of UPC-HONN model, UPC-HONN signal generator has the following formula:

$z = å\, c_{kj}{}^o*(x)^k*cos^j(j*y)$ $(k, j = 0,1,2,3,4,5,6,)$
$= c_{00}{}^o*(x)^0*cos^0(0*y) + c_{10}{}^o*(x)^1*cos^0(0*y) + c_{20}{}^o*(x)^2*cos^0(0*y) + c_{30}{}^o*(x)^3*cos^0(0*y)$
$+ c_{40}{}^o*(x)^4*cos^0(0*y) + c_{50}{}^o*(x)^5*cos^0(0*y) + c_{60}{}^o*(x)^6*cos^0(0*y)$
$+ c_{01}{}^o*(x)^0*cos^1(1*y) + c_{11}{}^o*(x)^1*cos^1(1*y) + c_{21}{}^o*(x)^2*cos^1(1*y) + c_{31}{}^o*(x)^3*cos^1(1*y)$
$+ c_{41}{}^o*(x)^4*cos^1(1*y) + c_{51}{}^o*(x)^5*cos^1(1*y) + c_{61}{}^o*(x)^6*cos^1(1*y)$
$+ c_{02}{}^o*(x)^0*cos^2(2*y) + c_{12}{}^o*(x)^1*cos^2(2*y) + c_{22}{}^o*(x)^2*cos^2(2*y) + c_{32}{}^o*(x)^3*cos^2(2*y)$
$+ c_{42}{}^o*(x)^4*cos^2(2*y) + c_{52}{}^o*(x)^5*cos^2(2*y) + c_{62}{}^o*(x)^6*cos^2(2*y)$
$+ c_{03}{}^o*(x)^0*cos^3(3*y) + c_{13}{}^o*(x)^1*cos^3(3*y) + c_{23}{}^o*(x)^2*cos^3(3*y) + c_{33}{}^o*(x)^3*cos^3(3*y)$
$+ c_{43}{}^o*(x)^4*cos^3(3*y) + c_{53}{}^o*(x)^5*cos^3(3*y) + c_{63}{}^o*(x)^6*cos^3(3*y)$

$+c_{04}{}^{o}*(x)^0*\cos^4(4*y) + c_{14}{}^{o}*(x)^1*\cos^4(4*y) + c_{24}{}^{o}*(x)^2*\cos^4(4*y) +$
$\quad c_{34}{}^{o}*(x)^3*\cos^4(4*y)$

$+ c_{44}{}^{o}*(x)^4*\cos^4(4*y) + c_{54}{}^{o}*(x)^5*\cos^4(4*y) + c_{64}{}^{o}*(x)^6*\cos^4(4*y)$

$+c_{05}{}^{o}*(x)^0*\cos^5(5*y) + c_{15}{}^{o}*(x)^1*\cos^5(5*y) + c_{25}{}^{o}*(x)^2*\cos^5(4*y) +$
$\quad c_{35}{}^{o}*(x)^3*\cos^5(5*y)$

$+ c_{45}{}^{o}*(x)^4*\cos^5(5*y) + c_{55}{}^{o}*(x)^5*\cos^5(5*y) + c_{65}{}^{o}*(x)^6*\cos^5(5*y)$

$+c_{06}{}^{o}*(x)^0*\cos^6(6*y) + c_{16}{}^{o}*(x)^1*\cos^6(6*y) + c_{26}{}^{o}*(x)^2*\cos^6(6*y) +$
$\quad c_{36}{}^{o}*(x)^3*\cos^6(6*y)$

$+ c_{46}{}^{o}*(x)^4*\cos^6(6*y) + c_{56}{}^{o}*(x)^5*\cos^6(6*y) + c_{66}{}^{o}*(x)^6*\cos^6(6*y)$

$= 1.4159*(x)^0*\cos^0(0*y) +(-1.6558)*(x)^1*\cos^0(0*y) +(-0.3245)$
$\quad *(x)^2*\cos^0(0*y)$

$+ (-1.0977)*(x)^3*\cos^0(0*y) +0.7113*(x)^4*\cos^0(0*y)$

$+ (-0.8844)*(x)^5*\cos^0(0*y) + 1.3532*(x)^6*\cos^0(0*y)$

$+0.9866*(x)^0*\cos^1(1*y)+0.8369*(x)^1*\cos^1(1*y)+(-0.9190)*(x)^2*\cos^1(1*y)$

$+ (-0.4566)*(x)^3*\cos^1(1*y) + 0.3243*(x)^4*\cos^1(1*y)$

$+ 0.5788*(x)^5*\cos^1(1*y) + (-1.0435)*(x)^6*\cos^1(1*y)$

$+0.1429*(x)^0*\cos^2(2*y)+0.4597*(x)^1*\cos^2(2*y)+(-0.3367)*(x)^2*\cos^2(2*y)$

$+ (-0.8323)*(x)^3*\cos^2(2*y) + (-0.2913)*(x)^4*\cos^2(2*y)$

$+ 8388*(x)^5*\cos^2(2*y) + (-1.0007)*(x)^6*\cos^2(2*y)$

$+ (-0.8385)*(x)^0*\cos^3(3*y) + (-0.1268)*(x)^1*\cos^3(3*y) + (-1.0272)$
$\quad *(x)^2*\cos^3(3*y)$

$+ 0.1983*(x)^3*\cos^3(3*y) + 1.1013*(x)^4*\cos^3(3*y)$

$+ (-0.8414)*(x)^5*\cos^3(3*y) + 0.1854*(x)^6*\cos^3(3*y)$

$+(-1.2526)*(x)^0*\cos^4(4*y) + 0.9644*(x)^1*\cos^4(4*y) + (-0.4672)$
$\quad *(x)^2*\cos^4(4*y)$

$+ 0.1435*(x)^3*\cos^4(4*y) + (-0.6709)*(x)^4*\cos^4(4*y)$

$+ 0.7575*(x)^5*\cos^4(4*y) + 1.4145*(x)^6*\cos^4(4*y)$

$+(-0.8143)*(x)^0*\cos^5(5*y)+0.4701*(x)^1*\cos^5(5*y)+0.3945*(x)^2*\cos^5(4*y)$

$+ 1.0986*(x)^3*\cos^5(5*y) + 0.7476*(x)^4*\cos^5(5*y)$

$+ (-0.6394)*(x)^5*\cos^5(5*y) + (-0.9793)*(x)^6*\cos^5(5*y)$

$+0.5673*(x)^0*\cos^6(6*y)+(-0.3724)*(x)^1*\cos^6(6*y)+1.0850*(x)^2*\cos^6(6*y)$

$+ (-0.3367)*(x)^3*\cos^6(6*y) + (-0.9272)*(x)^4*\cos^6(6*y)$

$+ (-0.1525)*(x)^5*\cos^6(6*y) + 0.4217*(x)^6*\cos^6(6*y)$

Table 1. UPS-HONN Signal Generator (n = 6, Model 0)

No.	UPS-HONN x	UPS-HONN y	UPS-HONN z	Desired Signal	Absolute Desired Signal	Difference	Absolute Difference	UPS-HONN Error %
1	1	0	0.00000000	0.000000	0.000000	0.00000000	0.00000000	0.000000%
2	1	0.1	-0.43642320	-0.436423	0.436423	-0.00000020	0.00000020	0.000019%
3	1	0.2	-0.81959500	-0.819595	0.819595	0.00000000	0.00000000	0.000000%
4	1	0.3	-1.10813896	-1.108139	1.108139	0.00000004	0.00000004	0.000004%
5	1	0.4	-1.28106187	-1.281062	1.281062	0.00000013	0.00000013	0.000012%
6	1	0.5	-1.34052178	-1.340522	1.340522	0.00000022	0.00000022	0.000021%
7	1	0.6	-1.30817427	-1.308174	1.308174	-0.00000027	0.00000027	0.000026%
8	1	0.7	-1.21630469	-1.216305	1.216305	0.00000031	0.00000031	0.000030%
9	1	0.8	-1.09648320	-1.096483	1.096483	-0.00000020	0.00000020	0.000020%
10	1	0.9	-0.96919948	-0.969199	0.969199	-0.00000048	0.00000048	0.000047%
11	1	1	-0.83763532	-0.837635	0.837635	-0.00000032	0.00000032	0.000031%
13	1	2	2.21472087	2.214721	2.214721	-0.00000013	0.00000013	0.000013%
14	1	3	-0.71285477	-0.712855	0.712855	0.00000023	0.00000023	0.000023%
15	1	4	-1.18563471	-1.185634	1.185634	-0.00000071	0.00000071	0.000069%
16	1	5	0.27836556	0.278366	0.278366	-0.00000044	0.00000044	0.000043%
17	1	6	1.06742608	1.067426	1.067426	0.00000008	0.00000008	0.000008%
18	1	7	-1.19736842	-1.197368	1.197368	-0.00000042	0.00000042	0.000041%
19	1	8	1.58517276	1.585173	1.585173	-0.00000024	0.00000024	0.000023%
Average					1.0363933		0.0000002470	0.00002383%

c_{kj}^{o}	k=0	k=1	k=2	k=3	k=4	k=5	k=6
j=0	0.7082	-0.5910	-0.7788	-0.6533	-1.3808	-0.6622	1.2421
j=1	0.1200	0.2814	-0.2746	-0.1233	0.1021	0.4677	-0.2658
j=2	0.0874	0.0153	-0.0034	-0.6101	-0.1802	0.0611	-0.3341
j=3	-0.3941	-0.0935	-0.8050	0.0872	0.3306	-0.1748	0.0299
j=4	-0.9193	0.7422	-0.3561	0.0324	-0.0043	0.2020	0.9701
j=5	-0.5921	0.3590	0.6168	0.4320	0.1921	-0.7954	-0.6462
j=6	0.4562	-0.1482	0.7517	-0.8923	-0.3717	-0.4859	0.6441

x=1, y=0.1	k =	k =	k =	k =	k =	k =	k =
$c_{kj}^{o}*(x)^{k}*\sin^{j}(j*y)$	0	1	2	3	4	5	6
j = 0	0.00000000	0.00000000	0.00000000	0.00000000	0.00000000	0.00000000	0.00000000
j = 1	0.01198001	0.02809312	-0.02741426	-0.01230946	0.01019299	0.04669209	-0.02653572
j = 2	0.01736370	0.00303964	-0.00067548	-0.12120816	-0.03580021	0.01213870	-0.06637542
j = 3	-0.11646451	-0.02763114	-0.23789377	0.02576936	0.09769898	-0.05165693	0.00883605
j = 4	-0.35799228	0.28902629	-0.13867187	0.01261715	-0.00167450	0.07866251	0.37777473
j = 5	-0.28386786	0.17211377	0.29570967	0.20711183	0.09209765	-0.38133507	-0.30980478
j = 6	0.25758990	-0.08368001	0.42444175	-0.50383048	-0.20987761	-0.27435978	0.36368622
Subtotal	-0.47139105	0.38096167	0.31549605	-0.39184975	-0.04736270	-0.56985849	0.34758108
$z = \Sigma c_{kj}^{o}*(x)^{k}*\sin^{j}(j*y)$		(k= 0, 1, 2, 3, 4, 5, 6		j = 0, 1, 2, 3, 4, 5, 6) =			-0.43642320

Figure 3. UPS-HONN signal generator

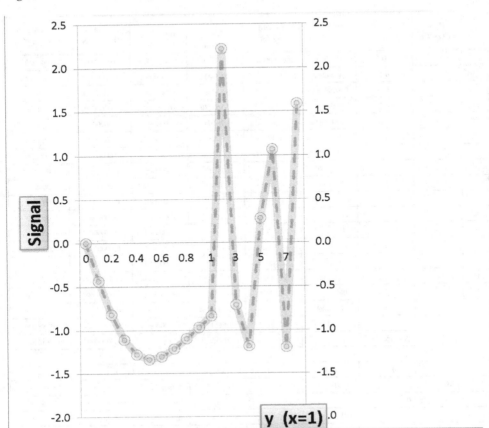

FUTHER RESEARCH DIRECTIONS

As the next step of HONN model research, more HONN models for different data control will be built to increase the pool of HONN models. Theoretically, the adaptive HONN models can be built and allow the computer automatically to choose the best model, order, and coefficients. Thus, making the adaptive HONN models easier to use is one of the future research topics.

HONNs can automatically select the initial coefficients for nonlinear data analysis. The next step of this study will also focus on how to allow people working in the control area to understand that HONNs are much easier to use and can have better results. Moreover, further research will develop

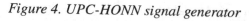

Figure 4. UPC-HONN signal generator

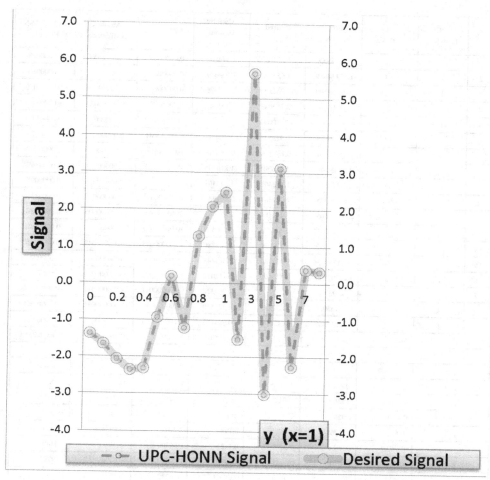

HONNs software packages for people working in the control area. HONNs will challenge classic procedures and change the research methodology that people are currently using in the control areas for the nonlinear data control application.

CONCLUSION

Two nonlinear neural network models, UPS-HONN and UPC-HONN, that are part of the Ultra High Frequency Polynomial and Trigonometric Higher

Table 2. UPC-HONN Signal Generator (n = 6, Model 0)

No.	UPC-HONN x	UPC-HONN y	UPC-HONN z	Desired Signal	Absolute Desired Signal	Difference	Absolute Difference	UPC-HONN Error %
1	1	0	-1.37456000	-1.374560	1.374560	0.00000000	0.00000000	0.000000%
2	1	0.1	-1.65434689	-1.654347	1.654347	0.00000011	0.00000011	0.000006%
3	1	0.2	-2.06259599	-2.062596	2.062596	0.00000001	0.00000001	0.000001%
4	1	0.3	-2.35404267	-2.354043	2.354043	0.00000033	0.00000033	0.000017%
5	1	0.4	-2.31009427	-2.310094	2.310094	-0.00000027	0.00000027	0.000014%
6	1	0.5	-0.92883259	-0.928833	0.928833	0.00000041	0.00000041	0.000021%
7	1	0.6	0.18761830	0.187618	0.187618	0.00000030	0.00000030	0.000016%
8	1	0.7	-1.21630469	-1.216305	1.216305	0.00000031	0.00000031	0.000016%
9	1	0.8	1.27246117	1.272461	1.272461	0.00000017	0.00000017	0.000009%
10	1	0.9	2.08134375	2.081344	2.081344	-0.00000025	0.00000025	0.000013%
11	1	1	2.46216605	2.462166	2.462166	0.00000005	0.00000005	0.000002%
13	1	2	-1.52657837	-1.526578	1.526578	-0.00000037	0.00000037	0.000019%
14	1	3	5.66527952	5.66528	5.665280	-0.00000048	0.00000048	0.000025%
15	1	4	-3.01334336	-3.0133433	3.013343	-0.00000006	0.00000006	0.000003%
16	1	5	3.11207179	3.112072	3.112072	-0.00000021	0.00000021	0.000011%
17	1	6	-2.26932211	-2.269322	2.269322	-0.00000011	0.00000011	0.000006%
18	1	7	0.37953036	0.37953	0.379530	0.00000036	0.00000036	0.000019%
19	1	8	0.32413459	0.324135	0.324135	-0.00000041	0.00000041	0.000022%
Average					1.8997015		0.0000002339	0.00001231%

$c_{kj}{}^o$	k=0	k=1	k=2	k=3	k=4	k=5	k=6
j=0	1.4159	-1.6558	-0.3245	-1.0977	0.7113	-0.8844	1.3532
j=1	0.9866	0.8369	-0.9190	-0.4566	0.3243	0.5788	-1.0435
j=2	0.1429	0.4597	-0.3367	-0.8323	-0.2913	0.8388	-1.0007
j=3	-0.8385	-0.1268	-1.0272	0.1983	1.1013	-0.8414	0.1854
j=4	-1.2526	0.9644	-0.4672	0.1435	-0.6709	0.7575	1.4145
j=5	-0.8143	0.4701	0.3945	1.0986	0.7476	-0.6394	-0.9793
j=6	0.5673	-0.3724	1.0850	-0.3367	-0.9272	-0.1525	0.4217

x=1, y=0.1	k =	k =	k =	k =	k =	k =	k =
$c_{kj}{}^{o*}(x)^{k*}\cos^j(j*y)$	0	1	2	3	4	5	6
j = 0	1.41590000	-1.65576000	-0.32450000	-1.09770000	0.71130000	-0.88440000	1.35320000
j = 1	0.98167111	0.83271899	-0.91440883	-0.45431890	0.03237598	0.57590841	-1.03828685
j = 2	0.14005151	0.45053661	-0.32998842	-0.81570941	-0.05787238	0.82207985	-0.98075262
j = 3	-0.80104965	-0.12113667	-0.98132164	0.18944323	0.32545640	-0.80382012	0.17711939
j = 4	-1.15372100	0.88827122	-0.43031970	0.13217225	-0.26126077	0.69770370	1.30284078
j = 5	-0.71461548	0.41255156	0.34620632	0.96411220	0.35841853	-0.56112629	-0.85941660
j = 6	0.46821289	-0.30735498	0.89548914	-0.27789050	-0.52353650	-0.12586368	0.34804403
Subtotal	0.33644939	0.49982673	-1.73884312	-1.35989114	0.58488127	-0.27951813	0.30274812
$z = \Sigma c_{kj}{}^{o*}(x)^{k*}\cos^j(j*y)$			(k= 0, 1, 2, 3, 4, 5, 6		j = 0, 1, 2, 3, 4, 5, 6) =		-1.65434689

Order Neural Networks (UPT-HONN), are developed. Based on the structures of UPT-HONN, this chapter provides two model learning algorithm formulae. This chapter tests the UPS-HONN model using ultra high frequency signals. Experimental results show that UPT-HONN models can generate any nonlinear signals with average error of 10^{-6}.

One of the topics for future research is to continue building models using UPT-HONN for different data series. The coefficients of the higher order models will be studied not only using artificial neural network techniques, but also statistical methods. Using nonlinear functions to model and analyze time series data will be a major goal in the future.

REFERENCES

Alanis, A. Y., Sanchez, E. N., & Loukianov, A. G. (2006). Discrete- Time Recurrent Neural Induction Motor Control using Kalman Learning. In *Proceedings of International Joint Conference on Neural Networks* (pp.1993 – 2000). Vancouver, Canada: Academic Press.

Alanis, A. Y., Sanchez, E. N., Loukianov, A. G., & Perez-Cisneros, M. A. (2010). Real-Time Discrete Neural Block Control Using Sliding Modes for Electric Induction Motors. *IEEE Transactions on Control Systems Technology, 18*(1), 11–21. doi:10.1109/TCST.2008.2009466

Arai, M., Kohon, R., Imai, H. (1991). Adaptive control of a neural network with a variable function of a unit and its application, *Transactions on Inst. Electronic Information Communication Engineering, J74-A*, 551-559.

Baruch, I. S., Galvan-Guerra, R., & Nenkova, B. (2008). Centralized Indirect Control of an Anaerobic Digestion Bioprocess Using Recurrent Neural Identifier. *Lecture Notes in Computer Science, 5253*, 297–310. doi:10.1007/978-3-540-85776-1_25

Boutalis, Y. S., Theodoridis, D. C., & Christodoulou, M. A. (2009). A new Neuro FDS definition for indirect adaptive control of unknown nonlinear systems using a method of parameter hopping. *IEEE Transactions on Neural Networks, 20*(4), 609–625. doi:10.1109/TNN.2008.2010772 PMID:19273046

Bukovsky, I., Bila, J., & Gupta, M. M. (2005). Linear Dynamic Neural Units with Time Delay for Identification and Control (in Czech). *Automatizace, 48*(10), 628-635.

Butt, N. R., & Shafiq, M. (2006). Higher-Order Neural Network Based Root-Solving Controller for Adaptive Tracking of Stable Nonlinear Plants. In *Proceedings of IEEE International Conference on Engineering of Intelligent Systems* (pp. 1–6). Islamabad, Pakistan: IEEE. 10.1109/ICEIS.2006.1703175

Campolucci, P., Capparelli, F., Guarnieri, S., Piazza, F., & Uncini, A. (1996). Neural networks with adaptive spline activation function. In *Proceedings of IEEE MELECON 96* (pp. 1442-1445). Bari, Italy: IEEE. 10.1109/MELCON.1996.551220

Campos, J., Loukianov, A. G., & Sanchez, E. N. (2003). Synchronous motor VSS control using recurrent high order neural networks. In *Proceedings of 42nd IEEE Conference on Decision and Control*, (vol. 4, pp.3894 – 3899). Maui, HI: IEEE. 10.1109/CDC.2003.1271757

Chen, F. C., & Khalil, H. K. (1992). Adaptive control of nonlinear systems using neural networks. *International Journal of Control, 55*(6), 1299–1317. doi:10.1080/00207179208934286

Chen, G., & Lewis, F. L. (2013). Cooperative Control of Unknown Networked Lagrange Systems Using Higher Order Neural Networks. In Artificial Higher Order Neural Networks for Modeling and Simulation (pp. 214-236). IGI Global.

Chen, L., & Narendra, K. S. (2002, June). Nonlinear Adaptive Control Using Neural Networks and Multiple Models. In *Proceedings of the 2000 American Control Conference* (pp. 4199-4203). Chicago, IL: Academic Press.

Das, A., & Lewis, F. (2013). Distributed Adaptive Control for Multi-Agent Systems with Pseudo Higher Order Neural Net. In Artificial Higher Order Neural Networks for Modeling and Simulation (pp. 194-213). IGI Global.

Das, A., Lewis, F. L., & Subbarao, K. (2010). Back-Stepping Control of Quadrotor: A Dynamically Tuned Higher Order Like Neural Network Approach. In Artificial Higher Order Neural Networks for Computer Science and Engineering – Trends for Emerging Applications (pp. 484-513). IGI Global.

Diao, Y., & Passino, K. M. (2002). Adaptive Neural/Fuzzy Control for Interpolated Nonlinear Systems. *IEEE Transactions on Fuzzy Systems, 10*(5), 583–595. doi:10.1109/TFUZZ.2002.803493

Farrell, J. A., & Polycarpou, M. M. (2006). *Adaptive approximation Based Control: Unifying Neural, Fuzzy and Traditional Adaptive Approximation Approaches*. John Wiley and Sons. doi:10.1002/0471781819

Ge, S. S., Zhang, J., & Lee, T. H. (2004). Adaptive neural network control for a class of MIMO nonlinear systems with disturbances in discrete-time. *IEEE Transactions on Systems, Man, and Cybernetics*, *34*, 1–4. PMID:15462431

Holubar, P., Zani, L., Hager, M., Froschl, W., Radak, Z., & Braun, R. (2002). Advanced controlling of anaerobic digestion by means of hierarchical neural networks. *Water Research*, *36*(10), 2582–2588. doi:10.1016/S0043-1354(01)00487-0 PMID:12153025

Hou, Z. G., Cheng, L., & Tan, M. (2009). Decentralized robust adaptive control for the multiagent system consensus problem using neural networks. *IEEE Transactions on Systems, Man, and Cybernetics. Part B, Cybernetics*, *39*(3), 636–647. doi:10.1109/TSMCB.2008.2007810 PMID:19174350

Hu, Z., & Shao, H. (1992). The study of neural network adaptive control systems. *Control and Decision*, *7*, 361–366.

Karnavas, Y. L. (2010). Electrical Machines Excitation Control via Higher Order Neural Networks. In *Artificial Higher Order Neural Networks for Computer Science and Engineering – Trends for Emerging Applications* (pp. 366-396). IGI Global.

Kumar, N., Panwar, V., Sukavanam, N., Sharma, S. P., & Borm, J. H. (2011). Neural Network-Based Nonlinear Tracking Control of Kinematically Redundant Robot Manipulators. *Mathematical and Computer Modelling*, *53*(9), 1889–1901. doi:10.1016/j.mcm.2011.01.014

Lee, M., Lee, S. Y., & Park, C. H. (1992). Neural controller of nonlinear dynamic systems using higher order neural networks. *Electronics Letters*, *28*(3), 276–277. doi:10.1049/el:19920170

Lewis, F. L., Jagannathan, S., & Yesildirek, A. (1998). *Neural Network Control of Robot Manipulators and Non-Linear Systems*. New York: Taylor & Francis.

Lewis, F. L., Yesildirek, A., & Liu, K. (1996). Multilayer neural-net robot controller with guaranteed tracking performance. *IEEE Transactions on Neural Networks*, *7*(2), 388–399. doi:10.1109/72.485674 PMID:18255592

Li, X., Chen, Z. Q., & Yuan, Z. Z. (2002). Simple Recurrent Neural Network-Based Adaptive Predictive Control for Nonlinear Systems. *Asian Journal of Control*, *4*(2), 31–239.

Narendra, K. S., & Parthasarathy, K. (1990). Identification and Control of Dynamical Systems Using Neural Networks. *IEEE Transactions on Neural Networks, 1*(1), 4–27. doi:10.1109/72.80202 PMID:18282820

Narendra, S., & Parthasarathy, K. (1990). Identification and control of dynamical systems using neural networks. *IEEE Transactions on Neural Networks, 1*(1), 4–27. doi:10.1109/72.80202 PMID:18282820

Norgaard, M., Ravn, O., Poulsen, N. K., & Hansen, L. K. (2000). *Neural Networks for Modelling and Control of Dynamic Systems: A practitioner's Handbook*. London, UK: Springer-Verlag. doi:10.1007/978-1-4471-0453-7

Pedro, J., & Dahunsi, O. (2011). Neural Network Based Feedback Linearization Control of a Servo-Hydraulic Vehicle Suspension System. *International Journal of Applied Mathematics and Computer Science, 21*(1), 137–147. doi:10.2478/v10006-011-0010-5

Plett, G. L. (2003). Adaptive Inverse Control of Linear and Nonlinear Systems Using Dynamic Neural Networks. *IEEE Transactions on Neural Networks, 14*(2), 360–376. doi:10.1109/TNN.2003.809412 PMID:18238019

Polycarpou, M. M. (1996). Stable adaptive neural control scheme for nonlinear systems. *IEEE Transactions on Automatic Control, 41*(3), 447–451. doi:10.1109/9.486648

Poznyak, A. S., Sanchez, E. N., & Yu, W. (2000). *Differential Neural Networks for Robust Nonlinear Control*. World Scientific.

Rovithakis, G., Gaganis, V., Perrakis, S., & Christodoulou, M. (1996). A recurrent neural network model to describe manufacturing cell dynamics. In *Proceedings of the 35th IEEE Conference on Decision and Control*, (vol.2, pp.1728 – 1733). Kobe, Japan: IEEE. 10.1109/CDC.1996.572808

Rovithakis, G. A., & Chistodoulou, M. A. (2000). *Adaptive Control with Recurrent High-Order Neural Networks*. Berlin, Germany: Springer Verlag. doi:10.1007/978-1-4471-0785-9

Rovithakis, G. A., Kosmatopoulos, E. B., & Christodoulou, M. A. (1993). Robust adaptive control of unknown plants using recurrent high order neural networks-application to mechanical systems. In *Proceedings of International Conference on Systems, Man and Cybernetics* (vol.4, pp.57 – 62). Le Touquet, France: Academic Press. 10.1109/ICSMC.1993.390683

Sanchez, E. N., Alanis, A. Y., & Loukianov, A. G. (2008). *Discrete Time High Order Neural Control Trained with Kalman Filtering*. Springer-Verlag. doi:10.1007/978-3-540-78289-6

Shannon, C. E. (1998, February). Communication in the presence of noise. *Proceedings of the IEEE, 86*(2), ●●●.

Shi, K. L., & Li, H. (2004). A Novel Control of a Small Wind Turbine Driven Generator Based on Neural Networks. *IEEE Power Engineering Society General Meeting, 2,* 1999-2005.

Theodoridis, D. C., Boutalis, Y. S., & Christodoulou, M. A. (2009). A new Neuro-Fuzzy Dynamical System Definition Based on High Order Neural Network Function Approximators. In *Proceedings of the European Control Conference ECC-09* (pp. 3305-3310). Budapest, Hungary: Academic Press. 10.23919/ECC.2009.7074915

Theodoridis, D. C., Christodoulou, M. A., & Boutalis, Y. S. (2010). Neuro-Fuzzy Control Schemes Based on High Order Neural Network Function Approximators. In Artificial Higher Order Neural Networks for Computer Science and Engineering – Trends for Emerging Applications (pp. 450-383). IGI Global.

Weidong, X., Yubing, L., & Xingpei, L. (2010). Short-Term Forecasting of Wind Turbine Power Generation Based on Genetic Neural Network. In *Proceedings of Eighth World Congress on Intelligent Control and Automation* (pp. 5943-5946). Jinan, China: Academic Press.

Yamada, T., & Yabuta, T. (1992). Remarks on a neural network controller which uses an auto-tuning method for nonlinear functions. *IJCNN, 2,* 775–780.

Yih, G. L., Wei, Y. W., & Tsu, T. L. (2005). Observer-based direct adaptive fuzzy-neural control for nonaffine nonlinear systems. *IEEE Transactions on Neural Networks, 16*(4), 853–861. doi:10.1109/TNN.2005.849824 PMID:16121727

Yu, W. (2010). Robust Adaptive Control Using Higher Order Neural Networks and Projection. In Artificial Higher Order Neural Networks for Computer Science and Engineering – Trends for Emerging Applications (pp. 99-137). IGI Global.

ADDITIONAL READING

Alanis, A. Y., Leon, B. S., Sanchez, E. N., & Ruiz-Velazquez, E. (2011). Blood Clucose Level Neural Model for Type 1 Diabetes Mellitus Patients. *International Journal of Neural Systems, 21*(6), 491–504. doi:10.1142/S0129065711003000 PMID:22131301

Amari, S. (1972). Characteristics of random nets of analog neuron-like elements. *IEEE Trans. SMC-2,* 5, 643-657.

Arai, M., Kohon, R., Imai, H. (1991). Adaptive control of a neural network with a variable function of a unit and its application, *Transactions on Inst. Electronic Information Communication Engineering,* J74-A, 551-559.

Baber, W., Kang, S., & Kumar, K. (1999). The Explanatory Power of Earnings Levels and Earnings Changes in the Context of Executive Compensation. *The Accounting Review, 74*(4), 459–472. doi:10.2308/accr.1999.74.4.459

Baruch, I. S., Galvan-Guerra, R., & Nenkova, B. (2008). Centralized Indirect Control of an Anaerobic Digestion Bioprocess Using Recurrent Neural Identifier. *Lecture Notes in Computer Science, 5253,* 297–310. doi:10.1007/978-3-540-85776-1_25

Boutalis, Y. S., Theodoridis, D. C., & Christodoulou, M. A. (2009). A new Neuro FDS definition for indirect adaptive control of unknown nonlinear systems using a method of parameter hopping. *IEEE Transactions on Neural Networks, 20*(4), 609–625. doi:10.1109/TNN.2008.2010772 PMID:19273046

Carlos-Hernandez, S., Sanchez, E. N., & Beteau, J.-F. (2009). Fuzzy observers for anaerobic wwtp: Synthesis and implementation. *Control Engineering Practice, 17*(6), 690–702. doi:10.1016/j.conengprac.2008.11.008

Chen, J. S. (1987). *Kinetic engineering modelling of co-current moving bed gasification reactors for carbonaceous material.* Unpublished doctoral dissertation, Cornell University.

Chopra, N., & Spong, M. W. (2006). Passivity-based control of multi-agent systems. In S. Kawamura & M. Svinin (Eds.), *Advances in Robot Control: From Everyday Physics to Human-Like Movements* (pp. 107–134). New York: Springer-Verlag. doi:10.1007/978-3-540-37347-6_6

Core, J., Guay, W., & Verrecchia, R. (2003). Price versus Non-Price Performance Measures in Optimal CEO Compensation Contracts. *The Accounting Review*, *78*(4), 957–981. doi:10.2308/accr.2003.78.4.957

Dayhoff, J. E. (1990). *Neural network architectures: an introduction*. New York, N.Y.: Van Nostrand Reinhold.

Do, K. D., Jiang, Z. P., & Pan, J. (2004). Simultaneous tracking and stabilization of mobile robots: An adaptive approach. *IEEE Transactions on Automatic Control*, *49*(7), 1147–1152. doi:10.1109/TAC.2004.831139

Dupont, D., Nocquet, T., Da Costa, J. A. Jr, & Verne-Tournon, C. (2011). Kinetic modeling of steam gasification of various woody biomass chars: Influence of inorganic elements. *Bioresource Technology*, *102*(20), 9743–9748. doi:10.1016/j.biortech.2011.07.016 PMID:21862327

Fallahnezhad, M., Moradi, M. H., & Zaferanlouei, S. (2011). A Hybrid Higher Order Neural Classifier for handling classification problems. *International Journal of Expert System and Application*, *38*(1), 386–393. doi:10.1016/j.eswa.2010.06.077

Gao, M., Lou, X., & Cui, B. (2008). Robust exponential stability of markovian jumping neural networks with time-varying delay. *International Journal of Neural Systems*, *18*(3), 207–218. doi:10.1142/S0129065708001531 PMID:18595150

Gøbel, B., Henriksen, U., Jensen, T. K., Qvale, B., & Houbak, N. (2007). The development of a computer model for a fixed bed gasifier and its use for optimization and control. *Bioresource Technology*, *98*(10), 2043–2052. doi:10.1016/j.biortech.2006.08.019 PMID:17055266

Gouze, J. L., Rapaport, A., & Hadj-Sadok, Z. (2000). Interval observers for uncertain biological systems. *Ecological Modelling*, *133*(1–2), 45–56. doi:10.1016/S0304-3800(00)00279-9

Hong, Y., Chen, G. R., & Bushnell, L. (2008). Distributed observers design for leader following control of multi-agent networks. *Automatica*, *44*(3), 846–850. doi:10.1016/j.automatica.2007.07.004

Hou, Z. G., Cheng, L., & Tan, M. (2009). Decentralized robust adaptive control for the multiagent system consensus problem using neural networks. *IEEE Transactions on Systems, Man, and Cybernetics. Part B, Cybernetics*, *39*(3), 636–647. doi:10.1109/TSMCB.2008.2007810 PMID:19174350

Huang, G. B., & Chen, L. (2007). Convex incremental extreme learning machine. *Neurocomputing, 70*(16-18), 3056–3062. doi:10.1016/j.neucom.2007.02.009

Jayah, T. H., Aye, L., Fuller, R. J., & Stewart, D. F. (2003). Computer simulation of a downdraft wood gasifier for tea drying. *Biomass and Bioenergy, 25*(4), 459–469. doi:10.1016/S0961-9534(03)00037-0

Kani, S. A. P., & Riany, G. H. (2008). A New ANN-Based Methodology for Very Short-Term Wind Speed Prediction Using Markov Chain Approach. *IEEE Electric Power Conference*. pp. 1-6. 10.1109/EPC.2008.4763386

Kawato, M., Uno, Y., Isobe, M., & Suzuki, R. (1987) A hierarchical model for voluntary movement and its application to robotics, *Proc. IEEE Int. Conf. Network, IV*, 573-582.

Kim, Y. H., & Lewis, F. L. (1998). *High-Level Feedback Control with Neural Networks*. Singapore: World Scientific. doi:10.1142/3701

Kros, J. F., Lin, M., & Brown, M. L. (2006). Effects of neural networks s-sigmoid function on KDD in the presence of imprecise data. *Computers & Operations Research, 33*(11), 3136–3149. doi:10.1016/j.cor.2005.01.024

Laurendeau, M. (1978). Kinetics of Coal Char Gasification and combustion. *Journal of Energy Combustion, 4*(4), 221–270. doi:10.1016/0360-1285(78)90008-4

Li, T. Y., & Yorke, J. A. (1975). Periodic three implies chaos. *The American Mathematical Monthly, 82*(10), 985–992. doi:10.1080/00029890.1975.119 94008

McEliece, R. J., Posner, E. C., Rodemich, E. R., & Venkatesh, S. S. (1987). The capacity of the Hopfield associative memory. *IEEE Transactions on Information Theory, 33*(4), 461–482. doi:10.1109/TIT.1987.1057328

McKee, T. E. (2009). A Meta-Learning Approach to Predicting Financial Statement Fraud. *Journal of Emerging Technologies in Accounting, 6*(1), 5–26. doi:10.2308/jeta.2009.6.1.5

Miyajima, H., & Yatsuki, S. (1994). On some dynamical properties of threshold and homogeneous networks. *IEICE Trans. Fundamentals, E77-A*(11), 1823–1830.

Mountouris, A., Voutsas, E., & Tassios, D. (2006). Plasma gasification of sewage sludge: Process development and energy optimization. *Energy Conversion and Management, 47*, 1723–1737. doi:10.1016/j.enconman.2005.10.015

Narendra, S., & Parthasarathy, K. (1990). Identification and control of dynamical systems using neural networks. *IEEE Transactions on Neural Networks, 1*(1), 4–27. doi:10.1109/72.80202 PMID:18282820

Plett, G. L. (2003). Adaptive Inverse Control of Linear and Nonlinear Systems Using Dynamic Neural Networks. *IEEE Transactions on Neural Networks, 14*(2), 360–376. doi:10.1109/TNN.2003.809412 PMID:18238019

Ren, W. (2009). Distributed leaderless consensus algorithms for networked Euler–Lagrange systems. *International Journal of Control, 82*(11), 2137–2149. doi:10.1080/00207170902948027

Rovithakis, G. A., & Chistodoulou, M. A. (2000). *Adaptive Control with Recurrent High -Order Neural Networks.* Berlin, Germany: Springer Verlag. doi:10.1007/978-1-4471-0785-9

Saad, E. W., Prokhorov, D. V., & Wunsch, D. C. II. (1998). Comparative Study of Stock Trend Prediction Using Time Delay Recurrent and Probabilistic Neural Networks. *IEEE Transactions on Neural Networks, 9*(6), 1456–1470. doi:10.1109/72.728395 PMID:18255823

Sanchez, E. N., Alanis, A. Y., & Loukianov, A. G. (2008). *Discrete-Time High Order Neural Control Trained with Kalman Filtering.* Berlin, Germany: Springer-Verlag. doi:10.1007/978-3-540-78289-6

Sethi, I. K., & Jan, A. K. (1991). Decision Tree Performance Enhancement Using an Artificial Neural Networks Implementation. In *Artificial Neural Networks and Statistical Pattern Recognition* (pp. 71–88). Amsterdam, the Netherlands: Elsevier.

Shie, J. D., & Chen, S. M. (2008). Feature subset selection based on fuzzy entropy measures for handling classification problems. *Journal of Applied Intelligence, 28*(1), 69–82. doi:10.100710489-007-0042-6

Sun, D., Shao, X., & Feng, G. (2007). A model-free cross-coupled control for position synchronization of multi-axis motions: Theory and experiments. *IEEE Transactions on Control Systems Technology, 15*(2), 306–314. doi:10.1109/TCST.2006.883201

Thangavel, P., & Gladis, D. (2007). Hopfield Hysteretic Hopfield network with dynamic tunneling for crossbar switch and N-queens problem. *Neurocomputing, 70*(13-15), 2544–2551. doi:10.1016/j.neucom.2006.06.006

Van Lier, J. B., Tilche, A., Ahring, B. K., Macarie, H., Moletta, R., Dohanyos, M., ... Verstraete, W. (2001). New perspectives in anaerobic digestion. *Water Science and Technology, 43*(1), 1–18. doi:10.2166/wst.2001.0001 PMID:11379079

Wang, Z., Ho, D. W. C., & Liu, X. (2005). State estimation for delayed neural networks. *IEEE Transactions on Neural Networks, 16*(1), 279–284. doi:10.1109/TNN.2004.841813 PMID:15732407

Xu, B., Liu, X., & Teoc, K. L. (2009). Global exponential stability of impulsive high-order Hopfield type neural networks with delays. *Computers & Mathematics with Applications (Oxford, England), 57*(3), 1959–1967. doi:10.1016/j.camwa.2008.10.001

Zaferanlouei, S., Rostamifard, D., & Setayeshi, S. (2010). Prediction of critical heat flux using ANFIS. *Annals of Nuclear Energy, 37*(6), 813–821. doi:10.1016/j.anucene.2010.02.019

Zhang, J. (2006). *Linear and nonlinear models for the power of chief elected officials and debt*. Pittsburgh, PA: Mid-Atlantic Region American Accounting Association.

KEY TERMS AND DEFINITIONS

ANN: Artificial neural network.

HONN: Artificial higher order neural network.

PHONN: Artificial polynomial higher order neural network.

THONN: Artificial trigonometric higher order neural network.

UPC-HONN: Artificial ultra-high frequency polynomial and cosine higher order neural network.

UPS-HONN: Artificial ultra-high frequency polynomial and sine higher order neural network.

UPT-HONN: Artificial ultra-high frequency polynomial and trigonometric higher order neural network.

Chapter 11

Data Pattern Recognition Based on Ultra–High Frequency Sigmoid and Trigonometric Higher Order Neural Networks

ABSTRACT

This chapter develops a new nonlinear model, ultra high frequency sigmoid and trigonometric higher order neural networks (UGT-HONN), for data pattern recognition. UGT-HONN includes ultra high frequency sigmoid and sine function higher order neural networks (UGS-HONN) and ultra high frequency sigmoid and cosine functions higher order neural networks (UGC-HONN). UGS-HONN and UGC-HONN models are used to recognition data patterns. Results show that UGS-HONN and UGC-HONN models are better than other polynomial higher order neural network (PHONN) and trigonometric higher order neural network (THONN) models, since UGS-HONN and UGC-HONN models can recognize data pattern with error approaching 10-6.

DOI: 10.4018/978-1-7998-3563-9.ch011

INTRODUCTION

The contributions of this chapter will be:

- Introduce the background of HONNs with the pattern recognition of HONNs.
- Develop a new UGT-HONN model for ultra-high frequency data pattern recognition.
- Provide the UGT-HONN learning algorithm and weight update formulae.
- Applications of UGT-HONN model for data pattern recognition.

This chapter is organized as follows: Section "BACKGROUND" gives the background knowledge of HONNs and pattern recognition applications using HONNs. Section "UGT-HONN MODELS" introduces UGT-HONN structure and different modes of the UGT-HONN model. Section LEARNING ALGORITHM OF UGT-HONN MODELS provides the UGT-HONN model update formula, learning algorithms, and convergence theories of HONN. Section "UGT-HONN TESTING" describes UGT-HONN computer software system and testing results for data pattern recognition.

BACKGROUND

Artificial Neural Network (ANN) techniques had been widely used in the pattern recognition area. Sankar and Mammone (1991) study speaker independent vowel recognition using neural tree networks. Sethi and Jan (1991) analyze decision tree performance enhancement using an artificial neural networks implementation. Yao, Freeman, Burke, and Yang (1991) experiment pattern recognition by a distributed neural network.

Artificial higher order neural networks have very successfully been used for invariant pattern recognition (Artyomov and Yadid-Pecht (2005); He and Siyal (1999); Kaita, Tomita, & Yamanaka (2002); Kanaoka, Chellappa, Yoshitaka, & Tomita (1992), and Lisboa & Perantonis (1991)). Reid, Spirkovska, and Ochoa (1989) demonstrate a second-order neural network that has learned to distinguish between two objects, regardless of their size or translational position, after being trained on only one view of each object. Spirkovska and Reid (1990a) present the results of experiments comparing the performance of the symbolic learning algorithm with a higher order neural network in the distortion invariant object recognition domain. Spirkovska and Reid (1990b) study the connectivity strategies for non-fully connected higher order neural networks and shown that by using such strategies an input field of 128×128 pixels can be attained while still achieving in-plane rotation and invariant recognition. Spirkovska and Reid (1991) present a coarsecoding applied to HONNs, in which the invariances are built directly into the architecture of a HONN, for object recognition. It is noted that a higher order neural network (HONN) can be easily designed for position, scale, and rotation invariant (PSRI) object recognition. Zhou, Koch, & Roberts (1991) find that selective attention can be used to reduce the number of inputs for a high-order neural network and, by selecting appropriate scanning mechanism, invariance to translation can be developed for invariant object recognition. Perantonis and Lisboa (1992) discuss the recognition of two-dimensional patterns independently of their position, orientation, and size by using high-order networks. A method is introduced for reducing and controlling the number of weights of a third-order neural network. Wu and Chang (1993) explore the use of the higher order neural networks to implement an invariant pattern recognition system that is insensitive to translation, rotation, and scaling. Kroner (1995) uses adaptive averaging in higher order neural networks for invariant pattern recognition, and found that, for the task of position invariant, scale invariant, and rotation invariant pattern recognition, higher order neural networks have shown good separation results for different object classes. He and Siyal (1998) try to recognize transformed English letters with modified higher order neural networks. The authors found that higher order neural networks (HONNs) are effective neural models for invariant pattern recognition. However, one of the main problems in HONNs is that they are sensitive to distortion of the input patterns. Wang, Sun, and Chen (2003) study the recognition of digital annotation with invariant HONN based on orthogonal Fourier-Mellin moments. A recently developed type of moments, Orthogonal Fourier-Mellin Moments (OFMMs) is applied to the specific problem of full scale and rotation invariant recognition of digital annotation. Zhang, Jing, and Li (2004) propose a new fast high-order neural network learning algorithm for invariant pattern recognition. The new learning algorithm uses some properties of trigonometry for reducing and controlling the number of weights of a third-order network used for invariant pattern recognition.

Artificial Higher Order Neural Network (HONN) had been widely used in the pattern recognition area too. Reid, Spirkovska, and Ochoa (1989) show rapid training of higher-order neural networks for invariant pattern recognition.

Spirkovska and Reid (1990) suggest connectivity strategies for higher-order neural networks applied to pattern recognition. Lisboa and Perantonis (1991) diusplay the invariant pattern recognition using third-order networks and zernlike moments. Kanaoka, Chellappa, Yoshitaka, and Tomita (1992) built an artificial higher order neural network for distortion un-variant pattern recognition. Perantonis and Lisboa (1992) test the rotation and scale invariant pattern recognition by high-order neural networks and moment classifiers. Schmidt and Davis (1993) check the pattern recognition properties of various feature spaces for higher order neural networks. Spirkovska and Reid (1994) try higher order neural networks to apply 2D and 3D object recognition. He, and Siyal (1999) operate Improvement on higher-order neural networks for invariant object recognition. Park, Smith, and Mersereau (2000) employ target recognition based on directional filter banks and higher-order neural network. Kaita, Tomita, and Yamanaka (2002) research on a higher-order neural network for distortion invariant pattern recognition. Voutriaridis, Boutalis, and Mertzios (2003) seek ridge polynomial networks in pattern recognition. Foresti and Dolso (2004) look into an adaptive high-order neural tree for pattern recognition. Artyomov and Yadid-Pecht (2005) provide modified high-order neural network for invariant pattern recognition.

Selviah (2009) focuses on high speed optical higher order neural networks for discovering data trends and patterns in very large database. Selviah describes the progress in using optical technology to construct high-speed artificial higher order neural network systems. The chapter reviews how optical technology can speed up searches within large databases in order to identify relationships and dependencies between individual data records, such as financial or business time-series, as well as trends and relationships within them. Two distinct approaches in which optics may be used are reviewed. In the first approach, the chapter reviews current research replacing copper connections in a conventional data storage system, such as a several terabyte RAID array of magnetic hard discs, by optical waveguides to achieve very high data rates with low crosstalk interference. In the second approach, the chapter reviews how high-speed optical correlators with feedback can be used to realize artificial higher order neural networks using Fourier Transform free space optics and holographic database storage.

Wang, Liu, and Liu (2009) investigate on complex artificial higher order neural networks for dealing with stochasticity, jumps and delays. This research deals with the analysis problem of the global exponential stability for a general class of stochastic artificial higher order neural networks with multiple mixed time delays and Markovian jumping parameters. The mixed time delays under consideration comprise both the discrete time-varying delays and the distributed time-delays. The main purpose of this chapter is to establish easily verifiable conditions under which the delayed high-order stochastic jumping neural network is exponentially stable in the mean square in the presence of both the mixed time delays and Markovian switching. By employing a new Lyapunov-Krasovskii functional and conducting stochastic analysis, a linear matrix nequality (LMI) approach is developed to derive the criteria ensuring the exponential stability. Furthermore, the criteria are dependent on both the discrete time-delay and distributed time-delay, hence less conservative. The proposed criteria can be readily checked by using some standard numerical packages such as the Matlab LMI Toolbox. A simple example is provided to demonstrate the effectiveness and applicability of the proposed testing criteria.

Zhang (2010) learn the rainfall estimation using neuron-adaptive higher order neural networks for rainfall estimation. Real world data is often nonlinear, discontinuous and may comprise high frequency, multi-polynomial components. Not surprisingly, it is hard to find the best models for modeling such data. Classical neural network models are unable to automatically determine the optimum model and appropriate order for data approximation. In order to solve this problem, Neuron-Adaptive Higher Order Neural Network (NAHONN) Models have been introduced. Definitions of one-dimensional, two-dimensional, and n-dimensional NAHONN models are studied. Specialized NAHONN models are also described. NAHONN models are shown to be "open box". These models are further shown to be capable of automatically finding not only the optimum model but also the appropriate order for high frequency, multi-polynomial, discontinuous data. Rainfall estimation experimental results confirm model convergence. This chapter further demonstrates that NAHONN models are capable of modeling satellite data. When the Xie and Scofield (1989) technique was used, the average error of the operator-computed IFFA rainfall estimates was 30.41%. For the Artificial Neural Network (ANN) reasoning network, the training error was 6.55% and the test error 16.91%, respectively. When the neural network group was used on these same fifteen cases, the average training error of rainfall estimation was 1.43%, and the average test error of rainfall estimation was 3.89%. When the neuron-adaptive artificial neural network group models were used on these same fifteen cases, the average training error of rainfall estimation was 1.31%, and the average test error of rainfall estimation was 3.40%. When the artificial neuron-adaptive higher order neural network model was used on these same fifteen cases, the average training error of rainfall estimation was 1.20%, and the average test error of rainfall estimation was 3.12%.

Murata (2010) presents the analysis and improvement of function approximation capabilities of pi-sigma higher order neural networks. Murata finds that A Pi-Sigma higher order neural network (Pi-Sigma HONN) is a type of higher order neural network, where, as its name implies, weighted sums of inputs are calculated first and then the sums are multiplied by each other to produce higher order terms that constitute the network outputs. This type of higher order neural networks has good function approximation capabilities. In this chapter, the structural feature of Pi-Sigma HONNs is discussed in contrast to other types of neural networks. The reason for their good function approximation capabilities is given based on pseudo-theoretical analysis together with empirical illustrations. Then, based on the analysis, an improved version of Pi-Sigma HONNs is proposed which has yet better functions approximation capabilities.

Ricalde, Sanchez, and Alanis (2010) propose recurrent higher order neural network control for output trajectory tracking with neural observers and constrained inputs. This study presents the design of an adaptive recurrent neural observer-controller scheme for nonlinear systems whose model is assumed to be unknown and with constrained inputs. The control scheme is composed of a neural observer based on Recurrent High Order Neural Networks which builds the state vector of the unknown plant dynamics and a learning adaptation law for the neural network weights for both the observer and identifier. These laws are obtained via control Lyapunov functions. Then, a control law, which stabilizes the tracking error dynamics is developed using the Lyapunov and the inverse optimal control methodologies. Tracking error boundedness is established as a function of design parameters.

Fallahnezhad and Zaferanlouei (2013) produce a hybrid higher order neural structure for pattern recognition. This project considers that high order correlations of selected features next to the raw features of input can facilitate target pattern recognition. In artificial intelligence, this is usually addressed by Higher Order Neural Networks (HONNs). In general, HHON structures provide superior specifications (e.g. resolving dilemma of choosing number of neurons and layers of network, better fitting specs, lesser timing process and open-box specificity) to traditional neural networks. This chapter introduces a hybrid structure of higher order neural networks which can be generally applied in various branches of pattern recognition. Structure, learning algorithm, and network configuration are introduced, and structure applied either as classifier (where is called HHONC) to different benchmark statistical data sets or as functional behavior approximation (where is called HHONN) to a heat and mass transfer dilemma. In each structure, results are compared with previous studies which imply on its superior performance next to other mentioned advantages.

UGT-HONN MODELS

The new HONN model, ultra-high frequency siGmoid and Trigonometric Higher Order Neural Network (UGT-HONN) has been developed. UGT-HONN includes two different models base on the different neuron functions. Ultra-high frequency siGmoid and Sine Trigonometric Higher Order Neural Network (UGS-HONN) has neurons with sigmoid and sine functions. Ultra-high frequency siGmoid and Cosine Trigonometric Higher Order Neural Network (UGC-HONN) has neurons with sigmoid and cosine functions. Except for the functions in the neuron all other parts of these three models are the same. The following section will discuss the UGS-HONN and UGC-HONN structures in detail.

UGS-HONN Model Structure can be seen in Figure 1. UGC-HONN Model Structure can be seen in Figure 2.

UGS-HONN Model

The Nyquist–Shannon sampling theorem, after Harry Nyquist and Claude Shannon, in the literature more commonly referred to as the Nyquist sampling theorem or simply as the sampling theorem, is a fundamental result in the field of information theory, telecommunications and signal processing. Shannon's version of the theorem states: [Shannon, 1998]

If a function $x(t)$ contains no frequencies higher than B hertz, it is completely determined by giving its ordinates at a series of points spaced 1/(2B) seconds apart.

In other words, a band limited function can be perfectly reconstructed from a countable sequence of samples if the band limit, B, is no greater than ½ the sampling rate (samples per second).

In simulating and predicting time series data, the new nonlinear models of UXS-HONN should have twice as high frequency as that of the ultra-high frequency of the time series data. To achieve this purpose, a new model should be developed to enforce high frequency of HONN in order to make the simulation and prediction error close to zero.

The different types of UGS-HONN models are shown as follows. Formula (1) (2) and (3) are for UGS-HONN model 2, 1 and 0 respectively. Model 2 has three layers of weights changeable; Model 1 has two layers of weights changeable, and model 0 has one layer of weights changeable. For models 2, 1 and 0, Z is the output while x and y are the inputs of UGS-HONN. $c_{kj}{}^{o}$ is the weight for the output layer, $c_{kj}{}^{hx}$ and $c_{kj}{}^{hy}$ are the weights for the second hidden layer, and $c_k{}^x$ and $c_j{}^y$ are the weights for the first hidden layer. Functions cosine and sine are the first and second hidden layer nodes of UGS-HONN. The output layer node of UGS-HONN is a linear function of $f^o(net^o) = net^o$, where net^o equals the input of output layer node. UGS-HONN is an open neural network model, each weight of HONN has its corresponding coefficient in the model formula, and each node of UGS-HONN has its corresponding function in the model formula. The structure of UGS-HONN is built by a nonlinear formula. It means, after training, there is rationale for each component of UGS-HONN in the nonlinear formula.

Based on Chapter 1 formulae from (1-113) to (1-117: UGS-HONN 2), the Ultra-high frequency siGmoid and Sine and Higher Order Neural Network (UGS-HONN) models are defined as follows:

Let

$$f_k{}^j\left(c_k{}^j x\right) = \left(1/\left(1+\exp(c_k{}^x(-x))\right)\right)^k \tag{11-1}$$

$$f_j{}^y\left(c_j{}^k y\right) = \sin^j(j * c_j{}^k y) \tag{11-2}$$

UGS – HONN Model 0:

$$z = \sum_{k,j=0}^{n} c_{kj}{}^{o}\left(1/\left(1+\exp(-x)\right)\right)^k\left(\sin^j(j * y)\right) \tag{11-3}$$

$$where : \left(c_{kj}{}^{hx}\right) = \left(c_{kj}{}^{hy}\right) = 1 \ \ and \ \ c_k{}^x = c_j{}^y = 1$$

UGS – HONN Model 1:

Figure 1. UGS-HONN architecture

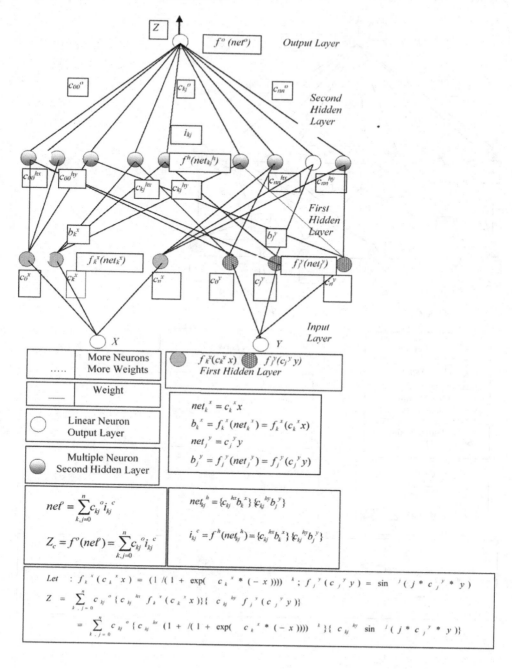

Figure 2. UGC-HONN architecture

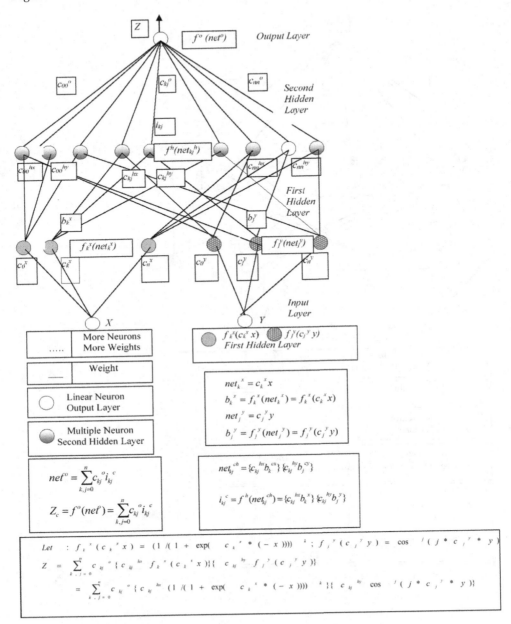

$$z = \sum_{k,j=0}^{n} c_{kj}{}^{o} \left(1 / \left(1 + \exp(c_k{}^x(-x))\right)\right)^k \left(\sin^j(j * c_j{}^y y)\right)$$

$$where : \left(c_{kj}{}^{hx}\right) = \left(c_{kj}{}^{hy}\right) = 1$$

(11-4)

UGS – HONN Model 2: Z=

$$\sum_{k,j=0}^{n} \left(c_{kj}{}^{o}\right) \{c_{kj}{}^{hx} \left(1 / \left(1 + \exp(c_k{}^x(-x))\right)\right)^k\} \{c_{kj}{}^{hy} \left(\sin^j(j * c_j{}^y y)\right)\}$$
(11-5)

For equations (11 -3: UGS-HONN 0), (11-4: UGS-HONN 1), and (11-5: UGS-HONN 2), values of k and j ranges from 0 to n, where n is an integer. The UGS-HONN model can simulate ultra-high frequency time series data, when n increases to a big number. This property of the model allows it to easily simulate and predicate ultra-high frequency time series data, since both k and j increase when there is an increase in n.

The following is an expansion of model UGS-HONN order two.

$$
\begin{aligned}
z = &\; c_{00}{}^{o} \, c_{00}{}^{hx} \, c_{00}{}^{hy} \sin^0(0 * c_0{}^y y) \\
&+ c_{01}{}^{o} \, c_{01}{}^{hx} \, c_{01}{}^{hy} \sin(1 * c_1{}^y y) \\
&+ c_{02}{}^{o} \, c_{02}{}^{hx} \, c_{02}{}^{hy} \sin^2(2 * c_2{}^y y) \\
&+ c_{10}{}^{o} \, c_{10}{}^{hx} \, c_{10}{}^{hy} \, (1/(1+\exp(c_1{}^x(-x)))) \sin^0(0 * c_0{}^y y) \\
&+ c_{11}{}^{o} \, c_{11}{}^{hx} \, c_{11}{}^{hy} \, (1/(1+\exp(c_1{}^x(-x)))) \sin(1 * c_1{}^y y) \\
&+ c_{12}{}^{o} \, c_{12}{}^{hx} \, c_{12}{}^{hy} \, (1/(1+\exp(c_1{}^x(-x))) \sin^2(2 * c_2{}^y y) \\
&+ c_{20}{}^{o} \, c_{20}{}^{hx} \, c_{20}{}^{hy} \, (1/(1+\exp(c_2{}^x(-x))))^2 \sin^0(0 * c_0{}^y y) \\
&+ c_{21}{}^{o} \, c_{21}{}^{hx} \, c_{21}{}^{hy} \, (1/(1+\exp(c_2{}^x(-x))))^2 \sin(1 * c_1{}^y y) \\
&+ c_{22}{}^{o} \, c_{22}{}^{hx} \, c_{22}{}^{hy} \, (1/(1+\exp(c_2{}^x(-x))))^2 \sin^2(2 * c_2{}^y y)
\end{aligned}
$$
(11–6))

The UGS-HONN Architecture is used to develop the model learning algorithm, which make sure the convergence of learning. This allows the deference between desired output and real output of UGS-HONN close to zero.

UGC-HONN Model

Based on Chapter 1 formulae from (1-118) to (1-122: UGC-HONN 2), the UGC-HONN models replace the sine functions from UGS-HONN with cosine functions models, and the UGC-HONN models are defined as follows.

Let

$$f_k^{\ j}\left(c_k^{\ j}x\right) = \left(1/\left(1+\exp(c_k^{\ x}\left(-x\right))\right)\right)^k \tag{11-7}$$

$$f_j^{\ y}\left(c_j^{\ k}y\right) = \cos^j\left(j * c_j^{\ k}y\right) \tag{11-8}$$

UGC – HONN Model 0:

$$z = \sum_{k,j=0}^{n} c_{kj}^{\ o}\left(1/\left(1+\exp(-x)\right)\right)^k\left(\cos^j\left(j * y\right)\right) \tag{11-9}$$

$$where:\left(c_{kj}^{\ hx}\right) = \left(c_{kj}^{\ hy}\right) = 1 \ and \ c_k^{\ x} = c_j^{\ y} = 1$$

UGC – HONN Model 1:

$$z = \sum_{k,j=0}^{n} c_{kj}^{\ o}\left(1/\left(1+\exp(c_k^{\ x}\left(-x\right))\right)\right)^k\left(\cos^j\left(j * c_j^{\ y}y\right)\right) \tag{11-10}$$

$$where:\left(c_{kj}^{\ hx}\right) = \left(c_{kj}^{\ hy}\right) = 1$$

UGC – HONN Model 2:

$$Z = \sum_{k,j=0}^{n}\left(c_{kj}^{\ o}\right)\{c_{kj}^{\ hx}\left(1/\left(1+\exp(c_k^{\ x}\left(-x\right))\right)\right)^k\}\{c_{kj}^{\ hy}\left(\cos^j\left(j * c_j^{\ y}y\right)\right)\} \tag{11-11}$$

LEARNING ALGORITHM OF UGT-HONN MODELS

The learning formula for the output layer weights in UGS-HONN models and UGC-HONN models are the same. The learning formula for the second-hidden layer weights in the UGS-HONN modes and UGC-HONN models are the same. The learning formula for the first-hidden layer weights in the UGS-HONN models and UGC-HONN models are different. Details are listed here.

Learning Formulae of Output Neurons in UGS-HONN Model and UGC-HONN Model (model 0, 1, and 2)

Based on Chapter 1 formulae from (1-133: A.1) to (1-145: A.13), UGS-HONN models and UGC-HONN models (model 0, 1, and 2) are rewritten as follows:

$$c_{kj}^{\ o}(t+1) = c_{kj}^{\ o}(t) - \eta\left(\partial E / \partial c_{kj}^{\ o}\right)$$
$$= c_{kj}^{\ o}(t) + \eta(d-z)f^{o}{}'\left(net^{o}\right)i_{kj}$$
$$= c_{kj}^{\ o}(t) + \eta\delta^{ol}i_{kj}$$

where: $\delta o^{l} = (d - z)$

$$f^{o'}\left(net^{o}\right) = 1 \quad (linear\ neuron) \tag{11-12}$$

Learning Formulae of Second-Hidden Layer Neurons in UGS-HONN Model and UGC-HONN Model (Model 2)

Based on Chapter 1 formulae from (1-146: B.1) to (1-160: B.15), UGS-HONN and UGC-HONN models (model 2) are rewritten as follows:

The weight update question for x input neurons is:

$$c_{kj}^{\ hx}(t+1) = c_{kj}^{\ hx}(t) - \eta\left(\partial E / \partial c_{kj}^{\ hx}\right)$$
$$= c_{kj}^{\ hx}(t) + \eta\left((d-z)f^{o}{}'\left(net^{o}\right)c_{kj}^{\ o}f^{h}{}'\left(net_{kj}^{\ hx}\right)c_{kj}^{\ hy}b_{j}^{\ y}b_{k}^{\ x}\right)$$
$$= c_{kj}^{\ hx}(t) + \eta\left(\delta^{ol}c_{kj}^{\ o}\delta_{kj}^{\ hx}b_{k}^{\ x}\right)$$

where: $\delta o^{l} = (d - z)$

$$\delta_{kj}^{\ hx} = c_{kj}^{\ hy}b_{j}^{\ y}$$

$$f^{o'}\left(net^{o}\right) = 1 \quad (linear\ neuron)$$

$$f^{h'}\left(net_{kj}^{\ hx}\right) = 1 \qquad (linear\ neuron) \qquad\qquad (11\text{-}13)$$

The weight update question for y input neurons is:

$$c_{kj}^{\ hy}\left(t+1\right) = c_{kj}^{\ hy}\left(t\right) - \eta\left(\partial E\ /\ \partial c_{kj}^{\ hy}\right)$$

$$= c_{kj}^{\ hy}\left(t\right) + \eta\left((d-z)f^{o\,\prime}\left(net^{o}\right)c_{kj}^{\ o}f^{h\,\prime}\left(net_{kj}^{\ hy}\right)c_{kj}^{\ hx}b_{k}^{\ x}b_{j}^{\ y}\right)$$

$$= c_{kj}^{\ hy}\left(t\right) + \eta\left(\delta^{ol}c_{kj}^{\ o}\delta_{kj}^{\ hy}b_{j}^{\ y}\right)$$

where: $\delta o^{l} = (d - z)$

$$\delta_{kj}^{\ hy} = c_{kj}^{\ hx}b_{k}^{\ x}$$

$$f^{o'}\left(net^{o}\right) = 1 \qquad (linear\ neuron)$$

$$f^{h'}\left(net_{kj}^{\ hy}\right) = 1 \qquad (linear\ neuron) \qquad\qquad (11\text{-}14)$$

General Learning Formulae of First Hidden Layer x Neurons in UGS-HONN Model and UGC-HONN Model (Model 1 and Model 2)

Based on Chapter 1 formulae from (1-161: C.1) to (1-177: C.17), UGS-HONN and UGC-HONN models (model 1 and 2) are rewritten as follows:

For a function of x input side:

$$b_{k}^{x} = f_{k}^{x}(net_{k}^{x})$$
$$f_{x}^{\ '}\left(net_{k}^{\ x}\right) = \partial b_{k}^{\ x}\ /\ \partial\left(net_{k}^{\ x}\right) \qquad\qquad (11\text{-}15)$$

$$c_k^x(t+1) = c_k^x(t) - \eta\left(\partial E_p / \partial c_k^x\right)$$

$$= c_k^x(t) + \eta(d-z) f^{o\,\prime}\left(net^o\right) c_{kj}^{\ o} * f^{h\,\prime}\left(net_{kj}^{\ h}\right) c_{kj}^{\ hy} b_j^{\ y} c_{kj}^{\ hx} f_x^{\,\prime}\left(net_k^x\right) x$$

$$= c_k^x(t) + \eta * \delta^{ol} * c_{kj}^{\ o} * \delta^{hx} * c_{kj}^{\ hx} * \delta^x * x$$

where

$$\delta^{ol} = (d-z) f^{o\,\prime}\left(net^o\right) = d-z \qquad (linear\ neuron)$$

$$\delta^{hx} = f^{h\,\prime}\left(net_{kj}^{\ h}\right) c_{kj}^{\ hy} b_j^{\ y} = c_{kj}^{\ hy} b_j^{\ y} \qquad (linear\ neuron)$$

$$\delta^x = f_x^{\,\prime}\left(net_k^x\right) \qquad\qquad\qquad\qquad (11\text{-}16)$$

General Learning Formulae of First Hidden Layer y Neurons in UGS-HONN Model and UGC-HONN Model (Model 1 and Model 2)

Based on Chapter 1 formulae from (1-178: D.1) to (1-194: D.17), UGS-HONN and UGC-HONN models (model 1 and 2) are rewritten as follows:

For a function of *y* input part:

$$b_j^{\ y} = f_j^{\ y}\left(net_j^{\ y}\right)$$

$$f_y^{\,\prime}\left(net_j^{\ y}\right) = \partial b_j^{\ y} / \partial\left(net_j^{\ y}\right) \qquad\qquad (11\text{-}17)$$

Using the above procedure:

$$c_j^y(t+1) = c_j^y(t) - \eta\left(\partial E_p / \partial c_j^y\right)$$

$$= c_j^y(t) + \eta(d-z) f^{o\,\prime}\left(net^o\right) c_{kj}^{o} * f^{h\,\prime}\left(net_{kj}^{h}\right) c_{kj}^{hx} b_k^{x} c_{kj}^{hy} f_y^{\,\prime}\left(net_j^y\right) y$$

$$= c_j^y(t) + \eta * \delta^{ol} * c_{kj}^{o} * \delta^{hy} * c_{kj}^{hy} * \delta^{y} * y$$

where

$$\delta^{ol} = (d-z) f^{o\,\prime}\left(net^o\right) = d - z \qquad \left(linear\ neuron\ \ f^{o\,\prime}\left(net^o\right) = 1\right)$$

$$\delta^{hy} = f^{h\,\prime}\left(net_{kj}^{h}\right) c_{kj}^{hx} b_k^{x} = c_{kj}^{hx} b_k^{x} \qquad \left(linear\ neuron\ \ f^{h\,\prime}\left(net_{kj}^{h}\right) = 1\right)$$

$$\delta^{y} = f_y^{\prime}\left(net_j^y\right) \tag{11-18}$$

Learning Formulae of UGS-HONN Model for the First Hidden Layer

The first hidden layer neurons in UGS-HONN (Model 1 and Model 2) use sigmoid and sine functions. Based on Chapter 1 formulae from (1-315) to (1-320: UGS-HONN D.17), update learning formulae of UGS-HONN models (model 1 and 2) are rewritten as follows:

Let

$$f_k^j\left(c_k^j x\right) = \left(1/\left(1 + \exp(c_k^x(-x))\right)\right)^k \tag{11-19}$$

$$f_j^y\left(c_j^k y\right) = \sin^j(j * c_j^k y) \tag{11-20}$$

For a sigmoid function of x input side:

$$b_k^{\;x} = f_k^{\;x}\left(net_k^{\;x}\right) = \left[1/\left(1+\exp(-net_k^{\;x})\right)\right]^k = \left[1/\left(1+\exp(c_k^{\;x}*(-x))\right)\right]^k$$

$$f_x'\left(net_k^{\;x}\right) = \partial b_k^{\;x}/\partial\left(net_k^{\;x}\right)$$

$$= \partial\left[1/\left(1+\exp(-net_k^{\;x})\right)\right]^k/\partial\left(net_k^{\;x}\right)$$

$$= k*\left[1/\left(1+\exp(-net_k^{\;x})\right)\right]^{k-1}*\left(1+\exp(-net_k^{\;x})\right)^{-2}*\exp(-net_k^{\;x})$$

$$= k*\left[1/\left(1+\exp(-c_k^{\;x}*x)\right)\right]^{k-1}*\left(1+\exp(-c_k^{\;x}*x)\right)^{-2}*\exp(-c_k^{\;x}*x)$$

$$(11\text{-}21)$$

$$c_k^{\;x}(t+1) = c_k^{\;x}(t)-\eta\left(\partial E_p/\partial c_k^{\;x}\right)$$

$$= c_k^{\;x}(t)+\eta(d-z)f^{o\,\prime}\left(net^o\right)c_{kj}^{\;o}*f^{h\,\prime}\left(net_{kj}^{\;h}\right)c_{kj}^{\;hy}b_j^{\;y}c_{kj}^{\;hx}f_x'\left(net_k^{\;x}\right)x$$

$$= c_k^{\;x}(t)+\eta*\delta^{ol}*c_{kj}^{\;o}*\delta^{hx}*c_{kj}^{\;hx}*f_x'\left(net_k^{\;x}\right)*x$$

$$= c_k^{\;x}(t)+\eta*\delta^{ol}*c_{kj}^{\;o}*\delta^{hx}*c_{kj}^{\;hx}$$

$$*\left[k*\left[1/\left(1+\exp(-c_k^{\;x}*x)\right)\right]^{k-1}*\left(1+\exp(-c_k^{\;x}*x)\right)^{-2}*\exp(-c_k^{\;x}*x)\right]*x$$

$$= c_k^{\;x}(t)+\eta*\delta^{ol}*c_{kj}^{\;o}*\delta^{hx}*c_{kj}^{\;hx}*\delta^x*x$$

$$(11\text{-}22)$$

where

$$\delta^{ol} = (d-z)f^{o\,\prime}\left(net^o\right) = d-z \qquad \left(linear\ neuron\ f^{o\,\prime}\left(net^o\right)=1\right)$$

$$\delta^{hx} = f^{h\,\prime}\left(net_{kj}^{\;h}\right)c_{kj}^{\;hy}b_j^{\;y} = c_{kj}^{\;hy}b_j^{\;y} \qquad \left(linear\ neuron\ f^{h\,\prime}\left(net_{kj}^{\;h}\right)=1\right)$$

$$\delta^x = f_x'\left(net_k^{\;x}\right) = k*\left[1/\left(1+\exp(-c_k^{\;x}*x)\right)\right]^{k-1}*\left(1+\exp(-c_k^{\;x}*x)\right)^{-2}*\exp(-c_k^{\;x}*x)$$

For an ultra-high frequency sine function of y input part:

$$b_j^{\;y} = f_j^{\;y}\left(net_j^{\;y}\right) = \sin^j(j*net_j^{\;y}) = \sin^j(j*c_j^{\;y}*y)$$

$$f_y'\left(net_j^y\right) = \partial b_j^y / \partial\left(net_j^y\right)$$

$$= \partial\left(\sin^j(j*net_j^y)\right)/\partial\left(net_j^y\right)$$

$$= j\sin^{j-1}(j*net_j^y)*\cos(j*net_j^y)*j \qquad (11\text{-}23)$$

$$= j^2 * \sin^{j-1}(j*net_j^y)*\cos(j*net_j^y)$$

$$= j^2 * \sin^{j-1}(j*c_j^y*y)*\cos(j*c_j^y*y)$$

Using the above procedure:

$$c_j^y(t+1) = c_j^y(t) - \eta\left(\partial E_p / \partial c_j^y\right)$$

$$= c_j^y(t) + \eta(d-z)f^{o\,\prime}\left(net^o\right)c_{kj}^o * f^{h\,\prime}\left(net_{kj}^h\right)c_{kj}^{hx}b_k^x c_{kj}^{hy} f_y'\left(net_j^y\right)y$$

$$= c_j^y(t) + \eta*\delta^{ol}*c_{kj}^o*\delta^{hy}*c_{kj}^{hy}*\left(j^2\right)\sin^{j-1}(j*c_j^y*y)\cos(j*c_j^y*y)*y$$

$$= c_j^y(t) + \eta*\delta^{ol}*c_{kj}^o*\delta^{hy}*c_{kj}^{hy}*\delta^y*y$$

$$(11\text{-}24)$$

where

$$\delta^{ol} = (d-z)f^{o\prime}\left(net^o\right) = d-z \qquad \left(linear\ neuron\ f^{o\,\prime}\left(net^o\right)=1\right)$$

$$\delta^{hy} = f^{h\prime}\left(net_{kj}^{hy}\right)c_{kj}^{hx}b_k^x = c_{kj}^{hx}b_k^x \qquad \left(linear\ neuron\ f^{h\,\prime}\left(net_{kj}^{hy}\right)=1\right)$$

$$\delta^y = f_y'\left(net_j^y\right) = \left(j^2\right)\sin^{j-1}(j*c_j^y*y)\cos(j*c_j^y*y)$$

Learning Formulae of UGC-HONN Model for the First Hidden Layer

The first hidden layer neurons in UGC-HONN (Model 1 and Model 2) use sigmoid and cosine functions. Based on Chapter 1 formulae from (1-321) to (1-326: UGC-HONN D.17), update learning formulae of UGC-HONN models (model 1 and 2) are rewritten as follows:

Let

$$f_k^{\ j}\left(c_k^{\ j}x\right)=\left(1/\left(1+\exp(c_k^{\ x}\left(-x\right)\right)\right)\right)^k \tag{11-25}$$

$$f_j^{\ y}\left(c_j^{\ k}y\right)=\cos^j\left(j*c_j^{\ k}y\right) \tag{11-26}$$

For a sigmoid function of x input side:

$$b_k^{\ x}=f_k^{\ x}\left(net_k^{\ x}\right)=\left[1/\left(1+\exp(-net_k^{\ x})\right)\right]^k=\left[1/\left(1+\exp(c_k^{\ x}*(-x))\right)\right]^k$$

$$f_x{}'\left(net_k^{\ x}\right)=\partial b_k^{\ x}/\partial\left(net_k^{\ x}\right)=\partial\left[1/\left(1+\exp(-net_k^{\ x})\right)\right]^k/\partial\left(net_k^{\ x}\right)$$

$$=k*\left[1/\left(1+\exp(-net_k^{\ x})\right)\right]^{k-1}*\left(1+\exp(-net_k^{\ x})\right)^{-2}*\exp(-net_k^{\ x})$$

$$=k*\left[1/\left(1+\exp(-c_k^{\ x}*x)\right)\right]^{k-1}*\left(1+\exp(-c_k^{\ x}*x)\right)^{-2}*\exp(-c_k^{\ x}*x) \tag{11-27}$$

$$c_k^{\ x}\left(t+1\right)=c_k^{\ x}\left(t\right)-\eta\left(\frac{\partial E_p}{\partial c_k^{\ x}}\right)$$

$$=c_k^{\ x}\left(t\right)+\eta\left(d-z\right)f^{o'}\left(net^o\right)c_{kj}^{\ o}*f^{h'}\left(net_{kj}^{\ h}\right)c_{kj}^{\ hy}b_j^{\ y}c_{kj}^{\ hx}f_x'\left(net_k^{\ x}\right)x$$

$$=c_k^{\ x}\left(t\right)+\eta*\delta^{ol}*c_{kj}^{\ o}*\delta^{hx}*c_{kj}^{\ hx}*f_x'\left(net_k^{\ x}\right)*x$$

$$=c_k^{\ x}\left(t\right)+\eta*\delta^{ol}*c_{kj}^{\ o}*\delta^{hx}*c_{kj}^{\ hx}$$

$$*\left[k*\left[1/\left(1+\exp(-c_k^{\ x}*x)\right)\right]^{k-1}*\left(1+\exp(-c_k^{\ x}*x)\right)^{-2}*\exp(-c_k^{\ x}*x)\right]*x$$

$$=c_k^{\ x}\left(t\right)+\eta*\delta^{ol}*c_{kj}^{\ o}*\delta^{hx}*c_{kj}^{\ hx}*\delta^x*x \tag{11-28}$$

where

$$\delta^{ol}=\left(d-z\right)f^{o'}\left(net^o\right)=d-z \qquad \left(linear\ neuron\ f^{o\,'}\left(net^o\right)=1\right)$$

$$\delta^{hx}=f^{h'}\left(net_{kj}^{\ h}\right)c_{kj}^{\ hy}b_j^{\ y}=c_{kj}^{\ hy}b_j^{\ y} \qquad \left(linear\ neuron\ f^{h\,'}\left(net_{kj}^{\ h}\right)=1\right)$$

$$\delta^x = f_x'\left(net_k^x\right) = k*\left[1/\left(1+\exp(-c_k^x*x)\right)\right]^{k-1}*\left(1+\exp(-c_k^x*x)\right)^{-2}*\exp(-c_k^x*x)$$

For an ultra-high frequency cosine function of y input part:

$$b_j^y = f_j^y\left(net_j^y\right) = \cos^j(j*net_j^y) = \cos^j(j*c_j^y*y)$$

$$
\begin{aligned}
f_y'\left(net_j^y\right) &= \partial b_j^y / \partial\left(net_j^y\right) \\
&= \partial\left(\cos^j(j*net_j^y)\right) / \partial\left(net_j^y\right) \\
&= j\cos^{j-1}(j*net_j^y)*\left(-\sin(j*net_j^y)\right)*j \\
&= -j^2*\cos^{j-1}(j*net_j^y)*\sin(j*net_j^y) \\
&= -j^2*\cos^{j-1}(j*c_j^y*y)*\sin(j*c_j^y*y)
\end{aligned}
\qquad (11\text{-}29)
$$

Using the above procedure:

$$
\begin{aligned}
c_j^y(t+1) &= c_j^y(t) - \eta\left(\frac{\partial E_p}{\partial c_j^y}\right) \\
&= c_j^y(t) + \eta(d-z) f^{o'}\left(net^o\right)c_{kj}^o * f^{h'}\left(net_{kj}^h\right)c_{kj}^{hx}b_k^x c_{kj}^{hy} f_y'\left(net_j^y\right)y \\
&= c_j^y(t) + \eta*\delta^{ol}*c_{kj}^o*\delta^{hy}*c_{kj}^{hy}*\left(-j^2\right)*\cos^{j-1}(j*c_j^y*y)*\sin(j*c_j^y*y)*y \\
&= c_j^y(t) + \eta*\delta^{ol}*c_{kj}^o*\delta^{hy}*c_{kj}^{hy}*\delta^y*y
\end{aligned}
$$

$$(11\text{-}30)$$

where

$$\delta^{ol} = (d-z) f^{o'}\left(net^o\right) = d-z \qquad \left(\text{linear neuron } f^{o\,'}\left(net^o\right)=1\right)$$

$$\delta^{hy} = f^{h'}\left(net_{kj}^{hy}\right)c_{kj}^{hx}b_k^x = c_{kj}^{hx}b_k^x \qquad \left(\text{linear neuron } f^{h\,'}\left(net_{kj}^{hy}\right)=1\right)$$

$$\delta^y = f_y'\left(net_j^y\right) = \left(-j^2\right)*\cos^{j-1}(j*c_j^y*y)*\sin(j*c_j^y*y)$$

UGT-HONN TESTING

UGS-HONN model is used to recognize the data pattern. Test results are shown in Table 1 and Figure 3 and Figure 4. UPC-HONN model is used to recognize the data pattern too. Test results are shown in Table 2 and Figure 5 and Figure 6

In Table 1, UGS-HONN

model 0 has been used. The order number for UGS-HONN model is 6. In the first table of Table 1, the "No." column shows total 19 points are chosen. The "UGS-HONN x" column displays the input x values, which are all "1" has been used. The "UGS-HONN y" column displays the input y values, which are 0, 0.1, 0.2, 0.3, 0.4, 05, 0.7, 0.8, 0.9, 1, 2, 3, 4, 5, 6, 7 and 8 are used. The "UGS-HONN z" column displays the output z values. The "Original Data" column displays the original data values. The "Absolute Original Data" column displays the absolute values for original data. The "Difference" column shows the difference between UGS-HONN output z and the original data (UPS-HONN z – Original Data). The "Absolute Difference" column shows the absolute difference between UGS-HONN output z and the original data (|UGS-HONN z – Original Data|). The "UGS-HONN Error %" column gives the error percentage for UGS-HONN Model (UGS-HONN error % = absolute difference / Absolute original Data * 100%). The average UGS-HONN error is 0.00005991%, which is very closed to zero. After training UGS-HONN model by using original data values, in the second table of Table 1, the UGS-HONN all coefficients are displayed. For examples, $c_{00}{}^{o}= 0.6858$, $c_{01}{}^{o}= 0.9365$, and $c_{10}{}^{o}= -0.4786$. In the third table of Table 1, gives the values for $c_{kj}{}^{o}*(1/(1+exp(-x)))^{k}*sin^{j}(j*y)$, when $x=1$, $y=0.1$, $k=0,1,2,3,4,5,6$, and $j=0,1,2,3,4,5,6$. For examples, $c_{01}{}^{o}*(1/(1+exp(-x)))^{0}*sin^{1}(1*0.1)=0.09349399$, $c_{02}{}^{o}*(1/(1+exp(-x)))^{0}*sin^{2}(2*0.1)=0.14757158$, and $c_{03}{}^{o}*(1/(1+exp(-x)))^{0}*sin^{3}(3*0.1)=-0.28027136$. And $z=\mathring{a} \ c_{kj}{}^{o}*(1/(1+exp(-x))) \ ^{k}*sin^{j}(j*y)=\mathring{a} \ c_{kj}{}^{o}*(1)^{k}*sin^{j}(j*0.1)=-0.01484859$.

The pattern recognition results for UGS-HONN data are provided in Figure 3. Figure 3 shows the original data, while Figure 4 presents the data pattern results for UGS-HONN recognition. Results from Figure 4 suggestions that the UGS-HONN model can recognize data pattern very well, since the average error percentage is close to 10^{-6}.

Based on the training of UGS-HONN model, UGS-HONN has the following formula to recognize the original data pattern:

$z = å\ c_{kj}{}^{o} * (1/(1+exp(-x)))^{k} * sin^{j}(j*y)\ (k, j = 0,1,2,3,4,5,6,)$

$= c_{00}{}^{o} * (1/(1+exp(-x)))^{0} * sin^{0}(0*y) + c_{10}{}^{o} * (1/(1+exp(-x)))^{1} * sin^{0}(0*y)$

$+ c_{20}{}^{o} * (1/(1+exp(-x)))^{2} * sin^{0}(0*y) + c_{30}{}^{o} * (1/(1+exp(-x)))^{3} * sin^{0}(0*y)$

$+ c_{40}{}^{o} * (1/(1+exp(-x)))^{4} * sin^{0}(0*y) + c_{50}{}^{o} * (1/(1+exp(-x)))^{5} * sin^{0}(0*y)$

$+ c_{60}{}^{o} * (1/(1+exp(-x)))^{6} * sin^{0}(0*y)$

$+ c_{01}{}^{o} * (1/(1+exp(-x)))^{0} * sin^{1}(1*y) + c_{11}{}^{o} * (1/(1+exp(-x)))^{1} * sin^{1}(1*y)$

$+ c_{21}{}^{o} * (1/(1+exp(-x)))^{2} * sin^{1}(1*y) + c_{31}{}^{o} * (1/(1+exp(-x)))^{3} * sin^{1}(1*y)$

$+ c_{41}{}^{o} * (1/(1+exp(-x)))^{4} * sin^{1}(1*y) + c_{51}{}^{o} * (1/(1+exp(-x)))^{5} * sin^{1}(1*y)$

$+ c_{61}{}^{o} * (1/(1+exp(-x)))^{6} * sin^{1}(1*y)$

$+ c_{02}{}^{o} * (1/(1+exp(-x)))^{0} * sin^{2}(2*y) + c_{12}{}^{o} * (1/(1+exp(-x)))^{1} * sin^{2}(2*y)$

$+ c_{22}{}^{o} * (1/(1+exp(-x)))^{2} * sin^{2}(2*y) + c_{32}{}^{o} * (1/(1+exp(-x)))^{3} * sin^{2}(2*y)$

$+ c_{42}{}^{o} * (1/(1+exp(-x)))^{4} * sin^{2}(2*y) + c_{52}{}^{o} * (1/(1+exp(-x)))^{5} * sin^{2}(2*y)$

$+ c_{62}{}^{o} * (1/(1+exp(-x)))^{6} * sin^{2}(2*y)$

$+ c_{03}{}^{o} * (1/(1+exp(-x)))^{0} * sin^{3}(3*y) + c_{13}{}^{o} * (1/(1+exp(-x00)^{1} * sin^{3}(3*y)$

$+ c_{23}{}^{o} * (1/(1+exp(-x)))^{2} * sin^{3}(3*y) + c_{33}{}^{o} * (1/(1+exp(-x)))^{3} * sin^{3}(3*y)$

$+ c_{43}{}^{o} * (1/(1+exp(-x)))^{4} * sin^{3}(3*y) + c_{53}{}^{o} * (1/(1+exp(-x)))^{5} * sin^{3}(3*y)$

$+ c_{63}{}^{o} * (1/(1+exp(-x)))^{6} * sin^{3}(3*y)$

$+ c_{04}{}^{o} * (1/(1+exp(-x)))^{0} * sin^{4}(4*y) + c_{14}{}^{o} * (1/(1+exp(-x)))^{1} * sin^{4}(4*y)$

$+ c_{24}{}^{o} * (1/(1+exp(-x)))^{2} * sin^{4}(4*y) + c_{34}{}^{o} * (1/(1+exp(-x)))^{3} * sin^{4}(4*y)$

$+ c_{44}{}^{o} * (1/(1+exp(-x)))^{4} * sin^{4}(4*y) + c_{54}{}^{o} * (1/(1+exp(-x)))^{5} * sin^{4}(4*y)$

$+ c_{64}{}^{o} * (1/(1+exp(-x)))^{6} * sin^{4}(4*y)$

$+ c_{05}{}^{o} * (1/(1+exp(-x)))^{0} * sin^{5}(5*y) + c_{15}{}^{o} * (1/(1+exp(-x)))^{1} * sin^{5}(5*y)$

$+ c_{25}{}^{o} * (1/(1+exp(-x)))^{2} * sin^{5}(4*y) + c_{35}{}^{o} * (1/(1+exp(-x)))^{3} * sin^{5}(5*y)$

$+ c_{45}{}^{o} * (1/(1+exp(-x)))^{4} * sin^{5}(5*y) + c_{55}{}^{o} * (1/(1+exp(-x)))^{5} * sin^{5}(5*y)$

$+ c_{65}{}^{o} * (1/(1+exp(-x)))^{6} * sin^{5}(5*y)$

$+ c_{06}{}^{o} * (1/(1+exp(-x)))^{0} * sin^{6}(6*y) + c_{16}{}^{o} * (1/(1+exp(-x)))^{1} * sin^{6}(6*y)$

$+ c_{26}{}^{o} * (1/(1+exp(-x)))^{2} * sin^{6}(6*y) + c_{36}{}^{o} * (1/(1+exp(-x)))^{3} * sin^{6}(6*y)$

$+ c_{46}{}^{o} * (1/(1+exp(-x)))^{4} * sin^{6}(6*y) + c_{56}{}^{o} * (1/(1+exp(-x)))^{5} * sin^{6}(6*y)$

$+ c_{66}{}^{o} * (1/(1+exp(-x)))^{6} * sin^{6}(6*y)$

$= 0.6858 * (1/(1+exp(-x)))^{0} * sin^{0}(0*y) + (-0.4786) * (1/(1+exp(-x)))^{1} * sin^{0}(0*y)$

$+ (-0.6554) * (1/(1+exp(-x)))^{2} * sin^{0}(0*y) + (-0.5309) * (1/(1+exp(-x)))^{3} * sin^{0}(0*y)$

$+ (-1.2674) * (1/(1+exp(-x)))^{4} * sin^{0}(0*y) + (-0.5498) * (1/(1+exp(-x)))^{5} * sin^{0}(0*y)$

$+ 0.1297 * (1/(1+exp(-x)))^{6} * sin^{0}(0*y)$

$+ 0.9365 * (1/(1+exp(-x)))^{0} * sin^{1}(1*y) + 0.0579 * (1/(1+exp(-x)))^{1} * sin^{1}(1*y)$

$+ (-0.0401) * (1/(1+exp(-x)))^{2} * sin^{1}(1*y) + (-0.9998) * (1/(1+exp(-x)))^{3} * sin^{1}(1*y)$

$+ 0.9786 * (1/(1+exp(-x)))^{4} * sin^{1}(1*y) + 0.2332 * (1/(1+exp(-x)))^{5} * sin^{1}(1*y)$

+ (-0.0313) *(1/(1+exp(-x)))^6*sin^1(1*y)

+0.7428*(1/(1+exp(-x)))^0*sin^2(2*y) + 0.7707*(1/(1+exp(-x)))^1*sin^2(2*y)

+ (-0.7688) *(1/(1+exp(-x)))^2*sin^2(2*y) + (-0.3755) *(1/(1+exp(-x)))^3*sin^2(2*y)

+(-0.8456)*(1/(1+exp(-x)))^4*sin^2(2*y)+0.7245*(1/(1+exp(-x)))^5*sin^2(2*y)

+ (-0.0995) *(1/(1+exp(-x)))^6*sin^2(2*y)

+(-0.9484) *(1/(1+exp(-x)))^0*sin^3(3*y) + (-0.6478) *(1/(1+exp(-x00)^1*sin^3(3*y)

+(-0.4593)*(1/(1+exp(-x)))^2*sin^3(3*y)+0.6315*(1/(1+exp(-x)))^3*sin^3(3*y)

+0.9849*(1/(1+exp(-x)))^4*sin^3(3*y)+(-0.7281)*(1/(1+exp(-x)))^5*sin^3(3*y)

+ 0.6732*(1/(1+exp(-x)))^6*sin^3(3*y)

+(-0.4525)*(1/(1+exp(-x)))^0*sin^4(4*y)+0.5854*(1/(1+exp(-x)))^1*sin^4(4*y)

+(-0.8993)*(1/(1+exp(-x)))^2*sin^4(4*y)+0.5756*(1/(1+exp(-x)))^3*sin^4(4*y)

+(-0.5475)*(1/(1+exp(-x)))^4*sin^4(4*y)+0.7442*(1/(1+exp(-x)))^5*sin^4(4*y)

+ 0.1133*(1/(1+exp(-x)))^6*sin^4(4*y)

+(-0.9242)*(1/(1+exp(-x)))^0*sin^5(5*y)+0.7811*(1/(1+exp(-x)))^1*sin^5(5*y)

+ 0.0489*(1/(1+exp(-x)))^2*sin^5(4*y) + 0.8641*(1/(1+exp(-x)))^3*sin^5(5*y)

+0.5242*(1/(1+exp(-x)))^4*sin^5(5*y)+(-0.1275)*(1/(1+exp(-x)))^5*sin^5(5*y)

+ (-0.1783) *(1/(1+exp(-x)))^6*sin^5(5*y)

+0.7771*(1/(1+exp(-x)))^0*sin^6(6*y)+(-0.3691)*(1/(1+exp(-x)))^1*sin^6(6*y)

+0.0726*(1/(1+exp(-x)))^2*sin^6(6*y)+(-0.1132)*(1/(1+exp(-x)))^3*sin^6(6*y)

+ (-0.6926) *(1/(1+exp(-x)))^4*sin^6(6*y) + (-0.7067)*(1/(1+exp(-x)))^5*sin^6(6*y)

+ 0.9651*(1/(1+exp(-x)))^6*sin^6(6*y)

In Table 2, UGC-HONN model 0 has been used. The order number for UGC-HONN model is 6. In the first table of Table 2, the "No." column shows a total of 19 points are chosen. The "UGC-HONN x" column displays the input x values, which are all "1" s are used. The "UGC-HONN y" column displays the input y values, which are 0, 0.1, 0.2, 0.3, 0.4, 05, 0.7, 0.8, 0.9, 1, 2, 3, 4, 5, 6, 7 and 8 are used. The "UGC-HONN z" column displays the output z values. The "Original Data" column displays the original data values. The "Absolute Original Data" column displays the absolute values for original data. The "Difference" column shows the difference between UGC-HONN output z and the original data (UPC-HONN z – Original Data). The "Absolute Difference" column shows the absolute difference between UGC-HONN output z and the original data (|UGC-HONN z – Original Datal). The "UGC-HONN Error %" column gives the error percentage for UGC-HONN Model (UGC-HONN error % = absolute difference / Absolute original Data * 100%). The average UGC-HONN error is 0.00002317%, which is very closed to zero. After training UGC-HONN model by using original data values, in the second table of Table 2, all coefficients in the UGS-HONN model are displayed. For examples, $c_{00}{}^o$= 0.0315, $c_{01}{}^o$= 0.4933, and $c_{10}{}^o$= -0.8243. In the third table of Table 2, gives the values for $c_{kj}{}^o*(1/(1+exp(-x)))^k*cos^j(j*y)$, when $x=1$, $y=0.1$, $k=0,1,2,3,4,5,6$, and $j=0,1,2,3,4,5,6$. For examples, $c_{01}{}^o*(1/(1+exp(-x)))^0*cos^1(1*0.1)=0.49083555$, $c_{02}{}^o*(1/(1+exp(-x)))^0*cos^2(2*0.1)=0.30450669$, and $c_{03}{}^o*(1/(1+exp(-x)))^0*cos^3(3*0.1)=-0.60138432$. And $z=å\ c_{kj}{}^o*(1/(1+exp(-x)))^k*cos^j(j*y)$ =å $c_{kj}{}^o*(1)^k*cos^j(j*0.1)=-0.73321663$.

The pattern recognition results for UGC-HONN data are provided Figure 4. The original data are displayed in Figure 5, while Figure 6 presents the data pattern results for UGC-HONN recognition. Results from Figure 6 show that the UGC-HONN model can recognize data pattern very well, since the average error percentage is close to 10^{-6}.

Based on the training of UGC-HONN model, UGC-HONN has the following formula to recognize the original data pattern:

z=å $c_{kj}{}^o*(1/(1+exp(-x)))^k*cos^j(j*y)$ $(k, j = 0,1,2,3,4,5,6,)$
$= c_{00}{}^o*(1/(1+exp(-x)))^0*cos^0(0*y) + c_{10}{}^o*(1/(1+exp(-x)))^1*cos^0(0*y)$
$+ c_{20}{}^o*(1/(1+exp(-x)))^2*cos^0(0*y) + c_{30}{}^o*(1/(1+exp(-x)))^3*cos^0(0*y)$
$+ c_{40}{}^o*(1/(1+exp(-x)))^4*cos^0(0*y) + c_{50}{}^o*(1/(1+exp(-x)))^5*cos^0(0*y)$
$+ c_{60}{}^o*(1/(1+exp(-x)))^6*cos^0(0*y)$
$+c_{01}{}^o*(1/(1+exp(-x)))^0*cos^1(1*y) + c_{11}{}^o*(1/(1+exp(-x)))^1*cos^1(1*y)$
$+ c_{21}{}^o*(1/(1+exp(-x)))^2*cos^1(1*y) + c_{31}{}^o*(1/(1+exp(-x)))^3*cos^1(1*y)$
$+ c_{41}{}^o*(1/(1+exp(-x)))^4*cos^1(1*y) + c_{51}{}^o*(1/(1+exp(-x)))^5*cos^1(1*y)$
$+ c_{61}{}^o*(1/(1+exp(-x)))^6*cos^1(1*y)$
$+c_{02}{}^o*(1/(1+exp(-x)))^0*cos^2(2*y) + c_{12}{}^o*(1/(1+exp(-x)))^1*cos^2(2*y)$
$+ c_{22}{}^o*(1/(1+exp(-x)))^2*cos^2(2*y) + c_{32}{}^o*(1/(1+exp(-x)))^3*cos^2(2*y)$
$+ c_{42}{}^o*(1/(1+exp(-x)))^4*cos^2(2*y) + c_{52}{}^o*(1/(1+exp(-x)))^5*cos^2(2*y)$
$+ c_{62}{}^o*(1/(1+exp(-x)))^6*cos^2(2*y)$
$+c_{03}{}^o*(1/(1+exp(-x)))^0*cos^3(3*y) + c_{13}{}^o*(1/(1+exp(-x00))^1*cos^3(3*y)$
$+ c_{23}{}^o*(1/(1+exp(-x)))^2*cos^3(3*y) + c_{33}{}^o*(1/(1+exp(-x)))^3*cos^3(3*y)$
$+ c_{43}{}^o*(1/(1+exp(-x)))^4*cos^3(3*y) + c_{53}{}^o*(1/(1+exp(-x)))^5*cos^3(3*y)$
$+ c_{63}{}^o*(1/(1+exp(-x)))^6*cos^3(3*y)$
$+c_{04}{}^o*(1/(1+exp(-x)))^0*cos^4(4*y) + c_{14}{}^o*(1/(1+exp(-x)))^1*cos^4(4*y)$
$+ c_{24}{}^o*(1/(1+exp(-x)))^2*cos^4(4*y) + c_{34}{}^o*(1/(1+exp(-x)))^3*cos^4(4*y)$
$+ c_{44}{}^o*(1/(1+exp(-x)))^4*cos^4(4*y) + c_{54}{}^o*(1/(1+exp(-x)))^5*cos^4(4*y)$
$+ c_{64}{}^o*(1/(1+exp(-x)))^6*cos^4(4*y)$

$+c_{05}{}^{o}*(1/(1+\exp(-x)))^{0}*\cos^{5}(5*y) + c_{15}{}^{o}*(1/(1+\exp(-x)))^{1}*\cos^{5}(5*y)$
$+ c_{25}{}^{o}*(1/(1+\exp(-x)))^{2}*\cos^{5}(4*y) + c_{35}{}^{o}*(1/(1+\exp(-x)))^{3}*\cos^{5}(5*y)$
$+ c_{45}{}^{o}*(1/(1+\exp(-x)))^{4}*\cos^{5}(5*y) + c_{55}{}^{o}*(1/(1+\exp(-x)))^{5}*\cos^{5}(5*y)$
$+ c_{65}{}^{o}*(1/(1+\exp(-x)))^{6}*\cos^{5}(5*y)$
$+c_{06}{}^{o}*(1/(1+\exp(-x)))^{0}*\cos^{6}(6*y) + c_{16}{}^{o}*(1/(1+\exp(-x)))^{1}*\cos^{6}(6*y)$
$+ c_{26}{}^{o}*(1/(1+\exp(-x)))^{2}*\cos^{6}(6*y) + c_{36}{}^{o}*(1/(1+\exp(-x)))^{3}*\cos^{6}(6*y)$
$+ c_{46}{}^{o}*(1/(1+\exp(-x)))^{4}*\cos^{6}(6*y) + c_{56}{}^{o}*(1/(1+\exp(-x)))^{5}*\cos^{6}(6*y)$
$+ c_{66}{}^{o}*(1/(1+\exp(-x)))^{6}*\cos^{6}(6*y)$
$=0.0315*(1/(1+\exp(-x)))^{0}*\cos^{0}(0*y)+(-0.8243)*(1/(1+\exp(-x)))^{1}*\cos^{0}(0*y)$
$+ (-0.0011)*(1/(1+\exp(-x)))^{2}*\cos^{0}(0*y) + (-0.9866)*(1/(1+\exp(-x)))^{3}*\cos^{0}(0*y)$
$+ (-0.6021)*(1/(1+\exp(-x)))^{4}*\cos^{0}(0*y) + (-0.9955)*(1/(1+\exp(-x)))^{5}*\cos^{0}(0*y)$
$+ 0.5754*(1/(1+\exp(-x)))^{6}*\cos^{0}(0*y)$
$+0.4933*(1/(1+\exp(-x)))^{0}*\cos^{1}(1*y) + 0.5147*(1/(1+\exp(-x)))^{1}*\cos^{1}(1*y)$
$+ (-0.5079)*(1/(1+\exp(-x)))^{2}*\cos^{1}(1*y) + (-0.4566)*(1/(1+\exp(-x)))^{3}*\cos^{1}(1*y)$
$+0.4354*(1/(1+\exp(-x)))^{4}*\cos^{1}(1*y) + 0.7900*(1/(1+\exp(-x)))^{5}*\cos^{1}(1*y)$
$+ (-0.5981)*(1/(1+\exp(-x)))^{6}*\cos^{1}(1*y)$
$+0.3107*(1/(1+\exp(-x)))^{0}*\cos^{2}(2*y) + 0.3486*(1/(1+\exp(-x)))^{1}*\cos^{2}(2*y)$
$+ (-0.3347)*(1/(1+\exp(-x)))^{2}*\cos^{2}(2*y) + (-0.6434)*(1/(1+\exp(-x)))^{3}*\cos^{2}(2*y)$
$+(-0.4135)*(1/(1+\exp(-x)))^{4}*\cos^{2}(2*y)+0.3924*(1/(1+\exp(-x)))^{5}*\cos^{2}(2*y)$
$+ (-0.6674)*(1/(1+\exp(-x)))^{6}*\cos^{2}(2*y)$
$+(-0.6295)*(1/(1+\exp(-x)))^{0}*\cos^{3}(3*y) + (-0.3269)*(1/(1+\exp(-x00))^{1}*\cos^{3}(3*y)$
$+(-0.1384)*(1/(1+\exp(-x)))^{2}*\cos^{3}(3*y)+0.3106*(1/(1+\exp(-x)))^{3}*\cos^{3}(3*y)$
$+0.6630*(1/(1+\exp(-x)))^{4}*\cos^{3}(3*y)+(-0.4072)*(1/(1+\exp(-x)))^{5}*\cos^{3}(3*y)$
$+ 0.3523*(1/(1+\exp(-x)))^{6}*\cos^{3}(3*y)$
$+(-0.2437)*(1/(1+\exp(-x)))^{0}*\cos^{4}(4*y)+0.3766*(1/(1+\exp(-x)))^{1}*\cos^{4}(4*y)$
$+(-0.6805)*(1/(1+\exp(-x)))^{2}*\cos^{4}(4*y)+0.3668*(1/(1+\exp(-x)))^{3}*\cos^{4}(4*y)$
$+(-0.3387)*(1/(1+\exp(-x)))^{4}*\cos^{4}(4*y)+0.5354*(1/(1+\exp(-x)))^{5}*\cos^{4}(4*y)$
$+ 0.9045*(1/(1+\exp(-x)))^{6}*\cos^{4}(4*y)$
$+(-0.8365)*(1/(1+\exp(-x)))^{0}*\cos^{5}(5*y)+0.6934*(1/(1+\exp(-x)))^{1}*\cos^{5}(5*y)$
$+0.9502*(1/(1+\exp(-x)))^{2}*\cos^{5}(4*y)+0.7764*(1/(1+\exp(-x)))^{3}*\cos^{5}(5*y)$
$+0.4365*(1/(1+\exp(-x)))^{4}*\cos^{5}(5*y)+(-0.0398)*(1/(1+\exp(-x)))^{5}*\cos^{5}(5*y)$
$+ (-0.0806)*(1/(1+\exp(-x)))^{6}*\cos^{5}(5*y)$
$+0.8902*(1/(1+\exp(-x)))^{0}*\cos^{6}(6*y)+(-0.4825)*(1/(1+\exp(-x)))^{1}*\cos^{6}(6*y)$
$+0.1950*(1/(1+\exp(-x)))^{2}*\cos^{6}(6*y)+(-0.5366)*(1/(1+\exp(-x)))^{3}*\cos^{6}(6*y)$

Figure 3. UGS-HONN data pattern recognition

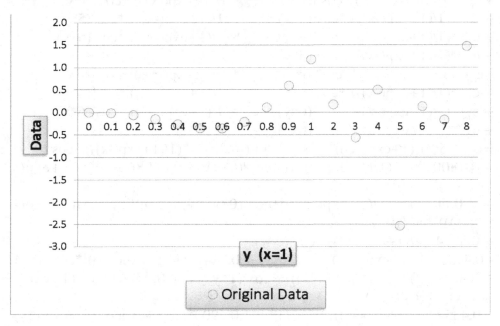

Figure 4. UGS-HONN data pattern recognition

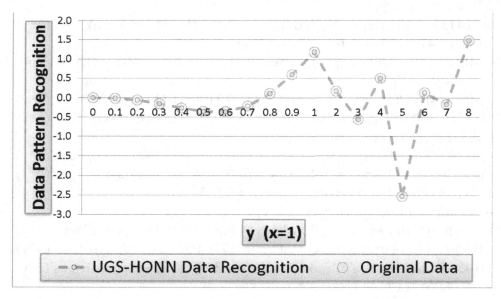

Table 1 UGS-HONN Data Pattern Recognition (n = 6, Model 0)

No.	UGS-HONN x	UGS-HONN y	UGS-HONN z	Original Data	Absolute Original Data	Difference	Absolute Difference	UGS-HONN Error %
1	1	0	0.00000000	0.000000	0.000000	0.00000000	0.00000000	0.000000%
2	1	0.1	-0.01484859	-0.014849	0.014849	0.00000041	0.00000041	0.000084%
3	1	0.2	-0.06048644	-0.060486	0.060486	-0.00000044	0.00000044	0.000091%
4	1	0.3	-0.14886556	-0.148866	0.148866	0.00000044	0.00000044	0.000090%
5	1	0.4	-0.26167745	-0.261677	0.261677	-0.00000045	0.00000045	0.000093%
6	1	0.5	-0.35110658	-0.351107	0.351107	0.00000042	0.00000042	0.000086%
7	1	0.6	-0.35314432	-0.353144	0.353144	-0.00000032	0.00000032	0.000066%
8	1	0.7	-0.20927225	-0.209272	0.209272	-0.00000025	0.00000025	0.000052%
9	1	0.8	0.11084710	0.110847	0.110847	0.00000010	0.00000010	0.000021%
10	1	0.9	0.59367746	0.593678	0.593678	-0.00000054	0.00000054	0.000111%
11	1	1	1.17898893	1.178989	1.178989	-0.00000007	0.00000007	0.000013%
13	1	2	0.17275166	0.172752	0.172752	-0.00000034	0.00000034	0.000070%
14	1	3	-0.56122411	-0.561224	0.561224	-0.00000011	0.00000011	0.000022%
15	1	4	0.49855874	0.498559	0.498559	-0.00000026	0.00000026	0.000053%
16	1	5	-2.53172894	-2.531729	2.531729	0.00000006	0.00000006	0.000012%
17	1	6	0.13139118	0.131391	0.131391	0.00000018	0.00000018	0.000036%
18	1	7	-0.16800261	-0.168003	0.168003	0.00000039	0.00000039	0.000079%
19	1	8	1.47238249	1.472382	1.472382	0.00000049	0.00000049	0.000099%
Average					0.4899419		0.0000002935	0.00005991%

$c_{kj}{}^o$	k=0	k=1	k=2	k=3	k=4	k=5	k=6
j=0	0.6858	-0.4786	-0.6554	-0.5309	-1.2674	-0.5498	0.1297
j=1	0.9365	0.0579	-0.0401	-0.9998	0.9786	0.2332	-0.0313
j=2	0.7428	0.7707	-0.7688	-0.3755	-0.8456	0.7245	-0.0995
j=3	-0.9484	-0.6478	-0.4593	0.6315	0.9849	-0.7281	0.6732
j=4	-0.4525	0.5854	-0.8993	0.5756	-0.5475	0.7442	0.1133
j=5	-0.9242	0.7811	0.0489	0.8641	0.5242	-0.1275	-0.1783
j=6	0.7771	-0.3691	0.0726	-0.1132	-0.6926	-0.7067	0.9651

x=1, y=0.1		k = 0	k = 1	k = 2	k = 3	k = 4	k = 5	k = 6
j =	0	0.00000000	0.00000000	0.00000000	0.00000000	0.00000000	0.00000000	0.00000000
j =	1	0.09349399	0.00422578	-0.00213956	-0.03899829	0.02790550	0.00486144	-0.00047702
j =	2	0.14757158	0.11193563	-0.08162977	-0.02914723	-0.04798489	0.03005593	-0.00301764
j =	3	-0.28027136	-0.13995238	-0.07254174	0.07291503	0.08313579	-0.04493028	0.03036997
j =	4	-0.17621180	0.16665613	-0.18716531	0.08757774	-0.06089887	0.06051555	0.00673534
j =	5	-0.44308508	0.27376630	0.01252952	0.16186081	0.07178387	-0.01276416	-0.01304925
j =	6	0.43878367	-0.15235958	0.02190859	-0.02497333	-0.11170298	-0.08332389	0.08318766
Subtotal		-0.21971901	0.26427188	-0.30903827	0.22923472	-0.03776157	-0.04558541	0.10374907
$z = \Sigma c_{kj}{}^{o*}(1/(1+exp(-x)))^{k*}sin^j(j*y)$			(k= 0, 1, 2, 3, 4, 5, 6			j = 0, 1, 2, 3, 4, 5, 6) =		-0.01484859

Figure 5. UGC-HONN data pattern recognition

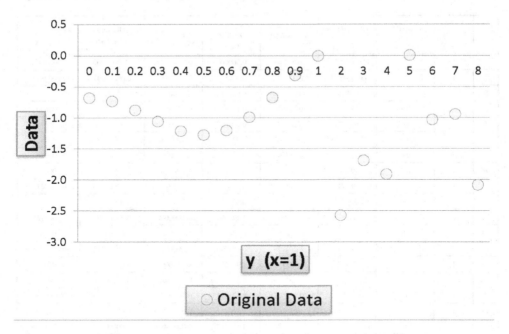

Figure 6. UGC-HONN data pattern recognition

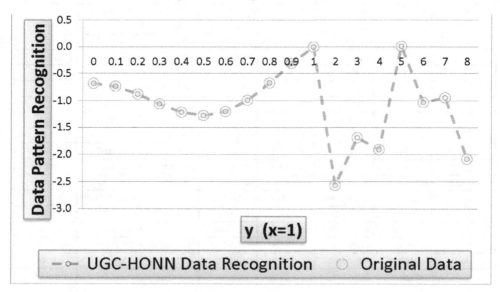

Table 2 UGC-HONN Data Pattern Recognition (n = 6, Model 0)

No.	UGC-HONN x	UGC-HONN y	UGC-HONN z	Original Data	Absolute Original Data	Difference	Absolute Difference	UGC-HONN Error %
1	1	0	-0.67901388	-0.679014	0.679014	0.00000012	0.00000012	0.000011%
2	**1**	**0.1**	**-0.73321663**	-0.733217	0.733217	0.00000037	0.00000037	0.000034%
3	1	0.2	-0.87717494	-0.877175	0.877175	0.00000006	0.00000006	0.000006%
4	1	0.3	-1.06038260	-1.060383	1.060383	0.00000040	0.00000040	0.000037%
5	1	0.4	-1.21528091	-1.215281	1.215281	0.00000009	0.00000009	0.000008%
6	1	0.5	-1.27727157	-1.277272	1.277272	0.00000043	0.00000043	0.000040%
7	1	0.6	-1.20433371	-1.204334	1.204334	0.00000029	0.00000029	0.000027%
8	1	0.7	-0.99075568	-0.990756	0.990756	0.00000032	0.00000032	0.000030%
9	1	0.8	-0.67113083	-0.671131	0.671131	0.00000017	0.00000017	0.000016%
10	1	0.9	-0.31345072	-0.313451	0.313451	0.00000028	0.00000028	0.000026%
11	1	1	-0.00309632	-0.003096	0.003096	-0.00000032	0.00000032	0.000030%
13	1	2	-2.56975825	-2.569758	2.569758	-0.00000025	0.00000025	0.000024%
14	1	3	-1.68937107	-1.689371	1.689371	-0.00000007	0.00000007	0.000007%
15	1	4	-1.91001454	-1.910015	1.910015	0.00000046	0.00000046	0.000043%
16	1	5	0.00849234	0.008492	0.008492	0.00000034	0.00000034	0.000032%
17	1	6	-1.02963976	-1.02964	1.029640	0.00000024	0.00000024	0.000023%
18	1	7	-0.94292615	-0.942926	0.942926	-0.00000015	0.00000015	0.000014%
19	1	8	-2.08157552	-2.0815756	2.081576	0.00000008	0.00000008	0.000007%
Average					1.0698271		0.0000002479	0.00002317%

$c_{kj}{}^o$	k=0	k=1	k=2	k=3	k=4	k=5	k=6
j=0	0.0315	-0.8243	-0.0011	-0.9866	-0.6021	-0.9955	0.5754
j=1	0.4933	0.5147	-0.5079	-0.4566	0.4354	0.7900	-0.5981
j=2	0.3107	0.3486	-0.3347	-0.6434	-0.4135	0.3924	-0.6674
j=3	-0.6295	-0.3269	-0.1384	0.3106	0.6630	-0.4072	0.3523
j=4	-0.2437	0.3766	-0.6805	0.3668	-0.3387	0.5354	0.9045
j=5	-0.8365	0.6934	0.9502	0.7764	0.4365	-0.0398	-0.0806
j=6	0.8902	-0.4825	0.1950	-0.5366	-0.7150	-0.8291	0.0885

x=1, y=0.1	k = 0	k = 1	k = 2	k = 3	k = 4	k = 5	k = 6
j = 0	0.03150000	-0.60261159	-0.00058789	-0.38547627	-0.17197976	-0.20787495	0.08783810
j = 1	0.49083555	0.37439604	-0.27008935	-0.17750776	0.12374340	0.16413941	-0.09084725
j = 2	0.30450669	0.24976705	-0.17531362	-0.24637303	-0.11575501	0.08030553	-0.09985156
j = 3	-0.60138432	-0.22830923	-0.07066377	0.11593494	0.18091668	-0.08123160	0.05137858
j = 4	-0.22446256	0.25358344	-0.33498154	0.13200010	-0.08910710	0.10297401	0.12717743
j = 5	-0.73409781	0.44486066	0.44566381	0.26621348	0.10941603	-0.00729343	-0.01079782
j = 6	0.73467250	-0.29112539	0.08601408	-0.17303653	-0.16855644	-0.14288887	0.01115031
Subtotal	0.00157004	0.20056098	-0.31995829	-0.46824506	-0.13132220	-0.09186989	0.07604779
$z = \Sigma c_{kj}{}^{o*}(1/(1+exp(-x)))^{k*}cos^j(j*y)$			(k= 0, 1, 2, 3, 4, 5, 6			j = 0, 1, 2, 3, 4, 5, 6) =	-0.73321663

+ (-0.7150) $*(1/(1+\exp(-x)))^4*\cos^6(6*y)$ + (-0.8291) $*(1/(1+\exp(-x)))^5*\cos^6(6*y)$

+ $0.0885*(1/(1+\exp(-x)))^6*\cos^6(6*y)$

CONCLUSION

Two nonlinear neural network models, UGS-HONN, UGC-HONN, that are part of the Ultra High Frequency Sigmoid and Trigonometric Higher Order Neural Networks (UGT-HONN), are developed. Based on the structures of UGS-HONN and UGC-HONN, this chapter provides two model learning algorithm formulae. This chapter tests the UGS-HONN and UGC-HONN models to recognize the data patterns. Experimental results show that UGS-HONN and UGC-HONN models can recognize data pattern very well. Using the UGS-HONN and UGC-HONN models, the average error can reach 10^{-6}.

One of the topics for future research is to continue building models using UGT-HONN for different data series. The coefficients of the higher order models will be studied not only using artificial neural network techniques, but also statistical methods. Using nonlinear functions to model and analyze time series data will be a major goal in the future.

REFERENCES

Artyomov, E., & Yadid-Pecht, O. (2005). Modified high-order neural network for invariant pattern recognition. *Pattern Recognition Letters*, *26*(6), 843–851. doi:10.1016/j.patrec.2004.09.029

Fallahnezhad, M., & Zaferanlouei, S. (2013). A Hybrid Higher Order Neural Structure for Pattern Recognition. In Artificial Higher Order Neural Networks for Modeling and Simulation (pp. 364-387). IGI Global.

Foresti, G. L., & Dolso, T. (2004). An adaptive high-order neural tree for pattern recognition. *IEEE Transactions on Systems, Man, and Cybernetics. Part B, Cybernetics*, *34*(2), 988–996. doi:10.1109/TSMCB.2003.818538 PMID:15376845

He, Z., & Siyal, M. Y. (1998). Recognition of transformed English letters with modified higher-order neural networks. *Electronics Letters, 34*(25), 2415–2416. doi:10.1049/el:19981654

He, Z., & Siyal, M. Y. (1999, August). Improvement on higher-order neural networks for invariant object recognition. *Neural Processing Letters, 10*(1), 49–55. doi:10.1023/A:1018610829733

Kaita, T., Tomita, S., & Yamanaka, J. (2002, June). On a higher-order neural network for distortion invariant pattern recognition. *Pattern Recognition Letters, 23*(8), 977 – 984.

Kanaoka, T., Chellappa, R., Yoshitaka, M., & Tomita, S. (1992). A Higher-order neural network for distortion unvariant pattern recognition. *Pattern Recognition Letters, 13*(12), 837–841. doi:10.1016/0167-8655(92)90082-B

Kroner, S. (1995). Adaptive averaging in higher order neural networks for invariant pattern recognition. *Neural Networks*, 2438 - 2435.

Lisboa, P., & Perantonis, S. (1991). Invariant pattern recognition using third-order networks and zernlike moments. In *Proceedings of the IEEE International Joint Conference on Neural Networks* (Vol. 2, pp. 1421-1425). Singapore: IEEE.

Murata, J. (2010). Analysis and Improvement of Function Approximation Capabilities of Pi-Sigma Higher Order Neural Networks. In *Artificial Higher Order Neural Networks for Computer Science and Engineering – Trends for Emerging Applications* (pp. 239-254). IGI Global.

Pao, Y. H. (1989). *Adaptive Pattern Recognition and Neural Networks*. Reading, MA: Addison-Wesley.

Park, S., Smith, M. J. T., & Mersereau, R. M. (2000, October). Target Recognition Based on Directional Filter Banks and higher-order neural network. *Digital Signal Processing, 10*(4), 297–308. doi:10.1006/dspr.2000.0376

Perantonis, S. J., & Lisboa, P. J. G. (1992). Translation, rotation, and scale invariant pattern recognition by high-order neural networks and moment classifiers. *IEEE Transactions on Neural Networks, 3*(2), 241–251. doi:10.1109/72.125865 PMID:18276425

Ragothaman, S., & Lavin, A. (2008). Restatements Due to Improper Revenue Recognition: A Neural Networks Perspective. *Journal of Emerging Technologies in Accounting, 5*(1), 129–142. doi:10.2308/jeta.2008.5.1.129

Reid, M. B., Spirkovska, L., & Ochoa, E. (1989). Rapid training of higher-order neural networks for invariant pattern recognition. *Proceedings of International Joint Conference on Neural Networks, 1,* 689–692.

Reid, M. B., Spirkovska, L., & Ochoa, E. (1989). Rapid training of higher-order neural networks for invariant pattern recognition. In *Proceedings of International Joint Conference on Neural Networks* (*vol.1,* pp.689 – 692). Academic Press.

Ricalde, L. J., Sanchez, E. N., & Alanis, A. Y. (2010). Recurrent Higher Order Neural Network Control for Output Trajectory Tracking with Neural Observers and Constrained Inputs. In Artificial Higher Order Neural Networks for Computer Science and Engineering – Trends for Emerging Applications (pp. 286-311). IGI Global.

Sankar, A., & Mammone, R. J. (1991). Speaker Independent Vowel Recognition using Neural Tree Networks. In *Proceedings of International Joint Conference on Neural Networks* (pp. 809-814). Seattle, WA: Academic Press.

Schmidt, W., & Davis, J. (1993). Pattern recognition properties of various feature spaces for higher order neural networks. *IEEE Transactions on Pattern Analysis and Machine Intelligence, 15,* 795–801.

Selviah, D. R. (2009). High Speed Optical Higher Order Neural Networks for Discovering Data Trends and Patterns in Very Large Databases. In Artificial Higher Order Neural Networks for Economics and Business (pp. 442-465). IGI Global.

Sethi, I. K., & Jan, A. K. (1991). Decision Tree Performance Enhancement Using an Artificial Neural Networks Implementation. In *Artificial Neural Networks and Statistical Pattern Recognition* (pp. 71–88). Amsterdam, The Netherlands: Elsevier.

Shannon, C. E. (1998), Communication in the presence of noise. In *Proceedings of Institute of Radio Engineers* (*vol. 37,* no. 1, pp. 10–21, Jan. 1949). IEEE.

Spirkovska, L., & Reid, M. B. (1990). Connectivity strategies for higher-order neural networks applied to pattern recognition. *Proceedings of International Joint Conference on Neural Networks, 1,* 21–26.

Spirkovska, L., & Reid, M. B. (1990a). An empirical comparison of ID3 and HONNs for distortion invariant object recognition. In *Proceedings of the 2nd International IEEE Conference on Tools for Artificial Intelligence* (pp. 577 – 582). 10.1109/TAI.1990.130402

Spirkovska, L., & Reid, M. B. (1990b). In Connectivity strategies for higher-order neural networks applied to pattern recognition. *Proceedings of International Joint Conference on Neural Networks* (vol.1, pp.21 – 26). 10.1109/IJCNN.1990.137538

Spirkovska, L., & Reid, M. B. (1991). Coarse coding applied to HONNs for PSRI object recognition. In *Proceedings of the International Joint Conference on Neural Networks* (vol.2, pp.931). 10.1109/IJCNN.1991.155519

Spirkovska L., & Reid, M. B. (1994). Higher-order neural networks applied to 2D and 3D object recognition. *Machine Learning, 15*(2), 169-199.

Voutriaridis, C., Boutalis, Y. S., & Mertzios, G. (2003). Ridge Polynomial Networks in pattern recognition. EC-VIP-MC 2003. In *Proceedings of 4th EURASIP Conference focused on Video / Image Processing and Multimedia Communications* (pp. 519-524). Academic Press.

Wang, J., Sun, Y., & Chen, Q. (2003). Recognition of digital annotation with invariant HONN based on orthogonal Fourier-Mellin moments. *Proceedings of 2003 International Conference on, 4*, 2261 – 2264.

Wang, Z., Liu, Y., & Liu, X. (2009). On Complex Artificial Higher Order Neural Networks: Dealing with Stochasticity Jumps and Delays. In *Artificial Higher Order Neural Networks for Economics and Business* (pp. 466-483). IGI Global.

Wu, J., & Chang, J. (1993). Invariant pattern recognition using higher-order neural networks. In *Proceedings of International Joint Conference on Neural Networks* (vol.2, pp.1273 – 1276). 10.1109/IJCNN.1993.716777

Yao, Y., Freeman, W. J., Burke, B., & Yang, Q. (1991). Pattern recognition by a distributed neural network: An industrial application. *Neural Networks, 4*(1), 103–121. doi:10.1016/0893-6080(91)90036-5

Zhang, M. (2010). Rainfall Estimation Using Neuron-Adaptive Artificial Higher Order Neural Networks. In *Artificial Higher Order Neural Networks for Computer Science and Engineering – Trends for Emerging Applications* (pp. 159-186). IGI Global.

Zhang, S.J., Jing, Z.L., & Li, J.X. (2004). *Fast learning high-order neural networks for pattern recognition*. Academic Press.

Zhou, X., Koch, M. W., & Roberts, M. W. (1991). Selective attention of high-order neural networks for invariant object recognition. In *Proceedings of International Joint Conference on Neural Networks* (vol. 2, pp.9378). 10.1109/IJCNN.1991.155533

ADDITIONAL READING

Abolhassani, N., Patel, R., & Moallem, M. (2007). Needle insertion into soft tissue: A survey. *International Journal of Medicine and Engineering Physics*, *29*(4), 413–431. doi:10.1016/j.medengphy.2006.07.003 PMID:16938481

Amari, S., & Maginu, K. (1988). Statistical neurodynamics of associative memories. *Neural Networks*, *1*(1), 63–73. doi:10.1016/0893-6080(88)90022-6

Aseltine, J. A., Mancini, A. R., & Sartune, C. W. (1958). A Survey of Adaptive Control Systems. *I.R.E. Transactions on Automatic Control*, *3*(6), 102–108. doi:10.1109/TAC.1958.1105168

Baber, W., Janakiraman, S., & Kang, S. (1996). Investment opportunities and the structure of performance-based executive compensation. *Journal of Accounting and Economics*, *21*(3), 297–318. doi:10.1016/0165-4101(96)00421-1

Baldi, P., & Venkatesh, S. S. (1993). Random interactions in higher order neural networks. *IEEE Transactions on Information Theory*, *39*(1), 274–283. doi:10.1109/18.179374

Barron, A. R. (1994). Approximation and Estimation Bounds for Artificial Neural Networks. *Machine Learning*, *14*(1), 115–133. doi:10.1007/BF00993164

Bebchuk, L. A., & Fried, J. M. (2003). Executive Compensation as an Agency Problem. *The Journal of Economic Perspectives*, *17*(3), 71–92. doi:10.1257/089533003769204362

Brachman, R. J., Khabaza, T., Kloesgen, W., Piatetsky-Shapiro, E., & Simoudis, E. (1996). Mining business databases. *Communications of the ACM*, *39*(11), 42–48. doi:10.1145/240455.240468

Browne, A., Hudson, B. D., Whitley, D. C., Ford, M. G., & Picton, P. (2004). Biological data mining with neural networks: Implementation and application of a flexible decision tree extraction algorithm to genomic problem domains. *Neurocomputing, Volume, 57*, 275–293. doi:10.1016/j.neucom.2003.10.007

Bushman, R. M., Indjejikian, R. J., & Smith, A. (1995). Aggregate Performance Measures in Business Unit Manager Compensation: The Role of Intrafirm Interdependencies. *Journal of Accounting Research, 33*(Supplement), 101–128. doi:10.2307/2491377

Campos, J., Loukianov, A. G., & Sanchez, E. N. (2003). Synchronous motor VSS control using recurrent high order neural networks. *Proceedings of 42nd IEEE Conference on Decision and Control*, vol. 4, pp.3894–3899. 10.1109/CDC.2003.1271757

Chatfield, C. (2000). *Time-Series Forecasting*. Chapman & Hall/CRC. doi:10.1201/9781420036206

Chen, G., & Lewis, F. L. (2011). Distributed adaptive tracking control for synchronization of unknown networked Lagrangian systems. *IEEE Transactions on Systems, Man, and Cybernetics. Part B, Cybernetics, 41*(3), 2011. PMID:21177157

Chen, Y., Yang, B., & Dong, J. (2004a). Nonlinear System Modeling via Optimal Design of Neural Trees. *International Journal of Neural Systems, 4*(2), 125–137. doi:10.1142/S0129065704001905 PMID:15112370

Chynoweth, D. P., Owens, J. M., & Legrand, R. (2001). Renewable methane from anaerobic digestion of biomass. *Renewable Energy, 22*(1-3), 1–8. doi:10.1016/S0960-1481(00)00019-7

Cooper, B. S. (1995). Higher order neural networks for combinatorial optimization improving the scaling properties of the hopfield network. *Proceedings of IEEE ICNN, 95*(4), 1855–1890.

DiMaio, S. P., & Salcudean, S. E. (2003). Needle insertion modeling and simulation. *IEEE Transactions on Robotics and Automation, 19*(5), 864–875. doi:10.1109/TRA.2003.817044

Dunis, C. L., Laws, J., & Evans, B. (2006b). Modelling and Trading the Soybean-Oil Crush Spread with Recurrent and Higher Order Networks: A Comparative Analysis. *Neural Network World, 3*(6), 193–213.

Fahlman, S. E., & Lebiere, C. (1990). The Cascade- Correlation Learning Architecture. *Advances in Neural Information Processing Systems, 2*, 524–532.

Farrell, J. A., & Polycarpou, M. M. (2006). *Adaptive approximation Based Control: Unifying Neural, Fuzzy and Traditional Adaptive Approximation Approaches*. John Wiley and Sons. doi:10.1002/0471781819

Fiori, S. (2003). Closed-form expressions of some stochastic adapting equations for nonlinear adaptive activation function neurons. *Neural Computation, Volume, 15*(12), 2909–2929. doi:10.1162/089976603322518795 PMID:14629873

Gasser, T. C., Gudmundson, P., & Dohr, G. (2009). Failure mechanisms of ventricular tissue due to deep penetration. *Journal of Biomechanics, 42*(5), 626–633. doi:10.1016/j.jbiomech.2008.12.016 PMID:19200998

Giles, C. L., & Maxwell, T. (1987). Learning, Invariance, and Generalization in High-Order Neural Networks. *Applied Optics, 26*(23), 4972–4978. doi:10.1364/AO.26.004972 PMID:20523475

Goodwin, G. C., & Mayne, D. Q. (1987). A parameter estimation perspective of continuous time model reference adaptive control. *Automatica, 23*(1), 57–70. doi:10.1016/0005-1098(87)90118-X

Gore, A., Kulp, S., & Li, Y. (2011). Golden handcuffs for bureaucrats? Ex ante severance contracts in the municipal sector. Working paper. The George Washington University.

Grover, R., & Hwang, P. Y. C. (1992). *Introduction to Random Signals and Applied Kalman Filtering* (2nd ed.). John Wiley and Sons.

Haykin, S. (1999). *Neural Networks: A Comprehensive Foundation*. Prentice Hall.

Hinton, G. E. (1989). Connectionist learning procedure. *Artificial Intelligence, 40*(1-3), 251–257. doi:10.1016/0004-3702(89)90049-0

Hjelmfelt, A., & Ross, J. (1994). Pattern recognition, chaos, and multiplicity in neural networks and excitable systems. *Proceedings of the National Academy of Sciences of the United States of America, 91*(1), 63–67. doi:10.1073/pnas.91.1.63 PMID:8278408

Hopfield, J. J. (1982). Neural networks and physical systems with emergent collective computational abilities. *Proceedings of the National Academy of Sciences of the United States of America, 79*(8), 2554–2558. doi:10.1073/pnas.79.8.2554 PMID:6953413

Hu, S., & Yan, P. (1992). Level-by-Level learning for artificial neural groups. *Tien Tzu Hsueh Pao, 20*(10), 39–43.

Huang, H. J., & Ramaswamy, S. (2009). Modeling Biomass Gasification Using Thermodynamic Equilibrium Approach. *Applied Biochemistry and Biotechnology, 154*(1-3), 193–204. doi:10.100712010-008-8483-x PMID:19172238

Ioannou, P., & Fidan, B. (2006). *Adaptive control tutorial.* SIAM: Advances in Design and Control Series.

Jain, B. A., & Nag, B. N. (1995). Artificial neural network models for pricing initial public offerings. *Decision Sciences, 26*(3), 283–302. doi:10.1111/j.1540-5915.1995.tb01430.x

Jensen, M., & Murphy, K. J. (1990). Performance pay and top management incentives. *Journal of Political Economy, 98*(2), 225–264. doi:10.1086/261677

Juang, C. F., & Lin, C. T. (1998). An on-line self-constructing neural fuzzy inference network and its applications. *IEEE Transactions on Fuzzy Systems, 6*(1), 12–32. doi:10.1109/91.660805

Karayiannis, N., & Venetsanopoulos, A. (1993). *Artificial Neural Networks: Learning Algorithms, Performance Evaluation and Applications.* Boston: Kluwer Academic. doi:10.1007/978-1-4757-4547-4

Katto, Y., & Ohno, H. (1984). An improved version of the generalized correlation of critical heat flux for the forced convective boiling in uniformly heated vertical tubes. *International Journal of Heat and Mass Transfer, 27*(9), 1641–1648. doi:10.1016/0017-9310(84)90276-X

Kendi, T. A., & Doyle, F. J. (1996). Nonlinear control of a fluidized bed reactor using approximate feedback linearization. *Industrial & Engineering Chemistry Research, 35*(3), 746–757. doi:10.1021/ie950334a

Khoo, S., Xie, L., & Man, Z. (2009). Robust finite-time consensus tracking algorithm for multirobot systems. *IEEE/ASME Transansactions Mechatronics, 14*(2), 219–228.

Kobayashi, Y., Onishi, A., Watanabe, H., Hoshi, T., Kawamura, K., Hashizume, M., & Fujie, M. G. (2010). Development of an integrated needle insertion system with image guidance and deformation simulation. *Computerized Medical Imaging and Graphics*, *34*(1), 9–18. doi:10.1016/j. compmedimag.2009.08.008 PMID:19815388

Kosmatopoulos, E. B., Polycarpou, M. M., Christodoulou, M. A., & Ioannou, P. A. (1995). High-order neural network structures for identification of dynamical systems. *Neural Networks*, *6*(2), 422–431. doi:10.1109/72.363477 PMID:18263324

Lambert, R., & Larcker, D. (1987). An Analysis of the Use of Accounting and Market Measures of Performance in Executive Compensation Contracts. *Journal of Accounting Research*, *25*(Supplement), 85–125. doi:10.2307/2491081

Lee, Y. C., Doolen, G., Chen, H., Sun, G., Maxwell, T., Lee, H., & Giles, C. L. (1986). Machine learning using a higher order correlation network. *Physica D. Nonlinear Phenomena*, *22*(1-3), 276–306. doi:10.1016/0167-2789(86)90300-6

Li, M. B., Huang, G.-B., Saratchandran, P., & Sundararajan, N. (2005). Fully complex extreme learning machine. *Neurocomputing*, *68*, 306–314. doi:10.1016/j.neucom.2005.03.002

Li, X. T., Grace, J. R., Lim, C. J., Watkinson, A. P., Chen, H. P., & Kim, J. R. (2004). Biomass gasification in a circulating fluidized bed. *Biomass and Bioenergy*, *26*(2), 171–193. doi:10.1016/S0961-9534(03)00084-9

LO, J. T-H. (1992). A New Approach to Global Optimization and its Applications to Neural Networks. *Neural Networks*, *2*(5), 367–373.

Lubitz, W. D. (2005). *Near Real Time Wind Energy Forecasting Incorporating Wind Tunnel Modeling*. Unpublished doctoral dissertation. University of California, Davis, California, USA.

Mahvash, M., & Dupont, P. E. (2010). Mechanics of Dynamic Needle Insertion into a Biological Material. *IEEE Transactions on Biomedical Engineering*, *57*(4), 934–943. doi:10.1109/TBME.2009.2036856 PMID:19932986

Manwell, J. F., McGowan, J. G., & Rogers, A. (2010). *Wind Energy Explained: Theory, Design and Application*. Wiley.

McCarty, P. L. (1964). Anaerobic waste treatment fundamentals. *Public Works*, *95*(9), 107–112.

Melgar, A., Pérez, J. F., Laget, H., & Horillo, A. (2007). Thermochemical equilibrium modelling of a gasifying process. *Energy Conversion and Management*, *48*(1), 59–67. doi:10.1016/j.enconman.2006.05.004

Misra, S., Macura, K., Ramesh, K., & Okamura, A. M. (2009). The importance of organ geometry and boundary constraints for planning of medical interventions. *Medical Engineering & Physics*, *31*(2), 195–206. doi:10.1016/j.medengphy.2008.08.002 PMID:18815068

Moon, S., & Chang, S. H. (1994). Classification and prediction of the critical heat flux using fuzzy clustering and artificial neural networks. *Nuclear Engineering and Design*, *150*(1), 151–161. doi:10.1016/0029-5493(94)90059-0

Morita, M. (1993). Associative memory with nonmonotone dynamics. *Neural Networks*, *6*(1), 115–126. doi:10.1016/S0893-6080(05)80076-0

Narendra, K. S., & Parthasarathy, K. (1990). Identification and Control of Dynamical Systems Using Neural Networks. *IEEE Transactions on Neural Networks*, *1*(1), 4–27. doi:10.1109/72.80202 PMID:18282820

Nath, S., Chen, Z., Yue, N., Trumpore, S., & Peschel, R. (2000). Dosimetric effects of needle divergence in prostate seed implant using 125I and 103Pd radioactive seeds. *Medical Physics*, *27*(5), 1058–1066. doi:10.1118/1.598971 PMID:10841410

Okamura, M., Simone, C., & O'Leary, M. D. (2004). Force Modeling for Needle Insertion into Soft Tissue. *IEEE Transactions on Biomedical Engineering*, *51*(10), 1707–1716. doi:10.1109/TBME.2004.831542 PMID:15490818

Pal, S. K., De, R. K., & Bsask, J. (2000). Unsupervised feature selection: A neuro-fuzzy approach. *IEEE Transactions on Neural Networks*, *11*(2), 366–376. doi:10.1109/72.839007 PMID:18249767

Park, J., & Sandberg, I. W. (1993). Approximation and radial-basis-fonction networks. *Neural Computation*, *5*(2), 305–316. doi:10.1162/neco.1993.5.2.305

Pedro, J., & Dahunsi, O. (2011). Neural Network Based Feedback Linearization Control of a Servo-Hydraulic Vehicle Suspension System. *International Journal of Applied Mathematics and Computer Science*, *21*(1), 137–147. doi:10.2478/v10006-011-0010-5

Pind, P. F., Angelidaki, I., Ahring, B. K., Stamatelatou, K., & Lyberato, G. (2003). Monitoring and control of anaerobic reactors. *Advances in Biochemical Engineering/Biotechnology*, *82*, 135–182. doi:10.1007/3-540-45838-7_4 PMID:12747567

Polycarpou, M. M. (1996). Stable adaptive neural control scheme for nonlinear systems. *IEEE Transactions on Automatic Control*, *41*(3), 447–451. doi:10.1109/9.486648

Psaltis, D., Park, C. H., & Hong, J. (1988). High order associative memories and their optical implementations. *Neural Networks*, *1*(2), 149–163. doi:10.1016/0893-6080(88)90017-2

Qu, Z., Wang, J., & Hull, R. A. (2008). Cooperative control of dynamical systems with application to autonomous vehicles. *IEEE Transactions on Automatic Control*, *53*(4), 894–911. doi:10.1109/TAC.2008.920232

Redding, N. J., Kowalczyk, A., & Downs, T. (1993). Constructive higher-order network algorithm that is polynomial time. *Neural Networks*, *6*(7), 997–1010. doi:10.1016/S0893-6080(09)80009-9

Reid, M. B., Spirkovska, L., & Ochoa, E. (1989). Simultaneous position, scale, rotation invariant pattern classification using third-order neural networks. *Int. J. Neural Networks*, *1*, 154–159.

Ren, W., & Beard, R. W. (2008). *Distributed Consensus in Multi-Vehicle Cooperative Control*. New York: Springer-Verlag. doi:10.1007/978-1-84800-015-5

Rong, H. J., Huang, G.-B., Sundararajan, N., & Saratchandran, P. (2009). Online sequential fuzzy extreme learning machine for function approximation and classification problems. *IEEE Transactions on Systems, Man, and Cybernetics. Part B, Cybernetics*, *39*(4), 1067–1072. doi:10.1109/TSMCB.2008.2010506 PMID:19336333

Rovithakis, G., Gaganis, V., Perrakis, S., & Christodoulou, M. (1996). A recurrent neural network model to describe manufacturing cell dynamics. *Proceedings of the 35th IEEE Conference on Decision and Control*, *2*, 1728–1733. 10.1109/CDC.1996.572808

Rumelhart, D. E., Hinton, G. E., & Williams, R. (1986). Learning representation by back-propagation errors. *Nature*, *323*(6088), 533–536. doi:10.1038/323533a0

Salcedo-Sanz, S., & Yao, X. (2004). A hybrid Hopfield network-genetic algorithm approach for the terminal assignment problem. *IEEE Transactions on Systems, Man, and Cybernetics, 34*(6), 2343–2353. doi:10.1109/TSMCB.2004.836471 PMID:15619934

Sanchez, E. N., Alanis, A. Y., & Loukianov, A. G. (2008). *Discrete Time High Order Neural Control Trained with Kalman Filtering*. Germany: Springer-Verlag. doi:10.1007/978-3-540-78289-6

Schmidt, W., & Davis, J. (1993). Pattern recognition properties of various feature spaces for higher order neural networks. *IEEE Transactions on Pattern Analysis and Machine Intelligence, 15*(8), 795–801. doi:10.1109/34.236250

Shi, K. L., & Li, H. (2004). A Novel Control of a Small Wind Turbine Driven Generator Based on Neural Networks. *IEEE Power Engineering Society General Meeting, 2*, 1999-2005.

Shin, Y., & Ghosh, J. (1995). Ridge Polynomial Networks. *IEEE Transactions on Neural Networks, 6*(3), 610–622. doi:10.1109/72.377967 PMID:18263347

Simpson, P. K. (1990). Higher-ordered and interconnected bidirectional associative memories. *IEEE Transactions on Systems, Man, and Cybernetics, 20*(3), 637–653. doi:10.1109/21.57276

Softky, R. W., & Kammen, D. M. (1991). Correlations in high dimensional or asymmetrical data sets: Hebbian neuronal processing. *Neural Networks, 4*(3), 337–347. doi:10.1016/0893-6080(91)90070-L

Song, Y., & Grizzle, J. W. (1995). The extended Kalman filter as a local asymptotic observer for discrete-time nonlinear systems, *Journal of Mathematical Systems, Estimation and Control. Birkhauser-Boston., 5*(1), 59–78.

Su, G., Fukuda, K., Jia, D., & Morita, K. (2002). Application of an artificial neural network in reactor thermo hydraulic problem: Prediction of critical heat flux. *Journal of Nuclear Science and Technology, 39*(5), 564–571. doi:10.1080/18811248.2002.9715235

Tai, H. M., & Jong, T. L. (1990). Information Storage in High-Order Neural Networks with Unequal Neural Activity. *Journal of the Franklin Institute, 327*(1), 129–141. doi:10.1016/0016-0032(90)90061-M

Tenti, P. (1996). Forecasting Foreign Exchange Rates Using Recurrent Neural Networks. *Applied Artificial Intelligence*, *10*(6), 567–581. doi:10.1080/088395196118434

Thibault, J., & Grandjean, B. P. A. (1991). A neural network methodology for heat transfer data analysis. *International Journal of Heat and Mass Transfer*, *34*(8), 2063–2070. doi:10.1016/0017-9310(91)90217-3

Utkin, V., Guldner, J., & Shi, J. (1999). *Sliding Mode Control in Electromechanical Systems*. Philadelphia: Taylor and Francis.

Vecci, L., Piazza, F., & Uncini, A. (1998). Learning and approximation capabilities of adaptive spline activation function neural networks. *Neural Networks*, *11*(2), 259–270. doi:10.1016/S0893-6080(97)00118-4 PMID:12662836

Wang, S. H. (2003). Application of self-organising maps for data mining with incomplete data sets. *Neural Computing & Applications*, *12*(1), 42–48. doi:10.100700521-003-0372-1

Williams, R. J., & Zipser, D. (1989). A learning algorithm for continually running fully recurrent neural networks. *Neural Computation*, *1*(2), 270–280. doi:10.1162/neco.1989.1.2.270

Wu, J., Chen, S., Zeng, J., & Gao, L. (2009). Control Technologies in Distributed Generation Systems Based on Renewable Energy. *Asian Power Electronics Journal*, *3*(1), 39–52.

Yao, X., & Liu, Y. (1997). A New Evolutionary System for Evolving Artificial Neural Networks. *IEEE Transactions on Neural Networks*, *8*(3), 694–713. doi:10.1109/72.572107 PMID:18255671

Yapo, T., Embrechets, S. T., & Cathey, S. T. (1992). Prediction of critical heat using a hybrid kohon-backpropagation neural network intelligent. Eng. *Systems through Artificial Neural Networks-proc. Artificial Neural Networks in Eng.*, *2*, 853–858.

Yi, X., Shao, J., & Yu, Y. (2008). Global exponential stability of impulsive high-order Hopfield type neural networks with delays. *Journal of Computational and Applied Mathematics*, *219*(3), 216–222. doi:10.1016/j.cam.2007.07.011

Zhang, B., Xu, S., & Li, Y. (2007). Delay-dependent robust exponential stability for uncertain recurrent neural networks with time-varying delays. *International Journal of Neural Systems, 17*(3), 207–218. doi:10.1142/S012906570700107X PMID:17640101

Zheng, T., Girgis, A. A., & Makram, E. B. (2000). A Hybrid Wavelet-Kalman Filter Method for Load Forecasting. *Electric Power Systems Research, 54*(1), 11–17. doi:10.1016/S0378-7796(99)00063-2

KEY TERMS AND DEFINITIONS

ANN: Artificial neural network.

HONN: Artificial higher order neural network.

PHONN: Artificial polynomial higher order neural network.

THONN: Artificial trigonometric higher order neural network.

UGC-HONN: Artificial ultra-high frequency sigmoid and cosine higher order neural network.

UGS-HONN: Artificial ultra-high frequency sigmoid and sine higher order neural network.

UGT-HONN: Artificial ultra-high frequency sigmoid and trigonometric higher order neural network.

Chapter 12

Face Recognition Based on Higher Order Neural Network Group-Based Adaptive Tolerance Trees

ABSTRACT

Recent artificial higher order neural network research has focused on simple models, but such models have not been very successful in describing complex systems (such as face recognition). This chapter presents the artificial higher order neural network group-based adaptive tolerance (HONNGAT) tree model for translation-invariant face recognition. Moreover, face perception classification, detection of front faces with glasses and/or beards models of using HONNGAT trees are presented. The artificial higher order neural network group-based adaptive tolerance tree model is an open box model and can be used to describe complex systems.

INTRODUCTION

Few Artificial Neural Network (ANN) research has concentrated on neural network group models. Naimark and Stern (1982) present a theory of group representations for face processing models. Matsuoka, Hamada, and Nakatsu[1989] studied the integrated neural network. Pentland and Turk [1989] provide holistic model. Tsao (1989) uses Lie group theory to the

DOI: 10.4018/978-1-7998-3563-9.ch012

computer simulation of 3D rigid motion. Unlike the research previously described, Yang (1990) concernes himself with the activities of neuron *groups*. Willcox (1991) devises the neural network hierarchical model which consists of binary-state neurons grouped into clusters, and can be analysed using a Renormalization Group (RG) approach. Lumer (1992) proposes a new mechanism of selective attention among perceptual groups as part of his computational model of early vision. Hu (1992) proposes a level-by-level learning scheme for artificial neural groups. Zhang, Fulcher, and Scofield (1997) develop artificial neural network group for rainfall estimation. This work in addition to other studies in this field, can be used as the basis for higher order neural network group theory.

Adaptive tree models have been widely studied. Armstrong and Gecsei (1979) develop an adaptation algorithm of binary tree networks for optical characters reconization, with each node of the tree performing the function *AND* or *OR*. Sanger (1991) proposes the Least Mean Square (LMS) tree, which is a new constructive neural network algorithm for image human face recognition. Zhang, Crowley, Dunstone, and Fulcher (1993) develop a Neural network Adaptive Tolerance (NAT) Tree technique for face recognition, in which every node is a neural network in tolerance space. NAT Tree can be connected and grown in tolerance space as well. Sankar (1993) provides a new pattern classification method called Neural Tree Networks (NTN). The NTN uses a neural network at each tree node. The results show that the NTN compares favourably to both neural networks and decision trees. But when use NTN to recognise complex pattern, the tolerance and accuracy are still problems. Because single neural network as a node is not good enough for complex pattern recognition. The decision function for complex pattern is always noncontinuous and nonsmooth. Single neural network can not simulate noncontinuous and nonsmooth function very well. Zhang & Fulcher (1996a) develope an artificial neural network group-based adaptive tolerance (GAT) trees for translation-invariant face recognition, which can used to describe complex system. GAT trees are black box models and are hard to use formular when modelling whole systems. Higher order neural networks are open box models and have potential feature for pattern recognition. A Higher Order Neural Network Group-based Adaptive Tolerance (HONNGAT) tree, which is open box model, will be presented for solving complex pattern recognition problem with noncontinuous and nonsmooth function.

This chapter gives the definitions of artificial higher order neural network sets, higher order neural network group, higher order neural group models, and higher order neural network group node of tree. The HONNGAT tree model and face recognition system are developed. By using HONNGAT tree, the experimental results of face perception recognition, recognition of front face with glasses and/or beards, and face recognition are provided. In the appendix, details of definitions of generalised artificial higher order neural network sets, proof of the inference, and HONNGAT tree definitions are described.

ARTIFICIAL HIGHER ORDER NEURAL NETWORK SETS

A *set* (Waerden, 1970) is defined as a collection of *elements* which possess the same properties. The symbol

$$a \in A \tag{12–1}$$

means: A is a set, and a is an element of set A.

The *artificial higher order neural network set* is a set in which every element is an HONN. The symbol

$$honn \in \textbf{\textit{HONNS}} \text{ (where: } honn = f{:}\textbf{\textit{R}}^{n} \rightarrow \textbf{\textit{R}}^{m}) \tag{12-2}$$

means: $\textbf{\textit{HONNS}}$ is an HONN set, and *honn*, which is one kind of artificial higher order neural network, is an element of set $\textbf{\textit{HONNS}}$. The domain of the artificial higher order neural network *honn* inputs is the n-dimensional real number $\textbf{\textit{R}}^{n}$. Likewise, the *honn* outputs belong to the m-dimensional real number $\textbf{\textit{R}}^{m}$. The neural network function f is a mapping from the inputs of *honn* to its outputs.

The set $\textbf{\textit{PHONN}}$ is a set whose elements are all artificial polynomial higher order neural networks. The set $\textbf{\textit{PHONN}}^{1,9,13,3}$ is one in which every element is an artificial polynomial higher order neural network comprising one output neuron, two hidden layers (of 9 neurons and 13 neurons respectively), and 3 input neurons. Moreover, $\textbf{\textit{PHONN}}$ is a subset of the artificial higher order neural network set $\textbf{\textit{HONNS}}$. We have:

$$\textbf{\textit{PHONN}}^{1,9,13,3} \text{ ì } \textbf{\textit{PHONN}} \text{ ì } \textbf{\textit{HONNS}} \tag{12–3}$$

Many other kinds of artificial higher order neural networks exist apart from the artificial polynomial higher order neural network - PHONN, such as (Zhang, 2009a and 2009b):

- Trigonomitrical Higher Orer Neural Netowrks (THONN);
- Ultra high frequency Cosine and Sine trigonometric Higher Order neural Network (UCSHONN);
- Sine and SINC Polynomial Higher Order Neural Netowrks (SSINCHONN);
- SINC Higher Order Neural Networks (SINCHONN);
- Sigmoid Polynomial Higher Order Neural Networks (SPHONN);

This list is not meant to be exhaustive; *new* HONN models continue to be reported in the literature on a regular basis.

We define the artificial higher order neural network set ***HONNS*** as the *union* of the *subsets* of ***PHONN, THONN, UCSHONN, SSINCHONN,***

Figure 1. The artifical higher order nueral network set HONNS and its subsets

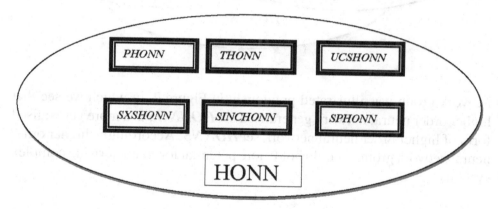

SINCHONN, SPHONN, ... and shown as follows. In formal notation, we write:

HONNS = PHONN⊂THONN∪UCSHONN⊂SXSPHONN⊂SINCHONN⊂SPHONN⊂ ....

We next introduce the concept of the *generalised* HONN *set*, prior to discussing higher order *neural network groups*. HONN Generalised Sets

(*HONNGS*) are defined as the union of additive HONN sets (*HONN*⁺) and product HONN sets (*HONN**), as detailed in Appendix A, which we write as:

$$HONNGS = HONN^* \subset HONN^+ \tag{12-5}$$

The elements of set *HONNS* are higher order neural networks; the elements of set *HONNGS*, by contrast, are higher order neural network *groups*. The difference between a higher order neural network and a higher order neural

Figure 2. Relationship between set HONNS and sets HONNGS (=HONN- HONN+)

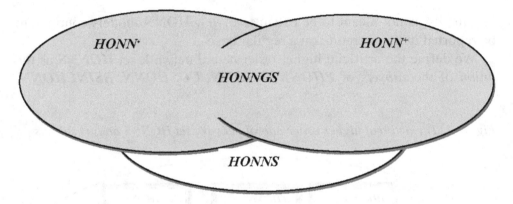

network group was illustrated previously in Figure 2, in which we see that higher order neural network generalised set *HONNGS* is a more generalised form of higher order neural network set *HONNS*. Accordingly, higher order neural network groups should hold more potential for characterising complex systems.

HIGHER ORDER NEURAL NETWORK GROUP

Following the group definitions by Inui (1978) and Naimark (1982), we have:
a nonempty set *HONNG* is called a *higher order neural network group*, if *HONNG* ∈ *HONNGS*(the higher order neural network generalised set), and either the product $h_i h_j$ or the sum $h_i + h_j$ is defined for every two elements $h_i, h_j \in$ *HONNG*.

Additive Notation of Higher Order Neural Network Groups

For a higher order neural network group defined in additive notation form, the following conditions must hold (associated law of composition):

(a) $h_i + h_j \in$ *HONNG*, $\forall\, h_i, h_j \in$ *HONNG*; (12-6)

(b) $(h_i + h_j) + h_k = h_i + (h_j + h_k)$, $\forall\, h_i, h_j, h_k \in$ *HONNG*; (12-7)

(c) $\exists$ a unique element h_0 in *HOONG* such that $h_0 + h = h + h_0 = h$

$\forall\, h \in$ *HONNG* (h_0 is called the identity element of the group *HONNG*); (12–8)

(d) for every element $h \in$ *HONN*, $\exists$ a unique element, designated $-h$,

for which $h + (-h) = (-h) + h = h_0$ (the element $-h$ is called the inverse of h); (12-10)

it is evident that h is the inverse of $-h$, so that $-(-h) = h$). (12–11)
There are two examples as follows:
    the additive generalised polynomial higher order neural network set *PHONN⁺* is a higher order neural network group if "addition" is taken to mean "plus". As another example, Boolean operator logical *OR* can be used as "addition". Then the additive generalised polynomial higher order neural network set *PHONN⁺* is a higher order neural network group as well.

Product Notation of Higher Order Neural Network Groups

For a higher order neural network group defined in product notation form, the following conditions must hold (associated law of composition):

(a) $h_i h_j \in$ *HONNG*, $\forall\, h_i, h_j \in$ *HONNG*; (12–12)

(b) $(h_i h_j) h_k = h_i (h_j h_k)$, $\forall\, h_i, h_j, h_k \in$ *HONNG*; (12–13)

(c) $\exists$ a unique element h_e in N such that $h_e h = h h_e = h \,\forall\, h \in$ *HONNG*;

(h_e is called the identity element of the group *HONNG*); (12-14)

(d) for every element $h \in HONN$, $\exists$ a unique element - designated h^{-1} - for which

$hh^{-1} = h^{-1}h = h_e$ (the element h^{-1} is called the inverse of h; it is obvious that h is the inverse of h^{-1}, so that $(h^{-1})^{-1} = h$). (12–15)

Two examples are as follows:

Consider for example the product generalised polynomial higher order neural network set **PHONN***. This is a higher order neural network group if "product" is taken to mean "multiplication" of the higher order neural network outputs. As another example, Boolean operator logical AND can be used as "product". Then the product generalised polynomial higher order neural network set **PHONN*** is a hogher order neural network group as well.

Higher Order Neural Network Algebra Sum Groups

Higher Order Neural Network Algebra Sum Groups - HONNASGs - are higher order neural network groups in which each addition $h_i + h_j$ is defined as an *Algebraic Sum* of every two elements h_i, $h_j \in HONNG$. Apart from Algebra Sum Groups, other higher order Neural Network Groups can be similarly defined, according to how each product $h_i h_j$ and/or addition $h_i + h_j$ is defined for every two elements h_i, $h_j \in HONN$ (such as Algebraic Product $[h_i h_j]$, Integral Operation, Differential Class, Boolean Algebraic, or Triangular Exponential, Logarithmic or Hyperbolic Functions, and so forth).

Higher Order Neural Network Piecewise Function Groups

We are particularly interested to the present the Higher Order Neurla Network Piecewise Function Groups (HONNPFGs). Higher Order Neural Network Piecewise Function Groups are defined as those in which each addition $h_i + h_j$ is a *Piecewise Function* for every two elements h_i, $h_j \in HONHHgNG$:

$$h_i + h_j = h_j + h_i = \begin{cases} h_i, & A < I <= B \\ h_i, & B < I <= C \end{cases} \quad (12\text{-}16)$$

$(h_i) + (h_j) + (h_k) = ((h_i) + (h_j)) + (h_k)$

$= (h_i) + ((h_j) + (h_k)) = h_j, \; B < I <$

$$= C \begin{cases} h_i, & A < I <= B \\ h_i, & C < I <= D \end{cases} \tag{12-17}$$

where: I input to the higher order neural networks; A, B, C, and D are constants

Such a piecewise function ensures that higher order neural networks satisfy the necessary conditions to be regarded as a higher order neural network group. Firstly, equation implies that piecewise function higher order neural networks satisfy condition (b). Furthermore, if we choose to build these higher order neural networks in the form of a *generalised* higher order neural network set, this automatically satisfies conditions (a), (c), and (d). Thus piecewise functions can be used to ensure that the higher order neural networks satisfy *all* of the necessary group conditions. The constants A, B, C, and D can be chose heuristically.

Inference of Higher Order Neural Network Piecewise Function Groups

Hornik (1991) proved the following general result: "Whenever the activation function is continuous, bounded and nonconstant, then for an arbitrary compact subset $X \acute{I} R^n$, standard multilayer feedforward networks can approximate any continuous function on X arbitrarily well with respect to uniform distance, provided that sufficiently many hidden units are available".

A more general result was proved by Leshno (1993): "A standard multilayer feedforward network with a locally bounded piecewise continuous activation function can approximate *any* continuous function to *any* degree of accuracy if and only if the network's activation function is not a polynomial".

Zhang, Fulcher, & Scofield (1997) provided a general result for neural network group: "Consider a neural network Piecewise Function *Group*, in which each member is a standard multilayer feedforward neural network, and which has a locally bounded, piecewise continuous (rather than polynomial) activation function and threshold. Each such group can approximate *any* kind of piecewise continuous function, and to *any* degree of accuracy."

An inference is provided as follows and proved by Appendix B: "Consider a higher order neural network Piecewise Function *Group*, in which each member is a standard multilayer feedforward higher order neural network, and which has a locally bounded, piecewise continuous (rather than polynomial) activation function and threshold. Each such group can approximate *any* kind of piecewise continuous function, and to *any* degree of accuracy."

In the real world, if the function being analysed varies in a discontinuous and nonsmooth fashion with respect to input variables, then such functions cannot be effectively simulated by a higher order neural network. By contrast, if we use higher order neural network *groups* to simulate these functions, it *is* possible to simulate discontinuous functions to any degree accuracy, even at points of discontinuity

HIGHER ORDER NEURAL NETWORK GROUP MODELS

Higher Order Neural Network models use trigonometric, linear, multiply, power and other neuron functions based on the following form:

$$z = \sum_{k1,k2,...,km=0}^{n} c \prod_{j=1}^{m} [\, f_1(c_1\, x_1)\,]^{\,k1}\, [\, f_2(c_2\, x_2)\,]^{\,k2}\, ...\, [\, f_j(c_j\, x_j)\,]^{\,kj}\, ...\, [\, f_m(c_m\, x_m)\,]^{\,km}$$

(12–18)

Let

$m=2$, $c = c_{k1k2}$, $c_1 = c_{k1k2}{}^x$, $c_2 = c_{k1k2}{}^y$, $x_1 = x$, and $x_2 = y$,

we have:

$$z = \sum_{k1,k2=0}^{n} c_{k1k2}[\, f_1(c_{k1k2}{}^x\, x)\,]^{\,k1}\, [\, f_2(c_{k1k2}{}^y\, y)\,]^{\,k2}$$

$$= \sum_{k1,k2=0}^{n} (c_{k1k2}{}^o)\{\, c_{k1k2}{}^{hx}[f_1(c_{k1k2}{}^x x)]^{k1}\, \}\{c_{k1k2}{}^{hy}[f_2(c_{k1k2}{}^y y)]^{k2}\, \}$$

(12-19)

where:

$$c_{k1k2} = (c_{k1k2}{}^o)(c_{k1k2}{}^{hx})(c_{k1k2}{}^{hy})$$

where: Output Layer Weights: $(c_{k1k2}{}^o)$
   Second Hidden Layer Weights: $(c_{k1k2}{}^x)$ and $(c_{k1k2}{}^y)$
   First Hidden Layer Weights: $(c_{k1k2}{}^{hx})$ and $(c_{k1k2}{}^{hy})$

Choosing a different function f_i, results in a different higher order neural network model.

Trigonometric Polynomial Higher Order Neural Network (THONN) Model

Let:

$$f_1(c_{k1k2}{}^x x) = sin(c_{k1k2}{}^x x); f_2(c_{k1k2}{}^y y) = cos(c_{k1k2}{}^y y)] \qquad (12-20)$$

then

$$z = \sum_{k1,k2=0}^{n} c_{k1k2}[f_1(c_{k1k2}{}^x x)]^{k1} [f_2(c_{k1k2}{}^y y)]^{k2}$$

$$= \sum_{k1,k2=0}^{n} (c_{k1k2}{}^o)\{ c_{k1k2}{}^{hx}[sin(c_{k1k2}{}^x x)]^{k1} \}\{c_{k1k2}{}^{hy}[cos(c_{k1k2}{}^y y)]^{k2} \} \qquad (12-21)$$

Polynomial Higher Order Neural Network (PHONN) Model

Let:

$$f_1(c_{k1k2}{}^x x) = (c_{k1k2}{}^x x); \text{ and } f_2(c_{k1k2}{}^y y) = (c_{k1k2}{}^y y) \qquad (12-22)$$

then

$$z = \sum_{k1,k2=0}^{n} c_{k1k2}[f_1(c_{k1k2}{}^x x)]^{k1} [f_2(c_{k1k2}{}^y y)]^{k2}$$

$$= \sum_{k1,k2=0}^{n} (c_{k1k2}{}^o)\{ c_{k1k2}{}^{hx}(c_{k1k2}{}^x x)^{k1} \}\{c_{k1k2}{}^{hy}(c_{k1k2}{}^y y)^{k2} \} \qquad (12-23)$$

Sigmoid polynomial Higher Order Neural Network (SPHONN) Model

Let:

$$f_1(c_{k1k2}{}^x x)] = 1/(1+exp(-c_{k1k2}{}^x x)) \; ; f_2(c_{k1k2}{}^y y) = (1/1+exp(-c_{k1k2}{}^y y))] \qquad (12\text{–}24)$$

then

$$z = \sum_{k1,k2=0}^{n} c_{k1k2}[f_1(c_{k1k2}{}^x x)]^{k1} [f_2(c_{k1k2}{}^y y)]^{k2}$$

$$= \sum_{k1,k2=0}^{n} (c_{k1k2}{}^o)\{ c_{k1k2}{}^{hx}[1/(1+exp(-c_{k1k2}{}^x x))]^{k1} \}\{c_{k1k2}{}^{hy}[(1/1+exp(-c_{k1k2}{}^y y))]^{k2} \}$$

$$(12-25)$$

Higher Order Neural network Group (***HONNG***) is one kind of neural network group, in which each element is a higher order neural network, such as PHONN, THONN, or SPHONN. We have:

HONNG Artificial Neural Network Group where:

$$HONNG = \{ \; PHONN, THONN, SPHONN, ...\} \qquad (12-26)$$

PHONN, ***THONN***, and ***SPHONN*** are subsets

In the following section, this chapter describe three different ***HONNG*** models.

Polynomial Higher Order Neural Network Group (PHONNG) Model

The ***PHONNG*** model is a PHONN model *Group*. It is a piecewise function group of Polynomial Higher Order Neural Networks, and is defined as follows:

$$Z = \{ \; z_1, z_2, z_3, ..., z_i, z_{i+1}, z_{i+2}, ...\} \qquad (12\text{–}27)$$

where

$z_i = \ln \left[(z_i')/(1-z_i') \right]$

$z_i \in K_i \grave{I} R^n, K_i$ is a compact set

$z_i' = 1/(1 + e^{-zi})$

$$z_i = \sum_{k1,k2=0}^{n} (c_{ik1k2}{}^o)[(c_{ik1k2}{}^x)x]^{k1}[(c_{ik1k2}{}^y)y]^{k2} = \sum_{k1,k2=0}^{n} c_{ik1k2}x^{k1}y^{k2} \qquad (12\text{--}28)$$

$$c_{ik1k2} = (c_{ik1k2}{}^o)[(c_{ik1k2}{}^x)^{k1}][(c_{ik1k2}{}^y)^{k2}]$$

In the **PHONNG** Model (Piecewise Function Group), group *addition* is defined as the *piecewise* function:

$$Z = \begin{cases} z_1, \ z_1 inputs \in K_1 \\ z_2, \ z_2 inputs \in K_2 \\ \dots \\ z_i, \\ z_{i+1}, \ z_{i+1} inputs \in K_{i+1} \\ \dots \end{cases} \qquad (12\text{-}29)$$

where:

z_i $inputs \in K_i \grave{I} R^n, K_i$ is a compact set

The **PHONNG** Model is an open and convergent model which can approximate any kind of piecewise continuous function *to any degree of accuracy*, even at discontinuous points (or regions).

Trigonometric Polynomial Higher Order Neural Network Group (THONNG) Model

In order to handle discontinuities in the input training data, the Trigonometric Polynomial Higher Order Neural Network *Group* (**THONNG**) model has also been developed. This is a model in which every element is a *trigonometric polynomial higher order neural network* - THONN (Zhang & Fulcher, 1996b).

509

The domain of the THONN inputs is the n-dimensional real number R^n. Likewise, the THONN outputs belong to the m-dimensional real number R^m. The higher order neural network function f constitutes a mapping from the inputs of THONN to its outputs.

THONN *THONNG*

where:

THONN $= f{:}R^n R^{m;\ THONNG}$is the group model $\qquad\qquad\qquad$ (12 – 30)

Based on the inference of Zhang, Fulcher & Scofield (1997), each such higher order neural network group can approximate any kind of piecewise continuous function, and to any degree of accuracy. Hence, *THONNG* is also able to simulate discontinuous data.

Sigmoid Polynomial Higher Order Neural Network Group (*SPHONNG*) Model

In order to handle discontinuities in the input training data, the sigmoid polynomial higher order neural network *Group* (**SPHONNG**) model has also been developed. This is a model in which every element is a *sigmoid* polynomial higher order neural network (SPHONN). The domain of the SHONN inputs is the n-dimensional real number R^n. Likewise, the SHONN outputs belong to the m-dimensional real number R^m. The higher order neural network function f constitutes a mapping from the inputs of SHONN to its outputs.

SPHONN *SPHONNG* $\qquad\qquad\qquad\qquad\qquad\qquad\qquad\qquad$ (12-31)

where:

SPHONN $= f{:}R^n R^{m;\ SPHOONG}$is group model

Each such higher order neural network group can approximate any kind of piecewise continuous function, and to any degree of accuracy. Hence, *SPHONNG* is also able to simulate discontinuous data.

Based on the discussion above, we have that Higher Order Neural Network Group (***HONNG***) is one kind of neural network group, in which each element is a higher order neural network, or higher order neural network group:

HONNGArtificial Neural Network Group (12-32)

where:

HONNG = { ***PHONN, THONN, SPHONN,... PHONNG, THONNG, SPHONNG*, ...}**

PHONN, THONN, and ***SPHONN*** are subsets

PHONNG, THONNG, and SPHONNG are group models

HIGHER ORDER NEURAL NETWORK GROUP NODE OF TREE

The structure of a HONNGAT Tree node shows as follows. The significant feature of this node is that it is neither an higher order artificial neuron nor an higher order artificial neural network, but rather a higher order neural network group ($HONN_1$, $HONN_2$, ..., $HONN_k$) in tolerance space. (Zeeman, 1962). The basic function of node is a classifier. Because the node is consisted of higher order neural network group. So higher order neural network group-based note is a complex pattern classifier. The basic function of node can be detail describes by a set of operator (See appendix C Artificial Higher order neural network Node Operator set):

HNO = { ***HNO0, HNO1,HNG, HNO2*** } (12–33)

The brief discuss about neural network group-based node are as follows:

(1) Inputs of node $I_f(H_{i,j})$ and $I_d(H_{i,j})$

   (1) Let:

$H_{i,j}$: HONN Group-Based (HONNGB) node, adaptive node and label node,

where

i: the level or deep of the HONNGAT Tree;
j: the *jth* node *n* the *i* level

The inputs of node are Fire Input-- $I_f(H_{i,j})$ and Data Input -- $I_d(H_{i,j})$. Fire Input has been connected to output of parent node. The Fire Input is a binary number (0 or 1). Data Input is the pattern data that is needed to be recognised or trained. For face recognition, Data Input is the face data matrix (we use 28*28 pixels matrix, each pixel has 256 grey level). In testing, Data Input -- $I_d(H_{i,j})$ is the *IMA(i,j)* pattern that we want to recognise. In the training, Input Data -- $I_d(H_{i,j})$ are translated training data *IMAu(i,j)* (see appendix C).

(2)   Higher order neural network Node Operator 0 --*HNO0*

In the testing, when Fire Input equals 1, the node is fired and the Data Input can accepted by node. Otherwise, the Data Input can not be input into the node. In the training, Data input can always be input into the node. We use *HNO0* (HONN Node Operator 0) to describe this function (see appendix C) . So in the training or fired cases, Input Data (Face, for example) has been input into the node and higher order neural network group input -- $I(H_{i,j})$ equals Input Data -- $I_d(H_{i,j})$.

(3)   Higher order neural network Node Operator 1 -- *HNO1*

All *K* higher order neural networks (a group of higher order neural networks) are used for training or testing using higher order neural network group input $I(H_{i,j})$. After training, the best weights are found and fixed for each higher order neural network (we use THONN as basic higher order neural network). In the training, one higher order neural network has been trained to suit a special case. For example, higher order neural network 1 ($HONN_1$) has been trained for recognising centre face of facial image $IMA_0(i,j)$, higher order neural network 2 ($HONN_2$) for lower-left face of facial image $IMA_1(i,j)$, and so on. Therefore, after training, the *K* higher order neural networks can recognise not only centre face but also lower-left face and so on. This model can solve shifting invariant problem very well. The trained *K* higher order neural networks can be used for testing. We use HONN Node Operator 1 --

Figure 3. HONN group-based node of tree

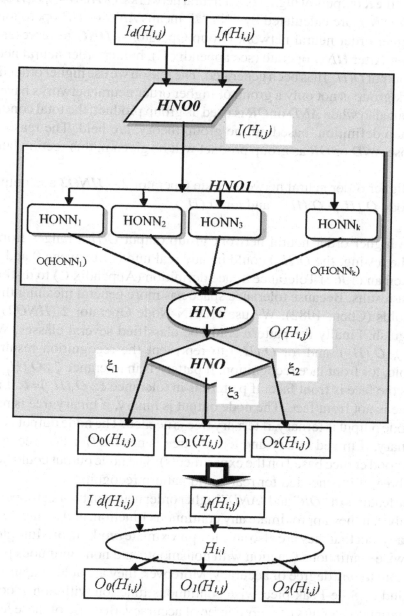

HNO1 describe this procedure. After **HNO1**, we got $O(HONN_1)$, $O(HONN_2)$, ... $O(HONN_k)$, the output of each K higher order neural networks.

(4)   Higherorder neural network Group Operator -- **HNG**

Then the K outputs of higher order neural networks, $O(HONN_1)$, $O(HONN_2)$, ... $O(HONN_k)$, are calculated by "*". "*" means *AND* or *OR* operation. We use Higher order neural network Group Operator -- **HNG** to represent this function. After **HNG** operate (see appendix C), higher order neural network group output $O(H_{i,j})$ has been generated. The reason we use higher order neural network group is not only a group of higher order neural networks have been used, but also when *AND* or *OR* is used as group product, the total conditions for group definition, based on the group theory, are held. The reason why we chose *AND* or *OR* as group product will be given in this section later on.

(5) Higher order neural network Node Operator 2 -- **HNO2** and outputs of node $O_0(H_{i,j})$, $O_1(H_{i,j})$, and /or $O_2(H_{i,j})$

The higher order neural network group output $O(H_{i,j})$ ranges from 0 to 1. In the testing, the $O(H_{i,j})$ could be any real number between 0 and 1. We use Zeeman (1962) Tolerance Space definition (Appendix C) to distinguish the test results. Because tolerance space has more general meaning than the thresholds (Chen, 1982). We use HONN Node Operator 2 (**HNO2**) to do distinguish. Finally the pattern could be classified several classes. We use $O_0(H_{i,j})$, $O_1(H_{i,j})$, and /or $O_2(H_{i,j})$ to represent the recognition results. For example, for front face recognition, if pattern is in tolerance ξ_1, $O_0(H_{i,j})=1$, it means the face is front face. If pattern is in tolerance ξ_2, $O_1(H_{i,j})=1$, it means the face is not front face. The node output is binary, if binary tree is needed. The node output is ternary, if ternary tree is needed. The node output is binary or ternary, if mixed binary and ternary tree is needed (for face recognition, this is good choice based on the experiments). The node output could be more than three, if it is needed for real world pattern recognition.

The features of "*OR*" and "*AND*" higher order neural network groups are that not only can they approximate any continuous function, and to any degree of accuracy, but that they are also able to approximate *any* kind of Multiple-Peak piecewise continuous function with nonsmooth and noncontinuous point(s), and again to *any* degree of accuracy. Moreover, they are able to approximate *any* kind of Sole-Peak piecewise continuous function with nonsmooth and noncontinuous point(s), to *any* degree of accuracy. Because of these features, higher order neural network groups render face recognition more accurate.

Two deductions follow directly from Leshno's result(1993) as the features of "*OR*" and "*AND*" higher order neural network groups are proved by the following:

Deduction 1:

Consider a higher order neural network "*OR*" Function *Group*, in which
each member is a higher order neural network, with a locally bounded,
piecewise continuous (rather than polynomial) activation function and
threshold. Each such group can approximate *any* kind of Multiple-Peak
piecewise continuous function with nonsmooth and non continuous
point(s), and to *any* degree of accuracy.

Deduction 2:

Consider a higher order neural network "*AND*" Function *Group*, in which
each member is a higher order neural network, with a locally bounded,
piecewise continuous (rather than polynomial) activation function and
threshold. Each such group can approximate *any* kind of Sole-Peak
piecewise continuous function with nonsmooth and noncontinuous
point(s), and to *any* degree of accuracy.

The features of higher order neural network groups in one dimension
shows as following describtion. The "*OR*" group of higher order neural
networks for approximating a multi-peak function with nonsmooth point
(x1) and noncontinuous point (x2). The "*AND*" group of higher order neural
networks for approximating a sole-peak function with nonsmooth point (x1)
and noncontinuous point (x2). A single higher order neural network cannot
approximate the multiple-peak function with nonsmooth and noncontinuous
points. Neither can a single higherorder neural network approximate a sole-
peak function with nonsmooth and noncontinuous points. This explains why
higher order neural network groups have more features than a single higher
order neural network.

For shifting invariant front face recognition, we use center front face as one
training case and left shift and right shift as other two training cases. We shift
center front face two pixels left as a left shift face and shift center front face
two pixels right as a right shift face. The center, left and right front face as
input data of higher order neural network. The output of higher order neural
network is the recognition function of the front face. After training, we have
three peaks represent each centre, left or right face. The peak 1 represents
the recognition function of left front face, peak 2 for centre front face, and
peak 3 for right front face. In this chapter, X is 1 dimension. In real world X
is 256 dimensions. Here we just want to use this as an example to explanation
why piecewise continuous functions with nonsmooth and noncontinuous
point(s) are true and existed in real world). The joint point(s) between peaks
is always nonsmooth and sometimes noncontinuous in the experiments. No

one higher order neural network can approximate the function with 3 peaks and nonsmooth and noncontinuous points.

When we recognise target face, target face could be made up, with or without beards, and with or without glasses. The target face without glasses and beards, target face with glasses, and target face with beards are as inputs into the higher order neural network. The output of higher order neural network for target face is the function of the target face. We found, in the experiments, The function of target face is always is sole-peak function but with nonsmooth and noncontinuous point(s). Here we still use 1 dimension to instate 256 dimensions, just for explanation why this case happened in real world. The part 1 is the function of target face without glasses and beards. The part 2 is the function of target face with glasses. The part 3 is the function of target face with beards. No one higher order neural network can approximate the sole-peak function with nonsmooth and noncontinuous points shown.

For face recognition, especially in real world conditions, we need to be able to approximate multiple-peak or sole peak functions with nonsmooth and noncontinuous points. In experiments, for example, the output of higher order neural network for front face recognition is a multiple-peak function which may have nonsmooth and/or noncontinuous point(s). Thus if the "*OR*" higher order neural network group has been used to approximate the front face function, the front face classification accuracy will be much better than if we were to use a single higher order neural network. The output of higher order neural network for target face recognition is always a sole-peak one, which may have nonsmooth and/or noncontinuous point(s). In this case, if the "*AND*" higher order neural network has been used for approximation, the accuracy is better than what would be obtained with one higher order neural network.

In this paper, "*OR*" and "*AND*" higher order neural network groups have been used as the nodes for HONNGAT Tree. This leads to more accurate and more efficient face recognition.

HONNGAT TREE MODEL

The basic HONNGAT Tree model is shown as follows, and comprises both binary and ternary trees. Adaptive connections and adaptively growing trees, the nodes of which are still higher order neural networks, have been developed for translation-invariant face recognition. Adaptive connection and growth can be described in terms of tolerance space theory (Zeeman, 1962).

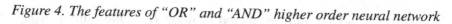

Figure 4. The features of "OR" and "AND" higher order neural network

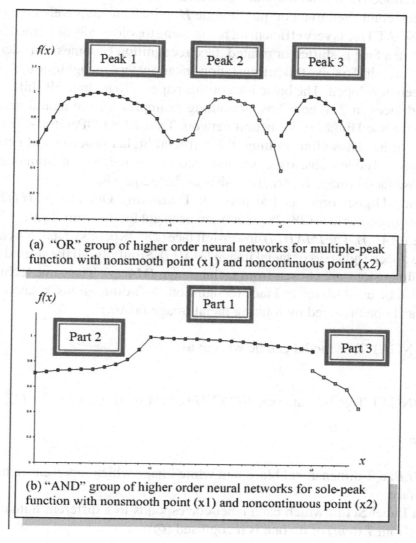

The adaptive growth of a HONNGAT Tree is shown as follows. We use Higher order neural network Adaptive Operator -- **HAO** to represent it. Because the output $O(H_{l,k})$ of node $H_{l,k}$ is within tolerance $\xi_3(H_{l,k})$, node Nm,n was added and fired. In such a manner the HONNGAT Tree has "grown" a node. The adaptively growing tree is therefore very useful for adding new faces which need to be recognised. These are adaptive connections within the HONNGAT Tree. Because output $O(H_{i,j})$ of node $H_{i,j}$ is within tolerance

$\xi_3(H_{i,j})$, node Nu,v is added and connected to node $H_{i,j}$. One output of $H_{u,v}$ has been connected to an output of node $H_{s,t}$. Such an adaptively connected HONNGAT Tree is very efficient for recognising topologically deformed faces.

When a face is shifted or rotated, face recognition becomes considerably more difficult. To solve this, a translation-invariant face recognition technique has been developed. The basic idea of this paper is to include all shifted and rotated faces in 2-dimensions as training examples for the neural network node (we use Higher order neural netwotk Translating OPerator -- **HTO** to represent it). Thus after training, the artificial higher order neural network group-based node is able to recognise shifted and rotated faces in 2-dimensions. Suppose facial image $IMA(i,j)$ consists of 32*32 pixels.

Using Higher order neural netwotk Translating Operator -- **HTO**, the $IMAo(i,j)$, center face (28*28 pixels) can been got for the central part of facial image $IMA(i,j)$. The $IMA1(i,j)$, lower-left face (28*28 pixels), has been chosen by the upper-right part of facial image $IMA(i,j)$. Similarly, all the shifted faces in 2-dimensions are chosen from facial image $IMA(i,j)$. The same technique can also be used for rotated face recognition. In 2-dimensions, rotated faces can easily be obtained by rotating facial image $IMA(i,j)$.

HONNGAT Tree model can be written as:

HONNGAT Tree operator set ***HONNGAT***: $IMA(i,j) \rightarrow LS$ $\qquad$ (12 – 34)

where:

$IMA(i,j)$: a 2-dimensional black and white image which represents a human face.

LS: a Label Set in which each label corresponds to a different human face (from *1* to *m*) or no one is recognised ($\oslash$);

$$LS = \{\oslash, 1, 2, 3, ..., i, ..., m\}. \qquad (12 - 35)$$

HONNGAT: Higher Order Neural Network Groug-based Adaptive Tolerance tree model operator set;

Figure 5. Higher order neural network group-based adaptive tolerance(HONNGAT) tree

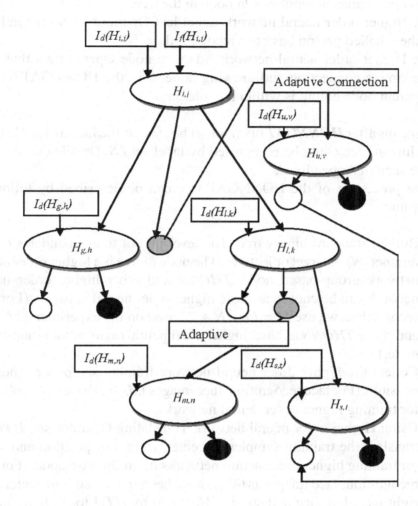

$$HONNGAT = \{ \; HTO, \; HNO, \; HPO, \; HLO, \; HAO \; \} \qquad (12-36)$$

Where:

HTO: Higher order neural network Translating OPerator that can translate facial image *IMA(i,j)* into centre face, left face, right face and so on -- shift and rotate the face image in 2 dimension.

HNO: Higher order neural network Node Operator set that is a complex pattern classifier.

HPO: Higher order neural network Path Operator set which let parent node's output equals to input of son node in the tree.

HLO: Higher order neural network Label leaf Operator set which indicate the labelled person has been recognised.

HAO: Higher order neural network Adaptive node Operator set that adds adaptive connection and growing node(s) in the HONNGAT Tree if parent node output is within the tolerance.

It means after **HONNGAT** operator set be used on the face image *IMA(i,j)*, The Human face could be recognised by label set *LS*. Detailed description can be seen in Appendix C.

The procedure of the HONNGAT tree can be described by following algorithm:

1) Build a standard binary tree. The level (*M*) of tree dependents on the number (*N*) of target objectives. The node of tree is a higher order neural network group-based node. *THONN* and other higher order neural network can be chosen as basic higher order neural network. (For face recognition, we use $M = log_2 N + 2$ based on the experimental results and chose *THONN* as basic higher order neural network for group-based node.)

2) Collect the higher order neural network training samples as more as possible. (For face recognition, face images *IMA(i,j)* have been collected for training higher order neural networks.)

3) Using Higher order neural network Translating Operator set, **HTO**, to translate the training samples to center, right, left position and so on for training higher order neural networks of group-base node. (For face recognition, face images *IMA(i,j)* have been translated into center face, right face, left face and so on (*IMAu(i,j)*) by **HTO** for training higher order neural networks of group-base node. For example, in 2 dimension, we move center face 2 pixels right to get right face.)

4) Training higher order neural networks of higher order neural network group-base note in the tree to find the bast weights for higher order neural networks. After training, all weights of higher order neural networks are fixed. Artificial Higher order neural network group Node Operator set -- **HNO** has been found. (For face recognition, The first level node has been trained for front face recognition. There are 9 *THONN* higher order neural networks in the node. Each higher order network has been trained for recognising one translated front face -- say $THONN_1$ for center front

face, *THONN₂* for right front face, *THONN₃* for left front face, and so on. After training, the first level node can classify front face and non-front face at 9 different positions. Then next level node has been trained to classify all target faces as class 1, other nontarget face as class 2. The following level node has been trained to divided all target face as two subclasses. One is class 1.1 and another is 1.2. This procedure continues until every lowest node of each branch in the tree represents one target face. After training, all weights are found and fixed. It means *HNO* has been found.)

5) Confirm the paths of tree. Let Fire Input of node equals to the output of parent node and get Higher order neural network Path Operator set -- *HPO*.

6) Chose label for each new target face and get Higher order neural network Label Operator -- *HLO*.

7) Testing object (testing face) has been input into Data Input of each fired node. If the testing objective (testing face) is the trained objective (face), one lowest node will be fired, the output of node is 1, and one label will be choose for represent this test object. It means this testing object (testing face) has been recognised. If no label appear, it means this object is not the one of objects been trained.

8) If no more training samples need to be added to the tree, Exit. If more training samples need to be added to the HONNGAT Tree, go to (9).

9) If new target objects (faces) needed to be recognised, using the Higher order neural network Adaptive node Operator -- *HAO* find the adaptive points in the tree. Then to grow tree and go to (3). If topologically deforming old target objects (faces) needed to be recognised, using the Higher order neural network Adaptive node Operator -- *HAO* find the adaptive points in the tree. Then build connection node and go to (3). If no new target objects (faces) needed to be recognised, go to (10).

10) Stop.

FACE RECOGNITION USING HONNGAT TREE MODELS

Face Recognition System

Machine face recognition system is difficult to build since a face is either deformed topologically, translated in 3-dimensions, or when the face environment and background is complicated. Figure 6 shows our face recognition system which organized as following components:

1) The camera captures images of people as they make their way to the check-in desk. Using higher order neural network techniques, faces are located within these captured images.
2) The face will be classified as a front face, tilted to the left, tilted right, rotated to the left, or rotated right.
3) At the same time, faces with glasses and/or beards will be classified using the HONNGAT Tree technique.
4) HONNGAT Trees are used for face recognition. Following successful classification, translation-invariant faces are recognised using adaptive connection and growth of HONNGAT Trees in tolerance space. Output of the system will show the face recognition result.

Face Perception Recognition Using HONNGAT Trees

28*28 pixels face image with 256 grey level are used and lighting condition is 60 *lux*. The experimental results for face perception recognition using HONNGAT trees are shown in Figure 7.

Recognition of Glasses and/or Beards Using HONNGAT Tree

HONNGAT Tree has been used for recognising front faces with glasses and beards. The 2-level HONNGAT Tree structure is shown in Figure 8.

Front Face Recognition Using HONNGAT Tree

The Model of the HONNGAT Tree used for front face recognition is shown in Figure 9. One HONNGAT Tree node is used for face perspective recognition, especially for picking up the front faces for next recognition procedure.

From Level 0 to Level 4, the basic HONNGAT Tree model is used to recognise the front face. Different faces will be recognised at the different label nodes. In order to recognize faces, each artificial neural network group based node needs to be trained prior to testing. Each node of the HONNGAT Tree is trigonometric higher order neural network group with the

Figure 6. Translation-invariant face recognition system using HONNGAT trees

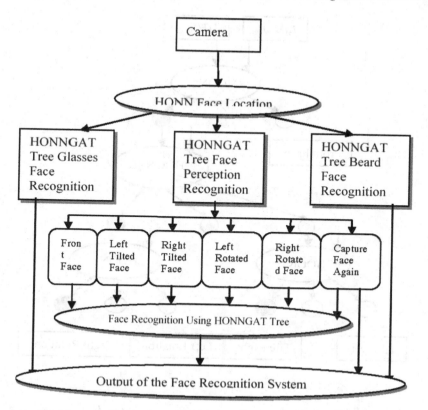

following configuration: input layer - 28*28 neurones; hidden layer; output layer - 1 neuron. The model of Figure 9 only describes the basic operation of the HONNGAT Tree. In order to recognise 1024 target faces, the basic HONNGAT Tree model only needs 12 Levels. This means that if a 12 level basic HONNGAT Tree model is chosen, recognising a specific person only takes about 2 seconds for recognise 1024 target face from million people by using the computer build in 2008.

In Figure 9, nodes *HONNG4,6* has been identified as the adaptive connection nodes from which the tree is to be connection. Such connection enables the system to recognize same people with deforming within the tolerance. Thus adaptive connection can also occur in a growing HONNGAT Tree.

In Figure 9, nodes *HONNG5,0* has been identified as the adaptive nodes from which the tree is to be grown. Such growth enables the system to

Figure 7. Face perspective classification using HONNGAT

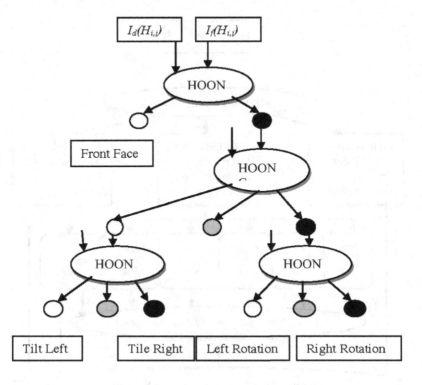

Figure 8. Front glasses and beard face classification using HONNGAT tree

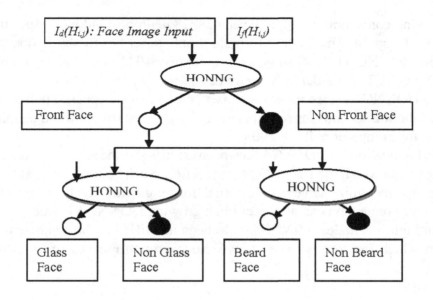

Figure 9. HONNGAT tree for front face recognition

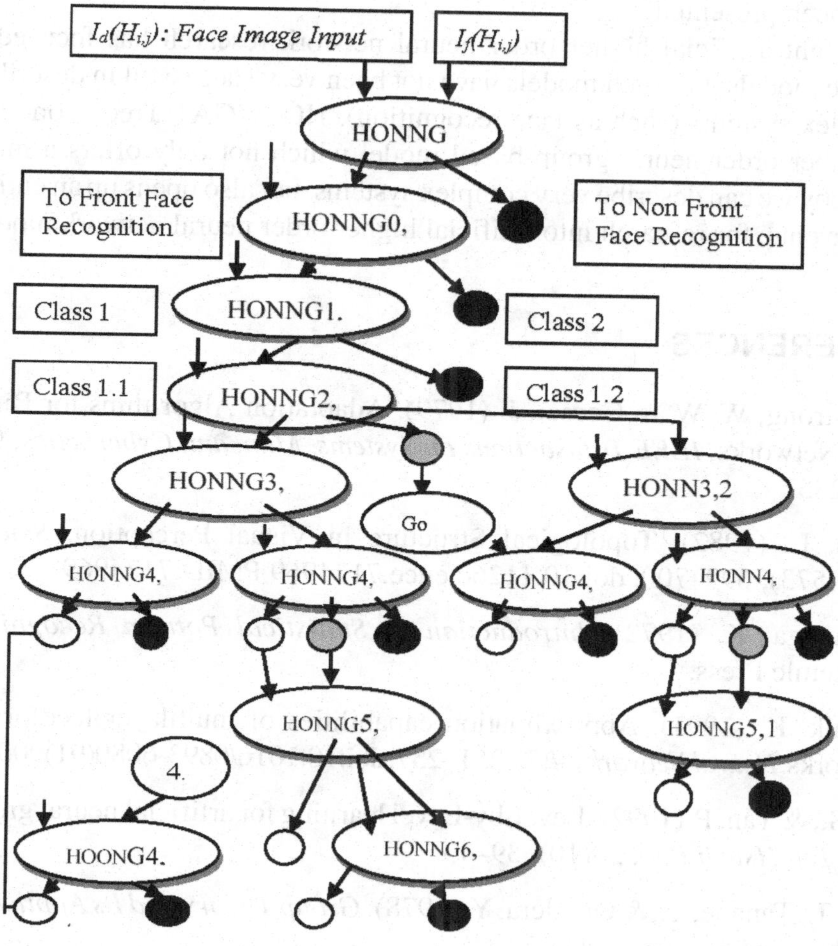

recognise new people. Thus adaptive growth can also occur in a growing HONNGAT Tree.

CONCLUSION

This paper presents the artificial higher order neural network group-based model - HONNGAT Tree for translation-invariant face recognition. The HONNGAT Tree models for face perception classification, distinguishing between front glasses faces and faces with beards under laboratory conditions have been presented.

Recent artificial higher order neural network research has focused on simple models, but such models have not been very successful in describing complex systems (such as face recognition). HONNGAT Tree is one kind of higher order neural group-based model which not only offers a means whereby we can describe very complex systems, but also opens up an entirely new avenue for research into artificial higher order neural network models.

REFERENCES

Armstrong, W. W. & Gecsei, J. (1979). Adaptation Algorithms for Binary Tree Networks. *IEEE Transactions on Systems, Man, and Cybernetics*, 9(5), 276-285.

Chen, L. (1982). Topological Structure in Visual Perception. *Science*, *218*(4573), 699–700. doi:10.1126cience.7134969 PMID:7134969

Fukunaga, K. (1972). *Introduction to Statistical Pattern Recognition*. Academic Press.

Hornik, K. (1991). Approximation capabilities of multilayer feedforward networks.*NeuralNetworks*,*4*(2),251–257.doi:10.1016/0893-6080(91)90009-T

Hu, S., & Yan, P. (1992). Level-by-Level learning for artificial neural groups. *Tien Tzu Hsueh Pao*, *20*(10), 39–43.

Inui, T., Tanabe, Y., & Onodera, Y. (1978). *Group Theory and Its Application in Physics*. Springer-Verlag.

Leshno, M., Lin, V. Y., Pinkus, A., & Schocken, S. (1993). Multilayer feedforward networks with a nonpolynomial activation function can approximate any function. *Neural Networks*, *6*(6), 861–867. doi:10.1016/S0893-6080(05)80131-5

Lumer, E. D. (1992). Selective attention to perceptual groups: The phase tracking mechanism. *International Journal of Neural Systems*, *3*(1), 1–17. doi:10.1142/S0129065792000024

Matsuoka, T., Hamada, H., & Nakatsu, R. (1989). Syllable Recognition Using Integrated Neural Networks. *Proc. Intl. Joint Conf. Neural Networks*, 251-258. 10.1109/IJCNN.1989.118588

Naimark, M. A., & Stern, A. I. (1982). *Theory of Group Representations.* Springer-Verlag. doi:10.1007/978-1-4613-8142-6

Pentland, A., & Turk, M. (1989). Face Processing: Models for Recognition. *Proc. SPIE - Intelligent Robots and Computer Vision VIII: Algorithms and Technology*, 20-35.

Reid, M. B., Spirkovska, L., & Ochoa, E. (1989). Simultaneous position, scale, rotation invariant pattern classification using third-order neural networks. *International Journal on Neural Networks, 1*, 154–159.

Sanger, T. D. (1991). A Tree-Structured Adaptive Network for Function Approximation in High-Dimensional Spaces. *IEEE Transactions on Neural Networks, 2*(2), 285–293. doi:10.1109/72.80339 PMID:18276382

Sankar, A., & Mammone, R. J. (1993). Growing and pruning neural network tree network. *IEEE Transactions on Computers, 42*(3), 291–299. doi:10.1109/12.210172

Tsao, T.-R., Shyu, & Libert. (1989). A group theory approach to neural network computing of 3D rigid motion. *Proceedings of International Joint Conference on Neural Networks, 2*, 275–280. doi:10.1109/IJCNN.1989.118710

van der Waerden, B. L. (1970). *Algebra.* New York: Frederick Ungar Publishing Co.

Voutriaridis, C., Boutalis, Y. S., & Mertzios, B. G. (2003). Ridge polynomial networks in pattern recognition. In *Proceedings of 4th EURASIP Conference on Video/Image Processing and Multimedia Communications* (vol.2, pp.519 – 524). Academic Press.

Wang, J., Sun, Y., & Chen, Q. (2003). Recognition of digital annotation with invariant HONN based on orthogonal Fourier-Mellin moments. *Proceedings of 2003 International Conference on, 4*, 2261 – 2264.

Willcox, C. R. (1991). Understanding hierarchical neural network behaviour: A renormalization group approach. *Journal of Physics. A. Mathematical Nuclear and General, 24*(11), 2655–2644. doi:10.1088/0305-4470/24/11/030

Yang, X. (1990). Detection and classification of neural signals and identification of neural networks (synaptic connectivity). *Dissertation Abstracts International - B, 50*(12), 5761.

Zeeman, E. C. (1962). The topology of the brain and visual perception. In M. K. Fork Jr., (Ed.), *Topology of 3-manifolds and related Topics* (pp. 240–256). Englewood Cliffs, NJ: Prentice-Hall, Inc.

Zhang, M. (2009a). Artificial Higher Order Neural Network Nonlinear Models: SAS NLIN or HONNs. In M. Zhang (Ed.), *Artificial Higher Order Neurla Networks for Economics and Business* (pp. 1–47). Hershey, PA: Information Science Publishing (an imprint of IGI Global). doi:10.4018/978-1-59904-897-0.ch001

Zhang, M. (2009b). Ultra Higher Frequency Trigonometric Higher Order Neural Networks for Time Series Data Analysis. In M. Zhang (Ed.), *Artificial Higher Order Neurla Networks for Economics and Business* (pp. 133–163). Hershey, PA: Information Science Publishing (an imprint of IGI Global). doi:10.4018/978-1-59904-897-0.ch007

Zhang, M., Crowley, J., Dunstone, E., & Fulcher, J. (1993, October). *Face Recognition. Australia Patent, No., PM1828*, 14.

Zhang, M., & Fulcher, J. (1996a). Face recognition using artificial neural network group-based adaptive tolerance (GAT) trees. *IEEE Transactions on Neural Networks*, *7*(3), 555–567. doi:10.1109/72.501715 PMID:18263454

Zhang, M., Fulcher, J., & Scofield, R. (1997). Rainfalll estimation using artificial neural network group. *International Journal of Neurlcomputing*, *16*(2), 97–115. doi:10.1016/S0925-2312(96)00022-7

Zhang, M., Xu, S., & Fulcher, J. (2007). ANSER: An Adaptive-Neuron artificial neural network System for Estimating Rainfall using satellite data. *International Journal of Computers and Applications*, *29*(3), 1–8. doi:10.1 080/1206212X.2007.11441850

ADDITIONAL READING

Alanis, A. Y., Sanchez, E. N., Loukianov, A. G., & Perez-Cisneros, M. A. (2011). Real-Time Neural-State Estimation. *IEEE Transactions on Neural Networks*, *22*(3), 497–505. doi:10.1109/TNN.2010.2103322 PMID:21245007

Hornik, K. (1991). Approximation capabilities of multilayer feedforward networks. *Neural Networks*, *4*(2), 251–257. doi:10.1016/0893-6080(91)90009-T

Munehisa, T., Kobayashi, M., & Yamazaki, H. (2001). Cooperative Updating in the Hopfield Model. *IEEE Trans on Neural Networks*, *12*(5), 1243–1251. doi:10.1109/72.950153 PMID:18249951

KEY TERMS AND DEFINITIONS

GAT: Group-based adaptive tolerance tree.

HONN: Artificial higher order neural network.

HONN⁺: Additive HONN sets.

HONN*: Product HONN sets.

HONNG: Artificial higher order neural network group.

HONNGAT: Artificial higher order neural network group-based adaptive tolerance tree.

HONNGS: Artificial higher order neural network grnrtslised set.

HONNS: Artificial higher order neural network set.

PHONN: Artificial polynomial higher order neural network.

PHONNG: Artificial polynomial higher order neural network group.

SINCHONN: Artificial SINC higher order neural network.

SPHONN: Artificial sigmoid polynomial higher order neural network.

SPHONNG: Artificial sigmoid polynomial higher order neural network group.

SSINCHONN: Artificial sine and SINC higher order neural network.

THONN: Artificial trigonometric higher order neural network.

THONNG: Artificial trigonometric higher order neural network group.

UCSHONN: Artificial ultra-high frequency trigonometric higher order neural network.

APPENDIX

The following definitions are needed in order to describe the HONNGAT Tree model:

A. Generalised Artificial Higher Order Neural Network Sets

Detaila definitions can be seen in Chapter 3, from Formulae (3-1) to (3-16) and from Formulae (3-36) to (3-53).

B. Proof of the Inference

Detail proof can be seen in Chapter 3, from formulae (3-24) to (3-35) and from formulae (3-57) to (3-60).

C. HONNGAT Tree Definitions

(1) Image Definitions:

Row index set: $Sr = \{1,2, ..., Nr\}$
Column index set: $Sc = \{1,2, ..., Nc\}$
Space field: $Sr\ Sc$
Grey set: N_i
$E_1, E_2, ..., E_k$ Euclidean space: $EE = \{E_1, E_2, ... E_i, ..., E_k\}$
Image Operator $IMAO$: $Sr\ Sc\ EE$ $\hspace{3cm}$ (12 – C1)

Let:

$E_i = \{1, 2, 3, ... N_i\}$
$N_i = 256$, $(i = 1,2,3)$
$EE = \{E_1, E_2, E_3\}$ $\hspace{4cm}$ (12 – C2)

then

$IMAO(i, j)$ is the colour image which can be described as a colour human
face. $\hspace{6cm}$ (12 - C3)

Let:

$i = 1$ for Ei and
$EE = E_1$
Digital Image Operator $\textbf{\textit{IMA}}$: Sr Sc (12- C4)

then

$IMA(i, j)$ is a black-and-white image which can be used to represent a human
face.   (12 – C5)

Let:
Label Set:

$LS= \{1, 2, ..., M\}$ (12 – C6)

each label corresponds to a different human face

(2) Tolerance Space Definitions:

The definitions for tolerance space are as follows (details, please see
Zeeman, 1962):
Given the Set: $\textbf{\textit{X, Y, Z}}$,

then tolerance is a type of relation in the set $\textbf{\textit{X}}$ or $\textbf{\textit{Y}}$ or $\textbf{\textit{Z}}$ (12 – C7)

We define Tolerance Space $(\textbf{\textit{X}},)$ as follows:
Let:

If $x\,\textbf{\textit{X}}$ (x, x) (12 – C8)
If $x\,\textbf{\textit{X}}$, $y\,\textbf{\textit{Y}}$, and (x, y)
then (y, x).   (12 – C9)
If $x\,\textbf{\textit{X}}$, $y\,\textbf{\textit{Y}}$, $z\,\textbf{\textit{Z}}$ and (x, y) , (y, z)
then (x, z) or (x, z) .   (12 – C10)

(3) Higher Order Neural Network Definitions:

$H_{i,j}$: Higher Order Neural Network Group-Based (HONNGB) node, adaptive
node and label node, where i: the level or deep of the HONNGAT Tree
         (12 – C11)

j: the *jth* node n the i level

$I_f(H_{i,j})$: The fire input of the node $H_{i,j}$ (12 – C12)
if $I_f(H_{i,j}) = 1$, the node has been fired
$I_d(H_{i,j})$: The data input of the node $H_{i,j}$ (12 – C13)
if $I_f(H_{i,j}) = 1$, $I_d(H_{i,j})$ can be input to node $H_{i,j}$
$I(H_{i,j})$: The input to HONNGB node $H_{i,j}$ (12 - C14)
$O(HONN_k)$: The output of higher order neural network $HONN_k$

     (12 – C15)

$O(H_{i,j})$: The output from HONNGB node $H_{i,j}$ (12 – C16)
$O_0(H_{i,j})$, $O_1(H_{i,j})$, $O_2(H_{i,j})$: Outputs of node $H_{i,j}$ (12 – C17)
binary outputs are: $O_0(H_{i,j})$ and $O_2(H_{i,j})$
ternary outputs are: $O_0(H_{i,j})$, $O_1(H_{i,j})$, and $O_2(H_{i,j})$
$P(H_{i,j}, H_{l,k})$: Path of the HONNGAT Tree between nodes $H_{i,j}$ and $H_{l,k}$
     (12 – C18)

     (4)   Higher Order Neural Network Group-based Adaptive Tolerance Tree operator

HONNGAT

Considering the above definitions, the Higher Order Neural Network Group-based Adaptive Tolerance Tree model can be written as:

Higher Order Neural Network Group-based Adaptive Tolerance Tree operator

HONNGAT: *IMA(i, j) LS*   (12 – C19)

This means that after *IMA(i, j)* has been operated upon by the *HONNGAT* operator -which incorporates an adaptive function and uses the translation invariant face recognition technique - an object (human face) can be recognised by label set *LS*.

The Higher Order Neural Network Groug-based Adaptive Tolerance tree operator *HONNGAT* is the operator set:

HONNGAT = { *HTO*, *HNO*, *HPO*, *HLO*, *HAO* }   (12 – C20)

Each operator or operator set belongs to one of the following four types:

     (4.1)   Higher Order Neural Network Translating Operator - **HTO**

Higher order neural network Translating Operator -- **HTO** uses the translation invariant face recognition technique and is defined as:

$$HTO\ (IMA(i,j)): IMA(i,j)\ IMA_u(i,j),\ u=0,1.2,\ ....N_u \qquad (12-C21)$$

where:

$IMA_0\ (i,j)$: centre face of facial image $IMA(i,j)$
$IMA_1(i,j)$: lower-left face of facial image $IMA(i,j)$
$IMA_2(i,j)$: lower face of facial image $IMA(i,j)$
$IMA_3(i,j)$: lower-right face of image $IMA(i,j)$
$IMA_4(i,j)$: right face of facial image $IMA(i,j)$
$IMA_5(i,j)$: upper-right face of facial image $IMA(i,j)$
$IMA_6(i,j)$: up face of facial image $IMA(i,j)$
$IMA_7(i,j)$: upper-left face of facial image $IMA(i,j)$
$IMA_8(i,j)$: left face of facial image $IMA(i,j)$

(4.2) Higher Order Neural Network Node Operator Set - **HNO**

The Higher order neural network Node Operator $HNO(H_{i,j})$, which has the adaptive function within tolerance space is the set of operators:

$$HNO(H_{i,j}) = \{\ HNO0(I_f(H_{i,j}),\ I_d(H_{i,j})),\ HNO1(H_{i,j},\ IMA(i,j)),\ HNG,$$
$$HNO2(O(H_{i,j}))\} \qquad (12-C22)$$

where:

$HNO0(I_f(H_{i,j}),\ I_d(H_{i,j}): I(H_{i,j})=I_d(H_{i,j})=IMA(i,j)$, if $I_f(H_{i,j})=1$ for testing
$HNO0(I_f(H_{i,j}),\ I_d(H_{i,j}): I(H_{i,j})=$, if $I_f(H_{i,j})=0$ for testing
$HNO0(I_f(H_{i,j}),\ I_d(H_{i,j}): I(H_{i,j})=I_d(H_{i,j})=IMAu(i,j)$, for training $\qquad (12-C23)$
$u=1,2,3,....,$ Nu
$HNO1(H_{i,j},\ I_d(H_{i,j})): I(H_{i,j})\ O(HONN_k)\ k=1,2\ ...,\ k \qquad (12-C24)$

Where **HNO1** is one kind of higher order neural network operator (for example **THONN**).

Higher Order Neural Netowrk Group operator -- **HNG** is used for all higher order neural networks in the group:

$$HNG:\ O(H_{i,j}) = O(HONN_1)\ *\ O(HONN_2)\ *\ O(HONN_3)*\ ......*\ O(HONN_k)$$
$$(12-C25)$$

Where: * means *AND* or *OR*.
For the binary case:

$$\textbf{HNO2}(O(H_{i,j})): (H_{i,j}) \{ O_0 (H_{i,j}), O_2(H_{i,j}) \} \tag{12 – C26}$$

The binary output is:

$O_0(H_{i,j}) = 1, O(H_{i,j}) \,_1(H_{i,j})$
$O_0(H_{i,j}) = 0$, otherwise $\tag{12 – C27}$
$O_1(H_{i,j}) = 1, O(H_{i,j}) \,_2(H_{i,j})$
$O_1(H_{i,j}) = 0$, otherwise $\tag{12 – C28}$

For the ternary case:

$$\textbf{HNO2}(O(H_{i,j})):O(H_{i,j}) \{ O_0(H_{i,j}), O_1(H_{i,j}), O_2(H_{i,j}) \} \tag{12 – C29}$$

The ternary output is:

$O_0(H_{i,j}) = 1, O(H_{i,j}) \,_1(H_{i,j})$
$O_0(H_{i,j}) = 0$, otherwise $\tag{12 - C30}$
$O_1(H_{i,j}) = 1, O(H_{i,j}) \,_3(H_{i,j})$
$O_1(H_{i,j}) = 0$, otherwise $\tag{12 – C31}$
$O_2(H_{i,j}) = 1, O(H_{i,j}) \,_2(H_{i,j})$
$O_2(H_{i,j}) = 0$, otherwise $\tag{12 – C32}$

where $_1(H_{i,j})$, $_2(H_{i,j})$, and $_3(H_{i,j})$ are tolerance values for node $H_{i,j}$.
Now let:
Higher order neural network Node Operator set $\textbf{HNO} = \{ \textbf{HNO}(H_{i,j}) \}$
$$\tag{12 – C33}$$

$i = 1,2,...,Nr; j = 1,2,...,Nc$

$H_{i,j}$ is the artificial higher order neural network node

(4.3)   Higher Order Neural Network Path Operator set - **HPO**

Higher order neural network Path Operator $\textbf{HPO}(H_{i,j}, H_{l,k})$:

$$I_f(H_{l,k}) = O_m(H_{i,j}), m = 0, \text{ or } 1, \text{ or } 2 \tag{12 – C34}$$

Now let:
Operator set

$$HPO=\{ \ HPO(H_{i,j}, \ H_{l,k}) \ \} \ \ i=1,2,...,Nr; \ \ j=1,2,...,Nc; \ \ l=1,2,...,Nr;$$
$$k=1,2,...,Nc \hspace{3cm} (12-C35)$$

(4.4)   Higher Order Neural Netowrk Label Operator - **HLO**

Higher order neural network Label Operator $HLO(H_{i,j})$:

if lowest level node in different branch $Om(H_{i,j}) = 1,$ $\hspace{1.5cm}$ (12 – C36)
m = 0, or 1, or 2

Now let:

$$HLO(H_{i,j}): LS \ i, \ i = 1,2,3, \ ......, \ m \hspace{2.5cm} (12-C37)$$

else

$$HLO(H_{i,j}): LS \hspace{4cm} (12-C38)$$

Now let:
Higher order neural network Node Operator Operator set

$$HLO=\{ \ HLO(H_{i,j}) \ \} \hspace{3.5cm} (12-C39)$$
i=1,2,...,Nr;
j=1,2,...,Nc

$H_{i,j}$ is label node of artificial higher order neural network

(4.5)   Higher Order Neural Network Adaptive node Operator set - **HAO**

Higher order neural network Adaptive node Operator $HAO(H_{i,j})$ means:

If $O(H_{l,k}) \in \xi_m(H_{l,k})$ and $O_m(H_{l,k}) = 1 \ (m = 0, 1, \ or \ 2)$ $\hspace{1cm}$ (12 – C40)

Add node $H_{i,j}$ that be connected to $O_m(H_{p,k})$ if needed, and

$$O_m(H_{i,j}) = I_f(H_{i,j}) = 1 \ (m = 0, 1, \ or \ 2) \hspace{2.5cm} (12-C41)$$

The function of **HAO(H_{i,j})** means that if the adaptive node is fired, its output will be 1.

Now Let:

Higher order neural network Node Operator set **HAO={ HAO(H_{i,j}) }**

$$(12 - C42)$$

$i=1,2,...,Nr; j=1,2,...,Nc, H_{i,j}$ is an adaptive node

About the Author

Ming Zhang received his M.S. degree in Information Processing and Ph.D. degree in the area of Computer Vision from East China Normal University, Shanghai, China, in 1982 and 1989, respectively. He held Postdoctoral Fellowships in artificial neural networks with the Chinese Academy of the Sciences from 1989 to 1991, and the USA National Research Council from 1991 to 1992. He worked as a project manager on face recognition for airport security system and Ph.D. co-supervisor at the University of Wollongong, Australia from 1992 to 1994. In 1994, he joined Monash University, Australia as a lecturer in the Computer Science department. From 1995 to 2000, he was a lecturer and then a senior lecturer and Ph.D. supervisor at the University of Western Sydney, Australia. He also held Senior Research Associate Fellowship in artificial neural networks with the USA National Research Council from 1999 to 2000. From 2000, he has been working as an associate professor and then, from 2008, as a full professor at the Christopher Newport University, Virginia, USA. He has published more than 100 papers in the top international journals and international conferences in the areas of face recognition, weather forecasting, financial data simulation by using artificial neural networks and artificial higher order neural networks.

Index

X

Y

Are You Ready to
Publish Your Research?

IGI Global
PUBLISHER of TIMELY KNOWLEDGE

IGI Global offers book authorship and editorship opportunities across 11 subject areas, including business, computer science, education, science and engineering, social sciences, and more!

Benefits of Publishing with IGI Global:

- Free one-on-one editorial and promotional support.
- Expedited publishing timelines that can take your book from start to finish in less than one (1) year.
- Choose from a variety of formats, including: Edited and Authored References, Handbooks of Research, Encyclopedias, and Research Insights.
- Utilize IGI Global's eEditorial Discovery® submission system in support of conducting the submission and double-blind peer review process.
- IGI Global maintains a strict adherence to ethical practices due in part to our full membership with the Committee on Publication Ethics (COPE).
- Indexing potential in prestigious indices such as Scopus®, Web of Science™, PsycINFO®, and ERIC – Education Resources Information Center.
- Ability to connect your ORCID iD to your IGI Global publications.
- Earn honorariums and royalties on your full book publications as well as complimentary copies and exclusive discounts.

Join Your Colleagues from Prestigious Institutions, Including:

Australian National University

MIT — Massachusetts Institute of Technology

JOHNS HOPKINS UNIVERSITY

HARVARD UNIVERSITY

TSINGHUA UNIVERSITY ~1911~

COLUMBIA UNIVERSITY IN THE CITY OF NEW YORK

Learn More at: www.igi-global.com/publish

or by Contacting the Acquisitions Department at: acquisition@igi-global.com